New Riverside Editions

General Editor for the American Volumes
Paul Lauter

STEPHEN CRANE, *The Red Badge of Courage, Maggie: A Girl of the Streets, and Other Selected Writings*
Edited by Phyllis Frus and Stanley Corkin

RALPH WALDO EMERSON, *Selected Writings* and MARGARET FULLER, *Woman in the Nineteenth Century*
Edited by John Carlos Rowe

OLAUDAH EQUIANO, MARY ROWLANDSON, AND OTHERS, *American Captivity Narratives*
Edited by Gordon M. Sayre

HENRY DAVID THOREAU, *Walden and Civil Disobedience*
Edited by Paul Lauter

MARK TWAIN, *Adventures of Huckleberry Finn*
Edited by Susan K. Harris

EDITH WHARTON, *The Age of Innocence*
Edited by Carol J. Singley

Other Riverside Literature Titles

Call and Response: The Riverside Anthology of the African American Literary Tradition
Edited by Patricia Liggins Hill et al.

The Riverside Anthology of Children's Literature, Sixth Edition
Edited by Judith Saltman

The Riverside Anthology of Literature, Third Edition
Edited by Douglas Hunt

The Riverside Anthology of Short Fiction: Convention and Innovation
Edited by Dean Baldwin

The Riverside Chaucer, Third Edition
Edited by Larry D. Benson

The Riverside Milton
Edited by Roy Flannagan

The Riverside Shakespeare, Second Edition
Edited by G. Blakemore Evans et al.

NEW RIVERSIDE EDITIONS

General Editor for the American Volumes
Paul Lauter, Trinity College

Edith Wharton

The Age of Innocence

Complete Text with Introduction
Historical Contexts • Critical Essays

edited by
Carol J. Singley
Rutgers University–Camden

HOUGHTON MIFFLIN COMPANY
Boston • *New York*

To my students at Rutgers–Camden

Senior Sponsoring Editor: Suzanne Phelps Weir
Associate Editor: Jennifer Roderick
Senior Project Editor: Kathryn Dinovo
Senior Cover Design Coordinator: Deborah Azerrad Savona
Manufacturing Manager: Florence Cadran
Senior Marketing Manager: Nancy Lyman
Associate Marketing Manager: Carla Gray

Cover design: Steven Cooley
Cover image: © Corbis-Bettmann

Library of Congress Cataloging-in-Publication Data is available on file.

ISBN: 0-395-98079-8

3456789-QW/F-06 05 04 03 02

As part of Houghton Mifflin's ongoing
commitment to the environment, this text
has been printed on recycled paper.

Contents

About This Series

Paul Lauter

The Riverside name dates back well over a century. Readers of this book may have seen—indeed, may own—Riverside Editions of works by the best-known nineteenth-century American writers, such as Emerson, Thoreau, Lowell, Longfellow, and Hawthorne. Houghton Mifflin and its predecessor, Ticknor & Fields, were the primary publishers of the New England authors who constituted much of the undisputed canon of American literature until well into the twentieth century. The Riverside Editions of works by these writers, and of some later writers such as Amy Lowell, became benchmarks for distinguished and useful editions of standard American authors for home, library, and classroom.

In the 1950s and 1960s, the Riverside name was used for another series of texts, primarily for the college classroom, of well-known American and British literary works. These paperback volumes, edited by distinguished critics of that generation, were among the most widely used and appreciated of their day. They provided carefully edited texts in a handsome and readable format, with insightful critical introductions. They were books one kept beyond the exam, the class, or even the college experience.

In the last quarter century, however, ideas about the American literary canon have changed. Many scholars want to see a canon that reflects a broader American heritage, including significant literary works by previously marginalized writers, many of them women or men of color. These changes began to be institutionalized in curricula as well as in textbooks such as *The Heath Anthology of American Literature,* which Houghton Mifflin started publishing in 1998. The older Riverside series, excellent in its day, ran the risk of appearing outdated; the editors were long retired or deceased, and the authors were viewed by some as too exclusive.

Yet the name Riverside and the ideas behind it continued to have appeal. The name stood for distinction and worth in the publication of America's literary heritage. Houghton Mifflin's New Riverside Series, initiated in the year 2000, is designed to uphold the Riverside reputation for excellence while offering a more inclusive range of authors. The Series also provides today's reader with books that contain, in addition to notable literary works, introductions by influential critics, as well as a variety of stimulating materials that bring alive the debates, the conversations, the social and cultural movements within which America's literary classics were formed.

Thus emerged the book you have in hand. Each volume of the New Riverside Editions will contain the basic elements that we think today's readers find interesting and useful: important literary works by significant authors, incisive introductions, and a variety of contextual materials to make the literary text fully engaging. These books will be useful in many kinds of classrooms, but they are also designed to offer the casual reader the enjoyment of a good read in a fresh and accessible format. Among the first group of New Riverside Editions are familiar titles, such as Henry David Thoreau's *Walden* and Mark Twain's *Adventures of Huckleberry Finn*. There are also works in fresh new combinations, such as the collection of early captivity narratives and the volume that pairs texts by Ralph Waldo Emerson and Margaret Fuller. And there are well-known works in distinctively interesting formats, such as the volume containing Edith Wharton's *The Age of Innocence* and the volume of writings by Stephen Crane. Future books will include classics as well as works drawing renewed attention.

The New Riverside Editions will provide discriminating readers with a wide range of important literary works, contextual materials that vividly illuminate those works, and the best of recent critical commentary and analysis. And because we have not confined our editors to a single monotonous format, we think our readers will find that each volume in this new series has a character appropriate to the literary work it presents.

We expect the New Riverside Editions to bring to the twenty-first century the same literary publishing distinction of its nineteenth- and twentieth-century predecessors.

Introduction

Carol J. Singley

The Age of Innocence, which won the Pulitzer Prize the year following its publication in 1920, is one of Edith Wharton's finest novels. She wrote it at the height of her career, when she was fifty-seven and living in Paris. Wharton knew the 1870s New York society that she depicts intimately, having grown up with the wealth and privilege that fill the pages of the novel. The Newbold Jones family into which Wharton was born in 1862 was one of the most prominent and social in old New York. Wharton looks backward at the aristocratic brownstones of Manhattan, leisurely summers in Newport, and the sojourns in Europe with a mixture of criticism and nostalgia. The novel is tinged by a profound, post–World War I sense of loss and disillusionment that Wharton felt after having led massive relief efforts for French and Belgian civilians, refugees, and soldiers. Tired, saddened, and somewhat wistful about the demise of civilization as she had known it, she sought to recapture in fiction a more stable and predictable past. Accordingly, *The Age of Innocence* somewhat sentimentally pays tribute to a bygone era—"an empty vessel into which no new wine would ever again be poured," as Wharton writes in her autobiography, *A Backward Glance*—whose virtue lay in "preserving a few drops of an old vintage too rare to be savoured by a youthful palate"(5). But the novel also indicts this antedated society for its "blind dread of innovation" and opposition to anything different from itself (22). Although Wharton portrays positive as well as negative aspects of old New York, readers have the impression that in the final analysis negative critique overrides appreciation. Wharton herself felt stifled by the prosaic, complacent aristocratic world of New York society and left it for Europe and a life of literature and the arts. She lived in France as an expatriate and continued writing fiction until her death in 1937.

The accuracy of Wharton's historic detail is remarkable, especially considering that she wrote the novel largely from memory. She based several characters—such as the obese and independent Mrs. Manson Mingott, the newly moneyed Mrs. Lemuel Struthers, the showy financier Julius

Beaufort—on people she had actually known. She had help from her niece, Beatrix (Minnie) Jones Farrand, who consulted books on upper-class society and back issues of the *New York Tribune* to provide dates and locations for some of the novel's events. But the heart of the novel emerged from Wharton's creative imagination, from a passion to "'make up' stories" that had seized her as a young girl (*Backward* 33) and eventually led to an internationally acclaimed career, beginning with her first bestseller, *The House of Mirth*, in 1905. Wharton had developed themes of infidelity in previous novels, particularly *Ethan Frome* (1911) and *The Reef* (1912), and explored clashes of personal desire and public mores in international novels such as *Madame de Treymes* (1907) and *The Custom of the Country* (1913). But in *The Age of Innocence,* setting, plot, and theme all come together in an exquisitely original, poignant, and beautiful way.

The achievement of *The Age of Innocence* derives in part from the novel's near-perfect structure: two books of equal length with the decisive wedding scene at the novel's midpoint; allusions to *Faust* in the opening and concluding chapters, to provide a framework for Newland Archer's seduction of and by the two women he loves; the insertion of a sentimental play, *The Shaughraun,* at the height of Archer's passion for Ellen Olenska; a series of brilliantly executed dinner scenes; and well-crafted chapters, each of which advances the plot toward its inevitable conclusion. The novel also dazzles with its exquisite detail. Readers can trace the steps of characters as they stroll on Manhattan, Newport, and Paris avenues and can vicariously enter theaters, museums, and shops that served patrons over a hundred years ago. Wharton's numerous references to literature, fashion, art, architecture, and decor not only enhance the realistic qualities of her art but also illuminate the characters' personalities. The books one keeps in a library, the styles of furniture or paintings one chooses for a drawing room, even the flowers one selects for a gift reveal subtle but important distinctions of taste, value, and temperament.

The novel owes its greatness not only to narrative technique and historical authenticity but also to its depth of characterization and to the timeless issues that it addresses. Wharton combines an ethnography of old New York with a powerful portrait of characters caught in perennial conflicts between desire and duty, freedom and restriction, passion and reason. Although few of today's readers can experience the kind of opulent, leisured society Wharton describes, and some may have difficulty even imagining such a world of elegant conventionality, none can finish the novel without being deeply touched by the characters' triumphs and disappointments. Wharton depicts an age-old problem of a younger generation struggling to honor an older generation's traditions and still blaze a path of its own. She juxtaposes the convenience and efficiency of following rules with the adventure and satisfaction of setting one's own standard of conduct. And she leaves provocatively open the answers to the complex social and moral questions she raises.

The New York society Wharton describes is a seemingly static, insular world that functions with clockwork predictability, but this charmed circle is on the brink of destruction. New York City as a whole was rapidly expanding in population after the Civil War, whereas the sheltered society Wharton describes was contracting—and vainly trying to close its ranks against commercialization and an onslaught from two different groups of people. First, newly arrived immigrants from Europe and African Americans from the South crowded into lower Manhattan. The unidentified cooks, mulatto maids, Sicilian bootblacks, and Irish vendors who serve the privileged classes in the novel are all part of this large working class. Although these characters have no voice in the text, they are important in signaling a late-nineteenth-century reconfiguration of American cities. Aristocratic families—who had lived in the Battery and on the East Side since settlement by their Dutch and Belgian ancestors in the 1600s— responded by moving northward or by further insulating themselves in fashionable neighborhoods around Washington Square. Second, newly moneyed classes eager to spend their way into social prominence invaded the ranks of the aristocracy. Ignorant of long-standing traditions and irreverently inventing new standards of behavior, the nouveaux riches threatened old New York with its relaxed mores and brash displays of wealth. Although the immigrant group could be contained, the magnitude of wealth—earned in industry and commerce—of the well-heeled newcomers made the threat to old New York immediate and alarming.

Wharton's skillful use of time in the novel helps readers take note of the enormousness and significance of this social change. Most of the novel (chaps. 1–33) takes place in the 1870s, the post–Civil War period when lingering gentility meets the aggression of finance and commerce. The last chapter (34) is set some thirty years later, when the transition to a modern society seems nearly complete. Finally, the novel as a whole is informed by the creative and critical intelligence of the author, who writes from a post–World War I perspective. Awareness of these three time periods can deepen readers' appreciation of the complexity of Wharton's fictional canvas, for these large-scale social developments have parallels on the personal level.

The problems of old New York are also Newland Archer's. There is an evolution of his life, beginning in the 1870s, when he is jarred out of complacency by the arrival from Europe of the beautiful, faintly exotic

Ellen Olenska. Not exactly an outsider, Ellen nevertheless disrupts the order and stability of Archer's world with her "Bohemian" behavior (215).[1] Her appearance on the eve of his betrothal to her conventional cousin, May Welland, presents Archer with a choice: he can either replicate the patterns of old New York and draw the circle tighter around himself and the society he knows, or he can risk opening to new and unfamiliar experiences of love and art. In the second phase, represented in the last chapter of the novel, Archer, now fifty-seven, contemplates changes in New York society over the past thirty years and tries to come to terms with decisions he has and has not made. Still, the full significance of life's victories and accommodations eludes him. But from the third perspective, readers— who enjoy Wharton's 1920 vantage point as well as their own—consider what Archer has lost and gained by his decision to be "a good citizen" (273). Wharton's readers measure the value of institutions for which Archer has sacrificed his dreams, contemplate the meaning of time and change, and realize the impossibility of recovering the lost innocence conveyed by the novel's title.

The unsettling effect of social change is felt in the very first scene of the novel, in which established New Yorkers attend the opera in their own boxes at the exclusive Academy of Music, a small theater they have arranged to build. There is already talk, however, about a larger "new Opera House" (13), the Metropolitan, that would open farther north some ten years later, constructed with the fortunes of the nouveaux riches who are piqued because they cannot obtain seats at the exclusive theater. Even as old New York contemplates this displacement, it has already capitulated to outsiders. Julius Beaufort, the boisterous financier with mysterious origins who has married into the reputable Dallas family, now hosts a ball that has become an annual event. Throughout the novel, concerned New Yorkers mumble about dangerous "trend[s]" in society (212), monitor attendance at dinner parties to keep out undesirables, and condemn those who wear Paris gowns as they arrive instead of packing them away for a year in order not to be in advance of the fashion. Given the small-mindedness of this society, it is no wonder that Ellen Olenska creates a stir when she appears in Mrs. Mingott's box. Equally predictable is Newland Archer's instinctive reaction to protect his beloved from the slightest hint of scandal by insisting that he and May Welland announce their engagement early.

New York society is highly stratified, like a pyramid. The aristocratic van der Luydens, with their direct Dutch ancestry, sit at the apex. Their

---

[1] All parenthetical references are to this New Riverside Edition.

position is so elevated that they rarely appear in society at all, and certainly not at the opera, where everyone comes to see and be seen by others. Their intervention is crucial, however, at times of crisis; like sovereigns performing a sacred rite, they grant pardons or mete out punishments in proportion to the magnitude of the social crime. Their elaborate dinner party for Ellen definitively settles the question of her membership in society, but inclusion is guaranteed only so long as Ellen conforms to expectations. When society perceives a lapse from standards of good taste, the van der Luydens literally escort her out of its ranks. The large middle section of the pyramid is occupied by the Archers, Lovells, Wellands, and other descendants of middle-class Dutch and Belgian merchants and bankers whose fortunes are made from real estate and other investments. Wealthy in a passive rather than active way, they use their abundantly free time to arrange dinners and marriages with one another; travel to Newport, London, and Paris; and update lists of social dos and don'ts. They complain the most loudly about the disintegration of values because they stand to lose so much from even the slightest fluctuation in social customs. Finally, the newcomers to society fill the lower tiers of the pyramid. Old New Yorkers studiously avoid the Sunday evening soirées of Mrs. Struthers, wife of a shoe polish magnate who slipped into society one winter during an epidemic. Although they grudgingly admire Julius Beaufort for "the way he carried things off" (28), they cannot forgive him for bringing disgrace on his family with questionable Wall Street investments.

Archer feels superior and immune to New York foibles, but in truth he is as much a creature of convention as anyone else in his narrow circle. Wharton uses anthropological terms to emphasize the similarity between New York society and earlier cultures, writing that "what was or was not 'the thing' played a part as important in Newland Archer's New York as the inscrutable totem terrors that had ruled the destinies of his forefathers thousands of years ago." Few things seem "more awful to him than an offense against 'Taste,'" which has become synonymous with moral principle (14, 24). Archer holds traditional, sentimental views of men's and women's roles, including those involving a double sexual standard. He loves May not only because of their shared, unspoken values but also because of her naive vacuity and malleability, which he sees as complements to his own worldly experience. Gazing at her innocent expression and youthful beauty at the opera, he draws "a breath of satisfied vanity" derived from the assurance that he is the only man in her life and that he will be the one to awaken her sexually: "He contemplated her absorbed young face with a thrill of possessorship in which pride in his own masculine initiation was mingled with a tender reverence for her abysmal purity." Archer takes May's chaste innocence for granted although he himself has gained sexual experience with a married woman. How the "miracle of fire and ice" by which his virginal May will be transformed into a sexually provocative partner as "worldly-wise and as eager to please" as the woman with whom he has had a two-year affair is a matter he has yet to consider. And how this model of sexual liberation is to be accomplished without a corresponding and disappointing emotional "frailty" that "nearly marred" the relationship with his mistress also remains a mystery (16–18).

May proves to be more enlightened and self-sufficient than Archer expects. Holding lilies of the valley and dressed in white in the opening scene, she appears pure, demure, and deferential. But she becomes more assertive as the plot progresses, leading readers to wonder whether her innocence is a mere facade that hides a potent capacity for calculation. May is, after all, savvy enough to know that her husband's attentions have wandered, and although she at first incorrectly guesses the object of his affections, she is confident enough to confront him and even offer to grant him his freedom. Remarkably determined and steadfast, May works quietly but surely to secure her marriage to Archer, even if it means a sacrifice of romantic ideals. By the end of the novel, she has achieved her goal, and Archer, who had occasionally felt "oppressed by this creation of factitious purity," comes to recognize her as the "tutelary divinity of all his old traditions and reverences" (48, 167).

Ellen Olenska also surpasses Archer's expectations of the opposite sex. She combines greater beauty, intelligence, and independence than he has ever known in a woman. Archer occasionally utters platitudes about the need for equality and freedom for women, but Ellen forces him to confront his prejudices, especially when, as her lawyer, he is enlisted for advice about her divorce. Her love of art, music, and conversation also revitalizes his intellectual and literary pursuits; simply viewing the paintings on the walls of her home challenges him to rethink aesthetic values and the European and American traditions that form them. Archer's overwhelming experience of Ellen is one of passion. Ironically, although he has been in love before and thinks of himself as May's awakener, it is Ellen who awakens him with a "passion that was closer than his bones [and] was not to be superficially satisfied" (203). Most important, however, is Ellen's "passionate honesty" (250). She leads Archer to view the society he takes for granted in a fresh, critical way; she gives him a reason to leave this world behind; and she remains a symbol of his life's ideals. In conversations throughout the novel, Ellen reminds Archer of the importance of forthrightness, and she is responsible—through her decision to reside in New York or Paris—for ending the escalating deception in Archer's marriage.

Ultimately, however, Ellen's effect on Archer is to reveal the person he has always been. "At heart a dilettante," he finds Ellen too "rich" for his blood (15, 283) and lacks the courage necessary to break social rules and strike a course of his own. His declarations about women's rights crumble under the weight of his family and firm, who maintain that regardless of circumstances, a woman's duty is with her husband. Archer is increasingly shown to be a romantic figure given to fantasies, not realities. From his minor error of mistaking the silly Blenker girl's umbrella for Ellen's, to his monumental plea that he and Ellen get away to "a world where words . . . categories . . . won't exist" (234), Archer ponders unrealistic solutions to real problems. And despite his desire for Ellen, each time he draws closer to her, he allows his bond to May to tighten. Wharton renders his situation with more irony than tragedy, but Archer evokes other ineffectual, self-absorbed literary heroes, such as Shakespeare's Hamlet, Henry James's John Marcher in "The Beast in the Jungle," and Arthur Miller's Willy Loman in *Death of a Salesman,* all of whom are dreamers rather than actors in their life dramas. This is not to say that Archer is contemptible or merely weak; on the contrary, he is one of the most sympathetic characters in all of Wharton's fiction. Given the strength of the social codes that bind him, it is impressive that he should come to question them at all.

Archer begins by thinking he is in control of his life—as any young man of his station would—but despite the privileges society accords to the male sex, he is no match for either May or Ellen and consistently underestimates their power. It is no accident that both women are related to Catherine Mingott, the feisty matriarch who manages New York society with all of the vigor and decisiveness worthy of her namesake, Catherine the Great. Mrs. Mingott is the only main character in the novel who lives life on her own terms. She reigns over a society that she also feels free to criticize. Her history suggests an unusual combination of traditional domesticity and creative rebellion from social norms. She becomes wealthy by making a good marriage despite her father's notorious abandonment of the family. She then gains control of her money when her husband dies. Capitalizing upon the opportunity for independence, she has the audacity to build a spectacular home far north of fashionable New York neighborhoods, preferring to let society come to her than to cater to it. A woman with the confidence to set trends rather than follow them, Mrs. Mingott instills strength of character in both May and Ellen, each of whom resembles her in different ways.

Although they may be seen as rivals, May and Ellen function as complements as well as competitors. Each represents a type of womanhood that Wharton respected but could not contain in a single character. May, athletic and domestic, embodies the qualities of physical nurturance and social continuity. Associated with the Roman goddess Diana—with nature, the hunt, fertility, and public virtue—she has a strong desire to marry and have children. She effortlessly attracts a network of family and friends necessary to help her reach this goal, and she keeps the force of society behind her throughout the novel, holding Archer accountable to the social contract he has made with her. She can even tell her husband, "you must be sure to go and see Ellen" (219) because she knows his marriage vows are a public promise that society will help him to keep.

Ellen, on the other hand, is aligned with artistic creativity. She is powerfully drawn to beauty and inspires it wherever she goes. Evoking the Roman goddess Venus and Helen of Troy, she is also aligned with love, both erotic and transcendent. The grace and originality of her fashions, home, and ideas are the offspring of her fertile mind and spirit. Ellen is modeled not after women Wharton knew from her childhood, but after Wharton herself—who left New York for Paris; spent twenty-eight years in an unhappy marriage; and devoted herself to the arts of literature, friendship, and conversation. Whereas May stands at the center of society, Ellen stands slightly outside it, her exoticism alluring but threatening to the status quo. Wharton brings the two women together not only by making them cousins and friends but by linking them at a pivotal point in the novel: May speaks first to Ellen about her pregnancy, and Ellen responds with characteristic integrity and loyalty. With the events that follow, Wharton makes the women inadvertent collaborators. Although different, each woman is faithful to her own nature, and each becomes more fully the person she was meant to be.

Archer misses the clues to May's and Ellen's true characters because he reads them according to conventional gender paradigms, and they resist easy classification. The result for Archer is a dilemma that ill fits him for either woman. With May, with whom he lives daily, he feels unreal or trapped like a prisoner. With Ellen, from whom he is estranged, he feels "real" (203) and free. Both May and Ellen ground Archer in realities that he cannot achieve on his own. Ellen answers his desire for escape with her question, "Oh, my dear—where is that country?" and her insistence on words like "mistress" to describe extramarital affairs (234). May similarly checks his plan for travel abroad with the announcement of their coming child. Yet years later, Archer still vacillates between reality and fantasy, between rootedness and flight, as he sits on a bench looking up at Ellen's apartment and imagines what it might be like to see her.

Wharton leaves the final assessment about her characters' choices with her readers, and such an assessment is not easy to make. The ambiguity is summed up in Archer's reflection that he had missed the "flower of life," but, "[a]fter all, there was good in the old ways. . . . [and] good in the new order too" (274–75). May acknowledges to their son that Archer has given up the one thing he most wanted, but she never speaks directly to Archer himself; Archer sacrifices his love of Ellen for a life with May, but his gift is extracted from him rather than selflessly given. Only Ellen seems to have pure motives, but Wharton complicates the reader's response to her by withholding important details—about her marriage, her relationship with Monsieur Rivière, and her life in Paris—and by making the consummation of her affair with Archer a decision based on coincidence as much as conscience.

The Age of Innocence makes a plea for open communication, for accepting women on their own terms, and for embracing change as a constant. The world is drastically altered by the time Archer's children reach maturity, and the values and institutions for which he has renounced his heart's desire are obsolete. Julius Beaufort, whom Archer once viewed as a rival, has proved to be the most resilient. No one remembers his financial disgrace anymore. He rebuilt his fortune, married his mistress after his wife died, and moved abroad. His daughter, reportedly as captivating and intriguing as Ellen Olenska, is now engaged to marry May and Archer's son, Dallas. Dallas faces the next century with buoyant optimism and moral relativism, fueled by an expanding economy and relaxed social rules. But even in this freer society, the past still influences the present, and the present still carries social expectations. Dallas will most likely base the millionaire's house he is designing on the eighteenth-century palace of Versailles, and his fiancee has made him promise to catch the latest Parisian trends by finding Debussy's music and visiting the Grand-Guignol Theater.

The truth that Wharton allows her readers to see—it is not clear that Archer ever sees it—is that we are always anchored to realities of one kind or another, but we can often choose the terms of our conformity to them. The difference between father and son is that Archer has made conformity a "dull duty" rather than an honorable joy. "Held fast by habit, by memories, by a sudden startled shrinking from new things," he has sadly "lost the habit of travel" (274–77). Wharton associates travel with her most successful characters; here she uses the term metaphorically to describe a process whereby characters set a course that allows them to sail safely around the barriers of social convention without going aground on them. Far from merely looking backward, then, Wharton's novel also welcomes the future. On the eve of marriage to the love of his life, on his way to visit the woman his father hesitates to see, young Dallas possesses the "self-confidence that [comes] of looking at fate not as a master but as an equal" (282). We can do no better, Wharton suggests in this final scene, than to embrace inevitable change and confront circumstances with creative choice.

A Note on the Text

Carol J. Singley

The Age of Innocence originally appeared in *The Pictorial Review* in four large installments that ran from July/August to November 1920. The magazine text included no chapter divisions. In the same year, the novel was published in New York and in London by D. Appleton and Company. Edith Wharton's habit was to revise extensively and to involve herself in every step of the publishing process. She heavily revised the magazine text of *The Age of Innocence,* making stylistic changes as well as corrections in spelling and punctuation.

Subsequent printings of the novel during Wharton's lifetime were from the Appleton edition, making it relatively easy to establish the authority of her text. Some thirty corrections were made before the third impression of the first printing, however. For example, Wharton changed a reference to "Guy de Maupassant's incomparable tales" to "the prolific Alphonse Daudet's brilliant tales" (123). Also, the later printings correctly set Dr. Agathon Carver's card (138) in "Gothic" type, as the text indicates. Most interesting—because it expresses Newland Archer's experience of marriage to May Welland as a kind of death—is Wharton's original misquotation of the marriage ceremony from the Book of Common Prayer. In the first two impressions, the Rector reads the words of the burial service: "Forasmuch as it hath pleased Almighty God—." Wharton later substituted the words of the marriage service: "Dearly beloved, we are gathered together here" (159).

The text of this edition of *The Age of Innocence* follows the Library of America edition (1985), which is based in turn on the sixth impression of the first edition of the novel. In preparing the explanatory footnotes for the New Riverside Edition, I have aimed to define language unfamiliar to today's readers; to describe items important to the settings, characterizations, and themes of Wharton's novel; and to provide as rich a cultural and historical background as possible in a short space. For their assistance, I gratefully acknowledge Julie Still, Robeson Library, Rutgers University–Camden; the reference staff at the Boston Public Library; Edward Fuller and Pamela Harris, McCabe Library, Swarthmore College; Bert Lippincott, Newport Historical Society; and Laura Harris, Metropolitan Museum of Art.

PART ONE

The Age of Innocence

THE AGE
OF INNOCENCE

Edith Wharton

BOOK I

I

On a January evening of the early seventies, Christine Nilsson was singing in Faust at the Academy of Music in New York.

Though there was already talk of the erection, in remote metropolitan distances "above the Forties," of a new Opera House which should compete in costliness and splendour with those of the great European capitals, the world of fashion was still content to reassemble every winter in the shabby red and gold boxes of the sociable old Academy. Conservatives cherished it for being small and inconvenient, and thus keeping out the "new people" whom New York was beginning to dread and yet be drawn to; and the sentimental clung to it for its historic associations, and the musical for its excellent acoustics, always so problematic a quality in halls built for the hearing of music.

Christine Nilsson A renowned Swedish soprano (1843–1921) who first appeared as Marguerite in Gounod's *Faust* at the Academy of Music in New York City on November 1, 1871.

Faust A legendary figure and the subject of many literary and musical works. *Faust,* a five-act opera written by French composer Charles François Gounod (1818–1893) and based on a German play by Johann Wolfgang von Goethe (1749–1832), was first performed in Italian in New York City in 1863. Gounod's *Faust* focuses on the love story of Faust and Marguerite, which was original with Goethe, rather than on the whole Faust story that appears in legends. Wharton, who admired Goethe, uses the Faust romance as a thematic touchstone for the love story in her novel. She also uses it as a structuring device: two years after meeting Ellen, Archer again attends the opera (chap. 32), where he sees the same scene of *Faust* performed. In both instances, Wharton describes Act 3, in which Faust—having sold his soul to the devil Mephistopheles in return for wealth, power, and youth—seduces the chaste maiden Marguerite.

Academy of Music An opera house that opened in 1854 on the corner of 14th Street and Irving Place, in Union Square, then an affluent New York neighborhood. Built by aristocratic New Yorkers, the lavish building had a stage large enough for grand opera, many private and stage boxes, and about four thousand crimson velvet upholstered seats. The white-and-gold interior was illuminated by thousands of gaslights. For thirty years, the Academy of Music was the principal venue for foreign opera singers visiting the city.

new Opera House Resentful of the small number of boxes at the Academy of Music, newly moneyed New Yorkers built the Metropolitan Opera House in 1883. Its opening dealt a serious blow to the Academy of Music. No longer able to compete, the latter closed its doors in 1886, the manager lamenting his inability "to fight Wall Street." By mentioning both opera houses, Wharton suggests the extraordinary transformation of New York in the 1870s. Society changed from a closely knit and modestly wealthy group

It was Madame Nilsson's first appearance that winter, and what the daily press had already learned to describe as "an exceptionally brilliant audience" had gathered to hear her, transported through the slippery, snowy streets in private broughams, in the spacious family landau, or in the humbler but more convenient "Brown *coupé*." To come to the Opera in a Brown *coupé* was almost as honourable a way of arriving as in one's own carriage; and departure by the same means had the immense advantage of enabling one (with a playful allusion to democratic principles) to scramble into the first Brown conveyance in the line, instead of waiting till the cold-and-gin congested nose of one's own coachman gleamed under the portico of the Academy. It was one of the great livery-stableman's most masterly intuitions to have discovered that Americans want to get away from amusement even more quickly than they want to get to it.

When Newland Archer opened the door at the back of the club box the curtain had just gone up on the garden scene. There was no reason why the young man should not have come earlier, for he had dined at seven, alone with his mother and sister, and had lingered afterward over a cigar in the Gothic library with glazed black-walnut bookcases and finial-topped chairs which was the only room in the house where Mrs. Archer allowed smoking. But, in the first place, New York was a metropolis, and perfectly aware that in metropolises it was "not the thing" to arrive early at the opera; and what was or was not "the thing" played a part as important in Newland Archer's New York as the inscrutable totem terrors that had ruled the destinies of his forefathers thousands of years ago.

---

of New Yorkers who could trace their ancestry to the first Dutch settlers of Manhattan to the "new people," such as the Vanderbilts, Goulds, Morgans, and Rockefellers, who were made fabulously rich by industry, commerce, and finance.

broughams   Closed, one-horse, four-wheeled carriages.

spacious family landau   A stylish, two-horse, four-wheeled carriage with front and back halves that could be independently raised and lowered to create a closed compartment.

"Brown *coupé*"   A coupé, from the French, is a type of two-horse, four-wheeled carriage with an inside seat for two and an outside seat for the driver. Isaac Brown, sexton of the fashionable Grace Church, operated a livery stable that supplied society's members with horses and carriages.

Gothic library   A room furnished in the style of architecture prevalent in western Europe from the twelfth to the sixteenth century, featuring ribbed vaults, pointed arches, and clustered pillars. The Gothic style experienced a revival in the mid-eighteenth and nineteenth centuries.

finial-topped   Decorative ornament or knob, often in the shape of an acorn or urn, placed on furniture or arched structures.

The second reason for his delay was a personal one. He had dawdled over his cigar because he was at heart a dilettante, and thinking over a pleasure to come often gave him a subtler satisfaction than its realisation. This was especially the case when the pleasure was a delicate one, as his pleasures mostly were; and on this occasion the moment he looked forward to was so rare and exquisite in quality that—well, if he had timed his arrival in accord with the prima donna's stage-manager he could not have entered the Academy at a more significant moment than just as she was singing: "He loves me—he loves me not—*he loves me!*" and sprinkling the falling daisy petals with notes as clear as dew.

She sang, of course, "*M'ama!*" and not "he loves me," since an unalterable and unquestioned law of the musical world required that the German text of French operas sung by Swedish artists should be translated into Italian for the clearer understanding of English-speaking audiences. This seemed as natural to Newland Archer as all the other conventions on which his life was moulded: such as the duty of using two silver-backed brushes with his monogram in blue enamel to part his hair, and of never appearing in society without a flower (preferably a gardenia) in his buttonhole.

"*M'ama . . . non m'ama . . .*" the prima donna sang, and "*M'ama!*", with a final burst of love triumphant, as she pressed the dishevelled daisy to her lips and lifted her large eyes to the sophisticated countenance of the little brown Faust-Capoul, who was vainly trying, in a tight purple velvet doublet and plumed cap, to look as pure and true as his artless victim.

Newland Archer, leaning against the wall at the back of the club box, turned his eyes from the stage and scanned the opposite side of the house. Directly facing him was the box of old Mrs. Manson Mingott, whose monstrous obesity had long since made it impossible for her to attend the Opera, but who was always represented on fashionable nights by some of

---

daisy petals In the garden scene, an infatuated Marguerite plucks petals from a daisy (*marguerite* is French for "daisy"), symbol of freshness and innocence, singing, "He loves me—he loves me not—he loves me!" The third act ends as the lovers agree to meet again; before departing, however, Faust sees Marguerite in her window, hears her avowal of love for him, and runs to her. The curtain falls on the lovers' passionate embrace. Acts 4 and 5 narrate Faust's betrayal and desertion of Marguerite, her death following imprisonment for killing their child, and Faust's prayerful remorse.

Faust-Capoul Joseph-Amédée-Victor Capoul (1839–1924) was a French tenor who played Faust in the 1871 production.

club box At the theater, members of Archer's club sit together in a box, a separate compartment that accommodates a small group. Membership in a social club was a principal way to proclaim one's position in elite society.

the younger members of the family. On this occasion, the front of the box was filled by her daughter-in-law, Mrs. Lovell Mingott, and her daughter, Mrs. Welland; and slightly withdrawn behind these brocaded matrons sat a young girl in white with eyes ecstatically fixed on the stage-lovers. As Madame Nilsson's *"M'ama!"* thrilled out above the silent house (the boxes always stopped talking during the Daisy Song) a warm pink mounted to the girl's cheek, mantled her brow to the roots of her fair braids, and suffused the young slope of her breast to the line where it met a modest tulle tucker fastened with a single gardenia. She dropped her eyes to the immense bouquet of lilies-of-the-valley on her knee, and Newland Archer saw her white-gloved finger-tips touch the flowers softly. He drew a breath of satisfied vanity and his eyes returned to the stage.

No expense had been spared on the setting, which was acknowledged to be very beautiful even by people who shared his acquaintance with the Opera houses of Paris and Vienna. The foreground, to the footlights, was covered with emerald green cloth. In the middle distance symmetrical mounds of woolly green moss bounded by croquet hoops formed the base of shrubs shaped like orange-trees but studded with large pink and red roses. Gigantic pansies, considerably larger than the roses, and closely resembling the floral pen-wipers made by female parishioners for fashionable clergymen, sprang from the moss beneath the rose-trees; and here and there a daisy grafted on a rose-branch flowered with a luxuriance prophetic of Mr. Luther Burbank's far-off prodigies.

---

brocaded   In a fabric enriched by a design made from additional weft threads, sometimes of precious metal, that run back and forth across each motif.

tulle tucker   A piece of lace or a thin, fine fabric worn inside or on top of the bodice of a woman's dress to fill in a low neckline.

lilies-of-the-valley   Delicately scented spring flowers that convey sweetness, virginity, and humility. In Christianity, they are the symbol of the Virgin Mary and the advent of new life. According to nineteenth-century books on the "language of flowers," lily of the valley meant a return of happiness. Most Victorian men and women were familiar with this elaborate language of flowers and could use a gift of blossoms to express a particular sentiment or quality. Wharton, a horticulturist as well as a novelist, would certainly have understood flowers' various meanings.

Mr. Luther Burbank's far-off prodigies   Burbank, a botanist and plant breeder (1849–1926), developed valuable hybrids and led the way for research in plant genetics. Influenced by Charles Darwin, he achieved results by introducing foreign species, carefully producing variations of a given plant, and selecting desirable modifications of ensuing hybrids. Wharton's description is "prophetic" in that Burbank did not develop the Shasta daisy, which he produced from crossbreeding American and European species and then crossing the resulting hybrids with a Japanese species, until 1901. In the 1870s

In the centre of this enchanted garden Madame Nilsson, in white cashmere slashed with pale blue satin, a reticule dangling from a blue girdle, and large yellow braids carefully disposed on each side of her muslin chemisette, listened with downcast eyes to M. Capoul's impassioned wooing, and affected a guileless incomprehension of his designs whenever, by word or glance, he persuasively indicated the ground floor window of the neat brick villa projecting obliquely from the right wing.

"The darling!" thought Newland Archer, his glance flitting back to the young girl with the lilies-of-the-valley. "She doesn't even guess what it's all about." And he contemplated her absorbed young face with a thrill of possessorship in which pride in his own masculine initiation was mingled with a tender reverence for her abysmal purity. "We'll read Faust together . . . by the Italian lakes . . ." he thought, somewhat hazily confusing the scene of his projected honey-moon with the masterpieces of literature which it would be his manly privilege to reveal to his bride. It was only that afternoon that May Welland had let him guess that she "cared" (New York's consecrated phrase of maiden avowal), and already his imagination, leaping ahead of the engagement ring, the betrothal kiss and the march from Lohengrin, pictured her at his side in some scene of old European witchery.

He did not in the least wish the future Mrs. Newland Archer to be a simpleton. He meant her (thanks to his enlightening companionship) to

---

he was beginning his career, having developed the Burbank potato in 1873. Wharton refers to Burbank's methods, and the evolutionary theories that inspired them, to explain changes in old New York society. From the 1870s on, the elite increasingly mingled and "crossbred" with those once considered outsiders.

reticule . . . girdle A reticule was a little bag that held a lady's personal toilet articles when her dress had no pockets. A girdle was a belt or cord worn around the waist.

muslin chemisette A short, sleeveless bodice made of a woven cotton fabric and worn either as an undergarment or as a blouse under a jumper.

Italian lakes The dozens of Alpine glacial lakes in northern Italy, known for their sparkling waters and beautiful, romantic settings. Lake Como is perhaps the most famous.

Lohengrin A three-act opera by German composer Richard Wagner (1813–1883) that includes the now-famous Wedding March. The opera tells the story of Lohengrin, a disguised Knight of the Holy Grail who arrives in a swan-drawn boat to champion the cause of Elsa, whose kingdom of Brabant is torn by strife. They marry on the condition that she not ask his name or origins. When Elsa is overcome by doubt instilled by her enemies, she asks the forbidden question, causing Lohengrin's disclosure of his true identity and departure from Brabant, and her own death. Archer entertains fantasies of himself as Lohengrin and May as the wife pledged to ignorance.

develop a social tact and readiness of wit enabling her to hold her own with the most popular married women of the "younger set," in which it was the recognised custom to attract masculine homage while playfully discouraging it. If he had probed to the bottom of his vanity (as he sometimes nearly did) he would have found there the wish that his wife should be as worldly-wise and as eager to please as the married lady whose charms had held his fancy through two mildly agitated years; without, of course, any hint of the frailty which had so nearly marred that unhappy being's life, and had disarranged his own plans for a whole winter.

How this miracle of fire and ice was to be created, and to sustain itself in a harsh world, he had never taken the time to think out; but he was content to hold his view without analysing it, since he knew it was that of all the carefully-brushed, white-waistcoated, buttonhole-flowered gentlemen who succeeded each other in the club box, exchanged friendly greetings with him, and turned their opera-glasses critically on the circle of ladies who were the product of the system. In matters intellectual and artistic Newland Archer felt himself distinctly the superior of these chosen specimens of old New York gentility; he had probably read more, thought more, and even seen a good deal more of the world, than any other man of the number. Singly they betrayed their inferiority; but grouped together they represented "New York," and the habit of masculine solidarity made him accept their doctrine on all the issues called moral. He instinctively felt that in this respect it would be troublesome—and also rather bad form— to strike out for himself.

"Well—upon my soul!" exclaimed Lawrence Lefferts, turning his opera-glass abruptly away from the stage. Lawrence Lefferts was, on the whole, the foremost authority on "form" in New York. He had probably devoted more time than any one else to the study of this intricate and fascinating question; but study alone could not account for his complete and easy competence. One had only to look at him, from the slant of his bald forehead and the curve of his beautiful fair moustache to the long patent-leather feet at the other end of his lean and elegant person, to feel that the knowledge of "form" must be congenital in any one who knew how to wear such good clothes so carelessly and carry such height with so much

---

Lawrence Lefferts . . . Sillerton Jackson   Wharton bases these two characters on Ward McAllister, a self-appointed arbiter of New York manners, philanderer, and author of the privately published memoir, *Society as I Have Found It.*

opera-glass   Small binoculars, especially for use at a theater.

patent-leather   Leather with a fine black varnished surface, then much in style.

lounging grace. As a young admirer had once said of him: "If anybody can tell a fellow just when to wear a black tie with evening clothes and when not to, it's Larry Lefferts." And on the question of pumps versus patent-leather "Oxfords" his authority had never been disputed.

"My God!" he said; and silently handed his glass to old Sillerton Jackson.

Newland Archer, following Lefferts's glance, saw with surprise that his exclamation had been occasioned by the entry of a new figure into old Mrs. Mingott's box. It was that of a slim young woman, a little less tall than May Welland, with brown hair growing in close curls about her temples and held in place by a narrow band of diamonds. The suggestion of this headdress, which gave her what was then called a "Josephine look," was carried out in the cut of the dark blue velvet gown rather theatrically caught up under her bosom by a girdle with a large old-fashioned clasp. The wearer of this unusual dress, who seemed quite unconscious of the at-tention it was attracting, stood a moment in the centre of the box, dis-cussing with Mrs. Welland the propriety of taking the latter's place in the front right-hand corner; then she yielded with a slight smile, and seated herself in line with Mrs. Welland's sister-in-law, Mrs. Lovell Mingott, who was installed in the opposite corner.

Mr. Sillerton Jackson had returned the opera-glass to Lawrence Lefferts. The whole of the club turned instinctively, waiting to hear what the old man had to say; for old Mr. Jackson was as great an authority on "family" as Lawrence Lefferts was on "form." He knew all the ramifica-tions of New York's cousinships; and could not only elucidate such com-plicated questions as that of the connection between the Mingotts (through the Thorleys) with the Dallases of South Carolina, and that of the re-lationship of the elder branch of Philadelphia Thorleys to the Albany Chiverses (on no account to be confused with the Manson Chiverses of University Place), but could also enumerate the leading characteristics of each family: as, for instance, the fabulous stinginess of the younger lines

---

pumps   A light shoe, usually without fastening and worn for dancing.

"Oxfords"   A low walking shoe laced over the instep.

"Josephine look"   A style named for Marie Rose Joséphine Tascher de la Pagerie (1763–1814), a Creole from Martinique who became the wife of Napoléon Bonaparte in 1796. Empress of the French from 1804 to 1809, she was divorced by Napoléon for reasons of state. The high waist, low neckline, and flowing skirt of the Empire dress contrasted with 1870s fashion, which featured restrictive corsets and bustles. Wharton links Ellen's "un-usual dress" to an older and beautiful European style.

of Leffertses (the Long Island ones); or the fatal tendency of the Rushworths to make foolish matches; or the insanity recurring in every second generation of the Albany Chiverses, with whom their New York cousins had always refused to intermarry—with the disastrous exception of poor Medora Manson, who, as everybody knew . . . but then her mother was a Rushworth.

In addition to this forest of family trees, Mr. Sillerton Jackson carried between his narrow hollow temples, and under his soft thatch of silver hair, a register of most of the scandals and mysteries that had smouldered under the unruffled surface of New York society within the last fifty years. So far indeed did his information extend, and so acutely retentive was his memory, that he was supposed to be the only man who could have told you who Julius Beaufort, the banker, really was, and what had become of handsome Bob Spicer, old Mrs. Manson Mingott's father, who had disappeared so mysteriously (with a large sum of trust money) less than a year after his marriage, on the very day that a beautiful Spanish dancer who had been delighting thronged audiences in the old Opera-house on the Battery had taken ship for Cuba. But these mysteries, and many others, were closely locked in Mr. Jackson's breast; for not only did his keen sense of honour forbid his repeating anything privately imparted, but he was fully aware that his reputation for discretion increased his opportunities of finding out what he wanted to know.

The club box, therefore, waited in visible suspense while Mr. Sillerton Jackson handed back Lawrence Lefferts's opera-glass. For a moment he silently scrutinised the attentive group out of his filmy blue eyes overhung by old veined lids; then he gave his moustache a thoughtful twist, and said simply: "I didn't think the Mingotts would have tried it on."

Julius Beaufort   Beaufort may be based on George Alfred Jones, Wharton's notorious cousin who embezzled money to support a mistress, or on August Belmont, a prominent financier of German Jewish origin who sponsored western frontier expansion and kept a mistress whom he transported in a yellow carriage.

old Opera-house on the Battery   Castle Garden, the converted fort Castle Clinton, was a center for popular entertainment from the 1820s through the 1850s. Castle Garden appealed to the masses in the same way that the Academy of Music appealed to the elite. It is best known for P. T. Barnum's presentation of singer Jenny Lind there in 1850. Located off the Battery, a public park at the southern tip of Manhattan, Castle Garden offered easy access to the New York harbor. Catherine Mingott's father presumably met his Spanish dancer at Castle Garden before running away with her to Cuba. By the 1870s, the building was used as the east coast federal immigration center, predating Ellis Island.

II

Newland Archer, during this brief episode, had been thrown into a strange state of embarrassment.

It was annoying that the box which was thus attracting the undivided attention of masculine New York should be that in which his betrothed was seated between her mother and aunt; and for a moment he could not identify the lady in the Empire dress, nor imagine why her presence created such excitement among the initiated. Then light dawned on him, and with it came a momentary rush of indignation. No, indeed; no one would have thought the Mingotts would have tried it on!

But they had; they undoubtedly had; for the low-toned comments behind him left no doubt in Archer's mind that the young woman was May Welland's cousin, the cousin always referred to in the family as "poor Ellen Olenska." Archer knew that she had suddenly arrived from Europe a day or two previously; he had even heard from Miss Welland (not disapprovingly) that she had been to see poor Ellen, who was staying with old Mrs. Mingott. Archer entirely approved of family solidarity, and one of the qualities he most admired in the Mingotts was their resolute championship of the few black sheep that their blameless stock had produced. There was nothing mean or ungenerous in the young man's heart, and he was glad that his future wife should not be restrained by false prudery from being kind (in private) to her unhappy cousin; but to receive Countess Olenska in the family circle was a different thing from producing her in public, at the Opera of all places, and in the very box with the young girl whose engagement to him, Newland Archer, was to be announced within a few weeks. No, he felt as old Sillerton Jackson felt; he did not think the Mingotts would have tried it on!

He knew, of course, that whatever man dared (within Fifth Avenue's limits) that old Mrs. Manson Mingott, the Matriarch of the line, would dare. He had always admired the high and mighty old lady, who, in spite of having been only Catherine Spicer of Staten Island, with a father mysteriously discredited, and neither money nor position enough to make people forget it, had allied herself with the head of the wealthy Mingott line, married two of her daughters to "foreigners" (an Italian marquis and an English banker), and put the crowning touch to her audacities by building

---

Fifth Avenue's limits   Fifth Avenue runs north and south in Manhattan. One of the most affluent and fashionable residential streets in New York City, it was governed by rigid social rules in the nineteenth century.

a large house of pale cream-coloured stone (when brown sandstone seemed as much the only wear as a frock-coat in the afternoon) in an inaccessible wilderness near the Central Park.

Old Mrs. Mingott's foreign daughters had become a legend. They never came back to see their mother, and the latter being, like many persons of active mind and dominating will, sedentary and corpulent in her habit, had philosophically remained at home. But the cream-coloured house (supposed to be modelled on the private hotels of the Parisian aristocracy) was there as a visible proof of her moral courage; and she throned in it, among pre-Revolutionary furniture and souvenirs of the Tuileries of Louis Napoleon (where she had shone in her middle age), as placidly as if there were nothing peculiar in living above Thirty-fourth Street, or in having French windows that opened like doors instead of sashes that pushed up.

Every one (including Mr. Sillerton Jackson) was agreed that old Catherine had never had beauty—a gift which, in the eyes of New York, justified every success, and excused a certain number of failings. Unkind people said that, like her Imperial namesake, she had won her way to suc-

---

brown sandstone   A dark brown or reddish brown sandstone quarried and used extensively in the eastern United States in the mid- to late nineteenth century. A brownstone is a house, often a row house, erected or faced with this material. In her autobiography, *A Backward Glance,* Wharton notes the "desperate uniformity" of these structures of her youth. New York, she writes, was "cursed with its universal chocolate-coloured coating of the most hideous stone ever quarried."

frock-coat   A single- or double-breasted man's coat with knee-length skirts joined at the waistline. The skirts of the coat met in the front, unlike the more formal cutaway, where they were "cut away" from the waistline to the knee.

wilderness . . . Central Park   Development of New York City began in lower Manhattan, at the Battery, and extended northward. By the 1870s, Central Park, bounded on the south by 59th Street, still marked the outermost limit of fashionable residential life. Anything north of Central Park, including the location of Mrs. Mingott's house, seemed "an inaccessible wilderness" to established New Yorkers.

pre-Revolutionary furniture   Made in France during the reign of Louis XVI, before the Revolution of 1789.

Tuileries   The Tuileries was the palace of French kings in central Paris and the site of parades, balls, and receptions. Dating from 1564, it was destroyed by fire in 1871. Only the formal gardens remain.

above Thirty-fourth Street   Stylish New York neighborhoods of this time were south of 34th Street. Wharton herself grew up in this fashionable area of Manhattan. She was born in 1862 at 14 West 23rd Street.

French windows   Windows, usually in a pair, that extend the full length to the floor.

Imperial namesake   Wharton compares Catherine Mingott with Catherine II, empress of Russia (1762–1796), known as Catherine the Great because she did much to trans-

cess by strength of will and hardness of heart, and a kind of haughty effrontery that was somehow justified by the extreme decency and dignity of her private life. Mr. Manson Mingott had died when she was only twenty-eight, and had "tied up" the money with an additional caution born of the general distrust of the Spicers; but his bold young widow went her way fearlessly, mingled freely in foreign society, married her daughters in heaven knew what corrupt and fashionable circles, hobnobbed with Dukes and Ambassadors, associated familiarly with Papists, entertained Opera singers, and was the intimate friend of Mme. Taglioni; and all the while (as Sillerton Jackson was the first to proclaim) there had never been a breath on her reputation; the only respect, he always added, in which she differed from the earlier Catherine.

Mrs. Manson Mingott had long since succeeded in untying her husband's fortune, and had lived in affluence for half a century; but memories of her early straits had made her excessively thrifty, and though, when she bought a dress or a piece of furniture, she took care that it should be of the best, she could not bring herself to spend much on the transient pleasures of the table. Therefore, for totally different reasons, her food was as poor as Mrs. Archer's, and her wines did nothing to redeem it. Her relatives considered that the penury of her table discredited the Mingott name, which had always been associated with good living; but people continued to come to her in spite of the "made dishes" and flat champagne, and in reply to the remonstrances of her son Lovell (who tried to retrieve the family credit by having the best *chef* in New York) she used to say laughingly: "What's the use of two good cooks in one family, now that I've married the girls and can't eat sauces?"

Newland Archer, as he mused on these things, had once more turned his eyes toward the Mingott box. He saw that Mrs. Welland and her sister-in-law were facing their semicircle of critics with the Mingottian *aplomb* which old Catherine had inculcated in all her tribe, and that only May Welland betrayed, by a heightened colour (perhaps due to the knowledge that he was watching her) a sense of the gravity of the situation. As for the cause of the commotion, she sat gracefully in her corner of the box, her eyes fixed on the stage, and revealing, as she leaned forward, a little more

---

form Russia into a modern country. Both women outlived their husbands and became strong absolute rulers. Catherine the Great deposed her husband Peter III with the help of her lover, whereas the widowed Catherine Mingott is reportedly uninvolved in romantic intrigue. Wharton based the character on her aunt, Mary Mason Jones, who defied convention by building a mansion in uptown Manhattan in the 1850s.

Mme. Taglioni Marie Taglioni (1804–1884), the most renowned ballerina of the Romantic period, was best known for her title role in *La Sylphide*.

shoulder and bosom than New York was accustomed to seeing, at least in ladies who had reasons for wishing to pass unnoticed.

Few things seemed to Newland Archer more awful than an offence against "Taste," that far-off divinity of whom "Form" was the mere visible representative and vicegerent. Madame Olenska's pale and serious face appealed to his fancy as suited to the occasion and to her unhappy situation; but the way her dress (which had no tucker) sloped away from her thin shoulders shocked and troubled him. He hated to think of May Welland's being exposed to the influence of a young woman so careless of the dictates of Taste.

"After all," he heard one of the younger men begin behind him (everybody talked through the Mephistopheles-and-Martha scenes), "after all, just *what* happened?"

"Well—she left him; nobody attempts to deny that."

"He's an awful brute, isn't he?" continued the young enquirer, a candid Thorley, who was evidently preparing to enter the lists as the lady's champion.

"The very worst; I knew him at Nice," said Lawrence Lefferts with authority. "A half-paralysed white sneering fellow—rather handsome head, but eyes with a lot of lashes. Well, I'll tell you the sort: when he wasn't with women he was collecting china. Paying any price for both, I understand."

There was a general laugh, and the young champion said: "Well, then—?"

"Well, then; she bolted with his secretary."

"Oh, I see." The champion's face fell.

"It didn't last long, though: I heard of her a few months later living alone in Venice. I believe Lovell Mingott went out to get her. He said she was desperately unhappy. That's all right—but this parading her at the Opera's another thing."

"Perhaps," young Thorley hazarded, "she's too unhappy to be left at home."

This was greeted with an irreverent laugh, and the youth blushed deeply, and tried to look as if he had meant to insinuate what knowing people called a *"double entendre."*

Mephistopheles-and-Martha scenes   In Act 3 of *Faust*, Mephistopheles seduces Marguerite's guardian Martha so that Faust can approach Marguerite.

"double entendre"   French: a word or phrase with a second meaning, especially one that is risqué.

"Well—it's queer to have brought Miss Welland, anyhow," some one said in a low tone, with a side-glance at Archer.

"Oh, that's part of the campaign: Granny's orders, no doubt," Lefferts laughed. "When the old lady does a thing she does it thoroughly."

The act was ending, and there was a general stir in the box. Suddenly Newland Archer felt himself impelled to decisive action. The desire to be the first man to enter Mrs. Mingott's box, to proclaim to the waiting world his engagement to May Welland, and to see her through whatever difficulties her cousin's anomalous situation might involve her in; this impulse had abruptly overruled all scruples and hesitations, and sent him hurrying through the red corridors to the farther side of the house.

As he entered the box his eyes met Miss Welland's, and he saw that she had instantly understood his motive, though the family dignity which both considered so high a virtue would not permit her to tell him so. The persons of their world lived in an atmosphere of faint implications and pale delicacies, and the fact that he and she understood each other without a word seemed to the young man to bring them nearer than any explanation would have done. Her eyes said: "You see why Mamma brought me," and his answered: "I would not for the world have had you stay away."

"You know my niece Countess Olenska?" Mrs. Welland enquired as she shook hands with her future son-in-law. Archer bowed without extending his hand, as was the custom on being introduced to a lady; and Ellen Olenska bent her head slightly, keeping her own pale-gloved hands clasped on her huge fan of eagle feathers. Having greeted Mrs. Lovell Mingott, a large blonde lady in creaking satin, he sat down beside his betrothed, and said in a low tone: "I hope you've told Madame Olenska that we're engaged? I want everybody to know—I want you to let me announce it this evening at the ball."

Miss Welland's face grew rosy as the dawn, and she looked at him with radiant eyes. "If you can persuade Mamma," she said; "but why should we change what is already settled?" He made no answer but that which his eyes returned, and she added, still more confidently smiling: "Tell

---

fan of eagle feathers An important fashion accessory in the nineteenth century, the lady's fan was useful for creating an appearance of modesty as well as for cooling. At one point demand was so great that the eagle, national bird of the United States, became an endangered species. Wharton may be suggesting that nature itself is sometimes sacrificed to satisfy requirements of fashion or convention.

satin A dressy silk fabric with a shiny surface on one side. Its stiffness makes a "creaky" sound.

my cousin yourself: I give you leave. She says she used to play with you when you were children."

She made way for him by pushing back her chair, and promptly, and a little ostentatiously, with the desire that the whole house should see what he was doing, Archer seated himself at the Countess Olenska's side.

"We *did* use to play together, didn't we?" she asked, turning her grave eyes to his. "You were a horrid boy, and kissed me once behind a door; but it was your cousin Vandie Newland, who never looked at me, that I was in love with." Her glance swept the horse-shoe curve of boxes. "Ah, how this brings it all back to me—I see everybody here in knickerbockers and pantalettes," she said, with her trailing slightly foreign accent, her eyes returning to his face.

Agreeable as their expression was, the young man was shocked that they should reflect so unseemly a picture of the august tribunal before which, at that very moment, her case was being tried. Nothing could be in worse taste than misplaced flippancy; and he answered somewhat stiffly: "Yes, you have been away a very long time."

"Oh, centuries and centuries; so long," she said, "that I'm sure I'm dead and buried, and this dear old place is heaven;" which, for reasons he could not define, struck Newland Archer as an even more disrespectful way of describing New York society.

III

It invariably happened in the same way.

Mrs. Julius Beaufort, on the night of her annual ball, never failed to appear at the Opera; indeed, she always gave her ball on an Opera night in order to emphasise her complete superiority to household cares, and her possession of a staff of servants competent to organise every detail of the entertainment in her absence.

The Beauforts' house was one of the few in New York that possessed a ball-room (it antedated even Mrs. Manson Mingott's and the Headly Chiverses'); and at a time when it was beginning to be thought "provincial" to put a "crash" over the drawing-room floor and move the furniture

---

knickerbockers and pantalettes Knickerbockers, worn by boys in the nineteenth century, were full pants gathered and banded just below the knee. Pantalettes, worn by girls or women at mid-century, were long underpants trimmed with ruffles and lace that extended below the skirt.

"crash" Coarse, light fabric of cotton or linen.

upstairs, the possession of a ball-room that was used for no other purpose, and left for three-hundred-and-sixty-four days of the year to shuttered darkness, with its gilt chairs stacked in a corner and its chandelier in a bag; this undoubted superiority was felt to compensate for whatever was regrettable in the Beaufort past.

Mrs. Archer, who was fond of coining her social philosophy into axioms, had once said: "We all have our pet common people—" and though the phrase was a daring one, its truth was secretly admitted in many an exclusive bosom. But the Beauforts were not exactly common; some people said they were even worse. Mrs. Beaufort belonged indeed to one of America's most honoured families; she had been the lovely Regina Dallas (of the South Carolina branch), a penniless beauty introduced to New York society by her cousin, the imprudent Medora Manson, who was always doing the wrong thing from the right motive. When one was related to the Mansons and the Rushworths one had a *"droit de cité"* (as Mr. Sillerton Jackson, who had frequented the Tuileries, called it) in New York society; but did one not forfeit it in marrying Julius Beaufort?

The question was: who *was* Beaufort? He passed for an Englishman, was agreeable, handsome, ill-tempered, hospitable and witty. He had come to America with letters of recommendation from old Mrs. Manson Mingott's English son-in-law, the banker, and had speedily made himself an important position in the world of affairs; but his habits were dissipated, his tongue was bitter, his antecedents were mysterious; and when Medora Manson announced her cousin's engagement to him it was felt to be one more act of folly in poor Medora's long record of imprudences.

But folly is as often justified of her children as wisdom, and two years after young Mrs. Beaufort's marriage it was admitted that she had the most distinguished house in New York. No one knew exactly how the miracle was accomplished. She was indolent, passive, the caustic even called her dull; but dressed like an idol, hung with pearls, growing younger and blonder and more beautiful each year, she throned in Mr. Beaufort's heavy brown-stone palace, and drew all the world there without lifting her jewelled little finger. The knowing people said it was Beaufort himself who trained the servants, taught the *chef* new dishes, told the gardeners what hot-house flowers to grow for the dinner-table and the drawing-rooms, selected the guests, brewed the after-dinner punch and dictated the little notes his wife wrote to her friends. If he did, these domestic activities were privately performed, and he presented to the world the appearance of a careless and hospitable millionaire strolling into his own drawing-room

---

"droit de cité"   French: right of citizenship, or acceptance.

with the detachment of an invited guest, and saying: "My wife's gloxinias are a marvel, aren't they? I believe she gets them out from Kew."

Mr. Beaufort's secret, people were agreed, was the way he carried things off. It was all very well to whisper that he had been "helped" to leave England by the international banking-house in which he had been employed; he carried off that rumour as casually as the rest—though New York's business conscience was no less sensitive than its moral standard—he carried everything before him, and all New York into his drawing-rooms, and for over twenty years now people had said they were "going to the Beauforts'" with the same tone of security as if they had said they were going to Mrs. Manson Mingott's, and with the added satisfaction of knowing they would get hot canvas-back ducks and vintage wines, instead of tepid Veuve Clicquot without a year and warmed-up croquettes from Philadelphia.

Mrs. Beaufort, then, had as usual appeared in her box just before the Jewel Song; and when, again as usual, she rose at the end of the third act, drew her opera cloak about her lovely shoulders, and disappeared, New York knew that meant that half an hour later the ball would begin.

The Beaufort house was one that New Yorkers were proud to show to foreigners, especially on the night of the annual ball. The Beauforts had been among the first people in New York to own their own red velvet carpet and have it rolled down the steps by their own footmen, under their own awning, instead of hiring it with the supper and the ball-room chairs. They had also inaugurated the custom of letting the ladies take their cloaks off in the hall, instead of shuffling up to the hostess's bedroom and recurling their hair with the aid of the gas-burner; Beaufort was understood to have said that he supposed all his wife's friends had maids who saw to it that they were properly *coiffées* when they left home.

Then the house had been boldly planned with a ball-room, so that, instead of squeezing through a narrow passage to get to it (as at the Chi-

---

gloxinias   A tropical plant with colorful, showy funnel-shaped flowers. In the nineteenth-century "language of flowers" (see note, p. 16), gloxinias conveyed a proud spirit.

Kew   The Royal Botanical Gardens at Kew, Surrey, near London, is considered one of the premiere gardens in the world.

canvas-back   A North American duck.

Veuve Cliquot   In Reims, France, the maker of fine champagne; also the name of this luxury wine.

Jewel Song   An aria Marguerite sings in Act 3 of *Faust* after receiving her suitor's gift of jewels and flowers.

coiffées   French: with hair properly done.

verses') one marched solemnly down a vista of enfiladed drawing-rooms, (the sea-green, the crimson and the *bouton d'or*), seeing from afar the many-candled lustres reflected in the polished parquetry, and beyond that the depths of a conservatory where camellias and tree-ferns arched their costly foliage over seats of black and gold bamboo.

Newland Archer, as became a young man of his position, strolled in somewhat late. He had left his overcoat with the silk-stockinged footmen (the stockings were one of Beaufort's few fatuities), had dawdled a while in the library hung with Spanish leather and furnished with Buhl and malachite, where a few men were chatting and putting on their dancing-gloves, and had finally joined the line of guests whom Mrs. Beaufort was receiving on the threshold of the crimson drawing-room.

Archer was distinctly nervous. He had not gone back to his club after the Opera (as the young bloods usually did), but, the night being fine, had walked for some distance up Fifth Avenue before turning back in the direction of the Beauforts' house. He was definitely afraid that the Mingotts might be going too far; that, in fact, they might have Granny Mingott's orders to bring the Countess Olenska to the ball.

From the tone of the club box he had perceived how grave a mistake that would be; and, though he was more than ever determined to "see the thing through," he felt less chivalrously eager to champion his betrothed's cousin than before their brief talk at the Opera.

Wandering on to the *bouton d'or* drawing-room (where Beaufort had had the audacity to hang "Love Victorious," the much-discussed nude of Bouguereau) Archer found Mrs. Welland and her daughter standing near

---

enfiladed drawing-rooms   Rooms situated in succession or a row so as to create a vista when the doors are open. The system obviated the need for corridors.

bouton d'or   French: a buttercup color suggesting gold or richness.

camellias   A plant from Asia with shiny evergreen leaves and showy, variously colored flowers. According to the "language of flowers," red camellias meant loveliness; white camellias meant unpretending excellence.

Buhl and malachite   Furniture either of ebony or painted black, made by André Charles Buhl (or Boulle, 1642–1732), a French cabinetmaker in the service of Louis XIV. The Buhl style, as it is known in England, relied on embellishing the wood with elaborate gilded mounts and metal, shell, pearl, or mineral inlays. Black furniture was equated with the venerable and was thought to go well with Gothic interiors. Buhl furniture connoted solid virtue based on sound tradition and reaffirmed authority over revolution and upheaval. Malachite is a bright green mineral that takes a high polish and is used as an inlay in Buhl.

"Love Victorious" . . . Bouguereau   William-Adolphe Bouguereau (1825–1905), a French painter influenced by the Renaissance masters and classical art, defended standard

the ball-room door. Couples were already gliding over the floor beyond: the light of the wax candles fell on revolving tulle skirts, on girlish heads wreathed with modest blossoms, on the dashing aigrettes and ornaments of the young married women's *coiffures,* and on the glitter of highly glazed shirt-fronts and fresh glacé gloves.

Miss Welland, evidently about to join the dancers, hung on the threshold, her lilies-of-the-valley in her hand (she carried no other bouquet), her face a little pale, her eyes burning with a candid excitement. A group of young men and girls were gathered about her, and there was much hand-clasping, laughing and pleasantry on which Mrs. Welland, standing slightly apart, shed the beam of a qualified approval. It was evident that Miss Welland was in the act of announcing her engagement, while her mother affected the air of parental reluctance considered suitable to the occasion.

Archer paused a moment. It was at his express wish that the announcement had been made, and yet it was not thus that he would have wished to have his happiness known. To proclaim it in the heat and noise of a crowded ball-room was to rob it of the fine bloom of privacy which should belong to things nearest the heart. His joy was so deep that this blurring of the surface left its essence untouched; but he would have liked to keep the surface pure too. It was something of a satisfaction to find that May Welland shared this feeling. Her eyes fled to his beseechingly, and their look said: "Remember, we're doing this because it's right."

No appeal could have found a more immediate response in Archer's breast; but he wished that the necessity of their action had been represented by some ideal reason, and not simply by poor Ellen Olenska. The group about Miss Welland made way for him with significant smiles, and after taking his share of the felicitations he drew his betrothed into the middle of the ball-room floor and put his arm about her waist.

---

academic training and generally restricted himself to classical, religious, and genre subjects. The sober nature of his 1860s work gave way to more playful portrayals in the 1870s, most notably *Nymphs and Satyr* (1873). English and American admirers widely collected his work, but it was devalued, especially by French critics who associated the academic style with sentimentality and bourgeois values. J. K. Huysmans called Bouguereau the "master in the hierarchy of mediocrity," opposed to all progressive ideas.

aigrettes   Plumage from an egret, a type of heron, used as a hair ornament.

coiffures   French: hairstyles.

glacé gloves   French: leather gloves with a smooth, shiny finish.

"Now we shan't have to talk," he said, smiling into her candid eyes, as they floated away on the soft waves of the Blue Danube.

She made no answer. Her lips trembled into a smile, but the eyes remained distant and serious, as if bent on some ineffable vision. "Dear," Archer whispered, pressing her to him: it was borne in on him that the first hours of being engaged, even if spent in a ball-room, had in them something grave and sacramental. What a new life it was going to be, with this whiteness, radiance, goodness at one's side!

The dance over, the two, as became an affianced couple, wandered into the conservatory; and sitting behind a tall screen of tree-ferns and camellias Newland pressed her gloved hand to his lips.

"You see I did as you asked me to," she said.

"Yes: I couldn't wait," he answered smiling. After a moment he added: "Only I wish it hadn't had to be at a ball."

"Yes, I know." She met his glance comprehendingly. "But after all—even here we're alone together, aren't we?"

"Oh, dearest—always!" Archer cried.

Evidently she was always going to understand; she was always going to say the right thing. The discovery made the cup of his bliss overflow, and he went on gaily: "The worst of it is that I want to kiss you and I can't." As he spoke he took a swift glance about the conservatory, assured himself of their momentary privacy, and catching her to him laid a fugitive pressure on her lips. To counteract the audacity of this proceeding he led her to a bamboo sofa in a less secluded part of the conservatory, and sitting down beside her broke a lily-of-the-valley from her bouquet. She sat silent, and the world lay like a sunlit valley at their feet.

"Did you tell my cousin Ellen?" she asked presently, as if she spoke through a dream.

He roused himself, and remembered that he had not done so. Some invincible repugnance to speak of such things to the strange foreign woman had checked the words on his lips.

"No—I hadn't the chance after all," he said, fibbing hastily.

"Ah." She looked disappointed, but gently resolved on gaining her point. "You must, then, for I didn't either; and I shouldn't like her to think—"

"Of course not. But aren't you, after all, the person to do it?"

She pondered on this. "If I'd done it at the right time, yes: but now that there's been a delay I think you must explain that I'd asked you to tell

---

Blue Danube "By the Beautiful Blue Danube," a waltz composed in 1867 by Johann Strauss II.

her at the Opera, before our speaking about it to everybody here. Otherwise she might think I had forgotten her. You see, she's one of the family, and she's been away so long that she's rather—sensitive."

Archer looked at her glowingly. "Dear and great angel! Of course I'll tell her." He glanced a trifle apprehensively toward the crowded ballroom. "But I haven't seen her yet. Has she come?"

"No; at the last minute she decided not to."

"At the last minute?" he echoed, betraying his surprise that she should ever have considered the alternative possible.

"Yes. She's awfully fond of dancing," the young girl answered simply. "But suddenly she made up her mind that her dress wasn't smart enough for a ball, though we thought it so lovely; and so my aunt had to take her home."

"Oh, well—" said Archer with happy indifference. Nothing about his betrothed pleased him more than her resolute determination to carry to its utmost limit that ritual of ignoring the "unpleasant" in which they had both been brought up.

"She knows as well as I do," he reflected, "the real reason of her cousin's staying away; but I shall never let her see by the least sign that I am conscious of there being a shadow of a shade on poor Ellen Olenska's reputation."

IV

In the course of the next day the first of the usual betrothal visits were exchanged. The New York ritual was precise and inflexible in such matters; and in conformity with it Newland Archer first went with his mother and sister to call on Mrs. Welland, after which he and Mrs. Welland and May drove out to old Mrs. Manson Mingott's to receive that venerable ancestress's blessing.

A visit to Mrs. Manson Mingott was always an amusing episode to the young man. The house in itself was already an historic document, though not, of course, as venerable as certain other old family houses in University Place and lower Fifth Avenue. Those were of the purest 1830, with a grim harmony of cabbage-rose-garlanded carpets, rosewood con-

---

University Place and lower Fifth Avenue   University Place runs parallel to Fifth Avenue, northeast of Washington Square. The southern end of Fifth Avenue was the oldest and most fashionable section of a neighborhood that expanded northward after 1850. Mrs. Mingott, with characteristic independence, moves ahead of the fashion, to an area near Central Park.

soles, round-arched fire-places with black marble mantels, and immense glazed book-cases of mahogany; whereas old Mrs. Mingott, who had built her house later, had bodily cast out the massive furniture of her prime, and mingled with the Mingott heirlooms the frivolous upholstery of the Second Empire. It was her habit to sit in a window of her sitting-room on the ground floor, as if watching calmly for life and fashion to flow northward to her solitary doors. She seemed in no hurry to have them come, for her patience was equalled by her confidence. She was sure that presently the hoardings, the quarries, the one-story saloons, the wooden green-houses in ragged gardens, and the rocks from which goats surveyed the scene, would vanish before the advance of residences as stately as her own—perhaps (for she was an impartial woman) even statelier; and that the cobblestones over which the old clattering omnibuses bumped would be replaced by smooth asphalt, such as people reported having seen in Paris. Meanwhile, as every one she cared to see came to *her* (and she could fill her rooms as easily as the Beauforts, and without adding a single item to the *menu* of her suppers), she did not suffer from her geographic isolation.

The immense accretion of flesh which had descended on her in middle life like a flood of lava on a doomed city had changed her from a plump active little woman with a neatly-turned foot and ankle into something as vast and august as a natural phenomenon. She had accepted this submergence as philosophically as all her other trials, and now, in extreme old age, was rewarded by presenting to her mirror an almost unwrinkled expanse of firm pink and white flesh, in the centre of which the traces of a small face survived as if awaiting excavation. A flight of smooth double chins led down to the dizzy depths of a still-snowy bosom veiled in snowy muslins that were held in place by a miniature portrait of the late Mr. Mingott; and around and below, wave after wave of black silk surged away over the edges of a capacious armchair, with two tiny white hands poised like gulls on the surface of the billows.

The burden of Mrs. Manson Mingott's flesh had long since made it impossible for her to go up and down stairs, and with characteristic

---

Second Empire   The period from 1852 to 1870, during the reign of Napoléon III. Characterized by ornamentation and eclecticism, it included classical, Gothic, and Baroque revival styles, gilded decoration, rich fabrics, and elaborate upholstery. The French style was undisputed until reformers such as Eastlake advocated more streamlined and craftsmanlike designs.

immense accretion of flesh . . . like a flood of lava   Pompeii, Italy, was buried by the eruption of Mount Vesuvius in 79 C.E. Volcanic ash preserved much of the city, which has since been excavated and is now an archaeological relic. Wharton describes natural processes that both destroy and preserve culture.

independence she had made her reception rooms upstairs and established herself (in flagrant violation of all the New York proprieties) on the ground floor of her house; so that, as you sat in her sitting-room window with her, you caught (through a door that was always open, and a looped-back yellow damask portière) the unexpected vista of a bedroom with a huge low bed upholstered like a sofa, and a toilet-table with frivolous lace flounces and a gilt-framed mirror.

Her visitors were startled and fascinated by the foreignness of this arrangement, which recalled scenes in French fiction, and architectural incentives to immorality such as the simple American had never dreamed of. That was how women with lovers lived in the wicked old societies, in apartments with all the rooms on one floor, and all the indecent propinquities that their novels described. It amused Newland Archer (who had secretly situated the love-scenes of "Monsieur de Camors" in Mrs. Mingott's bedroom) to picture her blameless life led in the stage-setting of adultery; but he said to himself, with considerable admiration, that if a lover had been what she wanted, the intrepid woman would have had him too.

To the general relief the Countess Olenska was not present in her grandmother's drawing-room during the visit of the betrothed couple. Mrs. Mingott said she had gone out; which, on a day of such glaring sunlight, and at the "shopping hour," seemed in itself an indelicate thing for a compromised woman to do. But at any rate it spared them the embarrassment of her presence, and the faint shadow that her unhappy past might seem to shed on their radiant future. The visit went off successfully, as was to have been expected. Old Mrs. Mingott was delighted with the engagement, which, being long foreseen by watchful relatives, had been carefully passed upon in family council; and the engagement ring, a large thick sapphire set in invisible claws, met with her unqualified admiration.

"It's the new setting: of course it shows the stone beautifully, but it looks a little bare to old-fashioned eyes," Mrs. Welland had explained, with a conciliatory side-glance at her future son-in-law.

---

looped-back yellow damask portière   Damask is a two-sided fabric woven so that the design on one side appears in reverse on the other side. The portière is a curtain hung over a doorway and pulled back to allow passage and a view of the room beyond.

"Monsieur de Camors"   A romance published in 1867 by popular French novelist and playwright Octave Feuillet (1821–1890). In this attack on aristocratic decadence, Louis de Camors has a secret rendezvous with the wife of his benefactor. The reference is ironic because Mrs. Mingott's chaste history is well known. It also suggests Archer's romantic tendencies.

"Old-fashioned eyes? I hope you don't mean mine, my dear? I like all the novelties," said the ancestress, lifting the stone to her small bright orbs, which no glasses had ever disfigured. "Very handsome," she added, returning the jewel; "very liberal. In my time a cameo set in pearls was thought sufficient. But it's the hand that sets off the ring, isn't it, my dear Mr. Archer?" and she waved one of her tiny hands, with small pointed nails and rolls of aged fat encircling the wrist like ivory bracelets. "Mine was modelled in Rome by the great Ferrigiani. You should have May's done: no doubt he'll have it done, my child. Her hand is large—it's these modern sports that spread the joints—but the skin is white.—And when's the wedding to be?" she broke off, fixing her eyes on Archer's face.

"Oh—" Mrs. Welland murmured, while the young man, smiling at his betrothed, replied: "As soon as ever it can, if only you'll back me up, Mrs. Mingott."

"We must give them time to get to know each other a little better, mamma," Mrs. Welland interposed, with the proper affectation of reluctance; to which the ancestress rejoined: "Know each other? Fiddlesticks! Everybody in New York has always known everybody. Let the young man have his way, my dear; don't wait till the bubble's off the wine. Marry them before Lent; I may catch pneumonia any winter now, and I want to give the wedding-breakfast."

These successive statements were received with the proper expressions of amusement, incredulity and gratitude; and the visit was breaking up in a vein of mild pleasantry when the door opened to admit the Countess Olenska, who entered in bonnet and mantle followed by the unexpected figure of Julius Beaufort.

There was a cousinly murmur of pleasure between the ladies, and Mrs. Mingott held out Ferrigiani's model to the banker. "Ha! Beaufort, this is a rare favour!" (She had an odd foreign way of addressing men by their surnames.)

"Thanks. I wish it might happen oftener," said the visitor in his easy arrogant way. "I'm generally so tied down; but I met the Countess Ellen in Madison Square, and she was good enough to let me walk home with her."

Lent   In Christian churches, the forty-day period from Ash Wednesday to Easter Eve spent in prayer, penance, and abstinence in commemoration of Jesus' fasting in the wilderness. Rituals of celebration, such as marriage, would not take place during Lent.

Madison Square   Originally a neighborhood on the east side of Manhattan named for President James Madison in 1814, bounded by 26th Street on the north, by Madison Avenue on the east, by 23rd Street on the south, and by Broadway and Fifth Avenue on the west. Soon all that remained was a square that opened in 1847 and was from the

"Ah—I hope the house will be gayer, now that Ellen's here!" cried Mrs. Mingott with a glorious effrontery. "Sit down—sit down, Beaufort: push up the yellow armchair; now I've got you I want a good gossip. I hear your ball was magnificent; and I understand you invited Mrs. Lemuel Struthers? Well—I've a curiosity to see the woman myself."

She had forgotten her relatives, who were drifting out into the hall under Ellen Olenska's guidance. Old Mrs. Mingott had always professed a great admiration for Julius Beaufort, and there was a kind of kinship in their cool domineering way and their short-cuts through the conventions. Now she was eagerly curious to know what had decided the Beauforts to invite (for the first time) Mrs. Lemuel Struthers, the widow of Struthers's Shoe-polish, who had returned the previous year from a long initiatory sojourn in Europe to lay siege to the tight little citadel of New York. "Of course if you and Regina invite her the thing is settled. Well, we need new blood and new money—and I hear she's still very good-looking," the carnivorous old lady declared.

In the hall, while Mrs. Welland and May drew on their furs, Archer saw that the Countess Olenska was looking at him with a faintly questioning smile.

"Of course you know already—about May and me," he said, answering her look with a shy laugh. "She scolded me for not giving you the news last night at the Opera: I had her orders to tell you that we were engaged—but I couldn't, in that crowd."

The smile passed from Countess Olenska's eyes to her lips: she looked younger, more like the bold brown Ellen Mingott of his boyhood. "Of course I know; yes. And I'm so glad. But one doesn't tell such things first in a crowd." The ladies were on the threshold and she held out her hand.

"Good-bye; come and see me some day," she said, still looking at Archer.

In the carriage, on the way down Fifth Avenue, they talked pointedly of Mrs. Mingott, of her age, her spirit, and all her wonderful attributes. No one alluded to Ellen Olenska; but Archer knew that Mrs. Welland was thinking: "It's a mistake for Ellen to be seen, the very day after her arrival, parading up Fifth Avenue at the crowded hour with Julius Beaufort—" and the young man himself mentally added: "And she ought to know that a man who's just engaged doesn't spend his time calling on married women.

1850s to 1870s the center of aristocratic brownstones where Edith Wharton, Theodore Roosevelt, and other old-line New Yorkers were born. Madison Square eventually became the home of newly moneyed residents—thus Ellen meets Beaufort there—whereas Washington Square remained the neighborhood of the aristocracy.

But I daresay in the set she's lived in they do—they never do anything else."
And, in spite of the cosmopolitan views on which he prided himself, he
thanked heaven that he was a New Yorker, and about to ally himself with
one of his own kind.

V

The next evening old Mr. Sillerton Jackson came to dine with the Archers.
   Mrs. Archer was a shy woman and shrank from society; but she liked
to be well-informed as to its doings. Her old friend Mr. Sillerton Jackson
applied to the investigation of his friends' affairs the patience of a collector and the science of a naturalist; and his sister, Miss Sophy Jackson, who
lived with him, and was entertained by all the people who could not secure
her much-sought-after brother, brought home bits of minor gossip that
filled out usefully the gaps in his picture.
   Therefore, whenever anything happened that Mrs. Archer wanted to
know about, she asked Mr. Jackson to dine; and as she honoured few
people with her invitations, and as she and her daughter Janey were an excellent audience, Mr. Jackson usually came himself instead of sending his
sister. If he could have dictated all the conditions, he would have chosen
the evenings when Newland was out; not because the young man was un-
congenial to him (the two got on capitally at their club) but because the
old anecdotist sometimes felt, on Newland's part, a tendency to weigh his
evidence that the ladies of the family never showed.
   Mr. Jackson, if perfection had been attainable on earth, would also
have asked that Mrs. Archer's food should be a little better. But then New
York, as far back as the mind of man could travel, had been divided into
the two great fundamental groups of the Mingotts and Mansons and all
their clan, who cared about eating and clothes and money, and the Archer-
Newland-van-der-Luyden tribe, who were devoted to travel, horticulture
and the best fiction, and looked down on the grosser forms of pleasure.
   You couldn't have everything, after all. If you dined with the Lovell
Mingotts you got canvas-back and terrapin and vintage wines; at Adeline
Archer's you could talk about Alpine scenery and "The Marble Faun";

---

terrapin   A turtle from the coasts of the Atlantic Ocean and Gulf of Mexico known for
its delicate flavor.

"The Marble Faun"   An 1860 romance novel by American author Nathaniel Hawthorne (1804–1864). Set in Rome, the novel examines Puritan morality in the context
of European art and faith. Donatello, a sensual, amoral admirer of the beautiful and

and luckily the Archer Madeira had gone round the Cape. Therefore when a friendly summons came from Mrs. Archer, Mr. Jackson, who was a true eclectic, would usually say to his sister: "I've been a little gouty since my last dinner at the Lovell Mingotts'—it will do me good to diet at Adeline's."

Mrs. Archer, who had long been a widow, lived with her son and daughter in West Twenty-eighth Street. An upper floor was dedicated to Newland, and the two women squeezed themselves into narrower quarters below. In an unclouded harmony of tastes and interests they cultivated ferns in Wardian cases, made macramé lace and wool embroidery on linen, collected American revolutionary glazed ware, subscribed to "Good Words," and read Ouida's novels for the sake of the Italian atmosphere. (They preferred those about peasant life, because of the descriptions of scenery and the pleasanter sentiments, though in general they liked novels about people in society, whose motives and habits were more comprehensible, spoke severely of Dickens, who "had never drawn a gentleman," and

---

mysterious Miriam, moves from innocence to experience after being driven to kill her stranger pursuer, Antonio. Witnessing the murder, the pale New England artist Hilda confesses to a Catholic priest and then marries an American sculptor, Kenyon. Miriam disappears into the shadowy realm from which she came.

Madeira   A fortified wine resembling sherry produced in Madeira, a Portuguese island off the west coast of Africa. The importation of the wine around Cape Horn, a considerable distance, attests to its quality.

Wardian cases   Dome-shaped glass cases under which ferns and other plants were grown indoors. Introduced in mid-century, they were popular items in Victorian furnishing. The cases were named after Nathaniel Bagshaw Ward (1791–1868), who in 1829 accidentally discovered this method of growing plants.

macramé lace   Coarse lacework made from weaving and knotting cords into a pattern.

"Good Words"   *Good Words,* edited by Scotsman and Queen's Chaplain Norman MacLeod, started as a weekly religious magazine in the 1860s. Later issued as a monthly, it was very successful, outselling even the popular *Cornhill Magazine*. The conservative, European-conscious Archer women would be likely subscribers to a magazine such as *Good Words*.

Ouida's novels   Ouida was the pseudonym of English writer Marie Louise de la Ramée (1839–1908), who wrote many novels of romantic exploits as well as the children's classic, *A Dog of Flanders* (1872).

Dickens   Charles Dickens (1812–1870) is considered one of the greatest English writers. His novels combine vast social panoramas, compassion for the lower classes, melodrama, and comic endurance. The conservative Archer women may speak "severely" of him because early novels such as *Oliver Twist* (1837–39) show Dickens's trust in a new commercial class rather than the old aristocracy. Later novels, such as *Bleak House* (1853), also reveal his disenchantment with the business ethic and a corrupt judicial system.

considered Thackeray less at home in the great world than Bulwer—who, however, was beginning to be thought old-fashioned.)

Mrs. and Miss Archer were both great lovers of scenery. It was what they principally sought and admired on their occasional travels abroad; considering architecture and painting as subjects for men, and chiefly for learned persons who read Ruskin. Mrs. Archer had been born a Newland, and mother and daughter, who were as like as sisters, were both, as people said, "true Newlands"; tall, pale, and slightly round-shouldered, with long noses, sweet smiles and a kind of drooping distinction like that in certain faded Reynolds portraits. Their physical resemblance would have been complete if an elderly *embonpoint* had not stretched Mrs. Archer's black brocade, while Miss Archer's brown and purple poplins hung, as the years went on, more and more slackly on her virgin frame.

Mentally, the likeness between them, as Newland was aware, was less complete than their identical mannerisms often made it appear. The long

---

Thackeray William Makepeace Thackeray (1811–1863) was an English novelist known for his satires of middle-class life. Born into a wealthy family, he lost his inheritance, whereupon he turned to painting and then to writing. He is best known for his sketches and his novel, *Vanity Fair* (1847–48), which depicts self-serving, pompous characters in competition with morally virtuous ones.

Bulwer Edward George Earle Lytton Bulwer-Lytton (1803–1873) was an English member of Parliament and a novelist and dramatist. He is best remembered for his historical novel, *The Last Days of Pompeii* (1834). Scholarly in detail and thrilling in plot, his books held the interest of generations of readers.

Ruskin John Ruskin (1819–1900) was an English art critic and social theorist with a national and international audience. Departing from classical frameworks, Ruskin stressed the active nature of the aesthetic process and argued for the artist's sense of the whole conception of truth rather than a mere "garland of thoughts." Creating not so much narratives about the work of art as stories of visual and kinesthetic journeys around a particular painting or sculpture, Ruskin urged his audience to read signs well and endeavor to change their environment in order that art may survive and beauty flow. He transformed the discussion of art in the nineteenth century, pointing his audience toward the empirical experience, emphasizing art's accessibility, and continually crossing boundaries between artistic and nonartistic disciplines. Although Ruskin occasionally addressed women directly (in his 1871 *Sesame and Lilies,* for example), Archer's conventional sister and mother may have found him too dynamic. In contrast, Archer, whose boyhood, Wharton writes in chap. 9, "had been saturated with Ruskin," prides himself on being current.

Reynolds English painter Sir Joshua Reynolds (1723–1792) was one of the most celebrated portrait painters of his time. He used a technique called the "grand manner," lectured on the value of academic art, and painted the literary and political elite of his age.

embonpoint French: stoutness.

poplins Dresses made of a ribbed fabric such as silk, wool, or cotton.

habit of living together in mutually dependent intimacy had given them the same vocabulary, and the same habit of beginning their phrases "Mother thinks" or "Janey thinks," according as one or the other wished to advance an opinion of her own; but in reality, while Mrs. Archer's serene unimaginativeness rested easily in the accepted and familiar, Janey was subject to starts and aberrations of fancy welling up from springs of suppressed romance.

Mother and daughter adored each other and revered their son and brother; and Archer loved them with a tenderness made compunctious and uncritical by the sense of their exaggerated admiration, and by his secret satisfaction in it. After all, he thought it a good thing for a man to have his authority respected in his own house, even if his sense of humour sometimes made him question the force of his mandate.

On this occasion the young man was very sure that Mr. Jackson would rather have had him dine out; but he had his own reasons for not doing so.

Of course old Jackson wanted to talk about Ellen Olenska, and of course Mrs. Archer and Janey wanted to hear what he had to tell. All three would be slightly embarrassed by Newland's presence, now that his prospective relation to the Mingott clan had been made known; and the young man waited with an amused curiosity to see how they would turn the difficulty.

They began, obliquely, by talking about Mrs. Lemuel Struthers.

"It's a pity the Beauforts asked her," Mrs. Archer said gently. "But then Regina always does what he tells her; and *Beaufort*—"

"Certain *nuances* escape Beaufort," said Mr. Jackson, cautiously inspecting the broiled shad, and wondering for the thousandth time why Mrs. Archer's cook always burnt the roe to a cinder. (Newland, who had long shared his wonder, could always detect it in the older man's expression of melancholy disapproval.)

"Oh, necessarily; Beaufort is a vulgar man," said Mrs. Archer. "My grandfather Newland always used to say to my mother: 'Whatever you do, don't let that fellow Beaufort be introduced to the girls.' But at least he's had the advantage of associating with gentlemen; in England too, they say. It's all very mysterious—" She glanced at Janey and paused. She and Janey

---

nuances   French: slight degrees of difference, as in meaning, color, or tone.

shad . . . roe   Shad is a herringlike fish that was abundant in the Hudson River in the nineteenth century. Roe is the egg-laden ovary or egg mass of the fish, considered a delicacy. Shad and roe were seasonal dishes served in the springtime, according to one nineteenth-century recipe, with asparagus.

knew every fold of the Beaufort mystery, but in public Mrs. Archer continued to assume that the subject was not one for the unmarried.

"But this Mrs. Struthers," Mrs. Archer continued; "what did you say *she* was, Sillerton?"

"Out of a mine: or rather out of the saloon at the head of the pit. Then with Living Wax-Works, touring New England. After the police broke *that* up, they say she lived—" Mr. Jackson in his turn glanced at Janey, whose eyes began to bulge from under her prominent lids. There were still hiatuses for her in Mrs. Struthers's past.

"Then," Mr. Jackson continued (and Archer saw he was wondering why no one had told the butler never to slice cucumbers with a steel knife), "then Lemuel Struthers came along. They say his advertiser used the girl's head for the shoe-polish posters; her hair's intensely black, you know—the Egyptian style. Anyhow, he—eventually—married her." There were volumes of innuendo in the way the "eventually" was spaced, and each syllable given its due stress.

"Oh, well—at the pass we've come to nowadays, it doesn't matter," said Mrs. Archer indifferently. The ladies were not really interested in Mrs. Struthers just then; the subject of Ellen Olenska was too fresh and too absorbing to them. Indeed, Mrs. Struthers's name had been introduced by Mrs. Archer only that she might presently be able to say: "And Newland's new cousin—Countess Olenska? Was *she* at the ball too?"

There was a faint touch of sarcasm in the reference to her son, and Archer knew it and had expected it. Even Mrs. Archer, who was seldom unduly pleased with human events, had been altogether glad of her son's engagement. ("Especially after that silly business with Mrs. Rushworth," as she had remarked to Janey, alluding to what had once seemed to Newland a tragedy of which his soul would always bear the scar.) There was no better match in New York than May Welland, look at the question from whatever point you chose. Of course such a marriage was only what Newland was entitled to; but young men are so foolish and incalculable—and some women so ensnaring and unscrupulous—that it was nothing short of a miracle to see one's only son safe past the Siren Isle and in the haven of a blameless domesticity.

All this Mrs. Archer felt, and her son knew she felt; but he knew also that she had been perturbed by the premature announcement of his

---

Siren Isle   In Greek mythology, the sirens were deceitful creatures, half-woman and half-bird, who lured sailors to their death with their singing. In Homer's *Odyssey*, Odysseus safely sails past the island by stopping the ears of his crew with wax and by having himself bound to the ship's mast when he hears the sirens' call.

engagement, or rather by its cause; and it was for that reason—because on the whole he was a tender and indulgent master—that he had stayed at home that evening. "It's not that I don't approve of the Mingotts' *esprit de corps;* but why Newland's engagement should be mixed up with that Olenska woman's comings and goings I don't see," Mrs. Archer grumbled to Janey, the only witness of her slight lapses from perfect sweetness.

She had behaved beautifully—and in beautiful behaviour she was unsurpassed—during the call on Mrs. Welland; but Newland knew (and his betrothed doubtless guessed) that all through the visit she and Janey were nervously on the watch for Madame Olenska's possible intrusion; and when they left the house together she had permitted herself to say to her son: "I'm thankful that Augusta Welland received us alone."

These indications of inward disturbance moved Archer the more that he too felt that the Mingotts had gone a little too far. But, as it was against all the rules of their code that the mother and son should ever allude to what was uppermost in their thoughts, he simply replied: "Oh, well, there's always a phase of family parties to be gone through when one gets engaged, and the sooner it's over the better." At which his mother merely pursed her lips under the lace veil that hung down from her grey velvet bonnet trimmed with frosted grapes.

Her revenge, he felt—her lawful revenge—would be to "draw" Mr. Jackson that evening on the Countess Olenska; and, having publicly done his duty as a future member of the Mingott clan, the young man had no objection to hearing the lady discussed in private—except that the subject was already beginning to bore him.

Mr. Jackson had helped himself to a slice of the tepid *filet* which the mournful butler had handed him with a look as sceptical as his own, and had rejected the mushroom sauce after a scarcely perceptible sniff. He looked baffled and hungry, and Archer reflected that he would probably finish his meal on Ellen Olenska.

Mr. Jackson leaned back in his chair, and glanced up at the candlelit Archers, Newlands and van der Luydens hanging in dark frames on the dark walls.

"Ah, how your grandfather Archer loved a good dinner, my dear Newland!" he said, his eyes on the portrait of a plump full-chested young man in a stock and a blue coat, with a view of a white-columned country-

---

esprit de corps   French: A show of solidarity.

stock   A broad scarf that men wore around the neck in the eighteenth and nineteenth centuries.

house behind him. "Well—well—well . . . I wonder what he would have said to all these foreign marriages!"

Mrs. Archer ignored the allusion to the ancestral *cuisine* and Mr. Jackson continued with deliberation: "No, she was *not* at the ball."

"Ah—" Mrs. Archer murmured, in a tone that implied: "She had that decency."

"Perhaps the Beauforts don't know her," Janey suggested, with her artless malice.

Mr. Jackson gave a faint sip, as if he had been tasting invisible Madeira. "Mrs. Beaufort may not—but Beaufort certainly does, for she was seen walking up Fifth Avenue this afternoon with him by the whole of New York."

"Mercy—" moaned Mrs. Archer, evidently perceiving the uselessness of trying to ascribe the actions of foreigners to a sense of delicacy.

"I wonder if she wears a round hat or a bonnet in the afternoon," Janey speculated. "At the Opera I know she had on dark blue velvet, perfectly plain and flat—like a night-gown."

"Janey!" said her mother; and Miss Archer blushed and tried to look audacious.

"It was, at any rate, in better taste not to go to the ball," Mrs. Archer continued.

A spirit of perversity moved her son to rejoin: "I don't think it was a question of taste with her. May said she meant to go, and then decided that the dress in question wasn't smart enough."

Mrs. Archer smiled at this confirmation of her inference. "Poor Ellen," she simply remarked; adding compassionately: "We must always bear in mind what an eccentric bringing-up Medora Manson gave her. What can you expect of a girl who was allowed to wear black satin at her coming-out ball?"

"Ah—don't I remember her in it!" said Mr. Jackson; adding: "Poor girl!" in the tone of one who, while enjoying the memory, had fully understood at the time what the sight portended.

"It's odd," Janey remarked, "that she should have kept such an ugly name as Ellen. I should have changed it to Elaine." She glanced about the table to see the effect of this.

Her brother laughed. "Why Elaine?"

"I don't know; it sounds more—more Polish," said Janey, blushing.

---

coming-out ball   The social occasion when a young woman, or débutante, makes her formal entry into society.

"It sounds more conspicuous; and that can hardly be what she wishes," said Mrs. Archer distantly.

"Why not?" broke in her son, growing suddenly argumentative. "Why shouldn't she be conspicuous if she chooses? Why should she slink about as if it were she who had disgraced herself? She's 'poor Ellen' certainly, because she had the bad luck to make a wretched marriage; but I don't see that that's a reason for hiding her head as if she were the culprit."

"That, I suppose," said Mr. Jackson, speculatively, "is the line the Mingotts mean to take."

The young man reddened. "I didn't have to wait for their cue, if that's what you mean, sir. Madame Olenska has had an unhappy life: that doesn't make her an outcast."

"There are rumours," began Mr. Jackson, glancing at Janey.

"Oh, I know: the secretary," the young man took him up. "Nonsense, mother; Janey's grown-up. They say, don't they," he went on, "that the secretary helped her to get away from her brute of a husband, who kept her practically a prisoner? Well, what if he did? I hope there isn't a man among us who wouldn't have done the same in such a case."

Mr. Jackson glanced over his shoulder to say to the sad butler: "Perhaps . . . that sauce . . . just a little, after all—"; then, having helped himself, he remarked: "I'm told she's looking for a house. She means to live here."

"I hear she means to get a divorce," said Janey boldly.

"I hope she will!" Archer exclaimed.

The word had fallen like a bombshell in the pure and tranquil atmosphere of the Archer dining-room. Mrs. Archer raised her delicate eyebrows in the particular curve that signified: "The butler—" and the young man, himself mindful of the bad taste of discussing such intimate matters in public, hastily branched off into an account of his visit to old Mrs. Mingott.

After dinner, according to immemorial custom, Mrs. Archer and Janey trailed their long silk draperies up to the drawing-room, where, while the gentlemen smoked below stairs, they sat beside a Carcel lamp with an engraved globe, facing each other across a rosewood work-table

---

Carcel lamp   An oil lamp invented by Frenchman Bernard Guillaume Carcel in 1798 (patented 1800). His spring-operated mechanism made operation of the lamp easier, but because the mechanism was delicate it could only be entrusted to the most careful, well-trained servants.

rosewood   A high-quality dark brown wood with a rose scent, taken from trees native to the tropics and used for furniture.

with a green silk bag under it, and stitched at the two ends of a tapestry band of field-flowers destined to adorn an "occasional" chair in the drawing-room of young Mrs. Newland Archer.

While this rite was in progress in the drawing-room, Archer settled Mr. Jackson in an armchair near the fire in the Gothic library and handed him a cigar. Mr. Jackson sank into the armchair with satisfaction, lit his cigar with perfect confidence (it was Newland who bought them), and stretching his thin old ankles to the coals, said: "You say the secretary merely helped her to get away, my dear fellow? Well, he was still helping her a year later, then; for somebody met 'em living at Lausanne together."

Newland reddened. "Living together? Well, why not? Who had the right to make her life over if she hadn't? I'm sick of the hypocrisy that would bury alive a woman of her age if her husband prefers to live with harlots."

He stopped and turned away angrily to light his cigar. "Women ought to be free—as free as we are," he declared, making a discovery of which he was too irritated to measure the terrific consequences.

Mr. Sillerton Jackson stretched his ankles nearer the coals and emitted a sardonic whistle.

"Well," he said after a pause, "apparently Count Olenski takes your view; for I never heard of his having lifted a finger to get his wife back."

VI

That evening, after Mr. Jackson had taken himself away, and the ladies had retired to their chintz-curtained bedroom, Newland Archer mounted thoughtfully to his own study. A vigilant hand had, as usual, kept the fire alive and the lamp trimmed; and the room, with its rows and rows of books, its bronze and steel statuettes of "The Fencers" on the mantelpiece and its many photographs of famous pictures, looked singularly home-like and welcoming.

As he dropped into his armchair near the fire his eyes rested on a large photograph of May Welland, which the young girl had given him in the first days of their romance, and which had now displaced all the other portraits on the table. With a new sense of awe he looked at the frank

---

Lausanne   A Swiss city on the north shore of Lake Geneva known as a popular tourist destination.

chintz   A cotton cloth printed with colored designs and usually glazed.

forehead, serious eyes and gay innocent mouth of the young creature whose soul's custodian he was to be. That terrifying product of the social system he belonged to and believed in, the young girl who knew nothing and expected everything, looked back at him like a stranger through May Welland's familiar features; and once more it was borne in on him that marriage was not the safe anchorage he had been taught to think, but a voyage on uncharted seas.

The case of the Countess Olenska had stirred up old settled convictions and set them drifting dangerously through his mind. His own exclamation: "Women should be free—as free as we are," struck to the root of a problem that it was agreed in his world to regard as non-existent. "Nice" women, however wronged, would never claim the kind of freedom he meant, and generous-minded men like himself were therefore—in the heat of argument—the more chivalrously ready to concede it to them. Such verbal generosities were in fact only a humbugging disguise of the inexorable conventions that tied things together and bound people down to the old pattern. But here he was pledged to defend, on the part of his betrothed's cousin, conduct that, on his own wife's part, would justify him in calling down on her all the thunders of Church and State. Of course the dilemma was purely hypothetical; since he wasn't a blackguard Polish nobleman, it was absurd to speculate what his wife's rights would be if he *were*. But Newland Archer was too imaginative not to feel that, in his case and May's, the tie might gall for reasons far less gross and palpable. What could he and she really know of each other, since it was his duty, as a "decent" fellow, to conceal his past from her, and hers, as a marriageable girl, to have no past to conceal? What if, for some one of the subtler reasons that would tell with both of them, they should tire of each other, misunderstand or irritate each other? He reviewed his friends' marriages—the supposedly happy ones—and saw none that answered, even remotely, to the passionate and tender comradeship which he pictured as his permanent relation with May Welland. He perceived that such a picture presupposed, on her part, the experience, the versatility, the freedom of judgment, which she had been carefully trained not to possess; and with a shiver of foreboding he saw his marriage becoming what most of the other marriages about him were: a dull association of material and social interests held together by ignorance on the one side and hypocrisy on the other. Lawrence Lefferts occurred to him as the husband who had most completely realised this enviable ideal. As became the high-priest of form, he had formed a wife so completely to his own convenience that, in the most conspicuous moments of his frequent love-affairs with other men's wives, she went about in smiling unconsciousness, saying that "Lawrence was so frightfully strict"; and had been known to blush indignantly, and avert her gaze, when some one alluded in her presence to the fact that Julius Beaufort (as became a "foreigner" of doubtful origin) had what was known in New York as "another establishment."

Archer tried to console himself with the thought that he was not quite such an ass as Larry Lefferts, nor May such a simpleton as poor Gertrude; but the difference was after all one of intelligence and not of standards. In reality they all lived in a kind of hieroglyphic world, where the real thing was never said or done or even thought, but only represented by a set of arbitrary signs; as when Mrs. Welland, who knew exactly why Archer had pressed her to announce her daughter's engagement at the Beaufort ball (and had indeed expected him to do no less), yet felt obliged to simulate reluctance, and the air of having had her hand forced, quite as, in the books on Primitive Man that people of advanced culture were beginning to read, the savage bride is dragged with shrieks from her parents' tent.

The result, of course, was that the young girl who was the centre of this elaborate system of mystification remained the more inscrutable for her very frankness and assurance. She was frank, poor darling, because she had nothing to conceal, assured because she knew of nothing to be on her guard against; and with no better preparation than this, she was to be plunged overnight into what people evasively called "the facts of life."

The young man was sincerely but placidly in love. He delighted in the radiant good looks of his betrothed, in her health, her horsemanship, her grace and quickness at games, and the shy interest in books and ideas that she was beginning to develop under his guidance. (She had advanced far enough to join him in ridiculing the Idyls of the King, but not to feel the beauty of Ulysses and the Lotus Eaters.) She was straightforward, loyal

---

hieroglyphic world Hieroglyphics (from the Greek, meaning "sacred carving" because of their frequent use in religious contexts) is a system of writing, such as that used in ancient Egypt, in which pictorial symbols represent meaning. By extension, *hieroglyphics* refers to language or codings that are difficult to understand. Wharton suggests that the conventions ruling old New York are as mysterious to outsiders as Egyptian hieroglyphics once were to western archaeologists.

books on Primitive Man Anthropology, the study of human origins and physical, social and cultural development, emerged as a discipline in the nineteenth century with developments in technology that allowed systematic research of remote people and places. Interest increased during this period in early nonwestern cultures; in archaeological excavation and preservation; and in comparative evaluations of cultures. Wharton mentions Archer's familiarity with anthropology again in chap. 9.

Idylls of the King ... Ulysses ... Lotus Eaters Poems by Alfred Tennyson (1809–1892), an English poet and national poet laureate in 1850. Influenced by the English Romantics, chiefly Keats, his poetry is considered representative of the Victorian era, reflecting the

and brave; she had a sense of humour (chiefly proved by her laughing at *his* jokes); and he suspected, in the depths of her innocently-gazing soul, a glow of feeling that it would be a joy to waken. But when he had gone the brief round of her he returned discouraged by the thought that all this frankness and innocence were only an artificial product. Untrained human nature was not frank and innocent; it was full of the twists and defences of an instinctive guile. And he felt himself oppressed by this creation of factitious purity, so cunningly manufactured by a conspiracy of mothers and aunts and grandmothers and long-dead ancestresses, because it was supposed to be what he wanted, what he had a right to, in order that he might exercise his lordly pleasure in smashing it like an image made of snow.

There was a certain triteness in these reflections: they were those habitual to young men on the approach of their wedding day. But they were generally accompanied by a sense of compunction and self-abasement of which Newland Archer felt no trace. He could not deplore (as Thackeray's heroes so often exasperated him by doing) that he had not a blank page to offer his bride in exchange for the unblemished one she was to give to him. He could not get away from the fact that if he had been brought up as she had they would have been no more fit to find their way about than the Babes in the Wood; nor could he, for all his anxious cogitations, see any honest reason (any, that is, unconnected with his own momentary pleasure, and the passion of masculine vanity) why his bride should not have been allowed the same freedom of experience as himself.

Such questions, at such an hour, were bound to drift through his mind; but he was conscious that their uncomfortable persistence and pre-

---

sensibilities and intellectual and moral values of the dominant social class. *Idylls of the King* (1859–85) is a sequence of poems that interprets the Arthurian legend. Tennyson focuses on the evil introduced into Camelot through Lancelot's sin of adulterous love for Guinevere, a choice some readers found lacking in substance. In her autobiography, Wharton describes these poems as "full of mystery and obscurity" and recalls "rhythmic raptures tingling through me" when she read them. "Ulysses" (1842), based on book IX of the *Odyssey* and canto XXVI of Dante's *Inferno*, describes Ulysses looking backward on his travels and forward to his last voyage. He summons the endurance and hope necessary to continue his adventures, filled with loss for what has passed as well as determination to face the future. "The Lotos-Eaters" (1832, 1842), based on book IX of the *Odyssey*, tells of sailors returning home from the fall of Troy who land on a strange island inhabited by people who eat only the fruit and flower of the lotus. Those who eat the plant are filled with languorous content and have no desire to continue their journey. Tennyson evokes the desire to withdraw from the world of work and competition.

Babes in the Wood An English literary folktale based on a ballad, the story is about two innocent children left in the woods to die by their guardian uncle who usurps their inheritance.

cision were due to the inopportune arrival of the Countess Olenska. Here he was, at the very moment of his betrothal—a moment for pure thoughts and cloudless hopes—pitchforked into a coil of scandal which raised all the special problems he would have preferred to let lie. "Hang Ellen Olenska!" he grumbled, as he covered his fire and began to undress. He could not really see why her fate should have the least bearing on his; yet he dimly felt that he had only just begun to measure the risks of the championship which his engagement had forced upon him.

A few days later the bolt fell.

The Lovell Mingotts had sent out cards for what was known as "a formal dinner" (that is, three extra footmen, two dishes for each course, and a Roman punch in the middle), and had headed their invitations with the words "To meet the Countess Olenska," in accordance with the hospitable American fashion, which treats strangers as if they were royalties, or at least as their ambassadors.

The guests had been selected with a boldness and discrimination in which the initiated recognised the firm hand of Catherine the Great. Associated with such immemorial standbys as the Selfridge Merrys, who were asked everywhere because they always had been, the Beauforts, on whom there was a claim of relationship, and Mr. Sillerton Jackson and his sister Sophy (who went wherever her brother told her to), were some of the most fashionable and yet most irreproachable of the dominant "young married" set; the Lawrence Leffertses, Mrs. Lefferts Rushworth (the lovely widow), the Harry Thorleys, the Reggie Chiverses and young Morris Dagonet and his wife (who was a van der Luyden). The company indeed was perfectly assorted, since all the members belonged to the little inner group of people who, during the long New York season, disported themselves together daily and nightly with apparently undiminished zest.

Forty-eight hours later the unbelievable had happened; every one had refused the Mingotts' invitation except the Beauforts and old Mr. Jackson and his sister. The intended slight was emphasised by the fact that even the Reggie Chiverses, who were of the Mingott clan, were among those inflicting it; and by the uniform wording of the notes, in all of which the

---

Roman punch   Victorian formal dinners often included mixed drinks such as the popular Roman punch. The alcohol content—1 cup champagne and 1 cup rum, combined with 3 cups lemonade, 2 beaten egg whites, 1/4 cup powdered sugar, and the juice of 2 oranges—made the drink strong enough to promote conviviality. Roman punch was reportedly the favorite of architect Stanford White and author Mark Twain. Here it is the choice of the Lovell Mingotts; it appears again in chap. 33, in which Mrs. Archer remarks that the inclusion of this punch in the menu "made all the difference."

writers "regretted that they were unable to accept," without the mitigating plea of a "previous engagement" that ordinary courtesy prescribed.

New York society was, in those days, far too small, and too scant in its resources, for every one in it (including livery-stable-keepers, butlers and cooks) not to know exactly on which evenings people were free; and it was thus possible for the recipients of Mrs. Lovell Mingott's invitations to make cruelly clear their determination not to meet the Countess Olenska.

The blow was unexpected; but the Mingotts, as their way was, met it gallantly. Mrs. Lovell Mingott confided the case to Mrs. Welland, who confided it to Newland Archer; who, aflame at the outrage, appealed passionately and authoritatively to his mother; who, after a painful period of inward resistance and outward temporising, succumbed to his instances (as she always did), and immediately embracing his cause with an energy redoubled by her previous hesitations, put on her grey velvet bonnet and said: "I'll go and see Louisa van der Luyden."

The New York of Newland Archer's day was a small and slippery pyramid, in which, as yet, hardly a fissure had been made or a foothold gained. At its base was a firm foundation of what Mrs. Archer called "plain people"; an honourable but obscure majority of respectable families who (as in the case of the Spicers or the Leffertses or the Jacksons) had been raised above their level by marriage with one of the ruling clans. People, Mrs. Archer always said, were not as particular as they used to be; and with old Catherine Spicer ruling one end of Fifth Avenue, and Julius Beaufort the other, you couldn't expect the old traditions to last much longer.

Firmly narrowing upward from this wealthy but inconspicuous substratum was the compact and dominant group which the Mingotts, Newlands, Chiverses and Mansons so actively represented. Most people imagined them to be the very apex of the pyramid; but they themselves (at least those of Mrs. Archer's generation) were aware that, in the eyes of the professional genealogist, only a still smaller number of families could lay claim to that eminence.

"Don't tell me," Mrs. Archer would say to her children, "all this modern newspaper rubbish about a New York aristocracy. If there is one, neither the Mingotts nor the Mansons belong to it; no, nor the Newlands or the Chiverses either. Our grandfathers and great-grandfathers were just respectable English or Dutch merchants, who came to the colonies to make their fortune, and stayed here because they did so well. One of your great-

---

English or Dutch merchants New York City was originally settled by the English and Dutch. Wharton's family, like the Archers, were initially merchants and bankers. She writes in her autobiography, *A Backward Glance,* "My mother, who had a hearty con-

grandfathers signed the Declaration, and another was a general on Washington's staff, and received General Burgoyne's sword after the battle of Saratoga. These are things to be proud of, but they have nothing to do with rank or class. New York has always been a commercial community, and there are not more than three families in it who can claim an aristocratic origin in the real sense of the word."

Mrs. Archer and her son and daughter, like every one else in New York, knew who these privileged beings were: the Dagonets of Washington Square, who came of an old English county family allied with the Pitts and Foxes; the Lannings, who had intermarried with the descendants of Count de Grasse, and the van der Luydens, direct descendants of the first Dutch governor of Manhattan, and related by pre-revolutionary marriages to several members of the French and British aristocracy.

The Lannings survived only in the person of two very old but lively Miss Lannings, who lived cheerfully and reminiscently among family portraits and Chippendale; the Dagonets were a considerable clan, allied to

---

tempt for the tardy discovery of aristocratic genealogies, always said that old New York was composed of Dutch and British middle-class families, and that only four or five could show a pedigree leading back to the aristocracy of their ancestral country"(10).

General Burgoyne's sword . . . Saratoga   The British general John Burgoyne (1723–1792) was sent to America in 1777, where he led an expedition from Canada. Burgoyne took Ticonderoga but was forced to surrender at Saratoga.

Washington Square   A nine-acre public park, bounded by Waverly Place (Washington Square Park North), University Place (Washington Square Park East), West 4th Street (Washington Park South), and MacDougal Street (Washington Square Park West). Site of parades and public executions in the early 1800s, it became the center of a fashionable neighborhood by mid-century.

Pitts   The family of Englishman William Pitt the Elder (1708–1778) and his son William Pitt the Younger (1759–1806), both of whom served as Britain's prime minister. The younger son was a Tory conservative and political rival of Charles Fox. (See the following note.)

Foxes   The family of Englishman Charles James Fox (1749–1806), a Whig politician who defended civil liberties, opposed the slave trade, and was known for his radical politics and disrespect for conventional morality.

Count de Grasse   François Joseph Paul, Comte de Grasse (1722–1788), was a French naval officer who commanded the French Atlantic fleet during the American Revolution. He ensured a Franco-American victory against General Charles Cornwallis in the Yorktown campaign.

first Dutch governor of Manhattan   This was Peter Minuit (1580–1638), who signed the treaty with the Indians that gave the Manhattan colony to the Dutch, reportedly for twenty-four dollars.

Chippendale   Furniture created by London cabinetmaker Thomas Chippendale (1718?–1779), fashionable during the mid-eighteenth century. By the nineteenth century,

the best names in Baltimore and Philadelphia; but the van der Luydens, who stood above all of them, had faded into a kind of super-terrestrial twilight, from which only two figures impressively emerged; those of Mr. and Mrs. Henry van der Luyden.

Mrs. Henry van der Luyden had been Louisa Dagonet, and her mother had been the granddaughter of Colonel du Lac, of an old Channel Island family, who had fought under Cornwallis and had settled in Maryland, after the war, with his bride, Lady Angelica Trevenna, fifth daughter of the Earl of St. Austrey. The tie between the Dagonets, the du Lacs of Maryland, and their aristocratic Cornish kinsfolk, the Trevennas, had always remained close and cordial. Mr. and Mrs. van der Luyden had more than once paid long visits to the present head of the house of Trevenna, the Duke of St. Austrey, at his country-seat in Cornwall and at St. Austrey in Gloucestershire; and his Grace had frequently announced his intention of some day returning their visit (without the Duchess, who feared the Atlantic).

Mr. and Mrs. van der Luyden divided their time between Trevenna, their place in Maryland, and Skuytercliff, the great estate on the Hudson which had been one of the colonial grants of the Dutch government to the famous first Governor, and of which Mr. van der Luyden was still "Patroon." Their large solemn house in Madison Avenue was seldom opened, and when they came to town they received in it only their most intimate friends.

"I wish you would go with me, Newland," his mother said, suddenly pausing at the door of the Brown *coupé*. "Louisa is fond of you; and of course it's on account of dear May that I'm taking this step—and also because, if we don't all stand together, there'll be no such thing as Society left."

Chippendale represented a style that combined rococo, Chinese, and Gothic designs in combination with Georgian classical forms.

Channel Island . . . Cornwallis . . . Cornwall . . . Gloucestershire   The Channel Islands are a group of islands under British governance in the English Channel. Charles Cornwallis, 1st Marquis (1738–1805), was a British general in the American Revolution. Personally opposed to taxing the colonies, he nevertheless defeated General Greene at Guilford Courthouse, North Carolina, but was forced to surrender at Yorktown (1781). Cornwall and Gloucestershire are counties in southwest and southwest-central England.

estate on the Hudson   The Hudson River, which borders the western edge of New York City, is one of the most important waterways in the world. Its striking beauty, especially along the Palisades and in the Hudson Highlands, inspired painters and writers in the nineteenth century and made it a popular summer destination for New Yorkers.

"Patroon"   A landholder in New York and New Jersey who was granted certain rights and powers under Dutch colonial rule.

VII

Mrs. Henry van der Luyden listened in silence to her cousin Mrs. Archer's narrative.

It was all very well to tell yourself in advance that Mrs. van der Luyden was always silent, and that, though non-committal by nature and training, she was very kind to the people she really liked. Even personal experience of these facts was not always a protection from the chill that descended on one in the high-ceilinged white-walled Madison Avenue drawing-room, with the pale brocaded armchairs so obviously uncovered for the occasion, and the gauze still veiling the ormolu mantel ornaments and the beautiful old carved frame of Gainsborough's "Lady Angelica du Lac."

Mrs. van der Luyden's portrait by Huntington (in black velvet and Venetian point) faced that of her lovely ancestress. It was generally considered "as fine as a Cabanel," and, though twenty years had elapsed since its execution, was still "a perfect likeness." Indeed the Mrs. van der Luyden

---

Madison Avenue   The major avenue in Manhattan between 23rd Street and 138th Street, it was an exclusive residential address in the last half of the nineteenth century. By the turn of the century, Madison Avenue was beginning to attract commercial establishments and later became associated with advertising.

ormolu   A gilded metal alloy of copper, zinc, and tin used to decorate candelabra, clocks, and other luxury objects.

Gainsborough's "Lady Angelica du Lac"   Thomas Gainsborough (1727–1788), an English landscapist and portraitist, was a poetic illustrator of the English personality who often situated his subjects in nature and established a fashionable clientele.

Huntington   Daniel Huntington (1816–1906), an American painter from a distinguished New England family, began painting landscapes and historical, religious subjects but progressed to portraiture in the 1850s, using family and social connections to attract prestigious subjects. Conservative in technique and principles, Huntington believed in art as a moral force, admired the Old Masters, and resisted late nineteenth-century artistic innovations. He was a founding member of the Century Club (of which Archer is a member) and exerted considerable influence in the academic establishment of his day.

velvet   An elegant, smooth, soft fabric with dense pile.

Venetian point   Lace of beautiful quality, with densely decorated flowers or scrolling patterns.

Cabanel   Alexandre Cabanel (1823–1889) was a French painter and winner of the Prix de Rome in 1845. He ranked with Bouguereau as one of the most successful and influential academic painters of the period. Best known for his *Birth of Venus* and his titillating yet ostensibly chaste nudes, he emphatically opposed Impressionism. By the end of the century, Cabanel's smooth, elegant style began to seem dated in comparison with the sharper, more contemporary manner of painting.

who sat beneath it listening to Mrs. Archer might have been the twin-sister of the fair and still youngish woman drooping against a gilt armchair before a green rep curtain. Mrs. van der Luyden still wore black velvet and Venetian point when she went into society—or rather (since she never dined out) when she threw open her own doors to receive it. Her fair hair, which had faded without turning grey, was still parted in flat overlapping points on her forehead, and the straight nose that divided her pale blue eyes was only a little more pinched about the nostrils than when the portrait had been painted. She always, indeed, struck Newland Archer as having been rather gruesomely preserved in the airless atmosphere of a perfectly irreproachable existence, as bodies caught in glaciers keep for years a rosy life-in-death.

Like all his family, he esteemed and admired Mrs. van der Luyden; but he found her gentle bending sweetness less approachable than the grimness of some of his mother's old aunts, fierce spinsters who said "No" on principle before they knew what they were going to be asked.

Mrs. van der Luyden's attitude said neither yes nor no, but always appeared to incline to clemency till her thin lips, wavering into the shadow of a smile, made the almost invariable reply: "I shall first have to talk this over with my husband."

She and Mr. van der Luyden were so exactly alike that Archer often wondered how, after forty years of the closest conjugality, two such merged identities ever separated themselves enough for anything as controversial as a talking-over. But as neither had ever reached a decision without prefacing it by this mysterious conclave, Mrs. Archer and her son, having set forth their case, waited resignedly for the familiar phrase.

Mrs. van der Luyden, however, who had seldom surprised any one, now surprised them by reaching her long hand toward the bell-rope.

"I think," she said, "I should like Henry to hear what you have told me."

A footman appeared, to whom she gravely added: "If Mr. van der Luyden has finished reading the newspaper, please ask him to be kind enough to come."

She said "reading the newspaper" in the tone in which a Minister's wife might have said: "Presiding at a Cabinet meeting"—not from any arrogance of mind, but because the habit of a life-time, and the attitude of her friends and relations, had led her to consider Mr. van der Luyden's least gesture as having an almost sacerdotal importance.

---

rep   A ribbed or corded fabric.

Her promptness of action showed that she considered the case as pressing as Mrs. Archer; but, lest she should be thought to have committed herself in advance, she added, with the sweetest look: "Henry always enjoys seeing you, dear Adeline; and he will wish to congratulate Newland."

The double doors had solemnly reopened and between them appeared Mr. Henry van der Luyden, tall, spare and frock-coated, with faded fair hair, a straight nose like his wife's and the same look of frozen gentleness in eyes that were merely pale grey instead of pale blue.

Mr. van der Luyden greeted Mrs. Archer with cousinly affability, proffered to Newland low-voiced congratulations couched in the same language as his wife's, and seated himself in one of the brocade armchairs with the simplicity of a reigning sovereign.

"I had just finished reading the Times," he said, laying his long fingertips together. "In town my mornings are so much occupied that I find it more convenient to read the newspapers after luncheon."

"Ah, there's a great deal to be said for that plan—indeed I think my uncle Egmont used to say he found it less agitating not to read the morning papers till after dinner," said Mrs. Archer responsively.

"Yes: my good father abhorred hurry. But now we live in a constant rush," said Mr. van der Luyden in measured tones, looking with pleasant deliberation about the large shrouded room which to Archer was so complete an image of its owners.

"But I hope you *had* finished your reading, Henry?" his wife interposed.

"Quite—quite," he reassured her.

"Then I should like Adeline to tell you—"

"Oh, it's really Newland's story," said his mother smiling; and proceeded to rehearse once more the monstrous tale of the affront inflicted on Mrs. Lovell Mingott.

"Of course," she ended, "Augusta Welland and Mary Mingott both felt that, especially in view of Newland's engagement, you and Henry *ought to know*."

"Ah—" said Mr. van der Luyden, drawing a deep breath.

There was a silence during which the tick of the monumental ormolu clock on the white marble mantelpiece grew as loud as the boom of a

---

the Times   The *New York Times* newspaper, begun in 1851 by bankers, became successful by offering comprehensive news reporting. It leaned politically toward the Republican and Whig parties and in the 1870s opposed William Marcy Tweed ("Boss Tweed").

minute-gun. Archer contemplated with awe the two slender faded figures, seated side by side in a kind of viceregal rigidity, mouth-pieces of some remote ancestral authority which fate compelled them to wield, when they would so much rather have lived in simplicity and seclusion, digging invisible weeds out of the perfect lawns of Skuytercliff, and playing Patience together in the evenings.

Mr. van der Luyden was the first to speak.

"You really think this is due to some—some intentional interference of Lawrence Lefferts's?" he enquired, turning to Archer.

"I'm certain of it, sir. Larry has been going it rather harder than usual lately—if cousin Louisa won't mind my mentioning it—having rather a stiff affair with the postmaster's wife in their village, or some one of that sort; and whenever poor Gertrude Lefferts begins to suspect anything, and he's afraid of trouble, he gets up a fuss of this kind, to show how awfully moral he is, and talks at the top of his voice about the impertinence of inviting his wife to meet people he doesn't wish her to know. He's simply using Madame Olenska as a lightning-rod; I've seen him try the same thing often before."

"The *Leffertses!*—" said Mrs. van der Luyden.

"The *Leffertses!*—" echoed Mrs. Archer. "What would uncle Egmont have said of Lawrence Lefferts's pronouncing on anybody's social position? It shows what Society has come to."

"We'll hope it has not quite come to that," said Mr. van der Luyden firmly.

"Ah, if only you and Louisa went out more!" sighed Mrs. Archer.

But instantly she became aware of her mistake. The van der Luydens were morbidly sensitive to any criticism of their secluded existence. They were the arbiters of fashion, the Court of last Appeal, and they knew it, and bowed to their fate. But being shy and retiring persons, with no natural inclination for their part, they lived as much as possible in the sylvan solitude of Skuytercliff, and when they came to town, declined all invitations on the plea of Mrs. van der Luyden's health.

Newland Archer came to his mother's rescue. "Everybody in New York knows what you and cousin Louisa represent. That's why Mrs. Mingott felt she ought not to allow this slight on Countess Olenska to pass without consulting you."

Mrs. van der Luyden glanced at her husband, who glanced back at her.

---

minute-gun   A gun fired at intervals, as at a funeral.

viceregal   Of a viceroy, a person who governed a colony or province.

Patience   A card game of solitaire. The van der Luydens play separate, parallel games rather than competing against each other.

"It is the principle that I dislike," said Mr. van der Luyden. "As long as a member of a well-known family is backed up by that family it should be considered—final."

"It seems so to me," said his wife, as if she were producing a new thought.

"I had no idea," Mr. van der Luyden continued, "that things had come to such a pass." He paused, and looked at his wife again. "It occurs to me, my dear, that the Countess Olenska is already a sort of relation—through Medora Manson's first husband. At any rate, she will be when Newland marries." He turned toward the young man. "Have you read this morning's Times, Newland?"

"Why, yes, sir," said Archer, who usually tossed off half a dozen papers with his morning coffee.

Husband and wife looked at each other again. Their pale eyes clung together in prolonged and serious consultation; then a faint smile fluttered over Mrs. van der Luyden's face. She had evidently guessed and approved.

Mr. van der Luyden turned to Mrs. Archer. "If Louisa's health allowed her to dine out—I wish you would say to Mrs. Lovell Mingott—she and I would have been happy to—er—fill the places of the Lawrence Leffertses at her dinner." He paused to let the irony of this sink in. "As you know, this is impossible." Mrs. Archer sounded a sympathetic assent. "But Newland tells me he has read this morning's Times; therefore he has probably seen that Louisa's relative, the Duke of St. Austrey, arrives next week on the Russia. He is coming to enter his new sloop, the Guinevere, in next summer's International Cup Race; and also to have a little canvasback shooting at Trevenna." Mr. van der Luyden paused again, and continued with increasing benevolence: "Before taking him down to Maryland we are inviting a few friends to meet him here—only a little dinner—with a reception afterward. I am sure Louisa will be as glad as I am if Countess Olenska will let us include her among our guests." He got up, bent his long body

---

Russia Built in 1867 by Cunard, the *Russia* was one of the most popular transatlantic ships of its day. It set a record in 1867 for traveling from New York to Queenstown in eight days and twenty-three minutes. The last mail Cunarder with clipper bow and figurehead, it was sold to Redstar, became the *Waesland,* and was lost in 1902 after a collision with a Houston liner. (See note to p. 276.)

sloop A single-masted, fore-and-aft rigged sailboat with only a headsail.

International Cup Race International yacht racing began in 1851 when a syndicate headed by New Yorker J. C. Stevens built the schooner yacht *America,* for which the America's Cup race is named. From the race's beginning until 1960, only England and the United States were contestants for the America's Cup. Various international competitions, some transatlantic, took place during the late nineteenth century.

with a stiff friendliness toward his cousin, and added: "I think I have Louisa's authority for saying that she will herself leave the invitation to dine when she drives out presently: with our cards—of course with our cards."

Mrs. Archer, who knew this to be a hint that the seventeen-hand chestnuts which were never kept waiting were at the door, rose with a hurried murmur of thanks. Mrs. van der Luyden beamed on her with the smile of Esther interceding with Ahasuerus; but her husband raised a protesting hand.

"There is nothing to thank me for, dear Adeline; nothing whatever. This kind of thing must not happen in New York; it shall not, as long as I can help it," he pronounced with sovereign gentleness as he steered his cousins to the door.

Two hours later, every one knew that the great C-spring barouche in which Mrs. van der Luyden took the air at all seasons had been seen at old Mrs. Mingott's door, where a large square envelope was handed in; and that evening at the Opera Mr. Sillerton Jackson was able to state that the envelope contained a card inviting the Countess Olenska to the dinner which the van der Luydens were giving the following week for their cousin, the Duke of St. Austrey.

Some of the younger men in the club box exchanged a smile at this announcement, and glanced sideways at Lawrence Lefferts, who sat carelessly in the front of the box, pulling his long fair moustache, and who remarked with authority, as the soprano paused: "No one but Patti ought to attempt the Sonnambula."

VIII

It was generally agreed in New York that the Countess Olenska had "lost her looks."

She had appeared there first, in Newland Archer's boyhood, as a brilliantly pretty little girl of nine or ten, of whom people said that she "ought

---

seventeen-hand chestnuts   Reddish-brown horses about 5 1/2 feet high (one hand equals 4 inches).

Esther interceding with Ahasuerus   Esther is the heroine of a biblical book bearing her name. A cousin and foster daughter of the Jew Mordecai, she was chosen to succeed Vashti as consort to King Ahasuerus. Esther prevailed on Ahasuerus to save her people from extermination ordered by Haman, the king's officer.

C-spring barouche   A four-wheeled, horse-drawn carriage with a seat for the driver and seats inside for two couples. The curved metal spring gave the carriage its name.

Patti . . . Sonnambula   Adelina Patti (1843–1919) was a famous Italian soprano who debuted in Europe at Covent Garden in 1861. She sang the role of Amina in *The Son-*

to be painted." Her parents had been continental wanderers, and after a roaming babyhood she had lost them both, and been taken in charge by her aunt, Medora Manson, also a wanderer, who was herself returning to New York to "settle down."

Poor Medora, repeatedly widowed, was always coming home to settle down (each time in a less expensive house), and bringing with her a new husband or an adopted child; but after a few months she invariably parted from her husband or quarrelled with her ward, and, having got rid of her house at a loss, set out again on her wanderings. As her mother had been a Rushworth, and her last unhappy marriage had linked her to one of the crazy Chiverses, New York looked indulgently on her eccentricities; but when she returned with her little orphaned niece, whose parents had been popular in spite of their regrettable taste for travel, people thought it a pity that the pretty child should be in such hands.

Every one was disposed to be kind to little Ellen Mingott, though her dusky red cheeks and tight curls gave her an air of gaiety that seemed unsuitable in a child who should still have been in black for her parents. It was one of the misguided Medora's many peculiarities to flout the unalterable rules that regulated American mourning, and when she stepped from the steamer her family were scandalised to see that the crape veil she wore for her own brother was seven inches shorter than those of her sisters-in-law, while little Ellen was in crimson merino and amber beads, like a gipsy foundling.

---

nambula (*The Sleepwalker*), a two-act opera by Vincenzo Bellini performed at the Academy of Music. Patti's voice was noted for its birdlike spontaneity.

"ought to be painted" Having one's portrait painted was a mark of distinction traditionally reserved for the aristocracy. By the late nineteenth century, portraiture received fresh interest as newly wealthy Americans sought to acquire social legitimacy by having their portraits painted.

American mourning Strict rules dictated the length of time and the type of dress during mourning. Men and women both wore black. Women's gowns were trimmed with dull, heavy black crepe. One came out of mourning gradually, in purple, lavender, and white for summer.

merino A high-quality soft wool, originally from sheep in Spain.

amber A fossilized resin from coniferous trees found near the Baltic Sea. Because of its bright golden color, amber was thought to be congealed sunlight, or, in western antiquity, tears shed over the death of Phaeton, the sun god's son. A prized material for jewelry, it reportedly warded off demons, ghosts, ailments, and bad dreams. In Victorian times, amber might connote decadence. Ellen wears amber beads in the novel's final dinner scene, chap. 33.

gipsy foundling Gipsies, or gypsies, are nomadic people whose origins are unknown. They are concentrated in southern Europe but found throughout the world. Many

But New York had so long resigned itself to Medora that only a few old ladies shook their heads over Ellen's gaudy clothes, while her other relations fell under the charm of her high colour and high spirits. She was a fearless and familiar little thing, who asked disconcerting questions, made precocious comments, and possessed outlandish arts, such as dancing a Spanish shawl dance and singing Neapolitan love-songs to a guitar. Under the direction of her aunt (whose real name was Mrs. Thorley Chivers, but who, having received a Papal title, had resumed her first husband's patronymic, and called herself the Marchioness Manson, because in Italy she could turn it into Manzoni) the little girl received an expensive but incoherent education, which included "drawing from the model," a thing never dreamed of before, and playing the piano in quintets with professional musicians.

Of course no good could come of this; and when, a few years later, poor Chivers finally died in a madhouse, his widow (draped in strange weeds) again pulled up stakes and departed with Ellen, who had grown into a tall bony girl with conspicuous eyes. For some time no more was heard of them; then news came of Ellen's marriage to an immensely rich Polish nobleman of legendary fame, whom she had met at a ball at the Tuileries, and who was said to have princely establishments in Paris, Nice and Florence, a yacht at Cowes, and many square miles of shooting in

---

gypsies speak the language of the country in which they live, or a combination of their own tongue, Romany, and the local language. They adapt to the culture in which they find themselves but preserve their own baptismal, marriage, and burial practices. Used colloquially, *gypsy* carries negative Bohemian connotations.

Spanish shawl dance   The shawl and flaring skirt are typical items of female dress in Spanish dances, known for their authenticity and spiritedness. Wharton may have had her own dance training by a French instructor in mind: she writes in *A Backward Glance,* that she was "persistently exercised in the *menuet* [minuet], the shawl dance (with a lace scarf) and the *cachucha* [a classical Spanish dance]—of course with castanets" (36–37).

Neapolitan love-songs   Music, chiefly opera, composed and performed in Naples, Italy, a significant music center in the eighteenth century.

Papal title   Legal right to assume a title.

Manzoni   Medora may choose this particular Italian form of her name because it is the same as that of Alessandro Manzoni (1785–1873), an acclaimed novelist.

"drawing from the model"   An artist's practice of using live models, usually nude. For reasons of modesty, Victorian female artists did not draw from nude models. Ellen's experience indicates an uncommon level of sophistication and freedom.

Cowes   A town on the Isle of Wight, off the southern coast of England, known as a yachting center.

Transylvania. She disappeared in a kind of sulphurous apotheosis, and when a few years later Medora again came back to New York, subdued, impoverished, mourning a third husband, and in quest of a still smaller house, people wondered that her rich niece had not been able to do something for her. Then came the news that Ellen's own marriage had ended in disaster, and that she was herself returning home to seek rest and oblivion among her kinsfolk.

These things passed through Newland Archer's mind a week later as he watched the Countess Olenska enter the van der Luyden drawing-room on the evening of the momentous dinner. The occasion was a solemn one, and he wondered a little nervously how she would carry it off. She came rather late, one hand still ungloved, and fastening a bracelet about her wrist; yet she entered without any appearance of haste or embarrassment the drawing-room in which New York's most chosen company was somewhat awfully assembled.

In the middle of the room she paused, looking about her with a grave mouth and smiling eyes; and in that instant Newland Archer rejected the general verdict on her looks. It was true that her early radiance was gone. The red cheeks had paled; she was thin, worn, a little older-looking than her age, which must have been nearly thirty. But there was about her the mysterious authority of beauty, a sureness in the carriage of the head, the movement of the eyes, which, without being in the least theatrical, struck him as highly trained and full of a conscious power. At the same time she was simpler in manner than most of the ladies present, and many people (as he heard afterward from Janey) were disappointed that her appearance was not more "stylish"—for stylishness was what New York most valued. It was, perhaps, Archer reflected, because her early vivacity had disappeared; because she was so quiet—quiet in her movements, her voice, and the tones of her low-pitched voice. New York had expected something a good deal more resonant in a young woman with such a history.

The dinner was a somewhat formidable business. Dining with the van der Luydens was at best no light matter, and dining there with a Duke who was their cousin was almost a religious solemnity. It pleased Archer to think that only an old New Yorker could perceive the shade of difference (to New York) between being merely a Duke and being the van der Luydens' Duke. New York took stray noblemen calmly, and even (except in the

---

Transylvania   A former province of Romania separated from Wallachia and Moldavia by the Carpathian Mountains.

Struthers set) with a certain distrustful *hauteur;* but when they presented such credentials as these they were received with an old-fashioned cordiality that they would have been greatly mistaken in ascribing solely to their standing in Debrett. It was for just such distinctions that the young man cherished his old New York even while he smiled at it.

The van der Luydens had done their best to emphasise the importance of the occasion. The du Lac Sèvres and the Trevenna George II plate were out; so was the van der Luyden "Lowestoft" (East India Company) and the Dagonet Crown Derby. Mrs. van der Luyden looked more than ever like a Cabanel, and Mrs. Archer, in her grandmother's seed-pearls and emeralds, reminded her son of an Isabey miniature. All the ladies had on their handsomest jewels, but it was characteristic of the house and the occasion that these were mostly in rather heavy old-fashioned settings; and old Miss Lanning, who had been persuaded to come, actually wore her mother's cameos and a Spanish blonde shawl.

The Countess Olenska was the only young woman at the dinner; yet, as Archer scanned the smooth plump elderly faces between their diamond

---

hauteur   French: haughtiness, arrogance.

Debrett   *Debrett's Peerage* is a list of the titled aristocracy of Great Britain. It also includes information on forms of address and etiquette.

Sèvres   Highly valued French porcelain manufactured in Sèvres, France, and known for its colored grounds, soft shapes, and pleasing bold colors. Sèvres was associated in the eighteenth century with sovereignty, as many European rulers bought their own distinctive services.

George II plate   Decorative or practical metalware gilded with silver, produced during the reign of George II, king of Great Britain from 1727 to 1760.

"Lowestoft" (East India Company)   A fine porcelain made in China for export to Britain and the United States in the eighteenth and nineteenth centuries. The East India Company was a British trading monopoly established in India in 1600 with strong political as well as economic power until the mid-nineteenth century. A family that owned Lowestoft most likely had profited from this often unregulated Eastern trade.

Crown Derby   Old Derby porcelain, known as "Crown Derby," was first made around 1748 in Derby, England. It is known for its Japanese, or imari, patterns that made particular use of red, blue, and gold. In the late eighteenth century, when the quality of Crown Derby was highest, the manufacturer's mark was a crown with the letter "D."

Isabey miniature   Jean-Baptiste Isabey (1767–1855), a French painter and the most brilliant miniaturist of his time, was the official painter in the government of Napoléon and the last miniaturist of consequence before the medium was eclipsed by photography.

cameos   Gemstones carved in relief, usually of two colors. A raised design, often a person's profile, is one color and the background is a different color. Cameos are usually worn as rings, pendants, or brooches.

necklaces and towering ostrich feathers, they struck him as curiously immature compared with hers. It frightened him to think what must have gone to the making of her eyes.

The Duke of St. Austrey, who sat at his hostess's right, was naturally the chief figure of the evening. But if the Countess Olenska was less conspicuous than had been hoped, the Duke was almost invisible. Being a well-bred man he had not (like another recent ducal visitor) come to the dinner in a shooting-jacket; but his evening clothes were so shabby and baggy, and he wore them with such an air of their being homespun, that (with his stooping way of sitting, and the vast beard spreading over his shirt-front) he hardly gave the appearance of being in dinner attire. He was short, round-shouldered, sunburnt, with a thick nose, small eyes and a sociable smile; but he seldom spoke, and when he did it was in such low tones that, despite the frequent silences of expectation about the table, his remarks were lost to all but his neighbours.

When the men joined the ladies after dinner the Duke went straight up to the Countess Olenska, and they sat down in a corner and plunged into animated talk. Neither seemed aware that the Duke should first have paid his respects to Mrs. Lovell Mingott and Mrs. Headly Chivers, and the Countess have conversed with that amiable hypochondriac, Mr. Urban Dagonet of Washington Square, who, in order to have the pleasure of meeting her, had broken through his fixed rule of not dining out between January and April. The two chatted together for nearly twenty minutes; then the Countess rose and, walking alone across the wide drawing-room, sat down at Newland Archer's side.

It was not the custom in New York drawing-rooms for a lady to get up and walk away from one gentleman in order to seek the company of another. Etiquette required that she should wait, immovable as an idol, while the men who wished to converse with her succeeded each other at her side. But the Countess was apparently unaware of having broken any rule; she sat at perfect ease in a corner of the sofa beside Archer, and looked at him with the kindest eyes.

"I want you to talk to me about May," she said.

Instead of answering her he asked: "You knew the Duke before?"

"Oh, yes—we used to see him every winter at Nice. He's very fond of gambling—he used to come to the house a great deal." She said it in the simplest manner, as if she had said: "He's fond of wild-flowers"; and after a moment she added candidly: "I think he's the dullest man I ever met."

This pleased her companion so much that he forgot the slight shock her previous remark had caused him. It was undeniably exciting to meet a lady who found the van der Luydens' Duke dull, and dared to utter the opinion. He longed to question her, to hear more about the life of which her careless words had given him so illuminating a glimpse; but he feared to touch on distressing memories, and before he could think of anything to say she had strayed back to her original subject.

"May is a darling; I've seen no young girl in New York so handsome and so intelligent. Are you very much in love with her?"

Newland Archer reddened and laughed. "As much as a man can be."

She continued to consider him thoughtfully, as if not to miss any shade of meaning in what he said, "Do you think, then, there is a limit?"

"To being in love? If there is, I haven't found it!"

She glowed with sympathy. "Ah—it's really and truly a romance?"

"The most romantic of romances!"

"How delightful! And you found it all out for yourselves—it was not in the least arranged for you?"

Archer looked at her incredulously. "Have you forgotten," he asked with a smile, "that in our country we don't allow our marriages to be arranged for us?"

A dusky blush rose to her cheek, and he instantly regretted his words.

"Yes," she answered, "I'd forgotten. You must forgive me if I sometimes make these mistakes. I don't always remember that everything here is good that was—that was bad where I've come from." She looked down at her Viennese fan of eagle feathers, and he saw that her lips trembled.

"I'm so sorry," he said impulsively; "but you *are* among friends here, you know."

"Yes—I know. Wherever I go I have that feeling. That's why I came home. I want to forget everything else, to become a complete American again, like the Mingotts and Wellands, and you and your delightful mother, and all the other good people here tonight. Ah, here's May arriving, and you will want to hurry away to her," she added, but without moving; and her eyes turned back from the door to rest on the young man's face.

The drawing-rooms were beginning to fill up with after-dinner guests, and following Madame Olenska's glance Archer saw May Welland entering with her mother. In her dress of white and silver, with a wreath of silver blossoms in her hair, the tall girl looked like a Diana just alight from the chase.

Diana . . . chase   Diana is the Roman equivalent of the Greek goddess Artemis. A complex figure, she is associated with the moon, the hunt, and virginity (although she is the goddess of childbirth and the protector of children as well). As a kind of universal god-

"Oh," said Archer, "I have so many rivals; you see she's already surrounded. There's the Duke being introduced."

"Then stay with me a little longer," Madame Olenska said in a low tone, just touching his knee with her plumed fan. It was the lightest touch, but it thrilled him like a caress.

"Yes, let me stay," he answered in the same tone, hardly knowing what he said; but just then Mr. van der Luyden came up, followed by old Mr. Urban Dagonet. The Countess greeted them with her grave smile, and Archer, feeling his host's admonitory glance on him, rose and surrendered his seat.

Madame Olenska held out her hand as if to bid him goodbye.

"Tomorrow, then, after five—I shall expect you," she said; and then turned back to make room for Mr. Dagonet.

"Tomorrow—" Archer heard himself repeating, though there had been no engagement, and during their talk she had given him no hint that she wished to see him again.

As he moved away he saw Lawrence Lefferts, tall and resplendent, leading his wife up to be introduced; and heard Gertrude Lefferts say, as she beamed on the Countess with her large unperceiving smile: "But I think we used to go to dancing-school together when we were children—." Behind her, waiting their turn to name themselves to the Countess, Archer noticed a number of the recalcitrant couples who had declined to meet her at Mrs. Lovell Mingott's. As Mrs. Archer remarked: when the van der Luydens chose, they knew how to give a lesson. The wonder was that they chose so seldom.

The young man felt a touch on his arm and saw Mrs. van der Luyden looking down on him from the pure eminence of black velvet and the family diamonds. "It was good of you, dear Newland, to devote yourself so unselfishly to Madame Olenska. I told your cousin Henry he must really come to the rescue."

He was aware of smiling at her vaguely, and she added, as if condescending to his natural shyness: "I've never seen May looking lovelier. The Duke thinks her the handsomest girl in the room."

---

dess with almost limitless power, she can be paradoxically compassionate and destructive. Although she is the object of men's affection, Diana has masculine qualities and seeks revenge on men who neglect to sacrifice to her or on women who fail her. She is often portrayed in hunting attire with bow and arrows. Wharton depicts May's skill in archery (chap. 21), and Archer remembers her as "tall and silver-shining," like the moon (245).

IX

The Countess Olenska had said "after five"; and at half after the hour
Newland Archer rang the bell of the peeling stucco house with a giant wis-
teria throttling its feeble cast-iron balcony, which she had hired, far down
West Twenty-third Street, from the vagabond Medora.

It was certainly a strange quarter to have settled in. Small dress-
makers, bird-stuffers and "people who wrote" were her nearest neighbours; and further down the dishevelled street Archer recognised a dilapidated wooden house, at the end of a paved path, in which a writer and
journalist called Winsett, whom he used to come across now and then, had
mentioned that he lived. Winsett did not invite people to his house; but he
had once pointed it out to Archer in the course of a nocturnal stroll, and
the latter had asked himself, with a little shiver, if the humanities were so
meanly housed in other capitals.

Madame Olenska's own dwelling was redeemed from the same appearance only by a little more paint about the window-frames; and as
Archer mustered its modest front he said to himself that the Polish Count
must have robbed her of her fortune as well as of her illusions.

The young man had spent an unsatisfactory day. He had lunched with
the Wellands, hoping afterward to carry off May for a walk in the Park.

---

stucco house   A house with an exterior of plaster, often made to resemble more expensive stone.

wisteria   A climbing woody vine with drooping clusters of white or purplish flowers.
According to the nineteenth-century "language of flowers," wisteria communicated "I
cling to thee."

far down West Twenty-third Street   Fashionable in the 1840s and 1850s, this neighborhood later became associated with artists, performers, and writers.

walk in the Park   Central Park, the first landscaped park in the United States, was developed through the efforts of many wealthy merchants and landowners who admired
the public grounds of London and Paris and desired comparable space in New York City.
They wanted the park to boost the city's international reputation, provide them with an
attractive setting for carriage rides, and give city workers more healthful recreation.
In 1853, the New York state legislature authorized the city to acquire more than 700
acres of land (later extended to 843 acres) unsuitable for development because of its
swamps and rocky terrain. Bounded by 110th Street on the north, Fifth Avenue on the
east, 59th Street on the south (Central Park South) and Central Park West on the west,
the park was designed by Frederick Law Olmsted and opened in 1859. In its first decade,
the park was used predominantly by the upper classes for strolls and afternoon carriage
parades. Immigrant groups and working-class residents were discouraged by rules that
banned group picnics and commercial vehicles for family use and that required special
permission to play on the grass. Later in the century, the park was opened to wider

He wanted to have her to himself, to tell her how enchanting she had looked the night before, and how proud he was of her, and to press her to hasten their marriage. But Mrs. Welland had firmly reminded him that the round of family visits was not half over, and, when he hinted at advancing the date of the wedding, had raised reproachful eye-brows and sighed out: "Twelve dozen of everything—hand-embroidered—"

Packed in the family landau they rolled from one tribal doorstep to another, and Archer, when the afternoon's round was over, parted from his betrothed with the feeling that he had been shown off like a wild animal cunningly trapped. He supposed that his readings in anthropology caused him to take such a coarse view of what was after all a simple and natural demonstration of family feeling; but when he remembered that the Wellands did not expect the wedding to take place till the following autumn, and pictured what his life would be till then, a dampness fell upon his spirit.

"Tomorrow," Mrs. Welland called after him, "we'll do the Chiverses and the Dallases"; and he perceived that she was going through their two families alphabetically, and that they were only in the first quarter of the alphabet.

He had meant to tell May of the Countess Olenska's request—her command, rather—that he should call on her that afternoon; but in the brief moments when they were alone he had had more pressing things to say. Besides, it struck him as a little absurd to allude to the matter. He knew that May most particularly wanted him to be kind to her cousin; was it not that wish which had hastened the announcement of their engagement? It gave him an odd sensation to reflect that, but for the Countess's arrival, he might have been, if not still a free man, at least a man less irrevocably pledged. But May had willed it so, and he felt himself somehow relieved of further responsibility—and therefore at liberty, if he chose, to call on her cousin without telling her.

As he stood on Madame Olenska's threshold curiosity was his uppermost feeling. He was puzzled by the tone in which she had summoned him; he concluded that she was less simple than she seemed.

The door was opened by a swarthy foreign-looking maid, with a prominent bosom under a gay neckerchief, whom he vaguely fancied to be

---

uses. In 1870, new facilities were added, including a carousel, goat rides, tennis, and bicycling; in 1871, the zoo opened.

"**Twelve dozen of everything . . .**"   The bride traditionally prepared a trousseau that included linens and clothing she would need for married life. The Wellands strictly follow the expectation that the number of items be exact.

Sicilian. She welcomed him with all her white teeth, and answering his enquiries by a head-shake of incomprehension led him through the narrow
hall into a low firelit drawing-room. The room was empty, and she left
him, for an appreciable time, to wonder whether she had gone to find her
mistress, or whether she had not understood what he was there for, and
thought it might be to wind the clocks—of which he perceived that the
only visible specimen had stopped. He knew that the southern races
communicated with each other in the language of pantomime, and was
mortified to find her shrugs and smiles so unintelligible. At length she
returned with a lamp; and Archer, having meanwhile put together a
phrase out of Dante and Petrarch, evoked the answer: *"La signora è fu-
ori; ma verrà subito"*; which he took to mean: "She's out—but you'll
soon see."

What he saw, meanwhile, with the help of the lamp, was the faded
shadowy charm of a room unlike any room he had known. He knew that
the Countess Olenska had brought some of her possessions with her—
bits of wreckage, she called them—and these, he supposed, were represented by some small slender tables of dark wood, a delicate little Greek
bronze on the chimney-piece, and a stretch of red damask nailed on the
discoloured wallpaper behind a couple of Italian-looking pictures in old
frames.

Newland Archer prided himself on his knowledge of Italian art. His
boyhood had been saturated with Ruskin, and he had read all the latest

---

maid . . . Sicilian   Newly arrived immigrants often held low-level, low-paying positions.
The number of Italians increased dramatically in last quarter of the nineteenth century.
In 1880, fewer than 20,000 Italians lived in New York City. Numbers increased to
220,000 in 1900 and to 545,000 in 1910, with heavy immigration from southern Italy.
Many Italians lived in the Lower East Side or in Greenwich Village, often within walking distance to work. Women labored in the garment industry or, like Nastasia, as do-
mestics in nearby fashionable neighborhoods. Men worked in construction, especially
on streets and subways; and as tailors, barbers, street vendors, bootblacks, or owners of
small shops. In Boston and other cities, immigrants performed similar work; Wharton
mentions a Sicilian bootblack on p. 199.

Dante and Petrarch   Archer relies on his knowledge of classical Italian literature to converse with the maid. Dante Alighieri (1265–1321), often acknowledged as the greatest
Italian poet, is the author of the *Divina Commedia* (Divine Comedy), a vision of hell,
heaven, and purgatory. Francesco Petrarca (1304–1374), or Petrarch, was an acclaimed
Italian poet and scholar. Both writers are known for their passionate yet platonic devotion to married women. Dante met Beatrice (c. 1265–1290) when he was nine years old,
remained enthralled with her despite both their marriages, and wrote of his passion for
her in the *Vita Nuova*. Petrarch first met Laura in his twenties and wrote a series of love
poems, *Canzoniere*, addressed to her.

books: John Addington Symonds, Vernon Lee's "Euphorion," the essays of
P. G. Hamerton, and a wonderful new volume called "The Renaissance"
by Walter Pater. He talked easily of Botticelli, and spoke of Fra Angelico
with a faint condescension. But these pictures bewildered him, for they
were like nothing that he was accustomed to look at (and therefore able to
see) when he travelled in Italy; and perhaps, also, his powers of observation were impaired by the oddness of finding himself in this strange empty
house, where apparently no one expected him. He was sorry that he had
not told May Welland of Countess Olenska's request, and a little disturbed
by the thought that his betrothed might come in to see her cousin. What
would she think if she found him sitting there with the air of intimacy implied by waiting alone in the dusk at a lady's fireside?

But since he had come he meant to wait; and he sank into a chair and
stretched his feet to the logs.

It was odd to have summoned him in that way, and then forgotten him;
but Archer felt more curious than mortified. The atmosphere of the room
was so different from any he had ever breathed that self-consciousness
vanished in the sense of adventure. He had been before in drawing-rooms

---

John Addington Symonds   An English poet and critic (1840–1893) best known for his
multivolume cultural history, *The Renaissance in Italy* (1875–86).

Vernon Lee's "Euphorion"   The title of a study of the Renaissance by an English aes-
thetician, critic, and novelist. Born Violet Paget, Lee (1856–1935) took a pseudonym,
believing no one would take a woman's work seriously. She is best known for *Studies of
the Eighteenth Century in Italy* (1893). Wharton met Lee in 1894, admired her work,
and helped her arrange an American speaking tour.

P. G. Hamerton   Philip Gilbert Hamerton (1834–1894) was a critic, editor, and novelist who wrote extensively on art, especially etching. He served as editor of the *Saturday
Review*, a conservative weekly review of politics, literature, science, and art, and
founded *Portfolio* magazine in 1869.

"The Renaissance" by Walter Pater   English essayist and critic Walter Horatio Pater
(1839–1894) was a leader in establishing renewed interest in the Renaissance. He was
first known for *Studies in the History of the Renaissance* (1873), which includes an essay
on the then neglected Botticelli. Presumably after reading this essay, Archer "talked easily" of the painter. Wharton may hint that Archer's knowledge is shallow or derivative.

Botticelli   The nickname of Alessandro di Mariano Filipepi (1444–1510), a leading
painter of the Florentine school. Botticelli painted for the Medici family and other
prominent members of Florentine society. Among his mythical and religious allegories
are *The Birth of Venus* and *Allegory of the Cross*.

Fra Angelico   The popular name of Fra Giovanni da Fiesole (c. 1400–1455), a painter
of the Florentine Renaissance. Preeminently a conventional painter, he is best known for
his religious and spiritual frescoes, such as the *Annunciation*.

hung with red damask, with pictures "of the Italian school"; what struck him was the way in which Medora Manson's shabby hired house, with its blighted background of pampas grass and Rogers statuettes, had, by a turn of the hand, and the skilful use of a few properties, been transformed into something intimate, "foreign," subtly suggestive of old romantic scenes and sentiments. He tried to analyse the trick, to find a clue to it in the way the chairs and tables were grouped, in the fact that only two Jacqueminot roses (of which nobody ever bought less than a dozen) had been placed in the slender vase at his elbow, and in the vague pervading perfume that was not what one put on handkerchiefs, but rather like the scent of some far-off bazaar, a smell made up of Turkish coffee and ambergris and dried roses.

His mind wandered away to the question of what May's drawing-room would look like. He knew that Mr. Welland, who was behaving "very handsomely," already had his eye on a newly built house in East Thirty-ninth Street. The neighbourhood was thought remote, and the house was built in a ghastly greenish-yellow stone that the younger architects were beginning to employ as a protest against the brownstone of which the uniform hue coated New York like a cold chocolate sauce; but the plumbing was perfect. Archer would have liked to travel, to put off the

---

pampas grass   A grass native to South America with arching bluish blades and tall stems. It grows up to 14 feet high and is commonly used as an ornamental.

Rogers statuettes   John Rogers (1829–1904) was an American sculptor whose small replicas of everyday life were mass produced in molded plaster and sold through mail-order catalogs. Selling for five to ten dollars, Rogers's inexpensive groupings of statues were very popular but were seen by critics as pandering to an uneducated public. By the time Rogers retired in 1894, changing tastes had made him obscure.

Jacqueminot roses   The Jacqueminot is a fine hybrid rose with very long stems and clear red flowers. Throughout history, the rose itself has been a complex symbol of both heavenly perfection and earthly passion, capturing the sense of time and eternity, of life and death, of fertility and virginity.

Turkish coffee   Very strong and usually very sweet black coffee. In this description Archer associates Ellen with the sensual, alluring, and exotic.

ambergris   A waxlike substance found in whale intestines and used in perfumes to make the scent last longer.

East Thirty-ninth Street   A fashionable residential neighborhood inhabited at the turn of century by such prominent families as the Belmonts, Rhinelanders, Tiffanys, Havemeyers, Phelpses, Delanos, and Morgans, all of whom owned brownstones along Fifth, Madison, and Park Avenues. This was also the area of influential professional, political, and social clubs such as the Union League Club, which was established in 1863 to support the Union cause and which later supported the Metropolitan Museum of Art.

housing question; but, though the Wellands approved of an extended European honeymoon (perhaps even a winter in Egypt), they were firm as to the need of a house for the returning couple. The young man felt that his fate was sealed: for the rest of his life he would go up every evening between the cast-iron railings of that greenish-yellow doorstep, and pass through a Pompeian vestibule into a hall with a wainscoting of varnished yellow wood. But beyond that his imagination could not travel. He knew the drawing-room above had a bay window, but he could not fancy how May would deal with it. She submitted cheerfully to the purple satin and yellow tuftings of the Welland drawing-room, to its sham Buhl tables and gilt vitrines full of modern Saxe. He saw no reason to suppose that she would want anything different in her own house; and his only comfort was to reflect that she would probably let him arrange his library as he pleased—which would be, of course, with "sincere" Eastlake furniture, and the plain new book-cases without glass doors.

The round-bosomed maid came in, drew the curtains, pushed back a log, and said consolingly: "*Verrà—verrà.*" When she had gone Archer stood up and began to wander about. Should he wait any longer? His position

---

Pompeian vestibule The excavation, beginning in 1755, of the volcano-buried town of Pompeii and the nearby towns of Herculaneum and Stabia had a profound effect on Neoclassical design. A Pompeian or Etruscan style emerged that featured bold blacks, reds, greens, and yellows, with finely drawn borders and grotesques. The vestibule—an entryway between the front door and the interior of the home—that Archer imagines is designed in this style.

wainscoting Wooden paneling or boarding usually applied to the lower part of a wall. The "varnished yellow wood" is probably oak.

tuftings A style of upholstery common in the Victorian era. The fabric has thread drawn through and pulled at regular intervals to produce a depression in its surface. Usually, each depression is ornamented with a tuft or button.

gilt vitrines Gold-leafed cabinets with glass doors. The vitrines contrast with the "plain new book-cases without glass doors" that Archer envisions for his own house.

modern Saxe A term used in France to describe the porcelain of the Meissen factory, located near Dresden. Modern Saxe replicates the porcelain made in the early 1700s.

"sincere" Eastlake furniture Englishman Charles Lock Eastlake (1836–1906) published the popular *Hints on Household Taste* (London, 1868; Boston, 1872), in which he argued for rich use of material but simple construction as the basis of artistic design. Eastlake considered solid wood furniture with rectangular joinery "honest" and advised discarding the ornate designs of the past in favor of crisper, more angular styles of furniture. In desiring "sincere" Eastlake furniture, Archer demonstrates taste for late rather than early styles.

"Verrà—verrà" Italian: "She will come—she will come."

was becoming rather foolish. Perhaps he had misunderstood Madame Olenska—perhaps she had not invited him after all.

Down the cobblestones of the quiet street came the ring of a stepper's hoofs; they stopped before the house, and he caught the opening of a carriage door. Parting the curtains he looked out into the early dusk. A street-lamp faced him, and in its light he saw Julius Beaufort's compact English brougham, drawn by a big roan, and the banker descending from it, and helping out Madame Olenska.

Beaufort stood, hat in hand, saying something which his companion seemed to negative; then they shook hands, and he jumped into his carriage while she mounted the steps.

When she entered the room she showed no surprise at seeing Archer there; surprise seemed the emotion that she was least addicted to.

"How do you like my funny house?" she asked. "To me it's like heaven."

As she spoke she untied her little velvet bonnet and tossing it away with her long cloak stood looking at him with meditative eyes.

"You've arranged it delightfully," he rejoined, alive to the flatness of the words, but imprisoned in the conventional by his consuming desire to be simple and striking.

"Oh, it's a poor little place. My relations despise it. But at any rate it's less gloomy than the van der Luydens'."

The words gave him an electric shock, for few were the rebellious spirits who would have dared to call the stately home of the van der Luydens gloomy. Those privileged to enter it shivered there, and spoke of it as "handsome." But suddenly he was glad that she had given voice to the general shiver.

"It's delicious—what you've done here," he repeated.

"I like the little house," she admitted; "but I suppose what I like is the blessedness of its being here, in my own country and my own town; and then, of being alone in it." She spoke so low that he hardly heard the last phrase; but in his awkwardness he took it up.

"You like so much to be alone?"

"Yes; as long as my friends keep me from feeling lonely." She sat down near the fire, said: "Nastasia will bring the tea presently," and signed to him to return to his armchair, adding: "I see you've already chosen your corner."

---

roan   A horse of mixed colors, especially a bay, sorrel, or chestnut mixed with gray or white. Wharton may imply that Beaufort himself lacks "true color."

Leaning back, she folded her arms behind her head, and looked at the fire under drooping lids.

"This is the hour I like best—don't you?"

A proper sense of his dignity caused him to answer: "I was afraid you'd forgotten the hour. Beaufort must have been very engrossing."

She looked amused. "Why—have you waited long? Mr. Beaufort took me to see a number of houses—since it seems I'm not to be allowed to stay in this one." She appeared to dismiss both Beaufort and himself from her mind, and went on: "I've never been in a city where there seems to be such a feeling against living in *des quartiers excentriques*. What does it matter where one lives? I'm told this street is respectable."

"It's not fashionable."

"Fashionable! Do you all think so much of that? Why not make one's own fashions? But I suppose I've lived too independently; at any rate, I want to do what you all do—I want to feel cared for and safe."

He was touched, as he had been the evening before when she spoke of her need of guidance.

"That's what your friends want you to feel. New York's an awfully safe place," he added with a flash of sarcasm.

"Yes, isn't it? One feels that," she cried, missing the mockery. "Being here is like—like—being taken on a holiday when one has been a good little girl and done all one's lessons."

The analogy was well meant, but did not altogether please him. He did not mind being flippant about New York, but disliked to hear any one else take the same tone. He wondered if she did not begin to see what a powerful engine it was, and how nearly it had crushed her. The Lovell Mingotts' dinner, patched up *in extremis* out of all sorts of social odds and ends, ought to have taught her the narrowness of her escape; but either she had been all along unaware of having skirted disaster, or else she had lost sight of it in the triumph of the van der Luyden evening. Archer inclined to the former theory; he fancied that her New York was still completely undifferentiated, and the conjecture nettled him.

"Last night," he said, "New York laid itself out for you. The van der Luydens do nothing by halves."

"No: how kind they are! It was such a nice party. Every one seems to have such an esteem for them."

---

des quartiers excentriques   French: eccentric or odd neighborhoods.
in extremis   Latin: at the point of death; in extreme circumstances.

The terms were hardly adequate; she might have spoken in that way of a tea-party at the dear old Miss Lannings'.

"The van der Luydens," said Archer, feeling himself pompous as he spoke, "are the most powerful influence in New York society. Unfortunately—owing to her health—they receive very seldom."

She unclasped her hands from behind her head, and looked at him meditatively.

"Isn't that perhaps the reason?"

"The reason—?"

"For their great influence; that they make themselves so rare."

He coloured a little, stared at her—and suddenly felt the penetration of the remark. At a stroke she had pricked the van der Luydens and they collapsed. He laughed, and sacrificed them.

Nastasia brought the tea, with handleless Japanese cups and little covered dishes, placing the tray on a low table.

"But you'll explain these things to me—you'll tell me all I ought to know," Madame Olenska continued, leaning forward to hand him his cup.

"It's you who are telling me; opening my eyes to things I'd looked at so long that I'd ceased to see them."

She detached a small gold cigarette-case from one of her bracelets, held it out to him, and took a cigarette herself. On the chimney were long spills for lighting them.

"Ah, then we can both help each other. But I want help so much more. You must tell me just what to do."

It was on the tip of his tongue to reply: "Don't be seen driving about the streets with Beaufort—" but he was being too deeply drawn into the atmosphere of the room, which was her atmosphere, and to give advice of that sort would have been like telling some one who was bargaining for attar-of-roses in Samarkand that one should always be provided with arctics for a New York winter. New York seemed much farther off than Samarkand, and if they were indeed to help each other she was rendering what might prove the first of their mutual services by making him look at his native city objectively. Viewed thus, as through the wrong end of a telescope, it looked disconcertingly small and distant; but then from Samarkand it would.

---

spills Pieces of paper or wood used for lighting a fire.

attar-of-roses in Samarkand Attar-of-roses is a fragrant essential oil or perfume obtained from the rose's petals. Samarkand is a city in Uzbekistan, south central Asia, known for its perfumes. Archer hesitates to offer Ellen irrelevant advice.

arctics Protective rubber coverings for shoes.

A flame darted from the logs and she bent over the fire, stretching her thin hands so close to it that a faint halo shone about the oval nails. The light touched to russet the rings of dark hair escaping from her braids, and made her pale face paler.

"There are plenty of people to tell you what to do," Archer rejoined, obscurely envious of them.

"Oh—all my aunts? And my dear old Granny?" She considered the idea impartially. "They're all a little vexed with me for setting up for my-self—poor Granny especially. She wanted to keep me with her; but I had to be free—" He was impressed by this light way of speaking of the for-midable Catherine, and moved by the thought of what must have given Madame Olenska this thirst for even the loneliest kind of freedom. But the idea of Beaufort gnawed him.

"I think I understand how you feel," he said. "Still, your family can advise you; explain differences; show you the way."

She lifted her thin black eyebrows. "Is New York such a labyrinth? I thought it so straight up and down—like Fifth Avenue. And with all the cross streets numbered!" She seemed to guess his faint disapproval of this, and added, with the rare smile that enchanted her whole face: "If you knew how I like it for just *that*—the straight-up-and-downness, and the big honest labels on everything!"

He saw his chance. "Everything may be labelled—but everybody is not."

"Perhaps. I may simplify too much—but you'll warn me if I do." She turned from the fire to look at him. "There are only two people here who make me feel as if they understood what I mean and could explain things to me: you and Mr. Beaufort."

Archer winced at the joining of the names, and then, with a quick readjustment, understood, sympathised and pitied. So close to the pow-ers of evil she must have lived that she still breathed more freely in their air. But since she felt that he understood her also, his business would be to make her see Beaufort as he really was, with all he represented—and abhor it.

He answered gently: "I understand. But just at first don't let go of your old friends' hands: I mean the older women, your Granny Mingott, Mrs. Welland, Mrs. van der Luyden. They like and admire you—they want to help you."

She shook her head and sighed. "Oh, I know—I know! But on con-dition that they don't hear anything unpleasant. Aunt Welland put it in those very words when I tried. . . . Does no one want to know the truth here, Mr. Archer? The real loneliness is living among all these kind people who only ask one to pretend!" She lifted her hands to her face, and he saw her thin shoulders shaken by a sob.

"Madame Olenska!—Oh, don't, Ellen," he cried, starting up and bending over her. He drew down one of her hands, clasping and chafing it like a child's while he murmured reassuring words; but in a moment she freed herself, and looked up at him with wet lashes.

"Does no one cry here, either? I suppose there's no need to, in heaven," she said, straightening her loosened braids with a laugh, and bending over the tea-kettle. It was burnt into his consciousness that he had called her "Ellen"—called her so twice; and that she had not noticed it. Far down the inverted telescope he saw the faint white figure of May Welland—in New York.

Suddenly Nastasia put her head in to say something in her rich Italian.

Madame Olenska, again with a hand at her hair, uttered an exclamation of assent—a flashing *"Già—già"*—and the Duke of St. Austrey entered, piloting a tremendous black-wigged and red-plumed lady in overflowing furs.

"My dear Countess, I've brought an old friend of mine to see you— Mrs. Struthers. She wasn't asked to the party last night, and she wants to know you."

The Duke beamed on the group, and Madame Olenska advanced with a murmur of welcome toward the queer couple. She seemed to have no idea how oddly matched they were, nor what a liberty the Duke had taken in bringing his companion—and to do him justice, as Archer perceived, the Duke seemed as unaware of it himself.

"Of course I want to know you, my dear," cried Mrs. Struthers in a round rolling voice that matched her bold feathers and her brazen wig. "I want to know everybody who's young and interesting and charming. And the Duke tells me you like music—didn't you, Duke? You're a pianist yourself, I believe? Well, do you want to hear Sarasate play tomorrow eve-

---

"Già—già"   Italian: "Of course, of course."

Mrs. Struthers   Wharton seems to draw on Mrs. Paran Stevens, the mother of a man to whom Wharton was briefly engaged, for her portrait of this nouveau riche socialite. Struthers was the widow of a shoe polish magnate (New York City was a center for shoe manufacturing in the nineteenth century). Stevens made her way into New York society just as Mrs. Struthers does in the novel. The undisputed mark of her new status was her purchase, in 1891, of the 58th Street Marble Row house owned by Wharton's aunt, Mary Mason Jones, who appears in the novel as Catherine Mingott.

Sarasate   Pablo de Sarasate (1844–1908) was a Spanish violinist and composer whose music was distinguished by its beauty and seemingly effortless technique.

ning at my house? You know I've something going on every Sunday evening—it's the day when New York doesn't know what to do with itself, and so I say to it: 'Come and be amused.' And the Duke thought you'd be tempted by Sarasate. You'll find a number of your friends."

Madame Olenska's face grew brilliant with pleasure. "How kind! How good of the Duke to think of me!" She pushed a chair up to the tea-table and Mrs. Struthers sank into it delectably. "Of course I shall be too happy to come."

"That's all right, my dear. And bring your young gentleman with you." Mrs. Struthers extended a hail-fellow hand to Archer. "I can't put a name to you—but I'm sure I've met you—I've met everybody, here, or in Paris or London. Aren't you in diplomacy? All the diplomatists come to me. You like music too? Duke, you must be sure to bring him."

The Duke said "Rather" from the depths of his beard, and Archer withdrew with a stiffly circular bow that made him feel as full of spine as a self-conscious school-boy among careless and unnoticing elders.

He was not sorry for the *dénouement* of his visit: he only wished it had come sooner, and spared him a certain waste of emotion. As he went out into the wintry night, New York again became vast and imminent, and May Welland the loveliest woman in it. He turned into his florist's to send her the daily box of lilies-of-the-valley which, to his confusion, he found he had forgotten that morning.

As he wrote a word on his card and waited for an envelope he glanced about the embowered shop, and his eye lit on a cluster of yellow roses. He had never seen any as sun-golden before, and his first impulse was to send them to May instead of the lilies. But they did not look like her—there was something too rich, too strong, in their fiery beauty. In a sudden revulsion of mood, and almost without knowing what he did, he signed to the florist to lay the roses in another long box, and slipped his card into a second envelope, on which he wrote the name of the Countess Olenska; then, just as he was turning away, he drew the card out again, and left the empty envelope on the box.

"They'll go at once?" he enquired, pointing to the roses.

The florist assured him that they would.

---

hail-fellow hand   A hand raised in a hearty, warm greeting.

dénouement   French: the outcome or conclusion of a series of events.

yellow roses   In the "language of flowers," the meaning of yellow roses varied according to their shade. Light or golden yellow roses conveyed the sense of the sun's light, intellect, intuition, faith, and goodness. Dark ones, on the other hand, connoted treachery, jealousy, ambition, secrecy, and betrayal.

X

The next day he persuaded May to escape for a walk in the Park after luncheon. As was the custom in old-fashioned Episcopalian New York, she usually accompanied her parents to church on Sunday afternoons; but Mrs. Welland condoned her truancy, having that very morning won her over to the necessity of a long engagement, with time to prepare a hand-embroidered trousseau containing the proper number of dozens.

The day was delectable. The bare vaulting of trees along the Mall was ceiled with lapis lazuli, and arched above snow that shone like splintered crystals. It was the weather to call out May's radiance, and she burned like a young maple in the frost. Archer was proud of the glances turned on her, and the simple joy of possessorship cleared away his underlying perplexities.

"It's so delicious—waking every morning to smell lilies-of-the-valley in one's room!" she said.

"Yesterday they came late. I hadn't time in the morning—"

"But your remembering each day to send them makes me love them so much more than if you'd given a standing order, and they came every morning on the minute, like one's music-teacher—as I know Gertrude Lefferts's did, for instance, when she and Lawrence were engaged."

"Ah—they would!" laughed Archer, amused at her keenness. He looked sideways at her fruit-like cheek and felt rich and secure enough to add: "When I sent your lilies yesterday afternoon I saw some rather gorgeous yellow roses and packed them off to Madame Olenska. Was that right?"

"How dear of you! Anything of that kind delights her. It's odd she didn't mention it: she lunched with us today, and spoke of Mr. Beaufort's having sent her wonderful orchids, and cousin Henry van der Luyden a whole hamper of carnations from Skuytercliff. She seems so surprised to

---

Episcopalian New York   Most old New Yorkers were Episcopalian, a Protestant denomination with similarities to the Church of England.

lapis lazuli   An opaque blue gemstone of lazurite, a relatively rare mineral. Wharton often associates May with white or blue colors and cool temperatures.

orchids   These delicate plants with irregular, showy flowers are native to the tropics. In the nineteenth century, an extraordinary number of Central and South American trees on which orchids grew were recklessly cut down in order to meet the demand of wealthy collectors. Orchids, which connoted a "belle," or beautiful woman, appear again in chap. 33, when Mr. van der Luyden sends them to May.

carnations   The meaning of these fringed, fragrant flowers varied according to their color. Red ones suggested "alas for my poor heart," white ones conveyed refusal, and

receive flowers. Don't people send them in Europe? She thinks it such a pretty custom."

"Oh, well, no wonder mine were overshadowed by Beaufort's, said Archer irritably. Then he remembered that he had not put a card with the roses, and was vexed at having spoken of them. He wanted to say: "I called on your cousin yesterday," but hesitated. If Madame Olenska had not spoken of his visit it might seem awkward that he should. Yet not to do so gave the affair an air of mystery that he disliked. To shake off the question he began to talk of their own plans, their future, and Mrs. Welland's insistence on a long engagement.

"If you call it long! Isabel Chivers and Reggie were engaged for two years: Grace and Thorley for nearly a year and a half. Why aren't we very well off as we are?"

It was the traditional maidenly interrogation, and he felt ashamed of himself for finding it singularly childish. No doubt she simply echoed what was said for her; but she was nearing her twenty-second birthday, and he wondered at what age "nice" women began to speak for themselves.

"Never, if we won't let them, I suppose," he mused, and recalled his mad outburst to Mr. Sillerton Jackson: "Women ought to be as free as we are—"

It would presently be his task to take the bandage from this young woman's eyes, and bid her look forth on the world. But how many generations of the women who had gone to her making had descended bandaged to the family vault? He shivered a little, remembering some of the new ideas in his scientific books, and the much-cited instance of the Kentucky cave-fish, which had ceased to develop eyes because they had no use for them. What if, when he had bidden May Welland to open hers, they could only look out blankly at blankness?

"We might be much better off. We might be altogether together—we might travel."

Her face lit up. "That would be lovely," she owned: she would love to travel. But her mother would not understand their wanting to do things so differently.

"As if the mere 'differently' didn't account for it!" the wooer insisted.

"Newland! You're so original!" she exulted.

His heart sank, for he saw that he was saying all the things that young men in the same situation were expected to say, and that she was making

---

yellow ones suggested disdain. Perhaps all three meanings are combined in this gift from the van der Luydens.

Kentucky cave-fish Organisms studied to support Darwin's theory of natural selection.

the answers that instinct and tradition taught her to make—even to the point of calling him original.

"Original! We're all as like each other as those dolls cut out of the same folded paper. We're like patterns stencilled on a wall. Can't you and I strike out for ourselves, May?"

He had stopped and faced her in the excitement of their discussion, and her eyes rested on him with a bright unclouded admiration.

"Mercy—shall we elope?" she laughed.

"If you would—"

"You *do* love me, Newland! I'm so happy."

"But then—why not be happier?"

"We can't behave like people in novels, though, can we?"

"Why not—why not—why not?"

She looked a little bored by his insistence. She knew very well that they couldn't, but it was troublesome to have to produce a reason. "I'm not clever enough to argue with you. But that kind of thing is rather—vulgar, isn't it?" she suggested, relieved to have hit on a word that would assuredly extinguish the whole subject.

"Are you so much afraid, then, of being vulgar?"

She was evidently staggered by this. "Of course I should hate it—so would you," she rejoined, a trifle irritably.

He stood silent, beating his stick nervously against his boot-top; and feeling that she had indeed found the right way of closing the discussion, she went on light-heartedly: "Oh, did I tell you that I showed Ellen my ring? She thinks it the most beautiful setting she ever saw. There's nothing like it in the rue de la Paix, she said. I do love you, Newland, for being so artistic!"

The next afternoon, as Archer, before dinner, sat smoking sullenly in his study, Janey wandered in on him. He had failed to stop at his club on the way up from the office where he exercised the profession of the law in the leisurely manner common to well-to-do New Yorkers of his class. He was out of spirits and slightly out of temper, and a haunting horror of doing the same thing every day at the same hour besieged his brain.

"Sameness—sameness!" he muttered, the word running through his head like a persecuting tune as he saw the familiar tall-hatted figures

---

rue de la Paix   A street on the Right Bank of Paris, famous for its luxurious shops, that runs from the southwest corner of the Place de l'Opéra to the Place Vendôme.

tall-hatted   A standard item of a gentleman's wardrobe, the tall hat was cylindrical; gray, fawn, or black in color; and often of silk, especially for formal occasions.

lounging behind the plate-glass; and because he usually dropped in at the club at that hour he had gone home instead. He knew not only what they were likely to be talking about, but the part each one would take in the discussion. The Duke of course would be their principal theme; though the appearance in Fifth Avenue of a golden-haired lady in a small canary-coloured brougham with a pair of black cobs (for which Beaufort was generally thought responsible) would also doubtless be thoroughly gone into. Such "women" (as they were called) were few in New York, those driving their own carriages still fewer, and the appearance of Miss Fanny Ring in Fifth Avenue at the fashionable hour had profoundly agitated society. Only the day before, her carriage had passed Mrs. Lovell Mingott's, and the latter had instantly rung the little bell at her elbow and ordered the coachman to drive her home. "What if it had happened to Mrs. van der Luyden?" people asked each other with a shudder. Archer could hear Lawrence Lefferts, at that very hour, holding forth on the disintegration of society.

He raised his head irritably when his sister Janey entered, and then quickly bent over his book (Swinburne's "Chastelard"—just out) as if he had not seen her. She glanced at the writing-table heaped with books, opened a volume of the "Contes Drôlatiques," made a wry face over the archaic French, and sighed: "What learned things you read!"

"Well—?" he asked, as she hovered Cassandra-like before him.

"Mother's very angry."

"Angry? With whom? About what?"

---

cobs   Thickset, stocky, short-legged horses.

Swinburne's "Chastelard"   Algernon Charles Swinburne (1837–1909) was an English poet and man of letters known for his rebellion against Victorian customs and religion, his sympathies with political revolutions of his time, and the light musical effects of his poetry. *Chastelard* (1865), the first play in his trilogy about Mary, Queen of Scots, describes a French poet who was executed for his love of the queen.

"Contes Drôlatiques"   Honoré de Balzac (1799–1850) was a French novelist and short story writer known for his meticulous detail, depictions of sweeping emotions, and sense of verbal comedy. His masterpiece is *La Comédie Humaine,* an attempt to give a social history of France. Balzac was an early realist, but his style looks back to Rabelais, whose sixteenth-century spelling and vocabulary he pastiches in *Contes Drôlatiques* (Droll Stories) (1832).

Cassandra-like   Bearing the unaccepted truth. In Greek mythology, Cassandra was the daughter of Priam, King of Troy. Apollo favored her and gave her the gift of prophecy, but because Cassandra did not return his love, he decreed that she would always tell the truth but never be believed. Archer prefers not to believe Janey's report of Ellen's unconventionality.

"Miss Sophy Jackson has just been here. She brought word that her brother would come in after dinner: she couldn't say very much, because he forbade her to: he wishes to give all the details himself. He's with cousin Louisa van der Luyden now."

"For heaven's sake, my dear girl, try a fresh start. It would take an omniscient Deity to know what you're talking about."

"It's not a time to be profane, Newland. . . . Mother feels badly enough about your not going to church . . ."

With a groan he plunged back into his book.

"*Newland!* Do listen. Your friend Madame Olenska was at Mrs. Lemuel Struthers's party last night: she went there with the Duke and Mr. Beaufort."

At the last clause of this announcement a senseless anger swelled the young man's breast. To smother it he laughed. "Well, what of it? I knew she meant to."

Janey paled and her eyes began to project. "You knew she meant to—and you didn't try to stop her? To warn her?"

"Stop her? Warn her?" He laughed again. "I'm not engaged to be married to the Countess Olenska!" The words had a fantastic sound in his own ears.

"You're marrying into her family."

"Oh, family—family!" he jeered.

"Newland—don't you care about Family?"

"Not a brass farthing."

"Nor about what cousin Louisa van der Luyden will think?"

"Not the half of one—if she thinks such old maid's rubbish."

"Mother is not an old maid," said his virgin sister with pinched lips.

He felt like shouting back: "Yes, she is, and so are the van der Luydens, and so we all are, when it comes to being so much as brushed by the wing-tip of Reality." But he saw her long gentle face puckering into tears, and felt ashamed of the useless pain he was inflicting.

"Hang Countess Olenska! Don't be a goose, Janey—I'm not her keeper."

"No; but you *did* ask the Wellands to announce your engagement sooner so that we might all back her up; and if it hadn't been for that cousin Louisa would never have invited her to the dinner for the Duke."

---

omniscient Deity   Archer uses a euphemism to swear, "God knows what you're talking about."

brass farthing   Something of little value. A farthing is a former British coin worth one-fourth of a penny.

"Well—what harm was there in inviting her? She was the best-looking woman in the room; she made the dinner a little less funereal than the usual van der Luyden banquet."

"You know cousin Henry asked her to please you: he persuaded cousin Louisa. And now they're so upset that they're going back to Skuytercliff tomorrow. I think, Newland, you'd better come down. You don't seem to understand how mother feels."

In the drawing-room Newland found his mother. She raised a troubled brow from her needlework to ask: "Has Janey told you?"

"Yes." He tried to keep his tone as measured as her own. "But I can't take it very seriously."

"Not the fact of having offended cousin Louisa and cousin Henry?"

"The fact that they can be offended by such a trifle as Countess Olenska's going to the house of a woman they consider common."

"*Consider—!*"

"Well, who is; but who has good music, and amuses people on Sunday evenings, when the whole of New York is dying of inanition."

"Good music? All I know is, there was a woman who got up on a table and sang the things they sing at the places you go to in Paris. There was smoking and champagne."

"Well—that kind of thing happens in other places, and the world still goes on."

"I don't suppose, dear, you're really defending the French Sunday?"

"I've heard you often enough, mother, grumble at the English Sunday when we've been in London."

"New York is neither Paris nor London."

"Oh, no, it's not!" her son groaned.

"You mean, I suppose, that society here is not as brilliant? You're right, I daresay; but we belong here, and people should respect our ways when they come among us. Ellen Olenska especially: she came back to get away from the kind of life people lead in brilliant societies."

Newland made no answer, and after a moment his mother ventured: "I was going to put on my bonnet and ask you to take me to see cousin Louisa for a moment before dinner." He frowned, and she continued: "I thought you might explain to her what you've just said: that society abroad is different . . . that people are not as particular, and that Madame

---

French Sunday A Sunday spent in pleasant family activity rather than in worship or prayer. In Catholic countries such as France, Sundays were to be enjoyed with relatives, whereas in predominantly Protestant countries such as England and the United States, they were to be devoted to more contemplative activities.

Olenska may not have realised how we feel about such things. It would be, you know, dear," she added with an innocent adroitness, "in Madame Olenska's interest if you did."

"Dearest mother, I really don't see how we're concerned in the matter. The Duke took Madame Olenska to Mrs. Struthers's—in fact he brought Mrs. Struthers to call on her. I was there when they came. If the van der Luydens want to quarrel with anybody, the real culprit is under their own roof."

"Quarrel? Newland, did you ever know of cousin Henry's quarrelling? Besides, the Duke's his guest; and a stranger too. Strangers don't discriminate: how should they? Countess Olenska is a New Yorker, and should have respected the feelings of New York."

"Well, then, if they must have a victim, you have my leave to throw Madame Olenska to them," cried her son, exasperated. "I don't see myself—or you either—offering ourselves up to expiate her crimes."

"Oh, of course you see only the Mingott side," his mother answered, in the sensitive tone that was her nearest approach to anger.

The sad butler drew back the drawing-room portières and announced: "Mr. Henry van der Luyden."

Mrs. Archer dropped her needle and pushed her chair back with an agitated hand.

"Another lamp," she cried to the retreating servant, while Janey bent over to straighten her mother's cap.

Mr. van der Luyden's figure loomed on the threshold, and Newland Archer went forward to greet his cousin.

"We were just talking about you, sir," he said.

Mr. van der Luyden seemed overwhelmed by the announcement. He drew off his glove to shake hands with the ladies, and smoothed his tall hat shyly, while Janey pushed an arm-chair forward, and Archer continued: "And the Countess Olenska."

Mrs. Archer paled.

"Ah—a charming woman. I have just been to see her," said Mr. van der Luyden, complacency restored to his brow. He sank into the chair, laid his hat and gloves on the floor beside him in the old-fashioned way, and went on: "She has a real gift for arranging flowers. I had sent her a few carnations from Skuytercliff, and I was astonished. Instead of massing them in big bunches as our head-gardener does, she had scattered them about loosely, here and there . . . I can't say how. The Duke had told me: he said: 'Go and see how cleverly she's arranged her drawing-room.' And she has. I should really like to take Louisa to see her, if the neighbourhood were not so—unpleasant."

A dead silence greeted this unusual flow of words from Mr. van der Luyden. Mrs. Archer drew her embroidery out of the basket into which she had nervously tumbled it, and Newland, leaning against the chimney-place and twisting a humming-bird-feather screen in his hand, saw Janey's gaping countenance lit up by the coming of the second lamp.

"The fact is," Mr. van der Luyden continued, stroking his long grey leg with a bloodless hand weighed down by the Patroon's great signet-ring, "the fact is, I dropped in to thank her for the very pretty note she wrote me about my flowers; and also—but this is between ourselves, of course—to give her a friendly warning about allowing the Duke to carry her off to parties with him. I don't know if you've heard—"

Mrs. Archer produced an indulgent smile. "Has the Duke been carrying her off to parties?"

"You know what these English grandees are. They're all alike. Louisa and I are very fond of our cousin—but it's hopeless to expect people who are accustomed to the European courts to trouble themselves about our little republican distinctions. The Duke goes where he's amused." Mr. van der Luyden paused, but no one spoke. "Yes—it seems he took her with him last night to Mrs. Lemuel Struthers's. Sillerton Jackson has just been to us with the foolish story, and Louisa was rather troubled. So I thought the shortest way was to go straight to Countess Olenska and explain—by the merest hint, you know—how we feel in New York about certain things. I felt I might, without indelicacy, because the evening she dined with us she rather suggested . . . rather let me see that she would be grateful for guidance. And she *was*."

Mr. van der Luyden looked about the room with what would have been self-satisfaction on features less purged of the vulgar passions. On his face it became a mild benevolence which Mrs. Archer's countenance dutifully reflected.

"How kind you both are, dear Henry—always! Newland will particularly appreciate what you have done because of dear May and his new relations."

---

humming-bird-feather screen   During the eighteenth century a new piece of furniture, the fire screen, was introduced. It both shielded the sitter from the fire's heat and served to display the needlework of the mistress of the house. The framed artwork could be raised and lowered on a pole attached to a carved base.

signet-ring   A finger ring with an engraved seal, originally used by sovereigns of England and Scotland for private purposes.

English grandees   Highest-ranking nobility.

She shot an admonitory glance at her son, who said: "Immensely, sir. But I was sure you'd like Madame Olenska."

Mr. van der Luyden looked at him with extreme gentleness. "I never ask to my house, my dear Newland," he said, "any one whom I do not like. And so I have just told Sillerton Jackson." With a glance at the clock he rose and added: "But Louisa will be waiting. We are dining early, to take the Duke to the Opera."

After the portières had solemnly closed behind their visitor a silence fell upon the Archer family.

"Gracious—how romantic!" at last broke explosively from Janey. No one knew exactly what inspired her elliptic comments, and her relations had long since given up trying to interpret them.

Mrs. Archer shook her head with a sigh. "Provided it all turns out for the best," she said, in the tone of one who knows how surely it will not. "Newland, you must stay and see Sillerton Jackson when he comes this evening: I really shan't know what to say to him."

"Poor mother! But he won't come—" her son laughed, stooping to kiss away her frown.

XI

Some two weeks later, Newland Archer, sitting in abstracted idleness in his private compartment of the office of Letterblair, Lamson and Low, attorneys at law, was summoned by the head of the firm.

Old Mr. Letterblair, the accredited legal adviser of three generations of New York gentility, throned behind his mahogany desk in evident perplexity. As he stroked his close-clipped white whiskers and ran his hand through the rumpled grey locks above his jutting brows, his disrespectful junior partner thought how much he looked like the Family Physician annoyed with a patient whose symptoms refuse to be classified.

"My dear sir—" he always addressed Archer as "sir"—"I have sent for you to go into a little matter; a matter which, for the moment, I prefer not to mention either to Mr. Skipworth or Mr. Redwood." The gentlemen he spoke of were the other senior partners of the firm; for, as was always the case with legal associations of old standing in New York, all the partners named on the office letter-head were long since dead; and Mr. Letterblair, for example, was, professionally speaking, his own grandson.

He leaned back in his chair with a furrowed brow. "For family reasons—" he continued.

Archer looked up.

"The Mingott family," said Mr. Letterblair with an explanatory smile and bow. "Mrs. Manson Mingott sent for me yesterday. Her grand-daughter the Countess Olenska wishes to sue her husband for divorce. Certain papers have been placed in my hands." He paused and drummed on his desk. "In view of your prospective alliance with the family I should like to consult you—to consider the case with you—before taking any farther steps."

Archer felt the blood in his temples. He had seen the Countess Olenska only once since his visit to her, and then at the Opera, in the Mingott box. During this interval she had become a less vivid and importunate image, receding from his foreground as May Welland resumed her rightful place in it. He had not heard her divorce spoken of since Janey's first random allusion to it, and had dismissed the tale as unfounded gossip. Theoretically, the idea of divorce was almost as distasteful to him as to his mother; and he was annoyed that Mr. Letterblair (no doubt prompted by old Catherine Mingott) should be so evidently planning to draw him into the affair. After all, there were plenty of Mingott men for such jobs, and as yet he was not even a Mingott by marriage.

He waited for the senior partner to continue. Mr. Letterblair unlocked a drawer and drew out a packet. "If you will run your eye over these papers—"

Archer frowned. "I beg your pardon, sir; but just because of the prospective relationship, I should prefer your consulting Mr. Skipworth or Mr. Redwood."

Mr. Letterblair looked surprised and slightly offended. It was unusual for a junior to reject such an opening.

He bowed. "I respect your scruple, sir; but in this case I believe true delicacy requires you to do as I ask. Indeed, the suggestion is not mine but Mrs. Manson Mingott's and her son's. I have seen Lovell Mingott; and also Mr. Welland. They all named you."

Archer felt his temper rising. He had been somewhat languidly drifting with events for the last fortnight, and letting May's fair looks and radiant nature obliterate the rather importunate pressure of the Mingott claims. But this behest of old Mrs. Mingott's roused him to a sense of what the clan thought they had the right to exact from a prospective son-in-law; and he chafed at the rôle.

"Her uncles ought to deal with this," he said.

"They have. The matter has been gone into by the family. They are opposed to the Countess's idea; but she is firm, and insists on a legal opinion."

The young man was silent: he had not opened the packet in his hand.

"Does she want to marry again?"

"I believe it is suggested; but she denies it."

"Then—"

"Will you oblige me, Mr. Archer, by first looking through these papers? Afterward, when we have talked the case over, I will give you my opinion."

Archer withdrew reluctantly with the unwelcome documents. Since their last meeting he had half-unconsciously collaborated with events in ridding himself of the burden of Madame Olenska. His hour alone with her by the firelight had drawn them into a momentary intimacy on which the Duke of St. Austrey's intrusion with Mrs. Lemuel Struthers, and the Countess's joyous greeting of them, had rather providentially broken. Two days later Archer had assisted at the comedy of her reinstatement in the van der Luydens' favour, and had said to himself, with a touch of tartness, that a lady who knew how to thank all-powerful elderly gentlemen to such good purpose for a bunch of flowers did not need either the private consolations or the public championship of a young man of his small compass. To look at the matter in this light simplified his own case and surprisingly furbished up all the dim domestic virtues. He could not picture May Welland, in whatever conceivable emergency, hawking about her private difficulties and lavishing her confidences on strange men; and she had never seemed to him finer or fairer than in the week that followed. He had even yielded to her wish for a long engagement, since she had found the one disarming answer to his plea for haste.

"You know, when it comes to the point, your parents have always let you have your way ever since you were a little girl," he argued; and she had answered, with her clearest look: "Yes; and that's what makes it so hard to refuse the very last thing they'll ever ask of me as a little girl."

That was the old New York note; that was the kind of answer he would like always to be sure of his wife's making. If one had habitually breathed the New York air there were times when anything less crystalline seemed stifling.

The papers he had retired to read did not tell him much in fact; but they plunged him into an atmosphere in which he choked and spluttered. They consisted mainly of an exchange of letters between Count Olenski's solicitors and a French legal firm to whom the Countess had applied for the settlement of her financial situation. There was also a short letter from the Count to his wife: after reading it, Newland Archer rose, jammed the papers back into their envelope, and re-ëntered Mr. Letterblair's office.

"Here are the letters, sir. If you wish, I'll see Madame Olenska," he said in a constrained voice.

"Thank you—thank you, Mr. Archer. Come and dine with me tonight if you're free, and we'll go into the matter afterward: in case you wish to call on our client tomorrow."

Newland Archer walked straight home again that afternoon. It was a winter evening of transparent clearness, with an innocent young moon above the house-tops; and he wanted to fill his soul's lungs with the pure radiance, and not exchange a word with any one till he and Mr. Letterblair were closeted together after dinner. It was impossible to decide otherwise than he had done: he must see Madame Olenska himself rather than let her secrets be bared to other eyes. A great wave of compassion had swept away his indifference and impatience: she stood before him as an exposed and pitiful figure, to be saved at all costs from farther wounding herself in her mad plunges against fate.

He remembered what she had told him of Mrs. Welland's request to be spared whatever was "unpleasant" in her history, and winced at the thought that it was perhaps this attitude of mind which kept the New York air so pure. "Are we only Pharisees after all?" he wondered, puzzled by the effort to reconcile his instinctive disgust at human vileness with his equally instinctive pity for human frailty.

For the first time he perceived how elementary his own principles had always been. He passed for a young man who had not been afraid of risks, and he knew that his secret love-affair with poor silly Mrs. Thorley Rushworth had not been too secret to invest him with a becoming air of adventure. But Mrs. Rushworth was "that kind of woman"; foolish, vain, clandestine by nature, and far more attracted by the secrecy and peril of the affair than by such charms and qualities as he possessed. When the fact dawned on him it nearly broke his heart, but now it seemed the redeeming feature of the case. The affair, in short, had been of the kind that most of the young men of his age had been through, and emerged from with calm consciences and an undisturbed belief in the abysmal distinction between the women one loved and respected and those one enjoyed—and pitied. In this view they were sedulously abetted by their mothers, aunts and other elderly female relatives, who all shared Mrs. Archer's belief that when "such things happened" it was undoubtedly foolish of the man, but somehow always criminal of the woman. All the elderly ladies whom Archer knew regarded any woman who loved imprudently as necessarily unscrupulous

---

Pharisees Hypocritically pretentious and self-righteous people. The Pharisees, an influential minority group in Palestinian Judaism before 70 C.E., were noted for their separation from common people and their strict observance of traditional and written laws regarding ritual purity, cleansing, and food.

and designing, and mere simple-minded man as powerless in her clutches. The only thing to do was to persuade him, as early as possible, to marry a nice girl, and then trust to her to look after him.

In the complicated old European communities, Archer began to guess, love-problems might be less simple and less easily classified. Rich and idle and ornamental societies must produce many more such situations; and there might even be one in which a woman naturally sensitive and aloof would yet, from the force of circumstances, from sheer defencelessness and loneliness, be drawn into a tie inexcusable by conventional standards.

On reaching home he wrote a line to the Countess Olenska, asking at what hour of the next day she could receive him, and despatched it by a messenger-boy, who returned presently with a word to the effect that she was going to Skuytercliff the next morning to stay over Sunday with the van der Luydens, but that he would find her alone that evening after dinner. The note was written on a rather untidy half-sheet, without date or address, but her hand was firm and free. He was amused at the idea of her week-ending in the stately solitude of Skuytercliff, but immediately afterward felt that there, of all places, she would most feel the chill of minds rigorously averted from the "unpleasant."

He was at Mr. Letterblair's punctually at seven, glad of the pretext for excusing himself soon after dinner. He had formed his own opinion from the papers entrusted to him, and did not especially want to go into the matter with his senior partner. Mr. Letterblair was a widower, and they dined alone, copiously and slowly, in a dark shabby room hung with yellowing prints of "The Death of Chatham" and "The Coronation of Napoleon." On the sideboard, between fluted Sheraton knife-cases, stood

---

"The Death of Chatham" *Death of the Earl of Chatham* (1779–81) was a painting by John Singleton Copley (1738–1815), the foremost American artist of the colonial period, that combined Copley's flair for portraiture and skill in history painting.

"The Coronation of Napoleon" A painting (1805–07) by French Neoclassical artist Jacques-Louis David (1748–1825), who became the official painter of Napoléon (1769–1821). His early work conveys the civic virtues of self-sacrifice, duty, and severity; this later painting, full of pageantry, is one of a series glorifying the exploits of the French emperor.

sideboard A piece of dining-room furniture with drawers and shelves for linens and tableware.

Sheraton A style created by Thomas Sheraton (1751–1806), an English furniture designer. The design originated about 1800 and was characterized by straight lines and graceful proportions.

a decanter of Haut Brion, and another of the old Lanning port (the gift of
a client), which the wastrel Tom Lanning had sold off a year or two before
his mysterious and discreditable death in San Francisco—an incident less
publicly humiliating to the family than the sale of the cellar.

After a velvety oyster soup came shad and cucumbers, then a young
broiled turkey with corn fritters, followed by a canvas-back with currant
jelly and a celery mayonnaise. Mr. Letterblair, who lunched on a sandwich
and tea, dined deliberately and deeply, and insisted on his guest's doing
the same. Finally, when the closing rites had been accomplished, the cloth
was removed, cigars were lit, and Mr. Letterblair, leaning back in his chair
and pushing the port westward, said, spreading his back agreeably to the
coal fire behind him: "The whole family are against a divorce. And I think
rightly."

Archer instantly felt himself on the other side of the argument. "But
why, sir? If there ever was a case—"

"Well—what's the use? *She's* here—he's there; the Atlantic's between
them. She'll never get back a dollar more of her money than what he's voluntarily returned to her: their damned heathen marriage settlements take
precious good care of that. As things go over there, Olenski's acted gener-
ously: he might have turned her out without a penny."

The young man knew this and was silent.

"I understand, though," Mr. Letterblair continued, "that she attaches
no importance to the money. Therefore, as the family say, why not let well
enough alone?"

Archer had gone to the house an hour earlier in full agreement with
Mr. Letterblair's view; but put into words by this selfish, well-fed and
supremely indifferent old man it suddenly became the Pharisaic voice of society wholly absorbed in barricading itself against the unpleasant.

"I think that's for her to decide."

"H'm—have you considered the consequences if she decides for
divorce?"

"You mean the threat in her husband's letter? What weight would that
carry? It's no more than the vague charge of an angry blackguard."

"Yes; but it might make some unpleasant talk if he really defends the
suit."

Haut Brion   Château Haut-Brion is a famous maker of red and white wines. The Haut-
Brion was the only red wine in the Graves district to be honored in the 1855 classification of wines.

blackguard   An unprincipled person; a scoundrel.

"Unpleasant—!" said Archer explosively.

Mr. Letterblair looked at him from under enquiring eyebrows, and the young man, aware of the uselessness of trying to explain what was in his mind, bowed acquiescently while his senior continued: "Divorce is always unpleasant."

"You agree with me?" Mr. Letterblair resumed, after a waiting silence.

"Naturally," said Archer.

"Well, then, I may count on you; the Mingotts may count on you; to use your influence against the idea?"

Archer hesitated. "I can't pledge myself till I've seen the Countess Olenska," he said at length.

"Mr. Archer, I don't understand you. Do you want to marry into a family with a scandalous divorce-suit hanging over it?"

"I don't think that has anything to do with the case."

Mr. Letterblair put down his glass of port and fixed on his young partner a cautious and apprehensive gaze.

Archer understood that he ran the risk of having his mandate withdrawn, and for some obscure reason he disliked the prospect. Now that the job had been thrust on him he did not propose to relinquish it; and, to guard against the possibility, he saw that he must reassure the unimaginative old man who was the legal conscience of the Mingotts.

"You may be sure, sir, that I shan't commit myself till I've reported to you; what I meant was that I'd rather not give an opinion till I've heard what Madame Olenska has to say."

Mr. Letterblair nodded approvingly at an excess of caution worthy of the best New York tradition, and the young man, glancing at his watch, pleaded an engagement and took leave.

XII

Old-fashioned New York dined at seven, and the habit of after-dinner calls, though derided in Archer's set, still generally prevailed. As the young man strolled up Fifth Avenue from Waverley Place, the long thoroughfare was deserted but for a group of carriages standing before the Reggie Chiverses' (where there was a dinner for the Duke), and the occasional figure of an elderly gentlemen in heavy overcoat and muffler ascending a brownstone doorstep and disappearing into a gas-lit hall. Thus, as Archer crossed Washington Square, he remarked that old Mr. du Lac was calling on his

---

Waverley Place [sic]   Waverly Street runs west from the northwest corner of Washington Square.

cousins the Dagonets, and turning down the corner of West Tenth Street he saw Mr. Skipworth, of his own firm, obviously bound on a visit to the Miss Lannings. A little farther up Fifth Avenue, Beaufort appeared on his doorstep, darkly projected against a blaze of light, descended to his private brougham, and rolled away to a mysterious and probably unmentionable destination. It was not an Opera night, and no one was giving a party, so that Beaufort's outing was undoubtedly of a clandestine nature. Archer connected it in his mind with a little house beyond Lexington Avenue in which beribboned window curtains and flower-boxes had recently appeared, and before whose newly painted door the canary-coloured brougham of Miss Fanny Ring was frequently seen to wait.

Beyond the small and slippery pyramid which composed Mrs. Archer's world lay the almost unmapped quarter inhabited by artists, musicians and "people who wrote." These scattered fragments of humanity had never shown any desire to be amalgamated with the social structure. In spite of odd ways they were said to be, for the most part, quite respectable; but they preferred to keep to themselves. Medora Manson, in her prosperous days, had inaugurated a "literary salon"; but it had soon died out owing to the reluctance of the literary to frequent it.

Others had made the same attempt, and there was a household of Blenkers—an intense and voluble mother, and three blowsy daughters who imitated her—where one met Edwin Booth and Patti and William Winter, and the new Shakespearian actor George Rignold, and some of the magazine editors and musical and literary critics.

Mrs. Archer and her group felt a certain timidity concerning these persons. They were odd, they were uncertain, they had things one didn't know about in the background of their lives and minds. Literature and art were

---

beyond Lexington Avenue   Lexington Avenue, which runs north–south between Park Avenue and Third Avenue, was the eastern boundary of fashionable society. The western boundary was Sixth Avenue.

blowsy   Blowzy: disheveled and frowzy; unkempt.

Edwin Booth   An actor (1833–1893) who regularly performed in New York City beginning in 1857 and who is best known for his role as Hamlet, which he performed a hundred times in 1864–65. During the period of the novel, he managed Booth's Theatre (1869–74). He was the brother of actor John Wilkes Booth, assassin of Abraham Lincoln.

William Winter   William Winter (1836–1917) was one of the most influential drama critics of his time. From 1865 to 1909, he wrote for the *New York Tribune*. Winter's early criticism was open minded, but he increasingly opposed the new realism and argued that no play had value unless it adhered to rigid standards of right and wrong.

George Rignold   An English actor who debuted in Shakespeare's *Henry V.*

deeply respected in the Archer set, and Mrs. Archer was always at pains to tell her children how much more agreeable and cultivated society had been when it included such figures as Washington Irving, Fitz-Greene Halleck and the poet of "The Culprit Fay." The most celebrated authors of that generation had been "gentlemen"; perhaps the unknown persons who succeeded them had gentlemanly sentiments, but their origin, their appearance, their hair, their intimacy with the stage and the Opera, made any old New York criterion inapplicable to them.

"When I was a girl," Mrs. Archer used to say, "we knew everybody between the Battery and Canal Street; and only the people one knew had carriages. It was perfectly easy to place any one then; now one can't tell, and I prefer not to try."

Only old Catherine Mingott, with her absence of moral prejudices and almost *parvenu* indifference to the subtler distinctions, might have bridged the abyss; but she had never opened a book or looked at a picture, and cared for music only because it reminded her of gala nights at the *Italiens,* in the days of her triumph at the Tuileries. Possibly Beaufort, who was her match in daring, would have succeeded in bringing about a fusion; but his grand house and silk-stockinged footmen were an obstacle to informal sociability. Moreover, he was as illiterate as old Mrs. Mingott, and considered

---

Washington Irving   A New York–born essayist, historian, and fiction writer, Washington Irving (1783–1859) was admired by upper-class New Yorkers, who considered him one of their own. He became famous for his *History of New York* (1809), a collection of satirical essays about the city's Dutch origins written under the pseudonym Diedrich Knickerbocker (the use of the term *Knickerbocker* to describe a New Yorker originated with Irving). He later moved to Europe, publishing two collections of short stories that included "Rip van Winkle" and "The Legend of Sleepy Hollow." Although American, Irving followed eighteenth-century British models, such as Scott, Addison, and Goldsmith, rather than developing a native idiom. Readers valued the charm, delicacy, and pictorial quality of his work.

Fitz-Greene Halleck . . . "The Culprit Fay"   An American banker and secretary to John Jacob Astor, Halleck (1790–1867) made literature his avocation. He is best known for his collaboration with Joseph Rodman Drake (1795–1820), an American poet and satirist. Their verse tale, *The Culprit Fay* (1835), is a nature fantasy about a fairy who loves a mortal maiden.

between the Battery and Canal Street   This area at the southern end of Manhattan was stylish through the early nineteenth century. But as fashionable New Yorkers moved northward, it became home to immigrants, food wholesalers and retailers, and other businesses.

parvenu   French: a person who has suddenly risen in economic or social class without the background or qualifications for this new status. From the verb meaning "to arrive."

Italiens   French: a European night spot.

"fellows who wrote" as the mere paid purveyors of rich men's pleasures; and no one rich enough to influence his opinion had ever questioned it.

Newland Archer had been aware of these things ever since he could remember, and had accepted them as part of the structure of his universe. He knew that there were societies where painters and poets and novelists and men of science, and even great actors, were as sought after as Dukes; he had often pictured to himself what it would have been to live in the intimacy of drawing-rooms dominated by the talk of Mérimée (whose "Lettres à une Inconnue" was one of his inseparables), of Thackeray, Browning or William Morris. But such things were inconceivable in New York, and unsettling to think of. Archer knew most of the "fellows who wrote," the musicians and the painters; he met them at the Century, or at the little musical and theatrical clubs that were beginning to come into existence. He enjoyed them there, and was bored with them at the Blenkers', where they were mingled with fervid and dowdy women who passed them about like captured curiosities; and even after his most exciting talks with Ned

---

Mérimée . . . "Lettres à une Inconnue"   Prosper Mérimée (1803–1870) was a French writer of novels, stories, plays, and historical and archaeological studies. His tersely written creative work usually depicts a ghastly tragic situation mediated by framing devices or various forms of irony. The volume Archer owns, *Letters to an Unknown Girl* (1874), is a collection of love letters. In chap. 20, Archer envies another character's conversations with Mérimée.

Browning   Robert Browning (1812–1889) was an English poet and dramatist whose work initially went unacknowledged, although *Men and Women* (1855) contains some of his best-known poems written in dramatic monologue. Acclaim followed publication of *The Ring and the Book* (1868–69). Browning is also known for his love of and marriage to poet Elizabeth Barrett.

William Morris   An admirer of Ruskin and Rossetti, William Morris (1834–1896) was an English poet, artisan, and socialist whose writing reflects his appreciation of Arthurian legend, classical subjects, and Icelandic sagas. Morris is largely responsible for the revival of the decorative arts. His wallpaper, damasks, embroideries, tapestries and carpets, which he made in his own shop, were much in demand during the Gothic revival period. (See note on Ruskin, p. 39, and "The House of Life," p. 123.)

the Century   One of the oldest and most prestigious social clubs in the United States, formed in 1846 by poet William Cullen Bryant and others to promote interest in literature and the arts. The Century Club originally limited its membership to 100 artists, writers, and their supporters but grew to 800 members by 1891.

musical and theatrical clubs   In the 1850s and 1860s, a string of minstrel halls developed along Broadway, harbingers of the flourishing theater district around Union Square in the last quarter of the nineteenth century. The phenomenal success of the musical production *The Black Crook* (1866) inspired many other musical and theatrical spectacles. There were also German music halls in the Bowery and theaters for Yiddish productions on Second Avenue.

Winsett he always came away with the feeling that if his world was small, so was theirs, and that the only way to enlarge either was to reach a stage of manners where they would naturally merge.

He was reminded of this by trying to picture the society in which the Countess Olenska had lived and suffered, and also—perhaps—tasted mysterious joys. He remembered with what amusement she told him that her grandmother Mingott and the Wellands objected to her living in a "Bohemian" quarter given over to "people who wrote." It was not the peril but the poverty that her family disliked; but that shade escaped her, and she supposed they considered literature compromising.

She herself had no fears of it, and the books scattered about her drawing-room (a part of the house in which books were usually supposed to be "out of place"), though chiefly works of fiction, had whetted Archer's interest with such new names as those of Paul Bourget, Huysmans, and the Goncourt brothers. Ruminating on these things as he approached her door, he was once more conscious of the curious way in which she reversed his values, and of the need of thinking himself into conditions incredibly different from any that he knew if he were to be of use in her present difficulty.

Nastasia opened the door, smiling mysteriously. On the bench in the hall lay a sable-lined overcoat, a folded opera hat of dull silk with a gold

---

"Bohemian" Free and easy in habits, manners, or morals. Derived from the mistaken belief that gypsies originally came from Bohemia, a region in south central Europe, the term was often applied to artists with unconventional lifestyles or to "fellows who wrote." In her autobiography, *A Backward Glance,* Wharton recalls being warned by a friend that "Bohemians" had been invited to a dinner party they had agreed to attend. She arrived only to find herself one of these rumored Bohemians (120).

Paul Bourget Paul Charles Joseph Bourget (1852–1935) was a French novelist and critic whose fiction helped to advance the development of the psychological novel. He and his wife Minnie were personal friends of Edith Wharton.

Huysmans French novelist Joris Karl Huysmans (1848–1907), of Dutch descent, was a writer in the post-Romantic, decadent style. Compared with Oscar Wilde and others who often displayed unconventional or sensational social behavior and hyperaesthetic temperaments, he was known for his vivid and concrete figures, fantastic description, and portrayals of the grotesque.

Goncourt brothers Edmond Goncourt (1822–1896) and Jules de Goncourt (1830–1870), French writers and collaborators, were leaders in the naturalist movement and forerunners of Emile Zola. Known as the Goncourt Brothers, they wrote episodic narratives that are impersonal in tone. They went to great lengths to ensure the accuracy of their depictions, spending time in hospitals or on the streets to gain knowledge of their subjects.

J. B. on the lining, and a white silk muffler: there was no mistaking the fact that these costly articles were the property of Julius Beaufort.

Archer was angry: so angry that he came near scribbling a word on his card and going away; then he remembered that in writing to Madame Olenska he had been kept by excess of discretion from saying that he wished to see her privately. He had therefore no one but himself to blame if she had opened her doors to other visitors; and he entered the drawing-room with the dogged determination to make Beaufort feel himself in the way, and to outstay him.

The banker stood leaning against the mantelshelf, which was draped with an old embroidery held in place by brass candelabra containing church candles of yellowish wax. He had thrust his chest out, supporting his shoulders against the mantel and resting his weight on one large patent-leather foot. As Archer entered he was smiling and looking down on his hostess, who sat on a sofa placed at right angles to the chimney. A table banked with flowers formed a screen behind it, and against the orchids and azaleas which the young man recognized as tributes from the Beaufort hot-houses, Madame Olenska sat half-reclined, her head propped on a hand and her wide sleeve leaving the arm bare to the elbow.

It was usual for ladies who received in the evenings to wear what were called "simple dinner dresses": a close-fitting armour of whale-boned silk, slightly open in the neck, with lace ruffles filling in the crack, and tight sleeves with a flounce uncovering just enough wrist to show an Etruscan gold bracelet or a velvet band. But Madame Olenska, heedless of tradition, was attired in a long robe of red velvet bordered about the chin and down the front with glossy black fur. Archer remembered, on his last visit to

---

azaleas   Native American shrubs with variously colored showy flowers, azaleas connoted temperance in the "language of flowers." They appear again in the final chapter, where Archer imagines Ellen seated next to azaleas.

armour of whale-boned silk   To achieve the slender waist in vogue during the Victorian period, women wore tightly laced corsets, often ribbed with whale bones that reached from the bosom to the hips.

flounce   A strip of gathered or pleated material attached to the edge of a garment, here a sleeve.

Etruscan gold bracelet   Jewelry inspired by Etruria, Italy, the home of a farming people about 1000 B.C.E. Archaeological discoveries prompted the revival of jewelry styles from ancient and medieval cultures; in particular, a mania for all things Italian in the 1860s and 1870s popularized Etruscan Revival jewelry, which copied Roman and Greek designs. Such a bracelet might be a bangle with wide borders, beaded edges, and bold designs or an elaborately coiled band shaped into figures or animals.

Paris, seeing a portrait by the new painter, Carolus Duran, whose pictures were the sensation of the Salon, in which the lady wore one of these bold sheath-like robes with her chin nestling in fur. There was something perverse and provocative in the notion of fur worn in the evening in a heated drawing-room, and in the combination of a muffled throat and bare arms; but the effect was undeniably pleasing.

"Lord love us—three whole days at Skuytercliff!" Beaufort was saying in his loud sneering voice as Archer entered. "You'd better take all your furs, and a hot-water-bottle."

"Why? Is the house so cold?" she asked, holding out her left hand to Archer in a way mysteriously suggesting that she expected him to kiss it.

"No; but the missus is," said Beaufort, nodding carelessly to the young man.

"But I thought her so kind. She came herself to invite me. Granny says I must certainly go."

"Granny would, of course. And *I* say it's a shame you're going to miss the little oyster supper I'd planned for you at Delmonico's next Sunday, with Campanini and Scalchi and a lot of jolly people."

She looked doubtfully from the banker to Archer.

"Ah—that does tempt me! Except the other evening at Mrs. Struthers's I've not met a single artist since I've been here."

Carolus Duran   Carolus-Duran was the pseudonym of French painter Charles Durand (1838–1917). Originally influenced by Courbet, he concentrated on portraiture from 1870 on and became a fashionable success. John Singer Sargeant was one of his many students.

the Salon   In Paris, an annual exhibition of art by members of the French Royal Academy. Established in 1667, the Salon conferred distinction and acceptance upon artists exhibited. In the nineteenth century, the selection jury refused to hang many of the Impressionist and post-Impressionist painters, who responded by showing their work in the Salon des Refusées.

Delmonico's   A restaurant opened in 1827 by Swiss brothers Giovanni and Pietro Delmonico, it became the best-known restaurant in the United States in the nineteenth century. The location changed several times. In 1861, it opened at Fifth Avenue at 14th Street; in 1876, it moved to 26th Street as the city expanded northward. Delmonico's attracted the city's elite and was the site of numerous social events, including the first débutante ball held outside a private home (1870).

Campanini   Italo Campanini (1845–1896) was an Italian tenor who debuted at the Academy of Music in 1873. He performed in *Faust* at the opening of the Metropolitan Opera House in 1883.

Scalchi   Sofia Scalchi (1850–1922) was an Italian mezzo-soprano whose voice was known for its great volume. She performed at New York City's Castle Garden for more than twenty years beginning in 1868.

"What kind of artists? I know one or two painters, very good fellows, that I could bring to see you if you'd allow me," said Archer boldly.

"Painters? Are there painters in New York?" asked Beaufort, in a tone implying that there could be none since he did not buy their pictures; and Madame Olenska said to Archer, with her grave smile: "That would be charming. But I was really thinking of dramatic artists, singers, actors, musicians. My husband's house was always full of them."

She said the words "my husband" as if no sinister associations were connected with them, and in a tone that seemed almost to sigh over the lost delights of her married life. Archer looked at her perplexedly, wondering if it were lightness or dissimulation that enabled her to touch so easily on the past at the very moment when she was risking her reputation in order to break with it.

"I do think," she went on, addressing both men, "that the *imprévu* adds to one's enjoyment. It's perhaps a mistake to see the same people every day."

"It's confoundedly dull, anyhow; New York is dying of dullness," Beaufort grumbled. "And when I try to liven it up for you, you go back on me. Come—think better of it! Sunday is your last chance, for Campanini leaves next week for Baltimore and Philadelphia; and I've a private room, and a Steinway, and they'll sing all night for me."

"How delicious! May I think it over, and write to you tomorrow morning?"

She spoke amiably, yet with the least hint of dismissal in her voice. Beaufort evidently felt it, and being unused to dismissals, stood staring at her with an obstinate line between his eyes.

"Why not now?"

"It's too serious a question to decide at this late hour."

"Do you call it late?"

She returned his glance coolly. "Yes; because I have still to talk business with Mr. Archer for a little while."

"Ah," Beaufort snapped. There was no appeal from her tone, and with a slight shrug he recovered his composure, took her hand, which he

---

imprévu   French: Unforeseen, unexpected.

Steinway   A high-quality piano designed and built by the German-born American Heinrich Engelhard Steinway (originally Steinweg, 1797–1871). The family opened an enormous factory at 53rd Street and Fourth Avenue (now Park Avenue) in 1860 and moved production to Queens between 1870 and 1873. Aspiring to build the very finest pianos, the company won prestigious competitions in Europe. Steinway pianos became a symbol of success and refinement for middle-class families.

kissed with a practised air, and calling out from the threshold: "I say, Newland, if you can persuade the Countess to stop in town of course you're included in the supper," left the room with his heavy important step.

For a moment Archer fancied that Mr. Letterblair must have told her of his coming; but the irrelevance of her next remark made him change his mind.

"You know painters, then? You live in their *milieu*?" she asked, her eyes full of interest.

"Oh, not exactly. I don't know that the arts have a *milieu* here, any of them; they're more like a very thinly settled outskirt."

"But you care for such things?"

"Immensely. When I'm in Paris or London I never miss an exhibition. I try to keep up."

She looked down at the tip of the little satin boot that peeped from her long draperies.

"I used to care immensely too: my life was full of such things. But now I want to try not to."

"You want to try not to?"

"Yes: I want to cast off all my old life, to become just like everybody else here."

Archer reddened. "You'll never be like everybody else," he said.

She raised her straight eyebrows a little. "Ah, don't say that. If you knew how I hate to be different!"

Her face had grown as sombre as a tragic mask. She leaned forward, clasping her knee in her thin hands, and looking away from him into remote dark distances.

"I want to get away from it all," she insisted.

He waited a moment and cleared his throat. "I know. Mr. Letterblair has told me."

"Ah?"

"That's the reason I've come. He asked me to—you see I'm in the firm."

She looked slightly surprised, and then her eyes brightened.

"You mean you can manage it for me? I can talk to you instead of Mr. Letterblair? Oh, that will be so much easier!"

Her tone touched him, and his confidence grew with his self-satisfaction. He perceived that she had spoken of business to Beaufort simply to get rid of him; and to have routed Beaufort was something of a triumph.

---

milieu Environment or surroundings.

"I am here to talk about it," he repeated.

She sat silent, her head still propped by the arm that rested on the back of the sofa. Her face looked pale and extinguished, as if dimmed by the rich red of her dress. She struck Archer, of a sudden, as a pathetic and even pitiful figure.

"Now we're coming to hard facts," he thought, conscious in himself of the same instinctive recoil that he had so often criticised in his mother and her contemporaries. How little practice he had had in dealing with unusual situations! Their very vocabulary was unfamiliar to him, and seemed to belong to fiction and the stage. In face of what was coming he felt as awkward and embarrassed as a boy.

After a pause Madame Olenska broke out with unexpected vehemence: "I want to be free; I want to wipe out all the past."

"I understand that."

Her face warmed. "Then you'll help me?"

"First—" he hesitated—"perhaps I ought to know a little more."

She seemed surprised. "You know about my husband—my life with him?"

He made a sign of assent.

"Well—then—what more is there? In this country are such things tolerated? I'm a Protestant—our church does not forbid divorce in such cases."

"Certainly not."

They were both silent again, and Archer felt the spectre of Count Olenski's letter grimacing hideously between them. The letter filled only half a page, and was just what he had described it to be in speaking of it to Mr. Letterblair: the vague charge of an angry blackguard. But how much truth was behind it? Only Count Olenski's wife could tell.

"I've looked through the papers you gave to Mr. Letterblair," he said at length.

"Well—can there be anything more abominable?"

"No."

She changed her position slightly, screening her eyes with her lifted hand.

"Of course you know," Archer continued, "that if your husband chooses to fight the case—as he threatens to—"

"Yes—?"

Protestant   The Catholic Church prohibits divorce. At this time, however, divorce was socially discouraged by both Protestants and Catholics.

"He can say things—things that might be unpl—might be disagreeable to you: say them publicly, so that they would get about, and harm you
even if—"

"If—?"

"I mean: no matter how unfounded they were."

She paused for a long interval; so long that, not wishing to keep his
eyes on her shaded face, he had time to imprint on his mind the exact
shape of her other hand, the one on her knee, and every detail of the three
rings on her fourth and fifth fingers; among which, he noticed, a wedding
ring did not appear.

"What harm could such accusations, even if he made them publicly,
do me here?"

It was on his lips to exclaim: "My poor child—far more harm than
anywhere else!" Instead, he answered, in a voice that sounded in his ears
like Mr. Letterblair's: "New York society is a very small world compared
with the one you've lived in. And it's ruled, in spite of appearances, by a
few people with—well, rather old-fashioned ideas."

She said nothing, and he continued: "Our ideas about marriage and
divorce are particularly old-fashioned. Our legislation favours divorce—
our social customs don't."

"Never?"

"Well—not if the woman, however injured, however irreproachable,
has appearances in the least degree against her, has exposed herself by any
unconventional action to—to offensive insinuations—"

She drooped her head a little lower, and he waited again, intensely
hoping for a flash of indignation, or at least a brief cry of denial. None
came.

A little travelling clock ticked purringly at her elbow, and a log broke
in two and sent up a shower of sparks. The whole hushed and brooding
room seemed to be waiting silently with Archer.

"Yes," she murmured at length, "that's what my family tell me."

He winced a little. "It's not unnatural—"

"*Our* family," she corrected herself; and Archer coloured. "For you'll
be my cousin soon," she continued gently.

"I hope so."

"And you take their view?"

He stood up at this, wandered across the room, stared with void eyes
at one of the pictures against the old red damask, and came back irreso-
lutely to her side. How could he say: "Yes, if what your husband hints is
true, or if you've no way of disproving it?"

"Sincerely—" she interjected, as he was about to speak.

He looked down into the fire. "Sincerely, then—what should you gain that would compensate for the possibility—the certainty—of a lot of beastly talk?"

"But my freedom—is that nothing?"

It flashed across him at that instant that the charge in the letter was true, and that she hoped to marry the partner of her guilt. How was he to tell her that, if she really cherished such a plan, the laws of the State were inexorably opposed to it? The mere suspicion that the thought was in her mind made him feel harshly and impatiently toward her. "But aren't you as free as air as it is?" he returned. "Who can touch you? Mr. Letterblair tells me the financial question has been settled—"

"Oh, yes," she said indifferently.

"Well, then: is it worth while to risk what my be infinitely disagreeable and painful? Think of the newspapers—their vileness! It's all stupid and narrow and unjust—but one can't make over society."

"No," she acquiesced; and her tone was so faint and desolate that he felt a sudden remorse for his own hard thoughts.

"The individual, in such cases, is nearly always sacrificed to what is supposed to be the collective interest: people cling to any convention that keeps the family together—protects the children, if there are any," he rambled on, pouring out all the stock phrases that rose to his lips in his intense desire to cover over the ugly reality which her silence seemed to have laid bare. Since she would not or could not say the one word that would have cleared the air, his wish was not to let her feel that he was trying to probe into her secret. Better keep on the surface, in the prudent old New York way, than risk uncovering a wound he could not heal.

"It's my business, you know," he went on, "to help you to see these things as the people who are fondest of you see them. The Mingotts, the Wellands, the van der Luydens, all your friends and relations: if I didn't show you honestly how they judge such questions, it wouldn't be fair of me, would it?" He spoke insistently, almost pleading with her in his eagerness to cover up that yawning silence.

She said slowly: "No; it wouldn't be fair."

The fire had crumbled down to greyness, and one of the lamps made a gurgling appeal for attention. Madame Olenska rose, wound it up and returned to the fire, but without resuming her seat.

Her remaining on her feet seemed to signify that there was nothing more for either of them to say, and Archer stood up also.

"Very well; I will do what you wish," she said abruptly. The blood rushed to his forehead; and, taken aback by the suddenness of her surrender, he caught her two hands awkwardly in his.

"I—I do want to help you," he said.

"You do help me. Good night, my cousin."

He bent and laid his lips on her hands, which were cold and lifeless. She drew them away, and he turned to the door, found his coat and hat under the faint gas-light of the hall, and plunged out into the winter night bursting with the belated eloquence of the inarticulate.

XIII

It was a crowded night at Wallack's theatre.

The play was "The Shaughraun," with Dion Boucicault in the title rôle and Harry Montague and Ada Dyas as the lovers. The popularity of the admirable English company was at its height, and the Shaughraun always packed the house. In the galleries the enthusiasm was unreserved; in the stalls and boxes, people smiled a little at the hackneyed sentiments and clap-trap situations, and enjoyed the play as much as the galleries did.

There was one episode, in particular, that held the house from floor to ceiling. It was that in which Harry Montague, after a sad, almost monosyllabic scene of parting with Miss Dyas, bade her good-bye, and turned to go. The actress, who was standing near the mantelpiece and looking

---

Wallack's   Wallack's Theatre, on Broadway at 13th Street, was a popular theater in the area of Union Square, where there were many other entertainment establishments.

"The Shaughraun"   The name of Dion Boucicault's three-act melodrama, which was produced by Lester Wallack and opened on November 14, 1874, in Wallack's Theatre. The play ran longer than any other plays of its time. Set in Ireland, it describes the romance between Captain Molineux, an English officer, and Claire Ffolliott, the sister of the Irishman Molineux is sent to capture. Archer thinks of the same scene in chap. 21, when he gazes at Ellen, who has her back to him.

Dion Boucicault   An Irish playwright and actor (1820?–1890) who came to the United States in 1853. The author of over 200 plays, he was the most successful and popular playwright of his era, known particularly for his "sensation" scenes. Boucicault played the role of Conn, the title character, in the Wallack production.

Harry Montague   Actor Henry James Mann Montague (1844–1878) was a late-nineteenth-century Valentino. Born in England, he came to the United States in 1874 to serve as the leading man in Wallack's ensemble. He played Captain Molineux in the premiere performance of *The Shaughraun.*

Ada Dyas   A leading actress in the Wallack Theatre Company, Dyas played opposite Captain Molineux in the role of Claire Ffolliott.

galleries   The highest and cheapest seats in the theater, in the balconies.

stalls   Seats in a theater closest to the stage.

boxes   Separate compartments or enclosed areas for a group of people in a theater.

down into the fire, wore a grey cashmere dress without fashionable loop-
ings or trimmings, moulded to her tall figure and flowing in long lines
about her feet. Around her neck was a narrow black velvet ribbon with the
ends falling down her back.

When her wooer turned from her she rested her arms against the
mantel-shelf and bowed her face in her hands. On the threshold he paused
to look at her; then he stole back, lifted one of the ends of velvet ribbon,
kissed it, and left the room without her hearing him or changing her attitude. And on this silent parting the curtain fell.

It was always for the sake of that particular scene that Newland
Archer went to see "The Shaughraun." He thought the adieux of Montague and Ada Dyas as fine as anything he had ever seen Croisette and
Bressant do in Paris, or Madge Robertson and Kendal in London; in its
reticence, its dumb sorrow, it moved him more than the most famous
histrionic outpourings.

On the evening in question the little scene acquired an added poignancy by reminding him—he could not have said why—of his leave-
taking from Madame Olenska after their confidential talk a week or ten
days earlier.

It would have been as difficult to discover any resemblance between
the two situations as between the appearance of the persons concerned.
Newland Archer could not pretend to anything approaching the young
English actor's romantic good looks, and Miss Dyas was a tall red-haired
woman of monumental build whose pale and pleasantly ugly face was
utterly unlike Ellen Olenska's vivid countenance. Nor were Archer and
Madame Olenska two lovers parting in heart-broken silence; they were
client and lawyer separating after a talk which had given the lawyer the
worst possible impression of the client's case. Wherein, then, lay the resemblance that made the young man's heart beat with a kind of retrospective excitement? It seemed to be in Madame Olenska's mysterious
faculty of suggesting tragic and moving possibilities outside the daily run
of experience. She had hardly ever said a word to him to produce this

---

Croisette and Bressant [sic]   Actress Sophie Croizette and actor Jean Baptiste Bressant
performed in the French theater, the Comédie Français. Croizette, as popular as her contemporary Sarah Bernhardt, retired in 1881. Bressant, whose health began failing after
1870, retired in 1875.

Madge Robertson and Kendal   Madge [Margaret] Sholto Robertson (1848–1935) was
an English actress. The daughter of an actor-manager, she first appeared on stage at age
five, debuted as Ophelia in *Hamlet* as an adult, and met and married William Hunter
Kendal (1843–1917), an English actor, in 1874. They were a famous acting team, performing together until 1908.

impression, but it was a part of her, either a projection of her mysterious and outlandish background or of something inherently dramatic, passionate and unusual in herself. Archer had always been inclined to think that chance and circumstance played a small part in shaping people's lots compared with their innate tendency to have things happen to them. This tendency he had felt from the first in Madame Olenska. The quiet, almost passive young woman struck him as exactly the kind of person to whom things were bound to happen, no matter how much she shrank from them and went out of her way to avoid them. The exciting fact was her having lived in an atmosphere so thick with drama that her own tendency to provoke it had apparently passed unperceived. It was precisely the odd absence of surprise in her that gave him the sense of her having been plucked out of a very maelstrom: the things she took for granted gave the measure of those she had rebelled against.

Archer had left her with the conviction that Count Olenski's accusation was not unfounded. The mysterious person who figured in his wife's past as "the secretary" had probably not been unrewarded for his share in her escape. The conditions from which she had fled were intolerable, past speaking of, past believing: she was young, she was frightened, she was desperate—what more natural than that she should be grateful to her rescuer? The pity was that her gratitude put her, in the law's eyes and the world's, on a par with her abominable husband. Archer had made her understand this, as he was bound to do; he had also made her understand that simple-hearted kindly New York, on whose larger charity she had apparently counted, was precisely the place where she could least hope for indulgence.

To have to make this fact plain to her—and to witness her resigned acceptance of it—had been intolerably painful to him. He felt himself drawn to her by obscure feelings of jealousy and pity, as if her dumbly-confessed error had put her at his mercy, humbling yet endearing her. He was glad it was to him she had revealed her secret, rather than to the cold scrutiny of Mr. Letterblair, or the embarrassed gaze of her family. He immediately took it upon himself to assure them both that she had given up her idea of seeking a divorce, basing her decision on the fact that she had understood the uselessness of the proceeding; and with infinite relief they had all turned their eyes from the "unpleasantness" she had spared them.

"I was sure Newland would manage it," Mrs. Welland had said proudly of her future son-in-law; and old Mrs. Mingott, who had summoned him for a confidential interview, had congratulated him on his cleverness, and added impatiently: "Silly goose! I told her myself what nonsense it was. Wanting to pass herself off as Ellen Mingott and an old maid, when she has the luck to be a married woman and a Countess!"

These incidents had made the memory of his last talk with Madame Olenska so vivid to the young man that as the curtain fell on the parting of the two actors his eyes filled with tears and he stood up to leave the theatre.

In doing so, he turned to the side of the house behind him, and saw the lady of whom he was thinking seated in a box with the Beauforts, Lawrence Lefferts and one or two other men. He had not spoken with her alone since their evening together, and had tried to avoid being with her in company; but now their eyes met, and as Mrs. Beaufort recognised him at the same time, and made her languid little gesture of invitation, it was impossible not to go into the box.

Beaufort and Lefferts made way for him, and after a few words with Mrs. Beaufort, who always preferred to look beautiful and not have to talk, Archer seated himself behind Madame Olenska. There was no one else in the box but Mr. Sillerton Jackson, who was telling Mrs. Beaufort in a confidential undertone about Mrs. Lemuel Struthers's last Sunday reception (where some people reported that there had been dancing). Under cover of this circumstantial narrative, to which Mrs. Beaufort listened with her perfect smile, and her head at just the right angle to be seen in profile from the stalls, Madame Olenska turned and spoke in a low voice.

"Do you think," she asked, glancing toward the stage, "he will send her a bunch of yellow roses tomorrow morning?"

Archer reddened, and his heart gave a leap of surprise. He had called only twice on Madame Olenska, and each time he had sent her a box of yellow roses, and each time without a card. She had never before made any allusion to the flowers, and he supposed she had never thought of him as the sender. Now her sudden recognition of the gift, and her associating it with the tender leave-taking on the stage, filled him with an agitated pleasure.

"I was thinking of that too—I was going to leave the theatre in order to take the picture away with me," he said.

To his surprise her colour rose, reluctantly and duskily. She looked down at the mother-of-pearl opera-glass in her smoothly gloved hands, and said, after a pause: "What do you do while May is away?"

"I stick to my work," he answered, faintly annoyed by the question.

In obedience to a long-established habit, the Wellands had left the previous week for St. Augustine, where, out of regard for the supposed susceptibility of Mr. Welland's bronchial tubes, they always spent the latter part of the winter. Mr. Welland was a mild and silent man, with no

---

St. Augustine   A city in northeast Florida, St. Augustine has a long and colorful history. It was settled by the Spanish in 1565, taken by the British in 1763, and returned to Spain before being sold to the United States in 1821. Five years later, a seven-year war with the

opinions but with many habits. With these habits none might interfere; and one of them demanded that his wife and daughter should always go with him on his annual journey to the south. To preserve an unbroken domesticity was essential to his peace of mind; he would not have known where his hair-brushes were, or how to provide stamps for his letters, if Mrs. Welland had not been there to tell him.

As all the members of the family adored each other, and as Mr. Welland was the central object of their idolatry, it never occurred to his wife and May to let him go to St. Augustine alone; and his sons, who were both in the law, and could not leave New York during the winter, always joined him for Easter and travelled back with him.

It was impossible for Archer to discuss the necessity of May's accompanying her father. The reputation of the Mingott's family physician was largely based on the attack of pneumonia which Mr. Welland had never had; and his insistence on St. Augustine was therefore inflexible. Originally, it had been intended that May's engagement should not be announced till her return from Florida, and the fact that it had been made known sooner could not be expected to alter Mr. Welland's plans. Archer would have liked to join the travellers and have a few weeks of sunshine and boating with his betrothed; but he too was bound by custom and conventions. Little arduous as his professional duties were, he would have been convicted of frivolity by the whole Mingott clan if he had suggested asking for a holiday in mid-winter; and he accepted May's departure with the resignation which he perceived would have to be one of the principal constituents of married life.

He was conscious that Madame Olenska was looking at him under lowered lids. "I have done what you wished—what you advised," she said abruptly.

"Ah—I'm glad," he returned, embarrassed by her broaching the subject at such a moment.

"I understand—that you were right," she went on a little breathlessly; "but sometimes life is difficult . . . perplexing . . ."

"I know."

"And I wanted to tell you that I *do* feel you were right; and that I'm grateful to you," she ended, lifting her opera-glass quickly to her eyes as the door of the box opened and Beaufort's resonant voice broke in on them.

Archer stood up, and left the box and the theatre.

---

indigenous Seminoles began over recovery of the latter's land. Seasonal northerners arrived shortly after Florida became a state in 1845, but St. Augustine did not become a fashionable resort destination until the turn of the century, through the efforts of developer and Standard Oil magnate Henry M. Flagler.

Only the day before he had received a letter from May Welland in which, with characteristic candour, she had asked him to "be kind to Ellen" in their absence. "She likes you and admires you so much—and you know, though she doesn't show it, she's still very lonely and unhappy. I don't think Granny understands her, or uncle Lovell Mingott either; they really think she's much worldlier and fonder of society than she is. And I can quite see that New York must seem dull to her, though the family won't admit it. I think she's been used to lots of things we haven't got; wonderful music, and picture shows, and celebrities—artists and authors and all the clever people you admire. Granny can't understand her wanting anything but lots of dinners and clothes—but I can see that you're almost the only person in New York who can talk to her about what she really cares for."

His wise May—how he had loved her for that letter! But he had not meant to act on it; he was too busy, to begin with, and he did not care, as an engaged man, to play too conspicuously the part of Madame Olenska's champion. He had an idea that she knew how to take care of herself a good deal better than the ingenuous May imagined. She had Beaufort at her feet, Mr. van der Luyden hovering above her like a protecting deity, and any number of candidates (Lawrence Lefferts among them) waiting their opportunity in the middle distance. Yet he never saw her, or exchanged a word with her, without feeling that, after all, May's ingenuousness almost amounted to a gift of divination. Ellen Olenska was lonely and she was unhappy.

XIV

As he came out into the lobby Archer ran across his friend Ned Winsett, the only one among what Janey called his "clever people" with whom he cared to probe into things a little deeper than the average level of club and chop-house banter.

He had caught sight, across the house, of Winsett's shabby round-shouldered back, and had once noticed his eyes turned toward the Beaufort box. The two men shook hands, and Winsett proposed a bock at a little German restaurant around the corner. Archer, who was not in the mood for the kind of talk they were likely to get there, declined on the plea that he had work to do at home; and Winsett said: "Oh, well so have I for that matter, and I'll be the Industrious Apprentice too."

---

chop-house   A restaurant that specializes in serving chops and steaks.

bock   A Bock beer, strong and dark because it is the first drawn from the vats in spring-time.

They strolled along together, and presently Winsett said: "Look here, what I'm really after is the name of the dark lady in that swell box of yours—with the Beauforts, wasn't she? The one your friend Lefferts seems so smitten by."

Archer, he could not have said why, was slightly annoyed. What the devil did Ned Winsett want with Ellen Olenska's name? And above all, why did he couple it with Lefferts's? It was unlike Winsett to manifest such curiosity; but after all, Archer remembered, he was a journalist.

"It's not for an interview, I hope?" he laughed.

"Well—not for the press; just for myself," Winsett rejoined. "The fact is she's a neighbour of mine—queer quarter for such a beauty to settle in— and she's been awfully kind to my little boy, who fell down her area chasing his kitten, and gave himself a nasty cut. She rushed in bareheaded, carrying him in her arms, with his knee all beautifully bandaged, and was so sympathetic and beautiful that my wife was too dazzled to ask her name."

A pleasant glow dilated Archer's heart. There was nothing extraordinary in the tale: any woman would have done as much for a neighbour's child. But it was just like Ellen, he felt, to have rushed in bareheaded, carrying the boy in her arms, and to have dazzled poor Mrs. Winsett into forgetting to ask who she was.

"That is the Countess Olenska—a granddaughter of old Mrs. Mingott's."

"Whew—a Countess!" whistled Ned Winsett. "Well, I didn't know Countesses were so neighbourly. Mingotts ain't."

"They would be, if you'd let them."

"Ah, well—" It was their old interminable argument as to the obstinate unwillingness of the "clever people" to frequent the fashionable, and both men knew that there was no use in prolonging it.

"I wonder," Winsett broke off, "how a Countess happens to live in our slum?"

"Because she doesn't care a hang about where she lives—or about any of our little social sign-posts," said Archer, with a secret pride in his own picture of her.

"H'm—been in bigger places, I suppose," the other commented. "Well, here's my corner."

He slouched off across Broadway, and Archer stood looking after him and musing on his last words.

Broadway   A street beginning at the Battery and extending north for seventeen miles through Manhattan. Now associated with entertainment, in the mid-nineteenth century

Ned Winsett had those flashes of penetration; they were the most interesting thing about him, and always made Archer wonder why they had
allowed him to accept failure so stolidly at an age when most men are still
struggling.

Archer had known that Winsett had a wife and child, but he had never
seen them. The two men always met at the Century, or at some haunt of
journalists and theatrical people, such as the restaurant where Winsett had
proposed to go for a bock. He had given Archer to understand that his
wife was an invalid; which might be true of the poor lady, or might merely
mean that she was lacking in social gifts or in evening clothes, or in both.
Winsett himself had a savage abhorrence of social observances: Archer,
who dressed in the evening because he thought it cleaner and more comfortable to do so, and who had never stopped to consider that cleanliness
and comfort are two of the costliest items in a modest budget, regarded
Winsett's attitude as part of the boring "Bohemian" pose that always made
fashionable people, who changed their clothes without talking about it,
and were not forever harping on the number of servants one kept, seem so
much simpler and less self-conscious than the others. Nevertheless, he was
always stimulated by Winsett, and whenever he caught sight of the journalist's lean bearded face and melancholy eyes he would rout him out of
his corner and carry him off for a long talk.

Winsett was not a journalist by choice. He was a pure man of letters,
untimely born in a world that had no need of letters; but after publishing
one volume of brief and exquisite literary appreciations, of which one hundred and twenty copies were sold, thirty given away, and the balance eventually destroyed by the publishers (as per contract) to make room for more
marketable material, he had abandoned his real calling, and taken a sub-
editorial job on a women's weekly, where fashion-plates and paper patterns alternated with New England love-stories and advertisements of temperance drinks.

On the subject of "Hearth-fires" (as the paper was called) he was in-
exhaustibly entertaining; but beneath his fun lurked the sterile bitter-
ness of the still young man who has tried and given up. His conversation
always made Archer take the measure of his own life, and feel how little it
contained; but Winsett's, after all, contained still less, and though their

---

it was the location of fashionable hotels and shops, including A. T. Stewart's well-known
department store.

"Hearth-fires"   A possible reference to the women's weekly periodical, *Hearth and
Home,* published in New York from 1868 to 1875.

common fund of intellectual interests and curiosities made their talks exhilarating, their exchange of views usually remained within the limits of a pensive dilettantism.

"The fact is, life isn't much a fit for either of us," Winsett had once said. "I'm down and out; nothing to be done about it. I've got only one ware to produce, and there's no market for it here, and won't be in my time. But you're free and you're well-off. Why don't *you* get into touch? There's only one way to do it: to go into politics."

Archer threw his head back and laughed. There one saw at a flash the unbridgeable difference between men like Winsett and the others—Archer's kind. Every one in polite circles knew that, in America, "a gentleman couldn't go into politics." But, since he could hardly put it in that way to Winsett, he answered evasively: "Look at the career of the honest man in American politics! They don't want us."

"Who's 'they'? Why don't you all get together and be 'they' yourselves?"

Archer's laugh lingered on his lips in a slightly condescending smile. It was useless to prolong the discussion: everybody knew the melancholy fate of the few gentlemen who had risked their clean linen in municipal or state politics in New York. The day was past when that sort of thing was possible: the country was in possession of the bosses and the emigrant, and decent people had to fall back on sport or culture.

"Culture! Yes—if we had it! But there are just a few little local patches, dying out here and there for lack of—well, hoeing and cross-fertilising: the last remnants of the old European tradition that your forebears brought with them. But you're in a pitiful little minority: you've got no centre, no competition, no audience. You're like the pictures on the walls of a deserted

---

"a gentleman couldn't go into politics" . . . bosses . . . emigrant In the 1870s, most members of elite society considered themselves above politics. However, by the end of the century, intellectual and social leaders, adopting the role of guardians of culture, became more involved in civic affairs and ran for political office. Affluent citizens, predominantly conservative and Republican, did work behind the scenes, especially in opposition to Tammany Hall, the Democratic political machine in power in New York City and state. The head of Tammany Hall, William Marcy Tweed (1823–1878), known as "Boss Tweed," swindled the city out of millions of dollars before being defeated and indicted in 1871. The Democratic party was generally favored by immigrant groups because it helped them find work and gain citizenship, and it opposed anti-Catholic and nativist sentiments.

patches, dying out . . . hoeing and cross-fertilising This horticultural image evokes the work of Darwin and Burbank. Winsett rather presciently cautions that a society that is too inbred cannot survive.

house: 'The Portrait of a Gentleman.' You'll never amount to anything, any of you, till you roll up your sleeves and get right down into the muck. That, or emigrate . . . God! If I could emigrate . . ."

Archer mentally shrugged his shoulders and turned the conversation back to books, where Winsett, if uncertain, was always interesting. Emigrate! As if a gentleman could abandon his own country! One could no more do that than one could roll up one's sleeves and go down into the muck. A gentleman simply stayed at home and abstained. But you couldn't make a man like Winsett see that; and that was why the New York of literary clubs and exotic restaurants, though a first shake made it seem more of a kaleidoscope, turned out, in the end, to be a smaller box, with a more monotonous pattern, than the assembled atoms of Fifth Avenue.

The next morning Archer scoured the town in vain for more yellow roses. In consequence of this search he arrived late at the office, perceived that his doing so made no difference whatever to any one, and was filled with sudden exasperation at the elaborate futility of his life. Why should he not be, at that moment, on the sands of St. Augustine with May Welland? No one was deceived by his pretense of professional activity. In old-fashioned legal firms like that of which Mr. Letterblair was the head, and which were mainly engaged in the management of large estates and "conservative" investments, there were always two or three young men, fairly well-off, and without professional ambition, who, for a certain number of hours of each day, sat at their desks accomplishing trivial tasks, or simply reading the newspapers. Though it was supposed to be proper for them to have an occupation, the crude fact of money-making was still regarded as derogatory, and the law, being a profession, was accounted a more gentlemanly pursuit than business. But none of these young men had much hope of really advancing in his profession, or any earnest desire to do so; and over many of them the green mould of the perfunctory was already perceptibly spreading.

It made Archer shiver to think that it might be spreading over him too. He had, to be sure, other tastes and interests; he spent his vacations in European travel, cultivated the "clever people" May spoke of, and generally tried to "keep up," as he had somewhat wistfully put it to Madame

---

'The Portrait of a Gentleman'   A painting by American artist John Singer Sargeant (1856–1925), who became well known for his portraits of wealthy and privileged members of society. Taught by Carolus-Duran (see note to p. 98), Sargeant captures the elegant opulence of his subjects' lives. Although his work was in demand, some critics noted its superficiality of character and lack of psychological penetration.

Olenska. But once he was married, what would become of this narrow margin of life in which his real experiences were lived? He had seen enough of other young men who had dreamed his dream, though perhaps less ardently, and who had gradually sunk into the placid and luxurious routine of their elders.

From the office he sent a note by messenger to Madame Olenska, asking if he might call that afternoon, and begging her to let him find a reply at his club; but at the club he found nothing, nor did he receive any letter the following day. This unexpected silence mortified him beyond reason, and though the next morning he saw a glorious cluster of yellow roses behind a florist's window-pane, he left it there. It was only on the third morning that he received a line by post from the Countess Olenska. To his surprise it was dated from Skuytercliff, whither the van der Luydens had promptly retreated after putting the Duke on board his steamer.

"I ran away," the writer began abruptly (without the usual preliminaries), "the day after I saw you at the play, and these kind friends have taken me in. I wanted to be quiet, and think things over. You were right in telling me how kind they were; I feel myself so safe here. I wish that you were with us." She ended with a conventional "Yours sincerely," and without any allusion to the date of her return.

The tone of the note surprised the young man. What was Madame Olenska running away from, and why did she feel the need to be safe? His first thought was of some dark menace from abroad; then he reflected that he did not know her epistolary style, and that it might run to picturesque exaggeration. Women always exaggerated; and moreover she was not wholly at her ease in English, which she often spoke as if she were translating from the French. "Je me suis évadée—" put in that way, the opening sentence immediately suggested that she might merely have wanted to escape from a boring round of engagements; which was very likely true, for he judged her to be capricious, and easily wearied of the pleasure of the moment.

It amused him to think of the van der Luyden's having carried her off to Skuytercliff on a second visit, and this time for an indefinite period. The doors of Skuytercliff were rarely and grudgingly opened to visitors, and a chilly week-end was the most ever offered to the few thus privileged. But Archer had seen, on his last visit to Paris, the delicious play of Labiche, "Le Voyage de M. Perrichon," and he remembered M. Perrichon's dogged and undiscouraged attachment to the young man whom he had pulled out of

---

Labiche, "Le Voyage de M. Perrichon"   Eugène Marin Labiche (1815–1888) was a French playwright during the Second Empire whose early plays are vaudeville-like; later ones pay more attention to characterization and manners, mocking bourgeois attitudes

the glacier. The van der Luydens had rescued Madame Olenska from a doom almost as icy; and though there were many other reasons for being attracted to her, Archer knew that beneath them all lay the gentle and obstinate determination to go on rescuing her.

He felt a distinct disappointment on learning that she was away; and almost immediately remembered that, only the day before, he had refused an invitation to spend the following Sunday with the Reggie Chiverses at their house on the Hudson, a few miles below Skuytercliff.

He had had his fill long ago of the noisy friendly parties at Highbank, with coasting, ice-boating, sleighing, long tramps in the snow, and a general flavour of mild flirting and milder practical jokes. He had just received a box of new books from his London book-seller, and had preferred the prospect of a quiet Sunday at home with his spoils. But he now went into the club writing-room, wrote a hurried telegram, and told the servant to send it immediately. He knew that Mrs. Reggie didn't object to her visitors' suddenly changing their minds, and that there was always a room to spare in her elastic house.

XV

Newland Archer arrived at the Chiverses' on Friday evening, and on Saturday went conscientiously through all the rites appertaining to a week-end at Highbank.

In the morning he had a spin in the ice-boat with his hostess and a few of the hardier guests; in the afternoon he "went over the farm" with Reggie, and listened, in the elaborately appointed stables, to long and impressive disquisitions on the horse; after tea he talked in a corner of the firelit hall with a young lady who had professed herself broken-hearted when his engagement was announced, but was now eager to tell him of her own matrimonial hopes; and finally, about midnight, he assisted in putting a gold-fish in one visitor's bed, dressed up a burglar in the bath-room of a nervous aunt, and saw in the small hours by joining in a pillow-fight that ranged from the nurseries to the basement. But on Sunday after luncheon he borrowed a cutter, and drove over to Skuytercliff.

---

toward money, marriage, and property. *Le Voyage de Monsieur Perrichon* (1860) is typical of Labiche's farces, with plots involving scheming lovers, hoodwinked husbands, and marital infidelity.

cutter A small sleigh, generally for two passengers. The most popular was the Albany cutter, distinguished by its round sides. The Portland (Maine) cutter, in contrast, had straighter sides.

People had always been told that the house at Skuytercliff was an Italian villa. Those who had never been to Italy believed it; so did some who had. The house had been built by Mr. van der Luyden in his youth, on his return from the "grand tour," and in anticipation of his approaching marriage with Miss Louisa Dagonet. It was a large square wooden structure, with tongued and grooved walls painted pale green and white, a Corinthian portico, and fluted pilasters between the windows. From the high ground on which it stood a series of terraces bordered by balustrades and urns descended in the steel-engraving style to a small irregular lake with an asphalt edge overhung by rare weeping conifers. To the right and left, the famous weedless lawns studded with "specimen" trees (each of a different variety) rolled away to long ranges of grass crested with elaborate cast-iron ornaments; and below, in a hollow, lay the four-roomed stone house which the first Patroon had built on the land granted him in 1612.

Against the uniform sheet of snow and the greyish winter sky the Italian villa loomed up rather grimly; even in summer it kept its distance, and the boldest coleus bed had never ventured nearer than thirty feet from its awful front. Now, as Archer rang the bell, the long tinkle seemed to echo through a mausoleum; and the surprise of the butler who at length responded to the call was as great as though he had been summoned from his final sleep.

Italian villa Americans adapted European styles throughout the nineteenth century, a practice that conveyed regard for Old World achievements as well as a belief in the Yankee ability to improve upon these models.

"grand tour" It was common practice for nineteenth-century Americans with the financial means to make pilgrimages, called the "grand tour," to view European art treasures and experience Old World culture.

Corinthian portico A portico is a colonnaded porch, or a walk with a roof supported by columns. The Corinthian column is the most elaborate of the three Greek styles. It has an elaborate cornice and a bell-shaped capital with volutes and two rows of acanthus leaves.

fluted pilaster A pier or pillar with flutes or grooves, often with a capital and base.

balustrades A rail and the posts that support it, as along a staircase.

steel-engraving style In printmaking, a technique of engraving introduced in the nineteenth century, in which steel plates—which were harder and longer lasting than copper ones—were used to meet the enormous demand for reproductions of popular pictures.

coleus A plant of Eurasia and Africa with vivid red, white, or yellow markings on its leaves.

Happily Archer was of the family, and therefore, irregular though his arrival was, entitled to be informed that the Countess Olenska was out, having driven to afternoon service with Mrs. van der Luyden exactly three quarters of an hour earlier.

"Mr. van der Luyden," the butler continued, "is in, sir; but my impression is that he is either finishing his nap or else reading yesterday's Evening Post. I heard him say, sir, on his return from church this morning, that he intended to look through the Evening Post after luncheon; if you like, sir, I might go to the library door and listen—"

But Archer, thanking him, said that he would go and meet the ladies; and the butler, obviously relieved, closed the door on him majestically.

A groom took the cutter to the stables, and Archer struck through the park to the high-road. The village of Skuytercliff was only a mile and a half away, but he knew that Mrs. van der Luyden never walked, and that he must keep to the road to meet the carriage. Presently, however, coming down a foot-path that crossed the highway, he caught sight of a slight figure in a red cloak, with a big dog running ahead. He hurried forward, and Madame Olenska stopped short with a smile of welcome.

"Ah, you've come!" she said, and drew her hand from her muff.

The red cloak made her look gay and vivid, like the Ellen Mingott of old days; and he laughed as he took her hand, and answered: "I came to see what you were running away from."

Her face clouded over, but she answered: "Ah, well—you will see, presently."

The answer puzzled him. "Why—do you mean that you've been overtaken?"

She shrugged her shoulders, with a little movement like Nastasia's, and rejoined in a lighter tone: "Shall we walk on? I'm so cold after the sermon. And what does it matter, now you're here to protect me?"

The blood rose to his temples and he caught a fold of her cloak. "Ellen—what is it? You must tell me."

"Oh, presently—let's run a race first: my feet are freezing to the ground," she cried; and gathering up the cloak she fled away across the snow, the dog leaping about her with challenging barks. For a moment Archer stood watching, his gaze delighted by the flash of the red meteor against the snow; then he started after her, and they met, panting and laughing, at a wicket that led into the park.

Evening Post   The *New York Post* was a widely read daily newspaper with conservative leanings.

wicket   A small door or gate.

She looked up at him and smiled. "I knew you'd come!"

"That shows you wanted me to," he returned, with a disproportionate joy in their nonsense. The white glitter of the trees filled the air with its own mysterious brightness, and as they walked on over the snow the ground seemed to sing under their feet.

"Where did you come from?" Madame Olenska asked.

He told her, and added: "It was because I got your note."

After a pause she said, with a just perceptible chill in her voice: "May asked you to take care of me."

"I didn't need any asking."

"You mean—I'm so evidently helpless and defenceless? What a poor thing you must all think me! But women here seem not—seem never to feel the need: any more than the blessed in heaven."

He lowered his voice to ask: "What sort of a need?"

"Ah, don't ask me! I don't speak your language," she retorted petulantly.

The answer smote him like a blow, and he stood still in the path, looking down at her.

"What did I come for, if I don't speak yours?"

"Oh, my friend—!" She laid her hand lightly on his arm, and he pleaded earnestly: "Ellen—why won't you tell me what's happened?"

She shrugged again. "Does anything ever happen in heaven?"

He was silent, and they walked on a few yards without exchanging a word. Finally she said: "I will tell you—but where, where, where? One can't be alone for a minute in that great seminary of a house, with all the doors wide open, and always a servant bringing tea, or a log for the fire, or the newspaper! Is there nowhere in an American house where one may be by one's self? You're so shy, and yet you're so public. I always feel as if I were in the convent again—or on the stage, before a dreadfully polite audience that never applauds."

"Ah, you don't like us!" Archer exclaimed.

They were walking past the house of the old Patroon, with its squat walls and small square windows compactly grouped about a central chimney. The shutters stood wide, and through one of the newly-washed windows Archer caught the light of a fire.

"Why—the house is open!" he said.

She stood still. "No; only for today, at least. I wanted to see it, and Mr. van der Luyden had the fire lit and the windows opened, so that we might stop there on the way back from church this morning." She ran up steps and tried the door. "It's still unlocked—what luck! Come in and we can have a quiet talk. Mrs. van der Luyden has driven over to see her old aunts at Rhinebeck and we shan't be missed at the house for another hour."

He followed her into the narrow passage. His spirits, which had dropped at her last words, rose with an irrational leap. The homely little house stood there, its panels and brasses shining in the firelight, as if magically created to receive them. A bid bed of embers still gleamed in the kitchen chimney, under an iron pot hung from an ancient crane. Rush-bottomed arm-chairs faced each other across the tiled hearth, and rows of Delft plates stood on shelves against the walls. Archer stooped over and threw a log upon the embers.

Madame Olenska, dropping her cloak, sat down in one the chairs. Archer leaned against the chimney and looked at her.

"You're laughing now; but when you wrote me you were unhappy," he said.

"Yes." She paused. "But I can't feel unhappy when you're here."

"I sh'n't be here long," he rejoined, his lips stiffening with the effort to say just so much and no more.

"No; I know. But I'm improvident: I live in the moment when I'm happy."

The words stole through him like a temptation, and to close his senses to it he moved away from the hearth and stood gazing out at the black tree-boles against the snow. But it was as if she too had shifted her place, and he still saw her, between himself and the trees, dropping over the fire with her indolent smile. Archer's heart was beating insubordinately. What if it were from him that she had been running away, and if she had waited to tell him so till they were here alone together in this secret room?

"Ellen, if I'm really a help to you—if you really wanted me to come—tell me what's wrong, tell me what it is you're running away from," he insisted.

Rhinebeck   A small village on the Hudson River where well-to-do Americans built summer homes. In *A Backward Glance*, Wharton remembers the "intolerable ugliness" of the Hudson River Gothic home owned by her aunt, "a ramrod-backed old lady compounded of steel and granite" (27–28).

rush-bottomed arm-chairs   Chairs with seats made of woven dried grass.

Delft   A style of glazed earthenware originally made in Delft, Netherlands. Usually blue and white, the decorations were inspired by Chinese porcelain that was imported by the Dutch East India Company.

tree-boles   Tree trunks.

He spoke without shifting his position, without even turning to look at her: if the thing was to happen, it was to happen in this way, with the whole width of the room between them, and his eyes still fixed on the outer snow.

For a long moment she was silent; and in that moment Archer imagined her, almost heard her, stealing up behind him to throw her light arms about his neck. While he waited, soul and body throbbing with the miracle to come, his eyes mechanically received the image of a heavily-coated man with his fur collar turned up who was advancing along the path to the house. The man was Julius Beaufort.

"Ah—!" Archer cried, bursting into a laugh.

Madame Olenska had sprung up and moved to his side, slipping her hand into his; but after a glance through the window her face paled and she shrank back.

"So that was it?" Archer said derisively.

"I didn't know he was here," Madame Olenska murmured. Her hand still clung to Archer's; but he drew away from her, and walking out into the passage threw open the door of the house.

"Hallo, Beaufort—this way! Madame Olenska was expecting you," he said.

During his journey back to New York the next morning, Archer relived with a fatiguing vividness his last moments at Skuytercliff.

Beaufort, though clearly annoyed at finding him with Madame Olenska, had, as usual, carried off the situation high-handedly. His way of ignoring people whose presence inconvenienced him actually gave them, if they were sensitive to it, a feeling of invisibility, of non-existence. Archer, as the three strolled back through the park, was aware of this odd sense of disembodiment; and humbling as it was to his vanity it gave him the ghostly advantage of observing unobserved.

Beaufort had entered the little house with his usual easy assurance; but he could not smile away the vertical line between his eyes. It was fairly clear that Madame Olenska had not known that he was coming, though her words to Archer had hinted at the possibility; at any rate, she had evidently not told him where she was going when she left New York, and her unexplained departure had exasperated him. The ostensible reason of his appearance was the discovery, the very night before, of a "perfect little house," not in the market, which was really just the thing for her, but would be snapped up instantly if she didn't take it; and he was loud in mock-reproaches for the dance she had led him in running away just as he had found it.

"If only this new dodge for talking along a wire had been a little bit nearer perfection I might have told you all this from town, and been toasting my toes before the club fire at this minute, instead of tramping after you through the snow," he grumbled, disguising a real irritation under the pretence of it; and at this opening Madame Olenska twisted the talk away to the fantastic possibility that they might one day actually converse with each other from street to street, or even—incredible dream!—from one town to another. This struck from all three allusions to Edgar Poe and Jules Verne, and such platitudes as naturally rise to the lips of the most intelligent when they are talking against time, and dealing with a new invention in which it would seem ingenuous to believe too soon; and the question of the telephone carried them safely back to the big house.

Mrs. van der Luyden had not yet returned; and Archer took his leave and walked off to fetch the cutter, while Beaufort followed the Countess Olenska indoors. It was probable that, little as the van der Luydens encouraged unannounced visits, he could count on being asked to dine, and sent back to the station to catch the nine o'clock train; but more than that he would certainly not get, for it would be inconceivable to his hosts that a gentleman travelling without luggage should wish to spend the night, and distasteful to them to propose it to a person with whom they were on terms of such limited cordiality as Beaufort.

Beaufort knew all this, and must have foreseen it; and his taking the long journey for so small a reward gave the measure of his impatience. He was undeniably in pursuit of the Countess Olenska; and Beaufort had only

---

new dodge Colloquial: a clever device or strategy; a contrivance.

talking along a wire Alexander Graham Bell articulated the principle of telephone communication in 1874 and patented the first telephone capable of practical use in 1876. Early telephones were extremely crude. It was almost impossible to talk or hear over them, there were no switchboards to interconnect numbers, and transmission was possible only over a few miles. Dramatic and immediate improvements soon made the telephone, at first a curiosity, a common tool of modern life, as chap. 34 suggests.

Edgar Poe Edgar Allan Poe (1809–1849) was an American Romantic poet, critic, and short story writer. Credited with helping to found the modern detective story, he was also a master of fantasy horror and is well known for tales such as "The Tell-Tale Heart" and "The Pit and the Pendulum." Wharton admired Poe's intensity and originality, but his subject matter and unconventional, drunken lifestyle made him anathema to the polite society of her parents' generation.

Jules Verne A French writer (1828–1905) whose imaginative, almost prescient stories predate modern science fiction. Best known for *A Journey to the Center of the Earth* (1864) and *Twenty Thousand Leagues under the Sea* (1870), Verne was immensely popular with young people.

one object in view in his pursuit of pretty women. His dull and childless home had long since palled on him; and in addition to more permanent consolations he was always in quest of amorous adventures in his own set. This was the man from whom Madame Olenska was avowedly flying: the question was whether she had fled because his importunities displeased her, or because she did not wholly trust herself to resist them; unless, indeed, all her talk of flight had been a blind, and her departure no more than a manœuvre.

Archer did not really believe this. Little as he had actually seen of Madame Olenska, he was beginning to think that he could read her face, and if not her face, her voice; and both had betrayed annoyance, and even dismay, at Beaufort's sudden appearance. But, after all, if this were the case, was it not worse than if she had left New York for the express purpose of meeting him? If she had done that, she ceased to be an object of interest, she threw in her lot with the vulgarest of dissemblers: a woman engaged in a love affair with Beaufort "classed" herself irretrievably.

No, it was worse a thousand times if, judging Beaufort, and probably despising him, she was yet drawn to him by all that gave him an advantage over the other men about her: his habit of two continents and two societies, his familiar association with artists and actors and people generally in the world's eye, and his careless contempt for local prejudices. Beaufort was vulgar, he was uneducated, he was purse-proud; but the circumstances of his life, and a certain native shrewdness, made him better worth talking to than many men, morally and socially his betters, whose horizon was bounded by the Battery and the Central Park. How should any one coming from a wider world not feel the difference and be attracted by it?

Madame Olenska, in a burst of irritation, had said to Archer that he and she did not talk the same language; and the young man knew that in some respects this was true. But Beaufort understood every turn of her dialect, and spoke it fluently: his view of life, his tone, his attitude, were merely a coarser reflection of those revealed in Count Olenski's letter. This might seem to be to his disadvantage with Count Olenski's wife; but Archer was too intelligent to think that a young woman like Ellen Olenska would necessarily recoil from everything that reminded her of her past. She might believe herself wholly in revolt against it; but what had charmed her in it would still charm her, even though it were against her will.

Thus, with a painful impartiality, did the young man make out the case for Beaufort, and for Beaufort's victim. A longing to enlighten her was strong in him; and there were moments when he imagined that all she asked was to be enlightened.

That evening he unpacked his books from London. The box was full of things he had been waiting for impatiently; a new volume of Herbert

Spencer, another collection of the prolific Alphonse Daudet's brilliant tales, and a novel called "Middlemarch," as to which there had lately been interesting things said in the reviews. He had declined three dinner invitations in favour of this feast; but though he turned the pages with the sensuous joy of the book-lover, he did not know what he was reading, and one book after another dropped from his hand. Suddenly, among them, he lit on a small volume of verse which he had ordered because the name had attracted him: "The House of Life." He took it up, and found himself plunged in an atmosphere unlike any he had ever breathed in books; so warm, so rich, and yet so ineffably tender, that it gave a new and haunting beauty to the most elementary of human passions. All through the night he pursued through those enchanted pages the vision of a woman who had the face of Ellen Olenska; but when he woke the next morning, and looked out at the brownstone houses across the street, and thought of his desk in Mr. Letterblair's office, and the family pew in Grace Church, his hour in the park of Skuytercliff became as far outside the pale of probability as the visions of the night.

Herbert Spencer Archer unwraps books that Wharton knew well. Herbert Spencer (1820–1903) was an English philosopher and social scientist known for his application of Darwinism to philosophy and ethics. Spencer's theory of social evolution was reassuring to Victorians, who sought in his ideas a confirmation of the continuing progress of humankind. He was immensely popular after the Civil War in the United States, where readers admired his comprehensive scope and scientific grounding.

Alphonse Daudet's brilliant tales A French novelist (1840–1897) of the naturalist school, Daudet is noted for his keen observation, sympathetic portrayal of character, and vivid presentation of incident. Daudet's novels deal with life in Provence, his birthplace, and with various Parisian social classes. His "prolific" output included *Tartarin de Tarascon* (1872), the volume Archer may be reading.

"Middlemarch" A novel by English realist George Eliot, the pen name of Mary Ann or Marian Evans (1819–1880). A committed woman of letters, Eliot gained notoriety for living with a man whose prior marriage prevented their legal union. Although *Middlemarch* (1871–1872) was praised as a masterpiece, some readers preferred the sentimental charm of her earlier novels to the critical, ironic tones of the later work. Eliot's dense social contexts and penetrating psychological portraits probe the complex moral territory that arises from conflict between personal desire and social good.

"The House of Life" A sonnet sequence by Dante Gabriel Rossetti (1828–1882), an English poet and painter of Italian parentage. *The House of Life,* written between 1848 and 1881, was chiefly autobiographical, inspired by Rossetti's love for his wife, Elizabeth Siddal.

Grace Church A famous Episcopal church on Broadway at East 10th Street and the site of many society weddings. Designed by James Renwick Jr., Grace Church was built in 1843–45 of white limestone in a decorated Gothic style (Wharton mentions its "imitation stone vaulting" on p. 155). It has an entrance framed by a handsome memorial porch and an eastern chancel window filled with English stained glass. Edith Wharton's

"Mercy, how pale you look, Newland!" Janey commented over the coffee-cups at breakfast; and his mother added: "Newland, dear, I've noticed lately that you've been coughing; I do hope you're not letting yourself be overworked?" For it was the conviction of both ladies that, under the iron despotism of his senior partners, the young man's life was spent in the most exhausting professional labours—and he had never thought it necessary to undeceive them.

The next two or three days dragged by heavily. The taste of the usual was like cinders in his mouth, and there were moments when he felt as if he were being buried alive under his future. He heard nothing of the Countess Olenska, or of the perfect little house, and though he met Beaufort at the club they merely nodded at each other across the whist-tables. It was not till the fourth evening that he found a note awaiting him on his return home. "Come late tomorrow: I must explain to you. Ellen." These were the only words it contained.

The young man, who was dining out, thrust the note into his pocket, smiling a little at the Frenchness of the "to you." After dinner he went to a play; and it was not until his return home, after midnight, that he drew Madame Olenska's missive out again and re-read it slowly a number of times. There were several ways of answering it, and he gave considerable thought to each one during the watches of an agitated night. That on which, when morning came, he finally decided was to pitch some clothes into a portmanteau and jump on board a boat that was leaving that very afternoon for St. Augustine.

XVI

When Archer walked down the sandy main street of St. Augustine to the house which had been pointed out to him as Mr. Welland's, and saw May Welland standing under a magnolia with the sun in her hair, he wondered why he had waited so long to come.

Here was the truth, here was reality, here was the life that belonged to him; and he, who fancied himself so scornful of arbitrary restraints, had been afraid to break away from his desk because of what people might think of his stealing a holiday!

Her first exclamation was: "Newland—has anything happened?" and it occurred to him that it would have been more "feminine" if she had in-

---

family and affluent members of her society attended this church, in which distinguished families occupied their own "family pews."

whist   A popular nineteenth-century card game that developed into bridge.

stantly read in his eyes why he had come. But when he answered: "Yes—I found I had to see you," her happy blushes took the chill from her surprise, and he saw how easily he would be forgiven, and how soon even Mr. Letterblair's mild disapproval would be smiled away by a tolerant family.

Early as it was, the main street was no place for any but formal greetings, and Archer longed to be alone with May, and to pour out all his tenderness and his impatience. It still lacked an hour to the late Welland breakfast-time, and instead of asking him to come in she proposed that they should walk out to an old orange-garden beyond the town. She had just been for a row on the river, and the sun that netted the little waves with gold seemed to have caught her in its meshes. Across the warm brown of her cheek her blown hair glittered like silver wire; and her eyes too looked lighter, almost pale in their youthful limpidity. As she walked beside Archer with her long swinging gait her face wore the vacant serenity of a young marble athlete.

To Archer's strained nerves the vision was as soothing as the sight of the blue sky and the lazy river. They sat down on a bench under the orange-trees and he put his arm about her and kissed her. It was like drinking at a cold spring with the sun on it; but his pressure may have been more vehement than he had intended, for the blood rose to her face and she drew back as if he had startled her.

"What is it?" he asked, smiling; and she looked at him with surprise, and answered: "Nothing."

A slight embarrassment fell on them, and her hand slipped out of his. It was the only time that he had kissed her on the lips except for their fugitive embrace in the Beaufort conservatory, and he saw that she was disturbed, and shaken out of her cool boyish composure.

"Tell me what you do all day," he said, crossing his arms under his tilted-back head, and pushing his hat forward to screen the sun-dazzle. To let her talk about familiar and simple things was the easiest way of carrying on his own independent train of thought; and he sat listening to her simple chronicle of swimming, sailing and riding, varied by an occasional dance at the primitive inn when a man-of-war came in. A few pleasant people from Philadelphia and Baltimore were picknicking at the inn, and the Selfridge Merrys had come down for three weeks because Kate Merry had had bronchitis. They were planning to lay out a lawn tennis court on the sands;

---

man-of-war   A combatant warship in a navy.

lawn tennis   Amateur lawn tennis—unlike real, or court, tennis, which required an elaborate indoor structure—could be played on well-rolled Victorian upper- and middle-class lawns. Invented in 1873 by Walter C. Wingfield, a British army officer, the game

but no one but Kate and May had racquets, and most of the people had
not even heard of the game.

All this kept her very busy, and she had not had time to do more than
look at the little vellum book that Archer had sent her the week before (the
"Sonnets from the Portuguese"); but she was learning by heart "How they
brought the Good News from Ghent to Aix," because it was one of the
first things he had ever read to her; and it amused her to be able to tell him
that Kate Merry had never even heard of a poet called Robert Browning.

Presently she started up, exclaiming that they would be late for breakfast; and they hurried back to the tumble-down house with its paintless
porch and unpruned hedge of plumbago and pink geraniums where the
Wellands were installed for the winter. Mr. Welland's sensitive domesticity shrank from the discomforts of the slovenly southern hotel, and at immense expense, and in face of almost insuperable difficulties, Mrs. Welland
was obliged, year after year, to improvise an establishment partly made
up of discontented New York servants and partly drawn from the local
African supply.

"The doctors want my husband to feel that he is in his own home; otherwise he would be so wretched that the climate would not do him any

---

rapidly became fashionable in England, Bermuda, and the United States. Unlike cricket,
tennis could be played by women, who had already been introduced to lawn play through
croquet. Although some thought it too vigorous and unladylike, tennis—involving
strength, skill, speed, and competition—signaled a new social and physical emancipation for women that was occurring in other walks of life as well. Athletic May is eager to
try her hand at this new game.

vellum   A fine-grained unsplit leather used for binding books.

"Sonnets from the Portuguese"   A sequence of love poems (1850) by Elizabeth Barrett
Browning (1806–1861) addressed to her husband, Robert Browning. The forty-third
sonnet begins with the well-known line, "How do I love thee? Let me count the ways."

"How they brought the Good News from Ghent to Aix"   A ballad in Robert Browning's *Dramatic Romances and Lyrics* (1845) describing an imaginary horseback ride.
The poem's onomatopoeic effects would make it appealing to memorize.

plumbago   A tropical plant known as leadwort, with broad leaves and spikes with clusters of blue, white, or red flowers.

pink geraniums   A popularly cultivated plant originally from Africa with variegated
leaves and showy round clusters of flowers. Pink geraniums conveyed preference in the
"language of flowers."

local African supply   In 1830, nine years after the United States purchased Florida
from Spain, St. Augustine had only 1,700 residents, one-third of them slaves. Wharton
refers to the large number of African Americans who continued to work as servants after emancipation.

good," she explained, winter after winter, to the sympathising Philadelphians and Baltimoreans; and Mr. Welland, beaming across a breakfast table miraculously supplied with the most varied delicacies, was presently saying to Archer: "You see, my dear fellow, we camp—we literally camp. I tell my wife and May that I want to teach them how to rough it."

Mr. and Mrs. Welland had been as much surprised as their daughter by the young man's sudden arrival; but it had occurred to him to explain that he had felt himself on the verge of a nasty cold, and this seemed to Mr. Welland an all-sufficient reason for abandoning any duty.

"You can't be too careful, especially toward spring," he said, heaping his plate with straw-coloured griddle-cakes and drowning them in golden syrup. "If I'd only been as prudent at your age May would have been dancing at the Assemblies now, instead of spending her winters in a wilderness with an old invalid."

"Oh, but I love it here, Papa; you know I do. If only Newland could stay I should like it a thousand times better than New York."

"Newland must stay till he has quite thrown off his cold," said Mrs. Welland indulgently; and the young man laughed, and said he supposed there was such a thing as one's profession.

He managed, however, after an exchange of telegrams with the firm, to make his cold last a week; and it shed an ironic light on the situation to know that Mr. Letterblair's indulgence was partly due to the satisfactory way in which his brilliant young junior partner had settled the troublesome matter of the Olenski divorce. Mr. Letterblair had let Mrs. Welland know that Mr. Archer had "rendered an invaluable service" to the whole family, and that old Mrs. Manson Mingott had been particularly pleased; and one day when May had gone for a drive with her father in the only vehicle the place produced Mrs. Welland took occasion to touch on a topic which she always avoided in her daughter's presence.

"I'm afraid Ellen's ideas are not at all like ours. She was barely eighteen when Medora Manson took her back to Europe—you remember the excitement when she appeared in black at her coming-out ball? Another of Medora's fads—really this time it was almost prophetic! That must have been at least twelve years ago; and since then Ellen has never been to America. No wonder she is completely Europeanised."

"But European society is not given to divorce: Countess Olenska thought she would be conforming to American ideas in asking for her freedom." It was the first time that the young man had pronounced her name since he had left Skuytercliff, and he felt the colour rise to his cheek.

Assemblies   Exclusive balls attended by elite members of society.

Mrs. Welland smiled compassionately. "That is just like the extraordinary things that foreigners invent about us. They think we dine at two o'clock and countenance divorce! That is why it seems to me so foolish to entertain them when they come to New York. They accept our hospitality, and then they go home and repeat the same stupid stories."

Archer made no comment on this, and Mrs. Welland continued: "But we do most thoroughly appreciate your persuading Ellen to give up the idea. Her grandmother and her uncle Lovell could do nothing with her; both of them have written that her changing her mind was entirely due to your influence—in fact she said so to her grandmother. She has an unbounded admiration for you. Poor Ellen—she was always a wayward child. I wonder what her fate will be?"

"What we've all contrived to make it," he felt like answering. "If you'd all of you rather she should be Beaufort's mistress than some decent fellow's wife you've certainly gone the right way about it."

He wondered what Mrs. Welland would have said if he had uttered the words instead of merely thinking them. He could picture the sudden decomposure of her firm placid features, to which a lifelong mastery over trifles had given an air of factitious authority. Traces still lingered on them of a fresh beauty like her daughter's; and he asked himself if May's face was doomed to thicken into the same middle-aged image of invincible innocence.

Ah, no, he did not want May to have that kind of innocence, the innocence that seals the mind against imagination and the heart against experience!

"I verily believe," Mrs. Welland continued, "that if the horrible business had come out in the newspapers it would have been my husband's death-blow. I don't know any of the details; I only ask not to, as I told poor Ellen when she tried to talk to me about it. Having an invalid to care for, I have to keep my mind bright and happy. But Mr. Welland was terribly upset; he had a slight temperature every morning while we were waiting to hear what had been decided. It was the horror of his girl's learning that such things were possible—but of course, dear Newland, you felt that too. We all knew that you were thinking of May."

"I'm always thinking of May," the young man rejoined, rising to cut short the conversation.

He had meant to seize the opportunity of his private talk with Mrs. Welland to urge her to advance the date of his marriage. But he could think of no arguments that would move her, and with a sense of relief he saw Mr. Welland and May driving up to the door.

His only hope was to plead again with May, and on the day before his departure he walked with her to the ruinous garden of the Spanish

Mission. The background lent itself to allusions to European scenes; and May, who was looking her loveliest under a wide-brimmed hat that cast a shadow of mystery over her too-clear eyes, kindled into eagerness as he spoke of Granada and the Alhambra.

"We might be seeing it all this spring—even the Easter ceremonies at Seville," he urged, exaggerating his demands in the hope of a larger concession.

"Easter in Seville? And it will be Lent next week!" she laughed.

"Why shouldn't we be married in Lent?" he rejoined; but she looked so shocked that he saw his mistake.

"Of course I didn't mean that, dearest; but soon after Easter—so that we could sail at the end of April. I know I could arrange it at the office."

She smiled dreamily upon the possibility; but he perceived that to dream of it sufficed her. It was like hearing him read aloud out of his poetry books the beautiful things that could not possibly happen in real life.

"Oh, do go on, Newland; I do love your descriptions."

"But why should they be only descriptions? Why shouldn't we make them real?"

"We shall, dearest, of course; next year." Her voice lingered over it.

"Don't you want them to be real sooner? Can't I persuade you to break away now?"

She bowed her head, vanishing from him under her conniving hat-brim.

"Why should we dream away another year? Look at me, dear! Don't you understand how I want you for my wife?"

For a moment she remained motionless; then she raised on him eyes of such despairing clearness that he half-released her waist from his hold. But suddenly her look changed and deepened inscrutably. "I'm not sure if I *do* understand," she said. "Is it—is it because you're not certain of continuing to care for me?"

Spanish Mission   A building or compound devoted to missionary work. Wharton may have in mind the Mission of Nombre de Dios, on San Marco Avenue and Old Mission Road. It was founded by the Spanish in 1565 and is believed to be the first permanent mission in the United States.

Granada and the Alhambra   The Alhambra, a thirteenth-century citadel and palace in Granada, Spain, is considered one of the finest examples of Moorish architecture. It became well known and acquired a sense of glamour and mystery through Washington Irving's tales and sketches, *Legends of the Alhambra* (1832, 1852).

Easter ceremonies at Seville   Throughout Spain, Holy Week is characterized by religious fervor and magnificent processions. Those in Seville surpass all others in their splendor and realism. After Easter begins the Seville Fair, which runs for six days. One of Spain's major spectacles, it includes singing, dancing, drinking, bullfights, and parades.

Archer sprang up from his seat. "My God—perhaps—I don't know," he broke out angrily.

May Welland rose also; as they faced each other she seemed to grow in womanly stature and dignity. Both were silent for a moment, as if dismayed by the unforeseen trend of their words: then she said in a low voice: "If that is it—is there some one else?"

"Some one else—between you and me?" He echoed her words slowly, as though they were only half-intelligible and he wanted time to repeat the question to himself. She seemed to catch the uncertainty of his voice, for she went on in a deepening tone: "Let us talk frankly, Newland. Sometimes I've felt a difference in you; especially since our engagement has been announced."

"Dear—what madness!" he recovered himself to exclaim.

She met his protest with a faint smile. "If it is, it won't hurt us to talk about it." She paused, and added, lifting her head with one of her noble movements: "Or even if it's true: why shouldn't we speak of it? You might so easily have made a mistake."

He lowered his head, staring at the black leaf-pattern on the sunny path at their feet. "Mistakes are always easy to make; but if I had made one of the kind you suggest, is it likely that I should be imploring you to hasten our marriage?"

She looked downward too, disturbing the pattern with the point of her sunshade while she struggled for expression. "Yes," she said at length. "You might want—once for all—to settle the question: it's one way."

Her quiet lucidity startled him, but did not mislead him into thinking her insensible. Under her hat-brim he saw the pallor of her profile, and a slight tremor of the nostril above her resolutely steadied lips.

"Well—?" he questioned, sitting down on the bench, and looking up at her with a frown that he tried to make playful.

She dropped back into her seat and went on: "You mustn't think that a girl knows as little as her parents imagine. One hears and one notices—one has one's feelings and ideas. And of course, long before you told me that you cared for me, I'd known that there was some one else you were interested in; every one was talking about it two years ago at Newport. And once I saw you sitting together on the verandah at a dance—and when she came back into the house her face was sad, and I felt sorry for her; I remembered it afterward, when we were engaged."

Her voice had sunk almost to a whisper, and she sat clasping and unclasping her hands about the handle of her sunshade. The young man laid

---

sunshade   An umbrella or parasol.

his upon them with a gentle pressure; his heart dilated with an inexpressible relief.

"My dear child—was *that* it? If you only knew the truth!"

She raised her head quickly. "Then there is a truth I don't know?"

He kept his hand over hers. "I meant, the truth about the old story you speak of."

"But that's what I want to know, Newland—what I ought to know. I couldn't have my happiness made out of a wrong—an unfairness—to somebody else. And I want to believe that it would be the same with you. What sort of a life could we build on such foundations?"

Her face had taken on a look of such tragic courage that he felt like bowing himself down at her feet. "I've wanted to say this for a long time," she went on. "I've wanted to tell you that, when two people really love each other, I understand that there may be situations which make it right that they should—should go against public opinion. And if you feel yourself in any way pledged . . . pledged to the person we've spoken of . . . and if there is any way . . . any way in which you can fulfill your pledge . . . even by her getting a divorce . . . Newland, don't give her up because of me!"

His surprise at discovering that her fears had fastened upon an episode so remote and so completely of the past as his love affair with Mrs. Thorley Rushworth gave way to wonder at the generosity of her view. There was something superhuman in an attitude so recklessly unorthodox, and if other problems had not pressed on him he would have been lost in wonder at the prodigy of the Wellands' daughter urging him to marry his former mistress. But he was still dizzy with the glimpse of the precipice they had skirted, and full of a new awe at the mystery of young-girlhood.

For a moment he could not speak; then he said: "There is no pledge— no obligation whatever—of the kind you think. Such cases don't always— present themselves quite as simply as . . . But that's no matter . . . I love your generosity, because I feel as you do about those things . . . I feel that each case must be judged individually, on its own merits . . . irrespective of stupid conventionalities . . . I mean, each woman's right to her liberty—" He pulled himself up, startled by the turn his thoughts had taken, and went on, looking at her with a smile: "Since you understand so many things, dearest, can't you go a little farther, and understand the uselessness of our submitting to another form of the same foolish conventionalities? If there's no one and nothing between us, isn't that an argument for marrying quickly, rather than for more delay?"

She flushed with joy and lifted her face to his; as he bent to it he saw that her eyes were full of happy tears. But in another moment she seemed to have descended from her womanly eminence to helpless and timorous girlhood; and he understood that her courage and initiative were all for others, and that she had none for herself. It was evident that the effort of speaking had been much greater than her studied composure betrayed, and that at his first word of reassurance she had dropped back into the usual, as a too-adventurous child takes refuge in its mother's arms.

Archer had no heart to go on pleading with her; he was too much disappointed at the vanishing of the new being who had cast that one deep look at him from her transparent eyes. May seemed to be aware of his disappointment, but without knowing how to alleviate it; and they stood up and walked silently home.

XVII

"Your cousin the Countess called on mother while you were away," Janey Archer announced to her brother on the evening of his return.

The young man, who was dining alone with his mother and sister, glanced up in surprise and saw Mrs. Archer's gaze demurely bent on her plate. Mrs. Archer did not regard her seclusion from the world as a reason for being forgotten by it; and Newland guessed that she was slightly annoyed that he should be surprised by Madame Olenska's visit.

"She had on a black velvet polonaise with jet buttons, and a tiny green monkey muff; I never saw her so stylishly dressed," Janey continued. "She came alone, early on Sunday afternoon; luckily the fire was lit in the drawing-room. She had one of those new card-cases. She said she wanted to know us because you'd been so good to her."

Newland laughed. "Madame Olenska always takes that tone about her friends. She's very happy at being among her own people again."

"Yes, so she told us," said Mrs. Archer. "I must say she seems thankful to be here."

"I hope you liked her, mother."

---

polonaise Popular from 1776 to 1787, the polonaise gown featured three panniers, or pockets, two on the sides and one on the back, that were drawn up on cords. They could also be let down for a "flying gown" effect.

jet buttons Made from dense English coal that takes a high polish, jet buttons were very fashionable in the 1870s and 1880s.

monkey muff Muffs, soft fur bags open at each end, were used for warming hands. They were popular for both sexes in the eighteenth century but were worn only by women in the nineteenth century. Long, silky, and lustrous, monkey fur became popular after it was displayed at the Great Exhibition in London in 1851. The fur was sometimes darkened with dye.

Mrs. Archer drew her lips together. "She certainly lays herself out to please, even when she is calling on an old lady."

"Mother doesn't think her simple," Janey interjected, her eyes screwed upon her brother's face.

"It's just my old-fashioned feeling; dear May is my ideal," said Mrs. Archer.

"Ah," said her son, "they're not alike."

Archer had left St. Augustine charged with many messages for old Mrs. Mingott; and a day or two after his return to town he called on her.

The old lady received him with unusual warmth; she was grateful to him for persuading the Countess Olenska to give up the idea of a divorce; and when he told her that he had deserted the office without leave, and rushed down to St. Augustine simply because he wanted to see May, she gave an adipose chuckle and patted his knee with her puff-ball hand.

"Ah, ah—so you kicked over the traces, did you? And I suppose Augusta and Welland pulled long faces, and behaved as if the end of the world had come? But little May—she knew better, I'll be bound?"

"I hoped she did; but after all she wouldn't agree to what I'd gone down to ask for."

"Wouldn't she indeed? And what was that?"

"I wanted to get her to promise that we should be married in April. What's the use of our wasting another year?"

Mrs. Manson Mingott screwed up her little mouth into a grimace of mimic prudery and twinkled at him through malicious lids. "'Ask Mamma,' I suppose—the usual story. Ah, these Mingotts—all alike! Born in a rut, and you can't root 'em out of it. When I built this house you'd have thought I was moving to California! Nobody ever *had* built above Fortieth Street—no, says I, nor above the Battery either, before Christopher Columbus discovered America. No, no; not one of them wants to be different; they're as scared of it as the small-pox. Ah, my dear Mr. Archer, I thank my stars I'm nothing but a vulgar Spicer; but there's not one of my own children that takes after me but my little Ellen." She broke off, still twinkling at him, and asked, with the casual irrelevance of old age: "Now, why in the world didn't you marry my little Ellen?"

---

adipose   Related to animal fat; fatty.

above Fortieth Street . . . above the Battery   Few fashionable people lived north of 40th Street until after the opening of Central Park at 59th Street in 1859. The development of Manhattan was northward, beginning at the southern end, at the Battery.

Archer laughed. "For one thing, she wasn't there to be married."

"No—to be sure; more's the pity. And now it's too late; her life is finished." She spoke with the cold-blooded complacency of the aged throwing earth into the grave of young hopes. The young man's heart grew chill, and he said hurriedly: "Can't I persuade you to use your influence with the Wellands, Mrs. Mingott? I wasn't made for long engagements."

Old Catherine beamed on him approvingly. "No; I can see that. You've got a quick eye. When you were a little boy I've no doubt you liked to be helped first." She threw back her head with a laugh that made her chins ripple like little waves. "Ah, here's my Ellen now!" she exclaimed, as the portières parted behind her.

Madame Olenska came forward with a smile. Her face looked vivid and happy, and she held out her hand gaily to Archer while she stooped to her grandmother's kiss.

"I was just saying to him, my dear: 'Now, why didn't you marry my little Ellen?'"

Madame Olenska looked at Archer, still smiling. "And what did he answer?"

"Oh, my darling, I leave you to find that out! He's been down to Florida to see his sweetheart."

"Yes, I know." She still looked at him. "I went to see your mother, to ask where you'd gone. I sent a note that you never answered, and I was afraid you were ill."

He muttered something about leaving unexpectedly, in a great hurry, and having intended to write to her from St. Augustine.

"And of course once you were there you never thought of me again!" She continued to beam on him with a gaiety that might have been a studied assumption of indifference.

"If she still needs me, she's determined not to let me see it," he thought, stung by her manner. He wanted to thank her for having been to see his mother, but under the ancestress's malicious eye he felt himself tongue-tied and constrained.

"Look at him—in such hot haste to get married that he took French leave and rushed down to implore the silly girl on his knees! That's something like a lover—that's the way handsome Bob Spicer carried off my poor mother; and then got tired of her before I was weaned—though they only had to wait eight months for me! But there—you're not a Spicer,

---

French leave   An informal, hasty, or secretive departure. From an eighteenth-century French custom of leaving a reception without properly saying goodbye to the host or hostess.

young man; luckily for you and for May. It's only my poor Ellen that has kept any of their wicked blood; the rest of them are all model Mingotts," cried the old lady scornfully.

Archer was aware that Madame Olenska, who had seated herself at her grandmother's side, was still thoughtfully scrutinising him. The gaiety had faded from her eyes, and she said with great gentleness: "Surely, Granny, we can persuade them between us to do as he wishes."

Archer rose to go, and as his hand met Madame Olenska's he felt that she was waiting for him to make some allusion to her unanswered letter.

"When can I see you?" he asked, as she walked with him to the door of the room.

"Whenever you like; but it must be soon if you want to see the little house again. I am moving next week."

A pang shot through him at the memory of his lamplit hours in the low-studded drawing-room. Few as they had been, they were thick with memories.

"Tomorrow evening?"

She nodded. "Tomorrow; yes; but early. I'm going out."

The next day was a Sunday, and if she were "going out" on a Sunday evening it could, of course, be only to Mrs. Lemuel Struthers's. He felt a slight movement of annoyance, not so much at her going there (for he rather liked her going where she pleased in spite of the van der Luydens), but because it was the kind of house at which she was sure to meet Beaufort, where she must have known beforehand that she would meet him— and where she was probably going for that purpose.

"Very well; tomorrow evening," he repeated, inwardly resolved that he would not go early, and that by reaching her door late he would either prevent her from going to Mrs. Struthers's, or else arrive after she had started— which, all things considered, would no doubt be the simplest solution.

It was only half-past eight, after all, when he rang the bell under the wisteria; not as late as he had intended by half an hour—but a singular restlessness had driven him to her door. He reflected, however, that Mrs. Struthers's Sunday evenings were not like a ball, and that her guests, as if to minimise their delinquency, usually went early.

The one thing he had not counted on, in entering Madame Olenska's hall, was to find hats and overcoats there. Why had she bidden him to come early if she was having people to dine? On a closer inspection of the garments besides which Nastasia was laying his own, his resentment gave way to curiosity. The overcoats were in fact the very strangest he had ever seen under a polite roof; and it took but a glance to assure himself that neither of them belonged to Julius Beaufort. One was a shaggy yellow ulster of "reach-me-down" cut, the other a very old and rusty cloak with a cape—something like what the French called a "Macfarlane." This garment, which appeared to be made for a person of prodigious size, had evidently seen long and hard wear, and its greenish-black folds gave out a moist sawdusty smell suggestive of prolonged sessions against bar-room walls. On it lay a ragged grey scarf and an odd felt hat of semiclerical shape.

Archer raised his eyebrows enquiringly at Nastasia, who raised hers in return with a fatalistic "Già!" as she threw open the drawing-room door.

The young man saw at once that his hostess was not in the room; then, with surprise, he discovered another lady standing by the fire. This lady, who was long, lean and loosely put together, was clad in raiment intricately looped and fringed, with plaids and stripes and bands of plain colour disposed in a design to which the clue seemed missing. Her hair, which had tried to turn white and only succeeded in fading, was surmounted by a Spanish comb and black lace scarf, and silk mittens, visibly darned, covered her rheumatic hands.

Beside her, in a cloud of cigar-smoke, stood the owners of the two overcoats, both in morning clothes that they had evidently not taken off since morning. In one of the two, Archer, to his surprise, recognised Ned Winsett; the other and older, who was unknown to him, and whose gigantic frame declared him to be the wearer of the "Macfarlane," had a feebly leonine head with crumpled grey hair, and moved his arms with large pawing gestures, as though he were distributing lay blessings to a kneeling multitude.

These three persons stood together on the hearth-rug, their eyes fixed on an extraordinarily large bouquet of crimson roses, with a knot of purple pansies at their base, that lay on the sofa where Madame Olenska usually sat.

"What they must have cost at this season—though of course it's the sentiment one cares about!" the lady was saying in a sighing staccato as Archer came in.

The three turned with surprise at his appearance, and the lady, advancing, held out her hand.

---

ulster   A heavy overcoat originally worn in Ulster, Ireland. It was long, loose fitting, and usually double breasted, with a belt.

"Macfarlane"   A cloth topcoat with separate sleeve capes and side slits to allow the wearer to reach into his pockets.

Spanish comb   A high comb, in the nineteenth century often of tortoise shell. A mantilla or lace scarf may be draped over it. It is still worn today in Spain and Spanish countries.

morning clothes   Daily wear consisting of shirt, frock coat, trousers, and top hat.

"Dear Mr. Archer—almost my cousin Newland!" she said. "I am the Marchioness Manson."

Archer bowed, and she continued: "My Ellen has taken me in for a few days. I came from Cuba, where I have been spending the winter with Spanish friends—such delightful distinguished people: the highest nobility of old Castile—how I wish you could know them! But I was called away by our dear great friend here, Dr. Carver. You don't know Dr. Agathon Carver, founder of the Valley of Love Community?"

Dr. Carver inclined his leonine head, and the Marchioness continued: "Ah, New York—New York—how little the life of the spirit has reached it! But I see you do know Mr. Winsett."

"Oh, yes—*I* reached him some time ago; but not by that route," Winsett said with his dry smile.

The Marchioness shook her head reprovingly. "How do you know, Mr. Winsett? The spirit bloweth where it listeth."

"List—oh, list!" interjected Dr. Carver in a stentorian murmur.

"But do sit down, Mr. Archer. We four have been having a delightful little dinner together, and my child has gone up to dress. She expects you; she will be down in a moment. We were just admiring these marvellous flowers, which will surprise her when she reappears."

Winsett remained on his feet. "I'm afraid I must be off. Please tell Madame Olenska that we shall all feel lost when she abandons our street. This house has been an oasis."

"Ah, but she won't abandon *you*. Poetry and art are the breath of life to her. It *is* poetry you write, Mr. Winsett?"

"Well, no; but I sometimes read it," said Winsett, including the group in a general nod and slipping out of the room.

"A caustic spirit—*un peu sauvage*. But so witty; Dr. Carver, you *do* think him witty?"

"I never think of wit," said Dr. Carver severely.

Marchioness The wife or widow of a marquis, or a woman who has the rank of marquis in her own right.

old Castile A region in central Spain. Not to be confused with New Castile, the name given to the former province of Toledo, once under Moorish rule.

Valley of Love Community In the nineteenth century, various leaders formed utopian communities in response to economic, social, and spiritual inequalities they saw in society. The Oneida Community, established by John Humphrey Noyes in 1848, flourished for over thirty years and may be the basis for Wharton's description of Dr. Carver's organization. Members of this unconventional group followed communal practices, believed in attaining perfection on earth, and followed a form of regulated polygamy.

un peu sauvage French: a bit unsociable. Literally, a little wild or savage.

"Ah—ah—you never think of wit! How merciless he is to us weak mortals, Mr. Archer! But he lives only in the life of the spirit; and tonight he is mentally preparing the lecture he is to deliver presently at Mrs. Blenker's. Dr. Carver, would there be time, before you start for the Blenkers' to explain to Mr. Archer your illuminating discovery of the Direct Contact? But no; I see it is nearly nine o'clock, and we have no right to detain you while so many are waiting for your message."

Dr. Carver looked slightly disappointed at this conclusion, but, having compared his ponderous gold time-piece with Madame Olenska's little travelling-clock, he reluctantly gathered up his mighty limbs for departure.

"I shall see you later, dear friend?" he suggested to the Marchioness, who replied with a smile: "As soon as Ellen's carriage comes I will join you; I do hope the lecture won't have begun."

Dr. Carver looked thoughtfully at Archer. "Perhaps, if this young gentleman is interested in my experiences, Mrs. Blenker might allow you to bring him with you?"

"Oh, dear friend, if it were possible—I am sure she would be too happy. But I fear my Ellen counts on Mr. Archer herself."

"That," said Dr. Carver, "is unfortunate—but here is my card." He handed it to Archer, who read on it, in Gothic characters:

Agathon Carver

The Valley of Love

Kittasquattamy, N. Y.

Dr. Carver bowed himself out, and Mrs. Manson, with a sigh that might have been either of regret or relief, again waved Archer to a seat.

Direct Contact Spiritualism, the belief that mortals can have "direct contact" with departed souls, was virtually unknown in the United States until 1848, when two New England sisters, Margaret and Kate Fox, claimed to have made contact, through a series of rappings, with the spirit of a peddler murdered by a previous owner of their house. Despite detractors, interest in spiritualism grew in the nineteenth century, both out of curiosity and out of need to find a spiritual balance to an increasingly scientific, materialistic, and industrial society.

"Ellen will be down in a moment; and before she comes, I am so glad of this quiet moment with you."

Archer murmured his pleasure at their meeting, and the Marchioness continued, in her low sighing accents: "I know everything, dear Mr. Archer—my child has told me all you have done for her. Your wise advice: your courageous firmness—thank heaven it was not too late!"

The young man listened with considerable embarrassment. Was there any one, he wondered, to whom Madame Olenska had not proclaimed his intervention in her private affairs?

"Madame Olenska exaggerates; I simply gave her a legal opinion, as she asked me to."

"Ah, but in doing it—in doing it you were the unconscious instrument of—of—what word have we moderns for Providence, Mr. Archer?" cried the lady, tilting her head on one side and drooping her lids mysteriously. "Little did you know that at that very moment I was being appealed to: being approached, in fact—from the other side of the Atlantic!"

She glanced over her shoulder, as though fearful of being overheard, and then, drawing her chair nearer, and raising a tiny ivory fan to her lips, breathed behind it: "By the Count himself—my poor, mad, foolish Olenski; who asks only to take her back on her own terms."

"Good God!" Archer exclaimed, springing up.

"You are horrified? Yes, of course; I understand. I don't defend poor Stanislas, though he has always called me his best friend. He does not defend himself—he casts himself at her feet: in my person." She tapped her emaciated bosom. "I have his letter here."

"A letter?— Has Madame Olenska seen it?" Archer stammered, his brain whirling with the shock of the announcement.

The Marchioness Manson shook her head softly. "Time—time; I must have time. I know my Ellen—haughty, intractable; shall I say, just a shade unforgiving?"

"But, good heavens, to forgive is one thing; to go back into that hell—"

"Ah, yes," the Marchioness acquiesced. "So she describes it—my sensitive child! But on the material side, Mr. Archer, if one may stoop to consider such things; do you know what she is giving up? Those roses there on the sofa—acres like them, under glass and in the open, in his matchless terraced gardens at Nice! Jewels—historic pearls: the Sobieski emeralds—

Sobieski   John Sobieski, or John III, King of Poland (1624–1696), reigned from 1674 to 1696. He was a champion of Christian Europe against the Turks; his death marked the virtual end of Polish independence.

sables—but she cares nothing for all these! Art and beauty, those she does care for, she lives for, as I always have; and those also surrounded her. Pictures, priceless furniture, music, brilliant conversation—ah, that, my dear young man, if you'll excuse me, is what you've no conception of here! And she had it all; and the homage of the greatest. She tells me she is not thought handsome in New York—good heavens! Her portrait has been painted nine times; the greatest artists in Europe have begged for the privilege. Are these things nothing? And the remorse of an adoring husband?"

As the Marchioness Manson rose to her climax her face assumed an expression of ecstatic retrospection which would have moved Archer's mirth had he not been numb with amazement.

He would have laughed if any one had foretold to him that his first sight of poor Medora Manson would have been in the guise of a messenger of Satan; but he was in no mood for laughing now, and she seemed to him to come straight out of the hell from which Ellen Olenska had just escaped.

"She knows nothing yet—of all this?" he asked abruptly.

Mrs. Manson laid a purple finger on her lips. "Nothing directly—but does she suspect? Who can tell? The truth is, Mr. Archer, I have been waiting to see you. From the moment I heard of the firm stand you had taken, and of your influence over her, I hoped it might be possible to count on your support—to convince you . . ."

"That she ought to go back? I would rather see her dead!" cried the young man violently.

"Ah," the Marchioness murmured, without visible resentment. For a while she sat in her arm-chair, opening and shutting the absurd ivory fan between her mittened fingers; but suddenly she lifted her head and listened.

"Here she comes," she said in a rapid whisper; and then, pointing to the bouquet on the sofa: "Am I to understand that you prefer *that*, Mr. Archer? After all, marriage is marriage . . . and my niece is still a wife. . . ."

XVIII

"What are you two plotting together, aunt Medora?" Madame Olenska cried as she came into the room.

She was dressed as if for a ball. Everything about her shimmered and glimmered softly, as if her dress had been woven out of candle-beams; and she carried her head high, like a pretty woman challenging a roomful of rivals.

"We were saying, my dear, that here was something beautiful to surprise you with," Mrs. Manson rejoined, rising to her feet and pointing archly to the flowers.

Madame Olenska stopped short and looked at the bouquet. Her colour did not change, but a sort of white radiance of anger ran over her like summer lightning. "Ah," she exclaimed, in a shrill voice that the young man had never heard, "who is ridiculous enough to send me a bouquet? Why a bouquet? And why tonight of all nights? I am not going to a ball; I am not a girl engaged to be married. But some people are always ridiculous."

She turned back to the door, opened it, and called out: "Nastasia!"

The ubiquitous handmaiden promptly appeared, and Archer heard Madame Olenska say, in an Italian that she seemed to pronounce with intentional deliberateness in order that he might follow it: "Here—throw this into the dustbin!" and then, as Nastasia stared protestingly: "But no—it's not the fault of the poor flowers. Tell the boy to carry them to the house three doors away, the house of Mr. Winsett, the dark gentleman who dined here. His wife is ill—they may give her pleasure . . . The boy is out, you say? Then, my dear one, run yourself; here, put my cloak over you and fly. I want the thing out of the house immediately! And, as you live, don't say they come from me!"

She flung her velvet opera cloak over the maid's shoulders and turned back into the drawing-room, shutting the door sharply. Her bosom was rising high under its lace, and for a moment Archer thought she was about to cry; but she burst into a laugh instead, and looking from the Marchioness to Archer, asked abruptly: "And you two—have you made friends!"

"It's for Mr. Archer to say, darling; he has waited patiently while you were dressing."

"Yes—I gave you time enough: my hair wouldn't go," Madame Olenska said, raising her hand to the heaped-up curls of her *chignon*. "But that reminds me: I see Dr. Carver is gone, and you'll be late at the Blenkers'. Mr. Archer, will you put my aunt in the carriage?"

She followed the Marchioness into the hall, saw her fitted into a miscellaneous heap of overshoes, shawls and tippets, and called from the doorstep: "Mind, the carriage is to be back for me at ten!" Then she returned to the drawing-room, where Archer, on re-entering it, found her standing by the mantelpiece, examining herself in the mirror. It was not

---

chignon Hair twisted into a knot at the nape of the neck.

tippets Fur or cloth scarves with long hanging ends, fashionable in the first half of the nineteenth century.

usual, in New York society, for a lady to address her parlour-maid as "my dear one," and send her out on an errand wrapped in her own opera-cloak; and Archer, through all his deeper feelings, tasted the pleasurable excitement of being in a world where action followed on emotion with such Olympian speed.

Madame Olenska did not move when he came up behind her, and for a second their eyes met in the mirror; then she turned, threw herself into her sofa-corner, and sighed out: "There's time for a cigarette."

He handed her the box and lit a spill for her; and as the flame flashed up into her face she glanced at him with laughing eyes and said: "What do you think of me in a temper?"

Archer paused a moment; then he answered with sudden resolution: "It makes me understand what your aunt has been saying about you."

"I knew she'd been talking about me. Well?"

"She said you were used to all kinds of things—splendours and amusements and excitements—that we could never hope to give you here."

Madame Olenska smiled faintly into the circle of smoke about her lips.

"Medora is incorrigibly romantic. It has made up to her for so many things!"

Archer hesitated again, and again took his risk. "Is your aunt's romanticism always consistent with accuracy?"

"You mean: does she speak the truth?" Her niece considered. "Well, I'll tell you: in almost everything she says, there's something true and something untrue. But why do you ask? What has she been telling you?"

He looked away into the fire, and then back at her shining presence. His heart tightened with the thought that this was their last evening by that fireside, and that in a moment the carriage would come to carry her away.

"She says—she pretends that Count Olenski has asked her to persuade you to go back to him."

Madame Olenska made no answer. She sat motionless, holding her cigarette in her half-lifted hand. The expression of her face had not changed; and Archer remembered that he had before noticed her apparent incapacity for surprise.

"You knew, then?" he broke out.

She was silent for so long that the ash dropped from her cigarette. She brushed it to the floor. "She has hinted about a letter: poor darling! Medora's hints—"

"Is it at your husband's request that she has arrived here suddenly?"

Madame Olenska seemed to consider this question also. "There again: one can't tell. She told me she had had a 'spiritual summons,' whatever that is, from Dr. Carver. I'm afraid she's going to marry Dr. Carver . . .

poor Medora, there's always some one she wants to marry. But perhaps the people in Cuba just got tired of her! I think she was with them as a sort of paid companion. Really, I don't know why she came."

"But you do believe she has a letter from your husband?"

Again Madame Olenska brooded silently; then she said: "After all, it was to be expected."

The young man rose and went to lean against the fireplace. A sudden restlessness possessed him, and he was tongue-tied by the sense that their minutes were numbered, and that at any moment he might hear the wheels of the returning carriage.

"You know that your aunt believes you will go back?"

Madame Olenska raised her head quickly. A deep blush rose to her face and spread over her neck and shoulders. She blushed seldom and painfully, as if it hurt her like a burn.

"Many cruel things have been believed of me," she said.

"Oh, Ellen—forgive me; I'm a fool and a brute!"

She smiled a little. "You are horribly nervous; you have your own troubles. I know you think the Wellands are unreasonable about your marriage, and of course I agree with you. In Europe people don't understand our long American engagements; I suppose they are not as calm as we are." She pronounced the "we" with a faint emphasis that gave it an ironic sound.

Archer felt the irony but did not dare to take it up. After all, she had perhaps purposely deflected the conversation from her own affairs, and after the pain his last words had evidently caused her he felt that all he could do was to follow her lead. But the sense of the waning hour made him desperate: he could not bear the thought that a barrier of words should drop between them again.

"Yes," he said abruptly; "I went south to ask May to marry me after Easter. There's no reason why we shouldn't be married then."

"And May adores you—and yet you couldn't convince her? I thought her too intelligent to be the slave of such absurd superstitions."

"She *is* too intelligent—she's not their slave."

Madame Olenska looked at him. "Well, then—I don't understand."

Archer reddened, and hurried on with a rush. "We had a frank talk—almost the first. She thinks my impatience a bad sign."

"Merciful heavens—a bad sign?"

"She thinks it means that I can't trust myself to go on caring for her. She thinks, in short, I want to marry her at once to get away from some one that I—care for more."

Madame Olenska examined this curiously. "But if she thinks that—why isn't she in a hurry too?"

"Because she's not like that: she's so much nobler. She insists all the more on the long engagement, to give me time—"

"Time to give her up for the other woman?"

"If I want to."

Madame Olenska leaned toward the fire and gazed into it with fixed eyes. Down the quiet street Archer heard the approaching trot of her horses.

"That *is* noble," she said, with a slight break in her voice.

"Yes. But it's ridiculous."

"Ridiculous? Because you don't care for any one else?"

"Because I don't mean to marry any one else."

"Ah." There was another long interval. At length she looked up at him and asked: "This other woman—does she love you?"

"Oh, there's no other woman; I mean, the person that May was thinking of is—was never—"

"Then, why, after all, are you in such haste?"

"There's your carriage," said Archer.

She half-rose and looked about her with absent eyes. Her fan and gloves lay on the sofa beside her and she picked them up mechanically.

"Yes; I suppose I must be going."

"You're going to Mrs. Struthers's?"

"Yes." She smiled and added: "I must go where I am invited, or I should be too lonely. Why not come with me?"

Archer felt that at any cost he must keep her beside him, must make her give him the rest of her evening. Ignoring her question, he continued to lean against the chimney-piece, his eyes fixed on the hand in which she held her gloves and fan, as if watching to see if he had the power to make her drop them.

"May guessed the truth," he said. "There is another woman—but not the one she thinks."

Ellen Olenska made no answer, and did not move. After a moment he sat down beside her, and, taking her hand, softly unclasped it, so that the gloves and fan fell on the sofa between them.

She started up, and freeing herself from him moved away to the other side of the hearth. "Ah, don't make love to me! Too many people have done that," she said, frowning.

Archer, changing colour, stood up also: it was the bitterest rebuke she could have given him. "I have never made love to you," he said, "and I never shall. But you are the woman I would have married if it had been possible for either of us."

"Possible for either of us?" She looked at him with unfeigned astonishment. "And you say that—when it's you who've made it impossible?"

He stared at her, groping in a blackness through which a single arrow of light tore its blinding way.

"*I've* made it impossible—?"

"You, you, *you!*" she cried, her lip trembling like a child's on the verge of tears. "Isn't it you who made me give up divorcing—give it up because you showed me how selfish and wicked it was, how one must sacrifice one's self to preserve the dignity of marriage . . . and to spare one's family the publicity, the scandal? And because my family was going to be your family—for May's sake and for yours—I did what you told me, what you proved to me that I ought to do. Ah," she broke out with a sudden laugh, "I've made no secret of having done it for you!"

She sank down on the sofa again, crouching among the festive ripples of her dress like a stricken masquerader; and the young man stood by the fireplace and continued to gaze at her without moving.

"Good God," he groaned. "When I thought—"

"You thought?"

"Ah, don't ask me what I thought!"

Still looking at her, he saw the same burning flush creep up her neck to her face. She sat upright, facing him with a rigid dignity.

"I do ask you."

"Well, then: there were things in that letter you asked me to read—"

"My husband's letter?"

"Yes."

"I had nothing to fear from that letter: absolutely nothing! All I feared was to bring notoriety, scandal, on the family—on you and May."

"Good God," he groaned again, bowing his face in his hands.

The silence that followed lay on them with the weight of things final and irrevocable. It seemed to Archer to be crushing him down like his own grave-stone; in all the wide future he saw nothing that would ever lift that load from his heart. He did not move from his place, or raise his head from his hands; his hidden eyeballs went on staring into utter darkness.

"At least I loved you—" he brought out.

On the other side of the hearth, from the sofa-corner where he supposed that she still crouched, he heard a faint stifled crying like a child's. He started up and came to her side.

"Ellen! What madness! Why are you crying? Nothing's done that can't be undone. I'm still free, and you're going to be." He had her in his arms, her face like a wet flower at his lips, and all their vain terrors shrivelling up like ghosts at sunrise. The one thing that astonished him now was that he should have stood for five minutes arguing with her across the width of the room, when just touching her made everything so simple.

She gave him back all his kiss, but after a moment he felt her stiffening in his arms, and she put him aside and stood up.

"Ah, my poor Newland—I suppose this had to be. But it doesn't in the least alter things," she said, looking down at him in her turn from the hearth.

"It alters the whole of life for me."

"No, no—it mustn't, it can't. You're engaged to May Welland; and I'm married."

He stood up too, flushed and resolute. "Nonsense! It's too late for that sort of thing. We've no right to lie to other people or to ourselves. We won't talk of your marriage; but do you see me marrying May after this?"

She stood silent, resting her thin elbows on the mantle-piece, her profile reflected in the glass behind her. One of the locks of her *chignon* had become loosened and hung on her neck; she looked haggard and almost old.

"I don't see you," she said at length, "putting that question to May. Do you?"

He gave a reckless shrug. "It's too late to do anything else."

"You say that because it's the easiest thing to say at this moment—not because it's true. In reality it's too late to do anything but what we'd both decided on."

"Ah, I don't understand you!"

She forced a pitiful smile that pinched her face instead of smoothing it. "You don't understand because you haven't yet guessed how you've changed things for me: oh, from the first—long before I knew all you'd done."

"All I'd done?"

"Yes. I was perfectly unconscious at first that people here were shy of me—that they thought I was a dreadful sort of person. It seems they had even refused to meet me at dinner. I found that out afterward; and how you'd made your mother go with you to the van der Luydens'; and how you'd insisted on announcing your engagement at the Beaufort ball, so that I might have two families to stand by me instead of one—"

At that he broke into a laugh.

"Just imagine," she said, "how stupid and unobservant I was! I knew nothing of all this till Granny blurted it out one day. New York simply meant peace and freedom to me: it was coming home. And I was so happy at being among my own people that every one I met seemed kind and good, and glad to see me. But from the very beginning," she continued, "I felt there was no one as kind as you; no one who gave me reasons that I understood for doing what at first seemed so hard and—unnecessary. The very good people didn't convince me; I felt they'd never been tempted.

But you knew; you understood; you had felt the world outside tugging at one with all its golden hands—and yet you hated the things it asks of one; you hated happiness bought by disloyalty and cruelty and indifference. That was what I'd never known before—and it's better than anything I've known."

She spoke in a low even voice, without tears or visible agitation; and each word, as it dropped from her, fell into his breast like burning lead. He sat bowed over, his head between his hands, staring at the hearth-rug, and at the tip of the satin shoe that showed under her dress. Suddenly he knelt down and kissed the shoe.

She bent over him, laying her hands on his shoulders, and looking at him with eyes so deep that he remained motionless under her gaze.

"Ah, don't let us undo what you've done!" she cried. "I can't go back now to that other way of thinking. I can't love you unless I give you up."

His arms were yearning up to her; but she drew away, and they remained facing each other, divided by the distance that her words had created. Then, abruptly, his anger overflowed.

"And Beaufort? Is he to replace me?"

As the words sprang out he was prepared for an answering flare of anger; and he would have welcomed it as fuel for his own. But Madame Olenska only grew a shade paler, and stood with her arms hanging down before her, and her head slightly bent, as her way was when she pondered a question.

"He's waiting for you now at Mrs. Struthers's; why don't you go to him?" Archer sneered.

She turned to ring the bell. "I shall not go out this evening; tell the carriage to go and fetch the Signora Marchesa," she said when the maid came.

After the door had closed again Archer continued to look at her with bitter eyes. "Why this sacrifice? Since you tell me that you're lonely I've no right to keep you from your friends."

She smiled a little under her wet lashes. "I shan't be lonely now. I *was* lonely; I *was* afraid. But the emptiness and the darkness are gone; when I turn back into myself now I'm like a child going at night into a room where there's always a light."

Her tone and her look still enveloped her in a soft inaccessibility, and Archer groaned out again: "I don't understand you!"

"Yet you understand May!"

He reddened under the retort, but kept his eyes on her. "May is ready to give me up."

"What! Three days after you've entreated her on your knees to hasten your marriage?"

"She's refused; that gives me the right—"

"Ah, you've taught me what an ugly word that is," she said.

He turned away with a sense of utter weariness. He felt as though he had been struggling for hours up the face of a steep precipice, and now, just as he had fought his way to the top, his hold had given way and he was pitching down headlong into darkness.

If he could have got her in his arms again he might have swept away her arguments; but she still held him at a distance by something inscrutably aloof in her look and attitude, and by his own awed sense of her sincerity. At length he began to plead again.

"If we do this now it will be worse afterward—worse for every one—"

"No—no—no!" she almost screamed, as if he frightened her.

At that moment the bell sent a long tinkle through the house. They had heard no carriage stopping at the door, and they stood motionless, looking at each other with startled eyes.

Outside, Nastasia's step crossed the hall, the outer door opened, and a moment later she came in carrying a telegram which she handed to the Countess Olenska.

"The lady was very happy at the flowers," Nastasia said, smoothing her apron. "She thought it was her *signor marito* who had sent them, and she cried a little and said it was a folly."

Her mistress smiled and took the yellow envelope. She tore it open and carried it to the lamp; then, when the door had closed again, she handed the telegram to Archer.

It was dated from St. Augustine, and addressed to the Countess Olenska. In it he read: "Granny's telegram successful. Papa and Mamma agree marriage after Easter. Am telegraphing Newland. Am too happy for words and love you dearly. Your grateful May."

Half an hour later, when Archer unlocked his own front-door, he found a similar envelope on the hall-table on top of his pile of notes and letters. The message inside the envelope was also from May Welland, and ran as follows: "Parents consent wedding Tuesday after Easter at twelve Grace Church eight bridesmaids please see Rector so happy love May."

Archer crumpled up the yellow sheet as if the gesture could annihilate the news it contained. Then he pulled out a small pocket-diary and turned over the pages with trembling fingers; but he did not find what he wanted, and cramming the telegram into his pocket he mounted the stairs.

---

signor marito   Italian: husband.

A light was shining through the door of the little hall-room which served Janey as a dressing-room and boudoir, and her brother rapped impatiently on the panel. The door opened, and his sister stood before him in her immemorial purple flannel dressing-gown, with her hair "on pins." Her face looked pale and apprehensive.

"Newland! I hope there's no bad news in that telegram? I waited on purpose, in case—" (No item of his correspondence was safe from Janey.)

He took no notice of her question. "Look here—what day is Easter this year?"

She looked shocked at such unchristian ignorance. "Easter? Newland! Why, of course, the first week in April. Why?"

"The first week?" He turned again to the pages of his diary, calculating rapidly under his breath. "The first week, did you say?" He threw back his head with a long laugh.

"For mercy's sake what's the matter?"

"Nothing's the matter, except that I'm going to be married in a month."

Janey fell upon his neck and pressed him to her purple flannel breast. "Oh Newland, how wonderful! I'm so glad! But, dearest, why do you keep on laughing? Do hush, or you'll wake Mamma."

END OF BOOK I

Edith Wharton, age 22, 1884. The photograph was taken three years after Wharton's social debut and one year before her marriage to Edward (Teddy) Wharton. By this time, she had written poems and a novella and had privately published one collection of poetry.

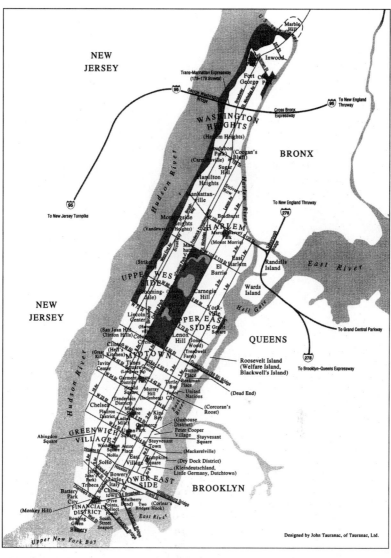

Map of Manhattan.

Parade of Brownstones, looking south along Fifth Avenue above 21st Street, 1865.
" . . . the old Fifth Avenue with its double line of low brown-stone houses, of a
desperate uniformity of style. . . . The Fifth Avenue of that day was a placid and
uneventful throughfare, along which genteel landaus, broughhams and victorias,
and more countrified vehicles of the 'carry-all' and 'surrey' type moved up and
down at decent intervals and a decorous pace." (Edith Wharton, *A Backward
Glance*, 2.)

*Looking north-west
from Madison
Avenue and 55th
Street, 1870.* On the
left is the home of
Wharton's great-
aunt, Mary Mason
Jones, inspiration
for the character
Mrs. Manson
Mingott, who
builds a house
far north of fash-
ionable New York
society "in an in-
accessible wilder-
ness near the
Central Park" (22).

Dinner at Haddo House, Alfred C. Emslie, 1884.

The Metropolitan Museum of Art, ca. 1880. Bypassing the popular Wolfe collection of paintings, Archer and Ellen "wandered down a passage to the room where the 'Cesnola antiquities' mouldered in unvisited loneliness. . . . 'It seems cruel,' she said, 'that after a while nothing matters . . . any more than these little things, that used to be necessary and important to forgotten people'" (247–48).

BOOK II

XIX

The day was fresh, with a lively spring wind full of dust. All the old ladies in both families had got out their faded sables and yellowing ermines, and the smell of camphor from the front pews almost smothered the faint spring scent of the lilies banking the altar.

Newland Archer, at a signal from the sexton, had come out of the vestry and placed himself with his best man on the chancel step of Grace Church.

The signal meant that the brougham bearing the bride and her father was in sight; but there was sure to be a considerable interval of adjustment and consultation in the lobby, where the bridesmaids were already hovering like a cluster of Easter blossoms. During this unavoidable lapse of time the bridegroom, in proof of his eagerness was expected to expose himself alone to the gaze of the assembled company; and Archer had gone through this formality as resignedly as through all the others which made of a nineteenth century New York wedding a rite that seemed to belong to the dawn of history. Everything was equally easy—or equally painful, as one chose to put it—in the path he was committed to tread, and he had obeyed the flurried injunctions of his best man as piously as other bridegrooms had obeyed his own, in the days when he had guided them through the same labyrinth.

So far he was reasonably sure of having fulfilled all his obligations. The bridesmaids' eight bouquets of white lilac and lilies-of-the-valley had been sent in due time, as well as the gold and sapphire sleeve-links of the eight ushers and the best man's cat's-eye scarf pin; Archer had sat up half the night trying to vary the wording of his thanks for the last batch of presents from men friends and ex-lady-loves; the fees for the Bishop and the Rector were safely in the pocket of his best man; his own luggage was already at Mrs. Manson Mingott's, where the wedding-breakfast was to

---

sables . . . ermines   Sable, the soft dark fur of a northern European and Asian mammal, is the most highly esteemed of all furs. Ermine is the valuable white fur of a northern weasel, which is brownish except in winter, when it turns white.

sexton   An officer of a church who is responsible for its care and upkeep.

camphor   A crystalline substance with a distinctive odor, used as an insect repellent.

gold and sapphire sleeve-links   Men's gold cufflinks set with blue gemstones.

cat's-eye   A semiprecious stone with a band of reflected light that shifts position as the gem is turned; at one angle, it resembles a cat's eye.

scarf-pin   A long, sticklike pin used to secure a scarf.

take place, and so were the travelling clothes into which he was to change; and a private compartment had been engaged in the train that was to carry the young couple to their unknown destination—concealment of the spot in which the bridal night was to be spent being one of the most sacred taboos of the prehistoric ritual.

"Got the ring all right?" whispered young van der Luyden Newland, who was inexperienced in the duties of a best man, and awed by the weight of his responsibility.

Archer made the gesture which he had seen so many bridegrooms make: with his ungloved right hand he felt in the pocket of his dark grey waistcoat, and assured himself that the little gold circlet (engraved inside: *Newland to May, April—, 187—*) was in its place; then, resuming his former attitude, his tall hat and pearl-grey gloves with black stitchings grasped in his left hand, he stood looking at the door of the church.

Overhead, Handel's March swelled pompously through the imitation stone vaulting, carrying on its waves the faded drift of the many weddings at which, with cheerful indifference, he had stood on the same chancel step watching other brides float up the nave toward other bridegrooms.

"How like a first night at the Opera!" he thought, recognising all the same faces in the same boxes (no, pews), and wondering if, when the Last Trump sounded, Mrs. Selfridge Merry would be there with the same towering ostrich feathers in her bonnet, and Mrs. Beaufort with the same diamond earrings and the same smile—and whether suitable proscenium seats were already prepared for them in another world.

After that there was still time to review, one by one, the familiar countenances in the first rows; the women's sharp with curiosity and excitement, the men's sulky with the obligation of having to put on their frockcoats before luncheon, and fight for food at the wedding-breakfast.

"Too bad the breakfast is at old Catherine's," the bridegroom could fancy Reggie Chivers saying. "But I'm told that Lovell Mingott insisted on its being cooked by his own *chef*, so it ought to be good if one can only get at it." And he could imagine Sillerton Jackson adding with authority: "My

---

Handel's March Marches were popular in the nineteenth century. This one was composed by George Frideric Handel (1685–1759), a highly acclaimed German-born English composer of operas, cantatas, and church music. He is best known for his oratorio, the *Messiah*.

nave The central part of a church, extending from the entrance to the altar.

proscenium seats Desirable seats in a theater located between the curtain and the orchestra.

dear fellow, haven't you heard? It's to be served at small tables, in the new English fashion."

Archer's eyes lingered a moment on the left-hand pew, where his mother, who had entered the church on Mr. Henry van der Luyden's arm, sat weeping softly under her Chantilly veil, her hands in her grandmother's ermine muff.

"Poor Janey!" he thought, looking at his sister, "even by screwing her head around she can see only the people in the few front pews; and they're mostly dowdy Newlands and Dagonets."

On the hither side of the white ribbon dividing off the seats reserved for the families he saw Beaufort, tall and red-faced, scrutinising the women with his arrogant stare. Beside him sat his wife, all silvery chinchilla and violets; and on the far side of the ribbon, Lawrence Lefferts's sleekly brushed head seemed to mount guard over the invisible deity of "Good Form" who presided at the ceremony.

Archer wondered how many flaws Lefferts's keen eyes would discover in the ritual of his divinity; then he suddenly recalled that he too had once thought such questions important. The things that had filled his days seemed now like a nursery parody of life, or like the wrangles of mediaeval schoolmen over metaphysical terms that nobody had ever understood. A stormy discussion as to whether the wedding presents should be "shown" had darkened the last hours before the wedding; and it seemed inconceivable to Archer that grown-up people should work themselves into a state of agitation over such trifles, and that the matter should have been decided (in the negative) by Mrs. Welland's saying, with indignant tears: "I should as soon turn the reporters loose in my house." Yet there was a time when Archer had had definite and rather aggressive opinions on all such problems, and when everything concerning the manners and customs of his little tribe had seemed to him fraught with world-wide significance.

"And all the while, I suppose," he thought, "real people were living somewhere, and real things happening to them . . ."

Chantilly veil   A veil of delicate silk or linen lace, usually black but sometimes white, made in Chantilly, France.

chinchilla   A soft, bluish-gray fur with black markings. The late-nineteenth-century fashion craze for the fur of this fragile, scarce South American animal almost made the species extinct.

wrangles of mediaeval schoolmen   A reference to medieval scholasticism, a system of philosophy that flourished during the Middle Ages and is colloquially thought of as tediously analytical and exacting.

"*There they come!*" breathed the best man excitedly; but the bridegroom knew better.

The cautious opening of the door of the church meant only that Mr. Brown the livery-stable keeper (gowned in black in his intermittent character of sexton) was taking a preliminary survey of the scene before marshalling his forces. The door was softly shut again; then after another interval it swung majestically open, and a murmur ran through the church: "The family!"

Mrs. Welland came first, on the arm of her eldest son. Her large pink face was appropriately solemn, and her plum-coloured satin with pale blue side-panels, and blue ostrich plumes in a small satin bonnet, met with general approval; but before she had settled herself with a stately rustle in the pew opposite Mrs. Archer's the spectators were craning their necks to see who was coming after her. Wild rumours had been abroad the day before to the effect that Mrs. Manson Mingott, in spite of her physical disabilities, had resolved on being present at the ceremony; and the idea was so much in keeping with her sporting character that bets ran high at the clubs as to her being able to walk up the nave and squeeze into a seat. It was known that she had insisted on sending her own carpenter to look into the possibility of taking down the end panel of the front pew, and to measure the space between the seat and the front; but the result had been discouraging, and for one anxious day her family had watched her dallying with the plan of being wheeled up the nave in her enormous Bath chair and sitting enthroned in it at the foot of the chancel.

The idea of this monstrous exposure of her person was so painful to her relations that they could have covered with gold the ingenious person who suddenly discovered that the chair was too wide to pass between the iron uprights of the awning which extended from the church door to the curbstone. The idea of doing away with this awning, and revealing the bride to the mob of dressmakers and newspaper reporters who stood outside fighting to get near the joints of the canvas, exceeded even old Catherine's courage, though for a moment she had weighed the possibility. "Why, they might take a photograph of my child *and put it in the papers!*" Mrs. Welland exclaimed when her mother's last plan was hinted to her; and from this unthinkable indecency the clan recoiled with a collective

---

plum-coloured satin with pale blue side-panels   Purple was a popular Victorian color. The side panels were rectangular shapes that could be sewn close to the body or left to hang.

Bath chair   A large, wheeled chair made popular in Bath, England, home to many health spas.

shudder. The ancestress had had to give in; but her concession was bought only by the promise that the wedding-breakfast should take place under her roof, though (as the Washington Square connection said) with the Wellands' house in easy reach it was hard to have to make a special price with Brown to drive one to the other end of nowhere.

Though all these transactions had been widely reported by the Jacksons a sporting minority still clung to the belief that old Catherine would appear in church, and there was a distinct lowering of the temperature when she was found to have been replaced by her daughter-in-law. Mrs. Lovell Mingott had the high colour and glassy stare induced in ladies of her age and habit by the effort of getting into a new dress; but once the disappointment occasioned by her mother-in-law's non-appearance had subsided, it was agreed that her black Chantilly over lilac satin, with a bonnet of Parma violets, formed the happiest contrast to Mrs. Welland's blue and plum-colour. Far different was the impression produced by the gaunt and mincing lady who followed on Mr. Mingott's arm, in a wild dishevelment of stripes and fringes and floating scarves; and as this last apparition glided into view Archer's heart contracted and stopped beating.

He had taken it for granted that the Marchioness Manson was still in Washington, where she had gone some four weeks previously with her niece, Madame Olenska. It was generally understood that their abrupt departure was due to Madame Olenska's desire to remove her aunt from the baleful eloquence of Dr. Agathon Carver, who had nearly succeeded in enlisting her as a recruit for the Valley of Love; and in the circumstances no one had expected either of the ladies to return for the wedding. For a moment Archer stood with his eyes fixed on Medora's fantastic figure, straining to see who came behind her; but the little procession was at an end, for all the lesser members of the family had taken their seats, and the eight tall ushers, gathering themselves together like birds or insects preparing for some migratory manoeuvre, were already slipping through the side doors into the lobby.

"Newland—I say: *she's here!*" the best man whispered.

Archer roused himself with a start.

A long time had apparently passed since his heart had stopped beating, for the white and rosy procession was in fact half way up the nave, the

---

Parma violets   From the Greeks on, violets have been associated with love, especially in its highest form. Elizabethans considered them a sign of innocent, unspoiled love, in part because violets do not propagate in the usual way through seeds. In nineteenth-century lore, they suggested faithfulness. Parma violets, named for the northern Italian city, are lavender in color. Here they appear at Archer and May's wedding; in chap. 31, Archer brings Ellen violets.

Bishop, the Rector and two white-winged assistants were hovering about the flower-banked altar, and the first chords of the Spohr symphony were strewing their flower-like notes before the bride.

Archer opened his eyes (but could they really have been shut, as he imagined?), and felt his heart beginning to resume its usual task. The music, the scent of the lilies on the altar, the vision of the cloud of tulle and orange-blossoms floating nearer and nearer, the sight of Mrs. Archer's face suddenly convulsed with happy sobs, the low benedictory murmur of the Rector's voice, the ordered evolutions of the eight pink bridesmaids and the eight black ushers: all these sights, sounds and sensations, so familiar in themselves, so unutterably strange and meaningless in his new relation to them, were confusedly mingled in his brain.

"My God," he thought, "*have* I got the ring?"—and once more he went through the bridegroom's convulsive gesture.

Then, in a moment, May was beside him, such radiance streaming from her that it sent a faint warmth through his numbness, and he straightened himself and smiled into her eyes.

"Dearly beloved, we are gathered together here," the Rector began ...

The ring was on her hand, the Bishop's benediction had been given, the bridesmaids were a-poise to resume their place in the procession, and the organ was showing preliminary symptoms of breaking out into the Mendelssohn March, without which no newly-wedded couple had ever emerged upon New York.

"Your arm—*I say, give her your arm!*" young Newland nervously hissed; and once more Archer became aware of having been adrift far off in the unknown. What was it that had sent him there, he wondered? Perhaps the glimpse, among the anonymous spectators in the transept, of a

---

Spohr symphony   Louis Spohr (1784–1859), a German composer and violinist who was especially popular in England.

orange-blossoms   Often worn on bridal gowns at this time, orange-blossoms signified chastity and fertility.

"Dearly beloved . . ."   In the first two impressions of the first edition of the novel, the Rector reads the words of the burial service: "Forasmuch as it hath pleased Almighty God—" rather than the words of the marriage service. Wharton corrected her error, but the mistake is an interesting expression of Archer's experience of marriage to May as a kind of death.

benediction   The blessing given at the end of a church service.

Mendelssohn March   A traditional wedding song by German composer Felix Mendelssohn (1809–1847). Revered in his lifetime, Mendelssohn became less popular with the ascension of Wagner.

transept   Either of two lateral arms of a cross-shaped church.

dark coil of hair under a hat which, a moment later, revealed itself as belonging to an unknown lady with a long nose, so laughably unlike the person whose image she had evoked that he asked himself if he were becoming subject to hallucinations.

And now he and his wife were pacing slowly down the nave, carried
forward on the light Mendelssohn ripples, the spring day beckoning to
them through widely opened doors, and Mrs. Welland's chestnuts, with
big white favours on their frontlets, curvetting and showing off at the far
end of the canvas tunnel.

The footman, who had a still bigger white favour on his lapel, wrapped
May's white cloak about her, and Archer jumped into the brougham at her
side. She turned to him with a triumphant smile and their hands clasped
under her veil.

"Darling!" Archer said—and suddenly the same black abyss yawned
before him and he felt himself sinking into it, deeper and deeper, while his
voice rambled on smoothly and cheerfully: "Yes, of course I thought I'd
lost the ring; no wedding would be complete if the poor devil of a bridegroom didn't go through that. But you *did* keep me waiting, you know! I
had time to think of every horror that might possibly happen."

She surprised him by turning, in full Fifth Avenue, and flinging her
arms about his neck. "But none ever *can* happen now, can it, Newland, as
long as we two are together?"

Every detail of the day had been so carefully thought out that the
young couple, after the wedding-breakfast, had ample time to put on their
travelling-clothes, descend the wide Mingott stairs between laughing bridesmaids and weeping parents, and get into the brougham under the traditional shower of rice and satin slippers; and there was still half an hour left
in which to drive to the station, buy the last weeklies at the bookstall with
the air of seasoned travellers, and settle themselves in the reserved compartment in which May's maid had already placed her dove-coloured travelling cloak and glaringly new dressing-bag from London.

The old du Lac aunts at Rhinebeck had put their house at the disposal
of the bridal couple, with a readiness inspired by the prospect of spending
a week in New York with Mrs. Archer; and Archer, glad to escape the
usual "bridal suite" in a Philadelphia or Baltimore hotel, had accepted
with an equal alacrity.

---

favours on their frontlets   Decorative ribbons on the horses' foreheads.
curvetting   Leaping lightly or prancing.

May was enchanted at the idea of going to the country, and childishly amused at the vain efforts of the eight bridesmaids to discover where their mysterious retreat was situated. It was thought "very English" to have a country-house lent to one, and the fact gave a last touch of distinction to what was generally conceded to be the most brilliant wedding of the year; but where the house was no one was permitted to know, except the parents of bride and groom, who, when taxed with the knowledge, pursed their lips and said mysteriously: "Ah, they didn't tell us—" which was manifestly true, since there was no need to.

Once they were settled in their compartment, and the train, shaking off the endless wooden suburbs, had pushed out into the pale landscape of spring, talk became easier than Archer had expected. May was still, in look and tone, the simple girl of yesterday, eager to compare notes with him as to the incidents of the wedding, and discussing them as impartially as a bridesmaid talking it all over with an usher. At first Archer had fancied that this detachment was the disguise of an inward tremor; but her clear eyes revealed only the most tranquil unawareness. She was alone for the first time with her husband; but her husband was only the charming comrade of yesterday. There was no one whom she liked as much, no one whom she trusted as completely, and the culminating "lark" of the whole delightful adventure of engagement and marriage was to be off with him alone on a journey, like a grown-up person, like a "married woman," in fact.

It was wonderful that—as he had learned in the Mission garden at St. Augustine—such depths of feeling could coexist with such absence of imagination. But he remembered how, even then, she had surprised him by dropping back to inexpressive girlishness as soon as her conscience had been eased of its burden; and he saw that she would probably go through life dealing to the best of her ability with each experience as it came, but never anticipating any by so much as a stolen glance.

Perhaps that faculty of unawareness was what gave her eyes their transparency, and her face the look of representing a type rather than a person; as if she might have been chosen to pose for a Civic Virtue or a Greek goddess. The blood that ran so close to her fair skin might have been a preserving fluid rather than a ravaging element; yet her look of indestructible youthfulness made her seem neither hard nor dull, but only primitive and pure. In the thick of this meditation Archer suddenly felt himself looking at her with the startled gaze of a stranger, and plunged into

---

a Civic Virtue or a Greek goddess   Wharton suggests that May's face has the admirable but impersonal qualities found in public statues, such as those that proclaim the virtues of good citizenship.

a reminiscence of the wedding-breakfast and of Granny Mingott's immense and triumphant pervasion of it.

May settled down to frank enjoyment of the subject. "I was surprised, though—weren't you?—that aunt Medora came after all. Ellen wrote that they were neither of them well enough to take the journey; I do wish it had been she who had recovered! Did you see the exquisite old lace she sent me?"

He had known that the moment must come sooner or later, but he had somewhat imagined that by force of willing he might hold it at bay.

"Yes—I—no: yes, it was beautiful," he said, looking at her blindly, and wondering if, whenever he heard those two syllables, all his carefully built-up world would tumble about him like a house of cards.

"Aren't you tired? It will be good to have some tea when we arrive— I'm sure the aunts have got everything beautifully ready," he rattled on, taking her hand in his; and her mind rushed away instantly to the magnificent tea and coffee service of Baltimore silver which the Beauforts had sent, and which "went" so perfectly with uncle Lovell Mingott's trays and side-dishes.

In the spring twilight the train stopped at the Rhinebeck station, and they walked along the platform to the waiting carriage.

"Ah, how awfully kind of the van der Luydens—they've sent their man over from Skuytercliff to meet us," Archer exclaimed, as a sedate person out of livery approached them and relieved the maid of her bags.

"I'm extremely sorry, sir," said this emissary, "that a little accident has occurred at the Miss du Lacs': a leak in the water-tank. It happened yesterday, and Mr. van der Luyden, who heard of it this morning, sent a house-maid up by the early train to get the Patroon's house ready. It will be quite comfortable, I think you'll find, sir; and the Miss du Lacs have sent their cook over, so that it will be exactly the same as if you'd been at Rhinebeck."

Archer stared at the speaker so blankly that he repeated in still more apologetic accents: "It'll be exactly the same, sir, I do assure you—" and May's eager voice broke out, covering the embarrassed silence: "The same as Rhinebeck? The Patroon's house? But it will be a hundred thousand times better—won't it, Newland? It's too dear and kind of Mr. van der Luyden to have thought of it."

Baltimore silver   Silverware made in Baltimore, Maryland, originally by immigrant silversmiths from England, Ireland, and Germany. A leading silversmith was Samuel Kirk (1793–1872), who is credited with introducing the *repoussé* technique, a method of raising patterns on metal by punching or hammering from the back. This silver is said to be in the Kirk, or Baltimore, style.

And as they drove off, with the maid beside the coachman, and their shining bridal bags on the seat before them, she went on excitedly: "Only fancy, I've never been inside it—have you? The van der Luydens show it to so few people. But they opened it for Ellen, it seems, and she told me what a darling little place it was: she says it's the only house she's seen in America that she could imagine being perfectly happy in."

"Well—that's what we're going to be, isn't it?" cried her husband gaily; and she answered with her boyish smile: "Ah, it's just our luck beginning—the wonderful luck we're always going to have together!"

XX

"Of course we must dine with Mrs. Carfry, dearest," Archer said; and his wife looked at him with an anxious frown across the monumental Britannia ware of their lodging house breakfast-table.

In all the rainy desert of autumnal London there were only two people whom the Newland Archers knew; and these two they had sedulously avoided, in conformity with the old New York tradition that it was not "dignified" to force one's self on the notice of one's acquaintances in foreign countries.

Mrs. Archer and Janey, in the course of their visits to Europe, had so unflinchingly lived up to this principle, and met the friendly advances of their fellow-travellers with an air of such impenetrable reserve, that they had almost achieved the record of never having exchanged a word with a "foreigner" other than those employed in hotels and railway-stations. Their own compatriots—save those previously known or properly accredited—they treated with an even more pronounced disdain; so that, unless they ran across a Chivers, a Dagonet or a Mingott, their months abroad were spent in an unbroken *tête-à-tête*. But the utmost precautions are sometimes unavailing; and one night at Botzen one of the two English ladies in the room across the passage (whose names, dress and social situation were already intimately known to Janey) had knocked on the door

---

Britannia ware   A metal used in place of more expensive silver. Discovered in Sheffield, England, around 1770, it is made of a pewterlike alloy of copper, tin, and antimony.

tête-à-tête   French: literally "head-to-head," it means a confidential or intimate conversation.

Botzen   Bozen, the German name for the northern Italian city of Bolzano, known as a tourist center.

and asked if Mrs. Archer had a bottle of liniment. The other lady—the intruder's sister, Mrs. Carfry—had been seized with a sudden attack of bronchitis; and Mrs. Archer, who never travelled without a complete family pharmacy, was fortunately able to produce the required remedy.

Mrs. Carfry was very ill, and as she and her sister Miss Harle were travelling alone they were profoundly grateful to the Archer ladies, who supplied them with ingenious comforts and whose efficient maid helped to nurse the invalid back to health.

When the Archers left Botzen they had no idea of ever seeing Mrs. Carfry and Miss Harle again. Nothing, to Mrs. Archer's mind, would have been more "undignified" than to force one's self on the notice of a "foreigner" to whom one had happened to render an accidental service. But Mrs. Carfry and her sister, to whom this point of view was unknown, and who would have found it utterly incomprehensible, felt themselves linked by an eternal gratitude to the "delightful Americans" who had been so kind at Botzen. With touching fidelity they seized every chance of meeting Mrs. Archer and Janey in the course of their continental travels, and displayed a supernatural acuteness in finding out when they were to pass through London on their way to or from the States. The intimacy became indissoluble, and Mrs. Archer and Janey, whenever they alighted at Brown's Hotel, found themselves awaited by two affectionate friends who, like themselves, cultivated ferns in Wardian cases, made macramé lace, read the memoirs of the Baroness Bunsen and had views about the occupants of the leading London pulpits. As Mrs. Archer said, it made "another thing of London" to know Mrs. Carfry and Miss Harle; and by the time that Newland became engaged the tie between the families was so firmly established that it was thought "only right" to send a wedding invitation to the two English ladies, who sent, in return, a pretty bouquet of pressed Alpine flowers under glass. And on the dock, when Newland and his wife sailed for England, Mrs. Archer's last word had been: "You must take May to see Mrs. Carfry."

Newland and his wife had had no idea of obeying this injunction; but Mrs. Carfry, with her usual acuteness, had run them down and sent them an invitation to dine; and it was over this invitation that May Archer was wrinkling her brows across the tea and muffins.

Brown's Hotel   A luxurious hotel located on Albemarle Street in the expensive Mayfair section of London.

Baroness Bunsen   Englishwoman Frances Bunsen (1791–1876) was a well-known supporter of the political and legal career of her husband, Baron Christian Bunsen. When he died in 1860, she published a two-volume tribute, *A Memoir of Baron Bunsen* (1868).

"It's all very well for you, Newland; you *know* them. But I shall feel so shy among a lot of people I've never met. And what shall I wear?"

Newland leaned back in his chair and smiled at her. She looked handsomer and more Diana-like than ever. The moist English air seemed to have deepened the bloom of her cheeks and softened the slight hardness of her virginal features; or else it was simply the inner glow of happiness, shining through like a light under ice.

"Wear, dearest? I thought a trunkful of things had come from Paris last week."

"Yes, of course. I meant to say that I shan't know *which* to wear." She pouted a little. "I've never dined out in London; and I don't want to be ridiculous."

He tried to enter into her perplexity. "But don't English-women dress just like everybody else in the evening?"

"Newland! How can you ask such funny questions? When they go to the theatre in old ball-dresses and bare heads."

"Well, perhaps they wear new ball-dresses at home; but at any rate Mrs. Carfry and Miss Harle won't. They'll wear caps like my mother's—and shawls; very soft shawls."

"Yes; but how will the other women be dressed?"

"Not as well as you, dear," he rejoined, wondering what had suddenly developed in her Janey's morbid interest in clothes.

She pushed back her chair with a sigh. "That's dear of you, Newland; but it doesn't help me much."

He had an inspiration. "Why not wear your wedding-dress? That can't be wrong, can it?"

"Oh, dearest! If I only had it here! But it's gone to Paris to be made over for next winter, and Worth hasn't sent it back."

"Oh, well—" said Archer, getting up. "Look here—the fog's lifting. If we made a dash for the National Gallery we might manage to catch a glimpse of the pictures."

The Newland Archers were on their way home, after a three months' wedding-tour which May, in writing to her girl friends, vaguely summarised as "blissful."

Worth The most influential of haute couture designers, located in Paris, the center of nineteenth-century women's fashion. Englishman Charles Frederick Worth (1826–1895) opened the city's first fashion salon on the rue de la Paix in the 1850s. He was also the first dressmaker to display his creations on live mannequins.

National Gallery Located on the north side of Trafalgar Square, the National Gallery is one of the finest museums of European art in the world.

They had not gone to the Italian Lakes: on reflection, Archer had not been able to picture his wife in that particular setting. Her own inclination (after a month with the Paris dressmakers) was for mountaineering in July and swimming in August. This plan they punctually fulfilled, spending July at Interlaken and Grindelwald, and August at a little place called Etretat, on the Normandy coast, which some one had recommended as quaint and quiet. Once or twice, in the mountains, Archer had pointed southward and said: "There's Italy"; and May, her feet in a gentian-bed, had smiled cheerfully, and replied: "It would be lovely to go there next winter, if only you didn't have to be in New York."

But in reality travelling interested her even less than he had expected. She regarded it (once her clothes were ordered) as merely an enlarged opportunity for walking, riding, swimming, and trying her hand at the fascinating new game of lawn tennis; and when they finally got back to London (where they were to spend a fortnight while he ordered *his* clothes) she no longer concealed the eagerness with which she looked forward to sailing.

In London nothing interested her but the theatres and the shops; and she found the theatres less exciting than the Paris *cafés chantants* where, under the blossoming horse-chestnuts of the Champs Élysées, she had had the novel experience of looking down from the restaurant terrace on an audience of "cocottes," and having her husband interpret to her as much of the songs as he thought suitable for bridal ears.

Archer had reverted to all his old inherited ideas about marriage. It was less trouble to conform with the tradition and treat May exactly as all

---

Interlaken   In the Swiss Alps between Lakes Thun and Brienz, Interlaken was one of the most popular tourist resorts in the nineteenth century.

Grindelwald   Just fourteen miles south of Interlaken, Grindelwald is an equally beautiful Alpine resort town.

Etretat   Étretat is an elegant tourist resort in Normandy, France, known for its steep cliffs.

gentian-bed   Clusters of a mountain plant with small blue or yellow flowers. According to the "language of flowers," gentians meant "you are unjust."

cafés chantants   French: a coffeehouse with musical entertainment. Literally, a singing café.

Champs Élysées   The Avenue des Champs-Élysées, on Paris's Right Bank, extends west from the Place de la Concorde to the Arc de Triomph. One of the most famous avenues in the world, it was flanked by wealthy mansions, large shops, and hotels at the west end and by fashionable cafés at the east end.

"cocottes"   French: "tarts" or prostitutes.

his friends treated their wives than to try to put into practice the theories with which his untrammelled bachelorhood had dallied. There was no use in trying to emancipate a wife who had not the dimmest notion that she was not free; and he had long since discovered that May's only use of the liberty she supposed herself to possess would be to lay it on the altar of her wifely adoration. Her innate dignity would always keep her from making the gift abjectly; and a day might even come (as it once had) when she would find strength to take it altogether back if she thought she were doing it for his own good. But with a conception of marriage so uncomplicated and incurious as hers such a crisis could be brought about only by something visibly outrageous in his own conduct; and the fineness of her feeling for him made that unthinkable. Whatever happened, he knew, she would always be loyal, gallant and unresentful; and that pledged him to the practice of the same virtues.

All this tended to draw him back into his old habits of mind. If her simplicity had been the simplicity of pettiness he would have chafed and rebelled; but since the lines of her character, though so few, were on the same fine mould as her face, she became the tutelary divinity of all his old traditions and reverences.

Such qualities were scarcely of the kind to enliven foreign travel, though they made her so easy and pleasant a companion; but he saw at once how they would fall into place in their proper setting. He had no fear of being oppressed by them, for his artistic and intellectual life would go on, as it always had, outside the domestic circle; and within it there would be nothing small and stifling—coming back to his wife would never be like entering a stuffy room after a tramp in the open. And when they had children the vacant corners in both their lives would be filled.

All these things went through his mind during their long slow drive from Mayfair to South Kensington, where Mrs. Carfry and her sister lived. Archer too would have preferred to escape their friends' hospitality: in conformity with the family tradition he had always travelled as a sight-seer and looker-on, affecting a haughty unconsciousness of the presence of his fellow-beings. Once only, just after Harvard, he had spent a few gay weeks at Florence with a band of queer Europeanised Americans, dancing all night with titled ladies in palaces, and gambling half the day with the rakes

---

tutelary   Being or serving as a guardian.

Mayfair   A district in London that became a fashionable residential area in the late nineteenth and early twentieth century.

South Kensington   A borough of greater London under transition in the nineteenth century from rural parish to residential neighborhood.

and dandies of the fashionable club; but it had all seemed to him, though the greatest fun in the world, as unreal as a carnival. These queer cosmopolitan women, deep in complicated love-affairs which they appeared to feel the need of retailing to every one they met, and the magnificent young officers and elderly dyed wits who were the subjects or the recipients of their confidences, were too different from the people Archer had grown up among, too much like expensive and rather malodorous hot-house exotics, to detain his imagination long. To introduce his wife into such a society was out of the question; and in the course of his travels no other had shown any marked eagerness for his company.

Not long after their arrival in London he had run across the Duke of St. Austrey, and the Duke, instantly and cordially recognising him, had said: "Look me up, won't you?"—but no proper-spirited American would have considered that a suggestion to be acted on, and the meeting was without a sequel. They had even managed to avoid May's English aunt, the banker's wife, who was still in Yorkshire; in fact, they had purposely postponed going to London till the autumn in order that their arrival during the season might not appear pushing and snobbish to these unknown relatives.

"Probably there'll be nobody at Mrs. Carfry's—London's a desert at this season, and you've made yourself much too beautiful," Archer said to May, who sat at his side in the hansom so spotlessly splendid in her sky-blue cloak edged with swansdown that it seemed wicked to expose her to the London grime.

"I don't want them to think that we dress like savages," she replied, with a scorn that Pocahontas might have resented; and he was struck again by the religious reverence of even the most unworldly American women for the social advantages of dress.

---

hot-house exotics   Wharton uses this term to describe Americans who become disenchanted with American life, feel affinities for Europe, and even relocate there. She applied the label to herself and other expatriate comrades in a letter to Sara Norton, 5 June 1903: "*we* are none of us Americans, we don't think or feel as the Americans do, we are the wretched exotics produced in a European glass-house, the most *déplacé* [displaced] & useless class on earth!" (*Letters* 84).

Yorkshire   A county in northern England.

hansom   A two-wheeled covered carriage with the driver's seat above and behind, named for Joseph Hansom (1803–1882).

swansdown   The underlying soft feathers of swan, used as a trim on women's clothing.

savages . . . Pocahontas   Pocahontas (c. 1595–1617) was the daughter of Powhatan, an Indian chief of Virginia. According to legend, she rescued English Captain John Smith when her father was about to kill him. She later married John Rolfe (1585–1622), a

"It's their armour," he thought, "their defence against the unknown, and their defiance of it." And he understood for the first time the earnestness with which May, who was incapable of tying a ribbon in her hair to charm him, had gone through the solemn rite of selecting and ordering her extensive wardrobe.

He had been right in expecting the party at Mrs. Carfry's to be a small one. Besides their hostess and her sister, they found, in the long chilly drawing-room, only another shawled lady, a genial Vicar who was her husband, a silent lad whom Mrs. Carfry named as her nephew, and a small dark gentleman with lively eyes whom she introduced as his tutor, pronouncing a French name as she did so.

Into this dimly-lit and dim-featured group May Archer floated like a swan with the sunset on her: she seemed larger, fairer, more voluminously rustling than her husband had ever seen her; and he perceived that the rosiness and rustlingness were the tokens of an extreme and infantile shyness.

"What on earth will they expect me to talk about?" her helpless eyes implored him, at the very moment that her dazzling apparition was calling forth the same anxiety in their own bosoms. But beauty, even when distrustful of itself, awakens confidence in the manly heart; and the Vicar and the French-named tutor were soon manifesting to May their desire to put her at her ease.

In spite of their best efforts, however, the dinner was a languishing affair. Archer noticed that his wife's way of showing herself at her ease with foreigners was to become more uncompromisingly local in her references, so that, though her loveliness was an encouragement to admiration, her conversation was a chill to repartee. The Vicar soon abandoned the struggle; but the tutor, who spoke the most fluent and accomplished English, gallantly continued to pour it out to her until the ladies, to the manifest relief of all concerned, went up to the drawing-room.

The Vicar, after a glass of port, was obliged to hurry away to a meeting, and the shy nephew, who appeared to be an invalid, was packed off to bed. But Archer and the tutor continued to sit over their wine, and suddenly Archer found himself talking as he had not done since his last

---

Jamestown settler; the marriage brought the colonists and Indians eight years of peace. In 1616, Pocahontas was brought to England, where she was viewed as a curiosity. Early America itself was considered by Europeans to be strange, uncivilized, and savage.

Vicar In the Church of England, the priest of a parish who receives a salary, not a portion of the parish's income.

repartee Witty, spirited conversation. Wharton valued good conversation above all social amenities and often used the ability to converse intelligently as a standard for judging character.

symposium with Ned Winsett. The Carfry nephew, it turned out, had been threatened with consumption, and had had to leave Harrow for Switzerland, where he had spent two years in the milder air of Lake Leman. Being a bookish youth, he had been entrusted to M. Rivière, who had brought him back to England, and was to remain with him till he went up to Oxford the following spring; and M. Rivière added with simplicity that he should then have to look out for another job.

It seemed impossible, Archer thought, that he should be long without one, so varied were his interests and so many his gifts. He was a man of about thirty, with a thin ugly face (May would certainly have called him common-looking) to which the play of his ideas gave an intense expressiveness; but there was nothing frivolous or cheap in his animation.

His father, who had died young, had filled a small diplomatic post, and it had been intended that the son should follow the same career; but an insatiable taste for letters had thrown the young man into journalism, then into authorship (apparently unsuccessful), and at length—after other experiments and vicissitudes which he spared his listener—into tutoring English youths in Switzerland. Before that, however, he had lived much in Paris, frequented the Goncourt *grenier,* been advised by Maupassant not to attempt to write (even that seemed to Archer a dazzling honour!), and had often talked with Mérimée in his mother's house. He had obviously always been desperately poor and anxious (having a mother and an unmarried sister to provide for), and it was apparent that his literary ambitions had failed. His situation, in fact, seemed, materially speaking, no more brilliant than Ned Winsett's; but he had lived in a world in which, as he said, no one who loved ideas need hunger mentally. As it was precisely of that love that poor Winsett was starving to death, Archer looked with a

---

Harrow   An elite private boys' school in Middlesex, England, founded in 1572.

Lake Leman   Lac Léman is the French name for Lake Geneva, Switzerland's largest lake.

Oxford   The oldest university in England, established in the twelfth century.

Goncourt *grenier*   French: Literally meaning attic or garret, the *grenier* refers to a literary salon presided over by writer Edmond Goncourt. Since it did not start until 1885, Wharton's reference appears anachronistic. However, the Goncourt brothers did come together at fortnightly "dîners Magny" at a Paris restaurant in the 1860s; Wharton may have had these gatherings in mind.

Maupassant   Guy de Maupassant (1850–1893), a French short story writer and novelist of the naturalist school, drew his subjects from peasant life, the Franco-Prussian war, and middle-class and fashionable Parisian life. Like his mentor, Gustave Flaubert, he paid careful attention to craft. Maupassant uses a direct, simple, and often ironic style to convey the toil and frequent suffering of his characters.

sort of vicarious envy at this eager impecunious young man who had fared so richly in his poverty.

"You see, Monsieur, it's worth everything, isn't it, to keep one's intellectual liberty, not to enslave one's powers of appreciation, one's critical independence? It was because of that that I abandoned journalism, and took to so much duller work: tutoring and private secretaryship. There is a good deal of drudgery, of course; but one preserves one's moral freedom, what we call in French one's *quant à soi*. And when one hears good talk one can join in it without compromising any opinions but one's own; or one can listen, and answer it inwardly. Ah, good conversation—there's nothing like it, is there? The air of ideas is the only air worth breathing. And so I have never regretted giving up either diplomacy or journalism—two different forms of the same self-abdication." He fixed his vivid eyes on Archer as he lit another cigarette. "*Voyez-vous*, Monsieur, to be able to look life in the face: that's worth living in a garret for, isn't it? But, after all, one must earn enough to pay for the garret; and I confess that to grow old as a private tutor—or a 'private' anything—is almost as chilling to the imagination as a second secretaryship at Bucharest. Sometimes I feel I must make a plunge: an immense plunge. Do you suppose, for instance, there would be any opening for me in America—in New York?"

Archer looked at him with startled eyes. New York, for a young man who had frequented the Goncourts and Flaubert, and who thought the life of ideas the only one worth living! He continued to stare at M. Rivière perplexedly, wondering how to tell him that his very superiorities and advantages would be the surest hindrance to success.

"New York—New York—but must it be especially New York?" he stammered, utterly unable to imagine what lucrative opening his native city could offer to a young man to whom good conversation appeared to be the only necessity.

A sudden flush rose under M. Rivière's sallow skin. "I—I thought it your metropolis: is not the intellectual life more active there?" he rejoined; then, as if fearing to give his hearer the impression of having asked a

---

quant à soi   French: dignity.

"*Voyez-vous . . .*"   French: "You see . . ."

Flaubert   The French novelist Gustave Flaubert (1821–1880) was associated with the naturalist school but also the Romantic tradition. Best known for the novel *Madame Bovary* (1856), he believed in the absolute value of art, the perfection of form, and the practice of craft. Flaubert's fiction is marked by exactness of observation, objectivity, and a precise, balanced style. Wharton considered him one of the greatest continental novelists.

favour, he went on hastily: "One throws out random suggestions—more to one's self than to others. In reality, I see no immediate prospect—" and rising from his seat he added, without a trace of constraint: "But Mrs. Carfry will think that I ought to be taking you upstairs."

During the homeward drive Archer pondered deeply on this episode. His hour with M. Rivière had put new air into his lungs, and his first impulse had been to invite him to dine the next day; but he was beginning to understand why married men did not always immediately yield to their first impulses.

"That young tutor is an interesting fellow: we had some awfully good talk after dinner about books and things," he threw out tentatively in the hansom.

May roused herself from one of the dreamy silences into which he had read so many meanings before six months of marriage had given him the key to them.

"The little Frenchman? Wasn't he dreadfully common?" she questioned coldly; and he guessed that she nursed a secret disappointment at having been invited out in London to meet a clergyman and a French tutor. The disappointment was not occasioned by the sentiment ordinarily defined as snobbishness, but by old New York's sense of what was due to it when it risked its dignity in foreign lands. If May's parents had entertained the Carfrys in Fifth Avenue they would have offered them something more substantial than a parson and a schoolmaster.

But Archer was on edge, and took her up.

"Common—common *where?*" he queried; and she returned with unusual readiness: "Why, I should say anywhere but in his school-room. Those people are always awkward in society. But then," she added disarmingly, "I suppose I shouldn't have known if he was clever."

Archer disliked her use of the word "clever" almost as much as her use of the word "common"; but he was beginning to fear his tendency to dwell on the things he disliked in her. After all, her point of view had always been the same. It was that of all the people he had grown up among, and he had always regarded it as necessary but negligible. Until a few months ago he had never known a "nice" woman who looked at life differently; and if a man married it must necessarily be among the nice.

"Ah—then I won't ask him to dine!" he concluded with a laugh; and May echoed, bewildered: "Goodness—ask the Carfry's tutor?"

"Well, not on the same day with the Carfrys, if you prefer I shouldn't. But I did rather want another talk with him. He's looking for a job in New York."

Her surprise increased with her indifference: he almost fancied that she suspected him of being tainted with "foreignness."

"A job in New York? What sort of a job? People don't have French tutors: what does he want to do?"

"Chiefly to enjoy good conversation, I understand," her husband retorted perversely; and she broke into an appreciative laugh. "Oh, Newland, how funny! Isn't that *French?*"

On the whole, he was glad to have the matter settled for him by her refusing to take seriously his wish to invite M. Rivière. Another after-dinner talk would have made it difficult to avoid the question of New York; and the more Archer considered it the less he was able to fit M. Rivière into any conceivable picture of New York as he knew it.

He perceived with a flash of chilling insight that in future many problems would be thus negatively solved for him; but as he paid the hansom and followed his wife's long train into the house he took refuge in the comforting platitude that the first six months were always the most difficult in marriage. "After that I suppose we shall have pretty nearly finished rubbing off each other's angles," he reflected; but the worst of it was that May's pressure was already bearing on the very angles whose sharpness he most wanted to keep.

XXI

The small bright lawn stretched away smoothly to the big bright sea.

The turf was hemmed with an edge of scarlet geranium and coleus, and cast-iron vases painted in chocolate colour, standing at intervals along the winding path that led to the sea, looped their garlands of petunia and ivy geranium above the neatly raked gravel.

Half way between the edge of the cliff and the square wooden house (which was also chocolate-coloured, but with the tin roof of the verandah striped in yellow and brown to represent an awning) two large targets had been placed against a background of shrubbery. On the other side of the lawn, facing the targets, was pitched a real tent, with benches and garden-seats about it. A number of ladies in summer dresses and gentlemen in grey frock-coats and tall hats stood on the lawn or sat upon the benches; and

---

scarlet geranium　Victorians attached a sense of comfort to the red geranium.

petunia　Petunias, native to South America, did not come to Europe until the nineteenth century, but by the mid-1880s they were popular garden flowers. Hardy, purple-flowered plants in their natural habitat, petunias meant "never despair."

ivy geranium　The stems of the ivy geranium hang or climb rather than grow upright. Nineteenth-century admirers attached the sense of bridal favor to the plant.

every now and then a slender girl in starched muslin would step from the tent, bow in hand, and speed her shaft at one of the targets, while the spectators interrupted their talk to watch the result.

Newland Archer, standing on the verandah of the house, looked curiously down upon this scene. On each side of the shiny painted steps was a large blue china flower-pot on a bright yellow china stand. A spiky green plant filled each pot, and below the verandah ran a wide border of blue hydrangeas edged with more red geraniums. Behind him, the French windows of the drawing-rooms through which he had passed gave glimpses, between swaying lace curtains, of glassy parquet floors islanded with chintz *poufs,* dwarf arm-chairs, and velvet tables covered with trifles in silver.

The Newport Archery Club always held its August meeting at the Beauforts'. The sport, which had hitherto known no rival but croquet, was beginning to be discarded in favour of lawn-tennis; but the latter game was still considered too rough and inelegant for social occasions, and as an opportunity to show off pretty dresses and graceful attitudes the bow and arrow held their own.

Archer looked down with wonder at the familiar spectacle. It surprised him that life should be going on in the old way when his own reactions to it had so completely changed. It was Newport that had first brought home

---

hydrangeas   Shrubs with large round clusters of pink, blue, or white flowers, hydrangeas, according to the "language of flowers," conveyed boastfulness or heartlessness.

parquet floors   Floors of different kinds of wood set in a pattern or mosaic.

poufs   French: low padded cushions or seats.

Newport Archery Club   Archery was introduced into the United States as a sport in the seventeenth century but did not become popular until the Victorian period, when American men and women followed England's lead in adopting it as a pastime of the leisured class. Clubs often had their beginnings on country-house lawns such as the one Wharton describes.

croquet   Croquet, a lawn game involving hitting balls through hoops, was popular until the mid- to late nineteenth century, when it was supplanted by tennis. Tennis, embraced by the younger set, was considered "too rough and inelegant" by older players.

Newport   Newport, Rhode Island, at the southern end of Aquidneck Island, was a famous resort town. As early as 1830, wealthy families from as far away as Virginia were spending summers there. Newport's reputation grew after the Civil War, when millionaires such as the August Belmonts, Ward McAllisters, Harry Lehrs, and William Astors built lavish palaces—called "cottages"—and hosted extravagant summer balls and parties. A hostess might spend as much as $300,000 (1890 dollars) entertaining her guests in a single season. The summer homes of old New Yorkers were modest in contrast to those built by these newly moneyed industrialists.

to him the extent of the change. In New York, during the previous winter, after he and May had settled down in the new greenish-yellow house with the bow-window and the Pompeian vestibule, he had dropped back with relief into the old routine of the office, and the renewal of this daily activity had served as a link with his former self. Then there had been the pleasurable excitement of choosing a showy grey stepper for May's brougham (the Wellands had given the carriage), and the abiding occupation and interest of arranging his new library, which, in spite of family doubts and disapprovals, had been carried out as he had dreamed, with a dark embossed paper, Eastlake book-cases and "sincere" arm-chairs and tables. At the Century he had found Winsett again, and at the Knickerbocker the fashionable young men of his own set; and what with the hours dedicated to the law and those given to dining out or entertaining friends at home, with an occasional evening at the Opera or the play, the life he was living had still seemed a fairly real and inevitable sort of business.

But Newport represented the escape from duty into an atmosphere of unmitigated holiday-making. Archer had tried to persuade May to spend the summer on a remote island off the coast of Maine (called, appropriately enough, Mount Desert), where a few hardy Bostonians and Philadelphians were camping in "native" cottages, and whence came reports of enchanting scenery and a wild, almost trapper-like existence amid woods and waters.

But the Wellands always went to Newport, where they owned one of the square boxes on the cliffs, and their son-in-law could adduce no good reason why he and May should not join them there. As Mrs. Welland rather tartly pointed out, it was hardly worth while for May to have worn herself out trying on summer clothes in Paris if she was not to be allowed to wear them; and this argument was of a kind to which Archer had as yet found no answer.

---

the Knickerbocker The Knickerbocker Club was an exclusive club formed in 1871 by eighteen members of the Union Club who were concerned about changes there. Its founding members included Alexander Hamilton (grandson of the Secretary of the Treasury), John Jacob Astor, Moses Lazarus, and August Belmont.

Mount Desert An island, much of which is now Acadia National Park, on the northern coast of Maine. Known for its dramatic natural setting—seaside cliffs, lakes, forested interior—it attracted summer residents in the 1850s, when steamboat service began running from the mainland. Hudson River School painter Thomas Cole and other artists came to the island for its spectacular scenery. By century's end, a number of the nation's richest families—the Astors, Vanderbilts, and Rockefellers—had built mansions on the island. Efforts to preserve the island as a national park were launched in the early twentieth century.

May herself could not understand his obscure reluctance to fall in with so reasonable and pleasant a way of spending the summer. She reminded him that he had always liked Newport in his bachelor days, and as this was indisputable he could only profess that he was sure he was going to like it better than ever now that they were to be there together. But as he stood on the Beaufort verandah and looked out on the brightly peopled lawn it came home to him with a shiver that he was not going to like it at all.

It was not May's fault, poor dear. If, now and then, during their travels, they had fallen slightly out of step, harmony had been restored by their return to the conditions she was used to. He had always foreseen that she would not disappoint him; and he had been right. He had married (as most young men did) because he had met a perfectly charming girl at the moment when a series of rather aimless sentimental adventures were ending in premature disgust; and she had represented peace, stability, comradeship, and the steadying sense of an unescapable duty.

He could not say that he had been mistaken in his choice, for she had fulfilled all that he had expected. It was undoubtedly gratifying to be the husband of one of the handsomest and most popular young married women in New York, especially when she was also one of the sweetest-tempered and most reasonable of wives; and Archer had never been insensible to such advantages. As for the momentary madness which had fallen upon him on the eve of his marriage, he had trained himself to regard it as the last of his discarded experiments. The idea that he could ever, in his senses, have dreamed of marrying the Countess Olenska had become almost unthinkable, and she remained in his memory simply as the most plaintive and poignant of a line of ghosts.

But all these abstractions and eliminations made of his mind a rather empty and echoing place, and he supposed that was one of the reasons why the busy animated people on the Beaufort lawn shocked him as if they had been children playing in a grave-yard.

He heard a murmur of skirts beside him, and the Marchioness Manson fluttered out of the drawing-room window. As usual, she was extraordinarily festooned and bedizened, with a limp Leghorn hat anchored to her head by many windings of faded gauze, and a little black velvet parasol on a carved ivory handle absurdly balanced over her much larger hat-brim.

---

festooned and bedizened   Decorated with garlands or ribbons and ornamented in a tasteless manner.

Leghorn hat   A hat made of fine plaited straw.

"My dear Newland, I had no idea that you and May had arrived! You yourself came only yesterday, you say? Ah, business—business—professional duties . . . I understand. Many husbands, I know, find it impossible to join their wives here except for the week-end." She cocked her head on one side and languished at him through screwed-up eyes. "But marriage is one long sacrifice, as I used often to remind my Ellen—"

Archer's heart stopped with the queer jerk which it had given once before, and which seemed suddenly to slam a door between himself and the outer world; but this break of continuity must have been of the briefest, for he presently heard Medora answering a question he had apparently found voice to put.

"No, I am not staying here, but with the Blenkers, in their delicious solitude at Portsmouth. Beaufort was kind enough to send his famous trotters for me this morning, so that I might have at least a glimpse of one of Regina's garden-parties; but this evening I go back to rural life. The Blenkers, dear original beings, have hired a primitive old farm-house at Portsmouth where they gather about them representative people . . ." She drooped slightly beneath her protecting brim, and added with a faint blush: "This week Dr. Agathon Carver is holding a series of Inner Thought meetings there. A contrast indeed to this gay scene of worldly pleasure— but then I have always lived on contrasts! To me the only death is monotony. I always say to Ellen: Beware of monotony; it's the mother of all the deadly sins. But my poor child is going through a phase of exaltation, of abhorrence of the world. You know, I suppose, that she has declined all invitations to stay at Newport, even with her grandmother Mingott? I could hardly persuade her to come with me to the Blenkers', if you will believe it! The life she leads is morbid, unnatural. Ah, if she had only listened to me when it was still possible . . . When the door was still open . . . But shall we go down and watch this absorbing match? I hear your May is one of the competitors."

Strolling toward them from the tent Beaufort advanced over the lawn, tall, heavy, too tightly buttoned into a London frock-coat, with one of his own orchids in its buttonhole. Archer, who had not seen him for two or

---

Portsmouth A summer resort town on the northern end of Aquidneck Island, as historic as Newport but less developed in the 1870s.

trotters Horses trained for harness racing, a sport that prospered at mid-century. In 1860, there were seven trotting tracks in the New York City area where Beaufort's horses may have run, including the Fashion Course in Newtown (1854) and Jerome Park in Fordham, site of the Belmont Stakes (1867). By 1879, the locus of racing had shifted to Coney Island.

three months, was struck by the change in his appearance. In the hot summer light his floridness seemed heavy and bloated, and but for his erect square-shouldered walk he would have looked like an over-fed and over-dressed old man.

There were all sorts of rumours afloat about Beaufort. In the spring he had gone off on a long cruise to the West Indies in his new steam-yacht, and it was reported that, at various points where he had touched, a lady resembling Miss Fanny Ring had been seen in his company. The steam-yacht, built in the Clyde, and fitted with tiled bath-rooms and other un-heard-of luxuries, was said to have cost him half a million; and the pearl necklace which he had presented to his wife on his return was as magnificent as such expiatory offerings are apt to be. Beaufort's fortune was substantial enough to stand the strain; and yet the disquieting rumours persisted, not only in Fifth Avenue but in Wall Street. Some people said he had speculated unfortunately in railways, others that he was being bled by one of the most insatiable members of her profession; and to every report of threatened insolvency Beaufort replied by a fresh extravagance: the building of a new row of orchid-houses, the purchase of a new string of race-horses, or the addition of a new Meissonnier or Cabanel to his picture-gallery.

He advanced toward the Marchioness and Newland with his usual half-sneering smile. "Hullo, Medora! Did the trotters do their business? Forty minutes, eh? . . . Well, that's not so bad, considering your nerves had to be spared." He shook hands with Archer, and then, turning back

---

the Clyde   The Clyde River, in southern Scotland, was famous for shipbuilding. Thomson on the Clyde built many of Cunard's finest ocean liners.

Wall Street   The location of the New York Stock Exchange and a term now synonymous with high finance, it is literally a small, once-walled street in Manhattan that runs for less than a mile between Broadway and the East River. Investing in the stock market in the mid-nineteenth century was a highly speculative activity, a bit like gambling, although trade was regulated. Old New Yorkers, who made their money from steady sources such as real estate investments and municipal bonds, tended to shy away from such market volatility. About her family and friends, Wharton writes in *A Backward Glance* that "great fortunes, originating in a fabulous increase of New York real estate values, had been fostered by judicious investments and prudent administration; but of feverish money-making, in Wall Street or in railway, shipping or industrial enterprises, I heard nothing in my youth" (56). Trading on the New York Stock Exchange picked up speed during the Civil War, with membership on the exchange increasing tenfold during the 1860s and growth continuing through the century.

Meissonnier [sic]   Ernest Meissonier (1814–1891) was the most famous of all Second Empire French painters. His depictions of Napoléon's campaigns as well as his genre pictures were known for their microscopic precision and attention to detail.

with them, placed himself on Mrs. Manson's other side, and said, in a low voice, a few words which their companion did not catch.

The Marchioness replied by one of her queer foreign jerks, and a "*Que voulez-vous?*" which deepened Beaufort's frown; but he produced a good semblance of a congratulatory smile as he glanced at Archer to say: "You know May's going to carry off the first prize."

"Ah, then it remains in the family," Medora rippled; and at that moment they reached the tent and Mrs. Beaufort met them in a girlish cloud of mauve muslin and floating veils.

May Welland was just coming out of the tent. In her white dress, with a pale green ribbon about the waist and a wreath of ivy on her hat, she had the same Diana-like aloofness as when she had entered the Beaufort ballroom on the night of her engagement. In the interval not a thought seemed to have passed behind her eyes or a feeling through her heart; and though her husband knew that she had the capacity for both he marvelled afresh at the way in which experience dropped away from her.

She had her bow and arrow in her hand, and placing herself on the chalk-mark traced on the turf she lifted the bow to her shoulder and took aim. The attitude was so full of a classic grace that a murmur of appreciation followed her appearance, and Archer felt the glow of proprietorship that so often cheated him into momentary well-being. Her rivals— Mrs. Reggie Chivers, the Merry girls, and divers rosy Thorleys, Dagonets and Mingotts, stood behind her in a lovely anxious group, brown heads and golden bent above the scores, and pale muslins and flower-wreathed hats mingled in a tender rainbow. All were young and pretty, and bathed in summer bloom; but not one had the nymph-like ease of his wife, when, with tense muscles and happy frown, she bent her soul upon some feat of strength.

"Gad," Archer heard Lawrence Lefferts say, "not one of the lot holds the bow as she does;" and Beaufort retorted: "Yes; but that's the only kind of target she'll ever hit."

Archer felt irrationally angry. His host's contemptuous tribute to May's "niceness" was just what a husband should have wished to hear said of his wife. The fact that a coarse-minded man found her lacking in

---

"*Que voulez-vous?*" French: "What do you want?"

wreath of ivy A wreath is often used as a mark of distinction or honor. In the "language of flowers," ivy connoted friendship, fidelity, and marriage.

nymph-like In Greek and Roman mythology, a nymph was a female spirit inhabiting and representing nature, especially woodlands and waters. The word can be used simply to mean a beautiful girl.

attraction was simply another proof of her quality; yet the words sent a faint shiver through his heart. What if "niceness" carried to that supreme degree were only a negation, the curtain dropped before an emptiness? As he looked at May, returning flushed and calm from her final bull's-eye, he had the feeling that he had never yet lifted that curtain.

She took the congratulations of her rivals and of the rest of the company with the simplicity that was her crowning grace. No one could ever be jealous of her triumphs because she managed to give the feeling that she would have been just as serene if she had missed them. But when her eyes met her husband's her face glowed with the pleasure she saw in his.

Mrs. Welland's basket-work poney-carriage was waiting for them, and they drove off among the dispersing carriages, May handling the reins and Archer sitting at her side.

The afternoon sunlight still lingered upon the bright lawns and shrubberies, and up and down Bellevue Avenue rolled a double line of victorias, dog-carts, landaus and "vis-à-vis," carrying well-dressed ladies and gentlemen away from the Beaufort garden-party, or homeward from their daily afternoon turn along the Ocean Drive.

"Shall we go to see Granny?" May suddenly proposed. "I should like to tell her myself that I've won the prize. There's lots of time before dinner."

Archer acquiesced, and she turned the ponies down Narragansett Avenue, crossed Spring Street and drove out toward the rocky moorland beyond. In this unfashionable region Catherine the Great, always indifferent to precedent and thrifty of purse, had built herself in her youth a many-peaked and cross-beamed *cottage-orné* on a bit of cheap land overlooking

---

Bellevue Avenue   A mansion-lined street that runs north and south through Newport. Kingscote, a Gothic revival built in 1839, is thought to be the nation's first summer "cottage." Mansions built later include Château-sur-Mer (1852), Belcourt Castle (1891), Marble House (1892), Rosecliff (1902), and The Elms (1901).

victorias   Light four-wheeled horse-drawn carriages for two people.

dog-carts   Light two-wheeled horse-drawn carriages.

"vis-à-vis"   French: a carriage in which two people face each other.

Ocean Drive   A scenic route that follows the coastline of southwestern Newport along Harrison Avenue, Ridge Road, and Ocean Avenue. The western side of the city was less developed than the eastern side.

Narragansett Avenue   A street that runs east and west, crossing Bellevue Avenue and Spring Street.

Spring Street   A north–south street running parallel to and west of Bellevue Avenue.

cottage-orné   French: an ornate country cottage.

the bay. Here, in a thicket of stunted oaks, her verandahs spread themselves above the island-dotted waters. A winding drive led up between iron
stags and blue glass balls embedded in mounds of geraniums to a front
door of highly-varnished walnut under a striped verandah-roof; and behind it ran a narrow hall with a black and yellow star-patterned parquet
floor, upon which opened four small square rooms with heavy flock-papers
under ceilings on which an Italian house-painter had lavished all the di-
vinities of Olympus. One of these rooms had been turned into a bedroom
by Mrs. Mingott when the burden of flesh descended on her, and in the ad-
joining one she spent her days, enthroned in a large armchair between the
open door and window, and perpetually waving a palm-leaf fan which the
prodigious projection of her bosom kept so far from the rest of her person
that the air it set in motion stirred only the fringe of the anti-macassars on
the chair-arms.

Since she had been the means of hastening his marriage old Catherine
had shown to Archer the cordiality which a service rendered excites toward the person served. She was persuaded that irrepressible passion was
the cause of his impatience; and being an ardent admirer of impulsiveness
(when it did not lead to the spending of money) she always received him
with a genial twinkle of complicity and a play of allusion to which May
seemed fortunately impervious.

She examined and appraised with much interest the diamond-tipped
arrow which had been pinned on May's bosom at the conclusion of
the match, remarking that in her day a filigree brooch would have been
thought enough, but that there was no denying that Beaufort did things
handsomely.

"Quite an heirloom, in fact, my dear," the old lady chuckled. "You
must leave it in fee to your eldest girl." She pinched May's white arm and
watched the colour flood her face. "Well, well, what have I said to make
you shake out the red flag? Ain't there going to be any daughters—only
boys, eh? Good gracious, look at her blushing again all over her blushes!
What—can't I say that either? Mercy me—when my children beg me to
have all those gods and goddesses painted out overhead I always say I'm
too thankful to have somebody about me that *nothing* can shock!"

---

flock-papers Wallpapers with wool or felt designs applied to create pattern or texture.
anti-macassars Protective covers for the backs of chairs and sofas, they were named for
the Macassar oil that men used on their hair. The antimacassar protected the upholstery.
filigree brooch A pin decorated with a fine gold or silver wire twisted into patterns.
in fee In absolute and legal possession.

Archer burst into a laugh, and May echoed it, crimson to the eyes.

"Well, now tell me all about the party, please, my dears, for I shall never get a straight word about it out of that silly Medora," the ancestress continued; and, as May exclaimed: "Cousin Medora? But I thought she was going back to Portsmouth?" she answered placidly: "So she is—but she's got to come here first to pick up Ellen. Ah—you didn't know Ellen had come to spend the day with me? Such fol-de-rol, her not coming for the summer; but I gave up arguing with young people about fifty years ago. Ellen—*Ellen!*" she cried in her shrill old voice, trying to bend forward far enough to catch a glimpse of the lawn beyond the verandah.

There was no answer, and Mrs. Mingott rapped impatiently with her stick on the shiny floor. A mulatto maid-servant in a bright turban, replying to the summons, informed her mistress that she had seen "Miss Ellen" going down the path to the shore; and Mrs. Mingott turned to Archer.

"Run down and fetch her, like a good grandson; this pretty lady will describe the party to me," she said; and Archer stood up as if in a dream.

He had heard the Countess Olenska's name pronounced often enough during the year and a half since they had last met, and was even familiar with the main incidents of her life in the interval. He knew that she had spent the previous summer at Newport, where she appeared to have gone a great deal into society, but that in the autumn she had suddenly sub-let the "perfect house" which Beaufort had been at such pains to find for her, and decided to establish herself in Washington. There, during the winter, he had heard of her (as one always heard of pretty women in Washington) as shining in the "brilliant diplomatic society" that was supposed to make up for the social short-comings of the Administration. He had listened to these accounts, and to various contradictory reports on her appearance,

---

fol-de-rol Foolishness, nonsense.

mulatto . . . bright turban *Mulatto* was the word used to designate a person of mixed Caucasian and Negro ancestry. Newport played a leading role in the history of slave trading. By 1730, Rhode Island had become the fifth wealthiest colony, largely through the "triangle trade": rum distilled in Rhode Island was exchanged for slaves in Africa, who were sold to West Indian sugar planters, who paid in molasses to make rum. Many African Americans remained in the Newport area; during the Revolutionary War, the town of Portsmouth put up the first African American regiment ever to fight under the American flag. However, the state was slow to give African Americans their rights. The legislature did not free all children born of slave mothers until 1784 and did not prohibit slave trading until 1787.

the Administration Republican Ulysses S. Grant served two terms as President, from 1868 to 1876. He was succeeded by Republican Rutherford B. Hayes, who served from 1876 to 1880. Both administrations were known for their widespread corruption.

her conversation, her point of view and her choice of friends, with the detachment with which one listens to reminiscences of some one long since dead; not till Medora suddenly spoke her name at the archery match had Ellen Olenska become a living presence to him again. The Marchioness's foolish lisp had called up a vision of the little fire-lit drawing-room and the sound of the carriage-wheels returning down the deserted street. He thought of a story he had read, of some peasant children in Tuscany lighting a bunch of straw in a wayside cavern, and revealing old silent images in their painted tomb . . .

The way to the shore descended from the bank on which the house was perched to a walk above the water planted with weeping willows. Through their veil Archer caught the glint of the Lime Rock, with its whitewashed turret and the tiny house in which the heroic light-house keeper, Ida Lewis, was living her last venerable years. Beyond it lay the flat reaches and ugly government chimneys of Goat Island, the bay spreading northward in a shimmer of gold to Prudence Island with its low growth of oaks, and the shores of Conanicut faint in the sunset haze.

From the willow walk projected a slight wooden pier ending in a sort of pagoda-like summer-house; and in the pagoda a lady stood, leaning against the rail, her back to the shore. Archer stopped at the sight as if he had waked from sleep. That vision of the past was a dream, and the reality was what awaited him in the house on the bank overhead: was Mrs. Welland's pony-carriage circling around and around the oval at the door, was May sitting under the shameless Olympians and glowing with secret hopes, was the Welland villa at the far end of Bellevue Avenue, and Mr. Welland, already dressed for dinner, and pacing the drawing-room floor, watch in hand, with dyspeptic impatience—for it was one of the houses in which one always knew exactly what is happening at a given hour.

Lime Rock   A lighthouse on a rock in Newport Harbor, well known for the rescue efforts of its lightkeeper Ida Lewis, who held her post from the mid-1870s to 1911.

turret   A small tower atop a larger tower or at the corner of a building.

Goat Island   An island in Newport Harbor, primarily devoted to defense. The "ugly government chimneys" are part of the military outpost.

Prudence Island   An island in Narragansett Bay, just north of Jamestown. Part of the town of Portsmouth, it had been inhabited since the settlement of Rhode Island.

Conanicut   Conanicut Island is the geographical name of Jamestown, the island just west of Newport.

pagoda-like   Resembling an Asian religious building with a tall tower of several stories, each with its own overhanging roof

dyspeptic   Suffering from indigestion.

"What am I? A son-in-law—" Archer thought.

The figure at the end of the pier had not moved. For a long moment the young man stood half way down the bank, gazing at the bay furrowed with the coming and going of sailboats, yacht-launches, fishing-craft and the trailing black coal-barges hauled by noisy tugs. The lady in the summer-house seemed to be held by the same sight. Beyond the grey bastions of Fort Adams a long-drawn sunset was splintering up into a thousand fires, and the radiance caught the sail of a cat-boat as it beat out through the channel between the Lime Rock and the shore. Archer, as he watched, remembered the scene in the Shaughraun, and Montague lifting Ada Dyas's ribbon to his lips without her knowing that he was in the room.

"She doesn't know—she hasn't guessed. Shouldn't I know if she came up behind me, I wonder?" he mused; and suddenly he said to himself: "If she doesn't turn before that sail crosses the Lime Rock light I'll go back."

The boat was gliding out on the receding tide. It slid before the Lime Rock, blotted out Ida Lewis's little house, and passed across the turret in which the light was hung. Archer waited till a wide space of water sparkled between the last reef of the island and the stern of the boat; but still the figure in the summer-house did not move.

He turned and walked up the hill.

"I'm sorry you didn't find Ellen—I should have liked to see her again," May said as they drove home through the dusk. "But perhaps she wouldn't have cared—she seems so changed."

"Changed?" echoed her husband in a colourless voice, his eyes fixed on the ponies' twitching ears.

"So indifferent to her friends, I mean; giving up New York and her house, and spending her time with such queer people. Fancy how hideously uncomfortable she must be at the Blenkers'! She says she does it to keep cousin Medora out of mischief: to prevent her marrying dreadful people. But I sometimes think we've always bored her."

Archer made no answer, and she continued, with a tinge of hardness that he had never before noticed in her frank fresh voice: "After all, I wonder if she wouldn't be happier with her husband."

---

yacht-launches Newport was and continues to be famous for boating and yachting.

Fort Adams Fort Adams, occupying twenty-one acres on a northern-facing peninsula in Newport Harbor, was the second largest bastioned fort in the United States between 1799 and 1945.

cat-boat A broad-beamed sailboat with a single sail on a forward mast.

He burst into a laugh. "*Sancta simplicitas!*" he exclaimed; and as she turned a puzzled frown on him he added: "I don't think I ever heard you say a cruel thing before."

"Cruel?"

"Well—watching the contortions of the damned is supposed to be a favourite sport of the angels; but I believe even they don't think people happier in hell."

"It's a pity she ever married abroad then," said May, in the placid tone with which her mother met Mr. Welland's vagaries; and Archer felt himself gently relegated to the category of unreasonable husbands.

They drove down Bellevue Avenue and turned in between the chamfered wooden gate-posts surmounted by cast-iron lamps which marked the approach to the Welland villa. Lights were already shining through its windows, and Archer, as the carriage stopped, caught a glimpse of his father-in-law, exactly as he had pictured him, pacing the drawing-room, watch in hand and wearing the pained expression that he had long since found to be much more efficacious than anger.

The young man, as he followed his wife into the hall, was conscious of a curious reversal of mood. There was something about the luxury of the Welland house and the density of the Welland atmosphere, so charged with minute observances and exactions, that always stole into his system like a narcotic. The heavy carpets, the watchful servants, the perpetually reminding tick of disciplined clocks, the perpetually renewed stack of cards and invitations on the hall table, the whole chain of tyrannical trifles binding one hour to the next, and each member of the household to all the others, made any less systematised and affluent existence seem unreal and precarious. But now it was the Welland house, and the life he was expected to lead in it, that had become unreal and irrelevant, and the brief scene on the shore, when he had stood irresolute, halfway down the bank, was as close to him as the blood in his veins.

All night he lay awake in the big chintz bedroom at May's side, watching the moonlight slant along the carpet, and thinking of Ellen Olenska driving home across the gleaming beaches behind Beaufort's trotters.

XXII

A party for the Blenkers—the Blenkers?"

Mr. Welland laid down his knife and fork and looked anxiously and incredulously across the luncheon-table at his wife, who, adjusting her

---

"*Sancta simplicitas!*"   Latin: "Holy simplicity!"

gold eye-glasses, read aloud, in the tone of high comedy: "Professor and Mrs. Emerson Sillerton request the pleasure of Mr. and Mrs. Welland's company at the meeting of the Wednesday Afternoon Club on August 25th at 3 o'clock punctually. To meet Mrs. and the Misses Blenker.

"Red Gables, Catherine Street.   R.S.V.P."

"Good gracious—" Mr. Welland gasped, as if a second reading had been necessary to bring the monstrous absurdity of the thing home to him.

"Poor Amy Sillerton—you never can tell what her husband will do next," Mrs. Welland sighed. "I suppose he's just discovered the Blenkers."

Professor Emerson Sillerton was a thorn in the side of Newport society; and a thorn that could not be plucked out, for it grew on a venerable and venerated family tree. He was, as people said, a man who had had "every advantage." His father was Sillerton Jackson's uncle, his mother a Pennilow of Boston; on each side there was wealth and position, and mutual suitability. Nothing—as Mrs. Welland had often remarked—nothing on earth obliged Emerson Sillerton to be an archaeologist, or indeed a Professor of any sort, or to live in Newport in winter, or do any of the other revolutionary things that he did. But at least, if he was going to break with tradition and flout society in the face, he need not have married poor Amy Dagonet, who had a right to expect "something different," and money enough to keep her own carriage.

No one in the Mingott set could understand why Amy Sillerton had submitted so tamely to the eccentricities of a husband who filled the house with long-haired men and short-haired women, and, when he travelled, took her to explore tombs in Yucatan instead of going to Paris or Italy. But there they were, set in their ways, and apparently unaware that they were different from other people; and when they gave one of their

---

Catherine Street   A street that runs perpendicular to Bellevue Avenue. Some of the first Newport cottages were built here, mostly by Bostonians before the arrival of New Yorkers.

archaeologist   A person who studies the material evidence of past cultures. The field of archaeology expanded in the nineteenth century as excavations of sites around the world yielded new information about human history and prehistory. Wharton's many references to primitive peoples; to artifacts of china, glass, furniture, and fashion; and to hieroglyphics and linguistic codings not only indicate her interest in this subject but point to the novel itself as an archaeological study of a past time and culture.

Yucatan   Located in eastern Mexico and home of the great Mayan civilization that flourished 2,500 years ago, the Yucatan Peninsula juts between the Gulf of Mexico and the Caribbean Sea. In the nineteenth century, these Mayan ruins, one of the world's richest archaeological zones, were just beginning to be excavated.

dreary annual garden-parties every family on the Cliffs, because of the Sillerton-Pennilow-Dagonet connection, had to draw lots and send an un-willing representative.

"It's a wonder," Mrs. Welland remarked, "that they didn't choose the Cup Race day! Do you remember, two years ago, their giving a party for a black man on the day of Julia Mingott's *thé dansant?* Luckily this time there's nothing else going on that I know of—for of course some of us will have to go."

Mr. Welland sighed nervously. "'Some of us,' my dear—more than one? Three o'clock is such a very awkward hour. I have to be here at half-past three to take my drops; it's really no use trying to follow Bencomb's new treatment if I don't do it systematically; and if I join you later, of course I shall miss my drive." At the thought he laid down his knife and fork again, and a flush of anxiety rose to his finely-wrinkled cheek.

"There's no reason why you should go at all, my dear," his wife an-swered with a cheerfulness that had become automatic. "I have some cards to leave at the other end of Bellevue Avenue, and I'll drop in at about half-past three and stay long enough to make poor Amy feel that she hasn't been slighted." She glanced hesitatingly at her daughter. "And if Newland's af-ternoon is provided for perhaps May can drive you out with the ponies, and try their new russet harness."

It was a principle in the Welland family that people's days and hours should be what Mrs. Welland called "provided for." The melancholy pos-sibility of having to "kill time" (especially for those who did not care for whist or solitaire) was a vision that haunted her as the spectre of the un-employed haunts the philanthropist. Another of her principles was that parents should never (at least visibly) interfere with the plans of their

---

the Cliffs   A three-and-a-half-mile rocky expanse on the eastern coast of Newport and a famous walk past impressive mansions. In 1892, Edith (Jones) Wharton and her hus-band, Edward (Teddy), bought a home along these cliffs called Land's End. Previously, they lived in Pencraig Cottage, which was owned by her parents—just as May and Archer spend their summers at the Welland cottage. Pencraig Cottage, across Harrison Avenue from the Jones family cottage, was on the western side of the island, on Newport Harbor. The purchase of Land's End placed Wharton among the more fashionable Newport soci-ety and marked a conscious separation from her parents and the Newport of her youth.

Cup Race   The America's Cup Race was not sailed out of Newport until 1930. During Wharton's time, it was sailed out of New York. During the 1870s, however, there were trial and qualifying races sailed in Newport in preparation for the America's Cup Race.

thé dansant   French: a tea dance; an afternoon party with dancing.

russet   Soft reddish-brown color.

married children; and the difficulty of adjusting this respect for May's independence with the exigency of Mr. Welland's claims could be overcome
only by the exercise of an ingenuity which left not a second of
Mrs. Welland's own time unprovided for.

"Of course I'll drive with Papa—I'm sure Newland will find something
to do," May said, in a tone that gently reminded her husband of his lack
of response. It was a cause of constant distress to Mrs. Welland that her
son-in-law showed so little foresight in planning his days. Often already,
during the fortnight that he had passed under her roof, when she enquired
how he meant to spend his afternoon, he had answered paradoxically:
"Oh, I think for a change I'll just save it instead of spending it—" and
once, when she and May had had to go on a long-postponed round of afternoon calls, he had confessed to having lain all the afternoon under a
rock on the beach below the house.

"Newland never seems to look ahead," Mrs. Welland once ventured
to complain to her daughter; and May answered serenely: "No; but you
see it doesn't matter, because when there's nothing particular to do he
reads a book."

"Ah, yes—like his father!" Mrs. Welland agreed, as if allowing for an
inherited oddity; and after that the question of Newland's unemployment
was tacitly dropped.

Nevertheless, as the day for the Sillerton reception approached, May
began to show a natural solicitude for his welfare, and to suggest a tennis
match at the Chiverses', or a sail on Julius Beaufort's cutter, as a means of
atoning for her temporary desertion. "I shall be back by six, you know,
dear: Papa never drives later than that—" and she was not reassured till
Archer said that he thought of hiring a run-about and driving up the island
to a stud-farm to look at a second horse for her brougham. They had been
looking for this horse for some time, and the suggestion was so acceptable
that May glanced at her mother as if to say: "You see he knows how to
plan out his time as well as any of us."

The idea of the stud-farm and the brougham horse had germinated in
Archer's mind on the very day when the Emerson Sillerton invitation had
first been mentioned; but he had kept it to himself as if there were something clandestine in the plan, and discovery might prevent its execution.
He had, however, taken the precaution to engage in advance a run-about
with a pair of old livery-stable trotters that could still do their eighteen

---

cutter   A sailing boat with one mast.

run-about   A small, light vehicle used to make short trips in towns.

miles on level roads; and at two o'clock, hastily deserting the luncheon-table, he sprang into the light carriage and drove off.

The day was perfect. A breeze from the north drove little puffs of white cloud across an ultramarine sky, with a bright sea running under it. Bellevue Avenue was empty at that hour, and after dropping the stable-lad at the corner of Mill Street Archer turned down the Old Beach Road and drove across Eastman's Beach.

He had the feeling of unexplained excitement with which, on half-holidays at school, he used to start off into the unknown. Taking his pair at an easy gait, he counted on reaching the stud-farm, which was not far beyond Paradise Rocks, before three o'clock; so that, after looking over the horse (and trying him if he seemed promising) he would still have four golden hours to dispose of.

As soon as he heard of the Sillertons' party he had said to himself that the Marchioness Manson would certainly come to Newport with the Blenkers, and that Madame Olenska might again take the opportunity of spending the day with her grandmother. At any rate, the Blenker habitation would probably be deserted, and he would be able, without indiscretion, to satisfy a vague curiosity concerning it. He was not sure that he wanted to see the Countess Olenska again; but ever since he had looked at her from the path above the bay he had wanted, irrationally and indescribably, to see the place she was living in, and to follow the movements of her imagined figure as he had watched the real one in the summer-house. The longing was with him day and night, an incessant undefinable craving, like the sudden whim of a sick man for food or drink once tasted and long since forgotten. He could not see beyond the craving, or picture what it might lead to, for he was not conscious of any wish to speak to Madame Olenska or to hear her voice. He simply felt that if he could carry away the vision of the spot of earth she walked on, and the way the sky and sea enclosed it, the rest of the world might seem less empty.

When he reached the stud-farm a glance showed him that the horse was not what he wanted; nevertheless he took a turn behind it in order to prove to himself that he was not in a hurry. But at three o'clock he shook out the reins over the trotters and turned into the by-roads leading to Portsmouth. The wind had dropped and a faint haze on the horizon showed

---

Old Beach Road . . . Eastman's Beach   [sic] Old Beach Road runs east–west from Belle-vue Avenue to Easton's Beach. Easton's Beach, also known as First Beach, extends from the northern end of the Cliff Walk to Middletown.

Sillerton's   Corrected; the first edition of Wharton's text reads "Sillerton's."

that a fog was waiting to steal up the Saconnet on the turn of the tide; but all about him fields and woods were steeped in golden light.

He drove past grey-shingled farm-houses in orchards, past hay-fields and groves of oak, past villages with white steeples rising sharply into the fading sky; and at last, after stopping to ask the way of some men at work in a field, he turned down a lane between high banks of goldenrod and brambles. At the end of the lane was the blue glimmer of the river; to the left, standing in front of a clump of oaks and maples, he saw a long tumble-down house with white paint peeling from its clapboards.

On the road-side facing the gateway stood one of the open sheds in which the New Englander shelters his farming implements and visitors "hitch" their "teams." Archer, jumping down, led his pair into the shed, and after tying them to a post turned toward the house. The patch of lawn before it had relapsed into a hay-field; but to the left an overgrown box-garden full of dahlias and rusty rose-bushes encircled a ghostly summer-house of trellis-work that had once been white, surmounted by a wooden Cupid who had lost his bow and arrow but continued to take ineffectual aim.

Archer leaned for a while against the gate. No one was in sight, and not a sound came from the open windows of the house: a grizzled New-foundland dozing before the door seemed as ineffectual a guardian as the arrowless Cupid. It was strange to think that this place of silence and decay was the home of the turbulent Blenkers; yet Archer was sure that he was not mistaken.

For a long time he stood there, content to take in the scene, and gradually falling under its drowsy spell; but at length he roused himself to the sense of the passing time. Should he look his fill and then drive away? He stood irresolute, wishing suddenly to see the inside of the house, so that he

---

Saconnet [sic]   The Sakonnet River, which runs north and south between Aquidneck Island and the Rhode Island mainland, flows into Rhode Island Sound between Newport and Little Compton.

goldenrod and brambles   Goldenrod, often growing wild, produces clusters of small yellow flowers in late summer. It was associated with precaution or encouragement in the "language of flowers." Brambles are prickly bushes, especially blackberry or raspberry.

dahlias   Native to Central America, dahlias have tuberous roots and brightly colored flowers. One dahlia suggested good taste, but several conveyed instability.

trellis-work   A light framework made by crossing strips of wood or other material and used as a support for climbing plants.

Newfoundland   A breed of large dog, usually with black hair.

might picture the room that Madame Olenska sat in. There was nothing to prevent his walking up to the door and ringing the bell; if, as he supposed, she was away with the rest of the party, he could easily give his name, and ask permission to go into the sitting-room to write a message.

But instead, he crossed the lawn and turned toward the box-garden. As he entered it he caught sight of something bright-coloured in the summer-house, and presently made it out to be a pink parasol. The parasol drew him like a magnet: he was sure it was hers. He went into the summer-house, and sitting down on the rickety seat picked up the silken thing and looked at its carved handle, which was made of some rare wood that gave out an aromatic scent. Archer lifted the handle to his lips.

He heard a rustle of skirts against the box, and sat motionless, leaning on the parasol handle with clasped hands, and letting the rustle come nearer without lifting his eyes. He had always known that this must happen . . .

"Oh, Mr. Archer!" exclaimed a loud young voice; and looking up he saw before him the youngest and largest of the Blenker girls, blonde and blowsy, in bedraggled muslin. A red blotch on one of her cheeks seemed to show that it had recently been pressed against a pillow, and her half-awakened eyes stared at him hospitably but confusedly.

"Gracious—where did you drop from? I must have been sound asleep in the hammock. Everybody else has gone to Newport. Did you ring?" she incoherently enquired.

Archer's confusion was greater than hers. "I—no—that is, I was just going to. I had to come up the island to see about a horse, and I drove over on a chance of finding Mrs. Blenker and your visitors. But the house seemed empty—so I sat down to wait."

Miss Blenker, shaking off the fumes of sleep, looked at him with increasing interest. "The house *is* empty. Mother's not here, or the Marchioness—or anybody but me." Her glance became faintly reproachful. "Didn't you know that Professor and Mrs. Sillerton are giving a garden-party for mother and all of us this afternoon? It was too unlucky that I couldn't go; but I've had a sore throat, and mother was afraid of the drive home this evening. Did you ever know anything so disappointing? Of course," she added gaily, "I shouldn't have minded half as much if I'd known you were coming."

Symptoms of a lumbering coquetry became visible in her, and Archer found the strength to break in: "But Madame Olenska—has she gone to Newport too?"

---

coquetry Flirtation.

Miss Blenker looked at him with surprise. "Madame Olenska—didn't you know she'd been called away?"

"Called away?—"

"Oh, my best parasol! I lent it to that goose of a Katie, because it matched her ribbons, and the careless thing must have dropped it here. We Blenkers are all like that . . . real Bohemians!" Recovering the sunshade with a powerful hand she unfurled it and suspended its rosy dome above her head. "Yes, Ellen was called away yesterday: she lets us call her Ellen, you know. A telegram came from Boston: she said she might be gone for two days. I do *love* the way she does her hair, don't you?" Miss Blenker rambled on.

Archer continued to stare through her as though she had been transparent. All he saw was the trumpery parasol that arched its pinkness above her giggling head.

After a moment he ventured: "You don't happen to know why Madame Olenska went to Boston? I hope it was not on account of bad news?"

Miss Blenker took this with a cheerful incredulity. "Oh, I don't believe so. She didn't tell us what was in the telegram. I think she didn't want the Marchioness to know. She's so romantic-looking, isn't she? Doesn't she remind you of Mrs. Scott-Siddons when she reads 'Lady Geraldine's Courtship'? Did you never hear her?"

Archer was dealing hurriedly with crowding thoughts. His whole future seemed suddenly to be unrolled before him; and passing down its endless emptiness he saw the dwindling figure of a man to whom nothing was ever to happen. He glanced about him at the unpruned garden, the tumble-down house, and the oak-grove under which the dusk was gathering. It had seemed so exactly the place in which he ought to have found Madame Olenska; and she was far away, and even the pink sunshade was not hers . . .

He frowned and hesitated. "You don't know, I suppose—I shall be in Boston tomorrow. If I could manage to see her—"

He felt that Miss Blenker was losing interest in him, though her smile persisted. "Oh, of course; how lovely of you! She's staying at the Parker House; it must be horrible there in this weather."

---

trumpery   Flashy but worthless finery.

Mrs. Scott-Siddons   Mary Frances Scott-Siddons (1844–1897) was an English actress.

'Lady Geraldine's Courtship'   A poem by Elizabeth Barrett Browning that pays tribute to the poetry of her husband, Robert Browning.

Parker House   Boston's most famous hotel, founded by Harvey Parker.

After that Archer was but intermittently aware of the remarks they ex-changed. He could only remember stoutly resisting her entreaty that he should await the returning family and have high tea with them before he drove home. At length, with his hostess still at his side, he passed out of range of the wooden Cupid, unfastened his horses and drove off. At the turn of the lane he saw Miss Blenker standing at the gate and waving the pink parasol.

XXIII

The next morning, when Archer got out of the Fall River train, he emerged upon a steaming midsummer Boston. The streets near the station were full of the smell of beer and coffee and decaying fruit and a shirt-sleeved popu-lace moved through them to the intimate abandon of boarders going down the passage to the bathroom.

Archer found a cab and drove to the Somerset Club for breakfast. Even the fashionable quarters had the air of untidy domesticity to which no excess of heat ever degrades the European cities. Care-takers in calico lounged on the door-steps of the wealthy, and the Common looked like a pleasure-ground on the morrow of a Masonic picnic. If Archer had tried to imagine Ellen Olenska in improbable scenes he could not have called up any into which it was more difficult to fit her than this heat-prostrated and deserted Boston.

He breakfasted with appetite and method, beginning with a slice of melon, and studying a morning paper while he waited for his toast and scrambled eggs. A new sense of energy and activity had possessed him ever since he had announced to May the night before that he had business in

---

Fall River An industrial town in Massachusetts, north of Newport and south of Boston.

Somerset Club An exclusive men's social club founded in Boston in 1851.

calico A printed cotton fabric, usually for casual wear.

Common Boston Common is a forty-eight-acre public park in Cambridge. Bounded by Massachusetts Avenue, Waterhouse Street, and Garden Street, it is the oldest public park in the United States.

Masonic Related to or like the Freemasons, a secret fraternal order associated with lib-eral and democratic principles and with elaborate ceremonies utilizing the tools of stone-masonry. Benjamin Franklin was a member of the first American lodge, founded in 1730. Other leaders of the American Revolution, including John Hancock and Paul Revere, were members of the St. Andrew's Lodge in Boston.

Boston, and should take the Fall River boat that night and go on to New York the following evening. It had always been understood that he would return to town early in the week, and when he got back from his expedition to Portsmouth a letter from the office, which fate had conspicuously placed on a corner of the hall table, sufficed to justify his sudden change of plan. He was even ashamed of the ease with which the whole thing had been done: it reminded him, for an uncomfortable moment, of Lawrence Lefferts's masterly contrivances for securing his freedom. But this did not long trouble him, for he was not in an analytic mood.

After breakfast he smoked a cigarette and glanced over the Commercial Advertiser. While he was thus engaged two or three men he knew came in, and the usual greetings were exchanged: it was the same world after all, though he had such a queer sense of having slipped through the meshes of time and space.

He looked at his watch, and finding that it was half-past nine got up and went into the writing-room. There he wrote a few lines, and ordered a messenger to take a cab to the Parker House and wait for the answer. He then sat down behind another newspaper and tried to calculate how long it would take a cab to get to the Parker House.

"The lady was out, sir," he suddenly heard a waiter's voice at his elbow; and he stammered: "Out?—" as if it were a word in a strange language.

He got up and went into the hall. It must be a mistake: she could not be out at that hour. He flushed with anger at his own stupidity: why had he not sent the note as soon as he arrived?

He found his hat and stick and went forth into the street. The city had suddenly become as strange and vast and empty as if he were a traveller from distant lands. For a moment he stood on the door-step hesitating; then he decided to go to the Parker House. What if the messenger had been misinformed, and she were still there?

He started to walk across the Common; and on the first bench, under a tree, he saw her sitting. She had a grey silk sunshade over her head—how could he ever have imagined her with a pink one? As he approached he was struck by her listless attitude: she sat there as if she had nothing else

---

Commercial Advertiser   Boston had no newspapers by this name, although there was a *Boston Daily Advertiser* and a weekly *Commercial Bulletin*. New York newspapers included the daily *New York Commercial Advertiser* and a weekly paper originally called the *New York Spectator and Weekly Commercial Advertiser* (changed in 1876 to the *Weekly Commercial Advertiser*). Archer may have brought a copy of this weekly New York paper with him. Mainly concerned with mercantile issues, it included information about the availability of commodities as well as lists of arrivals and departures of freight and passenger steamships.

to do. He saw her drooping profile, and the knot of hair fastened low in the neck under her dark hat, and the long wrinkled glove on the hand that held the sunshade. He came a step or two nearer, and she turned and looked at him.

"Oh"—she said; and for the first time he noticed a startled look on her face; but in another moment it gave way to a slow smile of wonder and contentment.

"Oh"—she murmured again, on a different note, as he stood looking down at her; and without rising she made a place for him on the bench.

"I'm here on business—just got here," Archer explained; and, without knowing why, he suddenly began to feign astonishment at seeing her. "But what on earth are *you* doing in this wilderness?" He had really no idea what he was saying; he felt as if he were shouting at her across endless distances, and she might vanish again before he could overtake her.

"I? Oh, I'm here on business too," she answered, turning her head toward him so that they were face to face. The words hardly reached him: he was aware only of her voice, and of the startling fact that not an echo of it had remained in his memory. He had not even remembered that it was low-pitched, with a faint roughness on the consonants.

"You do your hair differently," he said, his heart beating as if he had uttered something irrevocable.

"Differently? No—it's only that I do it as best I can when I'm without Nastasia."

"Nastasia; but isn't she with you?"

"No; I'm alone. For two days it was not worth while to bring her."

"You're alone—at the Parker House?"

She looked at him with a flash of her old malice. "Does it strike you as dangerous?"

"No; not dangerous—"

"But unconventional? I see; I suppose it is." She considered a moment. "I hadn't thought of it, because I've just done something so much more unconventional." The faint tinge of irony lingered in her eyes. "I've just refused to take back a sum of money—that belonged to me."

Archer sprang up and moved a step or two away. She had furled her parasol and sat absently drawing patterns on the gravel. Presently he came back and stood before her.

"Some one—has come here to meet you?"

"Yes."

"With this offer?"

She nodded.

"And you refused—because of the conditions?"

"I refused," she said after a moment.

He sat down by her again. "What were the conditions?"

"Oh, they were not onerous: just to sit at the head of his table now and then."

There was another interval of silence. Archer's heart had slammed itself shut in the queer way it had, and he sat vainly groping for a word.

"He wants you back—at any price?"

"Well—a considerable price. At least the sum is considerable for me."

He paused again, beating about the question he felt he must put.

"It was to meet him here that you came?"

She stared, and then burst into a laugh. "Meet him—my husband? *Here?* At this season he's always at Cowes or Baden."

"He sent some one?"

"Yes."

"With a letter?"

She shook her head. "No; just a message. He never writes. I don't think I've had more than one letter from him." The allusion brought the colour to her cheek, and it reflected itself in Archer's vivid blush.

"Why does he never write?"

"Why should he? What does one have secretaries for?"

The young man's blush deepened. She had pronounced the word as if it had no more significance than any other in her vocabulary. For a moment it was on the tip of his tongue to ask: "Did he send his secretary, then?" But the remembrance of Count Olenski's only letter to his wife was too present to him. He paused again, and then took another plunge.

"And the person?"—

"The emissary? The emissary," Madame Olenska rejoined, still smiling, "might, for all I care, have left already; but he has insisted on waiting till this evening . . . in case . . . on the chance . . ."

"And you came out here to think the chance over?"

"I came out to get a breath of air. The hotel's too stifling. I'm taking the afternoon train back to Portsmouth."

They sat silent, not looking at each other, but straight ahead at the people passing along the path. Finally she turned her eyes again to his face and said: "You're not changed."

He felt like answering: "I was, till I saw you again"; but instead he stood up abruptly and glanced about him at the untidy sweltering park.

"This is horrible. Why shouldn't we go out a little on the bay? There's a breeze, and it will be cooler. We might take the steamboat down to Point

---

Baden   A tourist town in northeastern Austria, just south of Vienna, known for its sulfurous springs.

Arley." She glanced up at him hesitatingly and he went on: "On a Monday morning there won't be anybody on the boat. My train doesn't leave till evening: I'm going back to New York. Why shouldn't we?" he insisted, looking down at her; and suddenly he broke out: "Haven't we done all we could?"

"Oh"—she murmured again. She stood up and re-opened her sun-shade, glancing about her as if to take counsel of the scene, and assure her-self of the impossibility of remaining in it. Then her eyes returned to his face. "You mustn't say things like that to me," she said.

"I'll say anything you like; or nothing. I won't open my mouth unless you tell me to. What harm can it do to anybody? All I want is to listen to you," he stammered.

She drew out a little gold-faced watch on an enamelled chain. "Oh, don't calculate," he broke out; "give me the day! I want to get you away from that man. At what time was he coming?"

Her colour rose again. "At eleven."

"Then you must come at once."

"You needn't be afraid—if I don't come."

"Nor you either—if you do. I swear I only want to hear about you, to know what you've been doing. It's a hundred years since we've met—it may be another hundred before we meet again."

She still wavered, her anxious eyes on his face. "Why didn't you come down to the beach to fetch me, the day I was at Granny's?" she asked.

"Because you didn't look round—because you didn't know I was there. I swore I wouldn't unless you looked round." He laughed as the childishness of the confession struck him.

"But I didn't look round on purpose."

"On purpose?"

"I knew you were there; when you drove in I recognised the ponies. So I went down to the beach."

"To get away from me as far as you could?"

She repeated in a low voice: "To get away from you as far as I could."

He laughed out again, this time in boyish satisfaction. "Well, you see it's no use. I may as well tell you," he added, "that the business I came here for was just to find you. But, look here, we must start or we shall miss our boat."

Point Arley   Wharton's reference, probably a destination in Boston Harbor or Massa-chusetts Bay, is unclear. From the 1830s until the Civil War, Gallop's Island was a pop-ular resort with an inn and restaurant famous for its chowder. Point Allerton, located on Hingham Island, was also a resort with a restaurant and observation post; it is still a popular summertime spot today.

"Our boat?" She frowned perplexedly, and then smiled. "Oh, but I must go back to the hotel first: I must leave a note—"

"As many notes as you please. You can write here." He drew out a note-case and one of the new stylographic pens. "I've even got an envelope—you see how everything's predestined! There—steady the thing on your knee, and I'll get the pen going in a second. They have to be humoured; wait—" He banged the hand that held the pen against the back of the bench. "It's like jerking down the mercury in a thermometer: just a trick. Now try—"

She laughed, and bending over the sheet of paper which he had laid on his note-case, began to write. Archer walked away a few steps, staring with radiant unseeing eyes at the passers-by, who, in their turn, paused to stare at the unwonted sight of a fashionably-dressed lady writing a note on her knee on a bench in the Common.

Madame Olenska slipped the sheet into the envelope, wrote a name on it, and put it into her pocket. Then she too stood up.

They walked back toward Beacon Street, and near the club Archer caught sight of the plush-lined "herdic" which had carried his note to the Parker House, and whose driver was reposing from this effort by bathing his brow at the corner hydrant.

"I told you everything was predestined! Here's a cab for us. You see!" They laughed, astonished at the miracle of picking up a public conveyance at that hour, and in that unlikely spot, in a city where cab-stands were still a "foreign" novelty.

Archer, looking at his watch, saw that there was time to drive to the Parker House before going to the steam-boat landing. They rattled through the hot streets and drew up at the door of the hotel.

Archer held out his hand for the letter. "Shall I take it in?" he asked; but Madame Olenska, shaking her head, sprang out and disappeared through the glazed doors. It was barely half-past ten; but what if the emissary, impatient for her reply, and not knowing how else to employ his time,

---

stylographic pens Pens developed by Alonzo Townsend Cross (1846–1922) that revolutionized the art of correspondence. Ink was supplied to the paper through a strong tubular needle and spindle that replaced the traditionally soft nib as the writing point, allowing the writer to bear down hard enough to make carbons. The stylographic pen was such a significant invention that the U.S. Postal Service almost immediately made its use mandatory.

Beacon Street One of the main streets in Boston, bordering Boston Common.

plush-lined "herdic" Plush is any fabric with a thick, deep pile. A herdic, named for Peter Herdic (1824–1888), was a small, horse-drawn cab with two wheels, side seats, and an entrance in the back.

were already seated among the travellers with cooling drinks at their elbows of whom Archer had caught a glimpse as she went in?

He waited, pacing up and down before the herdic. A Sicilian youth with eyes like Nastasia's offered to shine his boots, and an Irish matron to sell him peaches; and every few moments the doors opened to let out hot men with straw hats tilted far back, who glanced at him as they went by. He marvelled that the door should open so often, and that all the people it let out should look so like each other, and so like all the other hot men who, at that hour, through the length and breadth of the land, were passing continuously in and out of the swinging doors of hotels.

And then, suddenly, came a face that he could not relate to the other faces. He caught but a flash of it, for his pacings had carried him to the farthest point of his beat, and it was in turning back to the hotel that he saw, in a group of typical countenances—the lank and weary, the round and surprised, the lantern-jawed and mild—this other face that was so many more things at once, and things so different. It was that of a young man, pale too, and half-extinguished by the heat, or worry, or both, but somehow, quicker, vivider, more conscious; or perhaps seeming so because he was so different. Archer hung a moment on a thin thread of memory, but it snapped and floated off with the disappearing face—apparently that of some foreign business man, looking doubly foreign in such a setting. He vanished in the stream of passers-by, and Archer resumed his patrol.

He did not care to be seen watch in hand within view of the hotel, and his unaided reckoning of the lapse of time led him to conclude that, if Madame Olenska was so long in reappearing, it could only be because she had met the emissary and been waylaid by him. At the thought Archer's apprehension rose to anguish.

"If she doesn't come soon I'll go in and find her," he said.

The doors swung open again and she was at his side. They got into the herdic, and as it drove off he took out his watch and saw that she had been absent just three minutes. In the clatter of loose windows that made talk impossible they bumped over the disjointed cobblestones to the wharf.

Seated side by side on a bench of the half-empty boat they found that they had hardly anything to say to each other, or rather that what they had

---

Sicilian youth . . . Irish matron Thousands of immigrants from Ireland settled in Boston during the mid-nineteenth century, the first large ethnic group to arrive since the French Huguenots in the early eighteenth century. They quickly gained political power and elected their first Irish mayor in 1885. The Irish population was followed by European Jewish, Italian, and Portuguese immigrants.

to say communicated itself best in the blessed silence of their release and their isolation.

As the paddle-wheels began to turn, and wharves and shipping to re-cede through the veil of heat, it seemed to Archer that everything in the old familiar world of habit was receding also. He longed to ask Madame Olenska if she did not have the same feeling: the feeling that they were starting on some long voyage from which they might never return. But he was afraid to say it, or anything else that might disturb the delicate balance of her trust in him. In reality he had no wish to betray that trust. There had been days and nights when the memory of their kiss had burned and burned on his lips; the day before even, on the drive to Portsmouth, the thought of her had run through him like fire; but now that she was beside him, and they were drifting forth into this unknown world, they seemed to have reached the kind of deeper nearness that a touch may sunder.

As the boat left the harbour and turned seaward a breeze stirred about them and the bay broke up into long oily undulations, then into ripples tipped with spray. The fog of sultriness still hung over the city, but ahead lay a fresh world of ruffled waters, and distant promontories with light-houses in the sun. Madame Olenska, leaning back against the boat-rail, drank in the coolness between parted lips. She had wound a long veil about her hat, but it left her face uncovered, and Archer was struck by the tranquil gaiety of her expression. She seemed to take their adventure as a matter of course, and to be neither in fear of unexpected encounters, nor (what was worse) unduly elated by their possibility.

In the bare dining-room of the inn, which he had hoped they would have to themselves, they found a strident party of innocent-looking young men and women—school-teachers on a holiday, the landlord told them—and Archer's heart sank at the idea of having to talk through their noise.

"This is hopeless—I'll ask for a private room," he said; and Madame Olenska, without offering any objection, waited while he went in search of it. The room opened on a long wooden verandah, with the sea coming in at the windows. It was bare and cool, with a table covered with a coarse checkered cloth and adorned by a bottle of pickles and a blueberry pie under a cage. No more guileless-looking *cabinet particulier* ever offered its shelter to a clandestine couple: Archer fancied he saw the sense of its reas-surance in the faintly amused smile with which Madame Olenska sat down opposite to him. A woman who had run away from her husband—and re-putedly with another man—was likely to have mastered the art of taking things for granted; but something in the quality of her composure took the

---

cabinet particulier   French: a private dining-room.

edge from his irony. By being so quiet, so unsurprised and so simple she had managed to brush away the conventions and make him feel that to seek to be alone was the natural thing for two old friends who had so much to say to each other. . . .

XXIV

They lunched slowly and meditatively, with mute intervals between rushes of talk; for, the spell once broken, they had much to say, and yet moments when saying became the mere accompaniment to long duologues of silence. Archer kept the talk from his own affairs, not with conscious intention but because he did not want to miss a word of her history; and leaning on the table, her chin resting on her clasped hands, she talked to him of the year and a half since they had met.

She had grown tired of what people called "society"; New York was kind, it was almost oppressively hospitable; she should never forget the way in which it had welcomed her back; but after the first flush of novelty she had found herself, as she phrased it, too "different" to care for the things it cared about—and so she had decided to try Washington, where one was supposed to meet more varieties of people and of opinion. And on the whole she should probably settle down in Washington, and make a home there for poor Medora, who had worn out the patience of all her other relations just at the time when she most needed looking after and protecting from matrimonial perils.

"But Dr. Carver—aren't you afraid of Dr. Carver? I hear he's been staying with you at the Blenkers'."

She smiled. "Oh, the Carver danger is over. Dr. Carver is a very clever man. He wants a rich wife to finance his plans, and Medora is simply a good advertisement as a convert."

"A convert to what?"

"To all sorts of new and crazy social schemes. But do you know, they interest me more than the blind conformity to tradition—somebody else's tradition—that I see among our own friends. It seems stupid to have discovered America only to make it into a copy of another country." She smiled across the table. "Do you suppose Christopher Columbus would have taken all that trouble just to go to the Opera with the Selfridge Merrys?"

Archer changed colour. "And Beaufort—do you say these things to Beaufort?" he asked abruptly.

"I haven't seen him for a long time. But I used to; and he understands."

"Ah, it's what I've always told you; you don't like us. And you like Beaufort because he's so unlike us." He looked about the bare room and out at the bare beach and the row of stark white village houses strung along the shore. "We're damnably dull. We've no character, no colour, no variety.—I wonder," he broke out, "why you don't go back?"

Her eyes darkened, and he expected an indignant rejoinder. But she sat silent, as if thinking over what he had said, and he grew frightened lest she should answer that she wondered too.

At length she said: "I believe it's because of you."

It was impossible to make the confession more dispassionately, or in a tone less encouraging to the vanity of the person addressed. Archer reddened to the temples, but dared not move or speak: it was as if her words had been some rare butterfly that the least motion might drive off on startled wings, but that might gather a flock about it if it were left undisturbed.

"At least," she continued, "it was you who made me understand that under the dullness there are things so fine and sensitive and delicate that even those I most cared for in my other life look cheap in comparison. I don't know how to explain myself"—she drew together her troubled brows—"but it seems as if I'd never before understood with how much that is hard and shabby and base the most exquisite pleasures may be paid."

"Exquisite pleasures—it's something to have had them!" he felt like retorting; but the appeal in her eyes kept him silent.

"I want," she went on, "to be perfectly honest with you—and with myself. For a long time I've hoped this chance would come: that I might tell you how you've helped me, what you've made of me—"

Archer sat staring beneath frowning brows. He interrupted her with a laugh. "And what do you make out that you've made of me?"

She paled a little. "Of you?"

"Yes: for I'm of your making much more than you ever were of mine. I'm the man who married one woman because another one told him to."

Her paleness turned to a fugitive flush. "I thought—you promised—you were not to say such things today."

"Ah—how like a woman! None of you will ever see a bad business through!"

She lowered her voice. "*Is* it a bad business—for May?"

He stood in the window, drumming against the raised sash, and feeling in every fibre the wistful tenderness with which she had spoken her cousin's name.

"For that's the thing we've always got to think of—haven't we—by your own showing?" she insisted.

"My own showing?" he echoed, his blank eyes still on the sea.

"Or if not," she continued, pursuing her own thought with a painful application, "if it's not worth while to have given up, to have missed

things, so that others may be saved from disillusionment and misery—
then everything I came home for, everything that made my other life seem
by contrast so bare and so poor because no one there took account of
them—all these things are a sham or a dream—"

He turned around without moving from his place. "And in that
case there's no reason on earth why you shouldn't go back?" he concluded
for her.

Her eyes were clinging to him desperately. "Oh, *is* there no reason?"

"Not if you staked your all on the success of my marriage. My marriage," he said savagely, "isn't going to be a sight to keep you here." She
made no answer, and he went on: "What's the use? You gave me my first
glimpse of a real life, and at the same moment you asked me to go on with
a sham one. It's beyond human enduring—that's all."

"Oh, don't say that; when I'm enduring it!" she burst out, her eyes
filling.

Her arms had dropped along the table, and she sat with her face abandoned to his gaze as if in the recklessness of a desperate peril. The face exposed her as much as if it had been her whole person, with the soul behind
it: Archer stood dumb, overwhelmed by what it suddenly told him.

"You too—oh, all this time, you too?"

For answer, she let the tears on her lids overflow and run slowly
downward.

Half the width of the room was still between them, and neither made
any show of moving. Archer was conscious of a curious indifference to her
bodily presence: he would hardly have been aware of it if one of the hands
she had flung out on the table had not drawn his gaze as on the occasion
when, in the little Twenty-third Street house, he had kept his eye on it in
order not to look at her face. Now his imagination spun about the hand as
about the edge of a vortex; but still he made no effort to draw nearer. He
had known the love that is fed on caresses and feeds them; but this passion
that was closer than his bones was not to be superficially satisfied. His one
terror was to do anything which might efface the sound and impression of
her words; his one thought, that he should never again feel quite alone.

But after a moment the sense of waste and ruin overcame him. There
they were, close together and safe and shut in; yet so chained to their separate destinies that they might as well have been half the world apart.

"What's the use—when you will go back?" he broke out, a great hopeless *How on earth can I keep you?* crying out to her beneath his words.

She sat motionless, with lowered lids. "Oh—I shan't go yet!"

"Not yet? Some time, then? Some time that you already foresee?"

At that she raised her clearest eyes. "I promise you: not as long as you
hold out. Not as long as we can look straight at each other like this."

He dropped into his chair. What her answer really said was: "If you lift a finger you'll drive me back: back to all the abominations you know of, and all the temptations you half guess." He understood it as clearly as if she had uttered the words, and the thought kept him anchored to his side of the table in a kind of moved and sacred submission.

"What a life for you!" he groaned.

"Oh—as long as it's a part of yours."

"And mine a part of yours?"

She nodded.

"And that's to be all—for either of us?"

"Well; it *is* all, isn't it?"

At that he sprang up, forgetting everything but the sweetness of her face. She rose too, not as if to meet him or to flee from him, but quietly, as though the worst of the task were done and she had only to wait; so quietly that, as he came close, her outstretched hands acted not as a check but as a guide to him. They fell into his, while her arms, extended but not rigid, kept him far enough off to let her surrendered face say the rest.

They may have stood in that way for a long time, or only for a few moments; but it was long enough for her silence to communicate all she had to say, and for him to feel that only one thing mattered. He must do nothing to make this meeting their last; he must leave their future in her care, asking only that she should keep fast hold of it.

"Don't—don't be unhappy," she said, with a break in her voice, as she drew her hands away; and he answered: "You won't go back—you won't go back?" as if it were the one possibility he could not bear.

"I won't go back," she said; and turning away she opened the door and led the way into the public dining-room.

The strident school-teachers were gathering up their possessions preparatory to a straggling flight to the wharf; across the beach lay the white steam-boat at the pier; and over the sunlit waters Boston loomed in a line of haze.

XXV

Once more on the boat, and in the presence of others, Archer felt a tranquility of spirit that surprised as much as it sustained him.

The day, according to any current valuation, had been a rather ridiculous failure; he had not so much as touched Madame Olenska's hand with his lips, or extracted one word from her that gave promise of farther opportunities. Nevertheless, for a man sick with unsatisfied love, and parting for an indefinite period from the object of his passion, he felt himself almost humiliatingly calm and comforted. It was the perfect balance she had held between their loyalty to others and their honesty to themselves that had so stirred and yet tranquillized him; a balance not artfully calculated, as her tears and her falterings showed, but resulting naturally from her un-abashed sincerity. It filled him with a tender awe, now the danger was over, and made him thank the fates that no personal vanity, no sense of playing a part before sophisticated witnesses, had tempted him to tempt her. Even after they had clasped hands for good-bye at the Fall River station, and he had turned away alone, the conviction remained with him of having saved out of their meeting much more than he had sacrificed.

He wandered back to the club, and went and sat alone in the deserted library, turning and turning over in his thoughts every separate second of their hours together. It was clear to him, and it grew more clear under closer scrutiny, that if she should finally decide on returning to Europe— returning to her husband—it would not be because her old life tempted her, even on the new terms offered. No: she would go only if she felt her-self becoming a temptation to Archer, a temptation to fall away from the standard they had both set up. Her choice would be to stay near him as long as he did not ask her to come nearer; and it depended on himself to keep her just there, safe but secluded.

In the train these thoughts were still with him. They enclosed him in a kind of golden haze, through which the faces about him looked remote and indistinct: he had a feeling that if he spoke to his fellow-travellers they would not understand what he was saying. In this state of abstraction he found himself, the following morning, waking to the reality of a stifling September day in New York. The heat-withered faces in the long train streamed past him, and he continued to stare at them through the same golden blur; but suddenly, as he left the station, one of the faces detached itself, came closer and forced itself upon his consciousness. It was, as he instantly recalled, the face of the young man he had seen, the day before, passing out of the Parker House, and had noted as not conforming to type, as not having an American hotel face.

The same thing struck him now; and again he became aware of a dim stir of former associations. The young man stood looking about him with the dazed air of the foreigner flung upon the harsh mercies of American travel; then he advanced toward Archer, lifted his hat, and said in English: "Surely, Monsieur, we met in London?"

"Ah, to be sure: in London!" Archer grasped his hand with curiosity and sympathy. "So you *did* get here, after all?" he exclaimed, casting a wondering eye on the astute and haggard little countenance of young Carfry's French tutor.

"Oh, I got here—yes," M. Rivière smiled with drawn lips. "But not for long; I return the day after tomorrow." He stood grasping his light valise in one neatly gloved hand, and gazing anxiously, perplexedly, almost appealingly, into Archer's face.

"I wonder, Monsieur, since I've had the good luck to run across you, if I might—"

"I was just going to suggest it: come to luncheon, won't you? Down town, I mean: if you'll look me up in my office I'll take you to a very decent restaurant in that quarter."

M. Rivière was visibly touched and surprised. "You're too kind. But I was only going to ask if you would tell me how to reach some sort of conveyance. There are no porters, and no one here seems to listen—"

"I know: our American stations must surprise you. When you ask for a porter they give you chewing-gum. But if you'll come along I'll extricate you; and you must really lunch with me, you know."

The young man, after a just perceptible hesitation, replied, with profuse thanks, and in a tone that did not carry complete conviction, that he was already engaged; but when they had reached the comparative reassurance of the street he asked if he might call that afternoon.

Archer, at ease in the midsummer leisure of the office, fixed an hour and scribbled his address, which the Frenchman pocketed with reiterated thanks and a wide flourish of his hat. A horse-car received him, and Archer walked away.

Punctually at the hour M. Rivière appeared, shaved, smoothed-out, but still unmistakably drawn and serious. Archer was alone in his office, and the young man, before accepting the seat he proffered, began abruptly: "I believe I saw you, sir, yesterday in Boston."

The statement was insignificant enough, and Archer was about to frame an assent when his words were checked by something mysterious yet illuminating in his visitor's insistent gaze.

"It is extraordinary, very extraordinary," M. Rivière continued, "that we should have met in the circumstances in which I find myself."

"What circumstances?" Archer asked, wondering a little crudely if he needed money.

M. Rivière continued to study him with tentative eyes. "I have come, not to look for employment, as I spoke of doing when we last met, but on a special mission—"

---

horse-car   A horse-drawn conveyance that ran on rails and accommodated many passengers.

"Ah—!" Archer exclaimed. In a flash the two meetings had connected themselves in his mind. He paused to take in the situation thus suddenly lighted up for him, and M. Rivière also remained silent, as if aware that what he had said was enough.

"A special mission," Archer at length repeated.

The young Frenchman, opening his palms, raised them slightly, and the two men continued to look at each other across the office-desk till Archer roused himself to say: "Do sit down"; whereupon M. Rivière bowed, took a distant chair, and again waited.

"It was about this mission that you wanted to consult me?" Archer finally asked.

M. Rivière bent his head. "Not in my own behalf: on that score I—I have fully dealt with myself. I should like—if I may—to speak to you about the Countess Olenska."

Archer had known for the last few minutes that the words were coming; but when they came they sent the blood rushing to his temples as if he had been caught by a bent-back branch in a thicket.

"And on whose behalf," he said, "do you wish to do this?"

M. Rivière met the question sturdily. "Well—I might say *hers,* if it did not sound like a liberty. Shall I say instead: on behalf of abstract justice?"

Archer considered him ironically. "In other words: you are Count Olenski's messenger?"

He saw his blush more darkly reflected in M. Rivière's sallow countenance. "Not to *you,* Monsieur. If I come to you, it is on quite other grounds."

"What right have you, in the circumstances, to *be* on any other ground?" Archer retorted. "If you're an emissary you're an emissary."

The young man considered. "My mission is over: as far as the Countess Olenska goes, it has failed."

"I can't help that," Archer rejoined on the same note of irony.

"No: but you can help—" M. Rivière paused, turned his hat about in his still carefully gloved hands, looked into its lining and then back at Archer's face. "You can help, Monsieur, I am convinced, to make it equally a failure with her family."

Archer pushed back his chair and stood up. "Well—and by God I will!" he exclaimed. He stood with his hands in his pockets, staring down wrathfully at the little Frenchman, whose face, though he too had risen, was still an inch or two below the line of Archer's eyes.

M. Rivière paled to his normal hue: paler than that his complexion could hardly turn.

"Why the devil," Archer explosively continued, "should you have thought—since I suppose you're appealing to me on the ground of my relationship to Madame Olenska—that I should take a view contrary to the rest of her family?"

The change of expression in M. Rivière's face was for a time his only answer. His look passed from timidity to absolute distress: for a young man of his usually resourceful mien it would have been difficult to appear more disarmed and defenceless. "Oh, Monsieur—"

"I can't imagine," Archer continued, "why you should have come to me when there are others so much nearer to the Countess; still less why you thought I should be more accessible to the arguments I suppose you were sent over with."

M. Rivière took this onslaught with a disconcerting humility. "The arguments I want to present to you, Monsieur, are my own and not those I was sent over with."

"Then I see still less reason for listening to them."

M. Rivière again looked into his hat, as if considering whether these last words were not a sufficiently broad hint to put it on and be gone. Then he spoke with sudden decision. "Monsieur—will you tell me one thing? Is it my right to be here that you question? Or do you perhaps believe the whole matter to be already closed?"

His quiet insistence made Archer feel the clumsiness of his own bluster. M. Rivière had succeeded in imposing himself: Archer, reddening slightly, dropped into his chair again, and signed to the young man to be seated.

"I beg your pardon: but why isn't the matter closed?"

M. Rivière gazed back at him with anguish. "You do, then, agree with the rest of the family that, in face of the new proposals I have brought, it is hardly possible for Madame Olenska not to return to her husband?"

"Good God!" Archer exclaimed; and his visitor gave out a low murmur of confirmation.

"Before seeing her, I saw—at Count Olenski's request—Mr. Lovell Mingott, with whom I had several talks before going to Boston. I understand that he represents his mother's view; and that Mrs. Manson Mingott's influence is great throughout her family."

Archer sat silent, with the sense of clinging to the edge of a sliding precipice. The discovery that he had been excluded from a share in these negotiations, and even from the knowledge that they were on foot, caused him a surprise hardly dulled by the acuter wonder of what he was learn-

---

mien A person's appearance or bearing, especially as it communicates a mood.

ing. He saw in a flash that if the family had ceased to consult him it was because some deep tribal instinct warned them that he was no longer on their side; and he recalled, with a start of comprehension, a remark of May's during their drive home from Mrs. Manson Mingott's on the day of the Archery Meeting: "Perhaps, after all, Ellen would be happier with her husband."

Even in the tumult of new discoveries Archer remembered his indignant exclamation, and the fact that since then his wife had never named Madame Olenska to him. Her careless allusion had no doubt been the straw held up to see which way the wind blew; the result had been reported to the family, and thereafter Archer had been tacitly omitted from their counsels. He admired the tribal discipline which made May bow to this decision. She would not have done so, he knew, had her conscience protested; but she probably shared the family view that Madame Olenska would be better off as an unhappy wife than as a separated one, and that there was no use in discussing the case with Newland, who had an awkward way of suddenly not seeming to take the most fundamental things for granted.

Archer looked up and met his visitor's anxious gaze. "Don't you know, Monsieur—is it possible you don't know—that the family begin to doubt if they have the right to advise the Countess to refuse her husband's last proposals?"

"The proposals you brought?"

"The proposals I brought."

It was on Archer's lips to exclaim that whatever he knew or did not know was no concern of M. Rivière's; but something in the humble and yet courageous tenacity of M. Rivière's gaze made him reject this conclusion, and he met the young man's question with another. "What is your object in speaking to me of this?"

He had not to wait a moment for the answer. "To beg you, Monsieur— to beg you with all the force I'm capable of—not to let her go back.— Oh, don't let her!" M. Rivière exclaimed.

Archer looked at him with increasing astonishment. There was no mistaking the sincerity of his distress or the strength of his determination: he had evidently resolved to let everything go by the board but the supreme need of thus putting himself on record. Archer considered.

"May I ask," he said at length, "if this is the line you took with the Countess Olenska?"

M. Rivière reddened, but his eyes did not falter. "No, Monsieur: I accepted my mission in good faith. I really believed—for reasons I need not trouble you with—that it would be better for Madame Olenska to recover her situation, her fortune, the social consideration that her husband's standing gives her."

"So I supposed: you could hardly have accepted such a mission otherwise."

"I should not have accepted it."

"Well, then—?" Archer paused again, and their eyes met in another protracted scrutiny.

"Ah, Monsieur, after I had seen her, after I had listened to her, I knew she was better off here."

"You knew—?"

"Monsieur, I discharged my mission faithfully: I put the Count's arguments, I stated his offers, without adding any comment of my own. The Countess was good enough to listen patiently; she carried her goodness so far as to see me twice; she considered impartially all I had come to say. And it was in the course of these two talks that I changed my mind, that I came to see things differently."

"May I ask what led to this change?"

"Simply seeing the change in *her*," M. Rivière replied.

"The change in her? Then you knew her before?"

The young man's colour again rose. "I used to see her in her husband's house. I have known Count Olenski for many years. You can imagine that he would not have sent a stranger on such a mission."

Archer's gaze, wandering away to the blank walls of the office, rested on a hanging calendar surmounted by the rugged features of the President of the United States. That such a conversation should be going on anywhere within the millions of square miles subject to his rule seemed as strange as anything that the imagination could invent.

"The change—what sort of a change?"

"Ah, Monsieur, if I could tell you!" M. Rivière paused. "*Tenez*—the discovery, I suppose, of what I'd never thought of before: that she's an American. And that if you're an American of *her* kind—of your kind—things that are accepted in certain other societies, or at least put up with as part of a general convenient give-and-take—become unthinkable, simply unthinkable. If Madame Olenska's relations understood what these things were, their opposition to her returning would no doubt be as unconditional as her own; but they seem to regard her husband's wish to have her back as proof of an irresistible longing for domestic life." M. Rivière paused, and then added: "Whereas it's far from being as simple as that."

President of the United States Archer's glance at this portrait suggests a tension between the democratic experiment underway in the United States and more totalitarian systems of government in Europe. Wharton situates Ellen's bid for personal freedom within a larger concept of American liberty.

"*Tenez*— . . ."   French: "Look here."

Archer looked back to the President of the United States, and then down at his desk and at the papers scattered on it. For a second or two he could not trust himself to speak. During this interval he heard M. Rivière's chair pushed back, and was aware that the young man had risen. When he glanced up again he saw that his visitor was as moved as himself.

"Thank you," Archer said simply.

"There's nothing to thank me for, Monsieur: it is I, rather—" M. Rivière broke off, as if speech for him too were difficult. "I should like, though," he continued in a firmer voice, "to add one thing. You asked me if I was in Count Olenski's employ. I am at this moment: I returned to him, a few months ago, for reasons of private necessity such as may happen to any one who has persons, ill and older persons, dependent on him. But from the moment that I have taken the step of coming here to say these things to you I consider myself discharged, and I shall tell him so on my return, and give him the reasons. That's all, Monsieur."

M. Rivière bowed and drew back a step.

"Thank you," Archer said again, as their hands met.

XXVI

Every year on the fifteenth of October Fifth Avenue opened its shutters, unrolled its carpets and hung up its triple layer of window-curtains.

By the first of November this household ritual was over, and society had begun to look about and take stock of itself. By the fifteenth the season was in full blast, Opera and theatres were putting forth their new attractions, dinner-engagements were accumulating, and dates for dances being fixed. And punctually at about this time Mrs. Archer always said that New York was very much changed.

Observing it from the lofty stand-point of a non-participant, she was able, with the help of Mr. Sillerton Jackson and Miss Sophy, to trace each new crack in its surface, and all the strange weeds pushing up between the ordered rows of social vegetables. It had been one of the amusements of Archer's youth to wait for this annual pronouncement of his mother's, and to hear her enumerate the minute signs of disintegration that his careless gaze had overlooked. For New York, to Mrs. Archer's mind, never

---

the season   The New York social season spanned January to Lent.

strange weeds   As she does with the reference to Burbank's hybrids in chap. 1, Wharton uses a horticultural metaphor to describe fundamental changes in New York society.

changed without changing for the worse; and in this view Miss Sophy Jackson heartily concurred.

Mr. Sillerton Jackson, as became a man of the world, suspended his judgment and listened with an amused impartiality to the lamentations of the ladies. But even he never denied that New York had changed; and Newland Archer, in the winter of the second year of his marriage, was himself obliged to admit that if it had not actually changed it was certainly changing.

These points had been raised, as usual, at Mrs. Archer's Thanksgiving dinner. At the date when she was officially enjoined to give thanks for the blessings of the year it was her habit to take a mournful though not embittered stock of her world, and wonder what there was to be thankful for. At any rate, not the state of society; society, if it could be said to exist, was rather a spectacle on which to call down Biblical imprecations—and in fact, every one knew what the Reverend Dr. Ashmore meant when he chose a text from Jeremiah (chap. ii., verse 25) for his Thanksgiving sermon. Dr. Ashmore, the new Rector of St. Matthew's, had been chosen because he was very "advanced": his sermons were considered bold in thought and novel in language. When he fulminated against fashionable society he always spoke of its "trend"; and to Mrs. Archer it was terrifying and yet fascinating to feel herself part of a community that was trending.

"There's no doubt that Dr. Ashmore is right: there *is* a marked trend," she said, as if it were something visible and measurable, like a crack in a house.

"It was odd, though, to preach about it on Thanksgiving," Miss Jackson opined; and her hostess drily rejoined: "Oh, he means us to give thanks for what's left."

Archer had been wont to smile at these annual vaticinations of his mother's; but this year even he was obliged to acknowledge, as he listened to an enumeration of the changes, that the "trend" was visible.

"The extravagance in dress—" Miss Jackson began. "Sillerton took me to the first night of the Opera, and I can only tell you that Jane Merry's dress was the only one I recognised from last year; and even that had had

---

Jeremiah The biblical text reads: "Withhold thy foot from being unshod, and thy throat from thirst: but thou saidst, There is no hope: no; for I have loved strangers, and after them will I go." The minister ironically delivers a jeremiad, an elaborate lamentation, rather than a message of thankfulness: Rather than feeling gratitude at Thanksgiving, old New Yorkers feel besieged by the new people invading their ranks.

vaticinations Predictions or prophecies.

the front panel changed. Yet I know she got it out from Worth only two years ago, because my seamstress always goes in to make over her Paris dresses before she wears them."

"Ah, Jane Merry is one of *us*," said Mrs. Archer sighing, as if it were not such an enviable thing to be in an age when ladies were beginning to flaunt abroad their Paris dresses as soon as they were out of the Custom House, instead of letting them mellow under lock and key, in the manner of Mrs. Archer's contemporaries.

"Yes; she's one of the few. In my youth," Miss Jackson rejoined, "it was considered vulgar to dress in the newest fashions; and Amy Sillerton has always told me that in Boston the rule was to put away one's Paris dresses for two years. Old Mrs. Baxter Pennilow, who did everything handsomely, used to import twelve a year, two velvet, two satin, two silk, and the other six of poplin and the finest cashmere. It was a standing order, and as she was ill for two years before she died they found forty-eight Worth dresses that had never been taken out of tissue paper; and when the girls left off their mourning they were able to wear the first lot at the Symphony concerts without looking in advance of the fashion."

"Ah, well, Boston is more conservative than New York; but I always think it's a safe rule for a lady to lay aside her French dresses for one season," Mrs. Archer conceded.

"It was Beaufort who started the new fashion by making his wife clap her new clothes on her back as soon as they arrived: I must say at times it takes all Regina's distinction not to look like . . . like . . ." Miss Jackson glanced around the table, caught Janey's bulging gaze, and took refuge in an unintelligible murmur.

"Like her rivals," said Mr. Sillerton Jackson, with the air of producing an epigram.

"Oh—" the ladies murmured; and Mrs. Archer added, partly to distract her daughter's attention from forbidden topics: "Poor Regina! Her Thanksgiving hasn't been a very cheerful one, I'm afraid. Have you heard the rumours about Beaufort's speculations, Sillerton?"

---

front panel   A triangular piece of cloth, either part of the design of a dress or a replacement to give the dress a new look.

Custom House   The building with state and federal offices that collects duty payable on goods entering the country.

Symphony concerts   The Boston Symphony Orchestra was not founded until 1881. Symphony Hall opened in 1900 at Huntington Avenue and Massachusetts Avenue. Mrs. Pennilow would have attended the Boston Music Hall, built in 1852 at Winter Street and Bumstead Place.

Mr. Jackson nodded carelessly. Every one had heard the rumours in question, and he scorned to confirm a tale that was already common property.

A gloomy silence fell upon the party. No one really liked Beaufort, and it was not wholly unpleasant to think the worst of his private life; but the idea of his having brought financial dishonour on his wife's family was too shocking to be enjoyed even by his enemies. Archer's New York tolerated hypocrisy in private relations; but in business matters it exacted a limpid and impeccable honesty. It was a long time since any well-known banker had failed discreditably; but every one remembered the social extinction visited on the heads of the firm when the last event of the kind had happened. It would be the same with the Beauforts, in spite of his power and her popularity; not all the leagued strength of the Dallas connection would save poor Regina if there were any truth in the reports of her husband's unlawful speculations.

The talk took refuge in less ominous topics; but everything they touched on seemed to confirm Mrs. Archer's sense of an accelerated trend.

"Of course, Newland, I know you let dear May go to Mrs. Struthers's Sunday evenings—" she began; and May interposed gaily: "Oh, you know, everybody goes to Mrs. Struthers's now; and she was invited to Granny's last reception."

It was thus, Archer reflected, that New York managed its transitions: conspiring to ignore them till they were well over, and then, in all good faith, imagining that they had taken place in a preceding age. There was always a traitor in the citadel; and after he (or generally she) had surrendered the keys, what was the use of pretending that it was impregnable? Once people had tasted of Mrs. Struthers's easy Sunday hospitality they were not likely to sit at home remembering that her champagne was transmuted Shoe-Polish.

"I know, dear, I know," Mrs. Archer sighed. "Such things have to be, I suppose, as long as *amusement* is what people go out for; but I've never quite forgiven your cousin Madame Olenska for being the first person to countenance Mrs. Struthers."

A sudden blush rose to young Mrs. Archer's face; it surprised her husband as much as the other guests about the table. "Oh, *Ellen*—" she murmured, much in the same accusing and yet deprecating tone in which her parents might have said: "Oh, *the Blenkers*—."

It was the note which the family had taken to sounding on the mention of the Countess Olenska's name, since she had surprised and inconvenienced them by remaining obdurate to her husband's advances; but on May's lips it gave food for thought, and Archer looked at her with the sense of strangeness that sometimes came over him when she was most in the tone of her environment.

His mother, with less than her usual sensitiveness to atmosphere, still insisted: "I've always thought that people like the Countess Olenska, who have lived in aristocratic societies, ought to help us to keep up our social distinctions, instead of ignoring them."

May's blush remained permanently vivid: it seemed to have a significance beyond that implied by the recognition of Madame Olenska's social bad faith.

"I've no doubt we all seem alike to foreigners," said Miss Jackson tartly.

"I don't think Ellen cares for society; but nobody knows exactly what she does care for," May continued, as if she had been groping for something noncommittal.

"Ah, well—" Mrs. Archer sighed again.

Everybody knew that the Countess Olenska was no longer in the good graces of her family. Even her devoted champion, old Mrs. Manson Mingott, had been unable to defend her refusal to return to her husband. The Mingotts had not proclaimed their disapproval aloud: their sense of solidarity was too strong. They had simply, as Mrs. Welland said, "let poor Ellen find her own level"—and that, mortifyingly and incomprehensibly, was in the dim depths where the Blenkers prevailed, and "people who wrote" celebrated their untidy rites. It was incredible, but it was a fact, that Ellen, in spite of all her opportunities and her privileges, had become simply "Bohemian." The fact enforced the contention that she had made a fatal mistake in not returning to Count Olenski. After all, a young woman's place was under her husband's roof, especially when she had left it in circumstances that . . . well . . . if one had cared to look into them . . .

"Madame Olenska is a great favourite with the gentlemen," said Miss Sophy, with her air of wishing to put forth something conciliatory when she knew that she was planting a dart.

"Ah, that's the danger that a young woman like Madame Olenska is always exposed to," Mrs. Archer mournfully agreed; and the ladies, on this conclusion, gathered up their trains to seek the carcel globes of the drawing-room, while Archer and Mr. Sillerton Jackson withdrew to the Gothic library.

Once established before the grate, and consoling himself for the inadequacy of the dinner by the perfection of his cigar, Mr. Jackson became portentous and communicable.

"If the Beaufort smash comes," he announced, "there are going to be disclosures."

Archer raised his head quickly: he could never hear the name without the sharp vision of Beaufort's heavy figure, opulently furred and shod, advancing through the snow at Skuytercliff.

"There's bound to be," Mr. Jackson continued, "the nastiest kind of a cleaning up. He hasn't spent all his money on Regina."

"Oh, well—that's discounted, isn't it? My belief is he'll pull out yet," said the young man, wanting to change the subject.

"Perhaps—perhaps. I know he was to see some of the influential people today. Of course," Mr. Jackson reluctantly conceded, "it's to be hoped they can tide him over—this time anyhow. I shouldn't like to think of poor Regina's spending the rest of her life in some shabby foreign watering-place for bankrupts."

Archer said nothing. It seemed to him so natural—however tragic—that money ill-gotten should be cruelly expiated, that his mind, hardly lingering over Mrs. Beaufort's doom, wandered back to closer questions. What was the meaning of May's blush when the Countess Olenska had been mentioned?

Four months had passed since the midsummer day that he and Madame Olenska had spent together; and since then he had not seen her. He knew that she had returned to Washington, to the little house which she and Medora Manson had taken there: he had written to her once—a few words, asking when they were to meet again—and she had even more briefly replied: "Not yet."

Since then there had been no farther communication between them, and he had built up within himself a kind of sanctuary in which she throned among his secret thoughts and longings. Little by little it became the scene of his real life, of his only rational activities; thither he brought the books he read, the ideas and feelings which nourished him, his judgments and his visions. Outside it, in the scene of his actual life, he moved with a growing sense of unreality and insufficiency, blundering against familiar prejudices and traditional points of view as an absent-minded man goes on bumping into the furniture of his own room. Absent—that was what he was: so absent from everything most densely real and near to those about him that it sometimes startled him to find they still imagined he was there.

He became aware that Mr. Jackson was clearing his throat preparatory to farther revelations.

"I don't know, of course, how far your wife's family are aware of what people say about—well, about Madame Olenska's refusal to accept her husband's latest offer."

Archer was silent, and Mr. Jackson obliquely continued: "It's a pity—it's certainly a pity—that she refused it."

"A pity? In God's name, why?"

Mr. Jackson looked down his leg to the unwrinkled sock that joined it to a glossy pump.

"Well—to put it on the lowest ground—what's she going to live on now?"

"Now—?"

"If Beaufort—"

Archer sprang up, his fist banging down on the black walnut-edge of the writing-table. The wells of the brass double-inkstand danced in their sockets.

"What the devil do you mean, sir?"

Mr. Jackson, shifting himself slightly in his chair, turned a tranquil gaze on the young man's burning face.

"Well—I have it on pretty good authority—in fact, on old Catherine's herself—that the family reduced Countess Olenska's allowance considerably when she definitely refused to go back to her husband; and as, by this refusal, she also forfeits the money settled on her when she married— which Olenski was ready to make over to her if she returned—why, what the devil do *you* mean, my dear boy, by asking me what *I* mean?" Mr. Jackson good-humouredly retorted.

Archer moved toward the mantelpiece and bent over to knock his ashes into the grate.

"I don't know anything of Madame Olenska's private affairs; but I don't need to, to be certain that what you insinuate—"

"Oh, *I* don't: it's Lefferts, for one," Mr. Jackson interposed.

"Lefferts—who made love to her and got snubbed for it!" Archer broke out contemptuously.

"Ah—*did* he?" snapped the other, as if this were exactly the fact he had been laying a trap for. He still sat sideways from the fire, so that his hard old gaze held Archer's face as if in a spring of steel.

"Well, well: it's a pity she didn't go back before Beaufort's cropper," he repeated. "If she goes *now,* and if he fails, it will only confirm the general impression: which isn't by any means peculiar to Lefferts, by the way."

---

cropper   A disastrous failure or fiasco. Wharton may be alluding to the failure, in 1873, of Jay Cooke and Company, which caused such chaos that the New York Stock Exchange closed for ten days. Wharton's focus on opulence in this novel precludes her mention of a severe financial recession during this time. Immigrants and the working class were hit hardest; in the winter of 1873–1874, 25 percent of the city's labor force had lost their jobs, wages declined steadily, and hunger and homelessness spread across the city.

"Oh, she won't go back now: less than ever!" Archer had no sooner said it than he had once more the feeling that it was exactly what Mr. Jackson had been waiting for.

The old gentleman considered him attentively. "That's your opinion, eh? Well, no doubt you know. But everybody will tell you that the few pennies Medora Manson has left are all in Beaufort's hands; and how the two women are to keep their heads above water unless he does, I can't imagine. Of course, Madame Olenska may still soften old Catherine, who's been the most inexorably opposed to her staying; and old Catherine could make her any allowance she chooses. But we all know that she hates parting with good money; and the rest of the family have no particular interest in keeping Madame Olenska here."

Archer was burning with unavailing wrath: he was exactly in the state when a man is sure to do something stupid, knowing all the while that he is doing it.

He saw that Mr. Jackson had been instantly struck by the fact that Madame Olenska's differences with her grandmother and her other relations were not known to him, and that the old gentleman had drawn his own conclusions as to the reasons for Archer's exclusion from the family councils. This fact warned Archer to go warily; but the insinuations about Beaufort made him reckless. He was mindful, however, if not of his own danger, at least of the fact that Mr. Jackson was under his mother's roof, and consequently his guest. Old New York scrupulously observed the etiquette of hospitality, and no discussion with a guest was ever allowed to degenerate into a disagreement.

"Shall we go up and join my mother?" he suggested curtly, as Mr. Jackson's last cone of ashes dropped into the brass ashtray at his elbow.

On the drive homeward May remained oddly silent; through the darkness, he still felt her enveloped in her menacing blush. What its menace meant he could not guess: but he was sufficiently warned by the fact that Madame Olenska's name had evoked it.

They went upstairs, and he turned into the library. She usually followed him; but he heard her passing down the passage to her bedroom.

"May!" he called out impatiently; and she came back, with a slight glance of surprise at his tone.

"This lamp is smoking again; I should think the servants might see that it's kept properly trimmed," he grumbled nervously.

"I'm so sorry: it shan't happen again," she answered, in the firm bright tone she had learned from her mother; and it exasperated Archer to feel that she was already beginning to humour him like a younger Mr. Welland. She bent over to lower the wick, and as the light struck up on her white shoulders and the clear curves of her face he thought: "How young she is! For what endless years this life will have to go on!"

He felt, with a kind of horror, his own strong youth and the bounding blood in his veins. "Look here," he said suddenly, "I may have to go to Washington for a few days—soon; next week perhaps."

Her hand remained on the key of the lamp as she turned to him slowly. The heat from its flame had brought back a glow to her face, but it paled as she looked up.

"On business?" she asked, in a tone which implied that there could be no other conceivable reason, and that she had put the question automatically, as if merely to finish his own sentence.

"On business, naturally. There's a patent case coming up before the Supreme Court—" He gave the name of the inventor, and went on furnishing details with all Lawrence Lefferts's practised glibness, while she listened attentively, saying at intervals: "Yes, I see."

"The change will do you good," she said simply, when he had finished; "and you must be sure to go and see Ellen," she added, looking him straight in the eyes with her cloudless smile, and speaking in the tone she might have employed in urging him not to neglect some irksome family duty.

It was the only word that passed between them on the subject; but in the code in which they had both been trained it meant: "Of course you understand that I know all that people have been saying about Ellen, and heartily sympathise with my family in their effort to get her to return to her husband. I also know that, for some reason you have not chosen to tell me, you have advised her against this course, which all the older men of the family, as well as our grandmother, agree in approving; and that it is owing to your encouragement that Ellen defies us all, and exposes herself to the kind of criticism of which Mr. Sillerton Jackson probably gave you, this evening, the hint that has made you so irritable. . . . Hints have indeed not been wanting; but since you appear unwilling to take them from others, I offer you this one myself, in the only form in which well-bred people of our kind can communicate unpleasant things to each other: by letting you understand that I know you mean to see Ellen when you are in Washington, and are perhaps going there expressly for that purpose; and that, since you are sure to see her, I wish you to do so with my full and explicit approval—and to take the opportunity of letting her know what the course of conduct you have encouraged her in is likely to lead to."

Her hand was still on the key of the lamp when the last word of this mute message reached him. She turned the wick down, lifted off the globe, and breathed on the sulky flame.

"They smell less if one blows them out," she explained, with her bright housekeeping air. On the threshold she turned and paused for his kiss.

XXVII

Wall Street, the next day, had more reassuring reports of Beaufort's situation. They were not definite, but they were hopeful. It was generally understood that he could call on powerful influences in case of emergency, and that he had done so with success; and that evening, when Mrs. Beaufort appeared at the Opera wearing her old smile and a new emerald necklace, society drew a breath of relief.

New York was inexorable in its condemnation of business irregularities. So far there had been no exception to its tacit rule that those who broke the law of probity must pay; and every one was aware that even Beaufort and Beaufort's wife would be offered up unflinchingly to this principle. But to be obliged to offer them up would be not only painful but inconvenient. The disappearance of the Beauforts would leave a considerable void in their compact little circle; and those who were too ignorant or too careless to shudder at the moral catastrophe bewailed in advance the loss of the best ball-room in New York.

Archer had definitely made up his mind to go to Washington. He was waiting only for the opening of the law-suit of which he had spoken to May, so that its date might coincide with that of his visit; but on the following Tuesday he learned from Mr. Letterblair that the case might be postponed for several weeks. Nevertheless, he went home that afternoon determined in any event to leave the next evening. The chances were that May, who knew nothing of his professional life, and had never shown any interest in it, would not learn of the postponement, should it take place, nor remember the names of the litigants if they were mentioned before her; and at any rate he could no longer put off seeing Madam Olenska. There were too many things that he must say to her.

On the Wednesday morning, when he reached his office, Mr. Letterblair met him with a troubled face. Beaufort, after all, had not managed to "tide over"; but by setting afloat the rumour that he had done so he had reassured his depositors, and heavy payments had poured into the bank till the previous evening, when disturbing reports again began to predominate.

---

law of probity   Standard of complete integrity; uprightness. In *A Backward Glance*, Wharton writes that when "two or three men of high social standing were involved in a discreditable bank failure, their families were made to suffer to a degree that would seem merciless to our modern judgment." She speculates that "perhaps the New Yorkers of that day were unconsciously trying to atone for their culpable neglect of state and national politics, from which they had long disdainfully held aloof, by upholding the sternest principles of business probity, and inflicting the severest social penalties on whoever lapsed from them" (22).

In consequence, a run on the bank had begun, and its doors were likely to close before the day was over. The ugliest things were being said of Beaufort's dastardly manoeuvre, and his failure promised to be one of the most discreditable in the history of Wall Street.

The extent of the calamity left Mr. Letterblair white and incapacitated. "I've seen bad things in my time; but nothing as bad as this. Everybody we know will be hit, one way or another. And what will be done about Mrs. Beaufort? What *can* be done about her? I pity Mrs. Manson Mingott as much as anybody: coming at her age, there's no knowing what effect this affair may have on her. She always believed in Beaufort—she made a friend of him! And there's the whole Dallas connection: poor Mrs. Beaufort is related to every one of you. Her only chance would be to leave her husband—yet how can any one tell her so? Her duty is at his side; and luckily she seems always to have been blind to his private weaknesses."

There was a knock, and Mr. Letterblair turned his head sharply. "What is it? I can't be disturbed."

A clerk brought in a letter for Archer and withdrew. Recognising his wife's hand, the young man opened the envelope and read: "Won't you please come up town as early as you can? Granny had a slight stroke last night. In some mysterious way she found out before any one else this awful news about the bank. Uncle Lovell is away shooting, and the idea of the disgrace has made poor Papa so nervous that he has a temperature and can't leave his room. Mamma needs you dreadfully, and I do hope you can get away at once and go straight to Granny's."

Archer handed the note to his senior partner, and a few minutes later was crawling northward in a crowded horse-car, which he exchanged at Fourteenth Street for one of the high staggering omnibuses of the Fifth Avenue line. It was after twelve o'clock when this laborious vehicle dropped him at old Catherine's. The sitting-room window on the ground floor, where she usually throned, was tenanted by the inadequate figure of her daughter, Mrs. Welland, who signed a haggard welcome as she caught sight of Archer; and at the door he was met by May. The hall wore the unnatural appearance peculiar to well-kept houses suddenly invaded by illness: wraps and furs lay in heaps on the chairs, a doctor's bag and overcoat were on the table, and beside them letters and cards had already piled up unheeded.

May looked pale but smiling: Dr. Bencomb, who had just come for the second time, took a more hopeful view, and Mrs. Mingott's dauntless determination to live and get well was already having an effect on her family.

---

omnibuses   Horse-drawn street cars were first operated in New York City in 1831. The Fifth Avenue Coach Company operated a line toward the end of the century.

May led Archer into the old lady's sitting-room, where the sliding doors opening into the bedroom had been drawn shut, and the heavy yellow damask portières dropped over them; and here Mrs. Welland communicated to him in horrified undertones the details of the catastrophe. It appeared that the evening before something dreadful and mysterious had happened. At about eight o'clock, just after Mrs. Mingott had finished the game of solitaire that she always played after dinner, the doorbell had rung, and a lady so thickly veiled that the servants did not immediately recognise her had asked to be received.

The butler, hearing a familiar voice, had thrown open the sitting-room door, announcing: "Mrs. Julius Beaufort"—and had then closed it again on the two ladies. They must have been together, he thought, about an hour. When Mrs. Mingott's bell rang Mrs. Beaufort had already slipped away unseen, and the old lady, white and vast and terrible, sat alone in her great chair, and signed to the butler to help her into her room. She seemed, at that time, though obviously distressed, in complete control of her body and brain. The mulatto maid put her to bed, brought her a cup of tea as usual, laid everything straight in the room, and went away; but at three in the morning the bell rang again, and the two servants, hastening in at this unwonted summons (for old Catherine usually slept like a baby), had found their mistress sitting up against her pillows with a crooked smile on her face and one little hand hanging limp from its huge arm.

The stroke had clearly been a slight one, for she was able to articulate and to make her wishes known; and soon after the doctor's first visit she had begun to regain control of her facial muscles. But the alarm had been great; and proportionately great was the indignation when it was gathered from Mrs. Mingott's fragmentary phrases that Regina Beaufort had come to ask her—incredible effrontery!—to back up her husband, see them through—not to "desert" them, as she called it—in fact to induce the whole family to cover and condone their monstrous dishonour.

"I said to her: 'Honour's always been honour, and honesty honesty, in Manson Mingott's house, and will be till I'm carried out of it feet first,'" the old woman had stammered into her daughter's ear, in the thick voice of the partly paralysed. "And when she said: 'But my name, Auntie—my name's Regina Dallas,' I said: 'It was Beaufort when he covered you with jewels, and it's got to stay Beaufort now that he's covered you with shame.'"

So much, with tears and gasps of horror, Mrs. Welland imparted, blanched and demolished by the unwonted obligation of having at last to fix her eyes on the unpleasant and the discreditable. "If only I could keep it from your father-in-law: he always says: 'Augusta, for pity's sake, don't destroy my last illusions'—and how am I to prevent his knowing these horrors?" the poor lady wailed.

"After all, Mamma, he won't have *seen* them," her daughter suggested; and Mrs. Welland sighed: "Ah, no; thank heaven he's safe in bed. And Dr. Bencomb has promised to keep him there till poor Mamma is better, and Regina has been got away somewhere."

Archer had seated himself near the window and was gazing out blankly at the deserted thoroughfare. It was evident that he had been summoned rather for the moral support of the stricken ladies than because of any specific aid that he could render. Mr. Lovell Mingott had been telegraphed for, and messages were being despatched by hand to the members of the family living in New York; and meanwhile there was nothing to do but to discuss in hushed tones the consequences of Beaufort's dishonour and his wife's unjustifiable action.

Mrs. Lovell Mingott, who had been in another room writing notes, presently reappeared, and added her voice to the discussion. In *their* day, the elder ladies agreed, the wife of a man who had done anything disgraceful in business had only one idea: to efface herself, to disappear with him. "There was the case of poor Grandmamma Spicer; your great-grandmother, May. Of course," Mrs. Welland hastened to add, "your great-grandfather's money difficulties were private—losses at cards, or signing a note for somebody—I never quite knew, because Mamma would never speak of it. But she was brought up in the country because her mother had to leave New York after the disgrace, whatever it was: they lived up the Hudson alone, winter and summer, till Mamma was sixteen. It would never have occurred to Grandmamma Spicer to ask the family to 'countenance' her, as I understand Regina calls it; though a private disgrace is nothing compared to the scandal of ruining hundreds of innocent people."

"Yes, it would be more becoming in Regina to hide her own countenance than to talk about other people's," Mrs. Lovell Mingott agreed. "I understand that the emerald necklace she wore at the Opera last Friday had been sent on approval from Ball and Black's in the afternoon. I wonder if they'll ever get it back?"

Archer listened unmoved to the relentless chorus. The idea of absolute financial probity as the first law of a gentleman's code was too deeply ingrained in him for sentimental considerations to weaken it. An adventurer

---

Ball and Black's   Ball, Black and Company (later Black, Starr and Frost) was the oldest jeweler's firm in the United States. Founded in Savannah, Georgia, in 1801 and relocated to New York in 1810, the firm offered household and gift items such as porcelain, silver, paintings, and bronze statuary as well as gemstone jewelry. Shops opened at Broadway and Prince Street in 1860 and at several locations along Fifth Avenue, including one at 28th Street in 1876.

like Lemuel Struthers might build up the millions of his Shoe Polish on any number of shady dealings; but unblemished honesty was the *noblesse oblige* of old financial New York. Nor did Mrs. Beaufort's fate greatly move Archer. He felt, no doubt, more sorry for her than her indignant relatives; but it seemed to him that the tie between husband and wife, even if breakable in prosperity, should be indissoluble in misfortune. As Mr. Letterblair had said, a wife's place was at her husband's side when he was in trouble; but society's place was not at his side, and Mrs. Beaufort's cool assumption that it was seemed almost to make her his accomplice. The mere idea of a woman's appealing to her family to screen her husband's business dishonour was inadmissible, since it was the one thing the Family, as an institution, could not do.

The mulatto maid called Mrs. Lovell Mingott into the hall, and the latter came back in a moment with a frowning brow.

"She wants me to telegraph for Ellen Olenska. I had written to Ellen, of course, and to Medora; but now it seems that's not enough. I'm to telegraph to her immediately, and to tell her that she's to come alone."

The announcement was received in silence. Mrs. Welland sighed resignedly, and May rose from her seat and went to gather up some newspapers that had been scattered on the floor.

"I suppose it must be done," Mrs. Lovell Mingott continued, as if hoping to be contradicted; and May turned back toward the middle of the room.

"Of course it must be done," she said. "Granny knows what she wants, and we must carry out all her wishes. Shall I write the telegram for you, Auntie? If it goes at once Ellen can probably catch tomorrow morning's train." She pronounced the syllables of the name with a peculiar clearness, as if she had tapped on two silver bells.

"Well, it can't go at once. Jasper and the pantry-boy are both out with notes and telegrams."

May turned to her husband with a smile. "But here's Newland, ready to do anything. Will you take the telegram, Newland? There'll be just time before luncheon."

Archer rose with a murmur of readiness, and she seated herself at old Catherine's rosewood "Bonheur du Jour," and wrote out the message in her large immature hand. When it was written she blotted it neatly and handed it to Archer.

---

noblesse oblige   French: Benevolent and honorable behavior considered to be the responsibility of people of high birth or rank. From "nobility" and "obligates."
"Bonheur du Jour"   French: a small writing desk.

"What a pity," she said, "that you and Ellen will cross each other on the way!—Newland," she added, turning to her mother and aunt, "is obliged to go to Washington about a patent law-suit that is coming up before the Supreme Court. I suppose Uncle Lovell will be back by tomorrow night, and with Granny improving so much it doesn't seem right to ask Newland to give up an important engagement for the firm—does it?"

She paused, as if for an answer, and Mrs. Welland hastily declared: "Oh, of course not, darling. Your Granny would be the last person to wish it." As Archer left the room with the telegram, he heard his mother-in-law add, presumably to Mrs. Lovell Mingott: "But why on earth she should make you telegraph for Ellen Olenska—" and May's clear voice rejoin: "Perhaps it's to urge on her again that after all her duty is with her husband."

The outer door closed on Archer and he walked hastily away toward the telegraph office.

XXVIII

"Ol—Ol—Howjer spell it, anyhow?" asked the tart young lady to whom Archer had pushed his wife's telegram across the brass ledge of the Western Union office.

"Olenska—O-len-ska," he repeated, drawing back the message in order to print out the foreign syllables above May's rambling script.

"It's an unlikely name for a New York telegraph office; at least in this quarter," an unexpected voice observed; and turning around Archer saw Lawrence Lefferts at his elbow, pulling an imperturbable moustache and affecting not to glance at the message.

"Hallo, Newland: thought I'd catch you here. I've just heard of old Mrs. Mingott's stroke; and as I was on my way to the house I saw you turning down this street and nipped after you. I suppose you've come from there?"

Archer nodded, and pushed his telegram under the lattice.

"Very bad, eh?" Lefferts continued. "Wiring to the family, I suppose. I gather it *is* bad, if you're including Countess Olenska."

Archer's lips stiffened; he felt a savage impulse to dash his fist into the long vain handsome face at his side.

Western Union   The Western Union Telegraph Company receives and transmits telegraph messages. The building, located at Broadway and Dey Street, was at the time the nation's tallest office building.

"Why?" he questioned.

Lefferts, who was known to shrink from discussion, raised his eyebrows with an ironic grimace that warned the other of the watching damsel behind the lattice. Nothing could be worse "form," the look reminded Archer, than any display of temper in a public place.

Archer had never been more indifferent to the requirements of form; but his impulse to do Lawrence Lefferts a physical injury was only momentary. The idea of bandying Ellen Olenska's name with him at such a time, and on whatsoever provocation, was unthinkable. He paid for his telegram, and the two young men went out together into the street. There Archer, having regained his self-control, went on: "Mrs. Mingott is much better: the doctor feels no anxiety whatever"; and Lefferts, with profuse expressions of relief, asked him if he had heard that there were beastly bad rumours again about Beaufort. . . .

That afternoon the announcement of the Beaufort failure was in all the papers. It overshadowed the report of Mrs. Manson Mingott's stroke, and only the few who had heard of the mysterious connection between the two events thought of ascribing old Catherine's illness to anything but the accumulation of flesh and years.

The whole of New York was darkened by the tale of Beaufort's dishonour. There had never, as Mr. Letterblair said, been a worse case in his memory, nor, for that matter, in the memory of the far-off Letterblair who had given his name to the firm. The bank had continued to take in money for a whole day after its failure was inevitable; and as many of its clients belonged to one or another of the ruling clans, Beaufort's duplicity seemed doubly cynical. If Mrs. Beaufort had not taken the tone that such misfortunes (the word was her own) were "the test of friendship," compassion for her might have tempered the general indignation against her husband. As it was—and especially after the object of her nocturnal visit to Mrs. Manson Mingott had become known—her cynicism was held to exceed his; and she had not the excuse—nor her detractors the satisfaction—of pleading that she was "a foreigner." It was some comfort (to those whose securities were not in jeopardy) to be able to remind themselves that Beaufort *was;* but, after all, if a Dallas of South Carolina took his view of the case, and glibly talked of his soon being "on his feet again," the argument lost its edge, and there was nothing to do but to accept this awful evidence of the indissolubility of marriage. Society must manage to get on without the Beauforts, and there was an end of it—except indeed for such hapless victims of the disaster as Medora Manson, the poor old Miss Lannings, and certain other misguided ladies of good family who, if only they had listened to Mr. Henry van der Luyden . . .

"The best thing the Beauforts can do," said Mrs. Archer, summing it up as if she were pronouncing a diagnosis and prescribing a course of treatment, "is to go and live at Regina's little place in North Carolina. Beaufort has always kept a racing stable, and he had better breed trotting horses. I should say he had all the qualities of a successful horse-dealer." Every one agreed with her, but no one condescended to enquire what the Beauforts really meant to do.

The next day Mrs. Manson Mingott was much better: she recovered her voice sufficiently to give orders that no one should mention the Beauforts to her again, and asked—when Dr. Bencomb appeared—what in the world her family meant by making such a fuss about her health.

"If people of my age *will* eat chicken-salad in the evening what are they to expect?" she enquired; and, the doctor having opportunely modified her dietary, the stroke was transformed into an attack of indigestion. But in spite of her firm tone old Catherine did not wholly recover her former attitude toward life. The growing remoteness of old age, though it had not diminished her curiosity about her neighbours, had blunted her never very lively compassion for their troubles; and she seemed to have no difficulty in putting the Beaufort disaster out of her mind. But for the first time she became absorbed in her own symptoms, and began to take a sentimental interest in certain members of her family to whom she had hitherto been contemptuously indifferent.

Mr. Welland, in particular, had the privilege of attracting her notice. Of her sons-in-law he was the one she had most consistently ignored; and all his wife's efforts to represent him as a man of forceful character and marked intellectual ability (if he had only "chosen") had been met with a derisive chuckle. But his eminence as a valetudinarian now made him an object of engrossing interest, and Mrs. Mingott issued an imperial summons to him to come and compare diets as soon as his temperature permitted; for old Catherine was now the first to recognise that one could not be too careful about temperatures.

Twenty-four hours after Madame Olenska's summons a telegram announced that she would arrive from Washington on the evening of the following day. At the Wellands', where the Newland Archers chanced to be lunching, the question as to who should meet her at Jersey City was

---

valetudinarian   A person excessively preoccupied with his or her health.

Jersey City   Built largely on an island, New York City depended on ferries before it had bridges and tunnels. Service from the south provided by the Pennsylvania Railroad ended in Jersey City, New Jersey, where the New York and Erie Railroad built elaborate

immediately raised; and the material difficulties amid which the Welland household struggled as if it had been a frontier outpost, lent animation to the debate. It was agreed that Mrs. Welland could not possibly go to Jersey City because she was to accompany her husband to old Catherine's that afternoon, and the brougham could not be spared, since, if Mr. Welland were "upset" by seeing his mother-in-law for the first time after her attack, he might have to be taken home at a moment's notice. The Welland sons would of course be "down town," Mr. Lovell Mingott would be just hurrying back from his shooting, and the Mingott carriage engaged in meeting him; and one could not ask May, at the close of a winter afternoon, to go alone across the ferry to Jersey City, even in her own carriage. Nevertheless, it might appear inhospitable—and contrary to old Catherine's express wishes—if Madame Olenska were allowed to arrive without any of the family being at the station to receive her. It was just like Ellen, Mrs. Welland's tired voice implied, to place the family in such a dilemma. "It's always one thing after another," the poor lady grieved, in one of her rare revolts against fate; "the only thing that makes me think Mamma must be less well than Dr. Bencomb will admit is this morbid desire to have Ellen come at once, however inconvenient it is to meet her."

The words had been thoughtless, as the utterances of impatience often are; and Mr. Welland was upon them with a pounce.

"Augusta," he said, turning pale and laying down his fork, "have you any other reason for thinking that Bencomb is less to be relied on than he was? Have you noticed that he has been less conscientious than usual in following up my case or your mother's?"

It was Mrs. Welland's turn to grow pale as the endless consequences of her blunder unrolled themselves before her; but she managed to laugh, and take a second helping of scalloped oysters, before she said, struggling back into her old armour of cheerfulness: "My dear, how could you imagine such a thing? I only meant that, after the decided stand Mamma took about its being Ellen's duty to go back to her husband, it seems strange that she should be seized with this sudden whim to see her, when there are half a dozen other grandchildren that she might have asked for. But we must never forget that Mamma, in spite of her wonderful vitality, is a very old woman."

Mr. Welland's brow remained clouded, and it was evident that his perturbed imagination had fastened at once on this last remark. "Yes: your

---

terminal facilities in 1861. Access to New York was by boats that were double ended to obviate the need for turning at terminals and to accommodate horse-drawn carriages as well as pedestrians.

scalloped oysters   Scalloped foods are cooked in a casserole with milk and often bread crumbs. Oysters were a common dish in the late nineteenth century.

mother's a very old woman; and for all we know Bencomb may not be as successful with very old people. As you say, my dear, it's always one thing after another; and in another ten or fifteen years I suppose I shall have the pleasing duty of looking about for a new doctor. It's always better to make such a change before it's absolutely necessary." And having arrived at this Spartan decision Mr. Welland firmly took up his fork.

"But all the while," Mrs. Welland began again, as she rose from the luncheon-table, and led the way into the wilderness of purple satin and malachite known as the back drawing-room, "I don't see how Ellen's to be got here tomorrow evening; and I do like to have things settled for a least twenty-four hours ahead."

Archer turned from the fascinated contemplation of a small painting representing two Cardinals carousing, in an octagonal ebony frame set with medallions of onyx.

"Shall I fetch her?" he proposed. "I can easily get away from the office in time to meet the brougham at the ferry, if May will send it there." His heart was beating excitedly as he spoke.

Mrs. Welland heaved a sigh of gratitude, and May, who had moved away to the window, turned to shed on him a beam of approval. "So you see, Mamma, everything *will* be settled twenty-four hours in advance," she said, stooping over to kiss her mother's troubled forehead.

May's brougham awaited her at the door, and she was to drive Archer to Union Square, where he could pick up a Broadway car to carry him to the office. As she settled herself in her corner she said: "I didn't want to worry Mamma by raising fresh obstacles; but how can you meet Ellen tomorrow, and bring her back to New York, when you're going to Washington?"

"Oh, I'm not going," Archer answered.

"Not going? Why, what's happened?" Her voice was as clear as a bell, and full of wifely solicitude.

"The case is off—postponed."

"Postponed? How odd! I saw a note this morning from Mr. Letter-blair to Mamma saying that he was going to Washington tomorrow for the

---

Spartan   Simple and harsh, taken from the disciplined life of an ancient Greek people, the Spartans.

Union Square   An area located between Broadway and Park Avenue South, between 17th and 14th Streets. Originally part of a privately owned farm, it opened as a park in 1831 and was soon surrounded by elegant mansions, theaters, and concert halls, including the Academy of Music. Between 1860 and 1910, retail stores such as Tiffany's opened and Union Square became the midpoint of a fashionable shopping district known as the Ladies' Mile.

big patent case that he was to argue before the Supreme Court. You said it
was a patent case, didn't you?"

"Well—that's it: the whole office can't go. Letterblair decided to go
this morning."

"Then it's *not* postponed?" she continued, with an insistence so unlike her that he felt the blood rising to his face, as if he were blushing for
her unwonted lapse from all the traditional delicacies.

"No: but my going is," he answered, cursing the unnecessary ex-
planations that he had given when he had announced his intention of going to Washington, and wondering where he had read that clever liars give
details, but that the cleverest do not. It did not hurt him half as much to
tell May an untruth as to see her trying to pretend that she had not de-
tected him.

"I'm not going till later on: luckily for the convenience of your
family," he continued, taking base refuge in sarcasm. As he spoke he felt
that she was looking at him, and he turned his eyes to hers in order not to
appear to be avoiding them. Their glances met for a second, and perhaps
let them into each other's meanings more deeply than either cared to go.

"Yes; it *is* awfully convenient," May brightly agreed, "that you should
be able to meet Ellen after all; you saw how much Mamma appreciated
your offering to do it."

"Oh, I'm delighted to do it." The carriage stopped, and as he jumped
out she leaned to him and laid her hand on his. "Good-bye, dearest," she
said, her eyes so blue that he wondered afterward if they had shone on him
through tears.

He turned away and hurried across Union Square, repeating to himself, in a sort of inward chant: "It's all of two hours from Jersey City to old
Catherine's. It's all of two hours—and it may be more."

XXIX

His wife's dark blue brougham (with the wedding varnish still on it) met
Archer at the ferry, and conveyed him luxuriously to the Pennsylvania ter-
minus in Jersey City.

It was a sombre snowy afternoon, and the gas-lamps were lit in the big
reverberating station. As he paced the platform, waiting for the Washington
express, he remembered that there were people who thought there would
one day be a tunnel under the Hudson through which the trains of the
Pennsylvania railway would run straight into New York. They were of the
brotherhood of visionaries who likewise predicted the building of ships
that would cross the Atlantic in five days, the invention of a flying machine,

lighting by electricity, telephonic communication without wires, and other Arabian Night marvels.

"I don't care which of their visions comes true," Archer mused, "as long as the tunnel isn't built yet." In his senseless school-boy happiness he pictured Madame Olenska's descent from the train, his discovery of her a long way off, among the throngs of meaningless faces, her clinging to his arm as he guided her to the carriage, their slow approach to the wharf among slipping horses, laden carts, vociferating teamsters, and then the startling quiet of the ferry-boat, where they would sit side by side under the snow, in the motionless carriage, while the earth seemed to glide away under them, rolling to the other side of the sun. It was incredible, the number of things he had to say to her, and in what eloquent order they were forming themselves on his lips . . .

The clanging and groaning of the train came nearer, and it staggered slowly into the station like a prey-laden monster into its lair. Archer pushed forward, elbowing through the crowd, and staring blindly into window after window of the high-hung carriages. And then, suddenly, he saw Madame Olenska's pale and surprised face close at hand, and had again the mortified sensation of having forgotten what she looked like.

They reached each other, their hands met, and he drew her arm through his. "This way—I have the carriage," he said.

After that it all happened as he had dreamed. He helped her into the brougham with her bags, and had afterward the vague recollection of having properly reassured her about her grandmother and given her a summary of the Beaufort situation (he was struck by the softness of her: "Poor Regina!"). Meanwhile the carriage had worked its way out of the coil about the station, and they were crawling down the slippery incline to the wharf, menaced by swaying coal-carts, bewildered horses, dishevelled express-wagons, and an empty hearse—ah, that hearse! She shut her eyes as it passed, and clutched at Archer's hand.

"If only it doesn't mean—poor Granny!"

"Oh, no, no—she's much better—she's all right, really. There—we've passed it!" he exclaimed, as if that made all the difference. Her hand remained in his, and as the carriage lurched across the gang-plank onto the ferry he bent over, unbuttoned her tight brown glove, and kissed her palm

---

Arabian Night marvels *The Arabian Nights' Entertainments* or *A Thousand and One Nights* is a collection of fantasy-filled stories, originally in Arabic. They are narrated by Scheherazade, who postponed her execution by telling her royal husband a nightly tale and withholding the story's outcome until the following evening.

teamsters Drivers of teams of horses.

as if he had kissed a relic. She disengaged herself with a faint smile, and he said: "You didn't expect me today?"

"Oh, no."

"I meant to go to Washington to see you. I'd made all my arrangements—I very nearly crossed you in the train."

"Oh—" she exclaimed, as if terrified by the narrowness of their escape. "Do you know—I hardly remembered you?"

"Hardly remembered me?"

"I mean: how shall I explain? I—it's always so. *Each time you happen to me all over again.*"

"Oh, yes: I know! I know!"

"Does it—do I too: to you?" he insisted.

She nodded, looking out of the window.

"Ellen—Ellen—Ellen!"

She made no answer, and he sat in silence, watching her profile grow indistinct against the snow-streaked dusk beyond the window. What had she been doing in all those four long months, he wondered? How little they knew of each other, after all! The precious moments were slipping away, but he had forgotten everything that he had meant to say to her and could only helplessly brood on the mystery of their remoteness and their proximity, which seemed to be symbolised by the fact of their sitting so close to each other, and yet being unable to see each other's faces.

"What a pretty carriage! Is it May's?" she asked, suddenly turning her face from the window.

"Yes."

"It was May who sent you to fetch me, then? How kind of her!"

He made no answer for a moment; then he said explosively: "Your husband's secretary came to see me the day after we met in Boston."

In his brief letter to her he had made no allusion to M. Rivière's visit, and his intention had been to bury the incident in his bosom. But her reminder that they were in his wife's carriage provoked him to an impulse of retaliation. He would see if she liked his reference to Rivière any better than he liked hers to May! As on certain other occasions when he had expected to shake her out of her usual composure, she betrayed no sign of surprise: and at once he concluded: "He writes to her, then."

"M. Rivière went to see you?"

"Yes: didn't you know?"

"No," she answered simply.

"And you're not surprised?"

She hesitated. "Why should I be? He told me in Boston that he knew you; that he'd met you in England I think."

"Ellen—I must ask you one thing."

"Yes."

"I wanted to ask it after I saw him, but I couldn't put it in a letter. It was Rivière who helped you to get away—when you left your husband?"

His heart was beating suffocatingly. Would she meet this question with the same composure?

"Yes: I owe him a great debt," she answered, without the least tremor in her quiet voice.

Her tone was so natural, so almost indifferent, that Archer's turmoil subsided. Once more she had managed, by her sheer simplicity, to make him feel stupidly conventional just when he thought he was flinging convention to the winds.

"I think you're the most honest woman I ever met!" he exclaimed.

"Oh, no—but probably one of the least fussy," she answered, a smile in her voice.

"Call it what you like: you look at things as they are."

"Ah—I've had to. I've had to look at the Gorgon."

"Well—it hasn't blinded you! You've seen that she's just an old bogey like all the others."

"She doesn't blind one; but she dries up one's tears."

The answer checked the pleading on Archer's lips: it seemed to come from depths of experience beyond his reach. The slow advance of the ferryboat had ceased, and her bows bumped against the piles of the slip with a violence that made the brougham stagger, and flung Archer and Madam Olenska against each other. The young man, trembling, felt the pressure of her shoulder, and passed his arm about her.

"If you're not blind, then, you must see that this can't last."

"What can't?"

"Our being together—and not together."

"No. You ought not to have come today," she said in an altered voice; and suddenly she turned, flung her arms about his and pressed her lips to his. At the same moment the carriage began to move, and a gas-lamp at the head of the slip flashed its light into the window. She drew away, and they sat silent and motionless while the brougham struggled through the congestion of carriages about the ferry-landing. As they gained the street Archer began to speak hurriedly.

"Don't be afraid of me: you needn't squeeze yourself back into your corner like that. A stolen kiss isn't what I want. Look: I'm not even trying

---

Gorgon In Greek mythology, a loathsome serpent-haired monster whose gaze would turn to stone anyone who looked directly at her.

to touch the sleeve of your jacket. Don't suppose that I don't understand your reasons for not wanting to let this feeling between us dwindle
into an ordinary hole-and-corner love-affair. I couldn't have spoken like
this yesterday, because when we've been apart, and I'm looking forward
to seeing you, every thought is burnt up in a great flame. But then you
come; and you're so much more than I remembered, and what I want
of you is so much more than an hour or two every now and then, with
wastes of thirsty waiting between, that I can sit perfectly still beside you,
like this, with that other vision in my mind, just quietly trusting to it to
come true."

For a moment she made no reply; then she asked, hardly above a whisper: "What do you mean by trusting to it to come true?"

"Why—you know it will, don't you?"

"Your vision of you and me together?" She burst into a sudden hard
laugh. "You choose your place well to put it to me!"

"Do you mean because we're in my wife's brougham? Shall we get out
and walk, then? I don't suppose you mind a little snow?"

She laughed again, more gently. "No; I shan't get out and walk, because my business is to get to Granny's as quickly as I can. And you'll sit
beside me, and we'll look, not at visions, but at realities."

"I don't know what you mean by realities. The only reality to me is
this."

She met the words with a long silence, during which the carriage
rolled down an obscure side-street and then turned into the searching illumination of Fifth Avenue.

"Is it your idea, then, that I should live with you as your mistress—
since I can't be your wife?" she asked.

The crudeness of the question startled him: the word was one that
women of his class fought shy of, even when their talk flitted closest about
the topic. He noticed that Madame Olenska pronounced it as if it had a
recognised place in her vocabulary, and he wondered if it had been used
familiarly in her presence in the horrible life she had fled from. Her question pulled him up with a jerk, and he floundered.

"I want—I want somehow to get away with you into a world where
words like that—categories like that—won't exist. Where we shall be simply two human beings who love each other, who are the whole of life to
each other; and nothing else on earth will matter."

She drew a deep sigh that ended in another laugh. "Oh, my dear—
where is that country? Have you ever been there?" she asked; and as he remained sullenly dumb she went on: "I know so many who've tried to find
it; and, believe me, they all got out by mistake at wayside stations: at places

like Boulogne, or Pisa, or Monte Carlo—and it wasn't at all different from the old world they'd left, but only rather smaller and dingier and more promiscuous."

He had never heard her speak in such a tone, and he remembered the phrase she had used a little while before.

"Yes, the Gorgon *has* dried your tears," he said.

"Well, she opened my eyes too; it's a delusion to say that she blinds people. What she does is just the contrary—she fastens their eyelids open, so that they're never again in the blessed darkness. Isn't there a Chinese torture like that? There ought to be. Ah, believe me, it's a miserable little country!"

The carriage had crossed Forty-second Street: May's sturdy brougham-horse was carrying them northward as if he had been a Kentucky trotter. Archer choked with the sense of wasted minutes and vain words.

"Then what, exactly, is your plan for us?" he asked.

"For *us?* But there's no *us* in that sense! We're near each other only if we stay far from each other. Then we can be ourselves. Otherwise we're only Newland Archer, the husband of Ellen Olenska's cousin, and Ellen Olenska, the cousin of Newland Archer's wife, trying to be happy behind the backs of the people who trust them."

"Ah, I'm beyond that," he groaned.

"No, you're not! You've never been beyond. And *I* have," she said, in a strange voice, "and I know what it looks like there."

He sat silent, dazed with inarticulate pain. Then he groped in the darkness of the carriage for the little bell that signalled orders to the coachman. He remembered that May rang twice when she wished to stop. He pressed the bell, and the carriage drew up beside the curbstone.

"Why are we stopping? This is not Granny's," Madame Olenska exclaimed.

"No: I shall get out here," he stammered, opening the door and jumping to the pavement. By the light of a street-lamp he saw her startled face, and the instinctive motion she made to detain him. He closed the door, and leaned for a moment in the window.

"You're right: I ought not to have come today," he said, lowering his voice so that the coachman should not hear. She bent forward, and seemed

---

Boulogne   A seaport in northwestern France on the coast of the English Channel.

Pisa   An historic town in western Italy on the banks of the Arno River, site of the famous Leaning Tower.

Monte Carlo   A resort town on a rocky promontory in Monaco, on the Mediterranean Riviera.

about to speak; but he had already called out the order to drive on, and the carriage rolled away while he stood on the corner. The snow was over, and a tingling wind had sprung up, that lashed his face as he stood gazing. Suddenly he felt something stiff and cold on his lashes, and perceived that he had been crying, and that the wind had frozen his tears.

He thrust his hands in his pockets, and walked at a sharp pace down Fifth Avenue to his own house.

XXX

That evening when Archer came down before dinner he found the drawing-room empty.

He and May were dining alone, all the family engagements having been postponed since Mrs. Manson Mingott's illness; and as May was the more punctual of the two he was surprised that she had not preceded him. He knew that she was at home, for while he dressed he had heard her moving about in her room; and he wondered what had delayed her.

He had fallen into the way of dwelling on such conjectures as a means of tying his thoughts fast to reality. Sometimes he felt as if he had found the clue to his father-in-law's absorption in trifles; perhaps even Mr. Welland, long ago, had had escapes and visions, and had conjured up all the hosts of domesticity to defend himself against them.

When May appeared he thought she looked tired. She had put on the low-necked and tightly-laced dinner-dress which the Mingott ceremonial exacted on the most informal occasions, and had built her fair hair into its usual accumulated coils; and her face, in contrast, was wan and almost faded. But she shone on him with her usual tenderness, and her eyes had kept the blue dazzle of the day before.

"What became of you, dear?" she asked. "I was waiting at Granny's, and Ellen came alone, and said she had dropped you on the way because you had to rush off on business. There's nothing wrong?"

"Only some letters I'd forgotten, and wanted to get off before dinner."

"Ah—" she said; and a moment afterward: "I'm sorry you didn't come to Granny's—unless the letters were urgent."

"They were," he rejoined, surprised at her insistence. "Besides, I don't see why I should have gone to your grandmother's. I didn't know you were there."

She turned and moved to the looking-glass above the mantelpiece. As she stood there, lifting her long arm to fasten a puff that had slipped from its place in her intricate hair, Archer was struck by something languid and inelastic in her attitude, and wondered if the deadly monotony of their lives had laid its weight on her also. Then he remembered that, as he had left the house that morning, she had called over the stairs that she would meet him at her grandmother's so that they might drive home together. He had called back a cheery "Yes!" and then, absorbed in other visions, had forgotten his promise. Now he was smitten with compunction, yet irritated that so trifling an omission should be stored up against him after nearly two years of marriage. He was weary of living in a perpetual tepid honeymoon, without the temperature of passion yet with all its exactions. If May had spoken out her grievances (he suspected her of many) he might have laughed them away; but she was trained to conceal imaginary wounds under a Spartan smile.

To disguise his own annoyance he asked how her grandmother was, and she answered that Mrs. Mingott was still improving, but had been rather disturbed by the last news about the Beauforts.

"What news?"

"It seems they're going to stay in New York. I believe he's going into an insurance business, or something. They're looking about for a small house."

The preposterousness of the case was beyond discussion, and they went in to dinner. During dinner their talk moved in its usual limited circle; but Archer noticed that his wife made no allusion to Madame Olenska, nor to old Catherine's reception of her. He was thankful for the fact, yet felt it to be vaguely ominous.

They went up to the library for coffee, and Archer lit a cigar and took down a volume of Michelet. He had taken to history in the evenings since May had shown a tendency to ask him to read aloud whenever she saw him with a volume of poetry: not that he disliked the sound of his own voice, but because he could always foresee her comments on what he read. In the days of their engagement she had simply (as he now perceived) echoed what he told her; but since he had ceased to provide her with opinions she had begun to hazard her own, with results destructive to his enjoyment of the works commented on.

Seeing that he had chosen history she fetched her work-basket, drew up an arm-chair to the green-shaded student lamp, and uncovered a cushion she was embroidering for his sofa. She was not a clever needle-woman; her large capable hands were made for riding, rowing and open-air

---

Michelet   Jules Michelet (1798–1874) was a French historian whose nationalism, rejection of the central role of class conflict in history, and Romantic insistence on the organic unity of the nation made him seem old-fashioned and *petit-bourgeois* to some historians. Archer's preference for this book may indicate his own Romantic and conservative qualities.

activities; but since other wives embroidered cushions for their husbands she did not wish to omit this last link in her devotion.

She was so placed that Archer, by merely raising his eyes, could see her bent above her work-frame, her ruffled elbow-sleeves slipping back from her firm round arms, the betrothal sapphire shining on her left hand above her broad gold wedding-ring, and the right hand slowly and laboriously stabbing the canvas. As she sat thus, the lamplight full on her clear brow, he said to himself with a secret dismay that he would always know the thoughts behind it, that never, in all the years to come, would she surprise him by an unexpected mood, by a new idea, a weakness, a cruelty or an emotion. She had spent her poetry and romance on their short courting: the function was exhausted because the need was past. Now she was simply ripening into a copy of her mother, and mysteriously, by the very process, trying to turn him into a Mr. Welland. He laid down his book and stood up impatiently; and at once she raised her head.

"What's the matter?"

"The room is stifling: I want a little air."

He had insisted that the library curtains should draw backward and forward on a rod, so that they might be closed in the evening, instead of remaining nailed to a gilt cornice, and immovably looped up over layers of lace, as in the drawing-room; and he pulled them back and pushed up the sash, leaning out into the icy night. The mere fact of not looking at May, seated beside his table, under his lamp, the fact of seeing other houses, roofs, chimneys, of getting the sense of other lives outside his own, other cities beyond New York, and a whole world beyond his world, cleared his brain and made it easier to breathe.

After he had leaned out into the darkness for a few minutes he heard her say: "Newland! Do shut the window. You'll catch your death."

He pulled the sash down and turned back. "Catch my death!" he echoed; and he felt like adding: "But I've caught it already. I *am* dead— I've been dead for months and months."

And suddenly the play of the word flashed up a wild suggestion. What if it were *she* who was dead! If she were going to die—to die soon—and leave him free! The sensation of standing there, in that warm familiar room, and looking at her, and wishing her dead, was so strange, so fascinating and overmastering, that its enormity did not immediately strike him. He simply felt that chance had given him a new possibility to which his sick soul might cling. Yes, May might die—people

---

cornice   An ornamental horizontal molding or frame used to conceal rods, picture hooks, or other devices.

did: young people, healthy people like herself: she might die, and set him suddenly free.

She glanced up, and he saw by her widening eyes that there must be something strange in his own.

"Newland! Are you ill?"

He shook his head and turned toward his arm-chair. She bent over her work-frame, and as he passed he laid his hand on her hair. "Poor May!" he said.

"Poor? Why poor?" she echoed with a strained laugh.

"Because I shall never be able to open a window without worrying you," he rejoined, laughing also.

For a moment she was silent; then she said very low, her head bowed over her work: "I shall never worry if you're happy."

"Ah, my dear; and I shall never be happy unless I can open the windows!"

"In *this* weather?" she remonstrated; and with a sigh he buried his head in his book.

Six or seven days passed. Archer heard nothing from Madame Olenska, and became aware that her name would not be mentioned in his presence by any member of the family. He did not try to see her; to do so while she was at old Catherine's guarded bedside would have been almost impossible. In the uncertainty of the situation he let himself drift, conscious, somewhere below the surface of his thoughts, of a resolve which had come to him when he had leaned out from his library window into the icy night. The strength of that resolve made it easy to wait and make no sign.

Then one day May told him that Mrs. Manson Mingott had asked to see him. There was nothing surprising in the request, for the old lady was steadily recovering, and she had always openly declared that she preferred Archer to any of her other grandsons-in-law. May gave the message with evident pleasure: she was proud of old Catherine's appreciation of her husband.

There was a moment's pause, and then Archer felt it incumbent on him to say: "All right. Shall we go together this afternoon?"

His wife's face brightened, but she instantly answered: "Oh, you'd much better go alone. It bores Granny to see the same people too often."

Archer's heart was beating violently when he rang old Mrs. Mingott's bell. He had wanted above all things to go alone, for he felt sure the visit would give him the chance of saying a word in private to the Countess Olenska. He had determined to wait till the chance presented itself naturally; and here it was, and here he was on the doorstep. Behind the door, behind the curtains of the yellow damask room next to the hall, she was surely awaiting him; in another moment he should see her, and be able to speak to her before she led him to the sick-room.

He wanted only to put one question: after that his course would be clear. What he wished to ask was simply the date of her return to Washington; and that question she could hardly refuse to answer.

But in the yellow sitting-room it was the mulatto maid who waited. Her white teeth shining like a keyboard, she pushed back the sliding doors and ushered him into old Catherine's presence.

The old woman sat in a vast throne-like arm-chair near her bed. Beside her was a mahogany stand bearing a cast bronze lamp with an engraved globe, over which a green paper shade had been balanced. There was not a book or a newspaper in reach, nor any evidence of feminine employment: conversation had always been Mrs. Mingott's sole pursuit, and she would have scorned to feign an interest in fancywork.

Archer saw no trace of the slight distortion left by her stroke. She merely looked paler, with darker shadows in the folds and recesses of her obesity; and, in the fluted mob-cap tied by a starched bow between her first two chins, and the muslin kerchief crossed over her billowing purple dressing-gown, she seemed like some shrewd and kindly ancestress of her own who might have yielded too freely to the pleasures of the table.

She held out one of the little hands that nestled in a hollow of her huge lap like pet animals, and called to the maid: "Don't let in any one else. If my daughters call, say I'm asleep."

The maid disappeared, and the old lady turned to her grandson.

"My dear, am I perfectly hideous?" she asked gaily, launching out one hand in search of the folds of muslin on her inaccessible bosom. "My daughters tell me it doesn't matter at my age—as if hideousness didn't matter all the more the harder it gets to conceal!"

"My dear, you're handsomer than ever!" Archer rejoined in the same tone; and she threw back her head and laughed.

"Ah, but not as handsome as Ellen!" she jerked out, twinkling at him maliciously; and before he could answer she added: "Was she so awfully handsome the day you drove her up from the ferry?"

---

mulatto maid . . . teeth shining like a keyboard   Wharton emphasizes the dark skin of Mrs. Mingott's maid with a simile that disparages and stereotypes. The number of domestic positions available to African Americans shrank from mid-century on, as groups of Irish, German, and Italian immigrants took over these positions. The fact that Mrs. Mingott employs a person who is part African American at this time may further illustrate her tendency to depart from social norms.

mob-cap   A large round cotton cap that covers the hair, worn by women in the eighteenth century.

He laughed, and she continued: "Was it because you told her so that she had to put you out on the way? In my youth young men didn't desert pretty women unless they were made to!" She gave another chuckle, and interrupted it to say almost querulously: "It's a pity she didn't marry you; I always told her so. It would have spared me all this worry. But who ever thought of sparing their grandmother worry?"

Archer wondered if her illness had blurred her faculties; but suddenly she broke out: "Well, it's settled, anyhow: she's going to stay with me, whatever the rest of the family say! She hadn't been here five minutes before I'd have gone down on my knees to keep her—if only, for the last twenty years, I'd been able to see where the floor was!"

Archer listened in silence, and she went on: "They'd talked me over, as no doubt you know: persuaded me, Lovell, and Letterblair, and Augusta Welland, and all the rest of them, that I must hold out and cut off her allowance, till she was made to see that it was her duty to go back to Olenski. They thought they'd convinced me when the secretary, or whatever he was, came out with the last proposals: handsome proposals I confess they were. After all, marriage is marriage, and money's money—both useful things in their way . . . and I didn't know what to answer—" She broke off and drew a long breath, as if speaking had become an effort. "But the minute I laid eyes on her, I said: 'You sweet bird, you! Shut you up in that cage again? Never!' And now it's settled that she's to stay here and nurse her Granny as long as there's a Granny to nurse. It's not a gay prospect, but she doesn't mind; and of course I've told Letterblair that she's to be given her proper allowance."

The young man heard her with veins aglow; but in his confusion of mind he hardly knew whether her news brought joy or pain. He had so definitely decided on the course he meant to pursue that for the moment he could not readjust his thoughts. But gradually there stole over him the delicious sense of difficulties deferred and opportunities miraculously provided. If Ellen had consented to come and live with her grandmother it must surely be because she had recognised the impossibility of giving him up. This was her answer to his final appeal of the other day: if she would not take the extreme step he had urged, she had at last yielded to half-measures. He sank back into the thought with the involuntary relief of a man who has been ready to risk everything, and suddenly tastes the dangerous sweetness of security.

"She couldn't have gone back—it was impossible!" he exclaimed.

"Ah, my dear, I always knew you were on her side; and that's why I sent for you today, and why I said to your pretty wife, when she proposed to come with you: 'No, my dear, I'm pining to see Newland, and I don't want anybody to share out transports.' For you see, my dear—" she drew

her head back as far as its tethering chins permitted, and looked him full
in the eyes—"you see, we shall have a fight yet. The family don't want her
here, and they'll say it's because I've been ill, because I'm a weak old woman,
that she's persuaded me. I'm not well enough yet to fight them one by one,
and you've got to do it for me."

"I?" he stammered.

"You. Why not?" she jerked back at him, her round eyes suddenly as
sharp as pen-knives. Her hand fluttered from its chair-arm and lit on his
with a clutch of little pale nails like bird-claws. "Why not?" she search-
ingly repeated.

Archer, under the exposure of her gaze, had recovered his self-
possession.

"Oh, I don't count—I'm too insignificant."

"Well, you're Letterblair's partner, ain't you? You've got to get at them
through Letterblair. Unless you've got a reason," she insisted.

"Oh, my dear, I back you to hold your own against them all without
my help; but you shall have it if you need it," he reassured her.

"Then we're safe!" she sighed; and smiling on him with all her ancient
cunning she added, as she settled her head among the cushions: "I always
knew you'd back us up, because they never quote you when they talk
about its being her duty to go home."

He winced a little at her terrifying perspicacity, and longed to ask:
"And May—do they quote her?" But he judged it safer to turn the question.

"And Madame Olenska? When am I to see her?" he said.

The old lady chuckled, crumpled her lids, and went through the pantomime of archness. "Not today. One at a time, please. Madame Olenska's
gone out."

He flushed with disappointment, and she went on: "She's gone out,
my child: gone in my carriage to see Regina Beaufort."

She paused for this announcement to produce its effect. "That's what
she's reduced me to already. The day after she got here she put on her best
bonnet, and told me, as cool as a cucumber, that she was going to call on
Regina Beaufort. 'I don't know her; who is she?' says I. 'She's your grand-
niece, and a most unhappy woman,' she says. 'She's the wife of a scoundrel,'
I answered. 'Well,' she says, 'and so am I, and yet all my family want me
to go back to him.' Well, that floored me, and I let her go; and finally one
day she said it was raining too hard to go out on foot, and she wanted me
to lend her my carriage. 'What for?' I asked her; and she said: 'To go and
see cousin Regina'—cousin! Now, my dear, I looked out of the window,
and saw it wasn't raining a drop; but I understood her, and I let her have
the carriage . . . After all, Regina's a brave woman, and so is she; and I've
always liked courage above everything."

Archer bent down and pressed his lips on the little hand that still lay on his.

"Eh—eh—eh! Whose hand did you think you were kissing, young man—your wife's, I hope?" the old lady snapped out with her mocking cackle; and as he rose to go she called out after him: "Give her her Granny's love; but you'd better not say anything about our talk."

XXXI

Archer had been stunned by old Catherine's news. It was only natural that Madame Olenska should have hastened from Washington in response to her grandmother's summons; but that she should have decided to remain under her roof—especially now that Mrs. Mingott had almost regained her health—was less easy to explain.

Archer was sure that Madame Olenska's decision had not been influenced by the change in her financial situation. He knew the exact figure of the small income which her husband had allowed her at their separation. Without the addition of her grandmother's allowance it was hardly enough to live on, in any sense known to the Mingott vocabulary; and now that Medora Manson, who shared her life, had been ruined, such a pittance would barely keep the two women clothed and fed. Yet Archer was convinced that Madame Olenska had not accepted her grandmother's offer from interested motives.

She had the heedless generosity and the spasmodic extravagance of persons used to large fortunes, and indifferent to money; but she could go without many things which her relations considered indispensable, and Mrs. Lovell Mingott and Mrs. Welland had often been heard to deplore that any one who had enjoyed the cosmopolitan luxuries of Count Olenski's establishments should care so little about "how things were done." Moreover, as Archer knew, several months had passed since her allowance had been cut off; yet in the interval she had made no effort to regain her grandmother's favour. Therefore if she had changed her course it must be for a different reason.

He did not have far to seek for that reason. On the way from the ferry she had told him that he and she must remain apart; but she had said it with her head on his breast. He knew that there was no calculated coquetry in her words; she was fighting her fate as he had fought his, and clinging desperately to her resolve that they should not break faith with the people who trusted them. But during the ten days which had elapsed since her return to New York she had perhaps guessed from his silence, and from the fact of his making no attempt to see her, that he was meditating a decisive step, a step from which there was no turning back. At the thought, a sudden fear of her own weakness might have seized her, and she might have felt that, after all, it was better to accept the compromise usual in such cases, and follow the line of least resistance.

An hour earlier, when he had rung Mrs. Mingott's bell, Archer had fancied that his path was clear before him. He had meant to have a word alone with Madame Olenska, and failing that, to learn from her grandmother on what day, and by which train, she was returning to Washington. In that train he intended to join her, and travel with her to Washington, or as much farther as she was willing to go. His own fancy inclined to Japan. At any rate she would understand at once that, wherever she went, he was going. He meant to leave a note for May that should cut off any other alternative.

He had fancied himself not only nerved for this plunge but eager to take it; yet his first feeling on hearing that the course of events was changed had been one of relief. Now, however, as he walked home from Mrs. Mingott's, he was conscious of a growing distaste for what lay before him. There was nothing unknown or unfamiliar in the path he was presumably to tread; but when he had trodden it before it was as a free man, who was accountable to no one for his actions, and could lend himself with an amused detachment to the game of precautions and prevarications, concealments and compliances, that the part required. This procedure was called "protecting a woman's honour"; and the best fiction, combined with the after-dinner talk of his elders, had long since initiated him into every detail of its code.

Now he saw the matter in a new light, and his part in it seemed singularly diminished. It was, in fact, that which, with a secret fatuity, he had watched Mrs. Thorley Rushworth play toward a fond and unperceiving husband: a smiling, bantering, humouring, watchful and incessant lie. A lie by day, a lie by night, a lie in every touch and every look; a lie in every caress and every quarrel; a lie in every word and in every silence.

It was easier, and less dastardly on the whole, for a wife to play such a part toward her husband. A woman's standard of truthfulness was tacitly held to be lower: she was the subject creature, and versed in the arts of the enslaved. Then she could always plead moods and nerves, and the right not to be held too strictly to account; and even in the most strait-laced societies the laugh was always against the husband.

But in Archer's little world no one laughed at a wife deceived, and a certain measure of contempt was attached to men who continued their

---

Japan   While the European continent remained the most popular travel destination of post–Civil War Americans, there was increasing interest in visiting Africa and Asia.

philandering after marriage. In the rotation of crops there was a recognised season for wild oats; but they were not to be sown more than once.

Archer had always shared this view: in his heart he thought Lefferts despicable. But to love Ellen Olenska was not to become a man like Lefferts: for the first time Archer found himself face to face with the dread argument of the individual case. Ellen Olenska was like no other woman, he was like no other man: their situation, therefore, resembled no one else's, and they were answerable to no tribunal but that of their own judgment.

Yes, but in ten minutes more he would be mounting his own doorstep; and there were May, and habit, and honour, and all the old decencies that he and his people had always believed in . . .

At his corner he hesitated, and then walked on down Fifth Avenue.

Ahead of him, in the winter night, loomed a big unlit house. As he drew near he thought how often he had seen it blazing with lights, its steps awninged and carpeted, and carriages waiting in double line to draw up at the curbstone. It was in the conservatory that stretched its dead-black bulk down the side street that he had taken his first kiss from May; it was under the myriad candles of the ball-room that he had seen her appear, tall and silver-shining as a young Diana.

Now the house was as dark as the grave, except for a faint flare of gas in the basement, and a light in one upstairs room where the blind had not been lowered. As Archer reached the corner he saw that the carriage standing at the door was Mrs. Manson Mingott's. What an opportunity for Sillerton Jackson, if he should chance to pass! Archer had been greatly moved by old Catherine's account of Madame Olenska's attitude toward Mrs. Beaufort; it made the righteous reprobation of New York seem like a passing by on the other side. But he knew well enough what construction the clubs and drawing-rooms would put on Ellen Olenska's visits to her cousin.

He paused and looked up at the lighted window. No doubt the two women were sitting together in that room: Beaufort had probably sought consolation elsewhere. There were even rumours that he had left New York with Fanny Ring; but Mrs. Beaufort's attitude made the report seem improbable.

Archer had the nocturnal perspective of Fifth Avenue almost to himself. At that hour most people were indoors, dressing for dinner; and he was secretly glad that Ellen's exit was likely to be unobserved. As the thought passed through his mind the door opened, and she came out. Behind her was a faint light, such as might have been carried down the stairs to show her the way. She turned to say a word to some one; then the door closed, and she came down the steps.

"Ellen," he said in a low voice, as she reached the pavement.

She stopped with a slight start, and just then he saw two young men of fashionable cut approaching. There was a familiar air about their overcoats and the way their smart silk mufflers were folded over their white ties; and he wondered how youths of their quality happened to be dining out so early. Then he remembered that the Reggie Chiverses, whose house was a few doors above, were taking a large party that evening to see Adelaide Neilson in Romeo and Juliet, and guessed that the two were of the number. They passed under a lamp, and he recognised Lawrence Lefferts and a young Chivers.

A mean desire not to have Madame Olenska seen at the Beaufort's door vanished as he felt the penetrating warmth of her hand.

"I shall see you now—we shall be together," he broke out, hardly knowing what he said.

"Ah," she answered, "Granny has told you?"

While he watched her he was aware that Lefferts and Chivers, on reaching the farther side of the street corner, had discreetly struck away across Fifth Avenue. It was the kind of masculine solidarity that he himself often practised; now he sickened at their connivance. Did she really imagine that he and she could live like this? And if not, what else did she imagine?

"Tomorrow I must see you—somewhere where we can be alone," he said, in a voice that sounded almost angry to his own ears.

She wavered, and moved toward the carriage.

"But I shall be at Granny's—for the present that is," she added, as if conscious that her change of plans required some explanation.

"Somewhere where we can be alone," he insisted.

She gave a faint laugh that grated on him.

"In New York? But there are no churches . . . no monuments."

"There's the Art Museum—in the Park," he explained, as she looked puzzled. "At half-past two. I shall be at the door . . ."

---

mufflers Scarves worn around the neck for warmth.

Adelaide Neilson An English actress (1848–1880) who played the title role of Juliet in *Romeo and Juliet*.

Romeo and Juliet William Shakespeare's romantic tragedy (c. 1596) in which two lovers secretly marry and then die because of their feuding families.

Art Museum—in the Park The Metropolitan Museum of Art, on Fifth Avenue between 80th Street and 84th Street in Central Park, was formed in 1870. Wharton is confused about dates: construction at the site in Central Park began in 1874, but the building did not open until 1880. It was designed as a small red brick building in a new Gothic style with a steel and glass roof similar to that on the Crystal Palace, London (1851). The

She turned away without answering and got quickly into the carriage. As it drove off she leaned forward, and he thought she waved her hand in the obscurity. He stared after her in turmoil of contradictory feelings. It seemed to him that he had been speaking not to the woman he loved but to another, a woman he was indebted to for pleasures already wearied of: it was hateful to find himself the prisoner of this hackneyed vocabulary.

"She'll come!" he said to himself, almost contemptuously.

Avoiding the popular "Wolfe collection," whose anecdotic canvases filled one of the main galleries of the queer wilderness of cast-iron and encaustic tiles known as the Metropolitan Museum, they had wandered down a passage to the room where the "Cesnola antiquities" mouldered in unvisited loneliness.

They had this melancholy retreat to themselves, and seated on the divan enclosing the central steam-radiator, they were staring silently at the glass cabinets mounted in ebonised wood which contained the recovered fragments of Ilium.

"It's odd," Madame Olenska said, "I never came here before."

"Ah, well—. Some day, I suppose, it will be a great Museum."

"Yes," she assented absently.

She stood up and wandered across the room. Archer, remaining seated, watched the light movements of her figure, so girlish even under its heavy furs, the cleverly planted heron wing in her fur cap, and the way a dark curl lay like a flattened vine spiral on each cheek above the ear. His mind, as always when they first met, was wholly absorbed in the delicious details that made her herself and no other. Presently he rose and

---

Metropolitan's first important collection was 174 European paintings, mostly Dutch and Flemish.

"Wolfe collection" The Catharine Lorillard Wolfe Collection included Old Masters and modern paintings.

cast-iron and encaustic tiles Cast-iron architecture flourished from the mid-1850s to 1880s. Encaustic tiles were produced by baking inlaid colored clays on the surface of ceramic tiles.

"Cesnola antiquities" The Cesnola Collection was named for Luigi Palma di Cesnola, the first director of the museum. Its 6,000 mostly Cypriot objects were purchased in 1872 and filled the grand central hall of the museum.

divan A long, backless couch, especially one against a wall with pillows.

ebonised wood Wood painted black to resemble ebony.

Ilium Latin: Troy, the ancient city and site of the Trojan War.

approached the case before which she stood. Its glass shelves were crowded with small broken objects—hardly recognisable domestic utensils, ornaments and personal trifles—made of glass, of clay, of discoloured bronze and other time-blurred substances.

"It seems cruel," she said, "that after a while nothing matters . . . any more than these little things, that used to be necessary and important to forgotten people, and now have to be guessed at under a magnifying glass and labelled: 'Use unknown.'"

"Yes; but meanwhile—"

"Ah, meanwhile—"

As she stood there, in her long sealskin coat, her hands thrust in a small round muff, her veil drawn down like a transparent mask to the tip of her nose, and the bunch of violets he had brought her stirring with her quickly-taken breath, it seemed incredible that this pure harmony of line and colour should ever suffer the stupid law of change.

"Meanwhile everything matters—that concerns you," he said.

She looked at him thoughtfully, and turned back to the divan. He sat down beside her and waited; but suddenly he heard a step echoing far off down the empty rooms, and felt the pressure of the minutes.

"What is it you wanted to tell me?" she asked, as if she had received the same warning.

"What I wanted to tell you?" he rejoined. "Why, that I believe you came to New York because you were afraid."

"Afraid?"

"Of my coming to Washington."

She looked down at her muff, and he saw her hands stir in it uneasily.

"Well—?"

"Well—yes," she said.

"You *were* afraid? You knew—?"

"Yes: I knew . . ."

"Well, then?" he insisted.

"Well, then: this is better, isn't it?" she returned with a long questioning sigh.

"Better—?"

"We shall hurt others less. Isn't it, after all, what you always wanted?"

"To have you here, you mean—in reach and yet out of reach? To meet you in this way, on the sly? It's the very reverse of what I want. I told you the other day what I wanted."

She hesitated. "And you still think this—worse?"

"A thousand times!" He paused. "It would be easy to lie to you; but the truth is I think it detestable."

"Oh, so do I!" she cried with a deep breath of relief.

He sprang up impatiently. "Well, then—it's my turn to ask: what is it, in God's name, that you think better?"

She hung her head and continued to clasp and unclasp her hands in her muff. The step drew nearer, and a guardian in a braided cap walked listlessly through the room like a ghost stalking through a necropolis. They fixed their eyes simultaneously on the case opposite them, and when the official figure had vanished down a vista of mummies and sarcophagi Archer spoke again.

"What do you think better?"

Instead of answering she murmured: "I promised Granny to stay with her because it seemed to me that here I should be safer."

"From me?"

She bent her head slightly, without looking at him.

"Safer from loving me?"

Her profile did not stir, but he saw a tear overflow on her lashes and hang in a mesh of her veil.

"Safer from doing irreparable harm. Don't let us be like all the others!" she protested.

"What others? I don't profess to be different from my kind. I'm consumed by the same wants and the same longings."

She glanced at him with a kind of terror, and he saw a faint colour steal into her cheeks.

"Shall I—once come to you; and then go home?" she suddenly hazarded in a low clear voice.

The blood rushed to the young man's forehead. "Dearest!" he said, without moving. It seemed as if he held his heart in his hands, like a full cup that the least motion might over-brim.

Then her last phrase struck his ear and his face clouded.

"Go home? What do you mean by going home?"

"Home to my husband."

"And you expect me to say yes to that?"

She raised her troubled eyes to his. "What else is there? I can't stay here and lie to the people who've been good to me."

"But that's the very reason why I ask you to come away!"

"And destroy their lives, when they've helped me to remake mine?"

Archer sprang to his feet and stood looking down on her in inarticulate despair. It would have been easy to say: "Yes, come; come once." He knew the power she would put in his hands if she consented; there would be no difficulty then in persuading her not to go back to her husband.

---

necropolis   A cemetery, especially a large and elaborate one belonging to an ancient city.

But something silenced the word on his lips. A sort of passionate honesty in her made it inconceivable that he should try to draw her into that familiar trap. "If I were to let her come," he said to himself, "I should have to let her go again." And that was not to be imagined.

But he saw the shadow of the lashes on her wet cheek, and wavered.

"After all," he began again, "we have lives of our own. . . . There's no use attempting the impossible. You're so unprejudiced about some things, so used, as you say, to looking at the Gorgon, that I don't know why you're afraid to face our case, and see it as it really is—unless you think the sacrifice is not worth making."

She stood up also, her lips tightening under a rapid frown.

"Call it that, then—I must go," she said, drawing her little watch from her bosom.

She turned away, and he followed and caught her by the wrist. "Well, then: come to me once," he said, his head turning suddenly at the thought of losing her; and for a second or two they looked at each other almost like enemies.

"When?" he insisted. "Tomorrow?"

She hesitated. "The day after."

"Dearest—!" he said again.

She had disengaged her wrist; but for a moment they continued to hold each other's eyes, and he saw that her face, which had grown very pale, was flooded with a deep inner radiance. His heart beat with awe: he felt that he had never before beheld love visible.

"Oh, I shall be late—goodbye. No, don't come any farther than this," she cried, walking hurriedly away down the long room, as if the reflected radiance in his eyes had frightened her. When she reached the door she turned for a moment to wave a quick farewell.

Archer walked home alone. Darkness was falling when he let himself into his house, and he looked about at the familiar objects in the hall as if he viewed them from the other side of the grave.

The parlour-maid, hearing his step, ran up the stairs to light the gas on the upper landing.

"Is Mrs. Archer in?"

"No, sir; Mrs. Archer went out in the carriage after luncheon, and hasn't come back.

With a sense of relief he entered the library and flung himself down in his armchair. The parlour-maid followed, bringing the student lamp and shaking some coals onto the dying fire. When she left he continued to sit motionless, his elbows on his knees, his chin on his clasped hands, his eyes fixed on the red grate.

He sat there without conscious thoughts, without sense of the lapse of time, in a deep and grave amazement that seemed to suspend life rather than quicken it. "This was what had to be, then . . . this was what had to be," he kept repeating to himself, as if he hung in the clutch of doom. What he had dreamed of had been so different that there was a mortal chill in his rapture.

The door opened and May came in.

"I'm dreadfully late—you weren't worried, were you?" she asked, laying her hand on his shoulder with one of her rare caresses.

He looked up astonished. "Is it late?"

"After seven. I believe you've been asleep!" She laughed, and drawing out her hat pins tossed her velvet hat on the sofa. She looked paler than usual, but sparkling with an unwonted animation.

"I went to see Granny, and just as I was going away Ellen came in from a walk; so I stayed and had a long talk with her. It was ages since we'd had a real talk. . . ." She had dropped into her usual armchair, facing his, and was running her fingers through her rumpled hair. He fancied she expected him to speak.

"A really good talk," she went on, smiling with what seemed to Archer an unnatural vividness. "She was so dear—just like the old Ellen. I'm afraid I haven't been fair to her lately. I've sometimes thought—"

Archer stood up and leaned against the mantelpiece, out of the radius of the lamp.

"Yes, you've thought—?" he echoed as she paused.

"Well, perhaps I haven't judged her fairly. She's so different—at least on the surface. She takes up such odd people—she seems to like to make herself conspicuous. I suppose it's the life she's led in that fast European society; no doubt we seem dreadfully dull to her. But I don't want to judge her unfairly."

She paused again, a little breathless with the unwonted length of her speech, and sat with her lips slightly parted and a deep blush on her cheeks.

Archer, as he looked at her, was reminded of the glow which had suffused her face in the Mission Garden at St. Augustine. He became aware of the same obscure effort in her, the same reaching out toward something beyond the usual range of her vision.

"She hates Ellen," he thought, "and she's trying to overcome the feeling, and to get me to help her to overcome it."

The thought moved him, and for a moment he was on the point of breaking the silence between them, and throwing himself on her mercy.

"You understand, don't you," she went on, "why the family have sometimes been annoyed? We all did what we could for her at first; but she never seemed to understand. And now this idea of going to see Mrs. Beaufort, of going there in Granny's carriage! I'm afraid she's quite alienated the van der Luydens . . ."

"Ah," said Archer with an impatient laugh. The open door had closed between them again.

"It's time to dress; we're dining out, aren't we?" he asked, moving from the fire.

She rose also, but lingered near the hearth. As he walked past her she moved forward impulsively, as though to detain him: their eyes met, and he saw that hers were of the same swimming blue as when he had left her to drive to Jersey City.

She flung her arms about his neck and pressed her cheek to his.

"You haven't kissed me today," she said in a whisper; and he felt her tremble in his arms.

XXXII

"At the Court of the Tuileries," said Mr. Sillerton Jackson with his reminiscent smile, "such things were pretty openly tolerated."

The scene was the van der Luydens' black walnut dining-room in Madison Avenue, and the time the evening after Newland Archer's visit to the Museum of Art. Mr. and Mrs. van der Luyden had come to town for a few days from Skuytercliff, whither they had precipitately fled at the announcement of Beaufort's failure. It had been represented to them that the disarray into which society had been thrown by this deplorable affair made their presence in town more necessary than ever. It was one of the occasions when, as Mrs. Archer put it, they "owed it to society" to show themselves at the Opera, and even to open their own doors.

"It will never do, my dear Louisa, to let people like Mrs. Lemuel Struthers think they can step into Regina's shoes. It is just at such times that new people push in and get a footing. It was owing to the epidemic of chicken-pox in New York the winter Mrs. Struthers first appeared that the married men slipped away to her house while their wives were in the nursery. You and dear Henry, Louisa, must stand in the breach as you always have."

Mr. and Mrs. van der Luyden could not remain deaf to such a call, and reluctantly but heroically they had come to town, unmuffled the house, and sent out invitations for two dinners and an evening reception.

On this particular evening they had invited Sillerton Jackson, Mrs. Archer and Newland and his wife to go with them to the Opera, where Faust was being sung for the first time that winter. Nothing was done without ceremony under the van der Luyden roof, and though there were but four guests the repast had begun at seven punctually, so that the proper sequence of courses might be served without haste before the gentlemen settled down to their cigars.

Archer had not seen his wife since the evening before. He had left early for the office, where he had plunged into an accumulation of unimportant business. In the afternoon one of the senior partners had made an unexpected call on his time; and he had reached home so late that May had preceded him to the van der Luydens', and sent back the carriage.

Now, across the Skuytercliff carnations and the massive plate, she struck him as pale and languid; but her eyes shone, and she talked with exaggerated animation.

The subject which had called forth Mr. Sillerton Jackson's favourite allusion had been brought up (Archer fancied not without intention) by their hostess. The Beaufort failure, or rather the Beaufort attitude since the failure, was still a fruitful theme for the drawing-room moralist; and after it had been thoroughly examined and condemned Mrs. van der Luyden had turned her scrupulous eyes on May Archer.

"Is it possible, dear, that what I hear is true? I was told your grandmother Mingott's carriage was seen standing at Mrs. Beaufort's door." It was noticeable that she no longer called the offending lady by her Christian name.

May's colour rose, and Mrs. Archer put in hastily: "If it was, I'm convinced it was there without Mrs. Mingott's knowledge."

"Ah, you think—?" Mrs. van der Luyden paused, sighed, and glanced at her husband.

"I'm afraid," Mr. van der Luyden said, "that Madame Olenska's kind heart may have led her into the imprudence of calling on Mrs. Beaufort."

"Or her taste for peculiar people," put in Mrs. Archer in a dry tone, while her eyes dwelt innocently on her son's.

"I'm sorry to think it of Madame Olenska," said Mrs. van der Luyden; and Mrs. Archer murmured: "Ah, my dear—and after you'd had her twice at Skuytercliff!"

It was at this point that Mr. Jackson seized the chance to place his favourite allusion.

"At the Tuileries," he repeated, seeing the eyes of the company expectantly turned on him, "the standard was excessively lax in some respects; and if you'd asked where Morny's money came from—! Or who paid the debts of some of the Court beauties . . ."

Morny's money Auguste, Duc de Morny (1811–1865), was the half-brother of Napoléon III and an advisor during his reign. Involved in every sort of business venture,

"I hope, dear Sillerton," said Mrs. Archer, "you are not suggesting that we should adopt such standards?"

"I never suggest," returned Mr. Jackson imperturbably. "But Madame Olenska's foreign bringing-up may make her less particular—"

"Ah," the two elder ladies sighed.

"Still, to have kept her grandmother's carriage at a defaulter's door!" Mr. van der Luyden protested; and Archer guessed that he was remembering, and resenting, the hampers of carnations he had sent to the little house in Twenty-third Street.

"Of course I've always said that she looks at things quite differently," Mrs. Archer summed up.

A flush rose to May's forehead. She looked across the table at her husband, and said precipitately: "I'm sure Ellen meant it kindly."

"Imprudent people are often kind," said Mrs. Archer, as if the fact were scarcely an extenuation; and Mrs. van der Luyden murmured: "If only she had consulted some one—"

"Ah, that she never did!" Mrs. Archer rejoined.

At this point Mr. van der Luyden glanced at his wife, who bent her head slightly in the direction of Mrs. Archer; and the glimmering trains of the three ladies swept out of the door while the gentlemen settled down to their cigars. Mr. van der Luyden supplied short ones on Opera nights; but they were so good that they made his guests deplore his inexorable punctuality.

Archer, after the first act, had detached himself from the party and made his way to the back of the club box. From there he watched, over various Chivers, Mingott and Rushworth shoulders, the same scene that he had looked at, two years previously, on the night of his first meeting with Ellen Olenska. He had half-expected her to appear again in old Mrs. Mingott's box, but it remained empty; and he sat motionless, his eyes fastened on it, till suddenly Madame Nilsson's pure soprano broke out into "*M'ama, non m'ama . . .*"

Archer turned to the stage, where, in the familiar setting of giant roses and pen-wiper pansies, the same large blonde victim was succumbing to the same small brown seducer.

From the stage his eyes wandered to the point of the horseshoe where May sat between two older ladies, just as, on that former evening, she had sat between Mrs. Lovell Mingott and her newly-arrived "foreign"

---

often as developer or speculator, the Duc de Morny was known for his unscrupulous and immoral handling of finances, penchant for horse racing, gourmet tastes, and amateur love of painting and theater.

cousin. As on that evening, she was all in white; and Archer, who had not noticed what she wore, recognised the blue-white satin and old lace of her wedding dress.

It was the custom, in old New York, for brides to appear in this costly garment during the first year or two of marriage: his mother, he knew, kept hers in tissue paper in the hope that Janey might some day wear it, though poor Janey was reaching the age when pearl grey poplin and no bridesmaids would be thought more "appropriate."

It struck Archer that May, since their return from Europe, had seldom worn her bridal satin, and the surprise of seeing her in it made him compare her appearance with that of the young girl he had watched with such blissful anticipations two years earlier.

Though May's outline was slightly heavier, as her goddess-like build had foretold, her athletic erectness of carriage, and the girlish transparency of her expression, remained unchanged: but for the slight languor that Archer had lately noticed in her she would have been the exact image of the girl playing with the bouquet of lilies-of-the-valley on her betrothal evening. The fact seemed an additional appeal to his pity: such innocence was as moving as the trustful clasp of a child. Then he remembered the passionate generosity latent under that incurious calm. He recalled her glance of understanding when he had urged that their engagement should be announced at the Beaufort ball; he heard the voice in which she had said, in the Mission garden: "I couldn't have my happiness made out of a wrong—a wrong to some one else"; and an uncontrollable longing seized him to tell her the truth, to throw himself on her generosity, and ask for the freedom he had once refused.

Newland Archer was a quiet and self-controlled young man. Conformity to the discipline of a small society had become almost his second nature. It was deeply distasteful to him to do anything melodramatic and conspicuous, anything Mr. van der Luyden would have deprecated and the club box condemned as bad form. But he had become suddenly unconscious of the club box, of Mr. van der Luyden, of all that had so long enclosed him in the warm shelter of habit. He walked along the semicircular passage at the back of the house, and opened the door of Mrs. van der Luyden's box as if it had been a gate into the unknown.

"*M'ama!*" thrilled out the triumphant Marguerite; and the occupants of the box looked up in surprise at Archer's entrance. He had already broken one of the rules of his world, which forbade the entering of a box during a solo.

Slipping between Mr. van der Luyden and Sillerton Jackson, he leaned over his wife.

"I've got a beastly headache; don't tell any one, but come home, won't you?" he whispered.

May gave him a glance of comprehension, and he saw her whisper to his mother, who nodded sympathetically; then she murmured an excuse to Mrs. van der Luyden, and rose from her seat just as Marguerite fell into Faust's arms. Archer, while he helped her on with her Opera cloak, noticed the exchange of a significant smile between the older ladies.

As they drove away May laid her hand shyly on his. "I'm so sorry you don't feel well. I'm afraid they've been overworking you again at the office."

"No—it's not that: do you mind if I open the window?" he returned confusedly, letting down the pane on his side. He sat staring out into the street, feeling his wife beside him as a silent watchful interrogation, and keeping his eyes steadily fixed on the passing houses. At their door she caught her skirt in the step of the carriage, and fell against him.

"Did you hurt yourself?" he asked, steadying her with his arm.

"No; but my poor dress—see how I've torn it!" she exclaimed. She bent to gather up a mud-stained breadth, and followed him up the steps into the hall. The servants had not expected them so early, and there was only a glimmer of gas on the upper landing.

Archer mounted the stairs, turned up the light, and put a match to the brackets on each side of the library mantelpiece. The curtains were drawn, and the warm friendly aspect of the room smote him like that of a familiar face met during an unavowable errand.

He noticed that his wife was very pale, and asked if he should get her some brandy.

"Oh, no," she exclaimed with a momentary flush, as she took off her cloak. "But hadn't you better go to bed at once?" she added, as he opened a silver box on the table and took out a cigarette.

Archer threw down the cigarette and walked to his usual place by the fire.

"No; my head is not as bad as that." He paused. "And there's something I want to say; something important—that I must tell you at once."

She had dropped into an armchair, and raised her head as he spoke. "Yes, dear?" she rejoined, so gently that he wondered at the lack of wonder with which she received this preamble.

"May—" he began, standing a few feet from her chair, and looking over at her as if the slight distance between them were an unbridgeable abyss. The sound of his voice echoed uncannily through the homelike hush, and he repeated: "There is something I've got to tell you . . . about myself . . ."

She sat silent, without a movement or a tremor of her lashes. She was still extremely pale, but her face had a curious tranquillity of expression that seemed drawn from some secret inner source.

Archer checked the conventional phrases of self-accusal that were crowding to his lips. He was determined to put the case baldly, without vain recrimination or excuse.

"Madame Olenska—" he said; but at the name his wife raised her hand as if to silence him. As she did so the gaslight struck on the gold of her wedding-ring.

"Oh, why should we talk about Ellen tonight?" she asked, with a slight pout of impatience.

"Because I ought to have spoken before."

Her face remained calm. "Is it really worth while, dear? I know I've been unfair to her at times—perhaps we all have. You've understood her, no doubt, better than we did: you've always been kind to her. But what does it matter, now it's all over?"

Archer looked at her blankly. Could it be possible that the sense of unreality in which he felt himself imprisoned had communicated itself to his wife?

"All over—what do you mean?" he asked in an indistinct stammer.

May still looked at him with transparent eyes. "Why—since she's going back to Europe so soon; since Granny approves and understands, and has arranged to make her independent of her husband—"

She broke off, and Archer, grasping the corner of the mantelpiece in one convulsed hand, and steadying himself against it, made a vain effort to extend the same control to his reeling thoughts.

"I supposed," he heard his wife's even voice go on, "that you had been kept at the office this evening about the business arrangements. It was settled this morning, I believe." She lowered her eyes under his unseeing stare, and another fugitive flush passed over her face.

He understood that his own eyes must be unbearable, and turning away, rested his elbows on the mantel-shelf and covered his face. Something drummed and clanged furiously in his ears; he could not tell if it were the blood in his veins, or the tick of the clock on the mantel.

May sat without moving or speaking while the clock slowly measured out five minutes. A lump of coal fell forward in the grate, and hearing her rise to push it back, Archer at length turned and faced her.

"It's impossible," he exclaimed.

"Impossible—?"

"How do you know—what you've just told me?"

"I saw Ellen yesterday—I told you I'd seen her at Granny's."

"It wasn't then that she told you?"

"No; I had a note from her this afternoon. Do you want to see it?"

He could not find his voice, and she went out of the room, and came back almost immediately.

"I thought you knew," she said simply.

She laid a sheet of paper on the table, and Archer put out his hand and took it up. The letter contained only a few lines.

"May dear, I have at last made Granny understand that my visit to her could be no more than a visit; and she has been as kind and generous as ever. She sees now that if I return to Europe I must live by myself, or rather with poor Aunt Medora, who is coming with me. I am hurrying back to Washington to pack up, and we sail next week. You must be very good to Granny when I'm gone—as good as you've always been to me. Ellen.

"If any of my friends wish to urge me to change my mind, please tell them it would be utterly useless."

Archer read the letter over two or three times; then he flung it down and burst out laughing.

The sound of his laugh startled him. It recalled Janey's midnight fright when she had caught him rocking with incomprehensible mirth over May's telegram announcing that the date of their marriage had been advanced.

"Why did she write this?" he asked, checking his laugh with a supreme effort.

May met the question with her unshaken candour. "I suppose because we talked things over yesterday—"

"What things?"

"I told her I was afraid I hadn't been fair to her—hadn't always understood how hard it must have been for her here, alone among so many people who were relations and yet strangers; who felt the right to criticise, and yet didn't always know the circumstances." She paused. "I knew you'd been the one friend she could always count on; and I wanted her to know that you and I were the same—in all our feelings."

She hesitated, as if waiting for him to speak, and then added slowly: "She understood my wishing to tell her this. I think she understands everything."

She went up to Archer, and taking one of his cold hands pressed it quickly against her cheek.

"My head aches too; good-night, dear," she said, and turned to the door, her torn and muddy wedding-dress dragging after her across the room.

XXXIII

It was, as Mrs. Archer smilingly said to Mrs. Welland, a great event for a young couple to give their first big dinner.

The Newland Archers, since they had set up their household, had received a good deal of company in an informal way. Archer was fond of having three or four friends to dine, and May welcomed them with the beaming readiness of which her mother had set her the example in conjugal affairs. Her husband questioned whether, if left to herself, she would ever have asked any one to the house; but he had long given up trying to disengage her real self from the shape into which tradition and training had moulded her. It was expected that well-off young couples in New York should do a good deal of informal entertaining, and a Welland married to an Archer was doubly pledged to the tradition.

But a big dinner, with a hired *chef* and two borrowed footmen, with Roman punch, roses from Henderson's, and *menus* on gilt-edged cards, was a different affair, and not to be lightly undertaken. As Mrs. Archer remarked, the Roman punch made all the difference; not in itself but by its manifold implications—since it signified either canvas-backs or terrapin, two soups, a hot and a cold sweet, full *décolletage* with short sleeves, and guests of a proportionate importance.

It was always an interesting occasion when a young pair launched their first invitations in the third person, and their summons was seldom refused even by the seasoned and sought-after. Still, it was admittedly a triumph that the van der Luydens, at May's request, should have stayed over in order to be present at her farewell dinner for the Countess Olenska.

The two mothers-in-law sat in May's drawing-room on the afternoon of the great day, Mrs. Archer writing out the *menus* on Tiffany's thickest gilt-edged bristol, while Mrs. Welland superintended the placing of the palms and standard lamps.

Archer, arriving late from his office, found them still there. Mrs. Archer had turned her attention to the name-cards for the table, and Mrs. Welland was considering the effect of bringing forward the large gilt sofa, so that another "corner" might be created between the piano and the window.

---

décolletage   French: low-cut neckline, as in a formal evening dress.

Tiffany's . . . bristol   Jewelers formed in 1837 by Charles L. Tiffany (1812–1902) and John B. Young. Located at Union Square, it first offered stationery and fancy goods. In 1841, Tiffany's began selling jewelry and became internationally known for its innovative designs and precious gemstones. Bristol is a smooth, heavy pasteboard of fine quality.

May, they told him, was in the dining-room inspecting the mound of Jacqueminot roses and maidenhair in the centre of the long table, and the placing of the Maillard bonbons in openwork silver baskets between the candelabra. On the piano stood a large basket of orchids which Mr. van der Luyden had had sent from Skuytercliff. Everything was, in short, as it should be on the approach of so considerable an event.

Mrs. Archer ran thoughtfully over the list, checking off each name with her sharp gold pen.

"Henry van der Luyden—Louisa—the Lovell Mingotts—the Reggie Chiverses—Lawrence Lefferts and Gertrude—(yes, I suppose May was right to have them)—the Selfridge Merrys, Sillerton Jackson, Van Newland and his wife. (How time passes! It seems only yesterday that he was your best man, Newland)—and Countess Olenska—yes, I think that's all. . . ."

Mrs. Welland surveyed her son-in-law affectionately. "No one can say, Newland, that you and May are not giving Ellen a handsome send-off."

"Ah, well," said Mrs. Archer, "I understand May's wanting her cousin to tell people abroad that we're not quite barbarians."

"I'm sure Ellen will appreciate it. She was to arrive this morning, I believe. It will make a most charming last impression. The evening before sailing is usually so dreary," Mrs. Welland cheerfully continued.

Archer turned toward the door, and his mother-in-law called to him: "Do go in and have a peep at the table. And don't let May tire herself too much." But he affected not to hear, and sprang up the stairs to his library. The room looked at him like an alien countenance composed into a polite grimace; and he perceived that it had been ruthlessly "tidied," and prepared, by a judicious distribution of ash-trays and cedar-wood boxes, for the gentlemen to smoke in.

"Ah, well," he thought, "it's not for long—" and he went on to his dressing-room.

Ten days had passed since Madame Olenska's departure from New York. During those ten days Archer had had no sign from her but that conveyed by the return of a key wrapped in tissue paper, and sent to his office in a sealed envelope addressed in her hand. This retort to his last appeal might have been interpreted as a classic move in a familiar game; but the young man chose to give it a different meaning. She was still fighting against her fate; but she was going to Europe, and she was not returning to her husband. Nothing, therefore, was to prevent his following her; and

---

maidenhair A fern with fine stalks and delicate fronds.

once he had taken the irrevocable step, and had proved to her that it was irrevocable, he believed she would not send him away.

This confidence in the future had steadied him to play his part in the present. It had kept him from writing to her, or betraying, by any sign or act, his misery and mortification. It seemed to him that in the deadly silent game between them the trumps were still in his hands; and he waited.

There had been, nevertheless, moments sufficiently difficult to pass; as when Mr. Letterblair, the day after Madame Olenska's departure, had sent for him to go over the details of the trust which Mrs. Manson Mingott wished to create for her granddaughter. For a couple of hours Archer had examined the terms of the deed with his senior, all the while obscurely feeling that if he had been consulted it was for some reason other than the obvious one of his cousinship; and that the close of the conference would reveal it.

"Well, the lady can't deny that it's a handsome arrangement," Mr. Letterblair had summed up, after mumbling over a summary of the settlement. "In fact I'm bound to say she's been treated pretty handsomely all around."

"All around?" Archer echoed with a touch of derision. "Do you refer to her husband's proposal to give her back her own money?"

Mr. Letterblair's bushy eyebrows went up a fraction of an inch. "My dear sir, the law's the law; and your wife's cousin was married under the French law. It's to be presumed she knew what that meant."

"Even if she did, what happened subsequently—" But Archer paused. Mr. Letterblair had laid his pen-handle against his big corrugated nose, and was looking down it with the expression assumed by virtuous elderly gentlemen when they wish their youngers to understand that virtue is not synonymous with ignorance.

"My dear sir, I've no wish to extenuate the Count's transgressions; but—but on the other side . . . I wouldn't put my hand in the fire . . . well, that there hadn't been tit for tat . . . with the young champion. . . ." Mr. Letterblair unlocked a drawer and pushed a folded paper toward Archer. "This report, the result of discreet enquiries . . ." And then, as Archer made no effort to glance at the paper or to repudiate the suggestion, the lawyer somewhat flatly continued: "I don't say it's conclusive, you observe; far from it. But straws show . . . and on the whole it's eminently satisfactory for all parties that this dignified solution has been reached."

"Oh, eminently," Archer assented, pushing back the paper.

A day or two later, on responding to a summons from Mrs. Manson Mingott, his soul had been more deeply tried.

He had found the old lady depressed and querulous.

"You know she's deserted me?" she began at once; and without waiting for his reply: "Oh, don't ask me why! She gave so many reasons that I've forgotten them all. My private belief is that she couldn't face the boredom. At any rate that's what Augusta and my daughters-in-law think. And I don't know that I altogether blame her. Olenski's a finished scoundrel; but life with him must have been a good deal gayer than it is in Fifth Avenue. Not that the family would admit that: they think Fifth Avenue is Heaven with the rue de la Paix thrown in. And poor Ellen, of course, has no idea of going back to her husband. She held out as firmly as ever against that. So she's to settle down in Paris with that fool Medora. . . . Well, Paris is Paris; and you can keep a carriage there on next to nothing. But she was as gay as a bird, and I shall miss her." Two tears, the parched tears of the old, rolled down her puffy cheeks and vanished in the abysses of her bosom.

"All I ask is," she concluded, "that they shouldn't bother me any more. I must really be allowed to digest my gruel. . . ." And she twinkled a little wistfully at Archer.

It was that evening, on his return home, that May announced her intention of giving a farewell dinner to her cousin. Madame Olenska's name had not been pronounced between them since the night of her flight to Washington; and Archer looked at his wife with surprise.

"A dinner—why?" he interrogated.

Her colour rose. "But you like Ellen—I thought you'd be pleased."

"It's awfully nice—your putting it in that way. But I really don't see—"

"I mean to do it, Newland," she said, quietly rising and going to her desk. "Here are the invitations all written. Mother helped me—she agrees that we ought to." She paused, embarrassed and yet smiling, and Archer suddenly saw before him the embodied image of the Family.

"Oh, all right," he said, staring with unseeing eyes at the list of guests that she had put in his hand.

When he entered the drawing-room before dinner May was stooping over the fire and trying to coax the logs to burn in their unaccustomed setting of immaculate tiles.

The tall lamps were all lit, and Mr. van der Luyden's orchids had been conspicuously disposed in various receptacles of modern porcelain and knobby silver. Mrs. Newland Archer's drawing-room was generally thought a great success. A gilt bamboo *jardinière*, in which the primulas

---

jardinière   French: a window box for plants or flowers.

primulas   Primulas, or primroses, are plants with variously colored, five-lobed flowers. In the nineteenth century they were enthusiastically collected by the affluent. In the "language of flowers," they suggested diffidence, early youth, or sadness.

and cinerarias were punctually renewed, blocked the access to the bay window (where the old-fashioned would have preferred a bronze reduction of the Venus of Milo); the sofas and arm-chairs of pale brocade were cleverly grouped about little plush tables densely covered with silver toys, porcelain animals and efflorescent photograph frames; and tall rosy-shaded lamps shot up like tropical flowers among the palms.

"I don't think Ellen has ever seen this room lighted up," said May, rising flushed from her struggle, and sending about her a glance of pardonable pride. The brass tongs which she had propped against the side of the chimney fell with a crash that drowned her husband's answer; and before he could restore them Mr. and Mrs. van der Luyden were announced.

The other guests quickly followed, for it was known that the van der Luydens liked to dine punctually. The room was nearly full, and Archer was engaged in showing to Mrs. Selfridge Merry a small highly-varnished Verbeckhoven "Study of Sheep," which Mr. Welland had given May for Christmas, when he found Madame Olenska at his side.

She was excessively pale, and her pallor made her dark hair seem denser and heavier than ever. Perhaps that, or the fact that she had wound several rows of amber beads about her neck, reminded him suddenly of the little Ellen Mingott he had danced with at children's parties, when Medora Manson had first brought her to New York.

The amber beads were trying to her complexion, or her dress was perhaps unbecoming: her face looked lustreless and almost ugly, and he had never loved it as he did at that minute. Their hands met, and he thought he heard her say: "Yes, we're sailing tomorrow in the Russia—"; then there was an unmeaning noise of opening doors, and after an interval May's voice: "Newland! Dinner's been announced. Won't you please take Ellen in?"

Madame Olenska put her hand on his arm, and he noticed that the hand was ungloved, and remembered how he had kept his eyes fixed on it the evening that he had sat with her in the little Twenty-third Street drawing-room. All the beauty that had forsaken her face seemed to have taken refuge in the long pale fingers and faintly dimpled knuckles on his

---

cinerarias   A widely cultivated house plant with flat clusters of daisylike flowers, the cineraria meant "ever bright."

Venus of Milo   A marble statue of Aphrodite, best known of all ancient statues. Found on the island of Melos in 1820, it is housed in the Louvre.

Verbeckhoven "Study of Sheep" [sic]   Eugene Joseph Verboeckhoven (c. 1798–1881), a Belgian painter in the Romantic tradition, was known for his paintings of animals and country scenes.

sleeve, and he said to himself: "If it were only to see her hand again I should have to follow her—."

It was only at an entertainment ostensibly offered to a "foreign visitor" that Mrs. van der Luyden could suffer the diminution of being placed on her host's left. The fact of Madame Olenska's "foreignness" could hardly have been more adroitly emphasised than by this farewell tribute; and Mrs. van der Luyden accepted her displacement with an affability which left no doubt as to her approval. There were certain things that had to be done, and if done at all, done handsomely and thoroughly; and one of these, in the old New York code, was the tribal rally around a kinswoman about to be eliminated from the tribe. There was nothing on earth that the Wellands and Mingotts would not have done to proclaim their unalterable affection for the Countess Olenska now that her passage for Europe was engaged; and Archer, at the head of his table, sat marvelling at the silent untiring activity with which her popularity had been retrieved, grievances against her silenced, her past countenanced, and her present irradiated by the family approval. Mrs. van der Luyden shone on her with the dim benevolence which was her nearest approach to cordiality, and Mr. van der Luyden, from his seat at May's right, cast down the table glances plainly intended to justify all the carnations he had sent from Skuytercliff.

Archer, who seemed to be assisting at the scene in a state of odd imponderability, as if he floated somewhere between chandelier and ceiling, wondered at nothing so much as his own share in the proceedings. As his glance travelled from one placid well-fed face to another he saw all the harmless-looking people engaged upon May's canvas-backs as a band of dumb conspirators, and himself and the pale woman on his right as the centre of their conspiracy. And then it came over him, in a vast flash made up of many broken gleams, that to all of them he and Madame Olenska were lovers, lovers in the extreme sense peculiar to "foreign" vocabularies. He guessed himself to have been, for months, the centre of countless silently observing eyes and patiently listening ears, he understood that, by means as yet unknown to him, the separation between himself and the partner of his guilt had been achieved, and that now the whole tribe had rallied about his wife on the tacit assumption that nobody knew anything, or had ever imagined anything, and that the occasion of the entertainment was simply May Archer's natural desire to take an affectionate leave of her friend and cousin.

It was the old New York way of taking life "without effusion of blood": the way of people who dreaded scandal more than disease, who placed decency above courage, and who considered that nothing was more ill-bred than "scenes," except the behaviour of those who gave rise to them.

As these thoughts succeeded each other in his mind Archer felt like a prisoner in the centre of an armed camp. He looked about the table, and guessed at the inexorableness of his captors from the tone in which, over the asparagus from Florida, they were dealing with Beaufort and his wife. "It's to show me," he thought, "what would happen to *me*—" and a deathly sense of the superiority of implication and analogy over direct action, and of silence over rash words, closed in on him like the doors of the family vault.

He laughed, and met Mrs. van der Luyden's startled eyes.

"You think it laughable?" she said with a pinched smile. "Of course poor Regina's idea of remaining in New York has its ridiculous side, I suppose"; and Archer muttered: "Of course."

At this point, he became conscious that Madame Olenska's other neighbour had been engaged for some time with the lady on his right. At the same moment he saw that May, serenely enthroned between Mr. van der Luyden and Mr. Selfridge Merry, had cast a quick glance down the table. It was evident that the host and the lady on his right could not sit through the whole meal in silence. He turned to Madame Olenska, and her pale smile met him. "Oh, do let's see it through," it seemed to say.

"Did you find the journey tiring?" he asked in a voice that surprised him by its naturalness; and she answered that, on the contrary, she had seldom travelled with fewer discomforts.

"Except, you know, the dreadful heat in the train," she added; and he remarked that she would not suffer from that particular hardship in the country she was going to.

"I never," he declared with intensity, "was more nearly frozen than once, in April, in the train between Calais and Paris."

She said she did not wonder, but remarked that, after all, one could always carry an extra rug, and that every form of travel had its hardships; to which he abruptly returned that he thought them all of no account compared with the blessedness of getting away. She changed colour, and he added, his voice suddenly rising in pitch: "I mean to do a lot of travelling myself before long." A tremor crossed her face, and leaning over to Reggie Chivers, he cried out: "I say, Reggie, what do you say to a trip round the world: now, next month, I mean? I'm game if you are—" at which Mrs. Reggie piped up that she could not think of letting Reggie go till after the Martha Washington Ball she was getting up for the

---

Calais   A seaport in northwestern France on the Straits of Dover at the shortest crossing to England.

Blind Asylum in Easter week; and her husband placidly observed that by
that time he would have to be practising for the International Polo match.

But Mr. Selfridge Merry had caught the phrase "round the world,"
and having once circled the globe in his steam-yacht, he seized the opportunity to send down the table several striking items concerning the shal-
lowness of the Mediterranean ports. Though, after all, he added, it didn't
matter; for when you'd seen Athens and Smyrna and Constantinople, what
else was there? And Mrs. Merry said she could never be too grateful to
Dr. Bencomb for having made them promise not to go to Naples on account of the fever.

"But you must have three weeks to do India properly," her husband conceded, anxious to have it understood that he was no frivolous
globe-trotter.

And at this point the ladies went up to the drawing-room.

In the library, in spite of weightier presences, Lawrence Lefferts
predominated.

The talk, as usual, had veered around to the Beauforts, and even
Mr. van der Luyden and Mr. Selfridge Merry, installed in the honorary
arm-chairs tacitly reserved for them, paused to listen to the younger man's
philippic.

Never had Lefferts so abounded in the sentiments that adorn Christian manhood and exalt the sanctity of the home. Indignation lent him
a scathing eloquence, and it was clear that if others had followed his
example, and acted as he talked, society would never have been weak

---

Blind Asylum   Wharton may refer to the Society for the Relief of the Destitute Blind,
formed in 1869 and located at 219 West 14th Street, or to one of many asylums organized to help children and adults in the early twentieth century. In *A Backward Glance*,
she mentions that her father was on the board of such an asylum (57). Eye disease was
much feared at this time, especially as increasing numbers of immigrants entered the city.
Those passing through Ellis Island were subjected to the dreaded examination for glau-
coma or conjunctivitis, which accounted for half of all medical detentions.

International Polo match   The game of polo, originally played on small ponies with five
to seven players on each team, was at this time relatively new. The first English match
was played in 1871; the sport was introduced to the United States by multimillionaire
Gordon Bennett in the late 1870s and rapidly gained popularity among wealthy east-
erners. Until 1914, the leading polo nations were India, England, and the United States.

Athens and Smyrna and Constantinople   All located on or near the Aegean Sea. Wharton herself took an Aegean cruise in 1888 that included stops at Athens, Smyrna, and
parts of Turkey.

philippic   Speech that bitterly attacks; an invective.

enough to receive a foreign upstart like Beaufort—no, sir, not even if he'd married a van der Luyden or a Lanning instead of a Dallas. And what chance would there have been, Lefferts wrathfully questioned, of his marrying into such a family as the Dallases, if he had not already wormed his way into certain houses, as people like Mrs. Lemuel Struthers had managed to worm theirs in his wake? If society chose to open its doors to vulgar women the harm was not great, though the gain was doubtful; but once it got in the way of tolerating men of obscure origin and tainted wealth the end was total disintegration—and at no distant date.

"If things go on at this pace," Lefferts thundered, looking like a young prophet dressed by Poole, and who had not yet been stoned, "we shall see our children fighting for invitations to swindlers' houses, and marrying Beaufort's bastards."

"Oh, I say—draw it mild!" Reggie Chivers and young Newland protested, while Mr. Selfridge Merry looked genuinely alarmed, and an expression of pain and disgust settled on Mr. van der Luyden's sensitive face.

"Has he got any?" cried Mr. Sillerton Jackson, pricking up his ears; and while Lefferts tried to turn the question with a laugh, the old gentleman twittered into Archer's ear: "Queer, those fellows who are always wanting to set things right. The people who have the worst cooks are always telling you they're poisoned when they dine out. But I hear there are pressing reasons for our friend Lawrence's diatribe:—type-writer this time, I understand. . . ."

The talk swept past Archer like some senseless river running and running because it did not know enough to stop. He saw, on the faces about him, expressions of interest, amusement and even mirth. He listened to the younger men's laughter, and to the praise of the Archer Madeira, which Mr. van der Luyden and Mr. Merry were thoughtfully celebrating. Through it all he was dimly aware of a general attitude of friendliness toward himself, as if the guard of the prisoner he felt himself to be were trying to soften his captivity; and the perception increased his passionate determination to be free.

In the drawing-room, where they presently joined the ladies, he met May's triumphant eyes, and read in them the conviction that everything had "gone off" beautifully. She rose from Madame Olenska's side, and immediately Mrs. van der Luyden beckoned the latter to a seat on the gilt sofa

---

Poole Henry Poole and Co., a tailor located in Savile Row, London, a center of European men's fashion.

type-writer A typist.

where she throned. Mrs. Selfridge Merry bore across the room to join them, and it became clear to Archer that here also a conspiracy of rehabilitation and obliteration was going on. The silent organisation which held his little world together was determined to put itself on record as never for a moment having questioned the propriety of Madame Olenska's conduct, or the completeness of Archer's domestic felicity. All these amiable and inexorable persons were resolutely engaged in pretending to each other that they had never heard of, suspected, or even conceived possible, the least hint to the contrary; and from this tissue of elaborate mutual dissimulation Archer once more disengaged the fact that New York believed him to be Madame Olenska's lover. He caught the glitter of victory in his wife's eyes, and for the first time understood that she shared the belief. The discovery roused a laughter of inner devils that reverberated through all his efforts to discuss the Martha Washington ball with Mrs. Reggie Chivers and little Mrs. Newland; and so the evening swept on, running and running like a senseless river that did not know how to stop.

At length he saw that Madame Olenska had risen and was saying good-bye. He understood that in a moment she would be gone, and tried to remember what he had said to her at dinner; but he could not recall a single word they had exchanged.

She went up to May, the rest of the company making a circle about her as she advanced. The two young women clasped hands; then May bent forward and kissed her cousin.

"Certainly our hostess is much the handsomer of the two," Archer heard Reggie Chivers say in an undertone to young Mrs. Newland; and he remembered Beaufort's coarse sneer at May's ineffectual beauty.

A moment later he was in the hall, putting Madame Olenska's cloak about her shoulders.

Through all his confusion of mind he had held fast to the resolve to say nothing that might startle or disturb her. Convinced that no power could now turn him from his purpose he had found strength to let events shape themselves as they would. But as he followed Madame Olenska into the hall he thought with a sudden hunger of being for a moment alone with her at the door of her carriage.

"Is your carriage here?" he asked; and at that moment Mrs. van der Luyden, who was being majestically inserted into her sables, said gently: "We are driving dear Ellen home."

Archer's heart gave a jerk, and Madame Olenska, clasping her cloak and fan with one hand, held out the other to him. "Good-bye," she said.

"Good-bye—but I shall see you soon in Paris," he answered aloud— it seemed to him that he had shouted it.

"Oh," she murmured, "if you and May could come—!"

Mr. van der Luyden advanced to give her his arm, and Archer turned to Mrs. van der Luyden. For a moment, in the billowy darkness inside the big landau, he caught the dim oval of a face, eyes shining steadily—and she was gone.

As he went up the steps he crossed Lawrence Lefferts coming down with his wife. Lefferts caught his host by the sleeve, drawing back to let Gertrude pass.

"I say, old chap: do you mind just letting it be understood that I'm dining with you at the club tomorrow night? Thanks so much, you old brick! Good-night."

"It *did* go off beautifully, didn't it?" May questioned from the threshold of the library.

Archer roused himself with a start. As soon as the last carriage had driven away, he had come up to the library and shut himself in, with the hope that his wife, who still lingered below, would go straight to her room. But there she stood, pale and drawn, yet radiating the factitious energy of one who has passed beyond fatigue.

"May I come and talk it over?" she asked.

"Of course, if you like. But you must be awfully sleepy—"

"No, I'm not sleepy. I should like to sit with you a little."

"Very well," he said, pushing her chair near the fire.

She sat down and he resumed his seat; but neither spoke for a long time. At length Archer began abruptly: "Since you're not tired, and want to talk, there's something I must tell you. I tried to the other night—."

She looked at him quickly. "Yes, dear. Something about yourself?"

"About myself. You say you're not tired: well, I am. Horribly tired . . ."

In an instant she was all tender anxiety. "Oh, I've seen it coming on, Newland! You've been so wickedly overworked—"

"Perhaps it's that. Anyhow, I want to make a break—"

"A break? To give up the law?"

"To go away, at any rate—at once. On a long trip, ever so far off—away from everything—"

He paused, conscious that he had failed in his attempt to speak with the indifference of a man who longs for a change, and is yet too weary to welcome it. Do what he would, the chord of eagerness vibrated. "Away from everything—" he repeated.

"Ever so far? Where, for instance?" she asked.

"Oh, I don't know. India—or Japan."

She stood up, and as he sat with bent head, his chin propped on his hands, he felt her warmly and fragrantly hovering over him.

"As far as that? But I'm afraid you can't, dear . . ." she said in an unsteady voice. "Not unless you'll take me with you." And then, as he was silent, she went on, in tones so clear and evenly-pitched that each separate syllable tapped like a little hammer on his brain: "That is, if the doctors will let me go . . . but I'm afraid they won't. For you see, Newland, I've been sure since this morning of something I've been so longing and hoping for—"

He looked up at her with a sick stare, and she sank down, all dew and roses, and hid her face against his knee.

"Oh, my dear," he said, holding her to him while his cold hand stroked her hair.

There was a long pause, which the inner devils filled with strident laughter; then May freed herself from his arms and stood up.

"You didn't guess—?"

"Yes—I; no. That is, of course I hoped—"

They looked at each other for an instant and again fell silent; then, turning his eyes from hers, he asked abruptly: "Have you told any one else?"

"Only Mamma and your mother." She paused, and then added hurriedly, the blood flushing up to her forehead: "That is—and Ellen. You know I told you we'd had a long talk one afternoon—and how dear she was to me."

"Ah—" said Archer, his heart stopping.

He felt that his wife was watching him intently. "Did you *mind* my telling her first, Newland?"

"Mind? Why should I?" He made a last effort to collect himself. "But that was a fortnight ago, wasn't it? I thought you said you weren't sure till today."

Her colour burned deeper, but she held his gaze. "No; I wasn't sure then—but I told her I was. And you see I was right!" she exclaimed, her blue eyes wet with victory.

XXXIV

Newland Archer sat at the writing-table in his library in East Thirty-ninth Street.

He had just got back from a big official reception for the inauguration of the new galleries at the Metropolitan Museum, and the spectacle of

---

new galleries at the Metropolitan Museum   The museum expanded rapidly at the turn of the century, with building additions in 1888, 1894, and 1910. Gifts from wealthy

those great spaces crowded with the spoils of the ages, where the throng of fashion circulated through a series of scientifically catalogued treasures, had suddenly pressed on a rusted spring of memory.

"Why, this used to be one of the old Cesnola rooms," he heard some one say; and instantly everything about him vanished, and he was sitting alone on a hard leather divan against a radiator, while a slight figure in a long sealskin cloak moved away down the meagrely-fitted vista of the old Museum.

The vision had roused a host of other associations, and he sat looking with new eyes at the library which, for over thirty years, had been the scene of his solitary musings and of all the family confabulations.

It was the room in which most of the real things of his life had happened. There his wife, nearly twenty-six years ago, had broken to him, with a blushing circumlocution that would have caused the young women of the new generation to smile, the news that she was to have a child; and there their eldest boy, Dallas, too delicate to be taken to church in midwinter, had been christened by their old friend the Bishop of New York, the ample magnificent irreplaceable Bishop, so long the pride and ornament of his diocese. There Dallas had first staggered across the floor shouting "Dad," while May and the nurse laughed behind the door; there their second child, Mary (who was so like her mother), had announced her engagement to the dullest and most reliable of Reggie Chivers's many sons; and there Archer had kissed her through her wedding veil before they went down to the motor which was to carry them to Grace Church—for in a world where all else had reeled on its foundations the "Grace Church wedding" remained an unchanged institution.

It was in the library that he and May had always discussed the future of the children: the studies of Dallas and his young brother Bill, Mary's incurable indifference to "accomplishments," and passion for sport and philanthropy, and the vague leanings toward "art" which had finally landed the restless and curious Dallas in the office of a rising New York architect.

The young men nowadays were emancipating themselves from the law and business and taking up all sorts of new things. If they were not absorbed in state politics or municipal reform, the chances were that they were going in for Central American archæology, for architecture

---

philanthropists made new acquisitions possible such as the Crosby Collection of musical instruments, the Marquand and Altman Collection of paintings, the Garland Collection of Asian porcelains, additional European paintings, and works of decorative art.

architecture Architecture grew into a respected profession at the end of the century,

or landscape-engineering; taking a keen and learned interest in the pre-revolutionary buildings of their own country, studying and adapting Georgian types, and protesting at the meaningless use of the word "Colonial." Nobody nowadays had "Colonial" houses except the millionaire grocers of the suburbs.

But above all—sometimes Archer put it above all—it was in that library that the Governor of New York, coming down from Albany one evening to dine and spend the night, had turned to his host, and said, banging his clenched fist on the table and gnashing his eye-glasses: "Hang the professional politician! You're the kind of man the country wants, Archer. If the stable's ever to be cleaned out, men like you have got to lend a hand in the cleaning."

---

with the development of new professional associations, standards for education and licensing, and schools. Dallas's training is unclear, but he could have studied at Columbia, which launched its architecture program in 1881.

landscape-engineering   Throughout the nineteenth century, the profession of landscape architecture was defined by Frederick Law Olmsted, whose designs included Central Park. A second generation of landscape architects emerging at the end of the century founded the professional organization, the Society of Landscape Architects, in 1899. The development of cities and the desire of a growing middle class for leisure activities in open spaces led to the advancement of the profession in the early twentieth century. Wharton had close connections to the field, both through her interest in horticulture and through her relationship with her niece, Beatrix Jones Farrand (1872–1959), an internationally known landscape architect who created a number of outstanding gardens, including Dumbarton Oaks, in Washington, D.C., and the Abby Aldrich Rockefeller Garden at Sea Harbor, Maine.

Georgian   Architectural and interior design at the time of the British kings George I–IV (1714–1830). Styles varied but emphasized grace, balance, proportion, and refinement.

"Colonial"   In the last decade of the nineteenth century, a Colonial Revival began as a revolt against Victorian eclecticism and ornamentation. Looking to colonial America as a period of heroism, democracy, and craft, reformers revived all styles from 1620 to 1830. Wealthy families of long American ancestry especially favored the Colonial Revival style.

Governor of New York . . . "stable's ever to be cleaned out"   Theodore Roosevelt (1858–1919) served as governor of New York from 1899 to 1900, when he resigned to serve as William McKinley's vice presidential candidate. Born into a prominent old New York family, he was a friend of Edith Wharton. In 1882, he was elected to represent his mostly affluent Manhattan district in the state assembly, where he gained a reputation as a reformer and fighter of corruption—especially after accusing financier Jay Gould of attempting to influence a state supreme court judge. Roosevelt calls upon Archer to "clean out the stable" by helping to end the corruption of the Democratic machine, Tammany Hall, which Roosevelt had resisted as the city's civil service commissioner from 1889 to

"Men like you—" how Archer had glowed at the phrase! How eagerly he had risen up at the call! It was an echo of Ned Winsett's old appeal to roll his sleeves up and get down into the muck; but spoken by a man who set the example of the gesture, and whose summons to follow him was irresistible.

Archer, as he looked back, was not sure that men like himself *were* what his country needed, at least in the active service to which Theodore Roosevelt had pointed; in fact, there was reason to think it did not, for after a year in the State Assembly he had not been re-elected, and had dropped back thankfully into obscure if useful municipal work, and from that again to the writing of occasional articles in one of the reforming weeklies that were trying to shake the country out of its apathy. It was little enough to look back on; but when he remembered to what the young men of his generation and his set had looked forward—the narrow groove of money-making, sport and society to which their vision had been limited—even his small contribution to the new state of things seemed to count, as each brick counts in a well-built wall. He had done little in public life; he would always be by nature a contemplative and a dilettante; but he had had high things to contemplate, great things to delight in; and one great man's friendship to be his strength and pride.

He had been, in short, what people were beginning to call "a good citizen." In New York, for many years past, every new movement, philanthropic, municipal or artistic, had taken account of his opinion and wanted his name. People said: "Ask Archer" when there was a question of starting the first school for crippled children, reorganising the Museum of Art, founding the Grolier Club, inaugurating the new Library, or getting up a new society of chamber music. His days were full, and they were filled decently. He supposed it was all a man ought to ask.

1895 and as president of the police board in the reform administration of Mayor William L. Strong. In the 1870s, gentlemen of Archer's class refrained from entering politics, but by the turn of the century, partly through Roosevelt's example, the elite became more involved in public matters.

Grolier Club   A club formed in 1884 by business and cultural leaders who were also collectors of books and prints. Named for the sixteenth-century French bibliophile Jean Grolier, it sought to promote "literary study and the arts of the book."

new Library   The New York Public Library was "new" in the sense that it was formed in 1895 through consolidation of the Astor and Lenox Libraries and the Tilden Trust. Its first director, John S. Billings, combined the collections, reorganized staff, built new collections, and developed a unique classification system.

chamber music   Chamber music is composed for a group of instruments, such as a trio or quartet, and is performed in a private room or a small concert hall.

Something he knew he had missed: the flower of life. But he thought of it now as a thing so unattainable and improbable that to have repined would have been like despairing because one had not drawn the first prize in a lottery. There were a hundred million tickets in *his* lottery, and there was only one prize; the chances had been too decidedly against him. When he thought of Ellen Olenska it was abstractly, serenely, as one might think of some imaginary beloved in a book or a picture: she had become the composite vision of all that he had missed. That vision, faint and tenuous as it was, had kept him from thinking of other women. He had been what was called a faithful husband; and when May had suddenly died— carried off by the infectious pneumonia through which she had nursed their youngest child—he had honestly mourned her. Their long years together had shown him that it did not so much matter if marriage was a dull duty, as long as it kept the dignity of a duty: lapsing from that, it became a mere battle of ugly appetites. Looking about him, he honoured his own past, and mourned for it. After all, there was good in the old ways.

His eyes, making the round of the room—done over by Dallas with English mezzotints, Chippendale cabinets, bits of chosen blue-and-white and pleasantly shaded electric lamps—came back to the old Eastlake writing-table that he had never been willing to banish, and to his first photograph of May, which still kept its place beside his inkstand.

There she was, tall, round-bosomed and willowy, in her starched muslin and flapping Leghorn, as he had seen her under the orange-trees in the Mission Garden. As he had seen her that day, so she had remained; never quite at the same height, yet never far below it: generous, faithful, unwearied; but so lacking in imagination, so incapable of growth, that the world of her youth had fallen into pieces and rebuilt itself without her ever being conscious of the change. This hard bright blindness had kept her immediate horizon apparently unaltered. Her incapacity to recognise change made her children conceal their views from her as Archer concealed his; there had been, from the first, a joint pretence of sameness, a kind of in-

---

mezzotints   Prints made from a metal plate. Roughened surfaces result in a darker area; smooth surfaces result in a lighter area.

blue-and-white   An earthenware or porcelain pattern with a white background and blue design, such as Delft.

pleasantly shaded electric lamps   The first electric distribution system was put into place in London and in New York in 1882, although alternating current was not established until later in the decade. J. P. Morgan's house was the first private residence in the city to be lighted with electricity. The technology was so novel that early lighting fixtures were left unshaded and cords allowed to hang prominently in the room.

nocent family hypocrisy, in which father and children had unconsciously collaborated. And she had died thinking the world a good place, full of loving and harmonious households like her own, and resigned to leave it because she was convinced that, whatever happened, Newland would continue to inculcate in Dallas the same principles and prejudices which had shaped his parents' lives, and that Dallas in turn (when Newland followed her) would transmit the sacred trust to little Bill. And of Mary she was sure as of her own self. So, having snatched little Bill from the grave, and given her life in the effort, she went contentedly to her place in the Archer vault in St. Mark's, where Mrs. Archer already lay safe from the terrifying "trend" which her daughter-in-law had never even become aware of.

Opposite May's portrait stood one of her daughter. Mary Chivers was as tall and fair as her mother, but large-waisted, flat-chested and slightly slouching, as the altered fashion required. Mary Chivers's mighty feats of athleticism could not have been performed with the twenty-inch waist that May Archer's azure sash so easily spanned. And the difference seemed symbolic; the mother's life had been as closely girt as her figure. Mary, who was no less conventional, and no more intelligent, yet led a larger life and held more tolerant views. There was good in the new order too.

The telephone clicked, and Archer, turning from the photographs, unhooked the transmitter at his elbow. How far they were from the days when the legs of the brass-buttoned messenger boy had been New York's only means of quick communication!

"Chicago wants you."

Ah—it must be a long-distance from Dallas, who had been sent to Chicago by his firm to talk over the plan of the Lakeside palace they were to build for a young millionaire with ideas. The firm always sent Dallas on such errands.

"Hallo, Dad—Yes: Dallas. I say—how do you feel about sailing on Wednesday? Mauretania: Yes, next Wednesday as ever is. Our client wants

---

St. Mark's   A stately Episcopal church at Stuyvesant Street and East 10th Street.

large-waisted, flat-chested and slightly slouching   A reference to trends in early twentieth-century women's fashion. By the second decade, women had forsaken the corsetted waist and bustle for dress that allowed greater freedom of movement. The boyish flapper look included a low-waisted dress and a posture that tilted the pelvis forward to give the effect of a minimized bosom.

Lakeside palace   Dallas's Chicago client is building a mansion on Lake Michigan.

Mauretania   A passenger steamer and sister ship of the *Lusitania,* the *Mauretania* was built by the Cunard line in 1907. Nicknamed "speed queen of the Atlantic," it held the Blue Riband for twenty years for the fastest transatlantic crossing (less than five days). (See note on "Cunard," p. 276.)

me to look at some Italian gardens before we settle anything, and has asked me to nip over on the next boat. I've got to be back on the first of June—" the voice broke into a joyful conscious laugh—"so we must look alive. I say, Dad, I want your help: do come."

Dallas seemed to be speaking in the room: the voice was as near by and natural as if he had been lounging in his favourite arm-chair by the fire. The fact would not ordinarily have surprised Archer, for long-distance telephoning had become as much a matter of course as electric lighting and five-day Atlantic voyages. But the laugh did startle him; it still seemed wonderful that across all those miles and miles of country— forest, river, mountain, prairie, roaring cities and busy indifferent millions—Dallas's laugh should be able to say: "Of course, whatever happens, I must get back on the first, because Fanny Beaufort and I are to be married on the fifth."

The voice began again: "Think it over? No, sir: not a minute. You've got to say yes now. Why not, I'd like to know? If you can allege a single reason—No; I knew it. Then it's a go, eh? Because I count on you to ring up the Cunard office first thing tomorrow; and you'd better book a return on a boat from Marseilles. I say, Dad; it'll be our last time together, in this kind of way—. Oh, good! I knew you would."

Chicago rang off, and Archer rose and began to pace up and down the room.

It would be their last time together in this kind of way: the boy was right. They would have lots of other "times" after Dallas's marriage, his father was sure; for the two were born comrades, and Fanny Beaufort, whatever one might think of her, did not seem likely to interfere with their intimacy. On the contrary, from what he had seen of her, he thought she would be naturally included in it. Still, change was change, and differences were differences, and much as he felt himself drawn toward his future daughter-in-law, it was tempting to seize this last chance of being alone with his boy.

There was no reason why he should not seize it, except the profound one that he had lost the habit of travel. May had disliked to move except for valid reasons, such as taking the children to the sea or in the mountains: she could imagine no other motive for leaving the house in Thirty-ninth

---

long-distance telephoning   Continental long-distance service began in the United States as early as 1892.

Cunard   A passenger service across the Atlantic Ocean, founded by Sir Samuel Cunard, a Canadian shipowner.

Marseilles   A city and principal port in southern France, on the Mediterranean.

Street or their comfortable quarters at the Wellands' in Newport. After Dallas had taken his degree she had thought it her duty to travel for six months; and the whole family had made the old-fashioned tour through England, Switzerland and Italy. Their time being limited (no one knew why) they had omitted France. Archer remembered Dallas's wrath at being asked to contemplate Mont Blanc instead of Rheims and Chartres. But Mary and Bill wanted mountain-climbing, and had already yawned their way in Dallas's wake through the English cathedrals; and May, always fair to her children, had insisted on holding the balance evenly between their athletic and artistic proclivities. She had indeed proposed that her husband should go to Paris for a fortnight, and join them on the Italian lakes after they had "done" Switzerland; but Archer had declined. "We'll stick together," he said; and May's face had brightened at his setting such a good example to Dallas.

Since her death, nearly two years before, there had been no reason for his continuing in the same routine. His children had urged him to travel: Mary Chivers had felt sure it would do him good to go abroad and "see the galleries." The very mysteriousness of such a cure made her the more confident of its efficacy. But Archer had found himself held fast by habit, by memories, by a sudden startled shrinking from new things.

Now, as he reviewed his past, he saw into what a deep rut he had sunk. The worst of doing one's duty was that it apparently unfitted one for doing anything else. At least that was the view that the men of his generation had taken. The trenchant divisions between right and wrong, honest and dishonest, respectable and the reverse, had left so little scope for the unforeseen. There are moments when a man's imagination, so easily subdued to what it lives in, suddenly rises above its daily level, and surveys the long windings of destiny. Archer hung there and wondered. . . .

What was left of the little world he had grown up in, and whose standards had bent and bound him? He remembered a sneering prophecy of poor Lawrence Lefferts's, uttered years ago in that very room: "If things go on at this rate, our children will be marrying Beaufort's bastards."

It was just what Archer's eldest son, the pride of his life, was doing; and nobody wondered or reproved. Even the boy's Aunt Janey, who still

---

Mont Blanc   The highest mountain in Europe, in the Alps on the border between France and Italy.

Rheims   A historic town in northeastern France and former coronation site of French kings.

Chartres   A city in north central France and site of the cathedral, built in the thirteenth century and widely recognized as a masterpiece of Gothic architecture.

looked so exactly as she used to in her elderly youth, had taken her mother's emeralds and seed-pearls out of their pink cotton-wool, and carried them with her own twitching hands to the future bride; and Fanny Beaufort, instead of looking disappointed at not receiving a "set" from a Paris jeweller, had exclaimed at their old-fashioned beauty, and declared that when she wore them she should feel like an Isabey miniature.

Fanny Beaufort, who had appeared in New York at eighteen, after the death of her parents, had won its heart much as Madame Olenska had won it thirty years earlier; only instead of being distrustful and afraid of her, society took her joyfully for granted. She was pretty, amusing and accomplished: what more did any one want? Nobody was narrow-minded enough to rake up against her the half-forgotten facts of her father's past and her own origin. Only the older people remembered so obscure an incident in the business life of New York as Beaufort's failure, or the fact that after his wife's death he had been quietly married to the notorious Fanny Ring, and had left the country with his new wife, and a little girl who inherited her beauty. He was subsequently heard of in Constantinople, then in Russia; and a dozen years later American travellers were handsomely entertained by him in Buenos Ayres, where he represented a large insurance agency. He and his wife died there in the odour of prosperity; and one day their orphaned daughter had appeared in New York in charge of May Archer's sister-in-law, Mrs. Jack Welland, whose husband had been appointed the girl's guardian. The fact threw her into almost cousinly relationship with Newland Archer's children, and nobody was surprised when Dallas's engagement was announced.

Nothing could more clearly give the measure of the distance that the world had travelled. People nowadays were too busy—busy with reforms and "movements," with fads and fetishes and frivolities—to bother much about their neighbours. And of what account was anybody's past, in the huge kaleidoscope where all the social atoms spun around on the same plane?

Newland Archer, looking out of his hotel window at the stately gaiety of the Paris streets, felt his heart beating with the confusion and eagerness of youth.

---

reforms and "movements" Government corruption, industrialization, immigration, and urban expansion after the Civil War led to a number of social and economic crises that individuals and groups attempted to address through various programs. Among other goals, reformers hoped to curb crime, ensure fair labor practices, regulate monopolies, enfranchise minorities and women, improve public transportation and water, and ameliorate living conditions for the nation's poor.

It was long since it had thus plunged and reared under his widening waistcoat, leaving him, the next minute, with an empty breast and hot temples. He wondered if it was thus that his son's conducted itself in the presence of Miss Fanny Beaufort—and decided that it was not. "It functions as actively, no doubt, but the rhythm is different," he reflected, recalling the cool composure with which the young man had announced his engagement, and taken for granted that his family would approve.

"The difference is that these young people take it for granted that they're going to get whatever they want, and that we almost always took it for granted that we shouldn't. Only, I wonder—the thing one's so certain of in advance: can it ever make one's heart beat as wildly?"

It was the day after their arrival in Paris, and the spring sunshine held Archer in his open window, above the wide silvery prospect of the Place Vendôme. One of the things he had stipulated—almost the only one—when he had agreed to come abroad with Dallas, was that, in Paris, he shouldn't be made to go to one of the new-fangled "palaces."

"Oh, all right—of course," Dallas good-naturedly agreed. "I'll take you to some jolly old-fashioned place—the Bristol say—" leaving his father speechless at hearing that the century-long home of kings and emperors was now spoken of as an old-fashioned inn, where one went for its quaint inconveniences and lingering local colour.

Archer had pictured often enough, in the first impatient years, the scene of his return to Paris; then the personal vision had faded, and he had simply tried to see the city as the setting of Madame Olenska's life. Sitting alone at night in his library, after the household had gone to bed, he had evoked the radiant outbreak of spring down the avenues of horse-chestnuts, the flowers and statues in the public gardens, the whiff of lilacs from the flower-carts, the majestic roll of the river under the great bridges, and the life of art and study and pleasure that filled each mighty artery to bursting. Now the spectacle was before him in its glory, and as he looked out on it he felt shy, old-fashioned, inadequate: a mere grey speck of a man compared with the ruthless magnificent fellow he had dreamed of being. . . .

Dallas's hand came down cheerily on his shoulder. "Hullo, father: this is something like, isn't it?" They stood for a while looking out in silence, and then the young man continued: "By the way, I've got a message for you: the Countess Olenska expects us both at half-past five."

Place Vendôme An octagonal square on Paris's Right Bank, designed by Jules Hardouin-Mansart in the Louis XIV style.

Bristol One of a number of luxury hotels in grand buildings situated around Place Vendôme. The Bristol is at No. 3, the Ritz at No. 15.

He said it lightly, carelessly, as he might have imparted any casual item of information, such as the hour at which their train was to leave for Florence the next evening. Archer looked at him, and thought he saw in his gay young eyes a gleam of his great-grandmother Mingott's malice.

"Oh, didn't I tell you?" Dallas pursued. "Fanny made me swear to do three things while I was in Paris: get her the score of the last Debussy songs, go to the Grand-Guignol and see Madame Olenska. You know she was awfully good to Fanny when Mr. Beaufort sent her over from Buenos Ayres to the Assomption. Fanny hadn't any friends in Paris, and Madame Olenska used to be kind to her and trot her about on holidays. I believe she was a great friend of the first Mrs. Beaufort's. And she's our cousin, of course. So I rang her up this morning, before I went out, and told her you and I were here for two days and wanted to see her."

Archer continued to stare at him. "You told her I was here?"

"Of course—why not?" Dallas's eye brows went up whimsically. Then, getting no answer, he slipped his arm through his father's with a confidential pressure.

"I say, father: what was she like?"

Archer felt his colour rise under his son's unabashed gaze. "Come, own up: you and she were great pals, weren't you? Wasn't she most awfully lovely?"

"Lovely? I don't know. She was different."

"Ah—there you have it! That's what it always comes to, doesn't it? When she comes, *she's different*—and one doesn't know why. It's exactly what I feel about Fanny."

His father drew back a step, releasing his arm. "About Fanny? But, my dear fellow—I should hope so! Only I don't see—"

"Dash it, Dad, don't be prehistoric! Wasn't she—once—your Fanny?"

Dallas belonged body and soul to the new generation. He was the first-born of Newland and May Archer, yet it had never been possible to

***

Debussy   Claude Debussy (1862–1918) was a French composer who pioneered the use of the whole-tone scale. His musical compositions were compared to Impressionist paintings of the same period because of their dreamlike, lyrical quality.

Grand-Guignol   French: The Theatre du Grand-Guignol was a feature of Parisian life from 1897 to 1962. An evening's entertainment consisted of two short plays, two comedies, and two "blood curdlers," with realistic stage effects. It provided an arena within which the most sacred taboos surrounding violence and sexuality were breached.

Buenos Ayres [sic]   Buenos Aires, capital city of Argentina.

Assomption   A school associated with the Church of the Assumption, slightly north of Place de la Concorde.

inculcate in him even the rudiments of reserve. "What's the use of making mysteries? It only makes people want to nose 'em out," he always objected when enjoined to discretion. But Archer, meeting his eyes, saw the filial light under their banter.

"My Fanny—?"

"Well, the woman you'd have chucked everything for: only you didn't," continued his surprising son.

"I didn't," echoed Archer with a kind of solemnity.

"No: you date, you see, dear old boy. But mother said—"

"Your mother?"

"Yes: the day before she died. It was when she sent for me alone—you remember? She said she knew we were safe with you, and always would be, because once, when she asked you to, you'd given up the thing you most wanted."

Archer received this strange communication in silence. His eyes remained unseeingly fixed on the thronged sunlit square below the window. At length he said in a low voice: "She never asked me."

"No. I forgot. You never did ask each other anything, did you? And you never told each other anything. You just sat and watched each other, and guessed at what was going on underneath. A deaf-and-dumb asylum, in fact! Well, I back your generation for knowing more about each other's private thoughts than we ever have time to find out about our own.—I say, Dad," Dallas broke off, "you're not angry with me? If you are, let's make it up and go and lunch at Henri's. I've got to rush out to Versailles afterward."

Archer did not accompany his son to Versailles. He preferred to spend the afternoon in solitary roamings through Paris. He had to deal all at once with the packed regrets and stifled memories of an inarticulate lifetime.

After a little while he did not regret Dallas's indiscretion. It seemed to take an iron band from his heart to know that, after all, some one had guessed and pitied. . . . And that it should have been his wife moved him indescribably. Dallas, for all his affectionate insight, would not have understood that. To the boy, no doubt, the episode was only a pathetic instance of vain frustration, of wasted forces. But was it really no more? For a long time Archer sat on a bench in the Champs Elysées and wondered, while the stream of life rolled by. . . .

Versailles   A chateau built for Louis XIII at the village of Versailles, fourteen miles southwest of Paris, in the seventeenth century and transformed by Louis XIV into an opulent palace unequaled in its display of wealth.

A few streets away, a few hours away, Ellen Olenska waited. She had never gone back to her husband, and when he had died, some years before, she had made no change in her way of living. There was nothing now to keep her and Archer apart—and that afternoon he was to see her.

He got up and walked across the Place de la Concorde and the Tuileries gardens to the Louvre. She had once told him that she often went there, and he had a fancy to spend the intervening time in a place where he could think of her as perhaps having lately been. For an hour or more he wandered from gallery to gallery through the dazzle of afternoon light, and one by one the pictures burst on him in their half-forgotten splendour, filling his soul with the long echoes of beauty. After all, his life had been too starved. . . .

Suddenly, before an effulgent Titian, he found himself saying: "But I'm only fifty-seven—" and then he turned away. For such summer dreams it was too late; but surely not for a quiet harvest of friendship, of comradeship, in the blessed hush of her nearness.

He went back to the hotel, where he and Dallas were to meet; and together they walked again across the Place de la Concorde and over the bridge that leads to the Chamber of Deputies.

Dallas, unconscious of what was going on in his father's mind, was talking excitedly and abundantly of Versailles. He had had but one previous glimpse of it, during a holiday trip in which he had tried to pack all the sights he had been deprived of when he had had to go with the family to Switzerland; and tumultuous enthusiasm and cock-sure criticism tripped each other up on his lips.

As Archer listened, his sense of inadequacy and inexpressiveness increased. The boy was not insensitive, he knew; but he had the facility and self-confidence that came of looking at fate not as a master but as an equal.

Place de la Concorde   A large, open square located on the Right Bank, next to the Seine and midway between the Etoile and the Ile de la Cité. Skillfully landscaped and devoid of buildings on three sides, it offers impressive perspectives.

Louvre   The national museum of art in Paris, with one of the finest art collections in the world.

Titian   Tiziano Vecellio Titian (c. 1485–1576), a great painter of the Venetian school whose mastery of color allowed him to achieve an increased sense of movement, to model forms, and to describe lavish textures. Archer would have been able to view several of Titian's celebrated religious paintings, mythological allegories, and portraits at the Louvre.

Chamber of Deputies   A building that housed the lower house of Parliament. Archer and his son cross from the Right Bank to the Left Bank of the Seine River.

"That's it: they feel equal to things—they know their way about," he mused, thinking of his son as the spokesman of the new generation which had swept away all the old landmarks, and with them the sign-posts and the danger-signal.

Suddenly Dallas stopped short, grasping his father's arm. "Oh, by Jove," he exclaimed.

They had come out into the great tree-planted space before the Invalides. The dome of Mansart floated ethereally above the budding trees and the long grey front of the building: drawing up into itself all the rays of afternoon light, it hung there like the visible symbol of the race's glory.

Archer knew that Madame Olenska lived in a square near one of the avenues radiating from the Invalides; and he had pictured the quarter as quiet and almost obscure, forgetting the central splendour that lit it up. Now, by some queer process of association, that golden light became for him the pervading illumination in which she lived. For nearly thirty years, her life—of which he knew so strangely little—had been spent in this rich atmosphere that he already felt to be too dense and yet too stimulating for his lungs. He thought of the theatres she must have been to, the pictures she must have looked at, the sober and splendid old houses she must have frequented, the people she must have talked with, the incessant stir of ideas, curiosities, images and associations thrown out by an intensely social race in a setting of immemorial manners; and suddenly he remembered the young Frenchman who had once said to him: "Ah, good conversation—there is nothing like it, is there?"

Archer had not seen M. Rivière, or heard of him, for nearly thirty years; and that fact gave the measure of his ignorance of Madame Olenska's existence. More than half a lifetime divided them, and she had spent the long interval among people he did not know, in a society he but faintly guessed at, in conditions he would never wholly understand. During that time he had been living with his youthful memory of her; but she had doubtless had other and more tangible companionship. Perhaps she too had kept her memory of him as something apart; but if she had, it must have been like a relic in a small dim chapel, where there was not time to pray every day. . . .

Invalides   The Hôtel des Invalides, on the Right Bank, is a hospital founded by Louis XIV for the care of old and disabled soldiers. It is now also a museum.

dome of Mansart   The Dôme des Invalides, which sits atop the Church of St. Louis, was designed by architect Jules Hardouin-Mansart (1646–1708) and is thought to be the most splendid dome in Paris. Napoléon's tomb is located beneath the dome.

They had crossed the Place des Invalides, and were walking down one of the thoroughfares flanking the building. It was a quiet quarter, after all, in spite of its splendour and its history; and the fact gave one an idea of the riches Paris had to draw on, since such scenes as this were left to the few and the indifferent.

The day was fading into a soft sun-shot haze, pricked here and there by a yellow electric light, and passers were rare in the little square into which they had turned. Dallas stopped again, and looked up.

"It must be here," he said, slipping his arm through his father's with a movement from which Archer's shyness did not shrink; and they stood together looking up at the house.

It was a modern building, without distinctive character, but many-windowed, and pleasantly balconied up its wide cream-coloured front. On one of the upper balconies, which hung well above the rounded tops of the horse-chestnuts in the square, the awnings were still lowered, as though the sun had just left it.

"I wonder which floor—?" Dallas conjectured; and moving toward the *porte-cochère* he put his head into the porter's lodge, and came back to say: "The fifth. It must be the one with the awnings."

Archer remained motionless, gazing at the upper windows as if the end of their pilgrimage had been attained.

"I say, you know, it's nearly six," his son at length reminded him.

The father glanced away at an empty bench under the trees.

"I believe I'll sit there a moment," he said.

"Why—aren't you well?" his son exclaimed.

"Oh, perfectly. But I should like you, please, to go up without me."

Dallas paused before him, visibly bewildered. "But, I say, Dad: do you mean you won't come up at all?"

"I don't know," said Archer slowly.

"If you don't she won't understand."

"Go, my boy; perhaps I shall follow you."

Dallas gave him a long look through the twilight.

"But what on earth shall I say?"

"My dear fellow, don't you always know what to say?" his father rejoined with a smile.

"Very well. I shall say you're old-fashioned, and prefer walking up the five flights because you don't like lifts."

---

porte-cochère   French: a carriage entrance or porch.

porter's lodge   British English: a room at the entrance to a large building.

His father smiled again. "Say I'm old-fashioned: that's enough."

Dallas looked at him again, and then, with an incredulous gesture, passed out of sight under the vaulted doorway.

Archer sat down on the bench and continued to gaze at the awninged balcony. He calculated the time it would take his son to be carried up in the lift to the fifth floor, to ring the bell, and be admitted to the hall, and then ushered into the drawing-room. He pictured Dallas entering that room with his quick assured step and his delightful smile, and wondered if the people were right who said that his boy "took after him."

Then he tried to see the persons already in the room—for probably at that sociable hour there would be more than one—and among them a dark lady, pale and dark, who would look up quickly, half rise, and hold out a long thin hand with three rings on it. . . . He thought she would be sitting in a sofa-corner near the fire, with azaleas banked behind her on a table.

"It's more real to me here than if I went up," he suddenly heard himself say; and the fear lest that last shadow of reality should lose its edge kept him rooted to his seat as the minutes succeeded each other.

He sat for a long time on the bench in the thickening dusk, his eyes never turning from the balcony. At length a light shone through the windows, and a moment later a man-servant came out on the balcony, drew up the awnings, and closed the shutters.

At that, as if it had been the signal he waited for, Newland Archer got up slowly and walked back alone to his hotel.

THE END

PART TWO

Background Readings

Questions of Culture

The extraordinary growth of New York City after the Civil War—growth fueled by industrialization and the arrival of thousands of immigrants from Europe and freed slaves from the South—left intellectuals, reformers, and artists musing over the future of America. How was the face of American society changing? Who would take responsibility for its failures as well as its successes? What constituted American culture, and who could participate in its creation and expression? The commentaries that follow suggest a continuum of answers.

THE METROPOLITAN GENTRY: CULTURE AGAINST POLITICS

Thomas Bender

Thomas Bender's brief history of nineteenth-century New York City (1987) mentions developments that also appear in *The Age of Innocence*. Bender describes how society's elite, the self-appointed guardians of culture, worked to preserve customs and institutions that had been most valued in the past. [ED.]

During the third quarter of the nineteenth century, New York transformed itself into a metropolis that could be compared, at last, with Paris and London. New York's population, drawn from all parts of the world as well as from the American provinces, surged past the one million mark, and the city assumed a commanding and never again challenged position

From *New York Intellect*. New York: Knopf, 1987.

in the nation's economic and cultural life. Even in politics, this metropolis that was not a national capital was nonetheless a dominating force. Both the politics of the city and the political opinion of its journalists loomed large, decisively so, in national political affairs, in part because the New York Customs House was the primary source of federal revenue.

The city's aspirations toward metropolitan grandeur were increasingly realized in its architecture and thus visible to anyone who walked the city's streets or subscribed to the proliferating illustrated magazines that so often published pictures of New York. There were, for example, the rows upon rows of bourgeois brownstones extending north from Washington Square, the new Central Park, the enormous (for its time) Grand Central Depot on Forty-second Street, A. T. Stewart's grand department store at Broadway and Ninth Street or his marble mansion (the city's first) at Thirty-fourth Street and Fifth Avenue, the large and luxurious hotels that lined Broadway from Canal Street to Madison Square, where the elegant Fifth Avenue Hotel (built in 1859 and boasting the world's first hotel elevator) served as a New York home for visiting foreign dignitaries and for the American political elite.

The metropolitan quality of the city was reflected, as well, in the elaboration of economic, cultural, and philanthropic institutions on a new scale. Financial and communications industries led the way in business, organizing corporate headquarters from which they administered their national enterprises. Any walker in the city could immediately recognize the Broadway buildings that housed and symbolized, for example, the Equitable Life Assurance Society and the Western Union Company.

Private philanthropy, often with municipal assistance, now began to reform and consolidate both social welfare agencies and institutions of elite culture. The Association for Improving the Condition of the Poor (founded 1843) and the Charity Organization Society (founded 1882), for example, sought to coordinate the myriad of social welfare agencies serving the city's growing class of unfortunates, while the Children's Aid Society, founded in 1853, quickly established itself as the nation's most innovative urban philanthropy.

Some of the cultural philanthropies of this period still stand as major institutions. The scholarly, wealthy James Lenox endowed a great library (later combined with the Astor Library and Tilden Trust to form the New York Public Library). Lenox commissioned Richard Morris Hunt, the first American trained at the Ecole des Beaux Arts, to design a magnificent home for his library at Fifth Avenue and Seventy-first Street, while Peter B. Wight designed a new and impressive home for the National Academy of Design, a much-praised Venetian Gothic building located at Fourth Avenue and Twenty-third Street. Two privately organized and privately controlled not-for-profit corporations collaborated with the municipality to establish the Metropolitan Museum of Art and the American Museum of Natural History. In no other American city did civic leaders dare give such titles to local institutions. Only in New York did such use of "metropolitan" and "American" seem natural.

Such metropolitan progress was, of course, heartening to the men and women who concerned themselves with the city's cultural life. But political and social problems kept intruding onto the terrain of high culture, even with the last two institutions named. In order to obtain the charters necessary to incorporate the Museum of Natural History and the Metropolitan Museum, elite cultural reformers had to engage the political skills of William Marcy Tweed, "Boss Tweed." Their errand to Tweed presented them with something of a conundrum: How could their definition of culture relate to the diverse cultures of the city? It was difficult, all the more so because distaste for the city's working people—all of those who sustained Tweed in power—so easily overcame the rhetoric of uplift. Until the 1890s, when pressure from Tammany Hall forced a change, the private board that ran the Metropolitan Museum often talked about democratic culture but declined to open on Sunday, the only day when men and women of the city's working classes might, if they should so desire, take the time during the day to look at the pictures and sculpture in the museum.

If we allow it to, this little story about the museum points toward the underlying circumstance and the constant preoccupation of intellectual life in New York City in the second half of the nineteenth century. Before all is the overwhelming fact of inequality. Perhaps in no other great city, whether European or American, was social inequality so extreme.[1] By 1876, 50 percent of the city's population lived in tenements, many scandalously unhealthy; the residents of these tenements accounted for 65 percent of the city's deaths and an appalling 90 percent of the deaths of children under five years of age. Here we have the defining circumstance of life in Gilded Age New York.

The problem for intellectuals was to establish a place for themselves in a city whose politics and culture were conditioned by this troubling fact. What, they asked themselves, are the prerogatives of the cultivated in the politics of a city in which Tammany thrived as a link between a new and very rich class of crude capitalists and the ignorant masses? Was there, they worried, any place for learning, for the cultivated ideals that they so

---

[1] Diane Lindstrom, "The Growth of the New York City Economy," paper presented to SSRC conference, November 1983. Also her comments at SSRC workshop, September 14, 1984.

valued? What, they had to ask, is the role of elite culture in the larger culture of the city? Should they—could they—reach out to the masses, or was recoil in self-righteousness not only easier but more appropriate? They were troubled about the possibilities and implications of both extension and withdrawal. Perhaps they could redefine public life—or culture—in ways more congenial to themselves. What, after all, was their rightful authority? Their social responsibility? Their complicity in the social inequality of the city? These were the fundamental questions in Boss Tweed's New York. For the learned, these questions coalesced into a larger worry about whether either culture or democracy could survive the new conditions of metropolitan life in New York City. Because New York had become the center of American journalism and, thus, opinion making, these local concerns and worries informed the culture of the middle classes emerging in the cities and towns of the nation.

Certain words, those Raymond Williams has designated "keywords," gather into themselves and represent the structure of meaning and feeling that informs the social life and imagination of a historical period.[2] Neither the meaning nor the social salience of these words is fixed; they may change meaning over time, and they may move from the center to the periphery of discourse and back again. To track these changes in meaning and significance is to get very close to some basic facts of intellectual life— facts with considerable ideological significance.

Culture is a keyword, and its meaning was quite different, with profoundly different implications, in 1770 and 1870. We cannot trace the slow process of change, but one point is fundamental. The word was redefined in the context of emerging political democracy and expansive capitalism, and it came to distinguish itself from these developments. If for Clinton and Pintard culture meant improvement of all sorts, practical and intellectual, it now came to represent something higher, more refined, than ordinary life. Ideality, it was assumed, ought to dominate practice in economic and political life. For the individuals who embraced culture (and its cognates, cultivation, education, civilization), the prize was, it was presumed, special authority and, perhaps, responsibility. Something of Samuel Taylor Coleridge's dream of a national clerisy thus got involved with the notion of culture, and this association, though not formally acknowledged, colored American usage.[3]

---

[2] Raymond Williams, *Keywords* (New York: Oxford University Press, 1976).
[3] On Coleridge and culture, see Raymond Williams, *Culture and Society, 1780–1950* (New York: Harper & Row, 1966), part 1, chap. 3.

The post–Civil War writers and reformers in New York City of concern here, those I call the metropolitan gentry, took up a notion of culture that had its American origins in New England. It was largely derived from Ralph Waldo Emerson, though later the direct Anglo-French influence of Matthew Arnold would somewhat obscure this New England background.[4] The reforming ambitions of the metropolitan gentry were inspired by Emerson's observation that men could be turned away from their narrow pursuit of money and power only "by the gradual domestication of the idea of culture." Here, perhaps, Emerson had in mind self-culture rather than a model of social leadership, but he elsewhere translated his idea of culture into a justification for gentry leadership. He explained that every society "wants to be officered by a best class, who shall be masters instructed in all the great arts of life; shall be wise, temperate, brave, public men, adorned with dignity and accomplishments."[5]

Emerson's distaste for New York was great and his contacts there few, but Charles Eliot Norton, who by the 1880s had become Harvard's and Boston's "apostle of culture," extended Boston's influence through lines of friendship and an active, mentor-like correspondence with the rising generation of New York gentry.[6] Norton, who imbibed Emerson's ideas and combined them with a profoundly conservative concern for bolstering the leadership position of his class in the nation, forged a strong postwar link between Boston and New York. His *Considerations on Some Recent Social Theories,* published anonymously in 1853, was the definitive statement of Brahmin elitism, and by the time of the Civil War, Norton believed that the moment had come for the cultivated class to "seize control of society and give it practical direction."[7] Whatever the origins of these ideas, it was in New York that they got their test. New England's highly refined ideas came out of doors in New York and confronted American life in all its democratic complexity.

The culture of Emerson and Norton was exclusive; it separated or distinguished the elite more than it unified the masses. At the other extreme was Walt Whitman, whose *Democratic Vistas* we have already discussed.

---

[4] For Emerson and Arnold, see John H. Raleigh, *Matthew Arnold and American Culture* (Berkeley: University of California Press, 1957), pp. 1–13.

[5] Emerson quotes from ibid., p. 10. Peter G. Buckley, in "To the Opera House: Culture and Society in New York City, 1820–1860" (Ph.D. dissertation, SUNY–Stony Brook, 1984), p. 292, sees this redefinition emerging in the 1850s, in the wake of the Astor Place Riot of 1849.

[6] On Norton, see Kermit Vanderbilt, *Charles Eliot Norton* (Cambridge: Harvard University Press, 1959).

[7] George M. Fredrickson, *The Inner Civil War* (New York: Harper & Row, 1965), p. 32.

It is worth recalling, however, that in his plea for democratic culture, Whitman nervously acknowledged the tension between democracy and culture. With this word, he observed, we are in close quarters with the enemy, but he insisted upon an understanding of culture that was not divisive, not a basis for exclusion and class privilege.

As Whitman wrote, however, a new generation of New Yorkers, a metropolitan gentry, responding to broad changes that redefined the social position and weakened the intellectual authority of the traditional learned classes in America, embraced culture for precisely the reasons that worried Whitman. In the claims of culture they found the basis for reasserting gentry leadership outside of the traditional professions. Not yet glimpsing the authority that academic and disciplinary professions would later confer, they imagined themselves appointed to assume social leadership because of their cultivation, all in the interest of civilization. . . .

THE GENTEEL TRADITION
IN AMERICAN PHILOSOPHY

George Santayana

George Santayana (1863–1952), a philosopher and novelist whom Wharton knew and admired, articulated a fundamental division in American character in his 1911 address, "The Genteel Tradition in American Philosophy." Coining a phrase frequently applied to Wharton's work, he describes the genteel tradition in a society torn between faded propriety and capitalist venture— the same tensions Wharton incorporates in her portrayals of conflict between established New Yorkers and the newly moneyed classes. [ED.]

Address delivered before the Philosophical Union of the University of California, August 25, 1911.

. . . America is a young country with an old mentality: it has enjoyed the advantages of a child carefully brought up and thoroughly indoctrinated; it has been a wise child. But a wise child, an old head on young

From *The Winds of Doctrine.* New York: Scribner's, 1926.

shoulders, always has a comic and an unpromising side. The wisdom is a little thin and verbal, not aware of its full meaning and grounds; and physical and emotional growth may be stunted by it, or even deranged. Or when the child is too vigorous for that, he will develop a fresh mentality of his own, out of his observations and actual instincts; and this fresh mentality will interfere with the traditional mentality, and tend to reduce it to something perfunctory, conventional, and perhaps secretly despised. A philosophy is not genuine unless it inspires and expresses the life of those who cherish it. I do not think the hereditary philosophy of America has done much to atrophy the natural activities of the inhabitants; the wise child has not missed the joys of youth or of manhood; but what has happened is that the hereditary philosophy has grown stale, and that the academic philosophy afterwards developed has caught the stale odour from it. America is not simply, as I said a moment ago, a young country with an old mentality: it is a country with two mentalities, one a survival of the beliefs and standards of the fathers, the other an expression of the instincts, practice, and discoveries of the younger generations. In all the higher things of the mind—in religion, in literature, in the moral emotions—it is the hereditary spirit that still prevails, so much so that Mr. Bernard Shaw finds that America is a hundred years behind the times. The truth is that one-half of the American mind, that not occupied intensely in practical affairs, has remained, I will not say high-and-dry, but slightly becalmed; it has floated gently in the back-water, while, alongside, in invention and industry and social organisation, the other half of the mind was leaping down a sort of Niagara Rapids. This division may be found symbolised in American architecture: a neat reproduction of the colonial mansion—with some modern comforts introduced surreptitiously—stands beside the sky-scraper. The American Will inhabits the sky-scraper; the American Intellect inhabits the colonial mansion. The one is the sphere of the American man; the other, at least predominantly, of the American woman. The one is all aggressive enterprise; the other is all genteel tradition.

Now, with your permission, I should like to analyse more fully how this interesting situation has arisen, how it is qualified, and whither it tends. And in the first place we should remember what, precisely, that philosophy was which the first settlers brought with them into the country. In strictness there was more than one; but we may confine our attention to what I will call Calvinism, since it is on this that the current academic philosophy has been grafted. I do not mean exactly the Calvinism of Calvin, or even of Jonathan Edwards; for in their systems there was much that was not pure philosophy, but rather faith in the externals and history of revelation. Jewish and Christian revelation was interpreted by these men, however, in the spirit of a particular philosophy, which might have arisen under any sky, and been associated with any other religion as well as with Protestant Christianity. In fact, the philosophical principle of Calvinism appears also in the Koran, in Spinoza, and in Cardinal Newman; and persons with no very distinctive Christian belief, like Carlyle or like Professor Royce, may be nevertheless, philosophically, perfect Calvinists. Calvinism, taken in this sense, is an expression of the agonised conscience. It is a view of the world which an agonised conscience readily embraces, if it takes itself seriously, as, being agonised, of course it must. Calvinism, essentially, asserts three things: that sin exists, that sin is punished, and that it is beautiful that sin should exist to be punished. The heart of the Calvinist is therefore divided between tragic concern at his own miserable condition, and tragic exultation about the universe at large. He oscillates between a profound abasement and a paradoxical elation of the spirit. To be a Calvinist philosophically is to feel a fierce pleasure in the existence of misery, especially of one's own, in that this misery seems to manifest the fact that the Absolute is irresponsible or infinite or holy. Human nature, it feels, is totally depraved: to have the instincts and motives that we necessarily have is a great scandal, and we must suffer for it; but that scandal is requisite, since otherwise the serious importance of being as we ought to be would not have been vindicated.

To those of us who have not an agonised conscience this system may seem fantastic and even unintelligible; yet it is logically and intently thought out from its emotional premises. It can take permanent possession of a deep mind here and there, and under certain conditions it can become epidemic. Imagine, for instance, a small nation with an intense vitality, but on the verge of ruin, ecstatic and distressful, having a strict and minute code of laws, that paints life in sharp and violent chiaroscuro, all pure righteousness and black abominations, and exaggerating the consequences of both perhaps to infinity. Such a people were the Jews after the exile, and again the early Protestants. If such a people is philosophical at all, it will not improbably be Calvinistic. Even in the early American communities many of these conditions were fulfilled. The nation was small and isolated; it lived under pressure and constant trial; it was acquainted with but a small range of goods and evils. Vigilance over conduct and an absolute demand for personal integrity were not merely traditional things, but things that practical sages, like Franklin and Washington, recommended to their countrymen, because they were virtues that justified themselves visibly by their fruits. But soon these happy results themselves helped to relax the pressure of external circumstances, and indirectly the pressure of the agonised conscience within. The nation became numerous; it ceased to be either ecstatic or distressful; the high social morality which on the whole it preserved took another colour; people remained honest and helpful out of good sense and good will rather than out of scrupulous adherence to any fixed principles. They retained their instinct for order, and often created order with surprising quickness; but the sanctity of law, to be obeyed for its own sake, began to escape them; it seemed too unpractical a notion, and not quite serious. In fact, the second and native-born American mentality began to take shape. The sense of sin totally evaporated. Nature, in the words of Emerson, was all beauty and commodity; and while operating on it laboriously, and drawing quick returns, the American began to drink in inspiration from it æsthetically. At the same time, in so broad a continent, he had elbow-room. His neighbours helped more than they hindered him; he wished their number to increase. Good will become the great American virtue; and a passion arose for counting heads, and square miles, and cubic feet, and minutes saved—as if there had been anything to save them for. How strange to the American now that saying of Jonathan Edwards, that men are naturally God's enemies! Yet that is an axiom to any intelligent Calvinist, though the words he uses may be different. If you told the modern American that he is totally depraved, he would think you were joking, as he himself usually is. He is convinced that he always has been, and always will be, victorious and blameless.

Calvinism thus lost its basis in American life. Some emotional natures, indeed, reverted in their religious revivals or private searchings of heart to the sources of the tradition; for any of the radical points of view in philosophy may cease to be prevalent, but none can cease to be possible. Other natures, more sensitive to the moral and literary influences of the world, preferred to abandon parts of their philosophy, hoping thus to reduce the distance which should separate the remainder from real life. . . .

. . . [T]ranscendentalism had much to recommend it to American philosophers, for the transcendental method appealed to the individualistic and revolutionary temper of their youth, while transcendental myths enabled them to find a new status for their inherited theology, and to give what parts of it they cared to preserve some semblance of philosophical backing. This last was the use to which the transcendental method was put by Kant himself, who first brought it into vogue, before the terrible weapon had got out of hand, and become the instrument of pure romanticism. Kant came, he himself said, to remove knowledge in order to make room for faith, which in his case meant faith in Calvinism. In other words, he applied the transcendental method to matters of fact, reducing them thereby to human ideas, in order to give to the Calvinistic postulates of conscience a metaphysical validity. For Kant had a genteel tradition of his own, which he wished to remove to a place of safety, feeling that the empirical world had become too hot for it; and this place of safety was the region of transcendental myth. I need hardly say how perfectly this expedient suited the needs of philosophers in America, and it is no accident if the influence of Kant soon became dominant here. To embrace this philosophy was regarded as a sign of profound metaphysical insight, although the most mediocre minds found no difficulty in embracing it. In truth it was a sign of having been brought up in the genteel tradition, of feeling it weak, and of wishing to save it.

But the transcendental method, in its way, was also sympathetic to the American mind. It embodied, in a radical form, the spirit of Protestantism as distinguished from its inherited doctrines; it was autonomous, undismayed, calmly revolutionary; it felt that Will was deeper than Intellect; it focussed everything here and now, and asked all things to show their credentials at the bar of the young self, and to prove their value for this latest born moment. These things are truly American; they would be characteristic of any young society with a keen and discursive intelligence, and they are strikingly exemplified in the thought and in the person of Emerson. They constitute what he called self-trust. . . .

. . . Perhaps the prevalence of humour in America, in and out of season, may be taken as one more evidence that the genteel tradition is present pervasively, but everywhere weak. Similarly in Italy, during the Renaissance, the Catholic tradition could not be banished from the intellect, since there was nothing articulate to take its place; yet its hold on the heart was singularly relaxed. The consequence was that humorists could regale themselves with the foibles of monks and of cardinals, with the credulity of fools, and the bogus miracles of the saints; not intending to deny the theory of the church, but caring for it so little at heart that they could find it infinitely amusing that it should be contradicted in men's lives and that no harm should come of it. So when Mark Twain says, "I was born of poor but dishonest parents," the humour depends on the parody of the genteel Anglo-Saxon convention that it is disreputable to be poor; but to hint at the hollowness of it would not be amusing if it did not remain at bottom one's habitual conviction.

The one American writer who has left the genteel tradition entirely behind is perhaps Walt Whitman. For this reason educated Americans find him rather an unpalatable person, who they sincerely protest ought not to be taken for a representative of their culture; and he certainly should not, because their culture is so genteel and traditional. But the foreigner may sometimes think otherwise, since he is looking for what may have arisen in America to express, not the polite and conventional American mind, but the spirit and the inarticulate principles that animate the community, on which its own genteel mentality seems to sit rather lightly. When the foreigner opens the pages of Walt Whitman, he thinks that he has come at last upon something representative and original. In Walt Whitman democracy is carried into psychology and morals. The various sights, moods, and emotions are given each one vote; they are declared to be all free and equal, and the innumerable commonplace moments of life are suffered to speak like the others. . . .

But there is another distinguished man, lately lost to this country, who has given some rude shocks to this tradition and who, as much as Whitman, may be regarded as representing the genuine, the long silent American mind—I mean William James. . . .

For one thing, William James kept his mind and heart wide open to all that might seem, to polite minds, odd, personal, or visionary in religion and philosophy. He gave a sincerely respectful hearing to sentimentalists, mystics, spiritualists, wizards, cranks, quacks, and impostors—for it is hard to draw the line, and James was not willing to draw it prematurely. He thought, with his usual modesty, that any of these might have something to teach him. The lame, the halt, the blind, and those speaking with tongues could come to him with the certainty of finding sympathy; and if they were not healed, at least they were comforted, that a famous professor should take them so seriously; and they began to feel that after all to have only one leg, or one hand, or one eye, or to have three, might be in itself no less beauteous than to have just two, like the stolid majority. Thus William James became the friend and helper of those groping, nervous, half-educated, spiritually disinherited, passionately hungry individuals of which America is full. He became, at the same time, their spokesman and representative before the learned world; and he made it a chief part of his vocation to recast what the learned world has to offer, so that as far as possible it might serve the needs and interests of these people.

Yet the normal practical masculine American, too, had a friend in William James. There is a feeling abroad now, to which biology and Darwinism lend some colour, that theory is simply an instrument for practice, and intelligence merely a help toward material survival. Bears, it is said, have fur and claws, but poor naked man is condemned to be intelligent, or he will perish. This feeling William James embodied in that theory of thought and of truth which he called pragmatism. Intelligence, he thought, is no miraculous, idle faculty, by which we mirror passively any or everything that happens to be true, reduplicating the real world to no purpose. Intelligence has its roots and its issue in the context of events; it is one kind of practical adjustment, an experimental act, a form of vital tension. It does not essentially serve to picture other parts of reality, but to connect them. . . .

. . . The force of William James's new theology, or romantic cosmology, lies only in this: that it has broken the spell of the genteel tradition, and enticed faith in a new direction, which on second thoughts may prove no less alluring than the old. The important fact is not that the new fancy might possibly be true—who shall know that?—but that it has entered the heart of a leading American to conceive and to cherish it. The genteel tradition cannot be dislodged by these insurrections; there are circles to which it is still congenial, and where it will be preserved. But it has been challenged and (what is perhaps more insidious) it has been discovered. No one need be browbeaten any longer into accepting it. No one need be afraid, for instance, that his fate is sealed because some young prig may call him a dualist; the pint would call the quart a dualist, if you tried to pour the quart into him. We need not be afraid of being less profound, for being direct and sincere. The intellectual world may be traversed in many directions; the whole has not been surveyed; there is a great career in it open to talent. That is a sort of knell, that tolls the passing of the genteel tradition. Something else is now in the field; something else can appeal to the imagination, and be a thousand times more idealistic than academic idealism, which is often simply a way of white-washing—and adoring things as they are. The illegitimate monopoly which the genteel tradition had established over what ought to be assumed and what ought to be hoped for has been broken down by the first-born of the family, by the genius of the race. Henceforth there can hardly be the same peace and the same pleasure in hugging the old proprieties. Hegel will be to the next generation what Sir William Hamilton was to the last. Nothing will have been disproved, but everything will have been abandoned. An honest man has spoken, and the cant of the genteel tradition has become harder for young lips to repeat. . . .

DEMOCRATIC VISTAS

Walt Whitman

In this prose passage published in 1871, poet Walt Whitman (1819–1892) places himself outside the genteel tradition altogether. He defends egalitarian, democratic ideals and urges his readers toward a spirit of individualism and inclusiveness that will allow the United States to realize its vast potential. Despite apparent differences in their understanding of culture and cultivation, Wharton greatly admired Whitman. She wrote notes for

From *Prose Works 1892*. Vol. 2. New York: New York UP, 1964.

an essay about his poetry; lamented in 1923 that "there is no Whitman singing in this generation"; and borrowed the title of her autobiography, *A Backward Glance,* from his "A Backward Glance O'er Travel'd Roads." [ED.]

. . . The quality of BEING, in the object's self, according to its own central idea and purpose, and of growing therefrom and thereto—not criticism by other standards, and adjustments thereto—is the lesson of Nature. True, the full man wisely gathers, culls, absorbs; but if, engaged disproportionately in that, he slights or overlays the precious idiocrasy and special nativity and intention that he is, the man's self, the main thing, is a failure, however wide his general cultivation. Thus, in our times, refinement and delicatesse are not only attended to sufficiently, but threaten to eat us up, like a cancer. Already, the democratic genius watches, ill-pleased, these tendencies. Provision for a little healthy rudeness, savage virtue, justification of what one has in one's self, whatever it is, is demanded. Negative qualities, even deficiencies, would be a relief. Singleness and normal simplicity and separation, amid this more and more complex, more and more artificialized state of society—how pensively we yearn for them! how we would welcome their return!

In some such direction, then—at any rate enough to preserve the balance—we feel called upon to throw what weight we can, not for absolute reasons, but current ones. To prune, gather, trim, conform, and ever cram and stuff, and be genteel and proper, is the pressure of our days. While aware that much can be said even in behalf of all this, we perceive that we have not now to consider the question of what is demanded to serve a half-starved and barbarous nation, or set of nations, but what is most applicable, most pertinent, for numerous congeries of conventional, over-corpulent societies, already becoming stifled and rotten with flatulent, infidelistic literature, and polite conformity and art. In addition to establish'd sciences, we suggest a science as it were of healthy average personalism, on original-universal grounds, the object of which should be to raise up and supply through the States a copious race of superb American men and women, cheerful, religious, ahead of any yet known.

America has yet morally and artistically originated nothing. She seems singularly unaware that the models of persons, books, manners, &c., appropriate for former conditions and for European lands, are but exiles and exotics here. No current of her life, as shown on the surfaces of what is authoritatively called her society, accepts or runs into social or esthetic democracy; but all the currents set squarely against it. Never, in the Old

World, was thoroughly upholster'd exterior appearance and show, mental and other, built entirely on the idea of caste, and on the sufficiency of mere outside acquisition—never were glibness, verbal intellect, more the test, the emulation—more loftily elevated as head and sample—than they are on the surface of our republican States this day. The writers of a time hint the mottoes of its gods. The word of the modern, say these voices, is the word Culture.

We find ourselves abruptly in close quarters with the enemy. This word Culture, or what it has come to represent, involves, by contrast, our whole theme, and has been, indeed, the spur, urging us to engagement. Certain questions arise. As now taught, accepted and carried out, are not the processes of culture rapidly creating a class of supercilious infidels, who believe in nothing? Shall a man lose himself in countless masses of adjustments, and be so shaped with reference to this, that, and the other, that the simply good and healthy and brave parts of him are reduced and clipp'd away, like the bordering of box in a garden? You can cultivate corn and roses and orchards—but who shall cultivate the mountain peaks, the ocean, and the tumbling gorgeousness of the clouds? Lastly—is the readily-given reply that culture only seeks to help, systematize, and put in attitude, the elements of fertility and power, a conclusive reply?

I do not so much object to the name, or word, but I should certainly insist, for the purposes of these States, on a radical change of category, in the distribution of precedence. I should demand a programme of culture, drawn out, not for a single class alone, or for the parlors or lecture-rooms, but with an eye to practical life, the west, the working-men, the facts of farms and jack-planes and engineers, and of the broad range of the women also of the middle and working strata, and with reference to the perfect equality of women, and of a grand and powerful motherhood. I should demand of this programme or theory a scope generous enough to include the widest human area. It must have for its spinal meaning the formation of a typical personality of character, eligible to the uses of the high average of men—and *not* restricted by conditions ineligible to the masses. The best culture will always be that of the manly and courageous instincts, and loving perceptions, and of self-respect— aiming to form, over this continent, an idiocrasy of universalism, which, true child of America, will bring joy to its mother, returning to her in her own spirit, recruiting myriads of offspring, able, natural, perceptive, tolerant, devout believers in her, America, and with some definite instinct why and for what she has arisen, most vast, most formidable of historic births, and is, now and here, with wonderful step, journeying through Time. . . .

FROM *MERCHANTS AND MASTERPIECES:*
THE STORY OF THE METROPOLITAN
MUSEUM OF ART

Calvin Tomkins

Although twentieth-century patrons now take public art museums for granted, they are relatively new American institutions. The Metropolitan Museum of Art was one of many museums founded and supported after the Civil War by a handful of artists, writers, merchants, lawyers, and financiers inspired by a combined love of the arts and sense of civic responsibility. One such advocate was Frederic Rhinelander, related to Edith Wharton on her mother's side, who became treasurer of the Metropolitan's board of trustees in 1871 and remained involved for over thirty years. The founders envisioned a museum equal to those already established in great European cities. Such an institution, they believed, would elevate public appreciation of the arts and bring balance to a nation overly concerned with practicality. The founders' vision took form in 1870 with the purchase of 174 European paintings and an act of incorporation by the New York legislature, followed by the choice of a permanent site in Central Park.

Calvin Tomkins (1970) provides a lively history of the museum's early years, including the story of the acquisition of the Cesnola antiquities, among which Newland Archer and Ellen Olenska wander in chapter 31 of *The Age of Innocence.* Wharton sets her novel in the 1870s, coincident with the start of the museum's construction in Central Park in 1874; the actual building opened in 1880. [ED.]

. . . The civilizing lessons of art and beauty had not seemed particularly urgent to America's founding fathers. John Adams had looked upon the glories of French art and seen in them a threat to democratic liberties; painting and sculpture were essentially antidemocratic and "on the side of Despotism and Superstition," said Adams, who added that he "would not give sixpence for a picture by Raphael or a statue of Phidias." A few

New York: Dutton, 1970.

small, pioneering art galleries had been founded since Adams' time—the gallery of the Pennsylvania Academy of Fine Arts in 1805; the Wadsworth Atheneum in Hartford, the nation's first real art museum, in 1842. To most nineteenth century Americans, though, art remained something suspicious and European, and the word *museum* connoted natural science, not painting and sculpture.

Nearly every town of any consequence had its natural science museum, where science served as a pretext for catering to the national appetite for anything bizarre or grotesque, and where one could usually find, along with the bones of the woolly mammoth and the miniature steam engine carved from a cherry pit, the most lifelike waxwork tableau of some celebrated criminal in the act of committing his most celebrated crime, with the very hatchet or the very knife. These "dime museums," as they were called, reached their apogee in 1841 when Phineas T. Barnum opened his famous New York establishment at the corner of Broadway and Ann Street. Barnum had bought out the natural science collections of several earlier museums, including the original one started by the artist Charles Willson Peale in Philadelphia in 1805, but his principal asset was showmanship. His American Museum offered everything from "roaring baboons" to "interesting relics from the Holy Land," and Barnum claimed that it outdrew the British Museum. In his autobiography he tells of a Fourth of July holiday when the premises were so crowded that he was forced to stop selling tickets. "I pushed through the throng until I reached the roof of the building," Barnum wrote, "hoping to find room for a few more, but it was in vain. Looking down into the street it was a sad sight to see the thousands of people who stood with their money ready to enter the Museum, but who were actually turned away. It was exceedingly harrowing to my feelings."

The boisterous, commercial spirit of Barnum's New York had not kept the city from becoming a magnet for American artists, whose numbers were steadily increasing in spite of the absence of art museums. The New York Academy of Fine Arts, founded in 1802, was the country's first formally organized art institution. It had quickly ossified into a narrowly exclusive club dominated by the painter John Trumbull, whose idea of encouraging American art was to procure government commissions for himself. Trumbull's arrogance finally induced several of his associates to break away in 1826 and form the National Academy of Design; although this group soon became as exclusive and reactionary as the New York Academy, it in turn gave rise to more open-minded art schools and artist societies. New York's rapid growth, moreover, held out the promise of rich patronage. "The more I think of making a push at New York as a permanent place of residence in my profession, the more proper it seems to me that it should be pretty soon," the Massachusetts-born painter Samuel F. B. Morse (who would become better known as the inventor of the telegraph) confided to his diary in 1832. "New York does not yet feel the influx of wealth from the Western Canal but in a year or two she will feel it, and it will be advantageous for me to be previously identified among the citizens as a painter."

Morse's reasoning was sound, although at the time few New Yorkers were giving much thought to art. A single dealer, Michael Paff (known as "Old Paff") supplied the limited demand for "Old Masters"—usually with atrocious copies of dubious originals. The only significant collector of the period was Luman Reed, a wholesale grocery merchant who bought and commissioned paintings directly from the New York artists of his day, and who had converted the third floor of his house on Greenwich Street into a picture gallery to which the public was invited one day a week. After Reed's death in 1841 his collection became the nucleus of the New York Gallery of Fine Arts, one of the earliest efforts to establish an art museum in the city. The New York Gallery closed in 1854, plagued by chronic debts, but by this time the artists whom Reed had befriended and helped to support were receiving encouragement from other sources. Asher B. Durand, Thomas Cole, John F. Kensett, and other painters of what came to be called the Hudson River School were accepted and even lionized by upper-class New York society, more and more of whose members had come to feel that paintings and sculpture were a necessity for the well-appointed home.

These same artists were also beneficiaries of the American Art Union, whose astonishing success disclosed an unsuspected taste for art among the socially ambitious middle classes. The American Art Union began in 1838 as the Apollo Gallery, a nonprofit organization at 410 Broadway where artists could show their latest work and where the public paid a small entrance fee. It soon broadened its scope, becoming a cooperative association on a national scale. Subscribers to the Union paid an annual fee of $5.00, in return for which they received a steel engraving of an American painting, several issues of the Art Union *Bulletin,* and—the big attraction—a chance to win an original oil painting at the annual prize drawing in New York. Subscriptions poured in from every part of the country, more each year, until in the peak year 1849 cash receipts from 18,960 subscribers totaled more than $96,000—enough to buy four hundred and sixty paintings for distribution. Three years later the American Art Union was defunct, closed down by the courts as an illegal lottery. In its brief and spectacular career, though, it had distributed twenty-four hundred paintings (including such fine works as George Caleb Bingham's *Fur Traders Descending the Missouri,* now in the Metropolitan), and established New York as the marketplace and center of American art.

The public's growing interest in art was demonstrated anew in 1864 by the success of the Metropolitan Art Fair. This event was conceived as a benefit for the United States Sanitary Commission, a volunteer organization formed in 1861 to help care for sick and wounded Civil War soldiers. (Twenty years later its example would lead to the formation of the American Red Cross.) To raise money for the Sanitary Commission, several of its members evolved the idea of holding an auction of paintings and other works of art from New York private collections. One hundred and ninety-six paintings were donated, and more than a million dollars were raised for the Sanitary Commission. Never before had the "social and mercantile" advantages of art been so clearly demonstrated, and it is not surprising that several of the men who played an active part in the Metropolitan Fair should become, six years later, the prime movers on the Metropolitan Museum's founding board.

Like many of New York's more pleasant amenities, the idea for the Metropolitan Museum was first conceived in Paris. In the course of an after-dinner speech to a group of Americans celebrating their Fourth of July at the Pré Catalah, the fashionable garden restaurant in the Bois de Boulogne, John Jay, an eminent lawyer and a grandson of the first chief justice, remarked that it was "time for the American people to lay the foundations of a National Institution and Gallery of Art," and suggested that the American gentlemen then in Paris were the ones to inaugurate the plan. Among the Americans present that day were a number of New York citizens for whom Jay's proposal—coming at such a moment, and in a city that has traditionally stirred cultural longings in the mercantile soul—had the ring of a moral imperative. Before the evening was over, a group of these gentlemen approached Jay and pledged themselves to work toward such a goal.

The next steps took place inside the Union League Club, which at first blush might have seemed an inappropriate setting. The club had been established in 1863 to provide a focus for Unionist, pro-Lincoln sentiment in New York, and was thus politically rather than socially oriented. Its membership included most of the prominent men of the city, however, including Jay himself, William Cullen Bryant, Frederick Law Olmsted, William T. Blodgett, Joseph H. Choate, John Taylor Johnston, and the Reverend Henry W. Bellows. Bellows and Olmsted had been the principal organizers of the Sanitary Commission during the Civil War. Blodgett, Johnston, and others were largely responsible for the success of the Metropolitan Art Fair in 1864. These were all men of strong social conscience, so that when the little group that had responded so enthusiastically to Jay's speech in Paris (several of them were naturally Union Leaguers) returned from Europe and proposed that the Union League Club "might properly institute the best means for promoting this great object" of a major art museum, the social and moral advantages of the plan received a sympathetic hearing. By coincidence, John Jay was elected president of the club that fall, so that the proposal he had inspired came to him for action. Jay referred it to the club's art committee. . . .

The committee took its time deliberating. In fact, nearly three years elapsed before it reported to a meeting of the full membership that an art institution, provided it were "free alike from bungling government officials and from the control of a single individual," was surely worth the members' consideration. Events moved more quickly after that. Another meeting at the Union League Club was scheduled for November 23, 1869, with invitations going out to all those in the city who might be thought to have an active interest in the plan. A heavy downpour kept some potential sponsors from attending, but more than three hundred people showed up nonetheless, among them virtually the entire artist community, the leaders of most of the city's cultural and educational institutions, a sprinkling of municipal officials, and a liberal assortment of bankers, businessmen, and lawyers. John Jay was not there—he had become the United States ambassador to Austria in the meanwhile. In his absence William Cullen Bryant, the city's white-maned and white-bearded first citizen and its most elevated symbol of culture, had agreed to serve as presiding officer.

Bryant's opening address, which reverberated with organ tones and trumpet calls, played on the keys of civic and national pride. "Our city is the third great city of the civilized world," Bryant said. "Our republic has already taken its place among the great powers of the earth; it is great in extent, great in population, great in the activity and enterprise of her people. It is the richest nation in the world." And yet, Bryant added, its riches were too often diverted to mean or uncouth ends. "My friends, if a tenth part of what is every year stolen from us . . . in the city where we live, under the pretence of the public service, and poured profusely into the coffers of political rogues, were expended on a Museum of Art, we might have, reposited in spacious and stately buildings, collections formed of works left by the world's greatest artists, which would be the pride of the country."

In his austere and dignified voice, Bryant went on to state that virtually every country of Europe had its museums of fine arts, even Spain, "a third-rate power of Europe and poor besides." In America, however—and here he touched a sensitive nerve—"when the owner of a private gallery of art desires to leave his treasures where they can be seen by the public, he looks in vain for any institution to which he can send them." Great collections came on the market in Europe from time to time and could easily be acquired, but where, in America, could they be housed? American artists were growing in numbers and skills, but they still were obliged to go abroad to study because nowhere in their own country could they see the great works of the past. Bryant also mentioned "another view of the subject, and a most important one." New York was growing with unparalleled and chaotic speed, and attracting not only those who were "eminent in talent" but also the more sinister elements—those "most dexterous in villainy" and "most foul in guilt." "My friends," Bryant said gravely, "it is important that we should encounter the temptations to vice in this great and too rapidly growing capital by attractive entertainments of an innocent and improving character." Art, the great moral teacher, would redeem the wicked while refining the good.

Most of the other speakers provided glosses of one sort or another on Bryant's evangelical text. One speaker, however, presented a number of clear and concrete suggestions. This was George Fiske Comfort, a young lecturer at Princeton. Comfort had visited most of the major European museums, and for some time he had been urging the establishment in this country of art museums that differed essentially from the European model. "A great museum—one worthy of New York City and of our country— should represent the History of Art in all countries and in all ages, of art both pure and applied," Comfort told the audience at the Union League Club. He went on to discuss practically every aspect of museum work that would later be adopted by the Metropolitan and other museums—loan exhibitions, display techniques, the use of decorative and applied arts, museum lectures, and programs for schoolchildren. In each instance the underlying principle was clear: the museum must be an instrument of popular education. Its function was basically social and moral—aesthetics were secondary.

Comfort's ideas were really rooted in the revolutionary origins of Europe's museums. Art museums as we know them today are recent developments in Western society. They appeared at the same historical moment as the first encyclopedias, toward the end of the eighteenth century, and like the encyclopedias they were strongly influenced by the radical currents of French thought that helped to bring on the French Revolution. The first public museum was born in 1793, when the Louvre Palace with all its treasures, confiscated by the republican regime, was declared open to the people. In Europe, however, where centuries of private connoisseurship, royal patronage, and bourgeois family pride had gone into the accumulation of works of art, the Jacobin notion that art belonged to the people did not take firm hold. With a few important exceptions such as the South Kensington Museum in London, European museums had remained wedded to aristocratic ideals of connoisseurship. Even the Louvre, when it was opened to the public in 1793, limited admission on five days out of every ten to professional artists; as a result it has served ever since as the great laboratory for French art, but the majority of its visitors have been foreign tourists. Until well into the nineteenth century the British Museum, which was officially opened to the public in 1759, could be visited only by written appointment and by those who were able to qualify as "gentlemen." Today most European museums, the Louvre included, consider that their chief obligations are to the artist, the scholar, and the connoisseur. They tolerate but do not cultivate the public, and only in recent years have they given much thought to education.

The November meeting at the Union League Club was widely reported in the press, which saw evidence of high enthusiasm and sober purpose in the proceedings. A period of feverish activity now ensued. Legal documents were drawn and redrawn (mostly by Choate), potential trustees were sounded out, and advice was solicited. On January 31, 1870, the first board of trustees was elected. The ingredients of this twenty-seven-man founding board were predictable—a pomposity of businessmen and financiers, a clutch of lawyers, a nod of city officials, and a scintillation of writers and architects; less predictable, perhaps, was the inclusion of four practicing artists—the painters John F. Kensett, Frederick E. Church, and Eastman Johnson, and the sculptor J. Q. A. Ward. Choate, Comfort, Blodgett, Putnam, and the other "working trustees" were concentrated in the twelve-man executive committee. Bryant, who was seventy-six, had little time to give to the project, and soon resigned from the board. For president, the members selected a man who could be expected to give a great deal of his time, and who fitted almost ideally into that rare category of businessmen who were actively interested in art. He was John Taylor Johnston, the railroad executive and art collector whose private gallery, installed on the second floor of the stable behind his house at 8 Fifth Avenue, was considered one of the finest in the city.

Johnston had found that his presence was no longer continuously required by his railroad interests. In fact, on the evening his colleagues elected him the first president of the Metropolitan Museum, he happened to be in Egypt with his wife and daughter, drifting comfortably down the Nile. The Johnstons had rented a Nile steamer at Cairo and sailed up the river to Luxor, where Johnston negotiated with several native dealers for a collection of antiquities. The negotiation had ended abruptly when a dispute broke out among the dealers, a quarrel so loud and unseemly that Johnston felt obliged to hurry his family back on board the boat. The following day, docking at Gizah, Johnston found a large packet of mail waiting for him. In it was a cablegram from New York offering him the presidency of the prospective Metropolitan Museum of Art. As his daughter recalled the moment later, "He was very much pleased, sent an immediate acceptance, and made arrangements for hastening our return home."

New York has no enduring aristocratic traditions. Inherited money brings only its face value there, and defects of breeding have never kept an ambitious New York hostess from using her husband's spoils to establish her sway. In the absence of dynasties on the order of Boston's Lowells or Philadelphia's Biddles, however, there was once a social infrastructure known as Old New York, which managed to exert an influence on the behavior of those members of the wealthy class who were not quite rich or nervy enough to ignore it and do as they pleased. Old New York was upright, pious, hard-working, and smug, but at the same time it was more worldly than Boston, more interested in food and comfort and European travel. The Old New York families lent their names to the Manhattan topography and the Manhattan telephone book—Rhinelander and Schuyler, Beekman and Wickersham and Stuyvesant—and they did the work of founding its major institutions. They vanished about 1920, taking their cozy brownstone world with them.

John Taylor Johnston, while not Old New York himself, was a personification of the Old New York influence. His father was a Scot from the River Dee, who had come to America as a young man in 1804 and gone to work in the counting house of a fellow Scot named James Lenox (*his* son would one day found the Lenox Library). The elder Johnston had prospered gradually, built a brownstone house on Washington Square, and raised his four children in strict accordance with the requirements of Presbyterian conduct—requirements so unbending that the old gentleman, on a visit to Rome in his later years, declined to meet the Pope because his audience had been scheduled on a Sunday. Young John Taylor Johnston studied law at Yale and was admitted to the bar, but his interest soon shifted to the development of two small railroads, the Lehigh and Susquehanna and the Central of New Jersey. He devoted the next thirty years to the presidency of these lines, making in the process a substantial but not unseemly fortune. Johnston was no railroad buccaneer like E. H. Harriman or Jay Gould. His business methods were cautious, and he cared deeply about such matters as railroad safety, the cleanliness of terminals, and the churchgoing habits of his employees.

Johnston also came to care deeply about art. He began buying paintings before the Civil War, and like most of the collectors of the day he bought "modern," which meant, for the most part, pictures by contemporary French academicians. A discreet Bouguereau, historical scenes by

Meissonier and Gleyre, genre studies, landscapes, anecdotal pictures ("a most painful story in a picture by Hubner"), paintings of cattle—these were all very much to his taste, although Johnston sometimes showed more daring: Turner's great, impressionistic *The Slave Ship* entered his collection in 1872, and became one of his favorites. He was also the most active buyer of American paintings since Luman Reed. Other wealthy American collectors of this period looked almost exclusively to Europe for the cultural traditions that they had decided were their due, but Johnston also believed in encouraging native traditions. Frederick Church's huge *Niagara* and Winslow Homer's *Prisoners from the Front* hung prominently in his gallery, along with representative works by Kensett, Cole, Durand, and most of the New York painters of the time, all of whom were invited once a year to a reception at the Johnston home. The collection had long since overflowed the house that he had built in 1856 at the corner of Fifth Avenue and Eighth Street (the first private house in the city to be built of marble; people used to go out of their way to see it). Johnston displayed his pictures in a gallery built over the stable in back, and because he felt morally obligated to share the pleasure his collection gave him he opened his gallery to the public every Thursday afternoon, setting a precedent that was soon followed by August Belmont, William H. Vanderbilt, and several others. The diarist George Templeton Strong, who went by invitation in 1869, agreed with the general view that no collection in the city outshone the Johnston gallery, not even Belmont's. "How superb it is," Strong wrote, "how rich he must be, and how much wiser of him to spend his money this way than on race horses, four-in-hands, and great ostentatious parties."

When Johnston returned from Egypt to assume the presidency of the Metropolitan, he found much accumulated enthusiasm and goodwill but very little else. So far the museum existed only on paper. The New York Legislature voted an act of incorporation in the name of the Metropolitan Museum of Art on April 13, 1870. The museum thus had a charter, which gave its purpose as "encouraging and developing the study of the fine arts, and the application of the arts to manufacture, of advancing the general knowledge of kindred subjects, and, to that end, of furnishing popular instruction and recreation." It also had a constitution and a board of twenty-one elective and six ex-officio trustees (among them the mayor, the governor, and the head of the Department of Public Parks). Unlike the Boston Museum of Fine Arts or the Corcoran Gallery, however, the Metropolitan did not own a single work of art, nor did it have any space in which to exhibit future gifts or purchases.

Various remedies were suggested. "Order immediately from each middle-aged contemporary artist a masterpiece," one middle-aged enthusiast urged the trustees. Masterpieces cost money, however, and so far as most of the trustees were concerned they were only painted in Europe. That spring, Johnston and his colleagues addressed their major problem by launching a public subscription campaign for funds. They established three classes of membership in the museum corporation: one could become a Patron for $1,000, a Fellow in Perpetuity for $500, or a Fellow for Life for $200. The campaign goal was $250,000—remarkably modest even then—and the results were extremely discouraging. John Jacob Astor, August Belmont, and several other men of fortune and estate flatly refused to subscribe; they believed the new institution stood little chance of surviving without massive state aid. One year later only $110,000 had been raised, and in a city of millionaires the largest contribution was $10,000—it came from John Taylor Johnston. . . .

Acting entirely on his own initiative, [Trustee William T. Blodgett] secured the services of M. Etienne Leroy, art expert of the Royal Museum in Belgium, and through him negotiated for and bought in the summer of 1870 three important private collections of paintings—none of the owners were Germans, incidentally—which he then offered to the trustees of the Metropolitan for exactly what they had cost him.

One hundred and seventy-four pictures were involved, mostly Dutch and Flemish seventeenth century paintings, with a few Italian, French, English, and Spanish works ranging from the sixteenth to the nineteenth century. The cost, including expenses, came to $116,180.27. President Johnston thought the purchase "somewhat rash," but his confidence in Blodgett's judgment was so firm that he volunteered to assume half the cost, borrowing $100,000 from the Bank of America on joint account with Blodgett. . . .

The Metropolitan's trustees were not by any means convinced, in 1870, that their museum should be built in Central Park. The park was a long way out of town so far as most of them were concerned, and they doubted whether people could ever be persuaded to travel such a distance to see works of art. A majority on the executive committee favored another site, known then as Reservoir Square because it adjoined the site of the old city reservoir—it is now Bryant Park, the home of the New York Public Library. Johnston, the painter Frederick Church, and a few other trustees argued spiritedly for Central Park, but it was Andrew Haswell Green, the president of the Central Park Commission, who was primarily responsible for the final decision. . . .

The trustees of the two prospective museums [Metropolitan and American], working closely together, formulated a plan under which both institutions would occupy a building or buildings on what was known then as Manhattan Square—the present location of the American Museum. Joseph Choate, who served on both boards, framed a legal petition asking that the city be authorized to tax itself to the amount of $500,000 for this purpose. In the spring of 1871, having secured the signatures of a large number of prominent New Yorkers, the young Princeton professor George Fiske Comfort and a representative of the American Museum took the petition up to Albany and paid a call on the man himself—William Marcy Tweed.

"We arrived there and we were placed in seats behind Mr. Tweed as he sat at a table," Comfort recalled some years later, "and he said: 'We will see what the New York papers say about us today.'" The New York papers, led by *The Times,* had been attacking Tweed openly since early in 1870. The Boss had begun to feel a little uneasy, although he did not mind the press attacks as much as he did the vitriolic cartoons of Thomas Nast in *Harper's Weekly,* which even his nonliterate constituents had no trouble understanding. As Comfort sat watching, Tweed glanced at the newspapers and then his eye fell on the petition. He "looked at it a moment, saw the heading and instantly, with that celerity of action for which he was noted, he took it to a room, and said, 'You will see Mr. Sweeny. He will take charge of this.'" Peter Barr Sweeny, the city chamberlain, was known to be the brains of the Tweed Ring. He received the two petitioners without delay. Sweeny "took the paper and skipped the heading, and looked at the names, and when he saw the names attached to it, then he turned back and read the heading. And as I watched his face there was not the quiver of an eye, or twitch of the muscles, but he turned quickly and said: 'Please inform these gentlemen that we are the servants of the people. This is New York. New York wishes this and please inform them and say that they can see us on two or three details of the matter, and then this will go through.'"

There was no mystery about Tweed's sudden espousal of high culture. The names on the petition represented more than half the real estate of New York City, and a great many prominent businesses as well. Tweed needed the support of this element (curiously enough, six eminent New York citizens, including John Jacob Astor III and Moses Taylor, had examined the city's finances the previous year, at Tweed's invitation, and had returned Tweed's administration a clean bill of health), and he undoubtedly saw in the project new opportunities for the well-established shakedown. Tweed sought to persuade the trustees of the two museums that what they really needed was a huge, multimillion dollar structure— something on the order, perhaps, of the new County Court House, which had cost $3,000,000 to build but for which the city had actually paid $12,000,000, Tweed and his cronies pocketing the difference. The trustees made it clear that they would be quite satisfied with the $500,000 building originally proposed. On the prickly question of ownership—one of the "two or three details" Sweeny had mentioned—the trustees and the Tweed Ring settled for an ingenious compromise. Sweeny had said that if the city gave the money to build a museum on city property, then the city must control the building. Choate, the architect of the compromise, conceded the point: the city would retain legal ownership of the museum building. In return, Sweeny agreed to Choate's insistence that the trustees retain ownership and control of the contents of the building—i.e., the collections. This was an entirely new idea in municipal government, and it became the pattern followed by most of the major art museums in America (although not in Boston, where the Museum of Fine Arts neither solicited nor received any public funds at all).

Tweed's approval brought swift results. On April 5, 1871, the legislature passed an act enabling the Central Park Commissioners to authorize construction of a museum building on Manhattan Square, and to raise funds to the sum of $500,000 toward this end. The trustees had hoped to get funds from the city so that they could build for themselves; what they got, with Tweed's blessing, was a partnership with the city, under which the city was responsible for the construction and maintenance of the buildings and the trustees were responsible for everything else.

The following year a change of site was agreed upon. The American Museum would build separately on Manhattan Square; the Metropolitan's building, designed by the firm of Calvert Vaux and Jacob Wrey Mould, would be situated in the "Deer Park," the area between Seventy-ninth and Eighty-fourth streets, extending from Fifth Avenue west to the Park Drive. A number of trustees had argued up to the last in favor of Reservoir Square downtown, but Andrew Green and his fellow Park Commissioners wanted the museum in the park, and, since they held the purse strings, that is where it would be.

Long before the new building was even begun, however, Blodgett's one hundred and seventy-four Old Masters and a number of gifts and loans had made some sort of temporary exhibition space necessary. The Metropolitan's first home was at 681 Fifth Avenue, between Fifty-third and Fifty-fourth streets, in a house formerly known to New York matrons and their reluctant offspring as Allen Dodworth's Dancing Academy. . . .

[T]he museum moved at the end of 1873 into larger quarters and embarked on a program of expanded activities. What had made the move imperative was the purchase of the Cesnola Collection, an extensive group of antiquities excavated on the island of Cyprus by the American consul there, General Luigi Palma di Cesnola. Johnston had negotiated for and bought the collection for $60,000, in the hope that the trustees could raise the money to pay him back—as eventually, somewhat to their surprise, they did. There being no space in Dodworth's Dancing Academy to exhibit the more than six thousand stone sculptures, terracottas, glass, and other ancient objects that made up the collection, the trustees took a lease on a larger building on West Fourteenth Street, then a fashionable residential section. The Douglas Mansion, as it was formerly known, had five times as much wall space as the dancing academy, and the rent was lower—$8,000 a year instead of $9,000. . . .

Ground had been broken in 1874 for the new building in Central Park, and the work was proceeding on schedule. Relations with the city authorities, moreover, had become considerably more regular since the downfall of Boss Tweed. Indicted by a grand jury in December 1871, Tweed had eventually been convicted on one hundred and two counts, with most of the legal case against him being assembled by Joseph Choate. He had escaped from jail and fled to Spain, only to be arrested there, extradited back to New York, and clapped into jail where he died, a broken man, in 1878. The Tweed Ring's successors in Albany and City Hall were not exactly paragons of civic virtue, but municipal graft no longer took place on such a massive scale.

Meanwhile, private business had started to pick up a little [from the recession ensuing from the 1873 failure of Jay Cooke & Company]—by 1878 there would be a real upturn—and confidence was returning. New York's rich and fashionable society, moreover, had clasped the Metropolitan to its bosom. Most of the millionaire collectors were now willing to lend their support or at least their pictures—even August Belmont, as Johnston reported to Blodgett, had "forgotten his insulting note declining a post on the Museum board." The Metropolitan was developing an aura of respectability and success. George Templeton Strong, who remained unimpressed by the "alleged" Old Masters, conceded that "Twenty years hence it will probably have grown into a really instructive museum." In addition to these hopeful signs, the trustees had acquired in 1876 a second large collection of antiquities unearthed on the island of Cyprus by the "indefatigable and accomplished explorer," General Cesnola.

The indefatigable explorer came over in 1877, as he had done four years earlier, to supervise the unpacking, cataloguing, and placement of some ten thousand new objects that he had sold to the Metropolitan. Cesnola's boundless energy and military dash evidently made a strong impression on the trustees, some of whom had begun to feel that museum administration was a job for younger men. Several of the founding trustees had died—Putnam and Kensett in 1872, Blodgett in 1875. George Fiske Comfort had resigned to accept a teaching post at Syracuse University. As in most institutions, the board was made up of a minority of trustees who did the work and a majority who said yes, and the active minority—President Johnston, Frederick W. Rhinelander, who had succeeded the banker Robert Gordon as treasurer in 1871, Samuel Avery, Russell Sturgis, Jr., and William C. Prime, the editor of the *New York Journal of Commerce* and a trustee since 1871—had become increasingly aware that the museum was growing beyond their capacity to run it. Someone was needed, someone with practical wisdom and push and enterprise, who could give to the museum his full time and attention. The position of secretary to the board had recently become vacant when William J. Hoppin was appointed to the United States Legation in London. Could Cesnola be persuaded to take his place?

He could and was. Two years later, in 1879, Cesnola became the Metropolitan's first paid director, and the museum became a very different sort of place. . . .

Emanuele Pietro Paolo Maria Luigi Palma di Cesnola was born in 1832 at Rivarolo, a small Piedmontese town near Turin in northern Italy. . . . [He] volunteered for service in the Army of Sardinia for the war against Austria (Piedmont belonged then to the Kingdom of Sardinia). Cesnola was promoted to lieutenant on the battlefield of Novara, and his valor in that losing engagement also earned him a medal from the King. Further decorations honored his exploits in the Crimean War, during which he served as aide-de-camp to General Ansaldi and fought at the battle of Balaklava. Returning home again in 1856, Cesnola soon grew bored with peacetime military life. He resigned from the army, and in 1860, like so many other ambitious young Italians, sailed to seek his fortune in America. . . .

He served [in the Civil War] until the war ended, taking part in many battles, and received in 1865, from Lincoln's hand, the brevet rank of brigadier general. Cesnola had been looking ahead, though, and he used his meeting with Lincoln, which took place only a few days before the President's assassination, to secure for himself the trappings of a diplomatic career—specifically, the post of United States consul at Cyprus. . . .

Cesnola soon learned that the diplomatic duties of a consul took up practically no time at all. . . .

For a man of Cesnola's energetic temperament, it did not take long for archaeology to become an absorbing passion. At first he limited his excavations to the hundreds of hillside tombs in the vicinity of Larnaca, but by 1867 he was operating farther afield and spending much of his time away from home. At night he read voraciously everything he could find on the subject, including the works of Pliny, Strabo, and Ptolemy who had visited Cyprus in ancient times. Having tried and failed to get financial backing for his excavations, he soon ran through his own and his wife's savings. Now and then he sold a few objects, which helped to pay for further digging, and in 1869 he managed to get a loan from the Paris firm of Rollin & Feuardent, the leading European dealers in antiquities. Early in

1870 he made his first major discovery. Cesnola's native diggers had just started to work on a site near the ancient town of Golgoi (mentioned by Pliny as the center of the worship of Aphrodite on the island) when they uncovered a colossal limestone head. The crew sent a message to Cesnola, who dropped everything and rode out on muleback in the middle of the night. A large crowd of excited villagers had gathered at the site by the time he arrived. The diggers had unearthed several more large stone sculptures, and in the darkness and confusion there was danger that they might be damaged or, more likely, diminished by theft. Acting with military aplomb, Cesnola dispersed the villagers, loaded the colossal head and the other statutes on oxcarts and sent them back to Larnaca—"Thus I may say," as he wrote later, "that I rather captured than discovered these stone treasures."[1]

The Golgoi dig yielded a great many more monumental sculptures and smaller objects of all kinds. Cesnola succeeded in buying the property for £20 from the farmer who owned it, and for a month, despite orders from the Turkish authorities to desist, he kept more than a hundred diggers busy on the site. News of the discovery soon spread to Europe, and Cesnola's house in Larnaca, which he had transformed into a virtual museum, became the chief tourist attraction on the island. . . .

Cesnola had learned about the new museum in 1870 when he read an article on its founding in *Putnam's* magazine. Early in 1872 he had written to John Taylor Johnston, offering to sell his entire collection to the Metropolitan on very favorable terms—the price would be determined by arbitrators for both sides, and payment could be made over a period of time. The New York consignment was intended to further this negotiation. Unfortunately, the vessel carrying it ran into a violent storm off the coast of Syria and sank with all its cargo. The remainder, some six thousand objects including all the monumental statues found at Golgoi, reached London safely in the fall of 1872. It was received by an agent for the Paris firm of Rollin & Feuardent, which had recently established a branch in London, and negotiations began in earnest with the British Museum and various other institutions, including the Metropolitan. The British Museum offered £10,000 for all the sculptures and inscriptions from Golgoi. Cesnola refused, insisting that the collection must remain together as a whole. Into the breach stepped Johnston, who had not yet suffered the financial reverses that would decimate his fortune. The Metropolitan's president offered to buy the collection for $60,000 of his own money, in the hope that

---

[1] *Cyprus: Its Ancient Cities, Tombs, and Temples,* by General Louis Palma di Cesnola, Harper & Bros. New York, 1878.

his fellow trustees would raise that sum by public subscription. Cesnola accepted the offer. "What I desire above all," he had said, in words that would become all too familiar to Metropolitan trustees over the years, "is that my collection should remain all *together* and be known as the Cesnola Collection. . . . I have the pride of my race, and that of a Discoverer who wants his name perpetuated with his work if possible.". . .

THE LOCATION AND DECORATION OF HOUSES IN *THE AGE OF INNOCENCE*

Ada Van Gastel

Edith Wharton first gained fame, not for her novels, but for a co-authored book on architectural and interior design, *The Decoration of Houses* (1897). Drawing on models from the Renaissance through the eighteenth century and advocating classical principles of harmony, balance, and proportion, this informed study continues to influence professionals and serious amateurs today. Wharton's keen interest in houses is evident in *The Age of Innocence*, in which homes do more than provide settings for the novel's action. Ada Van Gastel explains how architecture and decoration play key roles in revealing characters' personalities. [ED.]

Although Lucretia Jones had some of her daughter's poems printed privately in 1878, the first book Edith Wharton wrote for the public was a book on interior decoration, *The Decoration of Houses* (1897). Throughout her life, Wharton remained interested in architecture and interior decoration, the latter being in her view a branch of the former.[1] Wharton was closely involved with the conceptualizing of her house The Mount in Lenox, Massachusetts, and spent much time and energy on the decoration of her other houses—Pencraig in Newport, the two Park Avenue townhouses in New York, the Rue de Varenne apartment in Paris,

Dutch Quarterly Review of Anglo-American Letters 20. 2 (1990).

[1] Edith Wharton and Ogden Codman, Introduction to *The Decoration of Houses*, New York, 1897, n.p. and p. 198, 64n.

Pavillon Colombe near St. Brice-sous-Fôret, and Ste. Claire Chateau near Hyères.[2] According to her biographer, R. W. B. Lewis, Wharton acquired a "nearly professional competence . . . regarding architectural design and interior decoration."[3] *The Decoration of Houses*—brought out in a beautifully stylized edition—was quite a success: the initial one thousand copies were sold within a few months.[4] Revolutionary was the book's censure of Victorian clutter, crammed rooms, and heavy draperies that kept out the natural light; in its place, the book advocated classical simplicity and appropriateness of design, "suitability."[5] "Suitability" not only meant good proportion between the various individual elements of the design, but—most interestingly—also a harmonious balance between the overall conception of the house and the living style of its inhabitants.

Edmund Wilson was one of the first critics to perceive that, when Wharton took up fiction writing, she carried over her extensive knowledge of architecture and interior decoration to the realm of literature. "The poet of interior decoration," he called her.[6] Many critics after Wilson have recognized the importance of houses in Wharton's fiction, but most studies focus either on Wharton's skill in evoking scenes—her "visualizing power" in the words of Blake Nevius—or on Wharton's use of "place" in its geographical sense—on, for instance, her use of New York, New England towns such as Starkville and North Dormer, or foreign countries such as France.[7]

---

[2] See R. W. B. Lewis, *Edith Wharton: A Biography*, New York, 1975, *passim*; and see Louis Auchincloss, *Edith Wharton: A Woman in Her Time*, New York, 1971, for photographs of all of Wharton's houses.

[3] Lewis, p. 78.

[4] Lewis, p. 79.

[5] Introduction to *The Decoration of Houses*, n.p.

[6] Edmund Wilson, "Justice to Edith Wharton," in *The Wound and the Bow*, New York, 1947, p. 163.

[7] Blake Nevius, *Edith Wharton*, Berkeley, CA, 1953, p. 180. R. W. B. Lewis treats Wharton's "exploitation of place as a basic fictional resource" by discussing Archer's pursuit of Ellen Olenska to Portsmouth and Boston only to hear there that she has just left her hotel (introd. to *The Age of Innocence*, New York, 1968, p. xi). In "Edith Wharton and Her New York," Louis Auchincloss discusses Wharton's use of her home town (in *Edith Wharton: A Collection of Critical Essays*, ed. Irving Howe, Englewood Cliffs, N.J., 1962, pp. 32–42). Blake Nevius defends Wharton's knowledge of Starkville against Alfred Kazin's charge that *Ethan Frome* was "not a New England story" ("Edith Wharton" in *Edith Wharton: A Collection of Critical Essays*, ed. Irving Howe, p. 27). Cynthia Griffin Wolff discusses Wharton's treatment of North Dormer (*A Feast of Words: The Triumph of Edith Wharton*, New York, 1977, pp. 270–91). Many critics discuss Wharton's use of France, amongst others Elizabeth Ammons in *Edith Wharton's Argument with America*, Athens, Georgia, 1980.

As yet, no study exists of the way in which Wharton employs both the location and decoration of houses as signs to convey information about the
dramatis personae in one of her greatest novels, *The Age of Innocence*
(1920).[8] This paper proposes to examine this issue.

In *The Age of Innocence,* Wharton is able to use the location and decoration of houses as signs about characters because the close-knit society
of New York in the 1870s possessed a fixed scale of values and operated
as much by way of signs as by way of words. "In reality they all lived in a
kind of hieroglyphic world, where the real thing was never said or done or
even thought, but only represented by a set of arbitrary signs," Wharton
writes (47).[9] Thus the van der Luydens' barouche delivering a large square
envelope to Mrs. Mingott's door "means" that countess Ellen Olenska is
accepted by the van der Luydens, which in turn "means" that she will soon
be accepted by the whole of New York society. The locations and the decorations of houses in *The Age of Innocence* similarly function as "signs"
in this "hieroglyphic world."

The house of Mr and Mrs Henry van der Luyden, for example, is
located in the fashionable section of Madison Avenue in the centre of
New York, reflecting the van der Luydens' position at the centre of New
York society. Being "direct descendants of the first Dutch governor of
Manhattan, and related by pre-revolutionary marriages to several members of the French and British aristocracy," the van der Luydens represent old, aristocratic New York (51). The size of the house ("large"), the
height of the rooms ("high-ceilinged"), the materials employed in the interior decoration (marble, ormulu, brocade) as well as the colour scheme
(white and various pale shades) all connote a stately, solemn formality.
So far does this solemn formality extend that most traces of life are removed from the interior. Upon entering the drawing room, Newland
Archer notices that the chairs are "obviously uncovered for the occasion,"
while the gauze is "still veiling" the mantel ornaments and the Gains-

----

[8] The following critics have written about the interiors of houses in Wharton's fiction, but not in such detail as I do in this paper; nor have they linked the locations of
houses to the *dramatis personae*: Louis Auchincloss in *Edith Wharton*, Minneapolis,
1961; Gary H. Lindberg, *Edith Wharton and the Novel of Manners,* Charlottesville,
1975; Margaret McDowell, *Edith Wharton,* Boston, 1976; Cynthia Griffin Wolff, *A
Feast of Words: The Triumph of Edith Wharton;* Carol Wershoven, *The Female Intruder in the Novels of Edith Wharton,* Rutherford, 1982; and especially Judith Fryer,
Felicitous Space: The Imaginative Structures of Edith Wharton and Willa Cather,
Chapel Hill, 1986.

[9] All parenthetical references are to this New Riverside Edition.

borough painting. Newland even feels a "chill" descend upon him (53). Others privileged to enter this mansion similarly "shivered there" (72). The dinner parties at the van der Luydens possess an aura of "religious solemnity" (61) (the forthright Ellen Olenska calls them "gloomy," 72). When Newland rings the doorbell at the van der Luydens's house at Skuytercliff, the sound echoes "as through a mausoleum," while the butler takes so long to respond that it is "as though he had been summoned from his final sleep" (116).

These mansions—grand but bereft of life—reflect the personalities of Mr and Mrs Henry van der Luyden. With their tall, spare frames, faded hair, pale eyes, and look of "frozen gentleness," the couple is majestic and imposing—but also pallid and aloof to the point of coldness. Newland never fails to be struck with the likeness of Mrs van der Luyden to a portrait of her painted twenty years earlier, for she appears to have been "rather gruesomely preserved in the airless atmosphere of a perfectly irreproachable existence, as bodies caught in glaciers keep for years a rosy life-in-death" (55, 54). Indeed, just as the van der Luydens attempt to protect their revered *objets d'art* by covering them with cloths and using them as little they can, they try to preserve their venerated selves by doing as little as possible: Mrs van der Luyden never goes out in public, the couple rarely comes to New York, and the two very seldom invite people to their home. Even in their daily conduct they exert themselves little, both being "shy and retiring" in their bearing (56).

However, there is more to the van der Luydens than this frosting of formality: deep down, buried below many layers of aloof irreproachability, the couple harbours feelings of warmth and love. It is Ellen Olenska—the outsider who catalyzes so many emotions—who brings these submerged feelings to the surface. It is for Ellen that the van der Luydens decide to break their semi-seclusion in order to arrange a select dinner party to ostentatiously welcome her to New York. Mr van der Luyden afterwards goes in person to visit Ellen in her townhouse. He also sends her on various occasions carnations from his orangeries. The couple even invites Ellen for a fortnight to their estate to visit Skuytercliff on the Hudson—a place where prior to that moment "a chilly week-end" was the most ever offered to some privileged few (114). Especially for Ellen do they open up the small ancient house of the original seventeenth-century Patroon. With its low squat walls, tiled hearth, rows of Delft plate, panels, brasses, rush-bottomed chairs, and iron pot hanging from an ancient crane in the kitchen chimney, the Patroon's house calls up scenes of friendly domesticity as depicted in old Dutch paintings (e.g. works of Johannes Vermeer, Pieter de Hooch, and Jan Steen). The house seems to be "magically created" as an idyllic place where Ellen and Newland can at last be alone. For a few brief but ideal moments they are alone. Ellen declares:

> "I can't feel unhappy when you're here."
> "I sh'n't be here long," he rejoined, his lips stiffening with the effort to say just so much and no more.
> "No; I know. But I'm improvident: I live in the moment when I'm happy" (119).

As esteemed vestiges of the past, the van der Luyden houses do not contain a single piece of modern furniture—which subtly reminds us that the couple has no modern scion in the form of offspring. Engrossed in fending off the emergence of new orders, the van der Luydens are unable to produce anything new: they can only guard salvages from the past; they can only keep the embers smouldering of a tradition that was once living, but which is now all but dead. Like their Delftware, Sèvres, George II plate, Lowestoft, and Crown Derby, the van der Luydens are antiques— fragile, valuable relics of a previous era.

In contrast to the van der Luydens, Julius Beaufort is very much a parvenu. Having only recently entered society, he still resides on the periphery; his house is located at the end of Fifth Avenue. The lower end, to be precise, just as Beaufort has risen from the lower classes: "the Beauforts were not exactly common; some people said they were even worse." Beaufort has besieged the bastion of society with the power of money. He has purchased an impressive mansion which

> was one of the few [houses] in New York that possessed a ball-room . . . ; this undoubted superiority was felt to compensate for whatever was regrettable in the Beaufort past. (26–27)

This archetypal self-made man refuses to use anything that has been touched by any one else: instead of renting the accoutrements for his annual ball (as all others do), Beaufort has bought his own chairs, his own awning, and his own red velvet carpet to be rolled down the steps by his own silk-stockinged footmen. Beaufort's actions vividly demonstrate that it is not enough for the *nouveau riche* to have money—he must display it as well. The more conspicuous the consumption, the better, to use Thorstein Veblen's famous phrase. Conspicuous consumption is evident in the very layout of Beaufort's house:

> [T]he house had been boldly planned with a ball-room, so that . . . one marched solemnly down a vista of enfiladed drawing-rooms (the sea-green, the crimson and the *bouton d'or*), seeing from afar the many-candled

lustres reflected in the polished parquetry, and beyond that the depths of a conservatory where camellias and tree-ferns arched their costly foliage over seats of black and gold bamboo. (28–29)

Furthermore, by hosting the annual meeting of the Newport Archery Club, Beaufort acquires the chance to show off his seaside resort—an immaculately kept mansion.

Conspicuous consumption necessarily demands an audience—one needs to be in the public's eye in order to use it as an inroad into the citadel of society. What better way to stay in the public's eye than by spurring talk? A well-proven method is shown by a passage from Wharton's autobiographical *A Backward Glance,* a passage in which she relates that in the New York of her youth, "Art and music and literature were rather timorously avoided (unless Trollope's last novel were touched upon, or a discreet allusion made to Mr. William Astor's audacious acquisition of a Bouguerean Venus)."[10] Partly in order to spur talk, Beaufort (who, according to R. W. B. Lewis, is a composite of William Astor and several other historical figures)[11] has acquired the painting "'Love Victorious,' the much-discussed nude of Bouguereau" (29). But this nude serves another function as well for it also alludes to a temperament trait of its owner: Beaufort likes the ladies a bit too much. He is "always in quest of amorous adventures" (122). He has taken up with Mrs Lemuel Struthers (widow of the shoe-polish king); is more than interested in Ellen Olenska; and, after his financial downfall, rumour has it that "he hasn't spent all his money on Regina [his wife]" (216).

As it is, it does not suffice to conspicuously display acquired wealth on some special occasions during the year. The Spanish-leather chairs in Beaufort's library, the heavy lusters, the blooming camellias, and the luscious ferns—these all demand continual upkeep. Even so, though Beaufort uses his wealth as an inroad into the citadel of New York society, once inside, he must pay continual homage to New York's financial code, to its code of "unblemished honesty" (224). A passage from Wharton's *A Backward Glance* illuminates this financial code:

> New York has always been a commercial community, and in my infancy the merits and defects of its citizens were those of a mercantile middle class. The first duty of such a class was to maintain a strict standard of uprightness in affairs; and the gentlemen of my father's day did maintain

---

[10] Wharton, *A Backward Glance* (1934; rpt. New York: Scribner's Sons, 1964), p. 61.
[11] Lewis, p. 431. [Lewis writes that financier August Belmont or Wharton's cousin, George Alfred Jones, was a possible model for the character of Beaufort. [ED.]

it, whether in law, in banking, shipping or wholesale commercial enterprises. I well remember the horror excited by any irregularity in affairs,
and the relentless social ostracism inflicted on the families of those who
lapsed from professional or business integrity.[12]

Beaufort's violation of this code of scrupulous honesty results in a prompt
expulsion from society—which in turn means that he has to give up his
Fifth Avenue mansion.

While Beaufort's house dominates one end of Fifth Avenue, the other
end is presided over by Mrs Manson Mingott's mansion. Catherine Mingott has situated herself on the periphery of the city, the upper end of Fifth
Avenue, reflecting the fact that she haughtily looks down upon the New
York society. Having travelled abroad in her youth, "Catherine the Great"
(as she is nicknamed) now finds New York too confining, too narrow for
her taste. She likes to defy its conventions, and, for example, delights in
having married her two daughters to foreigners (an Italian Marquis and an
English banker). She also enjoys associating familiarly with *personae non
gratae,* such as Papists and Opera singers. But, she put "the crowning
touch to her audacities by building a large house of pale cream-coloured
stone (when brown sandstone seemed as much the only wear as a frock-
coat in the afternoon) in an inaccessible wilderness near the Central Park"
(21–22). So crucial is this architectural sign that Wharton reiterates it a
moment later: "[T]he cream-coloured house (supposed to be modelled on
the private hotels of the Parisian aristocracy) was there as a visible proof
of her moral courage" (22). This Matriarch of the Mingott line refuses to
fit in the straight-jacket of convention. This is brought out most clearly by
her decision to establish herself on the ground floor—"in flagrant violation of all the New York proprieties"—in order not to have to ascend the
stairs with her voluminous mounds of flesh. Since she likes to display her
different views publicly, she does not attempt to cover up her idiosyncratic
living arrangement with screens or closed doors. Instead, she always leaves
open the door between her sitting-room and bedroom. Her visitors can
thus see her huge, low bed (upholstered like a sofa) and her "toilet-table
with frivolous lace flounces and a gilt-framed mirror." The "foreignness"
of this vista both "startled and fascinated her visitors, recalling to them

> scenes in French fiction, and architectural incentives to immorality such
> as the simple American had never dreamed of. That was how women
> with lovers lived in the wicked old societies, in apartments with all the

---

[12] *A Backward Glance,* pp. 21–22.

rooms on one floor, and all the indecent propinquities that their novels described. (34)

Having travelled abroad and seen more of the world, Mrs Mingott is one of the few who combines the foreign with the domestic, the old with the new. As the high and mighty Matriarch of the line, she resolutely advocates traditional family values such as solidarity; but she also declares (apropos the new setting of May Welland's engagement ring), "I like all the novelties" (35). In her house, she has "*mingled* with the Mingott heirlooms the frivolous upholstery of the Second Empire" (33; my italics). She similarly has *interspersed* American-made objects with "souvenirs of the Tuileries of Louis Napoleon" (22). The wide range and strong individuality of the interior of Mrs Mingott's house foreshadows that it is she who will become the most "devoted champion" of Ellen Olenska (215).

"[T]here's not one of my own children that takes after me but my little Ellen," Mrs Mingott declares (133). Indeed, Ellen Olenska has emulated her grandmother's foreign taste by marrying a Polish nobleman and settling abroad. Furthermore, she has emulated her grandmother's defiance of conventions by openly deserting her husband when her marriage did not work out and by now coming back to New York. However, when she left America some ten years earlier, she forfeited her "place" in New York— "place" in the literal sense of a house to live in as well as in the figurative sense of a position in New York's hierarchical society. As to the latter, Mrs Mingott and the van der Luydens take it upon themselves to marshal her back into the élite. In regard to the former, Ellen Olenska shows her independence by only temporarily accepting the shelter of relatives, and by then renting a house of her own. The house she takes is situated on West Twenty-third Street in a neighbourhood which is euphemistically labelled as "*des quartiers excentriques*" (73). The location of Countess Olenska's house thus reflects the fact that she is in the eyes of New York "eccentric." Ellen is surrounded by "small dress-makers, bird-stuffers and 'people who wrote'" (66). The circumlocutory phrase here as well as the quotation marks around the verb in "people who 'wrote'" well convey the snivel of snobbish New York which (as Wharton reports in *A Backward Glance*) grudgingly pronounced Washington Irving a gentleman "in spite of the disturbing fact that he 'wrote.'" [13]

The neighbourhood where Ellen Olenska settles has another function since it also points to her affinity with the arts and her own artistic talents. Varying the phrase she has used earlier, Wharton later describes the

---

[13] *A Backward Glance*, p. 67.

neighbourhood as inhabited by "artists, musicians and 'people who wrote'" (93). Ellen likes to meet artists, "dramatic artists, singers, actors, [and] musicians," and tells Newland she misses not seeing these in New York (99). Moreover, she herself possesses much artistic talent. Not a single one of her visitors fails to see this. "She has a real gift for arranging flowers," Henry van der Luyden declares. The English Duke of St Austrey is impressed with "how cleverly she's arranged her drawing-room" (84). And Newland, when he is let into her house, is struck with "the way in which Medora Manson's shabby hired house, with its blighted background of pampas grass and Rogers statuettes, had, by a turn of the hand, and the skilful use of a few properties, been transformed into something intimate, 'foreign', subtly suggestive of old romantic scenes and sentiments" (70). Wondering how Ellen Olenska has accomplished this, Newland "tried to analyze the trick, to find a clue to it in the way the chairs and tables were grouped, in the fact that only two Jacqueminot roses (of which nobody ever bought less than a dozen) had been placed in the slender vase at his elbow, and in the vague pervading perfume that was not what one put on handkerchiefs, but rather like the scent of some far-off bazaar, a smell made up of Turkish coffee and ambergris and dried roses" (70).

As all true works of art, Ellen's interior decorating in last instance defies analysis. However, it is noteworthy that in his attempt to describe it, Newland appeals to more than one sense organ: his visual sense is stimulated by the grouping of the chairs and tables as well as the arrangement of the flowers, and his olfactory as well as gustory senses are animated by the "perfume" of "dried roses" and "Turkish coffee." With its Italian paintings, Greek bronzes, Japanese cups, French novels by Bourget, Huysman, and the Goncourt brothers, and with the brief appearance of a "Sicilian"-looking maid who only speaks Italian, Ellen's room is as cultured and cosmopolitan as its mistress. It is "unlike any room" Newland has seen before (68). This is, among other reasons, because of the books: in the view of old New York the drawing room is a part of the house in which books are considered "out of place"—to say nothing of books being "scattered about," as they are in Ellen's room (96). As for this latter point, old New York is personified in Lucretia Jones's criticism of her twelve-year-old daughter's first attempt to write realistic fiction. Upon reading the opening lines of Edith Wharton's first story—"'Oh, how do you do, Mrs. Brown?' said Mrs. Tompkins. 'If only I had known you were going to call I should have tidied up the drawing-room.'"—Mrs Jones coldly observed: "Drawing-rooms are always tidy." [14]

---

[14] *A Backward Glance*, p. 73.

Since it is so unlike any other room he knows, Newland labels the room "foreign." And—just as the New Yorkers visiting Mrs Mingott's house—he associates it with "romantic scenes and sentiments," with "something intimate" (70). Indeed, Newland is "virtually seduced" by the room.[15] While the room arouses all of Archer's senses, he fails to grasp it rationally: not only does Ellen's decorative talent defy his analytic powers, the Italian paintings on the walls also do not figure in the books he has read, the studies of John Ruskin, John Addington Symonds, Vernon Lee, P. G. Hamerton, and Walter Pater. Archer is therefore unable to respond verbally to the room; he can only respond by sending the decorator of the room a bouquet of yellow roses, roses which likewise exceed the verbal realm as they are "too rich, too strong, in their fiery beauty" (77). Unable to find words for his feelings, Newland does not attach a card to the roses. This passage thus foreshadows the climactic carriage scene in which Newland exclaims: "I want—I want somehow to get away with you into a world where words like that—categories like that—won't exist. Where we shall be simply two human beings who love each other" (234).

So overpowering is the foreign and intimate atmosphere of Ellen's room that Newland cannot help but be drawn into it. The result is that New York seems very far away, as though seen "through the wrong end of a telescope" (74). Newland thus can no longer get himself to tell his cousin that New York believes that it is improper for her to be seen driving about the streets in Beaufort's carriage. The simile in which he expresses this to himself again evinces that it is Ellen's room which has effected this change:

> to give advice of that sort would have been like telling some one who was bargaining for attar-of-roses in Samarkand that one should always be provided with arctics for a New York winter. New York seemed much farther off than Samarkand. (74)

The "attar-of-roses" with its olfactory appeal, the foreignness of Samarkand, and the notion of sensuality presiding over rationality, all point to Ellen.

While waiting for the arrival of Ellen, Newland's thoughts turn to the architectural style of the house which his prospective father-in-law, Mr Welland, has selected, and he thinks about the manner in which his fiancee will decorate this house. This "transition" in Archer's thoughts has

---

[15] The phrase "virtually seduced" is Gary H. Lindberg's, p. 103.

puzzled critics such as Cynthia Griffin Wolff and Gary Lindberg.[16] However, if we assume that architecture and interior decoration function as signs conveying information about characters, there no longer is anything "curious" about this transition. Throughout the novel, Newland cannot help but compare Ellen to May, the dark lady to the blond lady. The foreignness and intimacy of Ellen's room, of Ellen, are all the more exciting to Newland when contrasted to the prim, proper, predictable life he can expect with May: "The young man felt that his fate was sealed: for the rest of his life he would go up every evening between the cast-iron railings of that greenish-yellow doorstep, and pass through a Pompeian vestibule into a hall with a wainscoting of varnished yellow wood" (71). The cast-iron railings connote severe restriction (the railings even conjure up prison bars). This image of confinement strikingly contrasts with the freedom and natural beauty suggested by the "giant wisteria" which adorns the facade of Ellen's house (66). Freedom is crucial to Ellen: "I had to be free," she declares (75). She is appalled when Newland suggests that she go back to her husband to avoid "a lot of beastly talk": "But my freedom—is that nothing?" (103). The wisteria also stands for Ellen's natural sense of beauty. Unlike Archer, Ellen does not need critical studies to guide her taste. Hers is a natural talent. She herself determines what she likes, what she does not like. To Newland's grim remark that she has located herself in a neighbourhood that is considered "not fashionable," she astonishedly replies: "Fashionable! Do you all think so much of that? Why not make one's own fashions?" (73).

Musing about the interior of his future home, Newland momentarily realizes that he is unable to fancy how May precisely will decorate the drawing room—only to reassure himself:

> She submitted cheerfully to the purple satin and yellow tuftings of the Welland drawing-room, to its sham Buhl tables and gilt vitrines full of modern Saxe. He saw no reason to suppose that she would want anything different in her own house. (71)

The Wellands' home on Bellevue Avenue is a house "in which one always knew exactly what [was] happening at a given hour" (183). Even an outsider always knows what is going on since the curtains are never closed at night. The "perpetually reminding tick of disciplined clocks" suit[s] Mr Welland, a man "with no opinions but with many habits." The "perpetually renewed stack of cards and invitations on the hall table" agree[s] with Mrs Welland, a woman whose chief concern in life is that every hour

---

[16] Wolff, p. 319; Lindberg, p. 103.

be always "provided for." This overregulated existence which buries itself in "tyrannical trifles" has the same effect on Newland as the Wellands' heavy carpets and voluminous cushions: it stultifies him as a narcotic does (185, 107–08, 187).

Interestingly enough, the reader later discovers that May does *not* decorate her drawing room in the style of her parents. Instead, she opts for sofas and armchairs of pale brocade; for little plush tables bedecked with silver toys, knobby vases, porcelain animals and efflorescent photograph frames; for tall rosy-shaded lamps which "sho[o]t up like tropical flowers among the palms"; and for "a gilt bamboo *jardinière*" with primulas and cinerarias (263, 262). Nature is brought indoors and, in the process, is tamed. May tames everything, from her waist which she squeezes into a twenty-inch girdle to Newland's secret passion for Ellen which she converts into overt family concern (she explicitly asks him to pay his respects to her cousin). The discrepancy between the picture Newland initially conjures up of May's drawing room and the way in which we later see her decorate it makes clear that Newland is slightly mistaken in May. Indeed, he never fully comes to know his wife. He is astounded when his son tells him after her death that, while he had always assumed May ignorant of his feelings for Ellen, in fact, she knew all along.

Newland's early thoughts on interior decoration provide yet more clues to personalities. Surrounded by the foreign atmosphere and books in Ellen's drawing room, Newland consoles himself for the way he erroneously expects his future home to look with the thought that May "would probably let him arrange his library as he pleased—which would be, of course, with 'sincere' Eastlake furniture, and the plain new bookcases without glass doors" (71). In her excellent *Felicitous Space,* Judith Fryer has called Newland's preference for Eastlake furniture a "devastating criticism." According to Fryer, it indicates that "he is a man of 'taste' rather than a man of principles."[17] Fryer here alludes to Wharton's distinction in *The Decoration of Houses* between persons of "taste"—people who divorce the aesthetic dimension from all other dimensions—and persons of "principle"—people who recognize that styles relate to a whole complex of social factors.[18] We have seen above that Wharton believed that decoration should be a branch of architecture, that there should be a harmonious balance between every element in the house and the overall structure. Wharton thus objected to the fact that Charles Eastlake merely looked at furniture as ornament; that he failed to take into account the

---

[17] Fryer, p. 121.
[18] *Decoration of Houses,* p. 198, 64n.

architectural design of the building. What Fryer does not mention, but what our analysis shows, is that Newland's preference for Eastlake suggests that he can only see parts of larger wholes—Newland only sees a part of the whole May, a part of the whole Ellen.

Newland's vision of his library with Eastlake furniture and bookcases reveals yet more of his personality. Eastlake's furniture being a vogue among the younger generations in the last quarter of the nineteenth century, Newland's intoxication with it signifies that he is not as rebellious, as independent of his surroundings, as he considers himself to be. Indeed, the choice of Eastlake foreshadows the fact that on the surface he will conform to New York and marry the New York May rather than the "foreign" Ellen. Moreover, Newland's longing to have the library as his own room, and in particular his interest in bookcases, foreshadows two additional things. While on the outside Newland will conform to New York, on the inside he will not do this but will instead create a private sanctuary for his innermost thoughts. In this private place, not the conventional May but the nonconformist Ellen will reign. In the course of the novel, Newland will retreat more and more often to his library to be alone with his dreams of Ellen:

> [H]e had built up within himself a kind of sanctuary in which she [Ellen] throned among his secret thoughts and longings. Little by little it became the scene of his real life, of his only rational activities; thither he brought the books he read, the ideas and feelings which nourished him, his judgments and his visions. (216)

Ellen, indeed, is connected in Newland's mind with books. Newland's first daydreams about Ellen were prompted by her drawing room with all its scattered books; his first dreams of her at night were induced by a volume of poetry which he had ordered because the title had attracted him. The volume significantly is entitled, *The House of Life* (123).[19] Later he no longer needs such a catalyst. With the passing of time, Newland even comes to think of Ellen "abstractly, serenely, as one might think of some imaginary beloved in a book or a picture" (274). Moreover, as seen in the quotation above, to Newland his mental life with Ellen becomes more "real" than his real life. This process of reversal—induced by the interior of Ellen's drawing room which made Samarkand seem closer than New York—gains momentum in the course of the novel until it culminates in the epilogue.

The epilogue takes place some thirty years later. Wharton indicates the passage of time by describing the changes in architectural and decora-

---

[19] Since Wharton does not mention this, I might add that *The House of Life* is a sonnet cycle by Dante Gabriel Rossetti, which first appeared in 1870.

tive taste. The pre-Revolutionary and Georgian styles have become fash-ionable again, while the Colonial style has fallen out of favour and is now only coveted by "the millionaire grocers of the suburbs" (the last phrase is a good example of Wharton's "trickle-down" theory of taste) (272).[20] Newland's own room has been "done over" by his son Dallas with "Eng-lish mezzotints, Chippendale cabinets, bits of chosen blue-and-white and pleasantly shaded electric lamps" (274). But, significantly, Newland has not been willing to give up his old Eastlake writing-table; he likewise has retained, and (will be seen to refuse to surrender) memories of three decades earlier. The location of Newland's house is again as telling as the interior decoration. While in the course of three decades others have moved away, Newland still resides in the small townhouse selected by Mr Welland at the time of his engagement, suggesting that Newland resists change. Further-more, it also shows—especially in combination with the place where Archer spends his summers, the Wellands' house in Newport—that he lacks the courage to break away from his father-in-law.

In imagining Ellen's life in Paris, Newland uses images he has come to associate with her on account of her New York house—that is, a foreign set-ting (the Italian paintings, Greek bronze, Japanese cups, and French nov-els), sensual natural vegetation (the giant wisteria outside and Jacqueminot roses inside), and intellectual stimulation (the new Huysmans novels and other books). Accordingly, Newland pictures Ellen in the City of Light with all its unique, Parisian landmarks (the "majestic" river, the public gardens with statues) amidst "the radiant outbreak of spring," blooming horse-chestnuts, an abundance of flowers, and the "whiff of lilacs from the flower-carts." The life he conjures up is full of "art and study and pleasure that filled each mighty artery to bursting" (279). Once he has arrived in Paris, he further discovers that Ellen lives close to the lively Champs-Elysees, the flowery Tuileries Gardens, and the cultural mecca of the Louvre.

How this location contrasts with the place Newland Archer has se-lected for his stay in Paris—the quiet stillness of the Place Vendôme (a place which was nearly deserted with the coming of the new century). As this location suggests, Newland has become a quiet, withdrawn, conser-vative man. Paris makes him realize this. When confronted with Ellen's many-windowed apartment above the flowering horse-chestnuts, near the golden splendour of the Mansart dome, Newland decides not to go up to meet her. Why? Because he would be forced to re-adjust his mental picture

---

[20] Wharton believed that trends pass on from the higher classes to the lower ones. See, Pierre Bourdieu, *Distinction: A Social Critique of the Judgment of Taste*, tr. Richard Nice, Cambridge, Mass., 1984, for a sociological study of the "trickle down" theory of taste.

of her, an image he has relished for nearly thirty years. By staying outside, Newland can keep his mental picture of Ellen intact. "It's more real to me here than if I went up," he announces. Archer thus completes the process of reversal of imagined life and real life instigated by Ellen's drawing room on Twenty-third Street (where "New York seemed much farther off than Samarkand" [74]). Now Archer only wants his imagined life, only wants his imagined, mental picture of Ellen in the drawing room of her Paris apartment, "with azaleas banked behind her on a table" (285).

FROM *HOW THE OTHER HALF LIVES*

Jacob A. Riis

Jacob A. Riis (1849–1914) was a social reformer and journalist. An immigrant from Denmark in 1870, he worked as a police re-porter for the *New York Tribune* from 1877 to 1888 and became known for his vivid descriptions of crime. The poverty and over-crowding Riis witnessed in tenements led him to become an ad-vocate for immigrants. He began to photograph tenements to il-lustrate his stories, forcing middle-class readers to confront the misery and filth of New York slums. In 1890, he became nation-ally known for his book, *How the Other Half Lives,* a graphic ac-count of the squalor of immigrant life on the Lower East Side, just blocks away from the fashionable neighborhoods inhabited by main characters in *The Age of Innocence.* Riis lectured to re-ligious and charitable organizations and worked for improved living conditions for the poor, such as tenement regulation, im-proved water supplies, care for needy children, and playgrounds. He gained the support of Theodore Roosevelt, who, as president of the New York City Board of Police Commissioners, worked to end police corruption and exploitation of the poor. ED.

The first tenement New York knew bore the mark of Cain from its birth, though a generation passed before the writing was deciphered. It was the "rear house," infamous ever after in our city's history. There had

---

New York: Dover, 1971.

been tenant-houses before, but they were not built for the purpose. Nothing would probably have shocked their original owners more than the idea of their harboring a promiscuous crowd; for they were the decorous homes of the old Knickerbockers, the proud aristocracy of Manhattan in the early days.

It was the stir and bustle of trade, together with the tremendous immigration that followed upon the war of 1812, that dislodged them. In thirty-five years the city of less than a hundred thousand came to harbor half a million souls, for whom homes had to be found. Within the memory of men not yet in their prime, Washington had moved from his house on Cherry Hill as too far out of town to be easily reached. Now the old residents followed his example; but they moved in a different direction and for a different reason. Their comfortable dwellings in the once fashionable streets along the East River front fell into the hands of real-estate agents and boarding-house keepers; and here, says the report to the Legislature of 1857, when the evils engendered had excited just alarm, "in its beginning, the tenant-house became a real blessing to that class of industrious poor whose small earnings limited their expenses, and whose employment in workshops, stores, or about the warehouses and thoroughfares, render a near residence of much importance." Not for long, however. As business increased, and the city grew with rapid strides, the necessities of the poor became the opportunity of their wealthier neighbors, and the stamp was set upon the old houses, suddenly become valuable, which the best thought and effort of a later age have vainly struggled to efface. Their "*large* rooms were partitioned into *several smaller ones,* without regard to light or ventilation, the rate of rent being lower in proportion to space or height from the street; and they soon became filled from cellar to garret with a class of tenantry living from hand to mouth, loose in morals, improvident in habits, degraded, and squalid as beggary itself." It was thus the dark bedroom, prolific of untold depravities, came into the world. It was destined to survive the old houses. In their new rôle, says the old report, eloquent in its indignant denunciation of "evils more destructive than wars," "they were not intended to last. Rents were fixed high enough to cover damage and abuse from this class, from whom nothing was expected, and the most was made of them while they lasted. Neatness, order, cleanliness, were never dreamed of in connection with the tenant-house system, as it spread its localities from year to year; while reckless slovenliness, discontent, privation, and ignorance were left to work out their invariable results, until the entire premises reached the level of tenant-house dilapidation, containing, but sheltering not, the miserable hordes that crowded beneath mouldering, water-rotted roofs or burrowed among the rats of clammy cellars." Yet so illogical is human greed that, at a later day, when called to account, "the proprietors frequently urged the filthy habits of the tenants as an excuse for the condition of their property, utterly losing sight of the fact that it was the tolerance of those habits which was the real evil, and that for this they themselves were alone responsible."

Still the pressure of the crowds did not abate, and in the old garden where the stolid Dutch burgher grew his tulips or early cabbages a rear house was built, generally of wood, two stories high at first. Presently it was carried up another story, and another. Where two families had lived ten moved in. The front house followed suit, if the brick walls were strong enough. The question was not always asked, judging from complaints made by a contemporary witness, that the old buildings were "often carried up to a great height without regard to the strength of the foundation walls." It was rent the owner was after; nothing was said in the contract about either the safety or the comfort of the tenants. The garden gate no longer swung on its rusty hinges. The shell-paved walk had become an alley; what the rear house had left of the garden, a "court." Plenty such are yet to be found in the Fourth Ward, with here and there one of the original rear tenements.

Worse was to follow. It was "soon perceived by estate owners and agents of property that a greater percentage of profits could be realized by the conversion of houses and blocks into barracks, and dividing their space into smaller proportions capable of containing human life within four walls. . . . Blocks were rented of real estate owners, or 'purchased on time,' or taken in charge at a percentage, and held for under-letting." With the appearance of the middleman, wholly irresponsible, and utterly reckless and unrestrained, began the era of tenement building which turned out such blocks as Gotham Court, where, in one cholera epidemic that scarcely touched the clean wards, the tenants died at the rate of one hundred and ninety-five to the thousand of population; which forced the general mortality of the city up from 1 in 41.83 in 1815, to 1 in 27.33 in 1855, a year of unusual freedom from epidemic disease. . . .

The dread of advancing cholera, with the guilty knowledge of the harvest field that awaited the plague in New York's slums, pricked the conscience of the community into action soon after the close of the war. A citizens' movement resulted in the organization of a Board of Health and the adoption of the "Tenement-House Act" of 1867, the first step toward remedial legislation. A thorough canvass of the tenements had been begun already in the previous year; but the cholera first, and next a scourge of small-pox, delayed the work, while emphasizing the need of it, so that it was 1869 before it got fairly under way and began to tell. The dark bedroom fell under the ban first. In that year the Board ordered the cutting of more than forty-six thousand windows in interior rooms, chiefly for ventilation—for little or no light was to be had from the dark hallways. Airshafts were unknown. The saw had a job all that summer; by early fall nearly all the orders had been carried out. Not without opposition; obstacles were thrown in the way of the officials on the one side by the owners of the tenements, who saw in every order to repair or clean up only an item of added expense to diminish their income from the rent; on the other side by the tenants themselves, who had sunk, after a generation of unavailing protest, to the level of their surroundings, and were at last content to remain there. The tenements had bred their Nemesis, a proletariat ready and able to avenge the wrongs of their crowds. Already it taxed the city heavily for the support of its jails and charities. The basis of opposition, curiously enough, was the same at both extremes; owner and tenant alike considered official interference an infringement of personal rights, and a hardship. It took long years of weary labor to make good the claim of the sunlight to such corners of the dens as it could reach at all. Not until five years after did the department succeed at last in ousting the "cave-dwellers" and closing some five hundred and fifty cellars south of Houston Street, many of them below tide-water, that had been used as living apartments. In many instances the police had to drag the tenants out by force. . . .

. . . [O]n the East Side . . . I actually lost my way once. There were thirty or forty rear houses in the heart of [the block], three or four on every lot, set at all sorts of angles, with odd, winding passages, or no passage at all, only "runways" for the thieves and toughs of the neighborhood. These yards are clear. There is air there, and it is about all there is. The view between brick walls outside is that of a stony street; inside, of rows of unpainted board fences, a bewildering maze of clothes-post and lines; underfoot, a desert of brown, hard-baked soil from which every blade of grass, every stray weed, every speck of green, has been trodden out, as much inevitably be every gentle thought and aspiration above the mere wants of the body in those whose moral natures such home surroundings are to nourish. In self-defence, you know, all life eventually accommodates itself to its environment, and human life is no exception. Within the house there is nothing to supply the want thus left unsatisfied. Tenement-houses have no æsthetic resources. If any are to be brought to bear on them, they must come from the outside. There is the common hall with doors opening softly on every landing as the strange step is heard on the stairs, the airshaft that seems always so busy letting out foul stenches from below that it has no time to earn its name by bringing down fresh air, the squeaking pumps that hold no water, and the rent that is never less than one week's wages out of the four, quite as often half of the family earnings. . . .

With the first hot night in June police despatches, that record the killing of men and women by rolling off roofs and window-sills while asleep, announce that the time of greatest suffering among the poor is at hand. It is in hot weather, when life indoors is well-nigh unbearable with cooking, sleeping, and working, all crowded into the small rooms together, that the tenement expands, reckless of all restraint. Then a strange and picturesque life moves upon the flat roofs. In the day and early evening mothers air their babies there, the boys fly their kites from the house-tops, undismayed by police regulations, and the young men and girls court and pass the growler. In the stifling July nights, when the big barracks are like fiery furnaces, their very walls giving out absorbed heat, men and women lie in restless, sweltering rows, panting for air and sleep. Then every truck in the street, every crowded fire-escape, becomes a bedroom, infinitely preferable to any the house affords. A cooling shower on such a night is hailed as a heaven-sent blessing in a hundred thousand homes. . . .

Every once in a while a case of downright starvation gets into the newspapers and makes a sensation. But this is the exception. Were the whole truth known, it would come home to the community with a shock that would rouse it to a more serious effort than the spasmodic undoing of its purse-strings. I am satisfied from my own observation that hundreds of men, women, and children are every day slowly starving to death in the tenements with my medical friend's complaint of "improper nourishment." Within a single week I have had this year three cases of insanity, provoked directly by poverty and want. One was that of a mother who in the middle of the night got up to murder her child, who was crying for food; another was the case of an Elizabeth Street truck-driver whom the newspapers never heard of. With a family to provide for, he had been unable to work for many months. There was neither food, nor a scrap of anything upon which money could be raised, left in the house; his mind gave way under the combined physical and mental suffering. In the third case I was just in time with the police to prevent the madman from murdering his whole family. He had the sharpened hatchet in his pocket when we seized him. He was an Irish laborer, and had been working in the sewers until the poisonous gases destroyed his health. Then he was laid off, and scarcely anything had been coming in all winter but the oldest child's earnings as cash-girl in a store, $2.50 a week. There were seven children to provide for, and the rent of the Mulberry Street attic in which the family lived was $10 a month. They had borrowed as long as anybody had a cent to lend. When at last the man got an odd job that would just buy the children bread, the week's wages only served to measure the depth of their misery. "It came in so on the tail-end of everything," said his wife in telling the story, with unconscious eloquence. The outlook worried him through sleepless nights until it destroyed his reason. In his madness he had only one conscious thought: that the town should not take the children. "Better that I take care of them myself," he repeated to himself as he ground the axe to an edge. Help came in abundance from many almost as poor as they when the desperate straits of the family became known through his arrest. The readiness of the poor to share what little they have with those who have even less is one of the few moral virtues of tenements. . . .

Marriage and Divorce

D ivorce has a long history in the United States—the first divorce was granted by a Quaker court in Boston in the 1640s on the grounds of adultery—but it has never found easy acceptance in American society. During the nineteenth century, the terms on which divorce was sought and granted were sharply contested. Divorce laws varied in restrictiveness from state to state and from decade to decade in response to changes brought about by such factors as industrialization, urbanization, westward expansion, immigration, weakening religious ties, increased rights of women, and a general diminution of older patriarchal patterns. Some individuals reacted by working to tighten bonds that kept couples together, whereas others welcomed new definitions of marriage that allowed for greater freedom and flexibility.

FROM *DOMESTIC REVOLUTIONS*

Steven Mintz and Susan Kellogg

In the following excerpt from their book on the social history of American families (1988), Steven Mintz and Susan Kellogg describe changing perspectives on marriage and divorce during the nineteenth century. They suggest reasons for increasing rates of divorce throughout the period and describe the rise of "companionate" marriage. The relatives who discourage Ellen Olenska's divorce seem intent merely on preserving appearances. However, their insistence that Ellen remain married, no matter how unsatisfying the union, speaks to deeper concerns about marriage as a sacrament and guarantor of social cohesion. Wharton knew well

New York: Free Press, 1988.

the issues she describes, having reluctantly obtained a divorce on grounds of adultery in 1913 from her husband of twenty-eight years. Her case was argued in a Parisian rather than New York court to avoid publicity. [ED.]

. . . During the years before the Civil War, in response to the nation's changing conceptions of the family, marriage, and sex roles, a fundamental revision of family law took place. A companionate conception of marriage demanded that husbands and wives be able to terminate unions that were not "true marriages" and that married women be given limited control over their property and earnings. The veneration of women's child-rearing role required that women be given new rights of custody over their children.[1]

. . . During the early decades of the nineteenth century, more and more people came to believe that if the primary objects of marriage were the promotion of personal happiness and the welfare of society, then divorce and remarriage were justified in instances of adultery, physical abuse, or failure of a marriage partner to fulfill his or her proper role. Before the nineteenth century, divorce was exceedingly difficult to obtain and the number of divorces granted was minuscule. Massachusetts records reveal that it granted only twenty-seven divorces in the period it was a colony. In a number of colonies, especially those in the South, divorce was unavailable, and in those colonies where legal divorce was possible, it could only be on the limited grounds of adultery, nonsupport, and abandonment or prolonged absence (usually after a period of seven years). Even in colonies that made provision for divorce, the law did not generally permit an injured spouse to remarry. Remarriage was only allowed in instances in which the marriage could be annulled (such as impotence or bigamy); otherwise the spouse could only obtain a legal separation. In many colonies divorce was only available through a special act of the colonial legislature. Given the difficulty of obtaining a divorce, unhappy couples were more likely to separate formally; in eighteenth-century Massachusetts, only 220 couples divorced, but 3,300 notices of separation were printed in the newspapers.[2]

---

[1] Lynne Carol Halem, *Divorce Reform: Changing Legal and Social Perspectives* (New York, 1980), 9–26; David Brion Davis, *Antebellum American Culture: An Interpretive Anthology* (University Park, PA, 1979), 7–8, 95–97.
[2] On the history of divorce, see Nelson Manfred Blake, *The Road to Reno: A History of Divorce in the United States* (New York, 1962); Halem, *Divorce Reform,* 9–26; Nancy F. Cott, "Eighteenth Century Family and Social Life Revealed in Massachusetts Divorce Records," *Journal of Social History,* 10 (1976), 32; Cott, "Divorce and the Changing Status of Women in Eighteenth Century Massachusetts," *William and Mary Quarterly,*

In the early nineteenth century, the availability of divorce as a remedy to intolerable marriages began to expand as states gave courts jurisdiction over divorce petitions. In the 1820s a growing number of reformers argued that the grounds for divorce should be expanded to include physical cruelty, willful desertion, intemperance, and temperamental incompatibility on the grounds that removing the barrier of indissolubility would promote individual happiness and discourage adultery. By the 1830s a number of states, led by Indiana, had adopted permissive divorce laws. Connecticut, for example, allowed a divorce to be granted for any misconduct that "permanently destroys the happiness of the petitioner and defeats the purposes of the marriage relation." But even in the states that did not liberalize divorce laws, the number of divorces began to rise after 1840. In 1867 the number of divorces granted in a single year reached 10,000.[3]

Of much greater importance than divorce in altering the position of women in the nineteenth-century American family was the adoption of laws guaranteeing married women's property rights. At the beginning of the nineteenth century, the basic principle guiding American law was that a husband was the natural guardian of his wife's interests. Her property, earnings, and services became his on marriage. A married woman was prohibited from bringing legal suits or being sued, from making contracts, and from owning property individually. She was not even permitted to control her own wages. By the Civil War, however, a crack had been made in the defenses of male prerogatives. Many states, beginning with those of the Deep South, adopted married women's property acts, which permitted married women to control their own property and earnings. . . .[4]

Over the course of the nineteenth century, a momentous transformation had taken place in the functions and expectations assigned to the middle-class American family. By the beginning of the twentieth century, middle-class families had been shorn of many traditional economic, educational, and welfare functions. The family's role in education, in health care, and in care of the aged, poor, and the mentally ill had increasingly been assumed by specialists and institutions outside the family. At the same time, however, the family had acquired new burdens and expectations.

3rd ser., 33 (1976), 586–614; Robert L. Griswold, *Family and Divorce in California, 1850–1890: Victorian Illusions and Everyday Realities* (Albany, N.Y., 1982).

[3] Refer to note 2; Davis, *Antebellum American Culture*, 7–8, 95–97.

[4] On married women's property rights, see Norma Basch, *In the Eyes of the Law: Women, Marriage, and Property in Nineteenth Century New York* (Ithaca, N.Y., 1982).

The middle-class family was assigned primary responsibilities for fulfilling the emotional and psychological needs of its members. Along with providing economic security and a stable environment for children, family life was now expected to provide romance, sexual fulfillment, companionship, and emotional sastisfaction.[5]

Many turn-of-the-century Americans believed the family to be in a unique state of crisis. Psychologist John B. Watson predicted, "In fifty years there will be no such thing as marriage." Critics denounced the family as "illimitably selfish, psychologically egocentric, spiritually dwarfish and decivilizing" and declared it a "factory of feeble-mindedness and insanity." Even defenders of the family were fearful of its future.[6]

Concern was provoked by a number of factors, one of which was a rapid upsurge in the number of divorces. Despite the efforts of late-nineteenth-century moral conservatives to make it difficult for couples to divorce, the divorce rate rose sharply after 1870. By 1916, in San Francisco, one out of every four marriages ended in divorce; in Los Angeles, one out of five; in Chicago, one out of seven.[7]

At the same time, a sharp decline in the birthrates of native-born, old-stock whites elicited deep concern. Birthrates had so decreased that the educated classes were failing to reproduce themselves, while the rate of childbearing among immigrant women was nearly twice that of native-born women. In 1903, Theodore Roosevelt expressed fear that the old-stock middle class was committing "race suicide."[8]

The drop in the nation's birthrate was merely one symptom of a dramatic change in traditional sex roles. More women were pursuing higher education, joining organizations, and working outside the home, and fewer

---

[5] On the changing functions and expectations assigned to the middle-class family, see David Brion Davis, "The American Family and Boundaries in Historical Perspective," in *From Homicide to Slavery: Studies in American Culture* (New York, 1986), 166–83; John Demos, "Images of the Family, Then and Now," in *Changing Images of the Family*, eds. Virginia Tufte and Barbara Myerhoff (New Haven, 1979), 56–59.

[6] On the turn-of-the-century crisis of the family, see Christopher Lasch, *Haven in a Heartless World: The Family Besieged* (New York, 1977), 8–9; Robert Briffault, ed., *Marriage: Past and Present* (Boston, 1956), 26; Peter Gabriel Filene, *Him/Her/Self: Sex Roles in Modern America* (New York, 1976), 36–39.

[7] On the rising turn of the century divorce rate, Lasch, *Haven in a Heartless World*, 8; Elaine Tyler May, *Great Expectations: Marriage and Divorce in Post-Victorian America* (Chicago, 1980), 2–5; J. P. Lichtenberger, *Divorce: A Social Interpretation* (New York, 1931), 154–86.

[8] On the shrinking middle-class birthrate, see Lasch, *Haven in a Heartless World*, 8–9; David Kennedy, *Birth Control in America: The Career of Margaret Sanger* (New Haven, 1971), 42–44.

young women seemed content to accept their traditional roles—caring for their homes, and tending their children. Many books, newspapers, and magazines bristled with alarm over this so-called revolution in morals and manners. Young women danced the fox-trot, smoked cigarettes openly and defiantly, read sex and confession magazines, watched lurid motion pictures, and, to an unprecedented extent, engaged in premarital sex. Alarm was expressed about how such radical changes would affect the cherished ideal of the family.[9]

The turn-of-the-century family was clearly an institution in flux, buffeted by stresses and pressures that have continued to confront twentieth-century families to this day. A rapidly rising divorce rate, an alarming fall in the birthrate, a sexual revolution, and a sharp increase in the numbers of women continuing their educations, joining women's organizations, and finding employment—each of these worked to transform the middle-class family. Many Americans believed that the family was being destroyed, but in fact a new kind of family was emerging from these demographic and cultural revolutions: It was the "companionate family," a new model and ideal of family function and behavior, which remains with us today.

Beginning in 1889, following the discovery that the United States had the highest divorce rate in the world, and continuing until 1906, state legislatures across the country sought to tighten divorce statutes to discourage marital separation. The statutory grounds for divorce were reduced from over four hundred to fewer than twenty, and only three states continued to allow courts to grant divorces on any grounds they deemed proper. New Jersey allowed divorce only on the grounds of adultery and desertion; New York only in cases of adultery; South Carolina prohibited divorce altogether.[10]

---

[9] On the alarm sparked by the changing position of women, see Lasch, *Haven in a Heartless World*, 8–9; Frederick Lewis Allen, *Only Yesterday: An Informal History of the Nineteen-Twenties* (New York, 1931), 89, 92–93, 103–08. On the changes taking place in women's lives, see Sallie Westwood, *All Day, Every Day: Factory and Family in the Making of Women's Lives* (Urbana, Ill., 1985). On the revolution in morals and manners, see James G. McGovern, "The American Woman's Pre-World War I Freedom in Manners and Morals," *Journal of American History*, 55 (1968), 315–33; Allen, *Only Yesterday*, 90–91, 100–01, 115; Henry F. May, *The End of American Innocence: A Study of the First Years of Our Own Time, 1912–1917* (New York, 1959), 340–47; John C. Burnham, "The Progressive Era Revolution in American Attitudes Toward Sex," *Journal of American History*, 59 (1972), 885–908.

[10] On turn-of-the-century efforts to tighten divorce laws, see May, *Great Expectations*, 4–7; Lichtenberger, *Divorce*, 154–86; Morton Keller, *Affairs of State: Public Life in Late Nineteenth Century America* (Cambridge, Mass., 1977), 471.

Not only was divorce granted on fewer grounds, but the process of applying for divorce was made more stringent. A number of states prolonged the waiting period between divorce and remarriage, prohibited the guilty party from remarrying for a period of time, imposed longer residency requirements before divorce could begin, and required more adequate notice to the defendants in divorce cases and more adequate defense of divorce suits. In most states, divorce laws were rewritten around the concept of "fault" or moral wrongdoing. To obtain a divorce, it had to be shown that one party had transgressed seriously against the other. The innocent party was to be rewarded economically, in many instances through the provision of lifelong alimony, while the guilty wrongdoer was to be punished.[11]

Despite their intent these restrictions made surprisingly little difference in the prevalence of divorce proceedings. In the half-century between 1870 and 1920, the number of divorces granted nationwide increased fifteen fold. By 1924 one marriage out of every seven ended in divorce. Legal restrictions made little difference when many couples were willing to participate in a charade to meet legal requirements for divorce in order to liberate themselves from unsatisfying marriages. . . .[12]

To moralists the most alarming symbol of change was the newly identified "restlessness" of the nation's women—the most conspicuous sign being a shift in their appearance. Before the turn of the century, most women, regardless of class, wore highly formal clothing designed to exaggerate their sexual distinctiveness. Irrespective of season, middle-class women covered their bodies with up to twenty-five pounds of petticoats, bustles, hats, and ankle-length skirts. Even before World War I, however, growing numbers of young women had begun to raise their hemlines; bob their hair; shed their bulky undergarments; and wear powder, rouge, lipstick, and eyeliner in public. A slender, boyish form quickly replaced the large-breasted, wide-hipped, nineteenth-century feminine ideal. By 1928 the amount of material used in a typical woman's dress had declined from nineteen yards to just seven. Women were shedding a familiar but cumbersome image.[13]

The symbol of the new woman was the flapper, the independent, assertive, pleasure-hungry young woman, "making love lightly, boldly,

---

[11] On the trend toward increasingly stringent divorce procedures, refer to note 10.
[12] On the ineffectuality of changes in divorce laws, see Lichtenberger, *Divorce*, 154–86; May, *Great Expectations*, 4–7.
[13] On changes in women's dress, see Eric Hobsbawm, *The Age of Capital* (London, England, 1975), 232–37; Filene, *Him/Her/Self*, 6–7, 68–71; Allen, *Only Yesterday*, 89, 103–08.

and promiscuously." Much more than her mother or grandmother, this new woman was likely to have attended high school or college, to be a member of a women's organization, or to hold a job in which she worked in the company of men. From 1890—when just one college-age woman in fifty continued her education—until 1910, female college enrollment tripled (doubling again during the teens). Extraordinary growth also took place in the membership of women's organizations. New women's organizations sprouted in large numbers during the last years of the nineteenth century, including the National Council of Women, founded in 1888; the General Federation of Women's Clubs and the Daughters of the American Revolution, formed in 1890; the National Congress of Parents and Teachers, established in 1897; and the National Consumer's League, set up in 1899. Membership in the leading woman suffrage organization shot upward from a few thousand members in the late nineteenth century to a hundred thousand members in 1910 and then to two million members in 1917. Women were seeking their own organizational outlets for their energies and aims, rather than using men's vehicles.[14]

Women's participation in the paid labor force in the late nineteenth century rocketed upward, doubling between 1880 and 1900 and then increasing by another 50 percent between 1900 and 1919. By the latter year, for the first time in the nation's history, more than a fourth of all women in the work force either were or had been married. Although most women continued to work in the traditional sectors of the economy, growing numbers of women were beginning to work in clerical, sales, and other service occupations, for the first time in the company of men. Clearly the boundaries of "woman's sphere" were shifting. During the first decades of the twentieth century, the educational attainments of women began to approximate those of men; growing legitimacy was extended to female activity outside of the home; and, most importantly, new realms of work opened up to women.[15]. . .

---

[14] On the Flapper, see McGovern, "American Woman's Pre-World War I Freedom in Manners and Morals." 322–33; May, *End of American Innocence,* 340–47. On women's increasing participation in roles outside the home, see Filene *Him/Her/Self,* 20–29.

[15] On changes in women's employment, see Alice Kessler-Harris, *Out to Work: A History of Wage-Earning Women in the United States* (New York, 1982), 217–49; Carl N. Degler, *At Odds: Women and the Family in America from the Revolution to the Present* (New York, 1978), 362–417. On the shifting boundaries of women's sphere, see Filene *Him/Her/Self,* 5–35.

FOR THE WEDDING NIGHT

J. Foote Bingham

In this passage published in 1871, a minister counsels the bride
and groom on marital happiness. He urges couples to commit
themselves to Christian principles and to practice restraint when
in conflict. His advice to refrain from argument—so different
from the confrontational approaches recommended today—
helps to explain the codes of silence that characterize many old
New York marriages, including Newland and May Archer's. [ED.]

Dear Bridegroom and Bride:

The most felicitous hour of your earthly existence has arrived. The
brightest goal of your youthful hopes is reached—a goal, too, which is not
quite so delusory as most other youthful hopes will be found. It is a real
and great attainment. We gladly lift the bridal wreath to your heads, and
crown you victors in this first honorable conquest in the battle of life.

Beyond all question, whatever of earthly bliss is to be found on this
round world, the sweetest, the noblest, the best is found in the joys that
flow like a perennial stream from the hallowed conjugal state. Beyond all
question, the stars that glitter in the sky, and garnish with their eternal fires
a celestial canopy over your nuptial festivities this night, as they did over
the first human pair who tasted the sweets of conjugal love in holy, happy
Eden, have looked down, in all their endless circuits, upon no other scene
in the affairs of men, which can for a moment be compared with this into
which you are now entering, whether in regard to the delicious joys of the
present, or the promise and possibility of life-long happiness unbroken
and unabated. The ground on which you are treading is Paradisaic. Enjoy
it with ecstacy. But, oh, tread softly, tread reverently, *for it is holy.*

Never forget (what many so easily and so soon after Marriage seem to
forget) that the atmosphere of Eden is always and only the aroma of love.
Given that, and you stand within the cherubic-guarded gates, the peaceful
zephyrs of the holy garden breathe joy around you, you dwell amidst the
beauties, you feed on the fruits, your soul is thrilled with the raptures of

---

From *The Christian Marriage Ceremony.* New York: Randolph, 1871.

Paradise—and this no matter how fortune may be buffeting the garden wall outside, what frosts may be biting, what storms may be tossing men's lives in the world abroad.

Never forget, also (it is yet more important still to remember and observe this) that love itself, which makes your Eden, is a tender tree, and an exotic in this blasted world. It will repay, and it will require the most tender guarding and most devoted nurture—this especially in its commencing life. Under storms of passion, under chills of neglect, or carelessly left to chance, it will be a miracle if it do not wither and die.

There are a thousand effective methods and means of this beautiful growth. We commend you to a life-long study of this horticulture of the domestic paradise. It is a worthy and a profitable engagement for every man and woman that breathes. But there is one principal artifice, which is at once so pre-eminently effective and yet so commonly disregarded, that we are content to name no other but that. It is stated in that famous stroke of Solomon, delineating a perfect wife, but which is in this respect equally felicitous and applicable in the perfect husband. "The law of kindness is in her tongue." [1]

It is impossible to over-estimate the efficiency of the tongue in this conjugal business. Could the momentary frettings of millions of husbands and wives be for that brief space, till the ordinary current of reason and affection had regained its sway, imprisoned in the silence of their own bosoms; could *one party* even, bear in silence the temporary frailty of the other's speech; what regrets, what jars, what breaches would be forestalled, and how great would be the calm! "If any man offend not in word, the same is a perfect man, and able to bridle the whole body." [2]

On the other hand, also, if "the tongue of the" *sometimes* "dumb" could *then* be "taught to speak"; if the thousand little thoughts of affection and kindness which are born in wedded hearts toward each other, were oftener spoken in the beloved ear; if the old vows of love, once so sweet to say and to hear, were to be oftener repeated in words, as they are still felt in secret, how it would serve to break up, as it were, the hardening earth around the roots of affection's tree, and soften the soil in which it stands to every other genial influence of growth and fruitage.

Still the former mischief is the greater, more generally at work, and more difficult to eradicate. We urge, therefore, for your bridal day, this one additional private rite. Assume this one extra-rubrical stipulation and vow.

---

[1] Prov. 31.26.
[2] James 3.2.

Solemnly resolve, and solemnly promise to God and to each other, that come what will, *the* FIRST *sharp word shall* NEVER *between you* BE SPOKEN. Keep that vow, though your partner break over his or hers, keep you your vow. Whatever sacrifice of momentary inclination or pride it may cost, keep your vow. Come what may, it will repay you.

Yet frail human hearts cannot make the most perfect attainments, by this or any other means of domestic felicity, without calling in the holy aids of religion, and of the God of love.

Whatever, therefore, be your methods of culture, plant your affections in that rich and holy soil. On your bridal night, when the bustle of congratulations and merriment has ceased, when you enter the nuptial chamber, and first find yourselves together alone, before you commit yourselves to each other's arms to sleep and dream of bliss which may or may not be realized, and which, alas! beyond your foresight and control, must be mingled with now unknown elements of anxiety and pain—at that interesting moment the like of which can never return, first of all, kneel together before Him who made you and gave you to each other; and to Him "who careth for the sparrows, and numbereth the hairs of your heads," commit your happiness and all your ways, in an act of solemn worship— an act to be nightly repeated, as steadily as your happy nights return. Do this, and you may rest assured that the habit will be worth more to you, in conjugal love and domestic peace, than all else which the gold of the Indies could buy. . . .

Travel and Sport

Edith Wharton was an avid European traveler. From ages four to ten (1867–1872), she lived abroad for the most "prosaic" of reasons: her parents, their income diminished by the post–Civil War recession, found it less expensive to live in France, Italy, Spain, Germany, and England. Liberated by the richness of European art, architecture, and culture, Wharton returned to the continent numerous times as an adult, eventually settling in France. Indeed, in *The Age of Innocence* she situates her expatriate heroine Ellen Olenska in the same quiet Parisian neighborhood that she chose for herself. Neither tourist nor ordinary traveler, Wharton became expert in eighteenth-century Italian and French architecture and decor, ran charities to aid France and Belgium during World War I, and authored six nonfictional books on European subjects.

The Age of Innocence also documents a historic change in women's relationship to games and sport, which had been largely male activities. Excluded from war, business, and politics, women traditionally played little or no role in competitive sports, although they are associated in thirteenth- and fourteenth-century England with games related to bowling, cricket, and, eventually, baseball—in which milkmaids threw a ball at a defended milking stool and scored a point if the stool were knocked down. In the latter half of the nineteenth century, as women increasingly entered the public sphere, their involvement in sports also increased. This was especially true for upper-class women, who had time and money to devote to leisure activities. Sports freed women from restrictive Victorian standards of passivity, helped them shed pounds of full skirts and tight corsets for looser-fitting clothing, and gave them freer use of their bodies. Wharton's portrayal of May as an accomplished athlete places her character at the forefront of one kind of social change. Wharton also captures the lively atmosphere that the new interest in sports generated among sponsors and spectators as well as players.

INTRODUCTION TO *AMERICAN TRAVEL WRITERS, 1850–1915*

Donald Ross and James J. Schramer

In the nineteenth century, the United States enjoyed a new political independence, but many Americans still felt strong attachments to Europe. The following essay describes the eagerness with which Wharton's contemporaries flocked to Europe and explains the range of meanings the Old World held for them. [ED.]

... During the infancy of the republic Americans traveled to Britain and the Continent for practical reasons related to diplomatic or commercial ventures. Later, in the two decades prior to the Civil War, Americans began to enjoy themselves more in Europe. The Civil War halted this discovery of the pleasures of European travel. With the end of the war and the emergence of new money, most of it from the industrial North and the developing West, Americans began to travel in increasing numbers to Europe. And while the Continent remained the primary destination for American travelers, there was also growing interest in other parts of the world, including Africa and Asia. "If the social history of the world is ever written," *Putnam's Magazine* declared in 1868, "the era in which we live will be called the nomadic period. With the advent of ocean steam navigation and the railway system, began a travelling mania which has gradually advanced until half of the earth's inhabitants, or least half of its civilized portion, are on the move."

One can get a rough notion of the increases in American travel abroad by the number of passports issued though the statistics understate the number of actual travelers since many traveled without official documents. Before the Civil War about twenty-five hundred passports were being issued per year; this figure doubled to about five thousand through the 1860s, 1870s, and early 1880s. The number rose to ten thousand a year in the mid 1880s, but this increase may be owing in large measure to more widespread passport requirements on the part of foreign countries as well as to the tightening of U.S. laws. Passports had to be reissued for each trip abroad and had to be renewed every two years if one stayed on. By the end of the century the number of issued passports rose to above fifteen thousand. The numbers then increased rapidly, reaching almost one hundred thousand for the year 1919.

Dictionary of Literary Biography. Vol. 189. Detroit: Gale, 1998.

Those bold enough to have made their fortunes from the steel mills and oil fields of the East or the forests and mines of the West were not shy about displaying their wealth. They flocked abroad to see and to be seen in the cities and spas of Europe. In *The American* (1877) Henry James fictionalizes and satirizes this exodus and its excesses. With the travail of the journey now removed from travel, the years of the tourist had begun. Like James's Christopher Newman, newly rich Americans were eager to sample all that Europe had to offer.

American travel writing during the latter half of the nineteenth century and the first years of the twentieth century reflects this appetite. In *Anglo-American Landscapes: A Study of Nineteenth-Century Anglo-American Travel Literature* (1983), Christopher Mulvey distinguishes between travel literature that focuses on the "authenticity of statement" and that which is more concerned with the "authenticity of feeling." He finds that "The English travel writer was preoccupied with the first; the American with the second. English travel literature was primarily directed at the intellect and the political imagination. American travel literature was primarily concerned with the sensibility and the cultural memory."

The emphasis on the sensory or the aesthetic experience in American travel literature seems perfectly in consonance with the experience of a people previously so taken up with the arduous and pragmatic concerns of building and then preserving a nation that they scarcely had any time to develop a more reflective sense of taste. As the nineteenth century came to a close, however, and the routine of European travel became more formulaic, Americans such as Meriwether began to abandon the rituals of the Grand Tour in favor of a more intimate level of person-to-person contact, an inquisitive rather than an appetitive approach to travel. This shift in the focus of American travel writing from the subjective, emotive, somewhat unreflective capturing of fleeting sensations to a more reflective, realistic, and other-directed reporting about people and places is one of the themes that emerges from the essays in *Dictionary of Literary Biography 189: American Travel Writers, 1850–1915*.

Literary travel accounts in the late nineteenth century must be seen in the light of decreased travel times and costs, which resulted in the growth of the middle-class tourist industry. Except for crossing into Mexico or Canada by horse or later by train, the only way out of the United States was by ship. In 1838 the *Great Western* (1,300 tons) won a transatlantic race between steam-driven paddle-wheel ships by crossing the ocean in fifteen days. The fare was $145, a princely sum when one considers that a laborer's wage at the time was about one dollar a day. By the late 1850s steamship technology had advanced but fares remained high: $160 for first class and $80 for cabin passengers. The American-owned Collins line had wooden ships of some 3,000 tons and 300 feet in length that could carry from 160 to 220 passengers. By the 1870s luxury liners, nearly all European, carrying several hundred passengers, made the crossing in a week; the Hamburg-America's *Deutschland* crossed in five days in 1900. Fares in the 1890s were from $100 to $200, an affordable price for the time.

Cutting down on the time and expense of the ocean crossing meant that more middle-class people could get to and from Europe and even Asia for a month or so, rather than having to commit themselves to at least six months for a trip. While many travelers went to business, conduct missionary work, or learn about fine art, many more went just for leisure, for a vacation. And many more could afford to take their families along. The growth of the American middle class and the rising standard of living helped to keep the berths of the ships full.

On the ground in Europe railroad service increased almost exponentially by the end of the century. Railroads not only connected the capital cities but also linked nearly all population centers as well as spas, mountains, and seaside resorts. Trains did much to change travel patterns, as visitors no longer confined themselves to a series of stops along the coast with only short side trips inland; instead, they were able to move freely into the interior of the Continent. Paul Baker in *The Fortunate Pilgrims: Americans in Italy, 1800–1860* (1964) shows how this transition took place in Italy at mid century.

Trains took much of the unpredictability out of travel so that, for example, one could make hotel bookings in advance. As opposed to carriage travel, which encouraged the traveler to tarry at a few spots, trains allowed travelers to move rapidly through a series of stops. This difference made it easier to "cover" the highlights without noticing much of what was between. As early as 1849 John Ruskin laments that the train "transmutes a man from a traveller into a living parcel."

Nostalgia about the good old days of difficult carriage transportation and unscheduled stops at uncomfortable inns was frequently voiced by English travel writers whose experience on the Continent went back to the first half of the century. This regret was not shared by Americans who mostly explored Europe after trains were established. During the bicycle craze of the 1880s and 1890s, the hardy, including Woodrow Wilson and Fanny Bullock Workman, chose to experience a closeness to the bumpy roads of Europe that surpassed even that experienced by the carriage passenger. For the truly adventurous, of course, there were more exotic destinations where the means of travel were still primitive.

In the 1880s Americans enjoyed favorable exchange rates and could budget between $250 to $300 for a comfortable ten weeks in Europe, with good hotels at $2.50 a day. They were anticipated at the Hotel du New York in Florence and the Hotel des États-Unis and Hotel de l'Oncle Tom in Paris. More and more, though, tourists were facing an increasing number of small fees to visit the important sights. In *The Beaten Track: European Tourism, Literature, and the Ways to Culture, 1800–1860* (1993) James Buzard, after pointing to the charges to see *The Last Supper,* Glastonbury Abbey, and Kenilworth Castle, notes "One could not turn back the turn-stiles through which historic and beautiful places had passed in becoming tourist attractions."

Both at the time and in retrospect, the development of tourism as a concept and as an industry affected ordinary travel, and it became a major theme in travel writing. Dean MacCannell in *Empty Meeting Grounds: The Tourist Papers* (1992) gives an often-cited definition: "[T]ourism is not just an aggregate of merely commercial activities; it is also an ideological framing of history, nature, and tradition; a framing that has the power to reshape culture and nature to its own needs." It is "a primary ground for the production of new cultural forms on a global base." Buzard comments on an 1848 *Blackwoods* article concerning "Modern Tourism" and characterizes the situation this way: "By mid-century the hyperbole so common to criticisms of tourists had set in: the tourists who were 'everywhere' in Europe were pictured as 'all pen in hand, all determined not to let a henroost remain undescribed.'" Tourists were feared to be pouring their writings on the "reading public," without compassion or conscience at the beginning of the "season."

Buzard explains that the traveler was seen to be good while the tourist was bad owing to his or her being the "dupe of fashion, following blindly where authentic travellers have gone with open eyes and free spirits." Citing Paul Fussell, he notes that tourists were a "pure cliché," who went "*en masse,* remaking whole regions in their homogeneous image." The contrast, now familiar, was between "the sensitive traveller" on the one hand and "vulgar tourist" on the other. As Baker explains, the real traveler conducted "truly perceptive studies of the land and the people" rather than making "repetition of the comments and responses of earlier travellers." Mulvey makes a similar point in the context of writing about travel: "Applied to others the term 'tourist' could be nasty, and it was used by most travel writers in the nineteenth century to separate the serious traveller from the frivolous and the serious writer from the superficial." Most readers probably make a similar distinction, for a guidebook is never thought of as literature whereas travel writing might be.

The greater accessibility of travel abroad for Americans had a profound influence on the audience for travel writing. Readers no longer picked up travel books just for vicarious experience but increasingly to help them to make their own travel plans. Some travel writers responded by becoming more informative to serve this need. Others varied their approach to make their writing more interesting. Some abandoned the worked-over field to report on more exotic adventures.

Following the Civil War, many Americans sought what Foster Rhea Dulles in *Americans Abroad: Two Centuries of European Travel* (1964) calls "new cultural ties." Buzard focuses on James as the spokesman for this change: "The great watershed of the Civil War having been passed, James saw both his nation and himself on the brink of new cultural accomplishments, which were to be won by Americans' converting their legacy of cultural impoverishment into an enabling freedom to 'pick and choose' the best among the separate national cultures of Europe." Like James, many believed that high culture had to be imported into the United States. Other Americans, however, did not find Europe so superior to their native land. Another important writer who also reported his visits to Europe, though not with the same reverence for its culture, was Samuel Langhorne Clemens, better known as Mark Twain. Other literary notables who recorded their experiences included Henry Adams, William Dean Howells, William Cullen Bryant, James Russell Lowell, Oliver Wendell Holmes, and Edith Wharton. . . .

While the United States officially supported the European colonial powers, especially England, with both rhetoric and attitude, the direct participation overseas of the United States was quite limited in the nineteenth century. With slavery and its aftermath, the long campaign against Native Americans, and an undercurrent of nativism, the country had plenty to do at home. Henry M. Stanley, who had gone to the American West before Africa, writes in *My Early Travels* (1895), "The lessons derived from the near extinction of the Indian are very applicable to Africa. . . . Savages have the minds of children and the passions of brutes, and to place breech-loaders in their hands is as cruel an act as to put razors in the hands of infants." To their contacts with people of color, most American travel writers brought a smug pride in their republican institutions as well as a strong belief in the benefits of capitalism and the blessings of Protestant Christianity.

With the notable exception of U.S. administrations in former Spanish colonies such as Puerto Rico, Guam, and the Philippines, Americans were only short-term visitors to Africa, Asia, and the Pacific rather than occupying forces with a stake and some responsibility in the colonial enterprise. Their observations were therefore likely to be superficial, their racism flippant, and their disdain often for both the colonial subjects and their rulers easily expressed. American travel writers joined the other Europeans in judging peoples of color as exotic or primitive and backward, or, in the Near East and part of Eastern Europe, medieval, and worthy of admiration or pity. While American travelers regretted that they could not get close to the ordinary citizens of Europe, on the other continents they rarely thought of closeness as being desirable, and thus did not even miss it. The flora and fauna and the natives all blended into the background for the traveler's transit across the landscape.

For practical purposes Americans were frozen out of both serious scholarly influence and political control over most parts of the world which were being colonized in the nineteenth century. In the Middle East, for example, scholarship and imperialism were dominated by the British and French and the Germans to some degree in scholarship. American travel writers in the area were amateur bit players, and the country did not have the kind of major oriental institutes that would sponsor significant studies or train scholars to conduct such studies. Thus, the United States in general could not take part in what Edward W. Said in *Orientalism* (1979) calls the "long and slow process of appropriation by which Europe, or the European awareness of the Orient, transformed itself from being textual and contemplative into being administrative, economic, and even military."

Travel books do play an important role in the textual phase of this process, and their apparent authority comes to define a place in ways that actual experience does not: "such texts can *create* not only knowledge but also the very reality they appear to describe. In time such knowledge and reality produce a tradition." For the United States, Said's "self-metamorphosis from a scholarly discourse to an imperial institution" shows up in the form of American travel writings about Cuba, Hawaii, and other islands of the South Pacific in the years surrounding the Spanish-American War. As David Spurr argues in *The Rhetoric of Empire* (1993), the colonial gaze "is never innocent or pure, never free of meditation by motives which might be judged noble or otherwise."

The most significant group of American travelers to exotic parts of the world were journalists—people who intentionally or accidentally arrived at "events"—war, revolutions, famine. Such a reporter becomes what David Porter calls a "political witness." Journalism, whether for daily newspapers or monthly magazines, takes on some of the intimacy of letters, although professional journalistic standards put a premium on combining accuracy with telling a good story. As with other retrospective evaluations of nineteenth-century travel writing, critics now recognize the pervasive cultural biases that affect the reporter's ability to see the complexities of "truth," however defined. It is also essential to recall that American newspapers were blatantly partisan, most being explicitly linked to political parties—William Randolph Hearst's role in the Spanish-American War, with Richard Harding Davis as one of the lead reporters, is the most famous symptom of this tendency.

The presence of hundreds of newspapers and magazines in the last third of the century made it possible for one to turn global travel writing into a lifelong career. These men and women, and a few wife-and-husband teams such as Fanny Bullock Workman and William Hunter Workman, managed to hit the correct, popular tone and were able to produce a successful series of books, built on previous publication in the periodicals. Bayard Taylor, for example, was the most famous professional traveler of the century. In 1890 Nellie Bly, on the staff of the *New York World,* went around the world in seventy-two days and wrote her own dispatches and book.

Observations by travel writers have often proved useful to twentieth-century historians and scientists. No matter how clearly postcolonial theories reveal the viciousness of the underlying ideology, ethnographic travel writing transformed the Western world's notions of the past and present. Perhaps more important, travel writing sought and found a mass audience. Aside from government reports and military dispatches, travel writing, whether through the work of amateurs, journalists, or travel professionals, enhanced Americans' awareness of peoples and natural environments in Africa, South America, central Asia, and the Middle East. . . .

AMERICANS ABROAD

Henry James

In this 1878 passage, Henry James, American author, expatriate, and close friend of Edith Wharton, ruminates on Europeans' impressions of American travelers. He repeats a term used by Europeans and frequently heard in the twentieth century, the "vulgar" American. [ED.]

. . . Americans in Europe are *outsiders;* that is the great point, and the point thrown into relief by all zealous efforts to controvert it. As a people we are out of European society; the fact seems to us incontestable, be it regrettable or not. We are not only out of the European circle politically and geographically; we are out of it socially, and for excellent reasons. We are the only great people of the civilized world that is a pure democracy, and

From *Collected Travel Writings.* New York: Literary Classics, 1993.

we are the only great people that is exclusively commercial. Add the remoteness represented by these facts to our great and painful geographical
remoteness, and it will be easy to see why to be known in Europe as an
American is to enjoy an imperfect reciprocity. It may be the Europeans
who are the losers by this absence of reciprocity; we do not prejudge that
point, and we do not know, indeed, who is to settle it. A great many Americans—by no means all—maintain that the Europeans *are* the losers, and
declare that if they don't know us and don't care about us, so much the
worse for them. This is in many ways a very proper and very natural attitude; but nothing can be more characteristic of our civilization than the
fact that an American may be almost defied to maintain it consistently. Let
him be even more patriotic than is necessary, he is constantly lapsing from
it, and, when he is in company with Europeans who do nothing to ruffle
his usually great good-nature, he constantly takes a tone which indicates
that he values their good opinion and that he is rather flattered than otherwise by possessing it. This, however, is a matter to be discussed apart. We
wish to mention the last fact which leads Europeans to look upon Americans as aliens—the fact that large and increasing numbers of them elect,
as the phrase is, to spend large parts of their lives in foreign lands. When
a European sees an American absentee settle down in the country of which
he himself is a native it is not surprising that, in the face of this practical
tribute, he should be found doubting whether the country the American has
left is as agreeable, as comfortable, as civilized, as desirable a one to belong
to as his own. The American may carefully explain that he is living abroad
for such and such special and limited reasons—for culture, for music, for
art, for the languages, for economy, for the education of his children; the
fact remains that in pursuit of some *agrément* or other he has forsaken his
native-land, and the European retains, ineffaceably, the impression that if
America were really a pleasant place he would never do so. He would come
to travel—yes, frequently and extensively; but he (or rather *she*, for as a
general thing, in this case, that is the proper pronoun) would never take up
an abode in a strange city and remain there year after year, looking about,
rather hungrily, for social diversion and "trying to get into society." Such
a spectacle makes the European take the American, as an American, by so
much the less *au sérieux*. An Englishman, a Frenchman, a German finds
his intellectual, his æsthetic ideal in living in his own country. . . .

   A very large proportion of the Americans who annually scatter themselves over Europe are by no means flattering to the national vanity. Their
merits, whatever they are, are not of a sort that strike the eye—still less
the ear. They are ill-made, ill-mannered, ill-dressed. A very good way to
get a collective impression of them is to go and sit for half an hour in the
waiting-room of any European banker upon whom Americans hold letters

of credit. During certain hours of the morning our compatriots swarm, getting their drafts cashed and asking for their letters—those letters which they apparently suspect the banker's clerks of a constitutional indisposition to surrender. The writer of these lines lately enjoyed on several occasions this oportunity of observation, and—from the point of view of amenity—the spectacle was not gratifying. *Are* we the worst-looking people in the world? the sophisticated spectator, on such an occasion, enquires; and lest he should be beguiled into giving an answer too monstrous he abstains from giving any at all. One American (of the "conscious" class) has a way of explaining these things—the common facial types, the vulgar manners, the "mean" voices, the want of acquaintance with the rudiments of the science of dress—to another. He says that in America "every one travels," and that the people at the bankers are much better than the corresponding class in Europe, who languish in downtrodden bondage and never have even a chance to show themselves to the world. The explanation is highly sufficient, for it is very certain that for many Americans a journey to Europe is the reward of a period of sordid toil. An American may take great satisfaction in this circumstance; he may be proud of belonging to a country in which the advantages of foreign travel are open to all, irrespective of "social standing"; instead of being, as in Europe (according, at least, to his theory), only within the reach of the luxurious and the privileged. But the European only perceives that a great many American travellers are remarkably "rough," and quite fails to congratulate either as his own country or theirs upon possessing them. . . .

NEWPORT

Henry James

Henry James's fondness for Newport dated to his adolescence, when he and his family lived there from 1858 to 1859 and from 1860 to 1864. He wrote the following passage in 1870 as a travel sketch for *The Nation;* it later appeared in his book, *The American Scene* (1907). Wharton echoes James's appreciation of Newport's natural beauty and gentility in her descriptions in *The Age of Innocence;* the two writers also share a lightly ironic tone. [ED.]

From *Collected Travel Writings*. New York, Literary Classics, 1993.

. . . I feel almost warranted in saying that here the background of life has sunk less in relative value and suffered less from the encroachments of pleasure-seeking man than the scenic dispositions of any other watering-place. For this, perhaps, we may thank rather the modest, incorruptible integrity of the Newport landscape than any very intelligent forbearance on the part of the summer colony. The beauty of this landscape is so subtle, so essential, so humble, so much a thing of character and expression, so little a thing of feature and pretension, that it cunningly eludes the grasp of the destroyer or the reformer, and triumphs in impalpable purity even when it seems to make concessions. I have sometimes wondered, in rational moods, why it is that Newport is so much appreciated by the votaries of idleness and pleasure. Its resources are few in number. It is extremely circumscribed. It has few drives, few walks, little variety of scenery. Its charms and its interest are confined to a narrow circle. It has of course the unlimited ocean, but seafaring idlers are not true Newporters, for any other sea would suit them as well. Last evening, it seemed to me, as I drove along the Avenue, that I guessed the answer to the riddle. The atmospheric tone, the careful selection of ingredients, your pleasant sense of a certain climatic ripeness—these are the real charm of Newport, and the secret of her supremacy. You are affected by the admirable art of the landscape, by seeing so much that is lovely and impressive achieved with such a frugality of means—with so little parade of the vast, the various, or the rare, with so narrow a range of colour and form. I could not help thinking, as I turned from the harmonies and purities which lay deepening on the breast of nature, with the various shades of twilight, to the heterogeneous procession in the Avenue, that, quite in their own line of effect, the usual performers in this exhibition might learn a few good lessons from the daily prospect of the great western expanse of rock and ocean in its relations with the declining sun. But this is asking too much. Many persons of course come to Newport simply because others come, and in this way the present brilliant colony has grown up. Let me not be suspected, when I speak of Newport, of the untasteful heresy of meaning primarily rocks and waves rather than ladies and gentlemen.

The ladies and gentlemen are in great force—the ladies, of course, especially. It is true everywhere, I suppose, that women are the animating element of "society;" but you feel this to be especially true as you pass along Bellevue Avenue. I doubt whether anywhere else so many women have a "good time" with so small a sacrifice of the luxury of self-respect. I heard a lady yesterday tell another, with a quiet ecstasy of tone, that she had been having a "most perfect time." This is the very poetry of pleasure. It is a part of our complacent tradition that in those foreign lands where women are supposed to be socially supreme, they maintain their empire by various clandestine and reprehensible arts. With us—we say it at Newport without bravado—they are both conspicuous and unsophisticated. You feel this most gratefully as you receive a confident bow from a pretty girl in her basket-phaeton. She is very young and very pretty, but she has a certain habitual assurance which is only a grace the more. She combines, you reflect with respectful tenderness, all that is possible in the way of modesty with all that is delightful in the way of facility. Shyness is certainly very pretty—when it is not very ugly; but shyness may often darken the bloom of genuine modesty, and a certain frankness and confidence may often incline it toward the light. Let us assume, then, that all the young ladies whom you may meet here are of the highest modern type. In the course of time they ripen into the delightful matrons who divide your admiration. It is easy to see that Newport must be a most agreeable sojourn for the male sex. The gentlemen, indeed, look wonderfully prosperous and well-conditioned. They gallop on shining horses or recline in a sort of coaxing Herculean submission beside the lovely mistress of a curricle. Young men—and young old men—I have occasion to observe, are far more numerous than at Saratoga, and of vastly superior quality. There is, indeed, in all things a striking difference in tone and aspect between these two great centres of pleasure. After Saratoga, Newport seems really substantial and civilised. Aesthetically speaking, you may remain at Newport with a fairly good conscience; at Saratoga you linger under passionate protest. At Newport life is public, if you will; at Saratoga it is absolutely common. The difference, in a word, is the difference between a group of undiscriminating hotels and a series of organised homes. Saratoga perhaps deserves our greater homage, as being characteristically democratic and American; let us, then, make Saratoga the heaven of our aspiration, but let us yet a while content ourselves with Newport as the lowly earth of our residence. . . .

THE LAWN SET

William J. Baker

After the Civil War, sports such as croquet, archery, and lawn tennis became very popular in the United States, attracting women as well as men. William J. Baker (1982) provides a brief history

From *Sports in the Western World*. Totowa: Rowman: 1982.

of the activities enjoyed by characters in Wharton's *The Age of Innocence*. [ED.]

. . . As Thorstein Veblen observed in *The Theory of the Leisure Class* (1899), "the lawn, or the close-cropped yard or park" appealed especially "to the taste of the well-to-do classes." Lawn and club games such as croquet, archery, badminton, and lawn tennis conspicuously served the purposes of middle-class affluence and respectability. All these activities were suitable for family participation, particularly for the newly emancipated woman. All evolving from ancient forms of play and competition, they provided both leisurely pastime and sporting rivalry for well-to-do westerners.

Croquet enjoyed the earliest popularity. A modernized version of the old French game of *le jeu de maille,* croquet was a favorite pastime of retired British army officers in Pau, France, following the Napoleonic Wars. In 1857 John Jaques manufactured the first set of equipment and composed a rudimentary set of rules. On the tidy suburban lawns of Victorian England, the game flourished. In 1867 the first championship tournament was held at Evesham, Worcestershire, and three years later moved to the new all-England Croquet Club at Wimbledon, where a group of croquet buffs drew up a set of rules and specifications that survive with few alterations to the present.

Shortly after the Civil War, croquet became the rage in the United States. According to *The Nation* (1866), "Of all the epidemics that have swept over our land, the swiftest and most infectious is croquet." For Americans eager to learn and display the manners of good society, croquet was a boon: "Grace in holding and using the mallet, easy and pleasing attitudes in playing, promptness in taking your turn, and gentlemanly and ladylike manners generally throughout the game, are points which it is unnecessary for us to enlarge on," observed the editor of an early American book of rules.

Most of all, like no other game at the time, croquet provided good family fun. Courtships ripened between the wickets on the late summer afternoons. Croquet revolutionized the relation of women to sport. Emerging from their stuffy parlors and confined domestic roles, women learned first to play and then to compete with men in outdoor exercise. So great was the vogue of croquet in the 1870s that manufacturers could not fill orders for equipment fast enough.

Archery, another genteel sport, similarly attracted women participants. From the beginning, Britain's Grand National Archery Society

(1861) and the National Archery Association of America (1870) included both male and female members. As archery became highly popular at private girls' schools, *Harper's Weekly* reported that "ladies and gentlemen from the cultured circles of society" competed in a large tournament in Chicago.

Yet widespread enthusiasm for archery, as for croquet, was short-lived. The novelty soon wore off. American men turned to a more exclusively male kind of target sport, rifle shooting, and in 1871 founded the National Rifle Association. By the time of the founding of the American National Croquet Association in 1882 and the British Croquet Association in 1896, the game had passed its zenith of popularity. The original appeal of archery and croquet—their gentle, sociable qualities—proved to be liabilities. Except for the occasional lawn party, only the old and the very young chose to play croquet instead of more vigorous new lawn games.

Badminton, for example, became highly popular in the English suburbs and seaside resorts in the 1870s. The game derived from an old exercise called battledore and shuttlecock, in which children wielded light wooden paddles to keep a feathered cork in the air. Around 1870 a strung racket and net began to be used, especially at the Duke of Beaufort's estate, Badminton, in Gloucestershire, where the name of the game originated. In 1873 the first badminton club was formed at Bath, a favorite resort for wealthy Britons.

At first three to five people played on each side of the net, the men in their Prince Albert suits and starched shirts, the women in long dresses, corsets, bustles, and high-buttoned shoes. Originally set indoors, the courts were in the shape of an hourglass, narrower at the net than at the four corners in order for the massive doors of Victorian salons to open in the center of the room beside the net. The court was not made rectangular until 1901. Also by the turn of the century the game was being played more on outdoor lawns than in indoor salons, under rules laid down by the Badminton Association, founded in 1893 in the seacoast town of Southsea, Hampshire.

Except in distant India, where British army officers promoted the game at leisurely lawn parties on humid afternoons, badminton never became popular outside the British Isles. It was introduced in the United States in the late 1870s, and in 1879 the Badminton Club of New York City was founded. But most wealthy Americans looked upon badminton as an inferior version of another new and much faster, more versatile racket-and-net game, lawn tennis.

Like many sports, lawn tennis has a popular myth of instant creation: Major Walter Clopton Wingfield supposedly invented the game in 1873. In truth, however, lawn tennis is yet another English middle-class adaptation of an ancient royal game, "real" tennis. In the egalitarian age of the nine-teenth century, the expensive indoor courts and aristocratic exclusiveness of real tennis made it as anachronistic as the traditional monarchies with which it was associated. More accessible was an outdoor game played with rackets and a cork ball. In a French version, *la longue paume,* and its English equivalent, "field tennis," players hit the ball over the net into the prescribed area rather than off indoor ceilings and walls in the old real ten-nis fashion. Once a rubber ball came into use during the Victorian era, ten-nis on grass became all the more attractive. Lawn tennis was more of an evolution than an invention.

In 1858 Major T. H. Gem, a clerk to the magistrates in Birmingham, England, and his Spanish friend, J. B. Perera, set up a net and established boundary lines on the back lawn of Gem's home in Edgbaston, a suburb of Birmingham, to the amusement of gawking neighbors. For years they played there, using the scoring system of the old royal game. In 1872 they joined with two local doctors to form the first lawn-tennis club at the Manor House in nearby Leamington Spa.

Major Wingfield's contribution to the early development of the game was both more eccentric and more widely publicized than Gem's. In 1873, to a gathering of upper-class friends at a house party in Nantclwyd Hall, Wales, Wingfield introduced equipment and a set of rules for a "new" game that he called "sphairistiké." He proposed a scoring system based on the old game of rackets rather than on royal tennis. Apparently having come in contact with badminton, he laid out the court in an hourglass design, with the net five feet from the ground at the posts. For a "serving box" he drew a small diamond-shaped box on each side of the net, in which the server had to stand. Never did a supposed "father" of a sport produce a design so unlike the finished product.

In 1874 Wingfield attempted to patent his "new and improved" ver-sion of "the ancient game of tennis," and in several articles and pamphlets propagated his scheme to the Victorian reading public. He struck a respon-sive chord in people tired of the tameness of croquet, archery, and bad-minton. In 1876 the essayist and playwright Oscar Wilde visited friends in Nottinghamshire and reported "some very pleasant garden parties and any amount of lawn tennis."

Yet early converts to lawn tennis were by no means uncritical of the details of Wingfield's game. In 1875 wealthy members of the All-England Croquet Club set aside an area for lawn tennis and badminton and imme-diately formed a subcommittee to codify the rules of tennis. Within two years they radically reshaped Wingfield's design. First they agreed to drop the name "sphairistiké" in favor of the simpler term, lawn tennis. Then they adopted a rectangular court in place of the hourglass shape, and the scoring system of real tennis (15–30–40) rather than rackets. Lowering the net to three feet, three inches at the center, they put the server back on the base line; to compensate for the increased distance, they allowed an extra serve if the first was not successful. Finally, they covered Wingfield's hollow rubber ball with white flannel for better control, an innovation of John Meyer Heathcote. By 1877 the rules and form of lawn tennis were largely fixed in a fashion that has remained intact to the present.

So was its oldest competitive tournament, Wimbledon. Adding "Tennis" to its name, the All-England Croquet Club sponsored the first Wimbledon matches in 1877. Twenty-two players competed for a trophy valued at twenty-five guineas. For the final championship match, won by Spencer W. Gore, 200 spectators looked on. The growth of the crowd for subsequent Wimbledon tournaments tells the story of the instant popularity of the game. Within one year the number of spectators jumped to 700 for the final, then to 1,100 in 1879, and to 3,500 by 1885. Never again did Wimbledon officials have to fear low turnouts at center court. As the crowds increased, the program enlarged. Women's singles were added in 1884; in the same year the men's doubles, begun at Oxford in 1879, moved to Wimbledon. Finally, in 1899 an unofficial women's doubles championship entered the picture, and in the following year mixed doubles completed the program.

The quality of play also increased rapidly during those early years. For the first Wimbledon, S. W. Gore won by methodically serving, charging the net, and slamming the ball back away from his opponents. In the following year, however, he was beaten by an opponent who consistently lobbed the ball over his head, thus popularizing a rather dreary lob game from the baselines. Not until the emergence in the early 1880s of the sparkling Renshaw brothers, William and Ernest, did the era of "pat ball" end. Dominating both the men's singles and doubles throughout the decade, the Renshaws perfected the hard, deep volley. Added to the overhead serve, which became standard for men (not women) in the late 1870s, the volley made the game a test of stamina as well as skill. From the beginning, Wimbledon displayed the best tennis in the world.

Lest Wimbledon obscure the social importance of lawn tennis in Victorian England, however, one must hasten to add that it was merely the competitive reflection of a widely popular pastime of middle-class Englishmen. As one commented in 1890, "A lawn, a racket, a soft ball, a net, a pot of paint, and an active member of either sex, here are all the materials needed for lawn tennis, and every country house and most suburban villas can supply them."...

Anthropology

Few scenes in literature are more powerful than the one describing the farewell dinner party for Ellen Olenska, when Archer realizes that he is attending "the tribal rally around a kinswoman about to be eliminated from the tribe" (264). Wharton uses anthropological language here and throughout *The Age of Innocence* to establish her novel as a "study" of old New York, in the same way that practitioners of the burgeoning field of anthropology were uncovering and documenting indigenous cultures throughout the world. She shows how New York's complex society is governed by unwritten rules and rituals, widely known and followed by its members but mysterious and even bizarre to outsiders. For example, it seems "natural" to Archer that a German text of a French opera sung by Swedes should be translated into English for an American audience, or that he should use two silver-backed brushes to part his hair and never go out in society without a flower in his buttonhole (15). Wharton's meticulous description of New York's customs and beliefs not only draws from a nineteenth-century interest in the origin and development of distant cultures but also demonstrates, by turning an investigative lens on a society close to home, the process by which arbitrary signs gain cultural significance.

FROM *VIOLENCE AND THE SACRED*

René Girard

Wharton frequently portrays old New York as a primitive society dependent on ritual to ensure order and continuity. In this excerpt from his book (1977), René Girard explains how a threatened so-

Baltimore: Johns Hopkins UP, 1977.

ciety takes steps—even violent ones—to cleanse and renew itself. It frequently chooses a symbolic victim of sacrifice, or scapegoat, in order to alleviate dissension and restore harmony within its ranks. From the perspective of old New York, Ellen Olenska is such a sacrificial victim; readers, however, may admire Ellen's exercise of free will throughout the novel. [ED.]

. . . Sacrifice plays a very real role in these [primitive] societies, and the problem of substitution concerns the entire community. The victim is not a substitute for some particularly endangered individual, nor is it offered up to some individual of particularly bloodthirsty temperament. Rather, it is a substitute for all the members of the community, offered up by the members themselves. The sacrifice serves to protect the entire community from *its own* violence; it prompts the entire community to choose victims outside itself. The elements of dissension scattered throughout the community are drawn to the person of the sacrificial victim and eliminated, at least temporarily, by its sacrifice. . . .

If we look at the extremely wide spectrum of human victims sacrificed by various societies, the list seems heterogeneous, to say the least. It includes prisoners of war, slaves, small children, unmarried adolescents, and the handicapped; it ranges from the very dregs of society, such as the Greek pharmakos, to the king himself.

Is it possible to detect a unifying factor in this disparate group? We notice at first glance beings who are either outside or on the fringes of society: prisoners of war, slaves, pharmakos. In many primitive societies children who have not yet undergone the rites of initiation have no proper place in the community; their rights and duties are almost nonexistent. What we are dealing with, therefore, are exterior or marginal individuals, incapable of establishing or sharing the social bonds that link the rest of the inhabitants. Their status as foreigners or enemies, their servile condition, or simply their age prevents these future victims from fully integrating themselves into the community. . . .

. . . All our sacrificial victims, whether chosen from one of the human categories enumerated above or, *a fortiori*, from the animal realm, are invariably distinguishable from the nonsacrificeable beings by one essential characteristic: between these victims and the community a crucial social link is missing, so they can be exposed to violence without fear of reprisal. Their death does not automatically entail an act of vengeance. . . .

The curative procedures employed by primitive societies appear rudimentary to us. We tend to regard them as fumbling efforts to improvise a judicial system. Certainly their pragmatic aspects are clearly visible, oriented as they are not toward the guilty parties, but toward the victims—since it is the latter who pose the most immediate threat. The injured parties must be accorded a careful measure of satisfaction, just enough to appease their own desire for revenge but not so much as to awaken the desire elsewhere. It is not a question of codifying good and evil or of inspiring respect for some abstract concept of justice; rather, it is a question of securing the safety of the group by checking the impulse for revenge. The preferred method involves a reconciliation between parties based on some sort of mutual compensation. If reconciliation is impossible, however, an armed encounter can be arranged in such a manner that the violence is wholly self-contained. This encounter can take place within an enclosed space and can involve prescribed regulations and specifically designated combatants. Its purpose is to cut violence short. . . .

FROM *PRIMITIVE CULTURE*

Edward B. Tylor

Victorians, influenced by Charles Darwin and Herbert Spencer, believed in an evolution or progression of societies from the most primitive to the most advanced, and they assumed that their own society was superior to those they studied. This view is represented in the following 1871 passage from *Primitive Culture* by Sir Edward Burnett Tylor (1832–1917), one of the most highly regarded anthropologists of his day. Writing from the perspective of 1920, however, Wharton also could incorporate newer insights of researchers such as Franz Boaz (1858–1942) and Bronislaw Malinowski (1884–1942). No longer equating evolution with progress toward some perfect goal, these anthropologists replaced a system of cultural hierarchies with a more empirically based approach that stressed the functions of custom and belief. Wharton's novel criticizes as well Victorian assumptions about levels of civilization. It asks readers to recognize the shifting meanings of such terms as *primitive* and *advanced* and to decide how a given cultural practice serves individual or group needs. [ED.]

London: Murray, and New York: Putnam's, 1920.

. . . The thesis which I venture to sustain, within limits, is simply this, that the savage state in some measure represents an early condition of mankind, out of which the higher culture has gradually been developed or evolved, by processes still in regular operation as of old, the result showing that, on the whole, progress has far prevailed over relapse.

On this proposition, the main tendency of human society during its long term of existence has been to pass from a savage to a civilized state. Now all must admit a great part of this assertion to be not only truth, but truism. Referred to direct history, a great section of it proves to belong not to the domain of speculation, but to that of positive knowledge. It is mere matter of chronicle that modern civilization is a development of mediæval civilization, which again is a development from civilization of the order represented in Greece, Assyria, or Egypt. Thus the higher culture being clearly traced back to what may be called the middle culture, the question which remains is whether this middle culture may be traced back to the lower culture, that is, to savagery. To affirm this, is merely to assert that the same kind of development in culture which has gone on inside our range of knowledge has also gone on outside it, its course of proceeding being unaffected by our having or not having reporters present. If any one holds that human thought and action were worked out in primæval times according to laws essentially other than those of the modern world, it is for him to prove by valid evidence this anomalous state of things, otherwise the doctrine of permanent principle will hold good, as in astronomy or geology. That the tendency of culture has been similar throughout the existence of human society, and that we may fairly judge from its known historic course what its prehistoric course may have been, is a theory clearly entitled to precedence as a fundamental principle of ethnographic research. . . .

The two theories which thus account for the relation of savage to cultured life may be contrasted according to their main character, as the progression-theory and the degradation-theory. Yet of course the progression-theory recognizes degradation, and the degradation-theory recognizes progression, as powerful influences in the course of culture. Under proper limitations the principles of both theories are conformable to historical knowledge, which shows us, on the one hand, that the state of the higher nations was reached by progression from a lower state, and, on the other hand, that culture gained by progression may be lost by degradation. If in this enquiry we should be obliged to end in the dark, at any rate we need not begin there. History, taken as our guide in explaining the different stages of civilization, offers a theory based on actual experience. This is a development-theory, in which both advance and relapse have their acknowledged places. But so far as history is to be our criterion, progression is primary and degradation secondary; culture must be gained before it can be lost. Moreover, in striking a balance between the effects of forward and backward movement in civilization, it must be borne in mind how powerfully the diffusion of culture acts in preserving the results of progress from the attacks of degeneration. A progressive movement in culture spreads, and becomes independent of the fate of its originators. What is produced in some limited district is diffused over a wider and wider area, where the process of effectual "stamping out" becomes more and more difficult. Thus it is even possible for the habits and inventions of races long extinct to remain as the common property of surviving nations; and the destructive actions which make such havoc with the civilizations of particular districts fail to destroy the civilization of the world. . . .

Arrest and decline in civilization are to be recognised as among the more frequent and powerful operations of national life. That knowledge, arts, and institutions should decay in certain districts, that peoples once progressive should lag behind and be passed by advancing neighbours, that sometimes even societies of men should recede into rudeness and misery— all these are phenomena with which modern history is familiar. In judging of the relation of the lower to the higher stages of civilization, it is essential to gain some idea how far it may have been affected by such degeneration. What kind of evidence can direct observation and history give as to the degradation of men from a civilized condition towards that of savagery? In our great cities, the so-called "dangerous classes" are sunk in hideous misery and depravity. If we have to strike a balance between the Papuans of New Caledonia and the communities of European beggars and thieves, we may sadly acknowledge that we have in our midst something worse than savagery. But it is not savagery; it is broken-down civilization. . . .

PART THREE

Other Writings by Edith Wharton

WRITING *THE AGE OF INNOCENCE*

Edith Wharton wrote *The Age of Innocence* during a time of profound loss. Not only had she lost friends and relatives to World War I, her close friend Henry James had died in 1916 and her friend Howard Sturgis in 1920. She was still reeling from the war's devastation and from the sense that civilization as the world knew it had been destroyed. Out of this period of mourning grew Wharton's reminiscence about the New York society of her childhood. The following passage is drawn from her autobiography, *A Backward Glance* (1934). [ED.]

. . . My spirit was heavy with these losses, but I could not sit still and brood over them. I wanted to put them into words, and in doing so I saw the years of the war, as I had lived them in Paris, with a new intensity of vision, in all their fantastic heights and depths of self-devotion and ardour, of pessimism, triviality and selfishness. A study of the world at the rear during a long war seemed to me worth doing, and I pondered over it till it took shape in "A Son at the Front." But before I could settle down to this tale, before I could begin to deal objectively with the stored-up emotions of those years, I had to get away from the present altogether; and though I began planning and brooding over "A Son at the Front" in 1917 it was not finished until four years later. Meanwhile I found a momentary escape in going back to my childish memories of a long-vanished America, and wrote "The Age of Innocence." I showed it chapter by chapter to Walter Berry; and when he had finished reading it he said: "Yes; it's good. But of course you and I are the only people who will ever read it. We are the last people left who can remember New York and Newport as they were then, and nobody else will be interested." . . .

From *A Backward Glance*. 1934. New York: Scribner's, 1964.

"A Son at the Front" *A Son at the Front* is Wharton's novel about World War I. First serialized in *Scribner's*, it appeared in 1923.

Walter Berry An international lawyer and intimate friend of Edith Wharton whom she often consulted for advice about her writing.

THE WAYS OF OLD NEW YORK

Wharton based *The Age of Innocence* on the cultured but prosaic world in which she was born and raised. In these excerpts
from her autobiography, *A Backward Glance,* she assesses the
strengths and weaknesses of this old New York society. She writes
appreciatively of her family's respect for good breeding and taste
but criticizes their lack of interest in serious intellectual or artistic pursuits. She also describes the exhilarating yet painful process
by which she began to break away from convention to become a
woman of letters. [ED.]

<hr>

. . . The readers (and I should doubtless have been among them) who
twenty years ago would have smiled at the idea that time could transform
a group of *bourgeois* colonials and their republican descendants into a sort
of social aristocracy, are now better able to measure the formative value of
nearly three hundred years of social observance: the concerted living up to
long-established standards of honour and conduct, of education and manners. The value of duration is slowly asserting itself against the welter of
change, and sociologists without a drop of American blood in them have
been the first to recognize what the traditions of three centuries have contributed to the moral wealth of our country. Even negatively, these traditions have acquired, with the passing of time, an unsuspected value. When
I was young it used to seem to me that the group in which I grew up was
like an empty vessel into which no new wine would ever again be poured.
Now I see that one of its uses lay in preserving a few drops of an old vintage too rare to be savoured by a youthful palate; and I should like to atone
for my unappreciativeness by trying to revive that faint fragrance.

If any one had suggested to me, before 1914, to write my reminiscences, I should have answered that my life had been too uneventful to be
worth recording. Indeed, I had never even thought of recording it for my
own amusement, and the fact that until 1918 I never kept even the briefest
of diaries has greatly hampered this tardy reconstruction. Not until the successive upheavals which culminated in the catastrophe of 1914 had "cut
all likeness from the name" of my old New York, did I begin to see its pathetic picturesqueness. The first change came in the 'eighties, with the earliest detachment of big money-makers from the West, soon to be followed

<hr>

From *A Backward Glance.* 1934. New York: Scribner's, 1964.

by the lords of Pittsburgh. But their infiltration did not greatly affect old manners and customs, since the dearest ambition of the newcomers was to assimilate existing traditions. Social life, with us as in the rest of the world, went on with hardly perceptible changes till the war abruptly tore down the old frame-work, and what had seemed unalterable rules of conduct became of a sudden observances as quaintly arbitrary as the domestic rites of the Pharaohs. Between the point of view of my Huguenot great-great-grandfather, who came from the French Palatinate to participate in the founding of New Rochelle, and my own father, who died in 1882, there were fewer differences than between my father and the post-war generation of Americans. That I was born into a world in which telephones, motors, electric light, central heating (except by hot-air furnaces), X-rays, cinemas, radium, aeroplanes and wireless telegraphy were not only unknown but still mostly unforeseen, may seem the most striking difference between then and now; but the really vital change is that, in my youth, the Americans of the original States, who in moments of crisis still shaped the national point of view, were the heirs of an old tradition of European culture which the country has now totally rejected. This rejection (which Mr. Walter Lippmann regards as the chief cause of the country's present moral impoverishment) has opened a gulf between those days and these. The compact world of my youth has receded into a past from which it can only be dug up in bits by the assiduous relic-hunter; and its smallest fragments begin to be worth collecting and putting together before the last of those who knew the live structure are swept away with it. . . .

When my grandfather died my father came into an independent fortune; but even before that my father and uncles seem to have had allowances permitting them to lead a life of leisure and amiable hospitality. The customs of the day were simple, and in my father's set the chief diversions were sea-fishing, boat-racing and wild-fowl shooting. There were no clubs as yet in New York, and my mother, whose view of life was incurably prosaic, always said that this accounted for the early marriages, as the young men of that day "had nowhere else to go." The young married couples, Langdons, Hones, Newbolds, Edgars, Joneses, Gallatins, etc., entertained each other a good deal, and my mother's sloping shoulders were often displayed above the elegant fringed and ruffled "berthas" of her Parisian dinner gowns. The amusing diary of Mr. Philip Hone gives a good idea of the simple but incessant exchange of hospitality between the young people who ruled New York society before the Civil War.

My readers, by this time, may be wondering what were the particular merits, private or civic, of these amiable persons. Their lives, as one looks back, certainly seem lacking in relief; but I believe their value lay in upholding two standards of importance in any community, that of education and good manners, and of scrupulous probity in business and private affairs. New York has always been a commercial community, and in my infancy the merits and defects of its citizens were those of a mercantile middle class. The first duty of such a class was to maintain a strict standard of uprightness in affairs; and the gentlemen of my father's day did maintain it, whether in the law, in banking, shipping or wholesale commercial enterprises. I well remember the horror excited by any irregularity in affairs, and the relentless social ostracism inflicted on the families of those who lapsed from professional or business integrity. In one case, where two or three men of high social standing were involved in a discreditable bank failure, their families were made to suffer to a degree that would seem merciless to our modern judgment. But perhaps the New Yorkers of that day were unconsciously trying to atone for their culpable neglect of state and national politics, from which they had long disdainfully held aloof, by upholding the sternest principles of business probity, and inflicting the severest social penalties on whoever lapsed from them. At any rate I should say that the qualities justifying the existence of our old society were social amenity and financial incorruptibility; and we have travelled far enough from both to begin to estimate their value.

The weakness of the social structure of my parents' day was a blind dread of innovation, an instinctive shrinking from responsibility. In 1824 (or thereabouts) a group of New York gentlemen who were appointed to examine various plans for the proposed laying-out of the city, and whose private sympathies were notoriously anti-Jeffersonian and undemocratic, decided against reproducing the beautiful system of squares, circles and radiating avenues which Major L'Enfant, the brilliant French engineer, had designed for Washington, because it was thought "undemocratic" for citizens of the new republic to own building-plots which were not all of exactly the same shape, size—and *value!* This naïf document, shown to me by Robert Minturn, a descendant of a member of the original committee, and doubtless often since published, typified the prudent attitude of a society of prosperous business men who have no desire to row against the current.

A little world so well-ordered and well-to-do does not often produce either eagles or fanatics, and both seem to have been conspicuously absent from the circle in which my forbears moved. In old-established and powerful societies originality of character is smiled at, and even encouraged to assert itself; but conformity is the bane of middle-class communities, and as far as I can recall, only two of my relations stepped out of the strait path of the usual. One was a mild and inoffensive old bachelor cousin, very small and frail, and reputed of immense wealth and morbid miserliness, who built himself a fine house in his youth, and lived in it for fifty or sixty years, in a state of negativeness and insignificance which made him proverbial even in our conforming class—and then, in his last years (so we children were told) *sat on a marble shelf, and thought he was a bust of Napoleon.*

Cousin Edmund's final illusion was not without pathos, but as a source of inspiration to my childish fancy he was a poor thing compared with George Alfred. George Alfred was another cousin, but one whom I had never seen, and could never hope to see, because years before he had—vanished. Vanished, that is, out of society, out of respectability, out of the safe daylight world of "nice people" and reputable doings. Before naming George Alfred my mother altered her expression and lowered her voice. Thank heaven *she* was not responsible for him—he belonged to my father's side of the family! But they too had long since washed their hands of George Alfred—had ceased even to be aware of his existence. If my mother pronounced his name it was solely, I believe, out of malice, out of the child's naughty desire to evoke some nursery hobgoblin by muttering a dark incantation like *Eena Meena Mina Mo,* and then darting away with affrighted backward looks to see if there is anything there.

My mother always darted away from George Alfred's name after pronouncing it, and it was not until I was grown up, and had acquired greater courage and persistency, that one day I drove her to the wall by suddenly asking: "But, Mamma, *what did he do?*" "Some woman"—my mother muttered; and no one accustomed to the innocuous word as now used can imagine the shades of disapproval, scorn and yet excited curiosity, that "some" could then connote on the lips of virtue.

George Alfred—and some woman! Who was she? From what heights had she fallen with him, to what depths dragged him down? For in those simple days it was always a case of "the woman tempted me." To her respectable sisters her culpability was as certain in advance as Predestination to the Calvinist. But I was not fated to know more—thank heaven I was not! For our shadowy Paolo and Francesca, circling together on the "accursèd air," somewhere outside the safe boundaries of our old New York, gave me, I verily believe, my earliest glimpse of the poetry that Goethe missed in the respectable world of the Hirschgraben, and that my ancestors assuredly failed to find, or to create, between the Battery and Union Square. The vision of poor featureless unknown Alfred and his siren, lurking in some cranny of my imagination, hinted at regions perilous, dark and yet lit with mysterious fires, just outside the world of copy-book axioms, and the old obediences that were in my blood; and the hint was useful—for a novelist. . . .

I remember once asking an old New Yorker why he never went abroad, and his answering: "Because I can't bear to cross Murray Street." It was indeed an unsavoury experience, and the shameless squalor of the purlieus

of the New York docks in the 'seventies dismayed my childish eyes, stored
with the glories of Rome and the architectural majesty of Paris. But it was
summer; we were soon at Newport, under the friendly gables of Pencraig;
and to a little girl long pent up in hotels and flats there was inexhaustible
delight in the freedom of a staircase to run up and down, of lawns and
trees, a meadow full of clover and daisies, a pony to ride, terriers to romp
with, a sheltered cove to bathe in, flower-beds spicy with "carnation, lily,
rose," and a kitchen-garden crimson with strawberries and sweet as honey
with Seckel pears.

The roomy and pleasant house of Pencraig was surrounded by a verandah wreathed in clematis and honeysuckle, and below it a lawn sloped
to a deep daisied meadow, beyond which were a private bathing-beach and
boat-landing. From the landing we used to fish for "scuppers" and "por-
gies," succulent little fish that were grilled or fried for high tea; and off the
rocky point lay my father's and brothers' "cat-boats," the graceful wide-
sailed craft that flecked the bay like sea-gulls. . . .

Most vivid is my memory of the picturesque archery club meetings of
which the grown daughters of the house, Margaret (afterward Mrs. Henry
White) and her sister Louisa were among the most brilliant performers.
When the club met we children were allowed to be present, and to circulate among the grown-ups (usually all three of us astride of one patient
donkey); and a pretty sight the meeting was, with parents and elders seated
in a semicircle on the turf behind the lovely archeresses in floating silks or
muslins, with their wide leghorn hats, and heavy veils flung back only at
the moment of aiming. These veils are associated with all the summer festivities of my childhood. In that simple society there was an almost pagan
worship of physical beauty, and the first question asked about any youthful newcomer on the social scene was invariably: "Is she pretty?" or: "Is
he handsome?"—for good looks were as much prized in young men as in
maidens. For the latter no grace was rated as high as "a complexion." It is
hard to picture nowadays the shell-like transparence, the luminous red-
and-white, of those young cheeks untouched by paint or powder, in which
the blood came and went like the lights of an aurora. Beauty was unthinkable without a "complexion," and to defend that treasure against
sun and wind, and the arch-enemy sea air, veils as thick as curtains (some
actually of woollen barège) were habitually worn. It must have been very
uncomfortable for the wearers, who could hardly see or breathe; but even
to my childish eyes the effect was dazzling when the curtain was drawn,
and young beauty shone forth. My dear friend Howard Sturgis used to
laugh at the "heavily veiled" heroines who lingered on so late in Victorian
fiction, and were supposed to preserve their incognito until they threw
back their veils; but if he had known fashionable Newport in my infancy

he would have seen that the novelists' formula was based on what was once a reality.

Those archery meetings greatly heightened my infantile desire to "tell a story," and the young gods and goddesses I used to watch strolling across the Edgerston lawn were the prototypes of my first novels. . . .

My parents' guests ate well, and drank good wine with discernment; but a more fastidious taste had shortened the enormous repasts and deep bumpers of colonial days, and in twenty minutes the whiskered gentlemen had joined the flounced ladies on the purple settees for another half hour of amiable chat, accompanied by the cup of tea which always rounded off the evening. How mild and leisurely it all seems in the glare of our new century! Small parochial concerns no doubt formed the staple of the talk. Art and music and literature were rather timorously avoided (unless Trollope's last novel were touched upon, or a discreet allusion made to Mr. William Astor's audacious acquisition of a Bouguereau Venus), and the topics chiefly dwelt on were personal: the thoughtful discussion of food, wine, horses ("high steppers" were beginning to be much sought after), the laying out and planting of country-seats, the selection of "specimen" copper beeches and fern-leaved maples for lawns just beginning to be shorn smooth by the new hand-mowers, and those plans of European travel which filled so large a space in the thought of old New Yorkers. From my earliest infancy I had always seen about me people who were either just arriving from "abroad" or just embarking on a European tour. The old New Yorker was in continual contact with the land of his fathers, and it was not until I went to Boston on my marriage that I found myself in a community of wealthy and sedentary people seemingly too lacking in intellectual curiosity to have any desire to see the world. . . .

. . . I was a healthy little girl who loved riding, swimming and romping; yet no children of my own age, and none even among the nearest of my grown-ups, were as close to me as the great voices that spoke to me from books. Whenever I try to recall my childhood it is in my father's library that it comes to life. I am squatting again on the thick Turkey rug, pulling open one after another the glass doors of the low bookcases, and dragging out book after book in a secret ecstasy of communion. I say "secret," for I cannot remember ever speaking to any one of these enraptured sessions. The child knows instinctively when it will be understood, and from the first I kept my adventures with books to myself. . . .

This ferment of reading revived my story-telling fever; but now I wanted to write and not to improvise. My first attempt (at the age of eleven) was a novel, which began: "'Oh, how do you do, Mrs. Brown?' said Mrs. Tompkins. 'If only I had known you were going to call I should have tidied up the drawing-room.'" Timorously I submitted this to my mother,

and never shall I forget the sudden drop of my creative frenzy when she returned it with the icy comment: "Drawing-rooms are always tidy."

This was so crushing to a would-be novelist of manners that it shook
me rudely out of my dream of writing fiction, and I took to poetry instead.
It was not thought necessary to feed my literary ambitions with foolscap,
and for lack of paper I was driven to begging for the wrappings of the
parcels delivered at the house. After a while these were regarded as belonging to me, and I always kept a stack in my room. It never occurred to
me to fold and cut the big brown sheets, and I used to spread them on
the floor and travel over them on my hands and knees, building up long
parallel columns of blank verse headed: "Scene: A Venetian palace," or
"Dramatis Personæ" (which I never knew how to pronounce). . . .

After this I withdrew to secret communion with the Muse. I continued to cover vast expanses of wrapping paper with prose and verse, but the
dream of a literary career, momentarily shadowed forth by one miraculous
adventure, soon faded into unreality. How could I ever have supposed I
could be an author? I had never even seen one in the flesh! . . .

THE CHILDISHNESS
OF AMERICAN WOMEN

When Edith Wharton left the United States, she chose France as
her permanent residence. She organized charities to benefit the
French people during World War I and published a group of essays, *French Ways and Their Meaning* (1919), praising France
as the epitome of culture and a source of intellectual freedom
for women. In the following passage, drawn from this book,
Wharton takes issue with dominant nineteenth-century ideolo-
gies that promoted separate social spheres for men and women.
Her unfavorable comparison of American women with their
French counterparts provides readers of *The Age of Innocence*
with hints about her views of her two protagonists, May Welland,
an "all-American girl," and Ellen Olenska, an expatriate like
Wharton living in France. [ED.]

From *French Ways and Their Meaning*. New York: Appleton, 1919.

. . . Compared with the women of France the average American woman is still in the kindergarten. The world she lives in is exactly like the most improved and advanced and scientifically equipped Montessori-method baby-school. At first sight it may seem preposterous to compare the American woman's independent and resonant activities—her "boards" and clubs and sororities, her public investigation of everything under the heavens from "the social evil" to baking-powder, and from "physical culture" to the newest esoteric religion—to compare such free and busy and seemingly influential lives with the artless exercises of an infant class. But what is the fundamental principle of the Montessori system? It is the development of the child's individuality, unrestricted by the traditional nursery discipline: a Montessori school is a baby world where, shut up together in the most improved hygienic surroundings, a number of infants noisily develop their individuality.

The reason why American women are not really "grown up" in comparison with the women of the most highly civilised countries—such as France—is that all their semblance of freedom, activity and authority bears not much more likeness to real living than the exercises of the Montessori infant. Real living, in any but the most elementary sense of the word, is a deep and complex and slowly-developed thing, the outcome of an old and rich social experience. It cannot be "got up" like gymnastics, or a proficiency in foreign languages; it has its roots in the fundamental things, and above all in close and constant and interesting and important relations between men and women. . . .

The Frenchwoman rules French life, and she rules it under a triple crown, as a business woman, as a mother, and above all as an artist. To explain the sense in which the last word is used it is necessary to go back to the contention that the greatness of France lies in her sense of the beauty and importance of living. As life is an art in France, so woman is an artist. She does not teach man, but she inspires him. As the Frenchwoman of the bread-winning class influences her husband, and inspires in him a respect for her judgment and her wishes, so the Frenchwoman of the rich and educated class is admired and held in regard for other qualities. But in this class of society her influence naturally extends much farther. The more civilised a society is, the wider is the range of each woman's influence over men, and of each man's influence over women. Intelligent and cultivated people of either sex will never limit themselves to communing with their own households. Men and women equally, when they have the range of interests that real cultivation gives, need the stimulus of different points of view, the refreshment of new ideas as well as of new faces. The long hypocrisy which Puritan England handed on to America concerning the danger of frank and free social relations between men and women has done more than anything else to retard real civilisation in America. . . .

THE VALLEY OF CHILDISH THINGS

In "The Valley of Childish Things," Wharton's early parable (1896) about a sophisticated woman who returns to the society of her youth only to be disappointed by her peers' immaturity, we can see not only Wharton herself but the sketch of the character who was to become Ellen Olenska. Inquisitive, intrepid, and alive to art and beauty, the protagonist hopes in vain for friends and a male partner to share her vision of life. [ED.]

Once upon a time a number of children lived together in the Valley of Childish Things, playing all manner of delightful games, and studying the same lesson books. But one day a little girl, one of their number, decided that it was time to see something of the world about which the lesson books had taught her; and as none of the other children cared to leave their games, she set out alone to climb the pass which led out of the valley.

It was a hard climb, but at length she reached a cold, bleak tableland beyond the mountains. Here she saw cities and men, and learned many useful arts, and in so doing grew to be a woman. But the tableland was bleak and cold, and when she had served her apprenticeship she decided to return to her old companions in the Valley of Childish Things, and work with them instead of with strangers.

It was a weary way back, and her feet were bruised by the stones, and her face was beaten by the weather; but halfway down the pass she met a man, who kindly helped her over the roughest places. Like herself, he was lame and weather-beaten; but as soon as he spoke she recognized him as one of her old playmates. He too had been out in the world, and was going back to the valley; and on the way they talked together of the work

From *Collected Short Stories of Edith Wharton*. Vol. 1. New York: Scribner's, 1968.

they meant to do there. He had been a dull boy, and she had never taken much notice of him; but as she listened to his plans for building bridges and draining swamps and cutting roads through the jungle, she thought to herself, "Since he has grown into such a fine fellow, what splendid men and women my other playmates must have become!"

But what was her surprise to find, on reaching the valley, that her former companions, instead of growing into men and women, had all remained little children. Most of them were playing the same old games, and the few who affected to be working were engaged in such strenuous occupations as building mudpies and sailing paper boats in basins. As for the lad who had been the favorite companion of her studies, he was playing marbles with all the youngest boys in the valley.

At first the children seemed glad to have her back, but soon she saw that her presence interfered with their games; and when she tried to tell them of the great things that were being done on the tableland beyond the mountains, they picked up their toys and went farther down the valley to play.

Then she turned to her fellow traveler, who was the only grown man in the valley; but he was on his knees before a dear little girl with blue eyes and a coral necklace, for whom he was making a garden out of cockleshells and bits of glass and broken flowers stuck in sand.

The little girl was clapping her hands and crowing (she was too young to speak articulately); and when she who had grown to be a woman laid her hand on the man's shoulder, and asked him if he did not want to set to work with her building bridges, draining swamps, and cutting roads through the jungle, he replied that at that particular moment he was too busy.

And as she turned away, he added in the kindest possible way, "Really, my dear, you ought to have taken better care of your complexion."

WINNING THE PULITZER PRIZE

In 1921, while living in France, Edith Wharton learned she had won the Pulitzer Prize for *The Age of Innocence*. The annual award was given by a jury at Columbia University for the American novel which shall "best present the wholesome atmosphere of American life and the highest standard of American manners and manhood" (Benstock 365). She received the news with mixed pride and irreverence: "Columbia has awarded me the—Pulitzer!!—

From *The Letters of Edith Wharton*. New York: Scribner's, 1988.

$1000—prize for the best novel of the year," she wrote a friend, "The which tainted money will come in particularly handy to polish off the gardens at Ste Claire [her Riviera home]" (*Letters*, 441–42).

Wharton was skeptical about the prize for several reasons. It came just after her novella, *The Old Maid,* had been rejected by *The Ladies' Home Journal* and *Metropolitan Magazine* on grounds of immorality, so Wharton was amused to be touted simultaneously "for uplifting American morals." (Following publicity surrounding the award ceremony, which Wharton declined to attend, *Red Book* offered an astounding $7,500 for *The Old Maid.*) She also chuckled over the fact that the judges apparently had missed all irony in her novel, not noticing how satirically she portrayed old New Yorkers. And finally, she was shocked and chagrined by the controversy surrounding the award. Originally, the prize had gone to Sinclair Lewis for his novel, *Main Street,* an exposé of small-town life in the Midwest, but it had been revoked because the novel was deemed offensive to Midwestern townspeople. In the following letter to Lewis, Wharton praises his work, reflects on her own reception in the United States, and complains—as she frequently did—about the dearth of genuine taste in American culture. [ED.]

Pavillon Colombe
August 6, 1921

My dear Mr. Lewis,

Your letter touched me very deeply; & I should have told you so sooner if it hadn't gone to America (where I have not been since the war), & then travelled back to me here.

What you say is so kind, so generous & so unexpected, that I don't know where to begin to answer. It is the first sign I have ever had—literally—that "les jeunes" at home had ever read a word of me. I had long since resigned myself to the idea that I was regarded by you all as the—say the Mrs. Humphry Ward of the Western Hemisphere; though at times I

"les jeunes"   French: young people.

Mrs. Humphry Ward   A popular English novelist (1851–1920) known for her philanthropic and religious polemics.

wondered why. Your book & Susan Lenox (unexpurgated) have been the only things out of America that have made me cease to despair of the republic—of letters; so you can imagine what a pleasure it is to know that you have read *me*, & cared, & understood. It gives me a "Nunc Dimittis" feeling—or would, if I hadn't still about a hundred subjects to deal with!

As for the Columbia Prize, the kind Appletons have smothered me in newspaper commentary; & when I discovered that I was being rewarded—by one of our leading Universities—for uplifting American morals, I confess I *did* despair.

Subsequently, when I found the prize shd really have been yours, but was withdrawn because your book (I quote from memory) had "offended a number of prominent persons in the Middle West," disgust was added to despair.—Hope returns to me, however, with your letter, & with the enclosed article, just received.—Some sort of standard *is* emerging from the welter of cant & sentimentality, & if two or three of us are gathered together, I believe we can still save fiction in America.

I wish I could talk to you of all this. Is there no chance of your coming to Paris? I'm only half an hour away—If not, let me at least tell you again how many hopes your book & your letter have waked in me. Believe me, Yrs very sincerely

E. Wharton

Susan Lenox   A posthumously published realistic novel by David Graham Phillips (1867–1911) about a country girl who becomes a prostitute and later a successful actress.

"Nunc Dimittis"   The canticle of Simeon Stylites, beginning *Nunc dimittis servum tuum* ("Now lettest thou thy servant depart"). By evoking this Syrian ascetic who lived for sixty-eight years on top of lofty pillars, Wharton toys with the idea of removing herself from the publishing world.

PART FOUR

Critical Readings

THE COMPOSITION
OF EDITH WHARTON'S
THE AGE OF INNOCENCE

Alan Price

Edith Wharton's notebook entitled "Subjects and Notes, 1918–1923"[1] reveals that she made significant revisions in writing *The Age of Innocence*. The entries for this novel begin on page 37 and continue for several pages. The original notes, in pencil, show that she at first called the story "Old New York (1875–80)" and planned the length of action as "about 18 months." Later notes indicate that writing was "Begun 1919" and "Finished 1920." Changes in the names of the characters appear not only on the first page but through the manuscript drafts. Newland Archer was at first called Langdon, then Lawrence; Ellen Olenska was variously Clementine and Clementina. Such indecision as to the names of her characters was not unusual for Mrs. Wharton: R. W. B. Lewis's research on the textual revisions of *The House of Mirth* (earlier titles for that novel had been "A Moment's Ornament" and "The Year of the Rose") reveals that Lily Bart had first been named Juliet Hurst.[2] These changes, however, may seem surprising to readers of *A Backward Glance* who recall the vigor with which Mrs. Wharton, in the dramatic chapter "The Secret Garden," insisted that her characters always appeared with their names attached:

> . . . Sometimes these names seem to me affected, sometimes almost ridiculous; but I am obliged to own that they are never fundamentally unsuitable. And the proof that they are not, that they really belong to the people, is the difficulty I have in trying to substitute other names. For many years the attempt always ended fatally; any character I unchristened instantly died on my hands, as if it were some kind of sensitive crustacean, and the name it brought with it were its shell. Only gradually, and in very

---

Yale University Literary Gazette 55 (1980).

[1] This is a French school copybook with marbled-paper covers and ruled pages. An "Index" on the last page offers a serial listing of the projects included. The notebook is part of the Wharton papers given to Yale (following the author's wishes) in 1938 by her literary executor, Gaillard Lapsley, and housed in the Collection of American Literature in the Beinecke Rare Book and Manuscript Library. (Hitherto unpublished writing by Mrs. Wharton is printed with the permission of her estate, A. Watkins, Inc., agent.) I am grateful to R. W. B. Lewis for calling my attention to the manuscript.

[2] R. W. B. Lewis, "Introduction," *The House of Mirth* by Edith Wharton (New York, New York University Press, 1977), p. xiv.

few cases, have I gained enough mastery over my creatures to be able to effect the change; and even now, when I do, I have to resort to hypodermics and oxygen, and not always successfully.[3]

In light of the frequent changes in names in her notebooks and manuscripts, her statements about her creative process become suspect; "The Secret Garden" should not be taken as an exact account of her creative method.

The pattern appears to have alternated between periods of passive receptivity and others of critical pruning and arrangement. In *A Backward Glance* she said of her plots, "But these people of mine, whose ultimate destiny I know so well, walk to it by ways unrevealed to me beforehand." [4] The three plot outlines made for *The Age of Innocence* show her working out the "subsidiary action" of the novel. All three begin with the appearance of the socially suspect Countess Olenska in New York and end with the impossibility of any successful marriage between her and Archer. But what takes place between appears to have been in process right up until the novel was printed.

The first of the three sketched plots, marked "1st Plan" in red pencil, is in pencil on leaves laid into the notebook. The Countess is the major character in this story, while "Lawrence" Archer recedes into the background:

> Lawrence   sees Countess X in the Wellands box. Horrified. The
> Ctess (Ellen   ) had married a Polish nobleman living in Paris &
> Nice. Reports of his debaucheries had come home; but it was also said
> that *she* had been "fast," & "talked about." Vague rumours were current, & some embarrassment was felt when she came home, saying simply that she had left her husband & obtained a divorce. Still, her behaviour was so discreet & retiring, & she seemed so genuinely glad to be at home, in a purer atmosphere, that every one became very friendly after the first recoil, & she was used as an Awful Warning to young girls with an inclination to "marry foreigners."
>
> Gradually Archer falls in love with her, & sees that life with May Welland, or any other young woman who has not had Ellen's initiation, would be unutterably dull.
>
> It is very painful to him to break his engagement, but he finally has the courage to do so, though he does not tell May why he no longer cares for her.
>
> She gives him up magnanimously [*cancelled:* but when she finds that Ellen is the cause she is very bitter, & reproaches Ellen for Ellen too is

---

[3] Edith Wharton, *A Backward Glance* (New York, London, D. Appleton-Century Co., 1934), p. 201.
[4] *Idem,* p. 204.

very much distressed but still] because she has been taught that "ladies do not make scenes," & she continues to pretend that she does not suspect Ellen of being her rival till the latter's engagement is announced. Even then May is heroically generous, & is among the first to bring her good wishes to her cousin.

Archer, his struggle over, is sublimely, supremely happy. He urges Ellen to marry him at once. She shocks him deeply by proposing that they should first "go off for a few weeks," so that he can be sure he is not making a mistake. He reproaches her for thinking that he "feels about her in that way," & she begins to feel ashamed of having made the suggestion, & to say to herself that the "European corruption" has tainted her soul. To efface this impression from her own mind & his, she consents to a hasty marriage; but then, when they come back from their honeymoon, & she realizes that for the next 30 or 40 years they are going to live in Madison Ave in winter & on the Hudson in the Spring & autumn, with a few weeks of Europe or Newport every summer, her whole soul recoils, & she knows at once that she has eaten of the Pomegranate Seed & can never never live without it.

She flies to Europe, & Archer consents to a separation. He realizes dimly that there is no use struggling with her. He arranges his own life as best he can, & occasionally goes to Europe, & usually calls on his wife, & is asked to dine with her. She is very poor, & very lonely, but she has a real life.

He grows more & more absorbed in business, more & more subdued to "New York." He returns to live with his mother & sister. May Welland marries some one else, & nothing ever happens to him again.

The most notable difference between this first plan and the published novel is that here Ellen is the one who initiates the action and undoubtedly would have become the central focus of the story. Much could have been made of the "European corruption" which has "tainted her soul"—a theme Henry James (had he lived to discuss the novel with Mrs. Wharton) might have pressed. One reason surely for the shift of focus from the Countess to Archer was that although Mrs. Wharton was sympathetic to Ellen, she could not be confident that her readers would share her sympathy for a woman who broke up the engagement of a nice girl, suggested a trial marriage, and then abandoned her husband because she thought New York's seasonal social life was dull. Also, Ellen's situation came dangerously close to that of Edith Wharton herself: she had divorced her husband seven years earlier, had long since chosen to live "a real life" in Paris rather than return to her own family in New York or Teddy Wharton's in Boston, and had been quite explicit about her distaste for a settled New York existence. Ellen as a heroine ran the risk of being seen as a woman who could not get along with a bad European husband and now cannot get along with a good American one. The novel with Ellen as a liberated heroine would have been an exciting, perhaps even a more interesting one, but Mrs. Wharton recognized the practical artistic problem of making her heroine acceptable to her readers.

"Lawrence" Archer is already provided with a mother and sister, but his profession here is business rather than law. Aside from his falling in love with Ellen and objecting to Ellen's offer to "go off for a few weeks," Archer does very little. Even in this early draft he is controlled by the conventions of New York society. Finally he is fatally written off: "nothing ever happens to him again."

May Welland has her name and her character firmly in place. In the cancelled passage she almost rises to complexity as she becomes bitter at Ellen's theft; but she is quickly pushed back into the pattern of the modest, generous young lady whom Howard Chandler Christy celebrated as "the American girl." Thus the three central characters were in Mrs. Wharton's mind from the beginning. Now it became a matter of finding a plot which would allow them to reveal themselves with the appropriate emphasis.

The second plan for the novel appears on pages 37 and 39 (page [38] is blank) of the notebook. While there are still some uncertainties about first names—Clementine becomes Clementina and finally Ellen—the plot and theme are moving much closer to the novel as we have it:

> Ellen Olenska (cousin of May) has married young. Lived in Paris, Nice, Rome [*cancelled:* Etrétat]. Glimpses of London. Husband charming gambler, drug-taker & debauché. Spends all her money, & marriage goes to smash. She comes back to America longing for virtue, innocence & "Old New York."
>
> Archer is engaged to May Welland. He falls in love with Ellen, but resists & marries May. (Conventional impossibility of a man's breaking his engagement in those days. Ellen enthusiastically converted to all that is "province," honour, decency, &c., applauds his resolution.) [*Cancelled:* finally goes back to her husband.
>
> In two or three years she reappears.]
>
> He goes on a wedding trip with May, comes back & settles down to married life in N.Y—Ellen still there—but less enthusiastic about New York. He sees a great deal of her. May is going to have a baby. At last he and Ellen fly together (contrast between bridal night with May & *this* one). Archer is fascinated & yet terrified. They [*cancelled:* go to Europ[e]] go to the South together—some little place in Florida.
>
> Arrange somehow that all this is done *very secretly*. No one knows they are there together. Both get tired—she of the idea of living in America, he of the idea of a scandal & a dislocation of his life.

He cannot live without New York & respectability, nor she without Europe & emotion.

They return to N.Y. separately, & the last scene is a dinner which the happy May (who has had a boy) insists on giving to her cousin Mme. Olenska before the latter sails.

Though in this second plan she has rejected the idea of a marriage between Ellen and Archer, Mrs. Wharton does give them a passionate interlude in Florida. With the publication of the "Beatrice Palmato" fragment and our knowledge of Mrs. Wharton's affair with Morton Fullerton,[5] it is fascinating to speculate on how she would have chosen to "contrast" Archer's supposedly bland bridal night with May and the presumably wild one with Ellen.

Mrs. Wharton's cancellations here are revealing. Some missteps are caught immediately, as when she decides that Ellen will *not* go back to her husband and that Ellen and Archer will *not* go to Europe to have their affair: the first was an attempt to have her characters' actions fit with behavior of their strongly felt personalities; the second, to head off complications which would prove distracting. (How could Archer go back to the tame May after having experienced Europe with Ellen as his guide?)

In this version of the plot Mrs. Wharton has introduced one of her big scenes: the farewell party given by May for Ellen. She has also shifted her emphasis from the freedom enjoyed by two passionate natures to the restraints implied by social conventions by moving the plot away from Ellen to action which is more or less balanced between her and Archer. This sketch ends with a dinner set in New York, just before Ellen's return to Europe and a life of "emotion."

What appears to have been Edith Wharton's final (through still tentative) plan before she began the actual writing of the novel precedes the first pages of the manuscript, also among the Wharton papers at Yale. At the top of the first page of this three-page summary Mrs. Wharton has noted that "The scene is laid in 1875." The title still is "Old New York," but many of the details of characterization and plot are more fully worked out than in either of the earlier plans:

Langdon Archer, a young man of very good "Old New York," is engaged to May Welland, a charming young girl of the same set, with whom he is deeply in love.

[5] R. W. B. Lewis, *Edith Wharton: A Biography* (New York [etc.], Harper & Row [1975]). The "Beatrice Palmato" material is in Appendix C, pp. 544–48; for her awakening sexuality in the affair with Fullerton, see pp. 205–31.

Her cousin, Clementine Welland, whose parents had lived in Paris and been popular at the court of Louis Napoleon, & in fashionable French society, has been married very young to Count Olenska, a [*cancelled:* a very rich] Polish nobleman of great family. She has led a brilliant cosmopolitan life in Paris, London, Florence & Nice, but her husband's extravagance & dissipation have obliged her to leave him, & she returns to N.Y. at 28, disillusioned & unhappy, & thirsting (as she imagines) for "the simple life," as represented by the quiet respectable "old New York" of the 'seventies.—Scenes at the Old Academy of Music, the "Assembly" balls, Christine Nilsson, Capoul, &c. Clementine Olenska & Langdon Archer meet & fall madly in love with each other.

He is almost carried off his feet; but in "Old New York" a girl is almost disgraced if her fiancé jilts her, & Archer dares not break with May. Mme. Olenska applauds his resolution, & with an aching heart he marries May, & they go on their tame colourless & eminently respectable wedding trip.

When they return they settle down in New York & begin to lead their life wh. is to go on till the grave. Clementine is there too, beginning to be bored with New York & virtue & renunciation, & thirsting for the freedom & variety of her European existence.

She falls into Archer's arms, & they go off secretly & meet in Florida, where they spend a few mad weeks. But Mme. Olenska cannot divorce as she & her husband are Roman Catholics.

Gradually Archer realizes that he cannot break with society & live as an outcast with [*cancelled:* an "immor[al"]] another man's wife. Mme. Olenska, on her side, is weary of their sentimental tête à tête & his scruples, & they finally go back, & the story ends by Mme. Olenska's returning to Europe.

Before she goes, May (who is going to have a baby, & who suspects nothing) insists on giving her cousin a farewell dinner, at which all of Old New York is present.

Archer's love for the Countess and his desire to fulfill his individual happiness are now in direct conflict with his duty to May and his need for the comfortable respectability of society's conventions. The focus is moving from Countess Olenska to Archer. In this plan the Countess seems almost a tempting siren who gives little thought to May's situation; in the published novel she is a more shadowy figure who wants to protect May's happiness at all costs.

In this plan the social accomplishments of the Countess's parents are indicated; the Count has money—until a stroke of the author's pen deprives him of it; and the Countess and Archer have a "few mad weeks" in Florida. Mrs. Wharton has arrived at the opening scene of the novel in which Christine Nilsson and Capoul perform *Faust* at the old Academy of

Music.[6] The final dinner given by May is now a fixed feature of the plot, even though here the Countess is rushing from New York to recapture "the freedom and variety of her European existence" rather than being driven away so that she can no longer tempt wandering husbands.

Mrs. Wharton now has her theme and her characters in much sharper focus. At this point in her career she had become an accomplished novelist who could allow her plots and characters to evolve naturally without pressing for quick solutions to artistic problems. Mrs. Wharton was especially sensitive to critical attacks upon the structure of her novels, as her introduction to *Ethan Frome* makes clear. In 1922 she wrote in a letter to Zona Gale:

> all through my early career [I have] been condemned by reviewers of my native land for "not knowing how to construct" a novel, I am now far more utterly banned by their descendants for "constructing."[7]

Whatever the value of the critics' claims, we have seen that Mrs. Wharton moved in stages in the construction of the plot of *The Age of Innocence* until she was ready to submit the broad outlines of her ideas to the refining process of actual composition. . . .

COOL DIANA AND THE BLOOD-RED MUSE
Edith Wharton on Innocence and Art

Elizabeth Ammons

For a number of reasons, Edith Wharton is unusually important to any feminist revision of American literary history. She is an author of the first rank and a woman. She spent her life writing about women and issues affecting women. Her career, because she did not publish in the mid-nineteenth century or begin her work in the 1920s, is underestimated in the current, rather skewed literary demography. Her fiction took a conservative

---

From *American Novelists Revisited*. Boston: Hall, 1982.

[6] The newspaper notices of Miss Nilsson's appearances in New York during the early 1870s do not mention her singing in *Faust*.

[7] Quoted in Eric LaGuardia, "Edith Wharton on Critics and Criticism," *Modern Language Notes*, LXXIII (Dec. 1958), p. 587.

turn after 1920, which, like similar shifts in the careers of Sinclair Lewis and Willa Cather, raises basic questions about war and misogyny in twentieth-century literature.

Wharton's career also is fascinating biographically. Her work, like that of many women artists, flowered when she was in the middle of life (around forty) rather than in her twenties or thirties. Also suggesting patterns that may be peculiar to female experience, gender and class clash at some important points in her life; and certainly her expatriation is connected both to being a woman and to the profession of writing. Not least important is untangling her complicated feelings (as opposed to her thoughts) about being female—how she felt about her mother, about being childless, about friendships with other women, about relationships with men.[1]

Indeed, there are so many issues that any short essay has to be selective. What I would like to do here, therefore, is talk in detail about one book, *The Age of Innocence,* a best-seller in 1920 and recipient of the Pulitzer Prize. I have chosen it because it is a pivotal book in Wharton's career and one in which several of the issues I have mentioned collect.[2]

After *The Age of Innocence,* critics agree, the quality of Wharton's long fiction changes. The line of exceptional work beginning with *The House of Mirth* in 1905 and running through *The Fruit of the Tree* (1907), *Ethan Frome* (1911), *The Reef* (1912), *The Custom of the Country* (1913), and *Summer* (1917) ends in 1920. After that there is an occasional book of extraordinary accomplishment (some argue that *The Mother's Recompense,* for instance, is one), but by and large the early books greatly overshadow the novels Wharton wrote in the twenties and thirties: *The Glimpses of the Moon* (1922), *The Mother's Recompense* (1925), *Twilight Sleep* (1927), *The Children* (1928), *Hudson River Bracketed* (1929), and *The Gods Arrive* (1932). *The Age of Innocence* marks the end of Edith Wharton's major period. It also marks the end of her Progressive Era fictions; and, as I hope to explain here in my discussion of the polarized portraits of the

---

[1] Biographies include R. W. B. Lewis's *Edith Wharton: A Biography* (New York: Harper & Row, 1975) and Cynthia Griffin Wolff's psychoanalytic and critical study, *A Feast of Words: The Triumph of Edith Wharton* (New York: Oxford University Press, 1977) [and Shari Benstock's *No Gifts from Chance: A Biography of Edith Wharton* (New York: Scribner's, 1994).—ED.]. For earlier biographies and criticism, see Marlene Springer's annotated bibliography, *Edith Wharton and Kate Chopin: A Reference Guide* (Boston: G. K. Hall, 1976).

[2] For full-length discussion of Wharton's work from a feminist perspective see my book, *Edith Wharton's Argument with America* (Athens: University of Georgia Press, 1980). My discussions of *The Age of Innocence* in the book and in this essay complement but do not duplicate each other.

American girl and the woman artist in *The Age of Innocence,* the novel comments significantly on its author's personal situation. *The Age of Innocence* is one of the clearest expressions we have of Edith Wharton's frustration as an American woman writer. . . .

As soon as Wharton named her hero Archer, she insisted upon comparison with her good friend Henry James's *The Portrait of a Lady* (1881). Both novels are set in the American 1870s, both contrast American and European values, both have as a central figure an American named Archer who is highly susceptible to Continental charm and mystery. Yet the comparison of most interest to me here is not between the two Archers, Isabel and Newland, but between the two American girls, Isabel and May, each of whom is, in a sense, the author's title character. Just as the "portrait" James paints applies most directly to Isabel Archer, so Wharton's title *The Age of Innocence,* which she took from a Reynolds portrait of a child, applies most directly to May, a character as frozen in endless childhood as the painter's little girl. As Cynthia Griffin Wolff notes, Wharton's painterly title strengthens this novel's connection to James.[3] But in its substitution of a little girl for a lady, it also, as I will go on to explain, emphasizes the great distance between them.

Henry James's American girl—adventurous, ignorant, virtuous, self-assured—was the pride of America by the time Wharton began publishing novels at the turn of the century. If the image had shocked the nation in *Daisy Miller* in the 1870s, by the late nineties the type was such a commonplace, imaginatively, that it was a staple of popular culture. The ingenuous American girl was the heroine of best-selling novels—Gertrude Atherton's *Patience Sparhawk and Her Times* (1894) is an excellent example—and she was so frequently the centerpiece of cultural analyses that in *Land of Contrasts: A Briton's View of His American Kin* (1898), James Fullarton Muirhead (author of Baedeker guides to Great Britain and the United States) could routinely remark on the type in his chapter, "An Appreciation of the American Woman":

> Put roughly, what chiefly strikes the stranger in the American woman is her candour, her frankness, her hail-fellow-well-met-edness, her apparent absence of consciousness of self or of sex, her spontaneity, her vivacity, her fearlessness. If the observer himself is not of specially refined or delicate type, he is apt at first to misunderstand the camaraderie of an American girl, to see in it suggestions of a possible coarseness of fibre. . . . But even to the obtuse stranger of this character it will become

---

[3] Wolff, *Feast of Words,* p. 312.

obvious—as to the more refined observer *ab initio*—that he can no more (if as much) dare to take a liberty with the American girl than with his own countrywoman. The plum may appear to be more easily handled, but its bloom will be found to be as intact and as ethereal as in the jealously guarded hothouse fruit of Europe. He will find that her frank and charming companionability is as far removed from masculinity as from coarseness; that the points in which she differs from the European lady do not bring her nearer either to a man on the one hand, or to a common woman on the other. He will find that he has to readjust his standards, to see that divergence from the best type of woman hitherto known to him does not necessarily mean deterioration; if he is of an open and susceptible mind, he may even come to the conclusion that he prefers the transatlantic type! [4]

Edith Wharton did not share Muirhead's enthusiasm. In *The Fruit of the Tree,* published thirteen years before *The Age of Innocence,* she first offered extended comment on the American girl in the character Bessy Westmore, who is vivacious, ignorant, brave, and, Wharton emphasizes, pathetically shallow. Bessy has energy but no knowledge, imagination but no depth. For all her robust self-confidence, she is an extremely limited creature. As Wharton has an attractive older woman ruefully observe, Bessy is "one of the most harrowing victims of the plan of bringing up our girls in double bondage of expediency and unreality . . . and leaving them to reconcile the two as best they can, or lose their souls in the attempt." [5] This description could as easily apply to Isabel Archer as to Bessy Westmore, with the major difference that, where James is fascinated to see how the reconciliation will be attempted, Wharton is disgusted by the problem's even existing. She does not see the American girl as America's noblest creation, the nation's most interesting contribution to modern civilization. She sees her as the nation's failure, the human victim of a deluded obsession with innocence.

May Welland is Wharton's rarefied version of the stereotype. Unsoiled by life, May is always connected with white: her virginity, mentally and emotionally, cannot be touched. She is permanently pure. Likewise, Wharton implies, she is permanently juvenile. She has a fresh "boyish" quality

---

[4] James Fullarton Muirhead, *Land of Contrasts* (Boston: Lanson, Wolffe & Co., 1898), pp. 50–51. James was so well known on the subject that Muirhead can casually refer to him: "The American girl, as Mr. Henry James says, is rarely negative; she is either (and usually) a most charming success or (and exceptionally) a most disastrous failure" (p. 48).

[5] Edith Wharton, *The Fruit of the Tree* (New York: Charles Scribner's Sons, 1907), p. 281.

that brings to mind the "invincible innocence" of her middle-aged mother, and suggests that May too will go through life sexually unaware and armed in innocence (125, 128).[6] To be sure, she is vigorous physically—she rides, rows, plays lawn tennis, wins archery competitions—but even this healthiness is deceptive, for the allusions Wharton surrounds May with are lifeless. She walks beside Archer and "her face wore the vacant serenity of a young marble athlete" (125); at another point her smile, we are told, is "Spartan" (237). Elsewhere and most pointedly, Wharton says, the "faculty of unawareness was what gave her eyes their transparency, and her face the look of representing a type rather than a person; as if she might have been chosen to pose for a Civic Virtue or a Greek goddess" (161).

The goddess Wharton associates with May is Diana, virgin deity of the hunt. Wearing a "white dress, with a pale green ribbon about the waist and a wreath of ivy on her hat," May wins her archery match with "Diana-like aloofness" (179). Later she enters a ballroom "tall and silver-shining as a young Diana" (245). Similarly, at the van der Luydens' reception for Ellen Olenska, "in her dress of white and silver, with a wreath of silver blossoms in her hair, the tall girl looked like a Diana just alight from the chase" (64). In May, Wharton takes selected virtues of the American girl: her innocence, her physical vigor, her cheerfulness and vivacity, her wholesomeness and self-confidence, and links them to a forever virginal goddess of death. Newland, with a shiver, wonders of May: "What if 'niceness' carried to that supreme degree were only a negation, the curtain dropped before an emptiness?" (180). May Welland *is* empty. She is, in addition, living at the pinnacle of American society, America's Dream Girl.

Wharton insists that innocent May is both ancient and artificial. In spite of her athletic freedom and bright modern cheeriness, she is as old as patriarchy itself. Newland is depressed as he tries to imagine a comradely marriage with the Wellands' daughter: "he perceived that such a picture presupposed, on her part, the experience, the versatility, the freedom of judgment, which she had been carefully trained not to possess" (46). He realizes further that, because "of this elaborate system of mystification" to which girls are subjected (which might well come from one of "the books on Primitive Man that people of advanced culture were beginning to read"), May has no depth: "she was frank, poor darling, because she had nothing to conceal, assured because she knew nothing to be on her guard against" (47). Yet Newland knows that "untrained human nature was not frank and innocent; it was full of the twists and

---

[6] All parenthetical references are to this New Riverside Edition.

defences of an instinctive guile. And he felt himself oppressed by this creation of factitious purity," which, ironically, has been manufactured solely for his pleasure (48).

In Wharton's version, the American girl is not spontaneous. She has been taught to be frank and self-assured as proof of her innocence (which is simply the ancient patriarchal value of virginity served up, or course, in nineteenth-century language). She is as manufactured an image of femininity as any other. She may look, in the guise of Isabel Archer or Daisy Miller, like a brand new independent creature; but take away James's infatuation with the American girl's illusion of freedom (and that is all Isabel or Daisy has, of course: the illusion of independence), and we have May Welland. The innocent American girl was a pernicious ideal, Wharton, looking back on the nineteenth century, felt compelled to say.

The issue here is larger, of course, than simply a difference of opinion between Edith Wharton and Henry James. Wharton was attacking an entire tradition when she entered May Welland in the lists of nineteenth-century American girls. Indeed, by the turn of the century, William Dean Howells, the most respected man of letters in America, was so convinced of the moral centrality of feminine virtue in fiction and life that he devoted two volumes to the study of women in nineteenth-century novels. His *Heroines of Fiction* (1901) argues, in his own words, "my prime position that the highest type of novelist is he who can most winningly impart the sense of womanhood."[7] That "sense of womanhood" most consistently admired by Howells in this book—as in his own fiction—always has the essential ingredients of the American girl. The preferred Howells heroine, who captures what *Heroines of Fiction* repeatedly calls the "Ever-Womanly," is fresh, intelligent, self-confident, and morally irradiating.

Subsequent criticism has followed Howells's lead. Paul John Eakin's *The New England Girl: Cultural Ideals in Hawthorne, Stowe, Howells, and James* (1976) maintains that in the nineteenth century, "woman functioned as an all-purpose symbol of the ideals of the culture: the official repository of its acknowledged moral code, and she appears accordingly as a redemptive figure in the era."[8] Eakin is building here, by his own admission, on William Wasserstrom's earlier study, *Heiress of All the Ages: Sex and Sentiment in the Genteel Tradition* (1959), which traces images

---

[7] William Dean Howells, *Heroines of Fiction,* 2 vols. (New York: Harper & Brothers, 1901), II:43.

[8] Paul John Eakin, *The New England Girl: Cultural Ideals in Hawthorne, Stowe, Howells, and James* (Athens: University of Georgia Press, 1976), p. 5. Although Eakin's announced focus is New England's version of the American girl, his inclusion of James's girls from New York State (Daisy, Isabel) indicates that the focus is not rigid.

of women in American novels from James through the twenties, looking in particular at the way the American girl is used symbolically, in fact messianically, to embody American idealism. As Eakin explains the premise he shares with Wasserstrom: "As the country moved toward more secular ways, a fiction arose which explicitly proposed its heroines as cult objects. . . . The value of these young women was measured by their power to redeem the individual, to regenerate society, through love."[9] Thus Wasserstrom, for example, concludes that Maggie Verver, the American girl of James's *The Golden Bowl* (1904), is the quintessential American heroine because she miraculously "combined the qualities of a nymph and a nun [and thus] finally reconciled all antitheses; she fulfilled the American dream of love, the dream of all the ages."[10]

It should not be surprising that Edith Wharton disliked *The Golden Bowl.*[11] In *The Age of Innocence,* she argues against the sentimentality of idealizing an "innocent" American woman; she argues against the masculine tradition celebrated by James and Howells and Wasserstrom and Eakin. In the first place, she knows that the price of innocence is diminished humanity for women. In the second place, she argues that the "natural" American girl May Welland (like Bessy Westmore before her) is in fact not natural at all; she is an artificial product, a manufactured symbol of patriarchal authority. Yet in their surveys of the subject, neither Eakin nor Wasserstrom takes Wharton's criticism into account. Eakin stops with James and does not discuss Edith Wharton. Wasserstrom cites Wharton's dislike for May[12] but fails to see that May is Maggie shown from a different angle than James's. The result, as has often occurred because of superficial (or non-) treatment of women writers, is perpetuation of a distorting thesis about American literature, in this case the idea that major nineteenth and early twentieth-century American novelists, except for Hawthorne, idealized a virginal American girl. In fact, Edith Wharton did not.

Ironically, it may be that the tradition Edith Wharton was more in sympathy with, whether she realized it or not, is the popular one described by Nina Baym in *Woman's Fiction: A Guide to Novels by and about Women in America, 1820–1870.* The novels Baym analyzes do not celebrate innocence or idealize ignorance. Nor do they abstract women into a cultural "value." Their objective is realism and the story they tell is pragmatic: how to create for oneself a healthy adult female identity. Typically

---

[9] Ibid., p. 6.
[10] William Wasserstrom, *Heiress of All the Ages: Sex and Sentiment in the Genteel Tradition* (Minneapolis: University of Minnesota Press, 1959), p. 98.
[11] See Lewis, *Edith Wharton,* p. 144.
[12] Wasserstrom, *Heiress of All the Ages,* p. 64.

these novels "chronicle the 'trials and triumph' (as the subtitle of one example reads) of a heroine who, beset with hardships, finds within herself the abilities of intelligence, will, resourcefulness, and courage sufficient to overcome them." [13] The goal of these women's novels, like Wharton's decades later, is to examine female experience in fact and in its full social context. The difference is that where earlier women customarily offered a happy resolution to the heroine's struggle to construct an identity that mediated between the extremes of perpetual passive dependence and total (and hence antisocial) independence, Wharton, writing from the vantage point of a world no longer nineteenth-century in its basic assumptions about the primacy of family and the home, repeatedly found no happy resolution to offer. Her heroines—Ellen Olenska is a good example—seek informed active adulthoods only to find that America insists on perpetual daughterhood, eternal innocence.

Wharton's disdain for innocence as a female ideal is passionately expressed in the characterization of Ellen Olenska. She is everything May is not. She is complicated, flawed, sensual, curious, and creative. In important ways, she reflects the artist Edith Wharton trying to make a place for herself in America and failing. . . .

As a rule, Edith Wharton avoided the subject of the woman writer. She was a proud and private person—she did not talk about her disastrous marriage to Edward Wharton; she kept her affair with Morton Fullerton so secret that not until her papers at Yale were opened in the late 1960s did biographers even know about it. She was similarly guarded about her feelings as an author. She did the ordinary things: sat for publicity photos, clipped reviews, fought with editors to get more money, wrote a memoir, *A Backward Glance* (1934), that is polite and uninformative. How she really *felt* about being a writer she expressed only very indirectly. If her first novel is remarkably direct—anger and anxiety are on the surface— it is the exception. After it, Wharton abandoned the woman writer as a character for long fiction. Perhaps she was afraid of revealing too many of her innermost feelings, perhaps she realized that writers writing about writers usually produce boring books. In any case, after *The Touchstone*, Edith Wharton continued to think about the woman artist in a few of her novels but the figure would not appear again as a writer. Sophy Viner in *The Reef* is an aspiring actress. Anne Clephane in *The Mother's Recompense* is a painter. And neither is an artist in the deepest sense. They are

---

[13] Nina Baym, *Woman's Fiction: A Guide to Novels by and about Women in America, 1820–1870* (Ithaca, N.Y.: Cornell University Press, 1978), p. 22.

young, gifted women whom Wharton wishes well but in whom she does not, as she had with Margaret Aubyn, invest herself. The only artist with whom she does that again, twenty years after she started writing novels, is Ellen Olenska.

Ellen is not an artist in any narrow, sheerly production-oriented sense of the word. She does not paint, sing, write, dance, or act—although as a child she did most of those things. Indeed, old New York vividly remembers her "gaudy clothes" and

> high colour and high spirits. She was a fearless and familiar little thing, who asked disconcerting questions, made precocious comments, and possessed outlandish arts, such as dancing a Spanish shawl dance and singing Neapolitan love-songs to a guitar. Under the direction of her aunt [Medora] . . . the little girl received an expensive but incoherent education, which included "drawing from the model," a thing never dreamed of before, and playing the piano in quintets with professional musicians. Of course no good could come of this. (60)

Small wonder that Ellen, who was as wild and gorgeous a child as Hawthorne's Pearl in *The Scarlet Letter,* shows up at the opera at the beginning of *The Age of Innocence* in, as Newland's grown sister describes it, a strange dress of "'dark blue velvet, perfectly plain and flat—like a nightgown.'" Newland's mother feigns shock at her daughter's reference to a bedroom and remarks, "'What can you expect of a girl who was allowed to wear black satin at her coming-out ball?'" (43). Ellen's opera costume offends because it is dramatic and sexy (one suspects the same was true of the earlier black satin). She sits engrossed in *Faust,* "revealing, as she leaned forward, a little more shoulder and bosom than New York was accustomed to seeing" (23–24).

As an artist Ellen's medium is life itself. She moves into her aunt's dilapidated house on unfashionable West Twenty-third Street and, without commotion or a lot of money, changes it into something original. Newland looks around him and

> what struck him was the way in which Medora Manson's shabby hired house, with its blighted background of pampas grass and Rogers statuettes, had, by a turn of the hand, and the skilful use of a few properties, been transformed into something intimate, "foreign," subtly suggestive of old romantic scenes and sentiments. He tried to analyse the trick, to find a clue to it in the way the chairs and tables were grouped, in the fact that only two Jacqueminot roses (of which nobody ever bought less than a dozen) had been placed in the slender vase at his elbow, and in the vague pervading perfume that was not what one put on handkerchiefs, but

rather like the scent of some far-off bazaar, a smell made up of Turkish coffee and ambergris and dried roses. (70)

Ellen Olenska, receiving Newland here in an erotic red-velvet gown (trimmed with black fur [97]), is exotic and passionate. Although she is not beautiful—she is thin and pale, on occasion haggard—she creates beauty around herself, automatically. She has the visual artist's instinct for interesting statement.

Ellen's life is also fertile intellectually. She prizes good conversation even more than the heirloom jewels and priceless antiques that she married into. Stimulating talk is for her (as it was for Wharton) a necessity of life, and she settles on West Twenty-third Street because she chooses to live among writers and actors. The odd move horrifies her relatives. They "had simply, as Mrs. Welland [May's mother] said, 'let poor Ellen find her own level'—and that, mortifyingly and incomprehensibly, was in the dim depths where . . . 'people who wrote' celebrated their untidy rites. It was incredible, but it was a fact, that Ellen, in spite of all her opportunities and her privileges, had become simply 'Bohemian'" (215). Unreclaimable in the opinion of conservative upper-class New York, the Countess Olenska is given a dinner—"the tribal rally around a kinswoman about to be eliminated from the tribe" (264)—and banished.

Her banishment, in keeping with old New York's impeccable good manners, is smooth and subtle. It even looks as if Ellen could stay in America and be happy if she wished. The family has tried to force her exit by forbidding divorce and then cutting her allowance severely—giving her no alternative but to return to her husband. Then at the last moment her grandmother, ignoring family pressure, offers Ellen a home with her. This may look appealing, but in fact, it is a sorry substitute for the freedom Ellen craved. She came to America to get a divorce, to live as an independent woman. The best she can achieve, however, is life as her grandmother's companion/dependent (with Newland propositioning her on the side). The only choice she has, in other words, is such a compromise that Wharton's point seems clear: there is no independent life available to this woman in America. The best she can do is grown-up little girlhood. Not surprisingly, Ellen turns down her grandmother's offer, and the original plan succeeds (with the help of a well-placed lie by May: she claims to be pregnant before she is positive in order to thoroughly close Ellen out of Newland's life). Forbidden a divorce and cut off from financial independence as long as she stays in the United States, Ellen is put in the position of having no good alternative but to leave. She is effectively—though politely, of course—gotten rid of.

With Ellen's exit Edith Wharton, living in France, repudiated the America of her youth and said important things about herself as an artist. Most obviously, Ellen's elimination exposes old New York as a barbaric and paranoid culture. Far from the model of genteel security that Wharton and others must have considered it during the nineteenth century, the New York of her girlhood is a frightened, primitive place in *The Age of Innocence*. And what is feared is Ellen Olenska. The woman of intellect and artistic disposition is such a threat that she must be expelled. Equally significant is the fact that Ellen is not alone. Behind her stands eccentric Aunt Medora, who raised her; behind Medora is her formidable grandmother, old Catherine Mingott. Medora is tolerated only because she lives on the fringe of society and is not as smart or creative as Ellen—also, she is no longer a sexual threat; Catherine is accepted because she has been assimilated through marriage (she has literally been incapacitated, being so fat that she can barely move without assistance). What is crucial is that these women—Catherine, Medora, Ellen (later Fanny Beaufort is added)—suggest a line of female unconventionality and vitality which has not been totally eradicated by the cultural preference for May Wellands, and one so powerful that, when irrepressible by co-option or ridicule (the methods used to keep Catherine and Medora within bounds), it requires the extreme remedy of exile. In this respect, the "matriarchal" line that Catherine Mingott heads is no sham. There is an implication of awesome female energy and creativity that, given a chance, could explode old New York. Wharton agrees with the established order on this: Ellen Olenska, and by association Wharton herself, *is* a threat.

Biographically, the identification between Wharton and Ellen Olenska is unmistakable. Both are women and passionate. Both are alienated from their old New York roots. Both value original, inquisitive conversation above all other sorts of social intercourse and need to create around themselves physical environments that are beautiful and interesting. Both are sexually experienced women who have had love affairs in Europe with slightly younger men while still married to men totally unsuited to them (this we know of Wharton and suspect of Ellen). Both seek divorces. Both—unlike their relatives—prize the life of artistic and intellectual achievement above all other lives. Both end up leaving America (in each case for Paris). The parallels are so strong that one must believe that Wharton spoke to one degree or another of her own situation, emotionally, when she wrote of Ellen's exile. At the very least, *The Age of Innocence,* published in 1920, says that in Wharton's opinion upper-class America had long ago made it impossible for the woman of sexual, intellectual, and artistic energy—that is, the woman such as Wharton herself—to live at home. . . .

BECOMING THE MASK
Edith Wharton's Ingenues

Judith P. Saunders

In Edith Wharton's presentation of ingenue heroines—upper-class, marriageable girls—she explores a clash between collective, cultural expectations and individual human needs. To what extent, she asks, is human nature susceptible to cultural alteration? For in attempting to mold its young women into proper ingenues—guileless and naive—the late nineteenth- and early twentieth-century society of Wharton's fiction undertakes a radical reshaping of its raw human material. Acting on the assumption that guile depends upon knowledge, this particular society enforces ignorance in its young girls, severely limiting their freedom and experience. Wharton investigates the effects of such limitations upon developing adults, discovering that the requirements of the ingenue role continue to affect women throughout their lives. The pernicious disparity between the real nature of young girls and their supposed nature as ingenues introduces an element of falsity into women's lives which they find difficult to escape thereafter.

In *The Age of Innocence* (1920) Wharton offers a clear and straightforward analysis of the ingenue and her situation. As its title indicates, the novel examines the concept of "innocence" which cultural forces have decreed to be the preponderant fact defining an unmarried young woman. She is perceived more as an embodiment of abstractions [whiteness, radiance, goodness] than as a highly individuated personality: "a type rather than a person" (161).[1] More important than any positive attributes she may possess are the qualities she is expected to be without. Her uniqueness resides in a lack, an absence, an incompleteness: her innocence consists of a systematic negation of certain aspects of her humanness. She is carefully denied access to knowledge and experience which might in any way be connected with sexuality, and thus she is excluded during her developmental years from a large and significant area of human life. Because so much of history and literature—as well as of everyday life—is concerned with the complexities and the consequences of human passion, the ingenue apparently grows up with an extremely narrow, artificially restricted view of the world. Her socially-imposed ignorance about personal and social inter-relationships is accompanied by a perhaps more appalling ignorance

Massachusetts Studies in English 8.4 (1982).

[1] All parenthetical references are to this New Riverside Edition.

about the cultural tradition to which she nominally belongs. Watching a seduction scene in an operatic version of Goethe's *Faust* with his fiancee, Newland Archer points out that the girl "doesn't even guess what it's all about." She is entirely unfamiliar with much of the greatest poetry, fiction, and drama ever written, "masterpieces of literature which it would be his [Archer's] manly privilege to reveal to his bride" (17).

The negations which define the ingenue are expected, in theory at least, to reverse themselves at the time of her marriage. Her husband "exercise[s] his lordly pleasure in smashing [her purity]," and with the help of his "enlightening companionship" the new bride is supposed to begin to think and feel in hitherto forbidden ways (48, 17). The trouble with such a dichotomized "before" and "after" is that it demands an impossible transition. Archer admits to himself that "the young girl who knew nothing," with "no past to conceal," cannot transform herself suddenly into a woman with "the experience, the versatility, the freedom of judgment, which she had been carefully trained not to possess" (46). Drawing on horrifying and compelling imagery, Archer acknowledges the possibility that the restrictive unawareness in which his bride has grown up may permanently warp her mind and spirit:

> It would presently be his task to take the bandage from this young woman's eyes, and bid her look forth on the world. But how many generations of the women who had gone to her making had descended bandaged to the family vault? He shivered a little, remembering some of the new ideas in his scientific books, and the much-cited instance of the Kentucky cave-fish, which had ceased to develop eyes because they had no use for them. What if, when he had bidden May Welland to open hers, they could only look out blankly at blankness? (79)

In this passage Wharton argues through her protagonist that the negative effects of the ingenue's education cannot be entirely undone: "innocence" here is the mental and spiritual equivalent of a bandage over the eyes. Powers neglected and stifled for eighteen years will necessarily be susceptible to atrophy. And indeed, many of the older New York matrons in the novel exhibit a narrow-minded, inappropriately childish response to their world which gives credence to Archer's fears about his fiancee. He observes in May Welland's own mother a "middle-aged image of invincible innocence," an "innocence that seals the mind against imagination and the heart against experience" (128).

Such constriction of character is, Wharton emphasizes, cultural rather than natural. In fact, we begin finally to realize that there is something intrinsically unreal and unconvincing about this notion of female innocence. Archer reasons that since "untrained human nature was not frank and innocent" but, rather, full of "instinctive guile," the ingenue's naivete must result from a "factitious purity, so cunningly manufactured by a conspiracy of mothers and aunts and grandmothers and long-dead ancestresses." Wharton's analysis of the ingenue's predicament is thus complicated by this recognition that the girl herself, together with all her female advisors, actually participates in the creation of the "artificial product" which she is (48). In refusing to present women as victims merely— blinded and crippled by their culture—Wharton gives her subject an extra dimension, documenting entrapment from within as well as from without. Events in the novel persistently indicate discrepancies between the woman and her role. Archer's sister Janey, for instance, is doomed as an unmarried woman to a lifetime of presumed innocence, since marriage is the only culturally legitimate way for a girl to make the transition into full adulthood.[2] Throughout her whole life, Janey must maintain a pose of unawareness concerning sexual matters, and endure the concommitant social humiliation. Wharton carefully points out that Janey is not in reality as ignorant as she must pretend to be; her status as aged ingenue is a kind of social fiction, preserved for decorum's sake. Her mother must refuse to allow certain forbidden subjects to be mentioned in her middle-aged daughter's hearing, but in private she drops the pretense of Janey's naivete: "She and Janey knew every fold of the Beaufort mystery, but in public Mrs. Archer continued to assume that the subject was not one for the unmarried" (40–41).

Archer's fiancee, May Welland, who appears to embody every characteristic of the ideal ingenue, provides still more dramatic evidence that the innocence required in young women is a mask more than a reality. Archer first begins to suspect the existence of a more sophisticated and worldly-wise side to May's character when she offers to release him from his engagement, revealing her knowledge of his prior involvement with an older, married woman: "'You mustn't think that a girl knows as little as her parents imagine,' she tells him; 'one hears and one notices—one has one's feelings and ideas'" (130). A girl's "blindness," then, in part represents an acquiescence to cultural expectations. Conformity to such expectations, as Wharton demonstrates in depicting this incident, impoverishes other lives besides those of the women themselves. Archer is "disappointed at the vanishing of the new being" he has just glimpsed within May, dis-

---

[2] To May Welland "the culminating 'lark' of the whole delightful adventure of engagement and marriage was to be off with him [her husband] alone on a journey, like a grown-up person, like a 'married woman,' in fact" (161); certainly this passage equates marriage with adulthood.

appointed when she sinks back into "helpless and timorous girlhood" (132, 131). He recognizes that with this "new being"—a girl not playing the prescribed role—he might have enjoyed a more profound and more adult attachment.

The hidden, less innocent side of May's character emerges again, in a more sinister fashion, at the climax of the novel's action when she successfully rids herself of her rival, Ellen Olenska. Not at all unaware of her husband's feelings for this woman, she maintains the façade of naivete while quietly arranging matters to suit her own ends. Archer is stunned when he realizes that his "pure" young bride not only guesses his feelings for Ellen but falsely assumes the two of them are "lovers, lovers in the extreme sense" (264). May fails to behave with the frankness which would be appropriate if her character were completely defined by the innocence in which she was reared. Instead she goes to Ellen Olenska behind her husband's back and announces, prematurely, that she is pregnant, invoking the idea of family to induce Ellen voluntarily to give up her affair with Archer. This successful and sophisticated maneuver proves to Archer and to the reader that May possesses more awareness and more "instinctive guile" than her everyday behavior has been trained to express. Two weeks after she has lied to Ellen about her condition, May finds herself pregnant in actual fact; with Ellen safely packed off to Europe, she acknowledges to her husband what she has done: " 'No; I wasn't sure then—but I told her I was. And you see I was right!' she exclaimed, her blue eyes wet with victory" (270).

May's shrewd lie and successful machinations pose significant questions: is women's "innocence" entirely feigned? Is it no more than a collective fiction, an elaborate pretense, like so much else in the New York world Wharton portrays? If so, how can she argue that women are permanently damaged, "blinded" like the Kentucky cave-fish, by something which is not even real? Wharton's point appears to be double-edged. The women in her fiction collaborate with their culture in manufacturing their own limitations. And the pernicious effects of those limitations are real, even though the idea they are based on—i.e., innocence—is not. A pretense long maintained finally assumes some of the force of fact. Role and reality blur and contaminate one another, as the women in Wharton's fiction shift uneasily between the two. . . .

The ingenue's innocence epitomizes both the artificiality and the power of cultural concepts, for without being at all valid as a statement about female human nature, the idea of innocence dominates women's lives, both before marriage and after. The young girl is trained to divorce herself from her own "underground" realities and so learns to live in special roles which regulate her behavior, her feelings, and her thoughts, but

fail to allow full expression of her inner self. Beginning by denying a girl's
right to sexual knowledge and experimentation, the culture portrayed in
Wharton's novels condemns women to live in a strange limbo, trapped between social fiction and human facts.

ANGEL OF DEVASTATION
Edith Wharton on the Arts
of the Enslaved

Sandra M. Gilbert and Susan Gubar

. . . Logically enough . . . the only woman in [*The Age of Innocence*]
who seems to have learned arts that are not the arts of the enslaved is, in
effect, a foreign lady: the Europeanized Ellen Olenska, once Ellen Mingott
of "old New York" but, by the time Newland Archer encounters her, a
woman of the world who is neither a fatal belle dame sans merci nor a
commodified objet d'art. But of course it is Ellen Olenska who must inevitably be exorcised from "good" New York society by what Veblen would
see as the necessary conservatism of its moral and economic laws.[1] Consistently referred to as "poor Ellen Olenska" from the first moment of her
return to her childhood home, she seems at first to prove that her compatriots are right to shudder at Europe's wicked ways. Her marriage to a
Polish count was an unhappy one—after her nuptials, Wharton comments
dryly, she disappeared "in a kind of sulphurous apotheosis"(61)[2]—and,
legally at least, she appears to be hopelessly doomed to a marital *"noyade"*
far more sinister than Newland Archer's could ever be.

Yet Ellen, and only Ellen in Wharton's major urban novels of manners,
can stand apart from the customs of her country and appraise them objectively. Neither destructive nor destroyed, she forces Archer to scrutinize
"his native city objectively" and, "viewed thus, as through the wrong end

From *No Man's Land: The Place of the Woman Writer in the Twentieth Century*. Vol. 2. New Haven, Yale UP, 1989.

[1] See Thorstein Veblen, *The Theory of the Leisure Class* (1899; New York: Modern Library, 1931): "The outcome of the [requirements of pecuniary reputability] is a strength-
ening of the general conservative attitude of the community" (205).
[2] All parenthetical references are to this New Riverside Edition.

of a telescope, it looked disconcertingly small and distant; but then from Samarkand it would" (74). Given both her moral clarity and her social alienation, therefore, Ellen represents—to use the anthropological rhetoric that permeates *The Age of Innocence*—that autonomy which is taboo, that objectivity which the tribe must ritually expel.[3] In a sense, like the women of France, her adopted country, she has become from Wharton's point of view a *"grown up"* who can no longer find a home in the happy valley of a childishly mercantile leisure class. For her individual adventure, then, no less than for Lily Bart's, [in *The House of Mirth*], there is no place in America's established order of things. . . .

Perhaps the most notable case in point is the extraordinary epiphany that concludes *The Age of Innocence*. After she has gone to live in France, outside the customs of her own country, Ellen Olenska seems to represent for author and characters alike an illicit, indeed taboo, force that has been in effect exorcised from the decorous society of "old New York."[4] But like Wharton herself—and unlike the variously imprisoned heroines of the two James novels (*The American* and *Portrait of a Lady*) that Wharton here revises—Ellen lives insouciantly on, in a glamorous expatriation. Claire de Cintré, the beloved of *The American*'s Christopher Newman, is theatrically immured in a convent, while Isabel Archer, in *Portrait of a Lady,* is locked in "the house of darkness, the house of dumbness, the house of suffocation" that is her marriage.[5] Ellen, however, escaping both virginal confinement and marital *couverture,* has become the mistress, rather than the victim, of "French ways and their meaning."

Along with Newland Archer, we discover this in the novel's poignant coda, when, more than a quarter century after their parting, Archer stands below Ellen's window in exactly the Paris *quartier*—perhaps, in fact, the very street[6]—where Wharton herself lived for many years,

[3] On the anthropological rhetoric of *The Age of Innocence,* see, among others, Elizabeth Ammons, *Edith Wharton's Argument with America* (Athens: University of Georgia Press, 1980), and Judith Fryer, *Felicitous Space: The Imaginative Structures of Edith Wharton and Willa Cather* (Chapel Hill and London: University of North Carolina Press, 1986), pp. 130–42, esp. Fryer's point that Ellen Olenska "is what anthropologist Mary Douglas would call a 'polluting person,' who is always in the wrong. She has 'simply crossed some line which should not have been crossed and this displacement unleashes danger for someone'" (pp. 138–39).

[4] On the "exorcism" of Ellen Olenska, see Ammons, pp. 143–45, and Fryer, pp. 138–39.

[5] Henry James, *The Portrait of a Lady,* ed. Leon Edel (Boston: Riverside, 1963), p. 353.

[6] See Fryer, p. 127. In addition, R. W. B. Lewis, in *Edith Wharton: A Biography* (New York: Harper & Row, 1975), notes that Archer finds himself below Ellen's window in

and mediates on the complex and, to him, alien existence that she has
had there:

> her life—of which he knew so strangely little—had been spent in this
> rich atmosphere that he already felt to be too dense and yet too stim-
> ulating for his lungs. . . . More than half a lifetime divided them, and she
> had spent the long interval among people he did not know, in a society
> he but faintly guessed at, in conditions he would never wholly under-
> stand. During that time he had been living with his youthful memory
> of her; but she had doubtless had other and more tangible companion-
> ship. (283)

In granting Archer an intuition of the *difference* that Ellen has experienced, Wharton also forces him to recognize that he himself has been
only an episode in the intricate narrative of this cosmopolitan exile's life,
a one time lover replaced by "other . . . more tangible" (and, in his society's terms, illicit) companionship. Thus, because he is at best no more
than "a relic in a small dim chapel, where there was not time to pray every
day" (283), Archer can neither understand nor analyze the larger architecture that dwarfs him.

At the same time, the novelist herself cannot (or will not) describe that
architecture, will not narrate Ellen's life, will not stipulate the details of its
radiant difference. With Newland Archer, she imagines but does not enter
the foreign room inhabited by "a dark lady, pale and dark, who would
look up quickly, half rise, and hold out a long thin hand with three rings
on it" (285): a dark lady who incarnates just the metamorphoses that
this writer herself underwent in her passage from a provincial origin as
"Pussy/Lily" Jones, New York debutante, to a brilliant career as Edith
Wharton, expatriate novelist. Like her hero, Wharton has no language for
such changes, even though they are, in her case, the transformations that
made her into Henry James's angel of devastation. " 'It's more real to me
here than if I went up,' " she has Newland say—and for the experienced
author of *The Age of Innocence,* too, the changes of rules and roles im-
plicitly demanded by her murderous assaults on the economy of sexuality
and the arts of the enslaved were evidently "more real" if they remained
unsaid, unsayable.

1907, just "the moment when Edith first settled in Paris," and that he "reminds himself . . .
that he is only fifty-seven years old—Edith Wharton's exact age in 1919 when she wrote
the larger part of the novel" (432).

THE AGE OF INNOCENCE
AND THE BOHEMIAN PERIL

Katherine Joslin

. . . Newland Archer . . . is attracted to two distinct and incompatible women. May Welland embodies the character of established Old New York, a safe, rigid, even icy and gravelike society. Ellen Olenska represents an outlying region, an eccentric, Bohemian culture that emanates fire and animates life. The two women function as Archer's muses, evoking conflicting responses. Over the course of the novel, the hero is forced by his passion for both women to consider risky questions about the social position of women. *The Age of Innocence* is a novel about womanhood because the plot turns on the Woman Question puzzled out by a male protagonist. . . .

The hero has been accustomed to the attraction of womanly beauty and sexuality, but nowhere in his training had he encountered female intellect, imagination, independence and aesthetic sensibility, the very traits that titillate him. When we first see Ellen Olenska at the opera, she wears an elaborate costume, the "Josephine look" including a headdress of diamonds and brown curls "carried out in the cut of the dark blue velvet gown rather theatrically caught up under her bosom by a girdle with a large old-fashioned clasp" (19),[1] a cut "revealing, as she leaned forward, a little more shoulder and bosom than New York was accustomed to seeing" (22–23).

Initially attracted, as the other men are, to Ellen's exposed bosom, Newland quickly cools to her physical self, "conscious of a curious indifference to her bodily presence" (203). He even mistakes a "blonde and blowsy" Blenker girl for her in a curious scene where he makes love to the wrong parasol. Later he forgets her voice, "that it was low-pitched, with a faint roughness on the consonants" (195). When they do meet, he explains that he continually experiences her anew: "*Each time you happen to me all over again*" (232). When she flings her arms about him and presses her lips to his, he pulls away. Physical passion, the feeling he has been trained to have for a woman, is not the source of his attraction: "A stolen kiss isn't what I want"(234), he tells her. When he last sees her at the dinner party, a ritual marking her ouster from New York, Newland finds her face

<hr>

From *Edith Wharton*. New York: St. Martin's, 1991.

[1] All parenthetical references are to this New Riverside Edition.

"lustreless and almost ugly" (263) and, at the same time, loves it more than ever.

At the heart of his dilemma, although he doesn't know it, is the Woman Question. If a woman does not follow convention and her abilities and talents develop more in line with men, who *is* she? As Vernon Lee put it in her review of [Charlotte Perkins] Gilman's *Women and Economics:* "We do not know what women *are.*" If passion and sensuality do not draw the male suitor, what does? Newland Archer, for all his philosophizing about the essential equality of men and women, had never before Ellen Olenska considered the concrete possibilities of his abstractions. In the fiery reality of her presence, not the physical but the intellectual dimensions of her being, Newland must reconsider all he has been taught about women.

His vanity is served a socially correct version of maidenhood in the "young girl in white," May Welland, with a name that more than suggests youthful health and wholesomeness.[2] As Christine Nilsson sings the Daisy Song in the opera *Faust,* May sits "slightly withdrawn," in pink modesty with her hair in "fair braids" and her youthful breasts fastened modestly in a "tulle tucker" (16). Archer has had his sexual initiation in a lengthy and mildly agitating affair with Mrs Thorley Rushworth; their liaison had been "a smiling, bantering, humouring, watchful and incessant lie" (244) that, as the double standard mandates, left her tainted and him experienced. Watching his fiancée at the opera, he is excited by her purity and proud of her innocence as his possession:

> "The darling!" thought Newland Archer, his glance flitting back to the young girl with the lilies-of-the-valley. "She doesn't even guess what it's all about." And he contemplated her absorbed young face with a thrill of possessorship in which pride in his own masculine initiation was mingled with a tender reverence for her abysmal purity. "We'll read Faust to-

---

[2] Critics have always pointed out the opposing qualities of the two heroines, the "light" and "dark" women of poetry and prose. From Cynthia Griffin Wolff's initial discussion of the importance of Wharton's early story "The Valley of Childish Things" in *A Feast of Words: The Triumph of Edith Wharton* (New York: Oxford University Press, 1977), pp. 82–84, later critics have read *The Age of Innocence* as a retelling of that tale, where the male prefers the innocent female to the experienced one. See Elizabeth Ammons, *Edith Wharton's Argument with America* (Athens: University of Georgia Press, 1980), pp. 131–43; and Carol Wershoven, *The Female Intruder in the Novels of Edith Wharton* (London: Associated University Press, 1982), pp. 75–93. Judith Fryer, *Felicitous Space* (Chapel Hill: University of North Carolina Press, 1986), p. 133, also considers this reading but concludes that there is no real choice for Newland Archer because he is trapped by the "sophisticated shrewdness" of the female culture that produced the supposedly "innocent" May Welland.

gether ... by the Italian lakes ... " he thought, somewhat hazily confusing the scene of his projected honey-moon with the masterpieces of literature which it would be his manly privilege to reveal to his bride. (17)

His smug male vanity over his supposedly superior social and intellectual
position will not go unpunished in the novel.

In the first pages, Wharton's narrator explains to the reader Newland's ambivalence. His vanity desires two conflicting attributes in his future wife: the innocence of the ingenuous and sexually naïve May Welland
and the experience of the "worldly-wise" and sexually accommodating
Mrs Thorley Rushworth. "How this miracle of fire and ice was to be created, and to sustain itself in a harsh world, he had never taken the time to
think out"(18), the narrator explains, using the dominant and conflicting
imagery of the novel. "Some say the world will end in fire," Robert Frost
put it, "Some say ice." Newland finds in May Welland that fire and ice in
such close proximity lose their power. After marrying and living with his
Diana-like May, Newland begins to feel the results: "He was weary of living in a perpetual tepid honeymoon, without the temperature of passion
yet with all its exactions" (237). The lesson the hero learns in the novel is
that what he thought was manly experience turns out in the end to have
been boyish innocence.

As the liberal intellectual he fancies himself to be, our hero is a portrait of an "armchair" feminist. He begins to contemplate radical ideas of
sexual equality during the homosocial male rite of smoking cigars after
dinner in the library. He argues with the gossiping, priggish Sillerton Jackson over Ellen Olenska's indiscretion with M. Rivière; she has apparently
lived with him for a year. Aggravated already by the impression Ellen has
made on him, Newland defends her right to live with whomever she
chooses: "I'm sick of the hypocrisy that would bury alive a woman at her
age if her husband prefers to live with harlots" (45). He seems not to understand his own hypocrisy: if women should be free to have sexual affairs
when they choose, why does he refer to the other women as "harlots"?
Why, we might also ask, the qualifier "at her age"? Or why should she be
free only if her husband fails to be monogamous? Archer, however, skims
the surface. His jealousy, spurred on by his cigar, leads him further along
the road to sexual equality than he had ever before wandered. 'Women
ought to be free—as free as we are,' he declared, making a discovery of
which he was too irritated to measure the terrific consequences" (45).

Later alone in his own library, comfortably seated in his familiar armchair, Newland ponders the inconsistencies between his egalitarian philosophy and the reality of his upcoming marriage to May Welland. Should
she also be free to find another male if he should follow Count Olenski's

example? Smugly certain, early in the novel, that adultery would never be his game, he pursues the imbalance between genders that has the potential of ruining his marriage. It all hinges on the double standard, the socially expected innocence of women and experience of men. May Welland, in his new analysis, becomes the "terrifying product" of his social code, "the young girl who knew nothing and expected everything."

But what about the question of compatibility? If he has had a "past" that he could not have had with her or even tell her about and if she, by the same code, had "no past" to tell, then how could they become truly intimate? It's a good question. Many of their past experiences would have to remain unuttered, his were indeed unutterable; they would live "in a kind of hieroglyphic world, where the real thing was never said or done or even thought" (46–47). But when he thought of his ideal marriage, he posited his mate as his equal partner in experience, intellect and judgment, an ideal his own social code forbids. The traits he desires are exactly those that have atrophied in the female to ready her as a respectable marital commodity. In his musings, much of the conflict comes clear to Newland:

> He perceived that such a picture [of passionate and tender comradeship] presupposed, on her part, the experience, the versatility, the freedom of judgment, which she had been carefully trained not to possess; and with a shiver of foreboding he saw his marriage becoming what most of the other marriages about him were: a dull association of material and social interests held together by ignorance on the one side and hypocrisy on the other. (46)

From his armchair he is able to pursue a feminist analysis that he never manages to use to shape his life. . . .

EDITH WHARTON
The Archeological Motive

James W. Tuttleton

In "Tradition and the Individual Talent," T. S. Eliot observed that the word "tradition" seldom appears except in a phrase of censure: "If otherwise, it is vaguely approbative, with the implication, as to the work approved, of some pleasing archeological reconstruction. You can hardly

Yale Review 61.4 (1972).

make the word agreeable to English ears without this comfortable reference to the reassuring science of archeology." Eliot's reference to the science of archeology is pleasantly facetious, but to anyone familiar with his thought it does not in any way obscure his profound respect for the significance of tradition—in art, religion, politics, and society. I wish to invoke this "censurable" term *tradition,* in relation to the science of archeology, as a means of exploring the fiction of Edith Wharton. Paradoxically, it provides one of the most meaningful approaches to her mind and art.

Edith Wharton conceived of the Western cultural tradition as a complex interrelation of legal, political, economic, and social structures, of art, morals, and religion. She thought of it as organic rather than as atomic and as fundamentally dynamic, in the evolutionary sense, rather than as static. She grew up with the first generation of American writers to experience the impact of evolutionary thought, and for her—as for many of her contemporaries—the figure of Darwin loomed large. In her autobiography, *A Backward Glance* (1934), she identified Darwin as one of her intellectual "Awakeners." She also spoke of her excitement at reading the physicist John Tyndall; the biologists T. H. Huxley, Alfred Russel Wallace, George John Romanes, and Ernst Haeckel; the evolutionary social philosopher Herbert Spencer; the Finnish sociologist Edvard Westermarck; and the archeologist Heinrich Schliemann. It is not my purpose to document the specific influence of these scientists on Edith Wharton—although she was a scientific horticulturalist herself, composed technical treatises on the development of landscape gardening styles in Italy, wrote a number of broadly sociological works, and went on numerous archeological expeditions in the Mediterranean area. Rather it is my intention to suggest that the notion of evolutionary development, advanced or implied in the work of these scientists, profoundly influenced Mrs. Wharton's general conception of individual human identity and of the cultural tradition which shapes it, deepened her sense of the meaning of the past for the present, and profoundly affected some of the thematic and technical choices she made in her own fiction.

In approaching her conception of what human identity is—in terms of how she believed character could be represented in fiction—it is instructive to recall her response to the familiar argument between Howells and Henry James as to the condition of American society as a field for fiction. James complained that the American novelist lacked those social forms and institutions available in Europe which help the European novelist to characterize his people and their manners—no State, barely a specific national name, no sovereign, no court, no aristocracy, no church, no clergy, no army, no diplomatic service, no country gentlemen, no palaces, parsonages, thatched cottages, ivied ruins, cathedrals, universities, no public schools, political society, no sporting class, no Epsom, no Ascot!

All of these phenomena, he argued, help the novelist to locate and materialize his people, to recreate exterior reality. The American novelist—Hawthorne is James's prime example—lacking a social field, is driven inward, forced to focus on the complexities of human psychology and to express his interior reality through the mode of romance. Howells reviewed James's biography of Hawthorne in 1880 and attacked James's view of the deficiencies of American society. Dispose of all of these social institutions, he argued, and the novelist still has the whole of human nature as his subject.

In this controversy Edith Wharton sided with Henry James and rebuked Van Wyck Brooks for taking the position Howells had espoused. For her, human nature consisted precisely *in* those forms and institutions which surround, enclose, and structure human life. Desmond Morris, the anthropologist, has reminded us that, for all our cultural overlay, man is basically a human animal, a "naked ape." Mrs. Wharton, as a student of Darwin, would have agreed. But despite the primacy of our biological existence, human life for her was principally a social phenomenon and it was life as a social phenomenon that mattered for the writer. In an essay entitled "The Great American Novel" (*The Yale Review*, Summer 1927), Mrs. Wharton asked what human nature does consist in if it is denuded of "the web of custom, manners, culture it has elaborately spun about itself." Her point was that very little of distinctively human nature can exist independent of society and its forms. If you strip away the web of custom and manners, she argued, the only thing left is "that hollow unreality, 'Man,' an evocation of the eighteenth-century demagogues who were the first inventors of 'standardization.'" She went on to assert that "human nature" and "man" are mere intellectual abstractions, whereas real men are bound up with the effects of climate, soil, laws, religion, wealth, and leisure.

In her best, most representative works, Mrs. Wharton continually returned to the idea of tradition and the need of viable modes of cultural transmission as important factors affecting the character of man's social history. She continually argued the necessity of the individual's commitment to the cultural tradition; the danger of alienation from it; the catastrophe which ensues when social upheavals like revolution, anarchy, and war destroy the slowly and delicately spun web of that tradition; and the necessity of imaginatively preserving—if necessary even reconstructing—the precious values of the past. Her artistic treatment of the theme of tradition usually involved two methods. The first was to dramatize the importance for men of the web of culture, manners, and mores which enclose them and to warn of the disaster in store for those who become culturally deracinated or alienated and for those who destroy the delicate web in a radical obsession to reform it. And the other method, evident in the final years of her life, was an impulse to reconstruct—archeologically, as it were—the social world of her youth: the traditions which vitalized the culture of Old New York in the period from about 1840 to 1880. She hoped to revive the memory of a set of slowly evolved cultural values suddenly wiped out by a succession of destructive changes in American life beginning in the 1880s—including the rise of the industrial plutocracy ("the lords of Pittsburgh," as she called them); massive immigration which totally altered the ethnic character of New York City; the First World War, the depression, and the New Deal; and the nationalistic hatreds, at the close of her life in 1937, building toward the Second World War. . . .

As she witnessed the Jazz Age spectacle after the war, Edith Wharton was moved to try to recover and imaginatively project some of the values expressed in the social and moral traditions of her youth in the 1870s. If the first method of her two approaches to the theme of tradition in her fiction was to portray (in the fate of Prince Odo's Pianura [*The Valley of Decision*, 1902], in Lily Bart [*The House of Mirth*, 1905], in Vance Weston [*Hudson River Bracketed*, 1929, and *The Gods Arrive*, 1932]) the ominous consequences of cultural deracination, the second was to provide the positive example of what a continuous social tradition could do for the lives of people who were fortunate enough to experience it. But none was conspicuous in the aftermath of the First World War and to give the positive example she had to turn to the past, to produce the archeological reconstruction. *The Age of Innocence* (1920) and *Old New York* (1924) were in large part an attempt to recapture from forgetfulness a social world swept away by the acceleration of historical forces which only Henry Adams, of her generation, had adequately foreseen. In these works she wished to show that Old New York in the age of innocence provided a certain kind of social norm for the modern world. There is no question, from her portrait of it, that Old New York was an imperfectly developed culture; indeed, it was marked by sexual hypocrisy, intellectual narrowness, civic irresponsibility, and class snobbery at its worst. But at its best it preserved the values of private dignity and personal decorum; a sensitivity to feeling and emotion, however bound in expression by conventional restraints; an appreciation for pictorial beauty and a feeling for the grandeur and sublimity of the English language; an unshakable belief in the civilizing power of education; a flair for the high (but modest) social style; and a commitment to the obligations of honor in public life—all of these qualities seemingly inconceivable in the age of flappers, jazz babies, flagpole sitters, and bathtub gin. At the end of *The Age of Innocence*, Newland Archer marvels at the greater openness and spontaneity, at the greater freedom in manners possible in turn-of-the-century New York society. But he also reaffirms the

goodness of the old established social and moral traditions of the 1870s
which have already begun to disappear in New York. Mrs. Wharton characterized the quaintness of Old New York moral standards in the age of
innocence by an expert use of the symbolic setting: Archer's last interview
with Ellen Olenska takes place in the Metropolitan Museum of Art. His
struggle with his conscience—over whether or not to leave his wife—takes
place in the room exhibiting the moldering Cesnola antiquities. As Archer
and Ellen explore this moral dilemma in the presence of the glass cabinets displaying "the recovered fragments of Ilium" and the "small broken
objects—hardly recognizable utensils, ornaments and personal trifles"
(247–48), it grows upon the reader that the scruples of conscience which
marked the 1870s are as meaningless to the generation of the 1920s as the
archeological antiquities Archer stares at—so rapidly and totally have the
foundations of moral life changed in the modern age.

Archer remains with his wife May, and Ellen returns to Paris alone.
The novel affirms Archer's decision—although Mrs. Wharton frankly
acknowledges that in giving up romantic love Newland Archer missed
"the flower of life." His decision to stay is affirmed because it constitutes a recognition that a man has institutional, familial, and social
responsibilities which cannot be abandoned simply for the gratification of
romantic passion. . . .

"HUNTING FOR THE REAL"
Wharton and the Science of Manners

Nancy Bentley

Edith Wharton was present at the famous 1913 debut of Stravinsky's
Le Sacre du Printemps when the Parisian ballet patrons erupted in protest
at the work's cacophonous sounds and sacrificial themes. She therefore
witnessed two ongoing dramas of early modernism: the absorption of
primitivism into the high arts, and the outrage it could provoke among the
arts establishment. It is not surprising that the cosmopolitan Wharton, by
this time a famous expatriate, was on hand for one of the signal events of
European art history. But her reputation as a cultural conservative dis-

From *The Cambridge Companion to Edith Wharton*. New York: Cambridge
UP, 1995.

trustful of avant-garde experimentation offers little to account for her deep admiration of the ballet: her notebook records that she found it "extraordinary."[1] The gap between reputation and reality here is provocative, for it hints at the complexity of Wharton's relation to her cultural context— and to the changing concept of culture itself, the subject at the heart of her fiction.

Of particular interest is the historical turn to primitivism reflected in both Stravinsky's score and Nijinsky's choreography, for this contemporary trend can also provide an illumination of Wharton's own art. Her intellectual interest in the subject of tribal or "primitive" culture is well known; R. W. B. Lewis writes that she was "passionately addicted" to anthropology from an early age, and it is easy to speculate that her ethnographic knowledge provided much of the pleasure she took in the ballet's harsh ritualism.[2] Like many contemporary artists Wharton had a taste for the exotic. At first glance, though, it may appear that ethnographic themes appear in Wharton's fiction merely as a marker of taste, only one among the hundreds that she records in her novels. Newland Archer in *The Age of Innocence,* for instance, is drawn to "books on Primitive Man that people of advanced culture were beginning to read," and, like his Eastlake furniture, anthropology is a sign of a new intellectual fashion (47).[3] Unlike Stravinsky, Wharton does not draw upon the ethnographic to radically refashion a traditional aesthetic form. Instead, she appears to subordinate the current vogue for the exotic to the conventions of a long-established genre, the novel of manners. One can imagine, indeed, that for Wharton it was Parisian manners that provided the most absorbing spectacle at the ballet premiere, that her ethnographic interest was drawn less to the exoticism of the dancers than to the remarkable behavior of the audience, a cultural performance equally as "extraordinary" as the strange species of ballet on the stage.

The behavior of audiences, in fact, is a favorite measure of manners in Wharton's novels. The first chapters of *The Age of Innocence* introduce

---

[1] Edith Wharton, Second Donnée Book, 6, in the Wharton Archives, Beinecke Library, Yale University. Wharton's response to the ballet is discussed in Cynthia Griffin Wolff, *A Feast of Words: The Triumph of Edith Wharton* (New York: Oxford University Press, 1977), 268–69.

[2] R. W. B. Lewis, *Edith Wharton: A Biography* (1975; rpt. New York: Fromm International, 1985), 108.

[3] All parenthetical references are to the present edition. Quotations from Wharton's other fiction and autobiography, included parenthetically in the text, are drawn from *Edith Wharton: Novels,* ed. R. W. B. Lewis (New York: Library of America, 1985) and the companion volume, *Edith Wharton: Novellas and Other Writings,* ed. Cynthia Griffin Wolff (New York: Library of America, 1990).

the reader to elite New York society by presenting the opera-house decorum of an "exceptionally brilliant audience"—the proper carriages for
transportation, the fashionable time for arrival, the seating arrangements within the opera box, the tacit rules for greetings and formal introductions. But as Wharton records these customs, we begin to see a
second dimension of primitivism that is crucial to the structure of the
narrative itself. The observances of opera decorum, for instance, are
described as tributes paid to "'Taste,' that far-off divinity" (24). As this
metaphor suggests, Wharton not only transcribes the manners of the
New York elite but glosses them as the anthropological rites and religion
of a "tribe." Manners and decorum "played as important a part in Newland Archer's New York as the inscrutable totem terrors that had ruled
the destinies of his forefathers thousands of years ago" (14). Wharton
records the customs and manners of the rich as an avowed novelist-
ethnographer, or a "drawing-room naturalist," to borrow her own phrase
from *The House of Mirth*. Thus Wharton not only recognizes ethnography as a reflection of taste, she makes taste ethnographic—the New York
tribal god of Taste. The method amounts to a superimposing of exotic
and civilized manners, a technique Wharton employs at several levels. The
device produces a deliberately whimsical effect, of course, but the implications are profound: far from subordinating the current interest in
primitivism to a traditional form, Wharton invokes the exotic to refashion
from within the established understanding of social form itself. Though
affixed to a narrow axis of elite manners, Wharton's fiction delineates the
broadest questions of culture addressed in early anthropology: what culture is, how it works, its power and its limits. In self-consciously exploring these questions, Wharton participated in the emergence of a whole
"science of manners."[4]

That label, from Wharton's contemporary Marcel Mauss, describes
the efforts of a wide range of contemporary writers and scientists to understand modern society through the lens of ethnographic estrangement, a
reciprocal mirroring of exotic and European customs of the kind we have
begun to see in Wharton's fiction. Thus what is a fictional technique for
Wharton is a critical method for leading theorists: for Thorstein Veblen,
who describes the practices of leisure-class "barbarians"; for Max Weber,
who analyzes modern classes as "castes" modeled after ethnic groups and
"anthropological types" (complete with their own "chiefs," "gods," and

---

[4] Marcel Mauss, *The Gift: Forms and Functions of Exchange in Archaic Societies,* trans.
Ian Cunnison (1925; rpt. New York: Norton, 1967), 81.

"laws of endogamy"); even for Freud, who used tribal "analogies" to describe the "pathology of cultural communities," as well as for a host of lesser-known names.[5] To place Wharton in this context is not to dispute that she is a novelist of manners; rather I aim to open the question of what it means to write about manners during this period. For Wharton, writing about manners had come to include work as different as portraits of small rural towns, essays on gardens and home interiors, eyewitness accounts of North African societies (including descriptions of a harem and the tribal blood rites of a Moroccan sect), even an unpublished erotic fragment that was composed for a project with the Conrad-like title "Powers of Darkness." What unifies this diverse range of Wharton materials is a disposition or posture of mind that anthropologist Ruth Benedict called "culture consciousness."[6]

"Culture" has long been one of our most overdetermined words, and the multiplication of its meanings began in earnest during just this era. Yet it is precisely the overtaxing of the concept that is instructive, for it points to new social contradictions that the idea of culture was called upon to suspend and mediate. In its multiple meanings, "culture" became a talisman for a transatlantic bourgeoisie that experienced a rapid growth of wealth at the same time that it faced a new and sometimes bewildering social heterogeneity in urban centers and colonial outposts. The culture consciousness articulated in Wharton's work, I shall argue, allows her writing both to critique and preserve the authority of the late-nineteenth-century elite class, a double strategy that finally serves to accommodate the very social changes that the class appeared to oppose. Like Benedict in her essay "The Science of Custom," Wharton presents culture as a "flexible instrument" for "divesting" a society of rigid absolutes while "reinstating and reshaping" the local values that sustain a particular social existence.[7] In this essay I trace some of the ways that Wharton's fiction embodies a new culture consciousness—not as a set of abstract axioms but as the intimate, subjective "feel" for the social that is fiction's most powerful resource. In turn, recognizing a historical context for contemporary concepts of manners and culture recasts many of the critical puzzles that still

---

[5] Thorstein Veblen, *The Theory of the Leisure Class* (1899; rpt. New York: Viking, 1983), 1; Max Weber, "Class, Status, Party," in *From Max Weber,* ed. H. H. Gerth and C. Wright Mills (New York: Oxford University Press, 1958), 180–95; Sigmund Freud, *Civilization and Its Discontents,* trans. James Strachey (New York: Norton, 1961), 103.
[6] The term appears in Ruth Benedict, "The Science of Custom: The Bearing of Anthropology on Contemporary Thought," *Century Magazine* 117 (April 1929), 641–49.
[7] Benedict, "Science of Custom," 642, 658, 649.

surround Wharton and her fiction: Is she an antimodernist or an innova-
tor? a feminist or a strict social conservative? These debates, important as
they are, cut us off from one of the fundamental achievements of her work.
Wharton's fiction is neither culturally subversive nor apologist; rather it effects a new representation of the sphere of culture itself in order to articulate, circulate, and finally acculturate the shocks of the modern. We should
not be surprised, in other words, that Wharton warmed to the "extraordinary" spectacle of *Le Sacre du Printemps,* nor that she replayed its
sacrificial rites in her literature as the "New York way of taking life 'without effusion of blood'" (264).[8]

"I go about this London hunting for the real." Written in a 1912
letter, Ezra Pound's striking description of "hunting for the real" echoes
a sentiment expressed widely in this period. Dramatic social changes
that were especially concentrated in cities had created a feeling of unreality for many writers and observers. Historian T. J. Jackson Lears has ana-
lyzed the sense of "weightlessness" and vertigo that began to appear in
the writings of educated Americans as official creeds of optimism were
broken up by fear of class and ethnic violence and by a changing urban
landscape. For many, the sanctuaries of home and church were little protection against the "modern doubt" that, as one minister put it, "destroys the sense of reality" and "envelopes all things in its puzzle." "Reality itself began to seem problematic," Lears writes, "something to be
sought rather than merely lived." What and where is the real? Many writers had taken these questions as a special challenge for art, and it was an
era that saw frequent manifestos declaring literature an agent for discovering and exhibiting reality. Some novelists, for instance, claimed for their
genre an unflinching scientific precision and power. Frank Norris called
the novel an "instrument with which we may go straight through the

---

[8] Among the critics who have remarked upon Wharton's ethnographic interests and
methods are James W. Tuttleton, "Edith Wharton: The Archeological Motive," *Yale Re-
view* 61 (1972), 562–74; Elizabeth Ammons, *Wharton's Argument with America*
(Athens: University of Georgia Press, 1980); Mary Ellis Gibson, "Edith Wharton and the
Ethnography of Old New York," *Studies in American Fiction* 13 (1985), 57–69; and
Katie Trumpener and James M. Nyce, "The Recovered Fragments: Archeological and
Anthropological Perspectives in Edith Wharton's *The Age of Innocence,*" in *Literary
Anthropology: A New Interdisciplinary Approach to People, Signs and Literature,* ed.
Fernando Poyatos (Philadelphia: Benjamins, 1988), 161–69. In addition to exploring
Wharton's ethnographic diction, in this essay I attempt to situate her fiction in a histor-
ical context that included the rise of anthropology and a vogue for primitivism among
the educated classes.

clothes and tissues and wrappings of flesh down into the red, living heart of things."[9]

Norris discards as superfluous "wrappings" what had long been a dominant subject for the novel: manners, the imprint of history and locality on the individual, the social signatures of clothing, speech, posture, gestures. Gazing at the individual, the naturalist novel discovers mass animated by instinct; at its most extreme, as one critic writes, it performs "the extinction of the social, civilized self in a frenzy of sensation." And yet for other contemporary thinkers, it was exactly that social self that had become a new object of scientific interest. Patterns of social habit and convention emerged as a "second nature," a reality unable to be stripped away and awaiting its own yet to be discovered causal laws. "Not incidental or subordinate," wrote one scholar, manners are "supreme and controlling," the "dominating force in history." William James famously called habit the "fly-wheel of society." Seeking the real, many scholars looked to the conventional: the sphere of customs, folkways, social habits and usages. The professional study of culture was established during just this period in the disciplines of anthropology, sociology, and social psychology. John Dewey's declaration that "man is a creature of habit, not of reason nor yet of instinct" describes the new cultural view of the human animal, echoed decades later by Claude Lévi-Strauss: "There is no doubt that, between instincts inherited from our genotype and the rules inspired by reason, the mass of unconscious rules remain more important and more effective."[10]

In this way, customs and manners, long the province of letters—conduct books, the novel, the travel essay—came under the scrutiny of science. And during the same period, the traditional novel of manners acquired a scientific inflection. Unlike novelists such as Norris, Wharton

---

[9]Ezra Pound, *Selected Letters, 1907–1914* (New York: 1971), 12; T. T. Munger, *The Appeal to Life* (Boston, 1887), 33–34; T. J. Jackson Lears, "From Salvation to Self-realization," in *The Culture of Consumption: Critical Essays in American History, 1880–1980,* ed. Richard Wight Fox and T. J. Jackson Lears (New York: Pantheon, 1983), 6, and Lears, *No Place of Grace: Antimodernism and the Transformation of American Culture, 1880–1920* (New York: Pantheon, 1981); Frank Norris, *Responsibilities of the Novelist* (New York: Doubleday, 1903), 7.

[10]Eric J. Sundquist, "Introduction: The Country of the Blue," in *American Realism: New Essays,* ed. Eric J. Sundquist (Baltimore: Johns Hopkins University Press, 1982), 13; William Graham Sumner, *Folkways* (1907; rpt. New York: Arno, 1979), 36, 38; William James, *The Principles of Psychology,* vol. 1 (1890; rpt. New York: Dover, 1950), 121–22; John Dewey, *Human Nature and Conduct* (New York: Holt, 1922), 32; Claude Lévi-Strauss, "The Anthropologist and the Human Condition," in Claude Lévi-Strauss, *The View from Afar,* trans. Joachim Neugroschel (New York: Basic, 1985), 34.

retained the "social, civilized self" as her primary subject, but she made the world of drawing rooms, parlors, and theaters as much a field for "hunting for the real" as the cruder settings—the wilderness, the marketplace, the battlefield—of Norris, Jack London, or Stephen Crane. Like the naturalists, Wharton was fascinated by biology and evolutionism, reading deeply in Darwin, Huxley, Ernst Haeckel, and in current studies of heredity and Mendelism. Favorite anthropological texts included works by Herbert Spencer, Edward Westermarck (probably his *History of Primitive Marriage*), James Frazer's *Golden Bough,* and the "remarkable books on tribal life in Melanesia" by Bronislaw Malinowski, whom she came to know socially. To Wharton, scientific knowledge was indispensable for discovering our "inward relation to reality." But crucially, reality included not only material forces and human instincts but the irreducible reality of social forms. In Durkheim's words, "man is human only because he is socialised." [11]

And yet the reality of social convention, Wharton recognized, is always both essential and equivocal. For although there is no human life outside of a web of mutual relations, still no *particular* social feature—this form of marriage, that division of labor or gender roles—is in itself either necessary, unalterable, or permanent. *The Age of Innocence* explores precisely this tension between the real and the conventional—or between nature and culture, the submerged fault line that was also at the heart of anthropological studies. Until the arrival of Ellen Olenska, Newland Archer accepts even the most baroque observances and distinctions of his circle as a natural, almost "congenital" inheritance (18). But when he falls in love with Ellen, the New York "tribal" customs and its rules of Taste begin to appear as an archaic formalism, a "parody of life." A gulf opens between the world of social convention and a private, alternative world he calls "reality":

> he had built up within himself a kind of sanctuary in which she throned among his secret thoughts and longings. Little by little it became the scene of his real life, of his only rational activities. . . . Outside it, in the scene of his actual life, he moved with a growing sense of unreality and

[11] On Wharton's reading, see Lewis, *Edith Wharton: A Biography,* 56, 108, 230, as well as *The Letters of Edith Wharton,* ed. R. W. B. Lewis and Nancy Lewis (New York: Simon & Schuster, 1988), 146, 15; Wharton's description of Malinowski's work and her comment on the "inward relation to reality" appear in *Letters,* 546 and 102; Emile Durkheim, *Selected Writings,* ed. and trans. Anthony Giddens (Cambridge: Cambridge University Press, 1972), 232.

insufficiency, blundering against familiar prejudices and traditional points of view as an absent-minded man goes on bumping into the furniture of his own room. (216)

Newland's crisis is a personal and emotional one, of course, but its repercussions have the broadest possible social range. His illicit desire triggers an estrangement at the level of the smallest details of social life and spreads into the very "structure of his universe" (95). And as the larger contours of the novel make clear, Newland's sense of "unreality" dramatizes the forces of dislocation pressuring a whole social era. . . .

What is real becomes intelligible precisely through a dialectic of the traditional and the personal, the arbitrary and the actual. And the medium for this dialectic is custom, the locally rooted but contingent forms which can be disowned or disobeyed but never transcended. When Newland Archer calls his very real passion for Ellen the "only reality," Ellen confronts him with the reality of bourgeois kinship terms: "Is it your idea, then, that I should live with you as your mistress—since I can't be your wife?" Newland's answer resists these social classifications: "I want somehow to get away with you into a world where words like that—categories like that—won't exist" (234). But Ellen's reply, "Where is that country? Have you ever been there?" returns the novel to its foundation in the cultural: the variable but irreducible categories of countries, classes, regions, and urban castes. Ellen's response acknowledges both their mutual desire and their mutual relation to New York kinship (we are "Newland Archer, the husband of Ellen Olenska's cousin," she recounts for him, "and Ellen Olenska, the cousin of Newland Archer's wife") and the novel's poignancy comes from the tension between the conflicting realities of kinship and illicit passion. Wharton thus uses a love story to generate a drama of cultural consciousness, the same drama Malinowski discloses in Trobriand society, where he represents an ethnographic reality by narrating "the power of tribal law, and of the passions which work against and in spite of these." [12]

Wharton underscores this doubleness of culture, at once conventional and actual, in the scene that places Newland and Ellen within the "queer wilderness of cast-iron and encaustic tiles known as the Metropolitan Museum," in front of the glass cases housing the "Cesnola antiquities" (247). The museum site is highly significant. As the lovers struggle

---

[12] Bronislaw Malinowski, *The Sexual Lives of Savages in North-Western Melanesia* (1929; rpt. Boston: Beacon, 1987), 13.

with a painful recognition of the real force of New York kinship taboos, Wharton stages the scene before a setting symbolic of culture in Tylor's "wide" ethnographic sense,[13] as represented by the exhibited fragments of a now-vanished ancient community. "Its glass shelves were crowded with small broken objects—hardly recognisable domestic utensils, ornaments and personal trifles—made of glass, of clay, of discoloured bronze and other time-blurred substances" (248). Gazing on the display, Ellen points to the tension that Wharton has built into the novel as a whole, noting that these reified, frozen pieces of an exotic world carry a life and meaning now inaccessible but once as real as her own: "these little things, that used to be necessary and important to forgotten people, and now have to be guessed at under a magnifying glass and labelled: 'Use unknown.'" While Ellen dwells on the historical contingency of cultural experience, Archer returns the novel's dialectic to its opposite pole of immediacy— "meanwhile everything matters"—though this declaration is ultimately framed by a "vista of mummies and sarcophagi" (248, 249), another reminder of the mutability of cultures and their customs. Shifting rapidly back and forth between the two perspectives, Wharton creates a wider consciousness of culture out of the reader's heightened experience of cultural difference. Fragments of experience from disparate worlds are made to represent a new totality. By juxtaposing the exotic and the immediate, Wharton turns the "unreality" of the New York scene into the stable category of culture in its professional sense, merging a drawing-room crisis into the institutional authority of the museum (Wharton has Newland announce proleptically the powerful prestige of civic museums like the Metropolitan: "Some day, I suppose, it will be a great Museum" [247]). The "queer wilderness" of the museum becomes the field for hunting for the real in the territory of culture. And significantly, it is precisely the odd, organized eclecticism of the museum, holding together a varied range of customs and cultural objects, that here provides Wharton with a center of authority from which to recover the realism of manners for a society facing modernity.

This seeming paradox requires a closer examination. Like the strange wilderness of the Metropolitan juxtaposing Cesnola antiquities with Egyptian mummies, Wharton's fiction is a kind of textual museum that recasts elite manners by representing them as carefully preserved artifacts. But what exactly is to be gained from this defamiliarizing perspective? In seeking the real, why look to institutions like anthropology and museums

---

[13]E. B. Tylor, *Primitive Culture*, vol. 1 (1871; rpt. New York: Putnam, 1920), 1.

and to what Paul Valéry called the "strange organized disorder" of disparate objects gathered and displayed in museum collections? Presenting a historical context for the large civic museums established in this era, Philip Fisher analyzes the role of the museum in institutionalizing forms of authenticity and cultural value for societies now fully committed to industrial production and bureaucratic systems. Museums, Fisher argues, are "counter-institutions to the factory":

> Museums became more and more central exactly in cultures touched most deeply by the modern system of mass-production. The British Museum in London and the Metropolitan Museum in New York represent a new kind of institution. No longer do they provide a visible history of the culture itself: that is, a display of objects rich with symbolic, local significance. Instead they are storage areas for authenticity and uniqueness per se, for objects from any culture or period whatever that were said to be irreplaceable.[14]

In modern museums, it is precisely the heterogeneity of varied artifacts— a medieval weapon, a tribal mask, an Impressionist painting—that guarantees authentic cultural value, for the museum exists to preserve and display what cannot be reproduced. A similar display of "relics" governs Wharton's fiction, allowing for the narrative juxtaposition of the manners of "Old New York" with prehistoric antiquities and tribal metaphors. Rather than amassing a rich surface of interlocking social details (the aim of earlier realists), Wharton creates a disjunctive view of manners. But this perspective in turn invokes an aura of authenticity out of the representation of mere fragments. A coherent narrative space unified under the concept of culture is produced from the very gaps between starkly different social worlds. . . .

It is not just the choice of the Metropolitan as a setting in *The Age of Innocence,* then, that links Wharton's fiction to the new institution of the museum. Many of Wharton's writings share the founding assumptions that made modern museums possible, assumptions that the authentic and the real are in some sense precarious, in need of preservation, and that they reveal their purest meaning in the form of special collections and related kinds of archival representation. Wharton is explicit about these assumptions in her memoir *A Backward Glance.* "The compact world of my

---

[14] Philip Fisher, *Making and Effacing Art: Modern American Art in a Culture of Museums* (New York: Oxford University Press, 1991), 29.

youth has receded into a past from which it can only be dug up in bits by the assiduous relic-hunter," she writes, "and its smallest fragments begin to be worth collecting and putting together before the last of those who knew the live structure are swept away with it" (781). Conceived as "relics" and "fragments," the past is reassembled according to dual principles of worth: cultural wholeness and cultural extinction. On one hand she points to a "live structure" that is analogous to E. B. Tylor's definition of culture as a "complex whole," and on the other hand she records the loss of that living whole. Extinction is the ultimate source of cultural value: "The small society into which I was born was 'good' in the most prosaic sense of the term, and its only interest, for the generality of readers, lies in the fact of its sudden and total extinction, and for the imaginative few in the recognition of the moral treasures that went with it" (781). Once suitably collected and framed by the idea of cultural extinction, "moral treasures" are recovered and preserved.

In passages such as these Wharton expresses an elegiac protest against the rationalizing forces of modernity that seemed to erode civic traditions and impose a deadening order of standardized production and bureaucracy (what Wharton in a letter once called "Fordian culture"). She echoes an antimodernism that was one of the keynotes of the decades of American "incorporation." [15] It was an age when antimodernists like Henry Adams and G. Stanley Hall sought a renewed cultural vitality by looking to pre-modern worlds and tribal societies. Adams, a close friend of Wharton, immersed himself in medieval Catholic art and native Samoan life, two islands of an authenticity lost to the modern bureaucratized society. But the paradox of antimodernism was that its "backward glance" (to borrow Wharton's borrowing of Whitman) ultimately may have helped to accommodate the new forces of modernity that it appeared to oppose. Lears argues that "American antimodernism unknowingly provided part of the psychological foundation for a streamlined liberal culture appropriate to twentieth-century consumer capitalism" and its "therapeutic ethos." [16] It promoted psychic adjustments, cults of individual vitalism, and a privatized spirituality that helped to refashion modern citizens for new forms of bureaucratic authority. The turn to primitivism was a distinctly modern phenomenon that served a modern purpose. Whether or not this precise

---

[15] *Letters of Edith Wharton*, 547; on the culture of incorporation, see Alan Trachtenberg, *The Incorporation of America: Culture and Society in the Gilded Age* (New York: Hill & Wang, 1982).
[16] Lears, *No Place of Grace*, 6.

historical argument holds true, the ethnographic turn in Wharton's fiction does indeed show us a paradoxical modernity that could be represented through a backward glance to a "vanished" society.

In *The Age of Innocence,* for instance, a relativistic view of the rites and customs of Old New York eases the narrative transition to a modern society of technology and bureaucracy. The novel's final chapter, set twenty-six years later in Paris, reveals the full implications of Wharton's ethnographic approach to manners. The flexible lens through which the novel has viewed customs and culture allows for both a recovered sense of realism and an adaptation to social change. In modern Paris, Newland himself is now a relic ("Don't be prehistoric!" his son tells him, 280). But it is precisely as an antiquarian object that Newland achieves a now-poignant sense of reality—though a reality now recognized as fragile, customary, and in need of preservation. Newland finds himself unable to cross the threshold to Ellen's apartment: "'It's more real to me here than if I went up,' he suddenly heard himself say; and the fear lest that last shadow of reality should lose its edge kept him rooted to his seat as the minutes succeeded each other" (285).

The moment is preserved in museumlike stillness. But with a precious sense of reality "rooted" with Archer in this scene, the chapter also embraces the opposing forces of modernity that had fostered the extinction of Old New York. Telephones and electric light, Roosevelt's new politics, and rapid overseas travel have been integrated into the lives of the next generation of leading New Yorkers. Even more important, the taboos against exogamous intermarriage with the sons and daughters of the worlds of business and politics have been lifted. Now society is a "huge kaleidoscope where all the social atoms spun around on the same plane" (278), but the disorder is a vital energy harnessed by Archer's children. Wharton's portrait of a class that, while fearing decline, in fact retained and strengthened its claim to power through the tumultuous social changes of fin-de-siècle America is demographically correct. In spite of apprehension about receding WASP powers, the northeastern elite expanded its social influence and helped to smooth the transition to a new corporate society. In this sense the novel deploys an adaptive culture consciousness that helped to refashion the social authority of the leadership classes for modern conditions. Like Newland Archer's haunting sense of "unreality," the uneasiness of a generation in pursuit of the real finally helped to put in place a new social reality.

I have been arguing that Wharton's realism, like Benedict's culture concept, is a "flexible instrument" for negotiating the conflicts of an emergent modern world. The elegiac preservation of fragile cultural relics, however, is only one side of Wharton's fiction of manners. Her realism also includes a fascinated obsession with what seemed to be the vital energies of social aggression in primitive cultures. It is fitting that the first ethnographic museum (founded by the Englishman L. F. Pitt Rivers) began as a collection of weapons, for even at its professional peak the discipline of anthropology retained the early explorers' interest in what Malinowski called "crime and custom in savage society." [17] Any reader of *The Age of Innocence* will recognize this interest in Wharton, for the novel's final reconciliation comes only after a climactic scene of ritualized violence, a dinner party glossed as "a tribal rally around a kinswoman about to be eliminated from the tribe" (264). The hunt for the real in Wharton's fiction of manners includes a complex attraction to contemporary notions of social coercion and power, and this romancing of aggression is equally important for understanding the workings of the culture concept in Wharton's fiction. . . .

A NOTE ON WHARTON'S USE OF *FAUST*

Linda W. Wagner

When Mephistopheles is tempting the young, innocent Margaret to take a lover, he prompts her use of the phrase "country's custom." This is the interchange:

> If not a husband, then a beau for you!
> It is to the greatest heavenly blessing,
> To have a dear thing for one's caressing! [1]

And Margaret replies, "The country's custom is not so." Mephistopheles' retort, "Custom, or not! It happens, though." With her characteristic irony, Wharton takes Margaret's suitably innocent defense (that unmarried women do not take lovers) and turns that maxim into its very opposite. . . .

If we take Newland Archer as a Faust figure—hungry for knowledge, superior to his peers, set on changing his existence and country—then all

---

[17] This is the title of one of Malinowski's monographs (1926; rpt. Totowa, N.J.: Rowman & Allanheld, 1985). [Margaret is referred to as Marguerite in the notes to pp. 13–15. Ed.]

Edith Wharton Newsletter 3.1 (Spring 1986).

[1] The B.Q. Morgan translation, Johann Wolfgang von Goethe, *Faust*, 1 (New York: Appleton-Century-Crofts, 1946).

the early passages in Wharton's novel, as Newland both scrutinizes his culture and meditates on his and May's roles in it, carry a double weight. They help to place Newland in the venerable tradition of "man who seeks knowledge," and may explain so many of the critics' tendencies to see Newland as the apparent narrative center of the book. In this reading, then, (which is suggested by the opening and closing scenes of the opera *Faust* used as frame for the novel), May becomes the epitome of innocence, Faust's Margaret; and Ellen Olenska becomes the Martha of Goethe's drama. But whereas Goethe sets innocence against experience in a conventional paradigm, Wharton embroiders that opposition with heavy irony. Margaret's pregnancy dooms her and leads to the murder of her child, and her incarceration and madness. May's, on the other hand, leads to her most obvious act of manipulation, telling Ellen that she is pregnant so that the would-be lovers' plans for a tryst are aborted. May knows only triumph.

For all his intentions, Newland fails to learn much beyond his own narrow boundaries of texts and life experiences. While Faust risks present-day life and eternal existence in his quest, Newland risks nothing. The tentative formulation of his relationship with Ellen shows his innate cowardice, just as the ending shows his reluctance to put anything of his—illusions as well as reputation—in danger. While Newland has known his Walpurgis Night before his marriage, he avoids any kind of sensual, physical involvement after it (leaving the carriage, touching Ellen's hands only).

The imagery of the novel, which is in some ways strangely melodramatic for Wharton, also suggests a Faustian concern. The New York world is termed "heaven" many times, by Ellen, early in the book (76).[2] Similarly, Newland describes Ellen's existence with the Count (about which he knows very little) as "hell." He is to be May's "soul's custodian" in their marriage, and she is to be his "possession." All these are locutions that form the basis of *Faust,* as Mephistopheles tempts Faust and is abetted by Wagner, the true innocent (Wagner: "to know all is my ambition"). Just as Faust has more insight than his younger protege, and replies, "every deed of ours, no less than every sorrow, / Impedes the onward march of life," so May becomes, in *The Age of Innocence,* the more knowledgeable of the pair. The tribal farewell dinner, a rite of sacrifice, fixes the readers' impression of May, victorious, and Newland, so bewildered he barely remembers to speak to Ellen on his right.

The close of the novel gives us Newland as Faust ("We dread the blows we never feel, and what we never lose is yet by us lamented"), professing

---

[2] All parenthetical references are to this New Riverside Edition.

a belief in Faith, Hope, and Patience, yet doing so in reality to save his own life. It is rather Ellen, who delights in living for the moment, who illustrates the Faustian, "he who grasps the Moment's gift, / He is the proper man." It is also fitting that Newland's moment of prime decision—whether or not to marry May—takes place around Easter, the Christian image for re-birth, and the point in *Faust* when Heaven's voices occur. That he does not really "make" that decision, but accepts her decision in the telegram as final, places him even more firmly in the Faustian pattern. Circumstances are Newland's Mephistopheles, but circumstances are often the machina-tions of the Welland/Newland tribe. Newland's mother is delighted that her son has gotten past "the Siren Isle"; May is imagined throughout as Diana, virginal nature and healing; and Newland consistently reverses all the associations with his (and May's) name, in circumstances much less fa-vorable to him than when they appear in Henry James's fiction. For New-land Archer, the journey to and through life has been anything but trium-phant. His existence goes on, as he walks away from any encounter with Ellen, but the words of Faust's Margaret echo in the motivations of both Wharton's women, May as well as Ellen: "I've done, else, all things for the love of thee." Suitably, Margaret—despite her murders—is saved. And Newland, like Faust, just continues his futile life.

THE MIND IN CHAINS
Public Plots and Personal Fables

Gary H. Lindberg

. . . In *The Age of Innocence* the same narrative strategy [as found in *The House of Mirth*] encloses the central moral decision of the novel, for in the transition between books 1 and 2 Archer chooses between Ellen Olenska and May Welland. Having declared his love to Ellen at the end of book 1, Archer asserts that his new self-awareness makes marriage to May unthinkable, whereas Ellen argues from Archer's own earlier pronounce-ments about duty to the community and in particular to May. It is not cer-tain that Ellen will be able to maintain her sincere reasoning, nor is it clear that Archer can even understand her argument. The arrival of May's tele-

From *Edith Wharton and the Novel of Manners*. Charlottesville: UP of Virginia, 1975.

gram, announcing an early wedding, breaks up the deliberation. Book 2 opens at the wedding. Here, instead of accounting for lapsed time by postulating a chain of consequences, the reader is forced into Archer's bewildered sense of what has happened. The very rapidity of the sequence leaves no time to consider whether May's telegram *should* have changed everything again for Archer; the sudden movement shows what power a simple public gesture, here a telegram, can have when backed by a network of social obligations and inward habits. Furthermore, the interval between the telegram and the wedding virtually vanishes, as if the latter were the immediate and the only recognizable consequence of the former. Momentarily, then, Wharton's arrangement of interstices engages the reader in Archer's own illusion that May's announcement eliminates moral choice entirely.

In its immediate implications this narrative strategy does not suggest an external doom hanging over the characters; rather it increases the moral seriousness of their conduct. The sequences begin in private moral dilemmas, and the hypothesized determinations and effects with which the reader fills in the narrative gaps simply measure the personal results of the implied decisions. But the choices made in each case can easily be construed as non-choices; to the character, the matter seems out of his hands, and even to author and reader the moral agent is not deliberating but following the course of least immediate difficulty. It is the power of social expectancies, reinforced by the pressure of public time, that creates for the character the illusion that only one line of action is even imaginable. Thus, insofar as Wharton's handling of narrative gaps makes us comply in projecting and understanding deterministic sequences, we tacitly acknowledge what personal strength and clarity of insight would be necessary before a character could even contemplate a course of action other than that determined by public pressure. The effect of these narrative gaps is often emphasized, as in the treatment of Archer's wedding, by their coinciding with a sudden passage from a private to a public scene, as if the character's implicit failure to accept his own accountability reduced him to a mere fragment of the communal world.

There are other strategies in Edith Wharton's overt plots, such as a series of contrived coincidences, that suggest more directly the existence of an outside force disposing the events, and this force can often be identified with certain movements of the communal machinery. The most serious and effective of these strategies involves her arrangement of narrative revelations. She constructs her plots so as to undermine the protagonists' moments of expansive meditation by developing earlier the very forces that will frustrate their expectations. As we read of a character's projected freedom and his new patterns of life, it is already clear that these rich possibilities are doomed. . . .

AMERICAN NATURALISM
IN ITS "PERFECTED" STATE
The Age of Innocence
and *An American Tragedy*

Donald Pizer

. . . One of the major assumptions about American naturalism is that it is a literature that is closely attuned to, and indeed derives from, "hard times."[1] The naturalist, it is believed, grounds his fiction in the social realities of his historical moment and he therefore cannot help being especially responsive to social reality when that reality impinges cruelly on the fates of most men. Or, to put the matter somewhat differently, the naturalistic ethos, which views man as circumscribed by conditions of life over which he has no control, appears to be confirmed during periods of social malaise and individual hardship. The history of American naturalism seems to support this interpretation of the movement. Naturalism first took hold in America during the economic hard times and social turmoil of the 1890s; it achieved a second major flowering during the 1930s depression; and it appeared as a significant force for a third time during the difficult political conditions occasioned by the onset of McCarthyism and the Cold War in the late 1940s and early 1950s. Indeed, many of the archetypal scenes of American naturalism—futilely looking for work, for example, as do Hurstwood and Studs Lonigan, or of being killed by a bullet or club that is the symbolic equivalent of an all-powerful economic or political force, as are Annixter and Jim Casy—derive from the contemporary social immediacies in which these works are set. Naturalism, in this assumption about its periodicity, is thus like a dermatological condition. Its appearance usually signifies a disturbance elsewhere in the organism. When the patient gets better, the spots disappear.

A second major belief about naturalism is that it is, to use Dreiserian slang, a young man's game, with both modifiers—young and man—operative. A moment's reflection produces evidence that appears to bear out

---

From *The Theory and Practice of American Literary Naturalism*. Carbondale: Southern Illinois UP, 1993.

[1] I myself adopt this approach to the history of American naturalism in my *Twentieth-Century American Literary Naturalism: An Interpretation* (Carbondale: Southern Illinois University Press, 1982).

this view. Frank Norris, Stephen Crane, and Theodore Dreiser were all in their twenties when they wrote important naturalistic novels, and John Dos Passos, James T. Farrell, and John Steinbeck were hardly much older when they published major naturalistic fiction in the 1930s. During the years following World War II, it was the very early fiction of Norman Mailer, William Styron, and Saul Bellow—novels such as *The Naked and the Dead, Lie Down in Darkness,* and *The Adventures of Augie March*—that are among the most naturalistic of their works. Two observations arise from these facts. The first is that naturalism appears to attract writers in their youth and then fade as an interest. Crane and Norris of course died when still very young, but otherwise all the writers I have named moved on to other kinds of fiction as their careers advanced. Even Dreiser, who wrote naturalistic novels in his 40s and 50s, went on to a very different kind of fiction in his last years in the semimystical allegories of *The Bulwark* and *The Stoic.* The second observation is that naturalism appears to be entirely the province of male authors. Together, the two observations constitute an implicit indictment of the quality and importance of naturalism. The naturalistic novel, it seems, is the product of a masculine late adolescence frame of mind that has overreacted both to the physical in life and to the deep disappointment that life as found is not as it was promised. An underlying premise of this indictment is that writers within the naturalistic movement lack the fine tuning of the imaginative temperament that women authors presumably have from birth and which the male author will gradually achieve, though some—like Dreiser—show an arrested development well into their careers. Naturalism is thus principally the expression of crass, youthful, male authors. To demonstrate the force of this assumption one need only recall the distaste that naturalism as a literary form occasioned among the followers of Henry James once James assumed—in the early 1940s—his position as the consummate artistic and moral sensibility.[2]

A third—and last—major assumption about naturalism as a literary movement is closely related to its presumed origins as a form of social realism written largely by young men. Naturalism, it has been believed for almost its entire history, is not conducive to artistic expression. Initially it was often denigrated as art by claims that it was a kind of photography in verbal form. But when photography itself emerged as a major art, the

---

[2] For a characteristically antinaturalistic position by a Jamesian, see Charles T. Samuels, "Mr. Trilling, Mr. Warren, and *An American Tragedy,*" *Yale Review* 53 (Summer 1964): 629–40.

notebook took its place as a metaphor of the naturalist's unmediated documentation of external experience. The naturalist might have an accurate sense of how to butcher a hog or of the workings of a Model T, but was the expression of this knowledge art? The answer was usually "no." Norris's often heavy-handed symbolism or Dreiser's disastrous ventures into purple prose were also frequently cited as sure evidence of the inadequacy of the naturalist when he sought to push beyond a documentary style. Thus a kind of naturalism/art inverse ratio was established in the historiography of American naturalism. Writers who were obviously self-conscious and innovative literary craftsmen—a Crane or Faulkner—could not be naturalists, while writers who appeared most clearly to have plowed the dull furrows of documentary realism—a Dreiser or Farrell—were consummate naturalists. And in the critical analysis of any one novel, the less naturalism found by the critic the more likely was he to praise the novel for its artistic strength. Naturalism, in brief, was not a technique but a literary bludgeon. And though bludgeons might create an effect, that effect was a different and lesser thing than the one obtained by a genuine work of art.

These historical and critical platitudes about naturalism that I have been describing do indeed have a certain truth. Naturalism has flourished among difficult social conditions, much naturalistic fiction is written by young men, and naturalism of the poorer sort does have its dull and blatant reaches. But the movement is also—and this is my central point—a far more complex critical and historical phenomenon than is implied by these clichés. The naturalistic novel, in other words, can also emerge during good times; it can be written by mature male *and* female authors; and it can express naturalistic themes with great fictional artistry.

Theodore Dreiser's *An American Tragedy* and Edith Wharton's *The Age of Innocence* are major examples of naturalistic fiction that lie outside of these clichés.[3] Both works appeared during the comparatively flush

---

[3] *An American Tragedy* has of course been frequently discussed as a naturalistic novel. For a representative sampling of such commentary, see *Critical Essays on Theodore Dreiser,* ed. Donald Pizer (Boston: G. K. Hall, 1981). Wharton's work, including *The Age of Innocence,* is far less frequently linked with naturalism. Two somewhat limited such efforts are Larry Rubin, "Aspects of Naturalism in Four Novels of Edith Wharton," *Twentieth Century Literature* 2 (January 1957): 182–97 and James A. Robinson, "Psychological Determinism in *The Age of Innocence,*" *Markham Review* 5 (Fall 1975): 1–5. In addition, Alan Price has briefly compared two earlier novels by Wharton and Dreiser in his "Lily Bart and Carrie Meeber: Cultural Sisters," *American Literary Realism* 13 (Autumn 1980): 238–45.

times of the 1920s—*The Age of Innocence* in 1920, *An American Tragedy* in 1925—and both were written when their authors were in full maturity. (Wharton was fifty-eight, Dreiser fifty-four.) And both works illustrate the highest fictional craftsmanship.

Given their obvious differences in subject matter and fictional form, it is perhaps difficult to recall that both *The Age of Innocence* and *An American Tragedy* are also historical novels of a special and essentially similar kind. Wharton's novel is set in upper-class New York of the 1870s. And *An American Tragedy,* though set in the 1920s, is based on a 1906 incident and, even more pertinently, was grounded in Dreiser's preoccupation since the 1890s in a distinctively late nineteenth-century configuration of the American dream of success.[4] Through the dramatization of an unconsummated love affair on the one hand and a sensational murder case on the other, Wharton and Dreiser seek to depict some of the limitations placed on human freedom by the social and moral nature of late nineteenth-century American life. . . .

In *An American Tragedy,* the capacity of the individual to be shaped by the ordinary world in which he lives can best by illustrated by Clyde's early experience as a bellhop in the Green-Davidson Hotel. Young, inexperienced, and eager for the pleasures and excitement of life, Clyde finds in the gauche luxuriousness of an American middle-class hotel of the 1920s a potential fulfillment of all he desires. In pursuing this fulfillment, he encounters and absorbs codes of behavior and belief that will condition his own actions and values for the remainder of his life. This process begins with his interview for the position of bellhop and his realization that he must make himself pleasing to his superiors within a hierarchical social structure if he is to climb within that structure. "For the first time in his life, it occurred to him that if he wanted to get on he ought to insinuate himself into the good graces of people—do or say something that would make them like him. So now he contrived an eager, ingratiating smile. . . ."[5]

Clyde also quickly encounters another condition of social power—that those in positions of strength exploit those beneath them. So Clyde is confronted during his first day by the convention of kickbacks that runs

---

[4] See my *Novels of Theodore Dreiser: A Critical Study* (Minneapolis: University of Minnesota Press, 1976), pp. 203–4.

[5] *An American Tragedy* (New York: Boni and Liveright, 1925), 1, 31. Citations from this edition will hereafter appear in the text.

through the hotel's economic structure—that he must pay a portion of his tips to his watch captain, another portion to those who supply ice water and drinks, while he himself receives money from hotel merchants to whom he brings trade. Yet these instances of hypocrisy and corruption are not questioned by Clyde, despite his moralistic upbringing, because they are a means toward the winning of a secular Eden far more immediate and desirable than any heavenly reward promised by his parents' faith. "What a realization of paradise!" (1, 37), Clyde cries, when he comes to understand that even a tiny part of the opulence of the Green-Davidson can be his.

The Green-Davidson as a microcosm of that aspect of American life in which power functions as deception and exploitation is even more sharply portrayed in the sexual ethic operative in the hotel. Well-to-do perverts and rich society women prey on the usually willing bellhops, and Clyde also learns of "a guy from St. Louis" who brings a young girl to the hotel, runs up a large bill, and then both deserts the girl and fails to pay the bill. In these instances, Clyde can still recoil with shock because of his sexual inexperience. But so powerful is the controlling ethic of the hotel that Clyde will eventually, in his relations with Roberta and Sondra in Book Two of the novel, act out this precise model of deception and exploitation, one in which Sondra now constitutes the Green-Davidson of his desires. For as he said to himself after his full absorption of the meaning of the hotel, "This, then, most certainly was what it meant to be rich, to be a person of consequence in the world—to have money. It meant that you did what you pleased. That other people, like himself, waited upon you. That you possessed all of these luxuries. That you went how, where, and when you pleased" (1, 45).

In *The Age of Innocence,* a parallel metaphor of entrapment within a powerful social institution is provided by the wedding ceremony of Archer and May. The right church for an upper middle-class New York wedding, the perfectly attired and correctly seated guests, the elaborately rehearsed and precisely orchestrated sequence of events—all constitute an acceptance by those participating in the occasion of a rigid code of life. Yet it is a code that is dead and meaningless—both in itself and in particular as it represents for Archer a death of the spirit that is about to engulf him. Whatever is fresh in the spring day is smothered by the smell of camphor from the "faded sable and yellowing ermines" of the "old ladies of both families." Archer has contributed "resignedly" to the gestures that make up the ceremony, gestures that make "a nineteenth century New York wedding a rite that seemed to belong to the dawn of history"[6] (154). He

---

[6] All parenthetical references are to this New Riverside Edition.

has provided flowers and presents for the bridesmaids and ushers, has thanked his male friends for their gifts, has paid the necessary fees, and has prepared his luggage—and each of these seemingly inconsequential acts constitutes his tacit acceptance of the more consequential rites and taboos that are at the heart of a middle-class marriage in his culture. For the remainder of his life, in short, he will be expected to play various prescribed roles and make various conventional provisions. . . .

Newland Archer's world is as much a system of limitations and prohibitions as is Clyde's. And though Archer in the end chooses to accept rather than to break through these barriers, the effect of the novel, as with *An American Tragedy*, is to demonstrate the power of the socially constraining over individual desire and destiny. Archer's world, as I have noted, is one in which tribal custom, discipline, and taboo are as prohibitive as engraved tablets of the law. But though little is permitted, even less is said. Communication rather—in what is perhaps the first fully intended semiotic novel—is by a system of signs. They all live, Archer reflects, "in a kind of hieroglyphic world, where the real thing was never said or done or even thought, but only represented by a set of arbitrary signs" (47). The "real thing" in *The Age of Innocence* is Archer's discovery of his love for Ellen Olenska during the course of his courtship, engagement, and marriage to May Welland.

Within the poles of duty and desire in *The Age of Innocence*, May is all that Newland's breeding and world deem most acceptable. She is young, pure, of excellent family, and—for good measure—attractive. She is also, Archer begins to realize, indescribably dull, conventional, and predictable. Ellen, on the other hand, is a thoroughly suspect commodity within tribal values. With a dissolute husband and a rumored love affair behind her in Europe, she is clearly shopworn and is available principally as a mistress—as indeed she is so pursued by the wealthy philanderer Beaufort. Moreover, she is bohemian and artistic and emotionally deep. Archer, seeing the long dull road before him which May represents, and fully engaged emotionally for the first time in his life by the pathos and beauty of Ellen's nature, contemplates escape from duty and fulfillment of desire. But at every turn he is silently but effectively anticipated, forestalled, and thwarted. His marriage to May is advanced, Ellen's divorce is blocked by family pressure, and—at a climactic moment—May uses her just-discovered pregnancy to drive off Ellen and hold Newland.

In one of the principal ironic devices of *The Age of Innocence*, Archer and Ellen serve as the major spokesmen for and agents of the system of moral and social taboos that keeps them apart. Neither wishes to descend to a clandestine affair; there must be a complete break with their world or nothing. And a complete break, Newland realizes, though it may gain love, will also mean the loss of "habit, and honour, and all the old decencies that he and his people had always believed in" (245). And so, in the end, when Newland is driven by the imminent loss of Ellen to project a possible escape—to find at last the emotional equivalent of the fresh air he is constantly seeking in stuffy drawing rooms and closed carriages—the "old decencies" he speaks for exert their greatest power in the compelling commitment represented by May's pregnancy.

The Age of Innocence, as I have noted, is a novel of inaction rather than, as is true of An American Tragedy, one of doing. Newland and Ellen never consummate their love. And though, in a scene remarkably evocative of An American Tragedy, Newland at one point wishes May dead (238–39), he does not harm her but rather settles into the placid but empty life with her that he had foreseen. But though it seldom expresses itself either in open prohibition or direct punishment, the social and moral world portrayed in The Age of Innocence—the world that Archer describes as a "silent organization" of habit, custom, and assumption—exerts a web of compulsion that powerfully shapes and controls individual belief and behavior in the most vital areas of human experience.

An American Tragedy and The Age of Innocence share another major characteristic of American naturalism in its fully mature form. In both works, the central figure consciously accepts the premise that he is free. For Clyde, freedom is expressed in his belief that he can fulfill the American dream—that he can move from the basement of the Griffiths factory to the ideal world of an unending summer with Sondra at Twelfth Lake. Indeed, much of the action of the novel emerges out of Clyde's effort to translate his sense of himself—that there is a better life than he has had and that he can gain it—into actuality in the face of his own limitations and an intractable world. In The Age of Innocence, Newland even more than Clyde accepts the proposition that he can mold his own life. It is his to choose, he believes almost to the end, whether he will elect to live with May or run away with Ellen. But both Clyde and Newland come to realize that their destinies were shaped outside of their conscious volition. In prison, awaiting execution, Clyde understands—as the world has not—how much his nature had been conditioned by "the ill-fate of his early life and training." And he realizes as well how devoid of any true freedom of choice was the seeming choice between Roberta's "determination that he marry her and thus ruin his whole life" and "the Sondra of his beautiful dream" (11, 392). And Newland, in Paris some thirty years after seemingly freely choosing to remain with May, is told by his son that May, on her deathbed, had spoken of the crisis represented by Newland's attraction to Ellen and of how May had asked Newland not to leave her, had asked him to give up "the thing [he] most wanted." After a long pause, Newland responds to his son, "She never asked me" (281). May did not have to ask, and Newland was not given a choice, because—with the announcement of her pregnancy—the choice was made for Newland, as May well knew and as Newland now fully realizes, so powerful were the constraints that all of them—including Ellen— fully accepted.

Both novels, therefore, dramatize not only that we live in a contingent universe, that our lives are largely shaped and conditioned by the distinctive social context in which we find ourselves, but also that we continue to share in the myth of the autonomous self that is capable of realizing and choosing its own fate. And in both works as well, though each in its own way, the dynamic aesthetic center of the novel is the tragic irony inherent in the conflict between a character's felt belief in his autonomy and a social contingency that does indeed shape his destiny. Clyde, thinking that he can somehow get out of his scrape and still have Sondra, Newland reaching out for a self-acceptance of his love for Ellen and what this requires of him—both figures are pursuing life as though it were malleable when it is they who have been and are being shaped.

Clyde and Newland are thus neither dumb brutes nor unthinking victims of grossly determining conditions. They are rather close to life as many of us suspect it is. They are less than strong figures who nevertheless wish to believe that they can control their lives and who discover that the ordinary worlds in which they exist—a commonplace factory town and an upper-class community—subtly but nevertheless powerfully are the controlling agents of their fates.

Novels such as *The Age of Innocence* are seldom discussed as naturalistic fiction because of the critic's assumption that if a novel is naturalistic in its central impulse it cannot be a successful novel and because *The Age of Innocence* is clearly successful. But another tack would be to recognize that most literary movements produce in their opening stages ungainly and awkward expressions of the movement—much pre-Shakespearean Elizabethan tragedy, for example—and that American naturalism is no exception to this general rule. The major naturalistic novels of the 1890s are indeed often crude and melodramatic both in theme and form. But in *An American Tragedy* and *The Age of Innocence* the movement comes to maturity both in the discovery of a fuller range of experience available for the representation of naturalistic themes and in the skill of the dramatization of these themes.

THE SCORSESE INTERVIEW
On Filming *The Age of Innocence*[1]

Ian Christie

. . . Ian Cristie: You quote in your book that accompanies the film a sentence from the novel: "They all lived in a hieroglyphic world, where the real thing was never said or done or even thought, but only represented by a set of arbitrary signs." Is this why you paid so much attention to period detail in the film—and why you're irritated by all the talk about "obsessive attention to detail," as if this comes from you?

Yes, it's all in the book. What seems to be description is in fact a clear picture of that culture, built up block by block—through every plate and glass and piece of silverware, all the sofas and what's on them. All this wealth of detail creates a wall around Newland Archer, and the longer he stays there, with these things becoming commonplace, the harder it will be for him to move out of that society.

Edith Wharton published the book in 1920, recalling a society that no longer existed after the war. Did you feel that you were showing Americans a period which most of them did not know existed?

Of course. And it was even more sumptuous than we show. I felt the film had to show a modern audience the blocks they put around Newland and people like him. But there's also an irony and a sarcasm in the presentation of that lifestyle—both in the way I tried to do it and in the way Wharton did it in the book. The decor had to become a character for me.

Jay Cocks showed the film to an audience of Wharton specialists which included R. W. B. Lewis, who wrote the Pulitzer Prize-winning biography. And he told me that their reaction was extraordinary, because every time a dinner service was shown or when Mrs. Mingott selected the silver plate, they laughed. They knew what the presentation of that particular piece meant. So when the van der Luydens create a dinner for Countess Olenska, they are making a statement and daring people to go against them.

Sight and Sound (Feb. 1994).

[1]In this article, Ian Christie interviews Martin Scorsese, who has just directed a film version of *The Age of Innocence*. Christie's questions and comments appear in italics; Scorsese's responses are in Roman type. [ED.]

In the book there's a fantastic build-up to that dinner that tells you just how important the van der Luydens are and how everyone in New York society acknowledges their status.

I tried to convey that by the attention given to the dinner itself—the centerpiece, the Roman punch—which is like having a triple high mass for a funeral rather than a regular low mass. They are saying, "Not only will we defend you, but we are going to do so on the highest level. If anyone has a problem with that, they are going to have to answer to us."

Just like in GoodFellas. . . .

Exactly. It's a matter of "You have a problem with that? Then you have a problem with me and let's settle it right now." Or in this case, "Oh very well. We're going to have to bring out the Crown Derby, aren't we?" I remember in *The Razor's Edge,* when Gene Tierney throws a plate at Herbert Marshall, he says, "My goodness, the Crown Derby."

It's the heavy artillery.

Absolutely. And the Wharton specialists loved it because they understood better than other people what those signals meant. It was important for me that real goodfellas would like *GoodFellas* and say that it was accurate—and they did. With *The Age of Innocence,* I think that even if ordinary people don't understand fully the significance of the different pieces of china, they will at least see that a lot of pomp and circumstance goes into certain sequences. And as it's not done by me, but by the characters, they get some understanding of the ritual.

Such occasions are the most official way they can sign someone on and make them credible in that society. For instance, when Ellen Olenska arrives late at the party given for her, it's not important to her. Next day Newland says, "You know all New York laid themselves at your feet last night." And she answers, "Yes, it was a wonderful party." The audience has to understand that this wasn't just a party, lady! Newland is in effect saying, "I'm getting married to your family, and we have agreed to take on the disgrace of your separation from your husband and we are going to do it with a stiff upper lip. So you really should know what we are doing for you by putting on a party."

There is something about social and professional ritual that fascinates you, whatever the setting or period. But now you seem to feel happier about moving away from your own experience.

One of the lines that led me to make *The Age of Innocence* was my interest in doing different kinds of genre film. I mean, there's a major part of me that says, "Let's do a Western," but it's not that easy. I have to find what's important for me in order to feel comfortable enough to wallow in the making of a film. So although this film deals with New York's "aristocracy" and a period of New York history that has been neglected, and although it deals with codes and ritual, and with love that's not unrequited but unconsummated—which pretty much covers all the themes I usually deal with—when I read it, I didn't say, "Oh, good—all those themes are here." I was just hit by the impact of the sequence near the end where Newland tries finally to tell his wife May he'd like to leave—and by her response.

It all came together in that scene, and I loved the way I was led by Wharton down the path of Newland's point of view, in which he underestimated all the women, and how he wound up checkmated by them, and how his wife becomes the strongest of them all. I find that admirable. Even though I may not agree with May totally, I like the growth of her character from a young girl to the person who takes control. You see how important her role is in the second opera house scene, which is the first time May has worn her wedding dress since the wedding. We see her seated between her mother and Mrs. van der Luyden—they have passed on the responsibility for continuing their lifestyle to her.

Ironically there seems to be more of you—your own desires and frustrations—in this movie than in some of your other films, even though it comes fully formed from Wharton and is set in such an apparently remote and artificial milieu.

There is. Sometimes when you fall in love you can't see what other people see. You become as passionate and obsessive as Newland, who can't see what's going on around him. That's the theme of *Taxi Driver* and of *Mean Streets*—it's a situation I've found myself in at times, and I've found the way it plays out so wonderful. But then Wharton goes beyond that and makes a case for a life that's not exactly well spent, but a life that happens to him. Newland has his children, then he finds out that his wife knew all along about his love for Ellen and even told his son about it. Basically he is what they call in America a stand-up guy—a man of principles who would not abandon his wife and children. When he really wanted something most, he gave it up because of his kid.

That's very interesting to me—I don't know if I could do the same. But I do know that there are a lot of people, even today, who would: it's about making a decision in life and sticking to it, making do with what you have. And then, of course, during the conclusion you realise that a generation has gone by. The children don't react in the same way; the First World War is looming ahead and they can't understand why everybody was angry. I don't say it's a happy ending, but it's a realistic and beautiful one. . . .

The Age of Innocence is a very literary film—deliberately so. But it's not theatrical, except where you bring in theatre and opera as part of the period texture and a dramatic counterpoint to the unspoken story being acted out among the characters.

I'm trying to get away from [the] three act approach. Over the last ten years, I've found everyone in Hollywood saying: "The script is good, but we need a new Act Two," or "Act Three just isn't there." Finally I said to a bunch of students: "Why are we using the term 'acts' when the damn thing is a movie?" I like theatre, but theatre is theatre and movies are movies. They should be separate. We should talk about sequences—and there are usually at least five or six sequences rather than three acts—which are broken up into sections and scenes. When I screened a few films for Elia Kazan back in 1992 and we discussed them afterwards, I found that he too was trying to get away from conventional theatrical dramaturgy in *East of Eden* and *Wild River*—neither of which, incidentally, he'd seen since he made them!

I certainly tried to find a different structure for *GoodFellas*, though that was more like a documentary on a lifestyle. For *The Age of Innocence* I wanted to find a way of making something literary—and you know how America is cowed by the tyranny of the word—also filmic. I also wanted a massive use of voiceover because I wanted to give the audience the impression I had while reading the book.

The experience of watching a film is often closer to reading than to watching a play. The Age of Innocence *made me think of Max Ophuls— the most literary and even theatrical of film-makers, but also the most filmic. It's about creating and manipulating the spectator's point of view, in time through voiceover and in space through those devastating camera movements.*

I adore Ophuls and we looked at the new print of *Lola Montès*. But for me, the major Ophuls film was *Letter from an Unknown Woman*. By a happy accident it seemed to be on television practically every afternoon when I was a child—that's the wonderful thing about Ophuls having made four American films—so when I was at home sick from school there would be *Letter from an Unknown Woman*. I couldn't tell at the time about camera moves, but I loved the romance and tragedy of it.

I thought that the way you move the camera so deliberately and elo- quently in The Age of Innocence *is like the way Ophuls tracks and cranes, as if you've entered into the characters' emotions and memory.*

That's what I was hoping. I'll never forget the arrival of the piano up the staircase in *Letter from an Unknown Woman*. And then the depiction of a whole life in miniature and the sense of romance in the sequence where Louis Jourdan takes Joan Fontaine to the fairground train ride, and the fake backgrounds just slide past them. Ophuls created a world that was unique. Even though I'd seen other films set in Vienna at the turn of the century, they didn't have the grace and truth that Ophuls had in that film, which stood repeated viewing. I used to have a still on my wall in Hollywood of Louis Jourdan at the end, when he decides to go to the duel—that wonderful shot of him at the desk as he's reading the letter.

You have worked with a wide range of collaborators during your career: perhaps only De Niro and Thelma Schoonmaker recur regularly. But even as personnel come and go according to the demands of each film, there is a sense of "family" about your method of working and a closeness with fellow-creators that you clearly seem to seek. Thelma Schoonmaker has always insisted that the Academy Award she got for the editing of Raging Bull *really belongs to you too, since you planned all the incredible distinctions and distortions in that film. I've seen the deluxe new editing suite you have, and I wonder how you work together in it?*

That's where the whole creative process happens. I sit in that chair behind her and we have worked out a system of red lights and buzzers to communicate with. It's set up for the way we like to work. Although I'm not in the editors' union, I did make my living as an editor for a while in the 70s, and I feel that working on the script and editing are my strong points, as opposed to understanding camera movement and lighting. I love editing. I love what you can do with a film, where you can cut and not cut. It's Eisenstein, really.

The way I work now is that I lay out the editing pattern, and pretty much all the time I decide where to cut and what not to cut. But what Thelma does is to focus on the characters in the film. She'll say, "Maybe we're losing some aspect of so-and-so here. Maybe we should change this performance of this one reading because it might indicate that she's not as sympathetic towards him and we want the audience to realise it at this point."

There's a lot of that kind of editing in *The Age of Innocence*. And in *Raging Bull* some scenes were written but there were also improvisations within the writing. So we would have ten good takes of Joe Pesci and twelve good takes of De Niro, and we would keep switching them around. "Why don't we use Take 4 again of Joe, because I think we lost something there," she would say. Or, "We lost something on De Niro there so maybe we should try Take 8 again." It has more to do with the spiritual quality of what's happening with the people in the film that she is able to perceive and help balance out for me.

The actual cutting—well, there's pure Eisenstein stuff in *The Age of Innocence*, like when the wife gets up and walks over to him, and you see three cuts of her rising. That's something I can imagine in my head, draw the pictures, and say, "Do this one here, that one there." Then Thelma puts it together and I ask her what she thinks, and often she'll suggest changes.

It took a little longer to edit *The Age of Innocence*, mainly because of the dialogue scenes—trying to work out how long a pause should be. But because there is such an appetite for stories about our business and I had taken between nine and ten months—working with only *one* editor!—they painted this picture of me as someone "obsessed with detail." But editing is the most important original element of the film-making process, so why short-change it? It's a sorry state of affairs when just doing my job properly is described as "obsessive."

Many people will be surprised to hear that you don't consider yourself a camera and lighting expert when your images are among the most precise and purposeful in contemporary cinema. Since you started working more or less regularly with the German cinematographer Michael Ballhaus, a former colleague of Fassbinder, there has been more tracking and an increased tendency towards formal overhead and big close-up shots, functioning like tableaux and still-lifes. You seem to enjoy creating special "mimetic" shots that encode an emotion or a vital plot point—like the famous experiments in variable camera speed for Raging Bull. *One such in* The Age of Innocence *is the opera-glass scan across the Met [sic: Academy of Music] audience which reveals Countess Olenska to one of Newland's circle, the supercilious Larry Lefferts.*

It's such an important move that I felt that just putting a binocular masking over it wasn't enough. Also, it didn't duplicate what you would actually see if you were looking through opera glasses—not that everything has to be literal. But I wanted to give it more of an edge and make it more important when you finally see Ellen slipping into the box, so Michael and I devised a kind of stop-action photography where we took just one frame at a time and panned. Then we realised that this was going to be too fast, so we decided to print each frame three times. However, this was still too choppy for me, so just when we were finishing negative cutting I finally decided to dissolve between each set of three frames. It took quite a lot of work, going back to the lab countless times—as Thelma can tell you.

Rock and classic American pop have played such a memorable part in your films from the start that you're not usually associated with the "symphonic" tradition of Hollywood music—unlike De Palma and Spielberg. But using Bernard Herrmann for Taxi Driver *was a deliberate homage—and after two collaborations with Elmer Bernstein it looks as though you have now been able to sign up fully to a tradition you admire.* Cape Fear

*had Bernstein reworking Herrmann's music for the original film, of
course, and Bernstein also did the score for* The Age of Innocence.

Using Bernstein is a matter of embracing the Hollywood tradition,
and *The Age of Innocence* is the closest to a traditional Hollywood score
I have ever worked with. I could have gone classical and scored the picture
with period music in the way I had used popular music before, but I
wanted to go the other way. It wasn't so much nostalgia for the sound of
all those romantic films as a remembrance of the skill and artistry that used
to be available—and still is with someone of Bernstein's stature.

*Another link with the Hollywood past is Saul Bass, creator of a range
of now classic title sequences which became indelibly linked with the image of the films they prefaced.*

For me Bass is one of the key figures in American movies. His title sequences don't just capture the spirit of the movie you are about to see—in
some cases they are better than the movie itself! He created a style and energy that give you a lift, prepare you for the picture and make you want to
see what is going to happen over the next two hours. And they don't feel
separate from the movie, they really seem part of it.

I didn't know that he was still working until I saw *The War of the
Roses* with his credit at the end. I thought the titles for that were simple
and interesting. At the time I was having a problem putting in the word
Goodfellas where I wanted it, because it was incorporated in the action.
When he slams down the trunk and says, "I want to be a gangster," the
lettering never seemed quite right. So I said, "The only man who can really work this out is a guy named Saul Bass." He did—and then we kept
him on to do *Cape Fear*.

How did you actually work with Bass and his wife Elaine on The Age
of Innocence?

We just sent them a tape of the first forty minutes that were edited.
The opera sequence made it very clear in his mind what he wanted to do:
opening on flowers and keeping text (which is from a book of etiquette of
that period) super-imposed over the images. And it was their idea to cut to
the *Faust* overture.

*Working with Bernstein, Bass, and with Freddie Francis as cinema-
tographer on* Cape Fear *isn't only because you admire these great names
from the past—it's more like making a bridge between your own work and
the period in which they gained their reputation.*

Exactly. Very often today you hear the phrase that someone has "been
round the block a lot" if they are over seventy. My view is that maybe we
should listen to what they have to say because they have more experience
to bring to what we need. . . .

OF WRITERS AND CLASS
In Praise of Edith Wharton

Gore Vidal

A few years ago I was asked by the publisher of a biography of Edith Wharton to provide him with what is elegantly known in the trade as a "blurb." Dutifully, I read the biography. There was new material about Mrs. Wharton's private life (after twenty-three years of marriage, she had her first sexual experience at forty-six). There was a good account of the ups and downs of the reputation of a writer who . . . well, herewith the blurb that eventually decorated the dust jacket of R. W. B. Lewis's *Edith Wharton.* "At best, there are only three or four American novelists who can be thought of as 'major' and Edith Wharton is one. Due to her sex, class (in every sense), and place of residence, she has been denied her proper place in the near-empty pantheon of American literature. Happily, Mr. Lewis's biography ought to convince the solemn of her seriousness; with much new material, he has illuminated a marvelous figure and her age." When, eventually, I collect in a single slender volume the various blurbs that I have produced over the years, I shall give, I hope not too immodestly, pride of place to this small but subtly cut zircon of the blurb-maker's tiny art.

Now, let us examine the points I raised in that blurb.

"At best, there are only three or four American novelists who can be thought of as 'major' and Edith Wharton is one." Who are the other two or three? I don't think I will go into that beyond noting that, to my mind, Henry James and Edith Wharton are the two great American masters of the novel. Most of our celebrated writers have not been, properly speaking, novelists at all. Hawthorne and Melville wrote romances. Hemingway and Crane and Fitzgerald were essentially short story writers (a literary form which Americans have always excelled at). Mark Twain was a memoirist. William Dean Howells was indeed a true novelist, but as Edith Wharton remarked (they were friendly acquaintances), Howells's "incurable moral timidity . . . again and again checked him on the verge of a masterpiece." She herself was never timid. Somehow in recent years a notion has got about that she was a stuffy, grand old lady who wrote primly decorous novels about upper-class people of a sort that is no longer supposed to exist. She was indeed a grand lady, but she was not at all stuffy. Quite

Atlantic Monthly (Feb. 1978).

the contrary. She was witty. She was tough as nails. As for those upper-class people, they are still very much with us. But as their age ceased to be gilded and became discreetly chromed, they decided wisely to stay out of sight. Nevertheless, they run the United States just as they did when Edith Wharton and her friend Henry James wrote about them.

"Due to her sex . . . she has been denied her proper place" as a great American writer. This seems to me to be altogether true, and sad. For a very long time it was an article of faith among American schoolteachers and writers of book chat for newspapers that no woman could be a major writer. Predictably, it was Norman Mailer who put the conservative case: "I have nothing to say about any of the talented women who write to-day. . . . Indeed I doubt if there will be a really exciting woman writer until the first whore becomes a call girl and tells her tale." If anyone can figure out what that last sentence means, drop me a line. For Mailer, women writers are "fey, old-hat, Quaintsy Goysy, tiny, too dykily psychotic, crip-pled, creepish, fashionable, frigid, outer-Baroque, *maquillé* mannequin's whimsy, or else bright and stillborn." He then adds a nervous footnote to the effect that, well, there are *three* contemporary women writers who are not too bad. But the point he has made reflects not only the Old Testament hatred that so many American men have for women (particularly notable in the fifties when the gabble that I've just quoted was written) but also the loony conviction that only men can do anything of major importance in literature, quite forgetting that the best novelist in the English language was a lady who was forced (partly by the Mailers of her day) to take the name George Eliot.

Edith Wharton was quite aware that her sex was held against her. There are hundreds of Mailers in every literary generation, and they write most of the book reviews. But I suspect that she was far more disturbed by the attitudes toward women of the class she was born into, where a woman . . . no, that word was not used . . . where a lady was expected to be supremely ornamental, and nothing else. From the beginning, Edith Jones (later Wharton) was far too clever. Or, as she ruefully noted, Boston thought her too fashionable to be clever while New York thought her too clever to be fashionable.

"Due to . . . her class . . . ," Edith Wharton was denied her proper place. Class is a delicate subject in the United States. We are not supposed to know anything about class because everyone is exactly like everyone else except, naturally, for those who are rich—and for those who are poor—and of course for the rest of us. Edith Newbold Jones was born in 1862. The Joneses were a large, proud New York family (it is said that the expression "keeping up with the Joneses" referred to them). Edith was related to almost everyone. And kinship is what society with a capital S is all about. For that matter, society with a small *s* (at least in small communities) tends to be pretty much the same thing. One of the reasons the American South produced so many good writers was that until recently each small town included a number of families who had become so involved with one another over the centuries that the often quite lurid stories of kin, passed on from generation to generation on slow, hot afternoons, were the very stuff of literature for any attentive child with a liking for stories, writing. One needs a well-defined society to make good novels. On the other hand, although the New York of Edith Jones's day was a splendid subject for a novelist, it was an article of faith that no one *in* Society could ever be a writer. Writers were "not like us." Of course they were brainy. But then so were chemists, and you did not have a chemist to dinner . . . or a writer.

Edith Jones's New York was still that of *The Age of Innocence.* There were dinner parties, appearances at the opera, Assembly balls; there was Newport in the summer, with the afternoon *passeggiata* along Ocean Drive; there was, best of all for her, Europe, where she spent much of her childhood because her father was suddenly obliged to economize and it was cheaper to live in Paris than in New York. When, finally, nervously, tentatively, she began to publish, her friends and family were deeply puzzled, and only one relative (a bedridden lady) ever admitted to having read her books. The making of literature in that world was like some wasting, sad disease which, luckily, was not thought to be contagious. Otherwise, she would have been locked up; kept permanently in quarantine.

In Edith Wharton's memoir *A Backward Glance,* she contemplated her long life (she died in 1937). Of her education: "I used to say that I had been taught only two things in my childhood: the modern languages and good manners. Now that I have lived to see both those branches of culture dispensed with, I perceive that there are worse systems of education." She also regarded with a sharp eye the New York gentry of her youth. They had bored her a good deal at the time. A girl who liked to read and think did not have many people to talk to in Old New York. But later, looking back, she was surprised at her own nostalgia. "Social life, with us as in the rest of the world, went on with hardly perceptible changes till the war [1917] abruptly tore down the old frame-work, and what had seemed unalterable rules of conduct became of a sudden observances as quaintly arbitrary as the domestic rites of the Pharaohs."

Although Edith Wharton professed a certain nostalgia for the customs of a class that after 1917 changed its style (but kept its money), she made certain that she herself was delivered, as soon as possible, into a happier world where not only was she admired as a writer but she could move among intellectual equals. Needless to say, such a world was to be found not in the United States of that day but in Europe. In Paris a woman could be taken seriously as an intellectual, and it was in Paris that she finally settled.

Owing to her place of residence, she was much criticized by those America Firsters who never seemed to mind the fact that writers such as Ernest Hemingway seldom lived in the United States. Some sort of double standard is obviously at work.

"With much new material, [Mr. Lewis] has illuminated a marvelous figure and her age." What was the new material? Well, some of it is fairly shocking even in these candid days. In 1885 Edith Jones married the charming but dim Edward Wharton. As was the custom in that far-off time, Edith went to the bridal bed a virgin. Whether or not she was still a virgin the next day is moot. We do know that whatever happened so traumatized her that that was that: no more sex. The marriage itself was not too bad (both of them liked animals). Eventually Teddy Wharton found friends elsewhere while Edith wrote, gardened, lived a full if not fulfilled life. Then, at forty-six, she had her first love affair with a clever, not entirely trustworthy bisexual. But the lover's shortcomings made no real difference. After all, it is not who or what one loves but the emotion itself that matters. In middle life, she was rejuvenated. More to the point, the honesty with which she had treated intimate relations between her characters now possessed a new authority. Despite her reputation as a stuffy grande dame, she had been the most direct and masculine (old sense of the word, naturally) of writers; far more so than her somewhat fussy and hesitant friend Henry James. Spades got called spades in Edith Wharton's novels. As a result, she was always at war with "editorial timidity." Early on, she was told by one of the few good editors of the day that no American magazine would publish anything that might offend "a non-existent clergyman in the Mississippi valley; . . . [I] made up my mind from the first that I would never sacrifice my literary conscience to this ghostly censor." But she lived long enough to find disquieting the explicitness of such writers as D. H. Lawrence and James Joyce.

With a certain dryness, she speaks of the difficulties that writers of her epoch had, turning "the wooden dolls of that literary generation into struggling suffering human-beings; but we have been avenged, and more than avenged, not only by life but by the novelists, and I hope the latter will see before long that it is as hard to get dramatic interest out of a mob of irresponsible criminals as out of the Puritan marionettes who formed our stock in trade. Authentic human nature lies somewhere between the two. . . ."

When the drunken Scott Fitzgerald tried to shock her by saying that he had just come from a bordello, old Mrs. Wharton silkily asked, "But what, Mr. Fitzgerald, did you *do* there?" Later, she complained of Fitzgerald's "insufficient data."

The four novellas that made up the volume *Old New York,* together with *The Age of Innocence,* can be read as a history of New York Society from the 1840s to the 1870s, all told from the vantage point of a brilliant middle-aged woman, looking back on a world that had already become as strange to her as that of the Pharaohs. *The Age of Innocence* was published in 1920 when Wharton was fifty-eight. *False Dawn, The Old Maid, The Spark,* and *New Year's Day* were published four years later.

With the four New York stories and *The Age of Innocence* we are back in a world that she knew as intimately as Proust knew the Paris of much the same era. The stories are precise and lucid, witty and passionate (there is no woman in American literature as fascinating as the doomed Madame Olenska). Not only does one live again in that lost world through Edith Wharton's art (and rather better to live in a far-off time through the medium of a great artist than to experience the real and probably awful age itself), but one is struck by the marvelous golden light that illuminates the world she reveals to us. How is this done? Through a total mastery of English. Now that our language is in trouble, one can, if not mourn the narrow world that she grew up in, at least respond with some sympathy when she observes: "My parents' ears were wounded by an unsuitable word as those of the musical are hurt by a false note." But then, "This feeling for good English was more than reverence, and nearer: it was love."

The Age of Innocence is unusually beautiful. That is to say, the prose is simple, straightforward, loved. When it comes to rounding off her great scene, where Madame Olenska is decorously destroyed by the Old New Yorkers at a dinner, Edith Wharton writes with the graceful directness of the Recording Angel: "It was the old New York way of taking life 'without effusion of blood': the way of people who dreaded scandal more than disease, who placed decency above courage, and who considered that nothing was more ill-bred than 'scenes'; except the behavior of those who gave rise to them."

Great writers are seldom great in everyday life. Edith Wharton seems to have been an exception. In World War I she remained in Paris. She worked hard for the refugees; visited the Front; was decorated by the French government. She was a loyal if tiring friend, as Henry James noted with awe: "Her powers of devastation are ineffable, her repudiation of repose absolutely tragic and she was never more brilliant and able and interesting."

Traditionally, Henry James has been placed slightly higher up the slope of Parnassus than Edith Wharton. But now that the prejudice against the female writer is on the wane, they look to be exactly what they are: giants, equals, the tutelary and benign gods of our American literature.

Works Cited

Benstock, Shari. *No Gifts from Chance: A Biography of Edith Wharton.* New York: Scribner's, 1994.

Wharton, Edith. *A Backward Glance.* 1934. New York: Scribner's, 1964.

———. *The Letters of Edith Wharton.* Ed. R. W. B. Lewis and Nancy Lewis. New York: Scribner's, 1988.

For Further Reading

By Wharton

Although many of Edith Wharton's writings are available in reprint editions, there is no complete edition of her work. Useful collections include:

The Collected Short Stories of Edith Wharton. Ed. R. W. B. Lewis. New York: Scribner's, 1968. 2 vols.

Edith Wharton Abroad: Selected Travel Writings, 1888–1920. Ed. Sarah Bird Wright. New York: St. Martin's, 1995.

Henry James and Edith Wharton: Letters, 1900–1915. Ed. Lyall H. Powers. New York: Scribner's, 1990.

The Letters of Edith Wharton. Ed. R. W. B. Lewis and Nancy Lewis. New York: Scribner's, 1988.

Novellas and Other Writings. Ed. Cynthia Griffin Wolff. Libr. of America Ser. New York: Literary Classics, 1990.

Novels. Ed. R. W. B. Lewis. Library of America Ser. New York: Literary Classics, 1985.

The Uncollected Critical Writings. Ed. Frederick Wegener. Princeton: Princeton UP, 1996.

Autobiography:

A Backward Glance. 1934. New York: Scribner's, 1964.

About Wharton

Many early studies examine Edith Wharton's work in light of the upper-class society in which she lived. More recently, a rapidly growing body of criticism explores a full range of her achievements, focusing, for example, on questions of literary style, period, and genre; on Wharton's relationship to other writers and literary traditions, and on her participation in cultural and intellectual developments of her time.

Ammons, Elizabeth. *Edith Wharton's Argument with America*. Athens: U of Georgia P, 1980.

Auchincloss, Louis. *Edith Wharton*. Minneapolis: U of Minnesota P, 1961.

Bauer, Dale M. *Edith Wharton's Brave New Politics*. Madison: U of Wisconsin P, 1994.

Beer, Janet. *Kate Chopin, Edith Wharton, and Charlotte Perkins Gilman: Studies in Short Fiction*. New York: St. Martin's, 1997.

Bell, Millicent. *Edith Wharton and Henry James: The Story of Their Friendship*. New York: Braziller, 1965.

———, ed. *The Cambridge Companion to Edith Wharton*. New York: Cambridge UP, 1995.

Bendixen, Alfred, and Annette Zilversmit, eds. *Edith Wharton: New Critical Essays*. New York: Garland, 1992.

Benstock, Shari. *No Gifts from Chance: A Biography of Edith Wharton*. New York: Scribner's, 1994.

———. *Women of the Left Bank: Paris, 1900–1940*. Austin: U of Texas P, 1986.

Bentley, Nancy. *The Ethnography of Manners: Hawthorne, James, Wharton*. New York: Cambridge UP, 1995.

Bloom, Harold, ed. *Modern Critical Views: Edith Wharton*. New York: Chelsea, 1986.

Brown, E. K. *Edith Wharton: Études Critiques*. Paris: Librarie Droz, 1935.

Colquitt, Clare, Susan Goodman, and Candace Waid, eds. *A Forward Glance: New Essays on Edith Wharton*. Newark: U of Delaware P, 1999.

Coolidge, Olivia E. *Edith Wharton, 1862–1937*. New York: Scribner's, 1964.

Donovan, Josephine. *After the Fall: The Demeter-Persephone Myth in Wharton, Cather, and Glasgow*. University Park: Pennsylvania State UP, 1989.

Dwight, Eleanor. *Edith Wharton: An Extraordinary Life*. New York: Abrams, 1995.

Erlich, Gloria C. *The Sexual Education of Edith Wharton*. Berkeley: U of California P, 1992.

Fedorko, Kathy A. *Gender and the Gothic in the Fiction of Edith Wharton.* Tuscaloosa: U of Alabama P, 1995.

Fryer, Judith. *Felicitous Space: The Imaginative Structures of Edith Wharton and Willa Cather.* Chapel Hill: U of North Carolina P, 1986.

Gimbel, Wendy. *Edith Wharton: Orphancy and Survival.* Landmark Dissertations in Women's Studies Ser. New York: Praeger, 1984.

Goodman, Susan. *Edith Wharton's Inner Circle.* Austin: U of Texas P, 1994.

———. *Edith Wharton's Women: Friends and Rivals.* Hanover: UP of New England, 1990.

Goodwyn, Janet Beer. *Edith Wharton: Traveller in the Land of Letters.* New York: St. Martin's, 1990.

Griffith, Grace Kellogg. *The Two Lives of Edith Wharton: The Woman and Her Work.* New York: Appleton-Century, 1965.

Howe, Irving, ed. *Edith Wharton: A Collection of Critical Essays.* Twentieth-Century Views Ser. Englewood Cliffs: Prentice-Hall, 1962.

Jessup, Josephine Lurie. *The Faith of Our Feminists: A Study in the Novels of Edith Wharton, Ellen Glasgow, Willa Cather.* New York: Smith, 1950.

Joslin, Katherine. *Edith Wharton.* Women Writers. New York: St. Martin's, 1991.

———, and Alan Price, eds. *Wretched Exotic: Essays on Edith Wharton in Europe.* New York: Lang, 1993.

Joslin-Jeske, Katherine. *The Social Thought and Literary Expression of Jane Addams and Edith Wharton.* Ann Arbor: U of Michigan P, 1984.

Killoran, Helen. *Edith Wharton: Art and Allusion.* Tuscaloosa: U of Alabama P, 1996.

Lewis, R. W. B. *Edith Wharton: A Biography.* New York: Harper, 1975.

Lindberg, Gary H. *Edith Wharton and the Novel of Manners.* Charlottesville: UP of Virginia, 1975.

Lovett, Robert Morss. *Edith Wharton.* New York: McBride, 1925.

Lubbock, Percy. *Portrait of Edith Wharton.* New York: Appleton-Century, 1947.

Lyde, Marilyn. *Edith Wharton: Convention and Morality in the Work of a Novelist.* Norman: U of Oklahoma P, 1959.

McDowell, Margaret B. *Edith Wharton.* Boston: Hall, 1976.

Montgomery, Maureen E. *Displaying Women: Spectacles of Leisure in Edith Wharton's New York*. New York: Routledge, 1998.

Nettels, Elsa. *Language and Gender in American Fiction: Howells, James, Wharton and Cather*. Charlottesville: UP of Virginia, 1997.

Nevius, Blake. *Edith Wharton: A Study of Her Fiction*. Berkeley: U of California P, 1953.

Preston, Claire. *Edith Wharton's Social Register*. New York: St. Martin's, 1999.

Price, Alan. *The End of the Age of Innocence: Edith Wharton and the First World War*. New York: St. Martin's, 1996.

Singley, Carol J. *Edith Wharton: Matters of Mind and Spirit*. New York: Cambridge UP, 1995.

Stange, Margit. *Wives, White Slaves, and the Market in Women*. Baltimore: Johns Hopkins UP, 1998.

Tuttleton, James W., Kristin O. Lauer, and Margaret P. Murray, eds. *Edith Wharton: The Contemporary Reviews*. New York: Cambridge UP, 1992.

Vita-Finzi, Penelope. *Edith Wharton and the Art of Fiction*. London: Pinter, 1990.

Waid, Candace. *Edith Wharton's Letters from the Underworld*. Chapel Hill: U of North Carolina P, 1991.

Walton, Geoffrey. *Edith Wharton: A Critical Interpretation*. Rutherford: Fairleigh Dickinson UP, 1970.

Wershoven, Carol. *The Female Intruder in the Novels of Edith Wharton*. Rutherford: Fairleigh Dickinson UP, 1982.

White, Barbara. *Edith Wharton: A Study of the Short Fiction*. New York: Twayne, 1991.

Wiser, William. *The Great Good Place: American Expatriate Women in Paris*. New York: Norton, 1991.

Wolff, Cynthia Griffin. *A Feast of Words: The Triumph of Edith Wharton*. New York: Oxford UP, 1977.

Wright, Sarah Bird. *Edith Wharton A to Z: The Essential Guide to the Life and Work of Edith Wharton*. New York: Facts on File, 1998.

———. *Edith Wharton's Travel Writing: The Making of a Connoisseur*. New York: St. Martin's, 1997.

Credits

"The Scorsese Interview" by Ian Christie. From *Sight and Sound* (February 1994), pp. 11–15. Reprinted by permission from Sight and Sound.

"Of Writers and Class: In Praise of Edith Wharton" by Gore Vidal. From *The Atlantic Monthly* (February 1978), pp. 64–67. Reprinted by permission from Gore Vidal.